WHY WE WATCHED

Theodore S. Hamerow

WHY WE
WATCHED

Europe, America, and the Holocaust

W. W. Norton & Company
New York • London

For information about permission to reproduce selections from this book,
write to Permissions, W. W. Norton & Company, Inc.,
500 Fifth Avenue, New York, NY 10110

For information about special discounts for bulk purchases, please contact
W. W. Norton Special Sales at specialsales@wwnorton.com or 800-233-4830

Manufacturing by RR Donnelley, Harrisonburg
Book design by Brooke Koven
Production manager: Andrew Marasia

Library of Congress Cataloging-in-Publication Data

Hamerow, Theodore S.
Why we watched : Europe, America, and the Holocaust / Theodore S.
Hamerow. — 1st ed.
p. cm.
Includes bibliographical references and index.
ISBN 978-0-393-06462-9 (hardcover)
1. Holocaust, Jewish (1939–1945)—Causes. 2. Antisemitism—Europe—
History—20th century. 3. Europe—Social conditions—20th century.
4. Europe—Ethnic relations—History—20th century. 5. Holocaust, Jewish
(1939–1945)—Public opinion. 6. Public opinion—United States. I. Title.
D804.3.H355 2008
940.53'18—dc22

2008004318

W. W. Norton & Company, Inc.
500 Fifth Avenue, New York, N.Y. 10110
www.wwnorton.com

W. W. Norton & Company Ltd.
Castle House, 75/76 Wells Street, London W1T 3QT

1 2 3 4 5 6 7 8 9 0

To my wife, Diane, with love

Contents

PART THREE: **The Destruction of European Jewery**

PART FOUR: **From Victimhood to Martyrdom**

Acknowledgments

I COULD NOT have written this book without assistance from a variety of sources, some of them close friends and colleagues, others casual acquaintances or even total strangers. To name all of them would require several pages of acknowledgments, but a few at least should not remain unmentioned. Richard Leffler of the University of Wisconsin–Madison and David Wetzel of the University of California–Berkeley read the finished manuscript and offered perceptive and constructive assessments. Among the many archivists whose help I sought, Paul Rood of the United States National Archives and Bob Clark of the Franklin D. Roosevelt Library were especially supportive, far beyond the requirements of their official positions. Judith L. Tuohy of the Memorial Library at the University of Wisconsin–Madison and Nancy Mulhern of the Wisconsin Historical Society worked tirelessly not only to locate needed materials among their own holdings but also to obtain many others through interlibrary loans. And finally, Anita Olson, a former staff member at the University of Wisconsin–Madison History Department, labored diligently and indefatigably to prepare the manuscript for publication. To them and all the others, my heartfelt thanks.

Introduction

M Y DECISION TO ADD one more book to the vast literature
dealing with the destruction of European Jewry is a result,
indirectly at least, of that very vastness. I have witnessed in the
course of the past fifty or sixty years the transformation of the Holocaust
from simply one of the many atrocities committed by a brutal totalitarian regime into a central feature of the Second World War. Today vivid
reminders of the Third Reich's murderous anti-Semitic policy are to be
found everywhere. There are museums, monuments, memorials, and
commemorations. There are remembrances, anniversaries, scholarly meetings, and academic conferences. There are monographs, periodicals, plays,
films, and television specials devoted exclusively to the Holocaust. It has
become part of the college and even the high school curriculum, with
various courses designed to explain its significance and entire departments
devoted to the study of its background. It is now as much a part of the history of the Second World War as the siege of Stalingrad or the invasion of
Normandy or the Battle of the Bulge. Is there anyone in the United States
and Europe who has never heard of Auschwitz?

The Holocaust has in fact become more than an object of remembrance and mourning. It has emerged as a significant element in our culture, attracting the attention of essayists, novelists, Broadway impresarios,
and Hollywood moguls. The memoirs of its survivors are being read today
with great avidity. Some of those who lived through the terrible years of
the Nazi occupation have achieved the status of living martyrs, Jeremiahs

warning the rest of us against the evils of racism, bigotry, cruelty, and indifference to human suffering. Movies portraying the brutalities inflicted on the Jews of Europe continue to attract large audiences. Sometimes high school students are urged or even required to see those movies, although the young viewers, bored or rebellious, do not always display the expected solemn respect for what is being shown on the screen. No matter. What counts is that an unspeakable horror that was once largely ignored, often deliberately, is now receiving the attention it deserves. Those who identify with the victims of the Holocaust find a deep psychological satisfaction in the knowledge that these victims, and thus they themselves, are finally receiving the recognition that was for so long denied to them.

Here is the key to the continuing and growing preoccupation with the Holocaust. What accounts for it is not only a resolve to memorialize those who perished so cruelly, scorned and abandoned, more than half a century ago. There is also the feeling that public acknowledgment of the atrocities committed against the victims of the Holocaust represents a tacit admission of injustices that may have been committed against those related to or descended from the victims. This, no doubt, is what the historian Charles S. Maier means by suggesting that the establishment of museums to commemorate the destruction of European Jewry is not motivated solely by an intellectual interest in history; it is also "part of a memory industry." The relationship between former perpetrators and former victims cannot be determined by paid debts or material compensations: "Confessional memory is demanded as the only valid reparation." The sense of guilt on one side and of victimhood on the other is an essential aspect of the collective remembrance of the Holocaust. It underlies the unremitting efforts to keep the past alive by various external, material reminders.[1]

The success of these efforts is attested to by the growing demand of other aggrieved minorities for acknowledgment of the sufferings they have had to endure and for some form of compensation for those sufferings. Such minorities often regard the original Holocaust, the Jewish one, as a model to be studied and emulated, sometimes with a touch of envy or even resentment. Here again Maier argues that "as a claim upon official memory, the victim's anguish comes to be seen as a valuable possession. Other peoples also want the status of victimhood."[2]

His argument sounds persuasive. After all, are the Jews the only ones who suffered discrimination, oppression, brutality, and mass murder? What about the ill treatment the African American minority had to endure during centuries of slavery and even afterward? Does it not call for public repentance and commemoration as well? Is it not also part of a holocaust, a "Black Holocaust"? And what about Native Americans, who once were the proud masters of a continent but are now forced to endure hardship and discrimination on desolate, impoverished reservations? And then there are the Armenian Americans, whose grandparents and great-grandparents were the victims of mass extermination during the First World War. Don't these victims deserve as much sympathy as those who perished in the Second World War? For that matter, there is no reason that the Irish peasants who died in the great famine of the 1840s, while the British government looked on in indifference, should not be recognized as victims of a holocaust as well. Was their fate any less tragic than that of other persecuted minorities in the Old World and the New?

In short, as Maier maintains, all oppressed groups have been encouraged by the example of the Jewish Holocaust to pursue the "general goal of seeking respect, attention and validation." The Jews are by no means the only ones "demanding attention from others." There are now many more. As a matter of fact, "modern American politics, it might be argued, has become a competition for enshrining grievances. Every group claims its share of public honor and public funds by pressing disabilities and injustices. National public life becomes the settlement of a collective malpractice suit in which all citizens are patients and physicians simultaneously."[3]

But if there is indeed a competition among various aggrieved minority groups for the acknowledgment of past injustices, the lead in that competition belongs indisputably to *the* Holocaust, the Jewish Holocaust. To be sure, not all countries regard it with the same reverential respect as the United States. There is general agreement that the extermination of European Jewry was a tragedy, an atrocity. But it is also sometimes compared to or lumped with other cruelties and barbarisms committed during the Second World War. There are even occasional grumbles, especially in Eastern Europe, that the Jews are monopolizing the compassion of posterity. What about the non-Jewish victims of Nazi brutality? Did not the Poles and the Czechs and the Greeks also endure heartbreaking losses under the occupation of the Third Reich? And should not their pain and sorrow be recognized as well? Others feel that their own sufferings, though not inflicted by the Nazi regime, deserve just as much recognition, just as much pity. "Does anyone think it was fun to be a Lithuanian or a Latvian or a Ukrainian living under the tyrannical rule of the Soviet Union?" they ask indignantly. Still, while in the Old World *the* Holocaust, the Jewish Holocaust, has to compete at times with other holocausts for public remorse, in the United States it continues to be viewed as the unparalleled atrocity of the twentieth century.

But it was not always that way. During the 1940s, while the extermination of European Jewry was still going on, and even in the early postwar years, the genocidal program of the Third Reich was generally portrayed by the American government and viewed by the American public as only one of the many brutalities for which National Socialism was responsible. Indeed, after it had been established beyond doubt that millions of Jews had perished simply because they were Jews, their death was still widely viewed as just one among the various unspeakable crimes committed by the Germans. After all, Nazi fury had been directed against many national, ethnic, religious, political, and ideological minorities regarded as hostile to the Third Reich. Why, then, should the Jews be singled out as the chief victims? The strategy generally adopted by the shapers of American public opinion was to insist that the war was being fought in defense of all nationalities, all races, all faiths. To have suggested that the heavy sacrifices, human and material, which the United States was forced to endure during the war were being incurred, even partly, in order to save European Jewry would undoubtedly have had an adverse effect on national morale.

In fact, the popular attitude toward Jews in America had from the outset not been entirely favorable. To a considerable extent, it resembled the popular attitude in Europe. The Jews seemed different, strange, alien. They were not like most Americans, like real Americans. They were often greedy, pushy, devious, and clannish. All the charges that had been leveled against them in the Old World could be heard, though not quite as loudly, in the New. Their admission to higher education and the learned professions was still restricted. They remained excluded from fancy social clubs and fashionable resorts and hotels. In short, the various forms of prejudice that Jewish emigrants hoped to escape by crossing the Atlantic continued to confront them, even if in a less blatant form, on the other side.

Surveys of public opinion show, moreover, that distrust of Jews actually increased during the war years. Asked which national, religious, or social groups in the United States were a threat to the country—Jews, Negroes, Catholics, Germans, or Japanese—a plurality of respondents consistently named the Jews, more even than the Germans. In August 1940, 17 percent of respondents regarded the Jews as a menace, as opposed to 14 percent for the Germans. In February 1941, the figures were 18 and 14, and in October 1941, 20 and 16. The entry of the United States into the war changed the proportions briefly: 15 percent for the Jews and 18 for the Germans in February 1942. But then the earlier pattern reemerged. By December 1942 the Jews were ahead once again, 15 to 14 percent, retaining their unenviable lead throughout the war period and beyond: 24 to 6 in June 1944, 19 to 4 in March 1945, 20 to 3 in June 1945, and 22 to 1 in February 1946.[4]

Members of the Jewish community in the United States may have taken some comfort in the knowledge that they were regarded by fewer than a fourth of their countrymen as a threat to the nation. But it is also clear that even among those who did not view them as disloyal there was distrust and suspicion of Jewish influence and ambition. Long-standing popular misgivings about the role of Jews in national life were aggravated by the hardships of daily existence in wartime. Such misgivings were in fact more prevalent than the suspicion that the Jews were a threat to America. Responses to a public opinion survey asking whether "you think the Jews have too much power in the United States" showed a steady increase in the popular perception of excessive Jewish influence in public affairs. During the immediate prewar years, a plurality of respondents declared—though sometimes by only a narrow margin—that they did not believe the Jews had too much power. In March 1938, the percentages were 41 "yes" and 46 "no"; in May 1938, they were 36 and 47; in November 1938, 35 and 49; and in February 1939, 41 and 48.

Then the balance began to change. The defeat of France in the spring of 1940, the decision of Great Britain to continue fighting, and the bitter debate in America over involvement in the war led to a growing belief that Jews did in fact exercise excessive influence and were using that influence to drag the United States into a dangerous military conflict. In April 1940, the weight of the responses shifted for the first time to the affirmative, 43 percent to 40 percent. In August 1940, the opposing views were still evenly divided, 42 to 42. But thereafter the "yes" answers grew more and more numerous, gaining first a plurality and then an absolute majority. In February 1941, they were ahead 45 percent to 41; in October 1941, the figures were 48 and 37; in February 1942, 47 and 38; and in December 1942, those responding that Jews did have too much power outnumbered the combined "noes" and "don't knows" by 51 percent to 33 and 16, respectively.

After that the American public became increasingly convinced that the Jews did indeed have excessive influence, although by then victory was beginning to look more and more likely. In May 1944, after the American triumph in North Africa, after the fall of Mussolini, and after the Allied occupation of southern Italy, popular distrust of Jewish influence in the United States actually grew, with 56 percent of the respondents in a survey expressing concern, while 30 percent saw no threat. In March 1945, following the liberation of France and during the invasion of the Third Reich, the percentages remained almost unchanged, 56 and 29. In June 1945, after the unconditional surrender of Germany and on the eve of victory against the Japanese in Okinawa, they were somewhat more one-sided, 58 to 29. In fact, as late as February 1946, six months after the end of the war, the popular perception of Jewish power had hardly changed. The percentage of those who thought it excessive was still 55, while those who disagreed had increased only moderately, to 33.[5]

Such statistics will probably come as no surprise to anyone who lived through the war years, especially if he had served as an enlisted man in the armed forces of the United States, for he would then have discovered, if he did not already know, that he did not have to cross the Atlantic to encounter the Brownshirts and the SS men. He could find them right here in America, wearing the familiar khaki uniform, in his own platoon, in his own barracks, eating at the next table, sleeping in the next bunk. It was easy to recognize them. They were the ones who would insist loudly that "we should be fighting those goddamn niggers instead of the Germans," or that "the only mistake Hitler made was not killing all the Jews." They would become especially vociferous in the evening, after consuming a few bottles of beer in the PX or a local bar, trying to relax after a hard day's marching and drilling.

Their numbers should not be exaggerated, to be sure. They were no more than a small minority. Yet the others seemed indifferent rather than shocked or surprised by what the hard-core bigots had to say. They had heard such sentiments before. In fact, many of them displayed a casual, unselfconscious bigotry of their own, which could at times turn quite ugly. They would tell jokes about the greediness of the Jews or the obtuseness of the Poles or the laziness of the Mexicans or the simplemindedness of the blacks. It never seemed to occur to them that what they were saying might be found objectionable. If anyone did protest, he was usually dismissed as lacking a sense of humor or being too touchy or interfering with the right of others to voice their opinions. Why should any reasonable person feel offended by a few harmless ethnic jokes or familiar racial stereotypes?

Here again, it is hard to tell how many Americans shared this scornful attitude toward various minorities. But it was a large enough number to be a source of concern to the government officials responsible for maintaining public morale in a time of war. They did not generally share the popular ethnic prejudices; in fact, most of them disapproved. But they also recognized that during a total military conflict, when the civilian population had to endure shortages and privations, when millions of young men were being conscripted and sent into battle, when day after day the newspapers were printing the names of soldiers who had been wounded or killed in combat, it was of the greatest importance to insist that these sacrifices were being made in the interest of everyone, in the defense of all Americans, for the security of the nation as a whole. To single out any particular group as the chief victim of the enemy's brutality could prove dangerous. The hardships that all were forced to endure had to be made to appear necessary for the protection of all. And conversely, to start making distinctions between the degree of danger or intensity of suffering facing various ethnic components of the American population might undermine the unity of purpose essential for victory.

That was why the Holocaust was generally portrayed as only one of the many atrocities committed by the Third Reich. At first, reports concerning the systematic extermination of European Jews were treated by the U.S. government and the press as unconfirmed rumors—rumors that had some basis in fact, no doubt, but that were probably exaggerated, perhaps deliberately so. Even late in the war, after the evidence that the Holocaust had not only taken place but that the number of its victims had been greatly underestimated became irrefutable, public opinion continued to group the atrocities committed against Jews with the atrocities committed against Poles, Russians, Czechs, Serbs, Greeks, Belgians, the French, and the Dutch.

The reason is clear. First of all, to emphasize the mass murder of European Jewry might lend credibility to the German claim that the war had been started by the Jews in order to defeat the efforts of the Hitler regime to free its people from alien domination. But even more important was an awareness by the American authorities of the undercurrent of native anti-Semitism, which had existed for a long time but which had been greatly intensified by the hardships of military conflict.

Only in the early 1960s did the extermination of the European Jews emerge as a unique aspect of the Second World War—indeed, as its central horror. Why this change in the public perception took place so long after the event itself is still not entirely clear. But its effect is obvious. A subject that had until then been consciously and deliberately deemphasized suddenly became the focus of popular interest as well as scholarly study. A vast literature now began to emerge dealing with life and death in the ghettos, the establishment and operation of the extermination camps, the submissiveness of some of the victims and the resistance of others, and the recollections and reflections of the survivors.

Yet while the Holocaust itself has been studied and analyzed and interpreted for more than forty years, the reasons for its relative neglect in the period immediately following the Second World War have only recently attracted attention, notably in Peter Novick's 1999 book, *The Holocaust in American Life*. The book is sharp, perceptive, and persuasive, though it becomes at times a little discursive, a little repetitious, hard to follow on some points, and given to musings or speculations on others. Still, it is the most systematic attempt so far to explain the emergence of the Holocaust as a focus of worldwide interest and sympathy.

According to Novick, the coming of the cold war had the effect of diverting public attention in the West from the brutalities committed by the Third Reich to those perpetrated by the Soviet Union. "The Russians were transformed from indispensable allies to implacable foes," he argues, "[and] the Germans from implacable foes to indispensable allies." The result was a relocation of "the apotheosis of evil—the epitome of limitless depravity" from Berlin to Moscow, from Hitler to Stalin. Since U.S.

public opinion had to be reoriented to accept this new perception of the dangers threatening the nation, symbols like the Holocaust, which had reinforced the earlier view, ceased to be "functional." In fact, they now became "seriously dysfunctional," because they reminded Americans that only yesterday "our new allies had been regarded as monsters." The need to maintain friendly relations with the recently established German Federal Republic thus led to an obscuration of the crimes committed by the Third Reich. The Holocaust became in a sense a victim of the cold war.[6]

Still, if the outbreak of the Soviet-American diplomatic conflict in the late 1940s had the effect of diverting public attention from the extermination of European Jewry, what led to its refocusing in the early 1960s? Here Novick points to several cultural and political developments which, in his opinion, helped arouse popular interest in a subject many had previously preferred to overlook. There was, first of all, the trial in Jerusalem of Adolf Eichmann, graphically reminding the world of the horrors of the Holocaust. A year later, in 1963, Hannah Arendt's book appeared, attracting a wide readership not only with its account of the trial but also with its sharp analysis of "the banality of evil." At the same time, Rolf Hochhuth's controversial play *The Deputy* accused the papacy of moral fainthearted-ness for failing to condemn the genocidal policies of the Third Reich publicly. The Holocaust began to emerge in American culture as "an event in its own right, not simply a subdivision of general Nazi barbarism."[7]

What completed the apotheosis of the destruction of European Jewry, Novick concluded, was the conflict between Israel and its Arab neighbors, especially the Six-Day War of 1967 and the Yom Kippur War of 1973. The successful struggle for survival of the Jewish community in the Middle East helped awaken memories of the doomed struggle for survival of the Jewish community in Europe. American Jews in particular became determined not to let the 1960s and 1970s become what the 1930s and 1940s had been. The Holocaust thus turned into a psychological weapon in the struggle over Israel. Jews and Gentiles alike were exhorted that this time there must be no deportations, no death marches, no extermination camps, no gas chambers. The Nazi genocide became a symbol and a warning. As such it attracted more and more attention, more and more reflection, inspiring not only memorials and monuments, convocations and commemorations, institutes and foundations, but also "a growing cadre of 'Holocaust professionals.' " The genocide of European Jewry became transformed from just another atrocity into an object of veneration.[8]

Still, Novick's argument, though eloquent and persuasive, cannot quite overcome some lingering doubts, some troubling questions. Could the reasons he gives for the rise of the Holocaust to prominence in American consciousness be viewed, in part at least, as effects rather than causes? Are they not perhaps consequences or manifestations rather than determinants? Could there be something else that transformed the familiar cruelties of the midcentury into the most horrifying atrocity of our age, perhaps of all time?

After all, there is little evidence that the cold war was primarily responsible for obscuring the brutalities of the Third Reich in dealing with the "Jewish question." The wartime alliance between the United States and the Soviet Union did not turn into outright hostility as soon as the Nazi regime collapsed. There was a period of three or four years during which it was hoped that the recent partners might still settle their differences and achieve some lasting compromise. The final break did not come until after the Communist coup in Czechoslovakia in February 1948, or perhaps after the introduction of a separate currency in West Germany in June 1948, or maybe even after the establishment of the German Federal Republic in May 1949 and the German Democratic Republic in October 1949. Yet there is no evidence that the popular perception of the Holocaust in either the United States or Europe was very different in the immediate postwar period from what it became after the coming of the cold war. The American government in the late 1940s made no effort to divert public attention from the atrocities of the Hitler regime. Nor did the newly established German Federal Republic, though inclined to minimize the number of those who contributed to or knew about the Holocaust, seek to obscure the horror of what had happened. In fact, it acknowledged a moral responsibility for it by offering financial compensation not only to the survivors but to the embattled state of Israel as well.

Conversely, the rise of the Holocaust in popular awareness during the early 1960s came at a time when the cold war was still at its height, with no sign of softening or abating. What, then, accounts for that rise? Why should the trial of Eichmann have made a deeper impression than the trials of other war criminals fifteen years earlier in Nuremberg and in various countries that had been occupied by the Third Reich? Why should Hochhuth's play have inspired more compassion than the 1952 English translation of Anne Frank's diary? And why should the Six-Day War or the Yom Kippur War have aroused greater interest in the tragic fate of European Jewry than the war of 1948 to establish the state of Israel? Those are questions that call for answers.

To say this is not to deny the importance of the events and developments at the heart of Novick's book. But there has to be something more that accounts for that importance. There has to be something that helps explain why mass brutalities, accepted as almost understandable, almost predictable while they were occurring, began little by little to be perceived as unspeakable atrocities. What was that something? The answer must be sought in the attitudes and events of the 1930s and 1940s that anticipated the destruction of the European Jewish community. To put it another way, there must be a careful examination of the widespread belief, not only in the Old World but in the New, that society had to deal with something called the "Jewish question"; that this was a question that could not be ignored, that demanded a solution; that it was not clear what that solution should be, that there might in fact be several solutions; but that whatever the final solution was, a solution had to be found.

My growing conviction that here is the key to an understanding of the way in which our perception of the Holocaust has changed in the course of the last half-century led me first to remembering, then to reflecting, then to reading and researching, and finally to writing this book.

WHY WE WATCHED

1

The Siren Song of Emancipation

Thou shalt keep thy blood pure. Consider it a crime to soil the noble Aryan breed of thy people by mingling it with the Jewish breed. For thou must know that Jewish blood is everlasting, putting the Jewish stamp on body and soul unto the farthest generation.

THEODOR FRITSCH, 1883

THE POPULAR PERCEPTION that the Holocaust was the tragic culmination of almost two thousand years of anti-Semitic oppression and persecution has a certain superficial logic to it—a deceptive and misleading logic, to be sure, but a logic nevertheless. After all, the Crusaders killing thousands of Jews in Germany and Bohemia as they started out on the long march to liberate the Holy Land from the Saracens can be seen as forerunners of the *Einsatzgruppen* killing hundreds of thousands of Jews in their campaign to save Europe from Bolshevism. The relentless hunt of the Spanish Inquisition for *marranos*, who, while pretending to embrace Christianity, remained secretly loyal to Judaism, seems to prefigure the relentless hunt of the Gestapo for Jews who tried to escape mass murder by hiding out among the "Aryans." And the bloody pogroms of Bogdan Chmielnicki's Cossacks in the seventeenth century do not appear very different from the pogroms by Nazi sympathizers in Lithuania or the Ukraine three hundred years later. The similarity between the persecution of Jews in the past and the persecution of Jews in the twentieth century looks obvious.

And yet that similarity can be misleading. At first glance, European anti-Semitism may seem like one long, uninterrupted succession of brutalities extending over two millennia. Its policies may appear unchanging, the reasons for those policies may appear unchanging as well, and the injustices resulting from those policies certainly appear unchanging. Only the scope of the hostility toward the Jews seems to have increased over time. And yet this widespread view of the anti-Semitic movement is oversimplified and superficial. There have actually been two distinct forms of anti-Semitism in Europe, one dominant for about fifteen hundred years, the other for only two hundred, the later one appearing at first glance to be just a continuation of the earlier, though in reality the two are separate and different in origin, motivation, and goal. A recognition of the crucial dissimilarities between them is essential for an understanding of the Holocaust.

The initial form of hostility toward Jews, prevalent during the Middle Ages and in the early modern period, was rooted essentially in religious faith. At a time when belief in Christianity was the chief cohesive force in European society and culture, members of the Jewish community were viewed as aliens, as perpetual outsiders. How could it have been otherwise? They were committed to doctrines and beliefs fundamentally different from those of the dominant religion, and that difference was the source of the distrust and dislike with which they were generally regarded by their Christian neighbors. Their unwillingness to accept the official faith was taken to mean civic disloyalty and social separateness. Although this perception did not as a rule lead to the expulsion of Jews, it did result in their segregation and isolation. The two communities, the Christian and the Jewish, remained divided by differences so basic as to be insurmountable.

Admittedly, behind the hostility toward Jews derived from religious differences were differences of another kind, generally disguised as disagreements over faith or ethics. Members of the Jewish community had to face a constant litany of complaints about their greediness, deviousness, dishonesty, and unscrupulousness. Their exclusion from the traditional occupations of medieval society forced them into marginal, questionable pursuits like commerce and moneylending, where popular disapproval of their economic role reinforced popular resentment of their religious nonconformity. Shylock was a well-known figure long before Shakespeare wrote about him. The widespread dislike for him and his coreligionists was expressed in perpetual grumbling about the sinister influence of those faithless Jews, about their rapacity or their cunning or their dishonesty or their mendacity. Jewish unscrupulousness was perceived as the natural result of Jewish infidelity. Those who were blind to the sacred teachings of the true religion could hardly be expected to observe its moral precepts. Their deviousness was the logical and inevitable result of their faith. Prejudice based on theological differences thus became reinforced by resentment arising out of economic hostility.

The anti-Semitism of medieval Christendom was most acute in times of political or military conflict, especially when the foe was an infidel. After all, what difference did it make whether that infidel was a Muslim or a Jew? Both were enemies of the true faith, some of them external, others internal, but both were dangerous, both had to be defeated. That was why the four hundred years from the end of the eleventh century to the end of the fifteenth were the most tragic period in the history of West European Jewry, at least prior to the Third Reich. Some 12,000 Jews were killed in Speyer, Worms, Mainz, and Cologne at the outset of the First Crusade. Each of the succeeding Crusades was accompanied by massacres as well, usually on a smaller scale, but inspired by the same zeal to settle scores with the infidels at home before seeking to defeat those abroad.

Such local, spontaneous attacks on the Jewish community often prepared the way for royal decrees expelling the Jews from one country or another. In 1180, Philip Augustus of France issued an order banishing them from the region under the direct control of the crown. In 1290, Edward I ordered them to leave England. And in 1492, Ferdinand and Isabella of Spain exiled more than 100,000 Jews, members of the largest and most influential Jewish community in Europe. By then anti-Semitism had reached a peak that was not exceeded until the twentieth century.

Still, the religious foundation of this hostility toward Jews made it possible for them to escape its consequences, though at a price. Conversion to Christianity meant exemption from the persecution to which the unyielding adherents of Judaism remained exposed. It is thus not surprising that in every country some Jews converted—usually not very many, but sometimes a substantial number—seeking to avoid the penalty for theological nonconformity. In 1492, for example, there were as many *conversos* as unconverted Jews in Castile, 150,000 in each category, while in Aragon the former actually outnumbered the latter, 40,000 to 30,000. Since these conversions were in most cases a result of expediency rather than conviction, it was to be expected that some of the new Christians would secretly continue to practice their old faith, exposing themselves to distrust and punishment by the Church authorities. Even those who accepted the teachings of their new religion without reservation were often viewed with suspicion. Were they really sincere? Had they become true Christians? And were they quite free of the greediness and deviousness fostered by their former faith? How could anyone be sure?

While hostility toward Jews was prevalent among all classes of society, significant differences related to economic position and social status could be found. In general, anti-Semitism was most pronounced among the masses, which often saw in the Jewish community the source of the bitter privations they had to endure. Village rustics and small-town artisans never met the wealthy aristocrats for whom they toiled or the royal administrators who imposed the taxes they had to pay, but they knew only too well the Jewish innkeeper who provided them with a brief escape from the drudgery of their daily existence. They had frequent encounters with the Jewish pawnbroker or moneylender in whose back room they would receive a small loan at what seemed to them an exorbitant rate of interest. They could see almost every day some prosperous Jewish banker or businessman riding by in his coach, appearing to look down with disdain at the dirty, ragged rabble crowding the streets. Was it fair that these aliens, these infidels, should prosper while devout, churchgoing Christians suffered and went hungry? Shouldn't the exploited turn against their exploiters? Shouldn't they try to take back what was rightly theirs? Were not the riots and massacres of Jews a form of rough justice? It is not hard to understand the anti-Semitism of the masses in medieval Europe.

The well-to-do classes, on the other hand—the princes, nobles, warlords, courtiers, landowners, and even many prelates—were in general less hostile. They still regarded Jews as aliens, as eternal outsiders. Being infidels, Jews could never be accepted into Christian society as equals. And yet they might prove useful as financiers and bureaucrats, performing tasks essential for the welfare of the state, tasks that members of the aristocracy would not or could not assume. Some patricians even felt that while the Jews remained disqualified by their religion from receiving the same honors and distinctions that Christians aspired to, they should at least be treated with some courtesy, some consideration, perhaps even humaneness.

Bishop Johannsen of Speyer, for example, opposed forced baptism during the First Crusade, going so far as to order the execution of some of the crusaders because of their brutality. At the same time Bishop Hermann III of Cologne was vainly trying to save the Jews of his city by providing them with refuge in neighboring towns and villages. In France during the Second Crusade, the famous Saint Bernard of Clairvaux urged the faithful to oppose the murder of Jews. The Jews should be spared so that at some future time they might be converted to Christianity. Abbot Suger of Saint-Denis, an influential adviser to Louis VII, opposed the anti-Semitic massacres that accompanied the eastward march of the crusading army. The same Philip Augustus who banished the Jews in 1180 readmitted them eighteen years later, almost as an afterthought, apparently as a gesture of defiance toward the clerical critics of his second marriage. The final expulsion of the Jews from France did not come until almost two hundred years later, in 1394, with the issuance of a decree of banishment by Charles VI.

In short, anti-Semitic prejudices were as a rule far less violent among the patrician classes than the plebeian ones. The Jews did not appear nearly as threatening to those in authority as to the oppressed and impoverished masses. The ups and downs of official policy regarding the Jewish community reflected expediency, indecisiveness, and sometimes simply indifference rather than a deep-seated hostility. In normal times, the issue just did not seem very important to the ruling patriciate.

Here lies the fundamental difference between European anti-Semitism before the French Revolution and the anti-Semitism underlying the Holocaust. In his widely read and widely debated study, *Hitler's Willing Executioners*, Daniel Jonah Goldhagen argues that those participating in the Third Reich's genocidal program were motivated by an "eliminationist" attitude toward Jews, which led logically to extermination. He writes, somewhat convolutedly, that "the elective affinity between the development of the notion of the unchanging and unchangeable nature of the Jews, conceptualized primarily in explicitly racial terms, and seeing the 'solution' to the 'Jewish Problem' to be their physical annihilation, is unmistakable." He concludes by emphasizing that *the eliminationist mind-set tended toward an exterminationist one.*" In other words, what distinguished the hostility toward Jews in the twentieth century from the hostility of the preceding fifteen hundred years was its logical and almost inevitable culmination in systematic mass murder.[1]

This distinction is crucial. It suggests that there is no direct connection between the murderous rampages of the Crusaders or the pogroms of Chmielnicki's followers and the gas chambers of Auschwitz. On the contrary, these manifestations of animosity toward Jews are entirely separate in motivation, justification, and purpose. If the anti-Semitism of the Third Reich can be characterized as "eliminationist" or "exterminationist," then the anti-Semitism of the medieval and early modern period is best described as "segregationist" or "exclusionary." At a time when prescribed piety was regarded as the most important cohesive force in the community, when civic loyalty was believed to be dependent on religious conformity, those who refused to accept Christianity were bound to be regarded as aliens and subversives. They could not be recognized as equal members of society, entitled to the same rights as the faithful. A sharp distinction between the two had to be maintained. Still, while the Jews must be treated differently from Christians, they should at least be permitted to lead a separate, semiautonomous existence, living in their own quarters, following their own customs, obeying their own leaders, and praying in their own houses of worship. The purpose of the restrictions imposed on them was segregation and subordination, not extermination.

The Jews themselves were in general agreement with the underlying assumptions of the official separation between them and the Christians. They too believed that civic loyalty was based on religious doctrine, that private behavior was bound to reflect spiritual faith, and that the unifying force of a community had to be a shared piety. What they objected to was not separation but discrimination. They thought it unjust that because of their religion, they were being denied the rights and opportunities that others enjoyed. They resented the indignities and insults they had to endure, the humiliations, provocations, taunts, and curses. But most of all they feared and condemned the sporadic violence directed against them, the riots, robberies, assaults, and massacres. They did not seek to tear down the barriers dividing them from the Christians but rather to lead undisturbed a separate collective existence based on beliefs and values different from those of the dominant community.

The end of feudalism in Western Europe and the emergence of absolute monarchy as the prevailing form of political authority seemed to make the Jews' attainment of a separate but equal status more likely. There were now fewer princes to appease, fewer authorities to conciliate, fewer warlords to flatter or bribe. The new rulers by divine right were more interested in service and obedience than in theological conformity. What they wanted from their subjects was revenue and compliance, and the Jewish community was prepared to provide both. Religious faith ceased to be a test of civic allegiance, becoming instead a largely formal, external expression of social conformity. There was no longer any reason that the absolute monarch and his Jewish subjects should not reach some mutually advantageous modus vivendi.

Such an arrangement was delayed for about a hundred years, however, by the religious wars that raged in Europe from the middle of the sixteenth century to the middle of the seventeenth century. When Catholics were denouncing Protestants as heretics and Protestants were condemning Catholics as idolaters, it was almost inevitable that both would turn against the infidels living among them who did not even believe in the divinity of Christ. The bitter conflict within the Christian community was bound to lead to an intensification of anti-Semitism.

Its most violent polemical expression was Luther's diatribe of 1543, *On the Jews and Their Lies*, attacking those sworn enemies of the true faith in terms that have a disturbingly twentieth-century ring. After describing the theological errors and distortions the Jews were guilty of, he went on to complain that "they let us work in the sweat of our brow to earn money and property while they sit behind the stove, idle away the time, fart, and roast pears. They stuff themselves, guzzle, and live in luxury and ease from our hard-earned goods. With their accursed usury they hold us and our property captive." Worse than that, "they mock and deride us because we work and let them play the role of lazy squires at our expense and in our land. Thus they are our masters and we are their servants, with our property, our sweat, and our labor." And worst of all, "by way of reward and thanks they curse our Lord and us!" Luther sounds here almost like Joseph Goebbels or Julius Streicher.[2]

Still, his attack on the Jews made a deeper impression on German public opinion in the 1930s than in the 1540s. While the religious wars were still going on, the usual anti-Semitic excesses did occur in many parts of Europe, but not nearly on the same scale as at the time of the Crusades, four centuries earlier. Moreover, once the Treaty of Westphalia was concluded in 1648, a new period of relative stability and tranquillity opened for the Jewry of Western Europe.

Farther to the east, beyond the Vistula and the Danube, the situation was different. Here the growing tension between the various distinct but intermingled ethnic communities—Poles and Ukrainians, Hungarians and Romanians, Lithuanians and Belarussians—had the effect of intensifying hostility toward the one minority whom they all viewed with distrust. Each suspected that the Jews were in collusion with its enemies.

But elsewhere in Europe the hundred and fifty years before the outbreak of the French Revolution produced a mood of rising hope and confidence in the Jewish community. In the last years of the Commonwealth, Oliver Cromwell opened the door slightly to the readmission of Jews to England after a banishment of almost four centuries, and under the Stuart Restoration the slow trickle became a steady stream. Even more exciting were developments on the other side of the Channel. Here the riots, assaults, confiscations, and expulsions that the Jews had had to endure in the past gradually diminished. They were now gaining acceptance, toleration, even grudging respect. They could move more freely outside the walls of the ghetto; they could mingle more easily with their Christian neighbors; they could even object more loudly to the restrictions and disabilities imposed on them.

A few Jews even managed to gain admission to the royal court as administrative experts or financial advisers. Their experience in commerce and banking could prove useful to a ruler seeking to establish a skilled professional bureaucracy in his newly centralized state. These *Hofjuden,* or "court Jews," as they were called in Germany, were generally regarded by the proud aristocrats in the ruler's entourage with condescension and even resentment. How could these coarse, pushy aliens be accepted as equals by noblemen who had dominated state and society throughout their nation's

history? Yet the newcomers could not be entirely ignored, either. Their expertise was valuable, their experience useful. Besides, they had access to the king, who was by no means free of prejudice but to whom usefulness was more important than aristocratic exclusivity. And while the "court Jews" were loyally serving the prince, they were also trying to use their newly acquired influence to improve the position of their coreligionists. Never did the Jewry of Western Europe seem as close to attaining the status of a separate but equal community as in the eighteenth century.

Yet an even more enticing prospect was now opening up. Why settle for segregation if they could achieve acceptance? Why be content with the position of tolerated aliens when the privileges of full citizenship were within reach? The liberal ideal emerging in European political thought, the ideal of an equality of rights for all, regardless of religion or ethnicity, was bound to prove irresistible to Jews.

The concept of an enlightened social order dissolving the distinctions of faith, class, custom, and origin in a common devotion to the progress of humanity was one that even some of the rulers of Europe, the "benevolent despots," were willing to accept. This concept did not threaten the principle of monarchical authority. On the contrary, it might strengthen that principle by transforming the ruler from a defender of tradition into a champion of progress. Nor did most members of the aristocracy or the bourgeoisie challenge the ideal of a better society based on justice, tolerance, kindness, and goodwill, especially since that ideal did not affect the existing distribution of power and wealth. The new secular faith was in fact vigorously propagated by a school of progressive intellectuals, the *philosophes*, most of them from the middle class but a few from the nobility, who denounced the prejudices bred by religious superstition and social intolerance, preaching instead faith in the essential harmony of all mankind.

No one embraced these teachings of the Enlightenment more eagerly than the Jews. How could they oppose the principle that all people were equal, regardless of faith or custom or ethnicity? Here was a philosophy that promised to end the injustices which they had been forced to endure for more than a thousand years. Once that philosophy triumphed, they would no longer have to fear riots, assaults, and massacres. They would no longer have to cajole or bribe those in power for the right to be left in

peace. They would even be free to emerge from the ghetto, to live wherever they liked, to practice any occupation they wanted, and to aspire to any position for which they were qualified.

Yet the emancipation that now seemed within reach did not come without cost. If Jews expected to be treated like Christians, they would have to start behaving like Christians. They might continue to attend religious services in a synagogue rather than a church, if that was what they wanted. But they would have to free themselves from all the moral blemishes and defects that had become deeply imbedded in their collective character. They would have to cease being greedy, cunning, bigoted, and clannish. They would have to become more honest in their dealings with Gentiles, more willing to associate with their Christian compatriots. While continuing to be Jews, they would have to stop behaving like Jews.

Even reformers who supported emancipation agreed that the Jewish character had become corrupted, that it displayed serious weaknesses and dangerous tendencies. Indeed, emancipation was desirable not only because it expressed some abstract principle of equality and justice but because it would make the Jews better, kinder, gentler, and nobler. And that the Jews needed to become better, kinder, gentler, and nobler seemed beyond dispute. Those opposing the discriminations that the Jewish community had to suffer did not as a rule deny the validity of the traditional accusations against that community, accusations of dishonesty or selfishness or exclusivity. Their argument was rather that failings in the behavior of the Jews were not really their fault but the result of the persecutions they had been forced to endure for so long. End the persecutions and you end the failings. It was that simple. The process of Jewish redemption might take time, to be sure. Some of the Christians waiting for this redemption might become impatient or discouraged. But sooner or later the Jews, having breathed the air of freedom, would turn into useful, productive citizens of the state, like their non-Jewish countrymen. Though perhaps still clinging to their ancestral faith, they would in a sense cease being Jews.

Such was the conviction of Christian Wilhelm von Dohm, scholar and civil servant, a familiar figure in the enlightened circles of Berlin society, who in 1781 argued that the widespread hostility toward Jews was not the result but the cause of their selfish and unscrupulous behavior. He conceded that "the Jews may be morally more corrupt than other nations,"

that "they are guilty of a relatively greater number of offenses than the Christians," that "their character is in general more inclined to usury and deceit in commerce," and that "their religious prejudice is more divisive and antisocial." But whose fault was that? Dohm explained the underlying assumption of his argument: "This supposed greater depravity of the Jews is an inevitable and natural result of the oppressive condition in which they have been living for so many centuries." Once the "oppressive condition" ended, the "greater depravity" would end as well.

How could it be otherwise? The Jew would obviously prove loyal to any state "in which he could freely acquire property and freely enjoy it, in which his taxes were no heavier than those of other citizens, and in which he too could gain honor and respect." He would stop hating people who no longer enjoyed "offensive privileges" that he was excluded from but who shared with him "equal rights and equal obligations." Clearly, "the novelty of this good fortune . . . would make it all the more precious to the Jew, and gratitude alone would necessarily transform him into a patriotic citizen." He would begin to look at his country differently, with the eyes of "a son who has until now been misjudged, and who only after a long banishment has regained his filial rights." Acceptance would end disloyalty; patriotism would replace clannishness. "These human emotions would speak louder in his heart than the sophistical reasonings of his rabbis." But Jewish emancipation would do more than fulfill some universal principle of civic justice. It would also provide the practical means for achieving ethnic rehabilitation. Everyone, Jew and Christian alike, would benefit.[3]

Voltaire, the most prominent of the *philosophes*, was less generous in his assessment of the Jews. To him, Judaism, even more than Christianity, embodied the myths and bigotries of supernatural religion. Those who embraced it were bound to become corrupted. Hence Voltaire's battle cry in the struggle for a better society became "*écrasez l'infâme*," crush the infamy of superstition. And nowhere could that infamy be seen more clearly than in Jewish history. His essay on the Jews, published originally in 1756 and included eight years later in his *Philosophical Dictionary*, is essentially a long list of the various distortions, fabrications, and prevarications that they had embraced, especially in Biblical times. No wonder that a nation with such a history had become debased and demoralized. "We find in [the Jews] only an ignorant and barbarous people," Voltaire maintained, "who have long united the most sordid avarice with the most detestable superstition and the most invincible hatred for every people by whom they are tolerated and enriched." Then he added a modest, grudging concession, almost as an afterthought. "Still, we ought not to burn them."[4]

In 1762, Voltaire offered an apology for the harsh things he had said about the Jews a few years earlier. Responding to the objections raised by Isaac de Pinto, a Jewish philosopher and economist living in Holland, he admitted that he might have been a little hasty. "The lines about which you complain, monsieur, are extreme and unfair." He assured de Pinto that he was convinced that in fact "there are among you very learned and very respectable men." Then came a little polite breast-beating. "When one is wrong, he must correct his mistake, and I was wrong to attribute to an entire nation the vices of several individuals." He did not retreat from the view that superstition, whether Jewish or Christian, was "the most abominable scourge on earth." Yet there was no need to prolong the dispute. "Remain a Jew, since that is what you are, . . . but be a philosopher. That is the best thing I can wish for you."[5]

Here was the gist of Voltaire's attitude toward organized religion in general. He was prepared to accept nominal adherence to Judaism or Christianity as a social convention, a ceremonial gesture. But the right-thinking person, especially the right-thinking Jew, should be a philosopher at heart, a deist, a rationalist. As such he would deserve admission to the company of other enlightened, progressive thinkers. But if he persisted in believing the fairy tales and superstitions of his ancestral faith, then he ought to be treated with scorn. For the Jews, in Voltaire's view, the only means of achieving liberation was the abandonment of Judaism, in spirit even more than in practice. Thereby they would become more rational, more understanding, more broad-minded, in short—more like Voltaire himself.

Actually, Jewish emancipation came much sooner than either the benevolent despots or the enlightened philosophers or even the Jews themselves had expected. The great revolutionary movement originating in France in 1789 and then spreading throughout the continent fundamentally altered the structure of state and society in Europe. Even many of the rulers who opposed the subversive principles of liberty, equality, and fraternity thought it expedient to make some concessions to a rising popular demand for reform. By adopting a policy of cautious liberalization they hoped to avoid the danger of democratic extremism. After all, acceptance of the doctrine that all citizens, regardless of class, wealth, or religion, are equal before the law would not alter the traditional distribution of property and power. The fate of Louis XVI, moreover, was a warning to every monarch against the danger of remaining too closely identified with the old order. Napoleon, in contrast, seemed to demonstrate that it was possible to maintain absolute power behind a facade of reformism and that the best defense against republican agitation was royal progressivism, or at least its appearance. There could be no doubt which course was preferable.

The result was that in the twenty years following the fall of the Bastille, most of the states on the continent embraced a policy of reform, varying in scope and intensity but generally intended to demonstrate the abandonment of absolutism, even enlightened absolutism. Some of the rulers genuinely believed in the progressive measures they were adopting. Others regarded them as a means of ingratiating themselves with the greatest power in Europe, the French empire. And a few even hoped secretly that reform would prepare the way for a future struggle against the Napoleonic hegemony. Whatever the reason, the growing acceptance of the principle that the rights of citizenship were independent of economic, social, or religious status led to the legal emancipation of European Jewry after more than a thousand years of hostility, discrimination, and oppression.

Once France opened the gates of acceptance in 1791, the other states followed in rapid succession, until by the late 1870s almost every one except the Russian empire had repealed the disabilities imposed on the Jews. In 1796, Holland, briefly renamed the Batavian Republic, led the way with a decree of Jewish emancipation. Next came several of the German states, all of them vassals of Napoleon: Baden and Hessen-Darmstadt in 1808, Frankfurt am Main in 1811, and Mecklenburg in 1813. Prussia, which secretly regarded reform as an ideological weapon in a coming struggle against Napoleon, granted the Jews legal equality in 1812. Denmark followed in 1814. The defeat of the French empire in 1814–15 temporarily put an end to the liberal reform movement, but Württemberg in 1828 and Hessen-Kassel in 1833 revived the policy of piecemeal Jewish emancipation in Germany. The revolutionary upheaval of 1848–49 promised to hasten the process of liberation, while the reaction that followed may have delayed it, but only for about a decade. Then came the final emancipatory spurt: England in 1858, Italy in 1859, Austria and Hungary in 1867, the North German Confederation in 1869, the German empire in 1871, Switzerland in 1874, and Spain—in a purely symbolic gesture, since no Jews had lived there for almost four hundred years—in 1876. Except for the stubbornly reactionary eastern regions of the continent, European Jewry was now free, or so it seemed.

It was an intoxicating moment for those who had waited so long and so impatiently for acceptance as equals. They were now witnessing a miraculous transformation, the most momentous change in the history of their people since the departure of the Jews from the Holy Land. How could they resist a sense of excitement and exhilaration, a feeling that they were at last free from the oppressions and injustices that they had been forced to endure for so many centuries? In the thousands and tens of thousands they came pouring out from the gates of the ghetto, from the mean streets of the Jewish quarter. They set out to realize the promise of liberation, the promise of equal rights, equal opportunities, and equal rewards.

They were not disappointed—at least, not at first. The long years of exclusion and segregation had fostered among them skills that proved highly useful in the changing economy of nineteenth-century Europe. Peddling and moneylending may have seemed demeaning occupations in an agricultural society, where landownership was the foundation of wealth and status. But in an age of emerging capitalism, of industrialization and commercialization, they provided valuable training for financial success. The penny-pinching Jewish shopkeeper and pawnbroker of the old order became transformed into the well-to-do Jewish merchant and banker of the new age. Not only that, the devotion to book learning and theological disputation which had characterized Judaism when its adherents were excluded from most of the important worldly occupations had prepared them for success in those same occupations during the era of emancipation. Soon many of them became prominent as physicians and lawyers, as scholars and teachers, as authors, musicians, composers, and artists, and as reporters, columnists, and publishers. Some even turned to politics, gaining influential positions in the liberal parties to whose ideology they owed their new freedom. The success that the Jews of Europe achieved in the course of the nineteenth century was far out of proportion to their number.

That helps explain the persistence of anti-Semitism in an age committed, in theory at least, to the principle of equal opportunity for all. The Jews, who were among the chief beneficiaries of that principle, soon discovered that more than a stroke of the pen or the promulgation of a decree was needed to overcome prejudices that had in the course of centuries become deeply imbedded in the popular consciousness. While enlightened rulers and liberal statesmen were proclaiming their faith in the universality of human rights, the masses remained skeptical. They resented the sight of those upstarts who only yesterday had been scorned and despised but who now were flaunting their newly acquired wealth, riding in fancy carriages, hobnobbing with aristocrats, attending exclusive dinner parties, and assuming the air of grand seigneurs while simple, ordinary folk, devout Christians, loyal subjects of the king, had to bow and scrape, wait cap in hand, and take orders from the sly, alien parvenus. Was that fair? Sometimes the undercurrent of popular resentment would rise to the surface in the form of mass assaults against the Jews not very different from those so common in the bad old days. Clearly, stirring declarations of liberty, equality, and fraternity were not enough to overcome the traditional bigotry of impoverished masses in need of scapegoats.

But more ominous than the persistence of the familiar lower-class animosity toward Jews was the emergence of a new form of anti-Semitism among members of the political, economic, and cultural elite. Before emancipation, noble landowners and prominent philosophers had regarded the Jews with disdain and distaste rather than outright hostility. After all, they had nothing to fear from these outlandish outsiders in their squalid ghettos, who were practicing such dubious, demeaning occupations. They did not have to haggle with the Jewish shopkeeper or borrow from the Jewish pawnbroker. It seemed best simply to ignore them.

After emancipation, however, that attitude began to change. Now the strange, foreign-looking figures emerging from the ghetto could no longer be ignored or dismissed as a minor or at times even useful annoyance. They were becoming rivals, competitors, often equals, occasionally superiors. Some of the Jewish bankers and merchants were richer than many of the noble landowners. Some of the Jewish physicians and jurists were acquiring a reputation equal to, sometimes greater than, that of their Christian colleagues. Jewish scholars, Jewish writers, and Jewish artists were beginning to play an increasingly important role in the culture of Europe, frequently at the expense of non-Jewish scholars, writers, and artists. Even national parties were being influenced more and more by Jewish journalists, publicists, orators, and members of the legislature. Was this what the enlightened statesmen and philosophers advocating the emancipation of the Jews had intended? Was the outcome of their progressive ideals and principles to be the Judaization of state and society? At first such doubts were expressed cautiously and only sporadically. They remained largely unspoken. But it was clear that beneath the surface there were growing resentments of the success achieved by the Jews following their emancipation.

What made this new form of anti-Semitism so much more dangerous than the old form was not only its different social basis—that is, its appeal to the affluent and educated rather than the poor and ignorant. It was also the new rationalization or justification of hostility toward the Jews. That hostility had traditionally been defended on theological grounds, as a result of the refusal of the adherents of Judaism to conform to the dominant faith of the community in which they lived. To be sure, the religious arguments were often reinforced, openly or covertly, by economic, social, or political considerations. But those Jews who were willing to abandon their faith could free themselves from the burden of anti-Semitic bigotry by becoming Christians. Even those who did not convert—and that meant the great majority of Jews—were slowly gaining a grudging tolerance as religious fervor cooled into religious conformity and conventionality.

The most important difference between the old form of anti-Semitism and the new was the abandonment of the theological justification for hostility toward Jews. In effect, those who formulated the basic tenets of the latter variety secularized, modernized, and rationalized anti-Semitism. They maintained that the fatal error of Judaism was not its adherence to false religious doctrines but its acceptance of greed, materialism, and clannishness as guiding principles. Its ultimate heresy, in other words, was not theological in nature but moral and cultural. That heresy had the effect of corrupting the spirit, debasing the mind. Consequently, a conversion to Christianity had little effect on the inherent character or mentality of the

Jews. Whether they worshipped in a synagogue or a church, their insidious influence on society remained unchanged.

The extent of this new anti-Semitism should not be exaggerated.
Throughout the nineteenth century the process of Jewish emancipation continued, not only in the form of legal equalization but in growing acceptance, acculturation, and assimilation. There was a widespread
expectation, among Christians as well as Jews, that the two would continue to draw closer together, work together, communicate with one
another, and eventually accept one another. The underlying assumption,
usually unspoken, was that the Jews would in time become indistinguishable from the Christians, except perhaps in the form of their worship,
constituting a small, independent religious community like the Quakers
or the Moravians or the Mennonites, different but respected, separate but
integrated. As late as 1914, that was the expectation of liberals, and especially of Jewish liberals.

Yet at the same time several eloquent and influential exponents of
the new anti-Semitism emerged, warning their countrymen against the
designs and machinations of world Jewry. They were most outspoken
in the east, where discriminatory legislation was still in force and where
genteel bigotry was regarded as one of the social graces of elegant society. In 1877, the great Russian writer Fyodor Dostoyevsky cried out in
anguish at what he perceived to be the steadily growing Judaization of
state and society:

> It is not for nothing that . . . the Jews are reigning everywhere
> over stock-exchanges; it is not for nothing that they control capi-
> tal, that they are the masters of credit, and it is not for nothing—
> I repeat—that they are also the masters of international politics,
> and what is going to happen in the future is known to the Jews
> themselves: their reign, their complete reign is approaching! We are
> approaching the complete triumph of ideas before which sentiments
> of humanity, thirst for truth, Christian and national feelings, and
> even those of national dignity, must bow. On the contrary, we are
> approaching materialism, a blind, carnivorous craving for personal
> material welfare, a craving for personal accumulation of money by
> any means—this is all that has been proclaimed as the supreme

aim, as the reasonable thing, as liberty, in lieu of the Christian idea
of salvation only through the closest moral and brotherly fellow-
ship of men.

Wherever Dostoyevsky looked, he saw the gradual erosion of traditional
spiritual and moral values through the corruptive influence of Judaism.[6]

Farther to the west, criticism of the Jews was much more restrained,
at least in the beginning. In Germany, for example, the common theme
of writers warning against the danger of Jewish emancipation was that the
Jews, though admittedly the victims of centuries of prejudice, were not
without fault for arousing that prejudice. There was Jewish as well as Christian bigotry, each reinforcing and aggravating the other. The intolerance
of the Christians intensified the clannishness of the Jews; the exclusivity of
the Jews exacerbated the bigotry of the Christians. Each should therefore
learn to be more understanding and sympathetic, more broad-minded,
more generous. But the Jews in particular must show greater tolerance.
They must learn to be like their non-Jewish countrymen in appearance,
manner, outlook, and behavior. In other words, they must renounce their
Jewishness, except perhaps as a form of worship. Once they ceased to
be different, they would cease to be treated differently. Assimilation was
surely not too high a price to pay for emancipation.

Bruno Bauer, theologian and philosopher, critic of both religious conservatism and political radicalism, maintained in the 1840s that emancipation was not a Jewish but a general problem; indeed, "it is *the* problem of
our age!" Both the Jews and the Christians had been struggling to achieve
liberation. At a time when no one else was free, the Jews could not expect
to be free either. "We all were surrounded by barriers." That was admittedly beginning to change. But if the Jews really wanted to gain acceptance, they would have to start behaving differently; they would have to
assimilate. "They cannot achieve [equality] in their chimerical nationality,
only in the real nations of our time living in history." Bauer reemphasized
this point because of its central importance. The Jews must give up "the
chimerical prerogative which will always alienate them from the other
nations and history." They must abandon "their disbelief in the other
nations and their exclusive belief in their own nationality." Only if they
renounced their self-centeredness would they be able "to participate sin-

cerely in national and state affairs." The Jews would have to earn equality by appropriate conduct, just as they had previously invited discrimination by inappropriate conduct.[7]

Karl Marx agreed with the contention that the achievement of Jewish emancipation depended to a considerable extent on the Jews themselves. He too believed that the oppression of the Jewish community could not be separated from the oppression of society as a whole. Yet while Bauer saw the source of that oppression in religious and political bigotry, Marx blamed the capitalistic system, which rested on economic exploitation and injustice. And capitalism in turn reflected the materialistic, acquisitive spirit of Judaism. Though born into an old rabbinical family, Marx, the grandson of Rabbi Marx Lewi of Trier, argued that the Jews had already become emancipated in a sense, not only by acquiring the "power of money" but by making money a "world power." The "practical spirit" of Jewry was now spreading among the Christian nations as well. "The Jews have become emancipated insofar as the Christians have become Jews." But for Marx, Judaism had ceased to be a religious, ethnic, or cultural concept. It had become transformed into an economic and social category transcending national boundaries. That is what he meant by declaring that "bourgeois society is constantly producing the Jew out of its own inner being."

Marx saw "practical concern and selfishness" as the secular basis of Judaism, usury as the secular object of its worship, and money as its secular god. He described it in summary form as "a generally present antisocial element which has been elevated to its present prominence by a historical development to whose unfortunate outcome the Jews have eagerly contributed." The anti-Semitism they were encountering was thus partly the result of impersonal economic forces that ranked profit above justice and wealth above compassion. But they themselves had encouraged it as well. By enlisting the destructive forces of commerce and banking to promote their own interests, they had aroused the resentment of those who were the victims of a rapacious capitalism. Jewish greed had bred anti-Jewish hostility.

Yet Marx did not condemn the Jews collectively as a distinct religious or ethnic community. What he criticized was the "spirit of Judaism," which, while common among Jews, was also gaining many adherents among

Christians. Jewishness, in other words, was not a manifestation of theological belief or cultural heritage: it was a form of social behavior which, despite its name, had little to do with the Jewish community. It was rather a product of the rapacious new forces of capitalism, which were enslaving Jews as well as Christians. Once capitalism, which seemed to Marx synonymous with Judaism, was abolished, anti-Semitism would disappear as well. That is what he meant by concluding that "the social emancipation of the Jew is the emancipation of society from Judaism." Marx, like Bruno Bauer, thus believed that the key to the acceptance of Jews by society was a change in the role of Jews in society. But while Bauer insisted that this change meant the renunciation of Jewish exclusiveness, Marx maintained that it meant the rejection of Jewish acquisitiveness.[8]

The contentions that though hostility toward the Jews was in theory incompatible with the fundamental principles of an enlightened society, the Jews themselves had contributed to it by their antisocial behavior, and that this hostility was bound to persist as long as the behavior persisted, appear over and over again in nineteenth-century writings about what was now increasingly called the "Jewish question." Even Theodor Mommsen, the eminent historian of ancient Rome, a liberal member of the Prussian legislature as well as the German parliament, a sharp critic of Bismarck, and an outspoken opponent of anti-Semitism, believed that the fault was not entirely one-sided. Writing in 1880 about "our Jewry," he asked his countrymen rhetorically: "What gives us the right . . . to exclude our fellow citizens who happen to belong to this or that [ethnic] category from the ranks of the Germans?" The only conclusion, based on logic as well as experience, was that the Jews should be recognized as Germans "who have had to bear a double burden of original sin." Citizenship should not be denied to anyone because of allegations of inherited collective shortcomings or transgressions. Equal treatment under the law was the only just principle for dealing with those seeking acceptance as members of the national community.

Yet Mommsen also felt that anti-Semitic prejudice was at least partly the fault of the Jews themselves. Why did they insist so stubbornly on clinging to their ancestral faith? Could they not see that the acceptance of Christianity had become more a token of national loyalty than of religious conviction? And even if they could not bring themselves to worship in a church instead of a synagogue, why did they have to continue to support various organizations and societies composed exclusively of Jews? After all, only a decade earlier the Hanoverians and the Hessians and the Schleswig-Holsteiners and all the other Germans had transferred their allegiance from their native states to the newly established national empire. Why couldn't the Jews do the same? Why couldn't they make the same sacrifice for the sake of the "common fatherland"? It was the duty of the Jews, Mommsen concluded, "insofar as they can do so without acting against their conscience," to abandon their tribalism, their exclusivity, and "to tear down resolutely all the barriers between them and their German fellow citizens." Surely assimilation was not too high a price to ask in return for emancipation.[9]

To many Jews, such advice was superfluous. As soon as the gates of the ghetto were opened, thousands of them, especially in Western and Central Europe, but even in the Russian empire, resolved to show themselves worthy of their new status as more or less equal citizens. Black caftans and skullcaps were replaced by cutaway coats and silk cravats. The dialects and jargons of the Jewish marketplace were supplanted by the elegant locutions of bourgeois society. The haggling and huckstering of the shopkeeper became only an embarrassing memory. Newly well-to-do merchants and financiers conducted their business affairs respectably, sedately, in tastefully furnished offices and conference rooms. And as for the familiar charge of clannishness, the new Jewish elite sought eagerly to be accepted by the old established Christian patriciate. There were dinners, balls, banquets, and parties at which the recent outsiders mingled with the established insiders, exchanging civilities and compliments, though not always with complete sincerity. If the cost of acceptance was acculturation, many of the recently emancipated Jews were willing to pay it.

Yet they soon discovered, like Tantalus in the underworld, that as they drew closer to their goal, their goal drew farther away from them, always almost within their reach, always just beyond their grasp. They always did something that was not quite right. They spoke a little too loudly, they gesticulated a little too vigorously, they dressed a little too ostentatiously, they behaved a little too familiarly. Usually behind their backs but sometimes within their hearing, those they were so assiduously courting would tell jokes, anecdotes, and stories about Jewish attempts to play the gentleman and how obvious the difference was between the authentic and the spurious members of the patriciate. Indeed, a genteel, drawing room form of anti-Semitic prejudice became one of the distinguishing marks of high society. Well-bred ladies and gentlemen would generally treat the parvenus with courtesy, but there could be no question of true equality between the two. Clearly, more than money was required to gain admission into the ranks of the social elite.

Well-to-do Jews who worked so hard to make themselves indistinguishable from well-to-do Christians were aware of the invisible barriers to their acceptance as equals by the upper classes. Many of them complained to each other about the discrimination they still had to face, not as blatant now as in the old days of the ghetto, but all the more insidious because it was less overt. Was this how the established order rewarded their efforts at assimilation? Was this how it kept its word that the end of Jewish exclusivity would lead to the achievement of Jewish equality?

Other Jews maintained, however, usually privately but sometimes openly, that their own people were at least partly responsible for the prejudices and discriminations that continued to confront them. There was something about the way they looked or talked or behaved or thought that invited Christian scorn. It was not enough to dress like Christians or socialize with Christians or live among Christians. The Jews must change their appearance as well as their character, their conduct as well as their mentality, before they could become fully accepted. In the face of continuing bigotry, subdued but widespread, some members of the Jewish community succumbed to a mood of self-deprecation or even self-contempt, to what might be called a Jewish form of anti-Semitism.

In 1897, Walter Rathenau, a well-known German industrialist, publicist, and statesman, who was assassinated twenty-five years later by anti-Semitic ultranationalists while serving as foreign minister under the Weimar Republic, published pseudonymously an article expressing this sense of guilt among Jews. "Look at yourselves in the mirror!" he urged his coreligionists. Nothing could be done about the fact that "you look frighteningly alike," so that the misdeeds of any one Jew were often attributed to all. Similarly, "your southeastern appearance does not appeal in any way to the northern tribes." Rathenau's advice to Jews was to avoid doing anything that might arouse scorn or ridicule on the part of their non-Jewish compatriots. They should be careful "not to make yourselves a laughingstock by a slouching and indolent way of walking amid a race which has been raised and bred in a strictly military fashion." They should become aware, moreover, of "your flabby build, your raised shoulders, your clumsy feet, [and] the soft rotundity of your shape." Indeed, it would take at least a few generations to change their outward appearance. In the meantime they should not try to look like "lean Anglo-Saxons," because that only made them resemble "a dachshund imitating a greyhound." They simply could not "alter nature" by wearing a sailor's costume on the beach or long stockings in the Alps. Rathenau was not sure what Jews had looked like in Biblical times, but it was obvious to him that "two thousand years of misery have left marks too deep to be washed away by eau de cologne."[10]

Forty years later, the National Socialists flaunted Rathenau's article as evidence that even Jews had to admit indirectly that the differences between Aryans and non-Aryans were ineradicable. But at the turn of the twentieth century, this view seemed to make sense to many of his coreligionists. After all, there was nothing wrong with the advice that Jews should behave with discretion and restraint, avoiding ostentatious displays of wealth or influence. Time was on their side. By simply exercising patience, they would sooner or later achieve the goal of acceptance and acculturation. In France, the struggle between monarchists and republicans culminating in the Dreyfus affair had ended with a decisive victory for the forces of democracy, which opposed religious discrimination. In Germany, the parties favoring parliamentary government and social reformism were gaining strength at the expense of the old-style traditionalists. Even in Russia, where royal absolutism had been most deeply entrenched, the revolution of 1905 revealed widespread dissatisfaction with the established order. By the time of the outbreak of the First World War, European Jews could look forward with confidence to the approaching hour of complete equality.

Yet in fact they were threatened by a far greater danger than ever before. By a cruel irony, their liberation had prepared the way for their destruction. By transforming the old-style anti-Semitism into a new form of anti-Semitism, emancipation produced a greater threat to European Jewry than any it had faced in almost two thousand years. But no one could have foreseen that. At the time all prospects seemed so bright, so inviting. Jews were gaining acceptance, not only in Western and Central Europe but even in Eastern Europe. They were becoming prominent in the economy, culture, and politics. They were acquiring influence in national and even international affairs. The future had never appeared so promising. The Jewish community in 1914 felt more hopeful, more confident, more secure than ever before.

But there were ominous signs that the growing importance of Jews was arousing growing hostility. Beneath the surface of civility and cordiality with which Jews were being widely received, there was noticeable uneasiness, even resentment of the role they were beginning to play in public life. Usually such feelings were expressed in whispers and mutters, but sometimes they could be heard with unmistakable clarity. Was it right that these newcomers, these pushy interlopers, should be competing more and more successfully with the traditional patriciate in the pursuit of wealth and influence? Was this how trusting, kindly, good-natured Germans or Austrians or Hungarians or Frenchmen were being rewarded for their willingness to accept the eternal aliens? Where was all this leading? How would it all end?

By the opening of the twentieth century, the uneasiness aroused by the Jews' talent for enhancing their wealth and influence under the capitalistic system was reinforced by the perception of another unwelcome Jewish talent. The socialist movement, with its advocacy of the collective ownership of the means of production and transportation, was finding support among the urban proletariat of an industrializing economy. Workers joining that movement saw in its doctrines the promise of a new social order free of oppression and exploitation. But for many Jews who had abandoned their ancestral faith, especially among the younger generation, socialism also seemed to be the key to ending ethnic bigotry, to establishing a society based on equality and justice in which they would be free at last of the eternal burden of anti-Semitism. A disproportionately large number of Jews were therefore attracted to the parties of the far left, and many of them rose to positions of leadership. This served only to reinforce uneasiness about the perceived excessive influence of world Jewry. Some of those who expressed alarm at Jewish success in using capitalism to acquire power now began to express alarm at Jewish success in using anticapitalism to acquire power. Whether as greedy capitalists or as rabble-rousing radicals, the Jews were increasingly seen as a threat to traditional social values and loyalties.

The most ominous sign of this persisting hostility was the increased militancy of the theorists of the new anti-Semitism. No longer content to dwell on the moral failings and deficiencies traditionally ascribed to the ghetto pawnbroker and marketplace peddler—greed, cunning, dishonesty, and obsequiousness—they began to emphasize the secret designs of world Jewry for domination over a society that had generously but naively opened its doors to these so-called victims of persecution. A realization that what the Jews really wanted was not acceptance and assimilation but influence and power would explain the seeming discrepancy between their simultaneous embrace of capitalism and anticapitalism. These were not really contradictory but complementary manifestations of a collective purpose. They were different strategies for achieving the same goal, namely, complete control over state and society. Unless the nations of Europe woke up to the danger confronting them, they would soon find themselves forced to abandon their time-honored traditions and submit to the rule of a cunning, ruthless, alien minority.

It was at this time that the "Jewish question" became a subject of serious discussion in many works dealing with the future of European society and culture. In his analysis *The Foundations of the Nineteenth Century*, Houston Stewart Chamberlain charged that "our governments, our law, our science, our commerce, our literature, our art . . . practically all branches of our life have become more or less willing slaves of the Jews." And this had happened in the space of barely a hundred years, only since the granting of Jewish emancipation. "The Indo-European," Chamberlain explained, "moved by ideal motives, opened the gates in friendship: the Jew rushed in like an enemy, stormed all positions and planted the flag of his, to us, alien nature—I will not say on the ruins, but on the breaches of our genuine individuality." If this situation were to continue, there would be in all of Europe "only one single people of pure race," namely, the Jews. All the others would become "a herd of pseudo-Hebraic mestizos," a hodgepodge of various races and nationalities, "degenerate physically, mentally and morally." The glory of Western civilization would come to an end in a society based on corruption and enslavement.[11]

What could be done to avert such a catastrophe? Chamberlain offered no solution, but a number of others did. In France, Édouard-Adolphe Drumont proposed a plan that seemed simple, obvious, and yet without risk of serious opposition: the expropriation of Jewish wealth by the state. No one, except of course the Jews themselves, could object to that. Such wealth was clearly of a "special character." It was essentially "parasitic and usurious." It was the fruit not of "the labor of countless generations" but of "speculation and fraud" by Jewish businesses, which "have enriched their founders while ruining their stockholders." And yet it would take so little to confiscate those ill-gotten riches. All that was required was "an officer who is brave," perhaps "five hundred determined men," and "a regiment surrounding the Jewish banks." It would all be over in a single day. And as for the public reaction, "people would embrace in the streets" at the news that the economic tyranny of the Jews had come to an end. It would be so easy.[12]

The most prophetic of the spokesmen for the new anti-Semitism, however, was the German philosopher and economist Eugen Dühring. What made his views regarding the "Jewish question" so ominous was his contention that the pernicious qualities in the Jewish character were not the result of religious belief or historical experience or cultural tradition; they were hereditary, rooted in the genetic composition of the Jews, reflecting on unchangeable racial character. These qualities could not be overcome or modified by adaptation or acculturation or assimilation. They could only be obscured or disguised. However compliant the behavior of the Jews might appear, however familiar their appearance, however conventional their discourse, in their inner being they would always remain unalterably and incorrigibly alien. To ignore this hard reality, to embrace the generous but naive belief that all people were essentially the same, to pretend that there were no irreconcilable differences between Jews and non-Jews, must lead to the corruption of the innocent majority by an unscrupulous minority. It must end in social disaster.

Dühring argued that the Jews were "not a religion but a racial tribe" whose true nature had been "hidden to some extent by the admixture of religion." In fact, a "Jewish question" would exist even if "all Jews had turned their back on their religion and had gone over to one of the leading churches among us," for experience had shown that baptized Jews were precisely the ones who penetrated furthest into the various branches of society and politics. Their conversion to Christianity had provided a "master key" that enabled them to enter those areas of public life which had remained closed to religious Jews. The result was "the spread of racial Jewry through the seams and crevices of our national structures." But that could not go on indefinitely. Sooner or later there would be a reaction. Sooner or later the Germans were bound to realize "how irreconcilable with our best impulses is the infusion of the qualities of the Jewish race into our [national] environment." It was only a question of time.[13]

Half a century later, these views would serve as a justification for an official policy of racial extermination. But when Dühring was expounding them, they seemed to most Jews and to many non-Jews as well to be simply the fulminations of a dying social order. The future clearly belonged to a new and different vision of society, more generous, more understanding, more humane. Such optimism seemed justified in light of the momentous changes that had taken place in the previous hundred years: the growth of the economy, the rise of social welfare, the spread of representative government, and the advance of religious toleration. There was no reason that the nations of Europe should not continue on the road to freedom and equality.

What destroyed this optimistic view of the future was the First World War. Unforeseeably, paradoxically, tragically, a military conflict that Woodrow Wilson had described as a struggle to make the world safe for democracy made the world disillusioned with democracy. The hopeful outlook of the years before 1914 was replaced by insecurity and disenchantment after 1918. The losers were embittered by their defeat; the winners became disappointed in their victory. Whereas peace and prosperity had fostered the growth of liberalism in the nineteenth century, war and depression led to a revival of authoritarianism in the twentieth. As for the Jews, their fate was linked to doctrines and policies that seemed in the ascendant before the outbreak of war but came to be increasingly challenged after the return of peace. The question can thus be legitimately asked whether the emancipation of the Jews, which had been greeted with such high hopes and expectations, did not lead ultimately to the destruction of the Jews.

To be sure, the disastrous consequences of the First World War were not immediately apparent. At first it looked as if the world, or at least Europe, had indeed been made safe for democracy. In the defeated nations of Central Europe—in Germany, Austria, and briefly in Hungary—republican regimes replaced the traditional semiauthoritarian monarchical system. Russia, now governed by Communists, who denounced bourgeois liberalism, proclaimed its unequivocal rejection of racial and ethnic discrimination as well. Equally encouraging were the constitutions adopted by the succession states of Eastern Europe—Poland, Lithuania, and Latvia—which granted freedom and equality to all citizens regardless of origin or religion. Even Romania at last bestowed full rights of citizenship on the Jews. Admittedly, many of these reforms were inspired less by democratic conviction than by a desire to win the approval of great powers like England, France, and the United States. But whatever their motivation, to European Jewry they appeared to represent the final step in emancipation.

Yet beneath the appearance of the new, seemingly tolerant republicanism, the old anti-Semitic prejudices persisted and actually gained strength. The 1920s were a decade of economic insecurity, social conflict, and political upheaval. A mood of growing disillusionment spread, not only among the losers in the war but among the winners as well. Was this what they had fought and suffered and sacrificed for? The only ones to have profited appeared to be the Jews, jubilant at their achievement of full equality, at least on paper, who were assuming an increasingly important role in national life. Was this what democracy meant?

The growing postwar undercurrent of anti-Semitism was further intensified by the disproportionately large number of Jews who, aware of the hostility they were arousing among their non-Jewish compatriots, became supporters of the Communist movement. This in turn reinforced anti-Semitic fears among those who felt threatened by Bolshevism. Was this how the Jews were showing their gratitude for being accepted as equals? Was there no limit to their appetites and ambitions? Was their real goal not toleration or emancipation but domination? The questions, doubts, and resentments continued to mount.

Even many liberals, in theory believers in the equality of all citizens regardless of ethnic origin, began to wonder whether the growing prominence of the Jews was really a good thing. Perhaps it would be better for everyone if they were less ambitious, less aggressive, less successful. Twenty years later, after the Second World War, the eminent German historian Friedrich Meinecke, who had been a cautious supporter of the Weimar Republic, explained and even half justified this growing suspicion of Jewish influence during the 1920s. "Among those who drank too hastily and greedily of the cup of power which had come to them were many Jews," he recalled. "They appeared in the eyes of persons with anti-Semitic feeling to be the beneficiaries of the German defeat and revolution. Everyone else in Germany, aside from these beneficiaries, seemed irrevocably consigned to misery." No wonder that more and more people, including some who had previously been generous and tolerant, were beginning to turn against "these beneficiaries" of the national misery.[14]

A growing feeling that the Jews were gaining wealth and power at the expense of non-Jews was not confined to Germany. It appeared even stronger farther to the east, where anti-Semitic prejudice was often regarded as a manifestation of national pride and religious devotion. There was throughout Europe a rough correlation between the proportion of Jews in the total population and the intensity of the hostility toward them. Poland, where Jews constituted 10.4 percent of all inhabitants, was at the top of the list. There anti-Semitism had become a widespread and deep-rooted popular attitude, especially since the end of the eighteenth century. Not far behind were Hungary, with a Jewish population amounting to 5.9 percent of the total, and Romania, with 4.8. Then came countries in the middle range of anti-Semitic prejudice, like Austria, with 3.5 percent, and Czechoslovakia, with 2.4 percent. The states in which hostility toward Jews seemed least intense were those with the lowest proportion of Jews: the Netherlands, with 1.7 percent; Great Britain and Belgium, with 0.7 percent each; France, with 0.5; and—though this may seem hard to believe in light of what was to happen later—Germany, with 0.9. But in all countries, distrust and fear of what was perceived as growing Jewish influence continued to mount throughout the 1920s.[15]

What finally persuaded both public opinion and governmental bureaucracy that something had to be done to solve the "Jewish question" was the financial crash of 1929 and the ensuing Great Depression. Amid the mounting problems of unemployment and impoverishment, economic insecurity and social unrest, the rhetoric of anti-Semitism began to sound increasingly plausible. Perhaps it was true after all that the crisis facing European society was a result of Jewish speculation, that it was enlarging Jewish wealth through the exploitation of Christian misfortune, that it had in fact been deliberately started to increase Jewish power by encouraging class conflict and political instability. To more and more people in the early 1930s, those contentions did not sound far-fetched. Some governments, moreover, under growing public pressure to adopt drastic measures to restore stability, agreed, whether out of conviction or expediency, that something must be done to find a solution to the "Jewish question." That solution would have to be credible, it would have to be effective, but above all it would have to deal with the matter once and for all. At last, one way or another, Europe had to arrive at a final solution.

PART ONE

———⟩⟩⟨⟨———

The Great Depression and Anti-Semitism

People in those democracies deplore the "unspeakable cruelty" with which Germany . . . is trying to get rid of the Jewish element. . . . Now that complaints [against the Jews] have at last become very loud and our nation is no longer willing to let itself be further impoverished by those parasites, people are wailing about it. But they are not trying to solve the so-called problem once and for all by some constructive action on the part of those democratic countries. Quite the contrary, they inform us very coolly that there is of course no room [for Jews] over there. . . . They offer no help, but, oh, the moralizing!

ADOLF HITLER, NUREMBERG,
SEPTEMBER 12, 1938

2

Eastern Europe in Crisis

THE 1930S BECAME the decade in which the last remaining illusions regarding the inevitable triumph of the democratic ideal vanished. Those illusions, widely accepted as realities at the turn of the century, were first challenged by the experience of the devastating war that broke out a few years later. The enormous sacrifices of life and property exacted by that war gradually began to arouse doubts about a political system that had led to such a vast international catastrophe. No amount of propaganda regarding the sinister plots and cruel atrocities of the enemy could overcome the feeling that the fault was not entirely one-sided, that all the belligerents had contributed in some measure to the calamity now confronting them. The greater the hardship a country had to endure, the greater its disillusionment with the established order. The overthrow of czarism in Russia and the establishment of the Bolshevik regime while the conflict was still going on demonstrated that what had started out as a war against a foreign enemy was beginning to turn into a rejection of the existing system of authority.

The end of the war seemed at first to quiet this dissatisfaction with the status quo, at least among the victor states. After all, the parliamentary democracies had succeeded in defeating the conservative empires. The new constitutions adopted by several European nations after 1918 seemed to reflect a growing commitment to liberal policies and principles. Statesmen in almost every country were now proclaiming their resolve to reject the inherited dogmas and prejudices of the past and pursue the path of political freedom and social justice. Perhaps all the wartime sacrifices of manpower and wealth had not been in vain after all. Perhaps the world was really becoming or about to become better. There was a brief revival of optimism regarding the future of Europe during the 1920s, an optimism that was not always unshakable or spontaneous or entirely sincere. Still, the mood of despair that had become widespread during the latter stages of the war seemed to be dissipating.

Yet there were troubling signs that the victory of the democratic ideal had been less than complete. Although the revolution in Russia failed to spread to other states and its supporters in Poland, Hungary, and the Baltic states had been defeated in their efforts to establish a similar regime, the Communist movement continued to gain support among urban workers throughout the world. At the other end of the political spectrum, the Fascist Party came to power in Italy on a program embracing nationalism, militarism, and authoritarianism. Hungary, after brief experiments with a democratic republic and a Communist dictatorship, turned to what was in theory a monarchy but in reality a traditional oligarchy under Admiral Nicholas Horthy. These were troubling signs that the victory of democracy had not been quite as complete as its adherents would like to believe.

To be sure, manifestations of an undercurrent of authoritarianism in the political sympathies of Europe could be explained away as the last gasps of an old order refusing to admit defeat. The Russians had always been backward, submissive, and superstitious. It would have been too much to expect such a people to go directly from unquestioning acceptance of traditional authority to a commitment to democratic principles. There were bound to be relapses and setbacks. Moreover, there were already signs that even the Russians were beginning to see the light. The defeat of the Kremlin's attempt to export communism by military force had served to isolate the Bolshevik regime, to make it less aggressive, less dangerous. Now the emerging struggle between pragmatists and militants in the Soviet Union, between the followers of Stalin and the supporters of Trotsky, between the advocates of "socialism in one state" and the proponents of "permanent revolution," was evidence that the Communist system was in trouble. Sooner or later it would make way for a more tolerant and democratic form of government.

Many liberals expressed a similar optimism, sometimes genuine, sometimes merely professed, about the future of Fascist Italy. Here again, they maintained, was a nation whose bark was worse than its bite, whose militant rhetoric was designed to disguise a cautious policy. Mussolini might continue for a while to strut and posture, declaim and bellow. But little by little he was becoming more moderate, more reasonable. In time he would turn into just another middle-of-the-road Italian prime minister like those of the prewar period, Francesco Crispi and Giovanni Giolitti: prudent, reasonable, and flexible; a little calculating, perhaps, a little shifty at times, but willing to accept the constraints of a parliamentary system. Besides, had not Mussolini succeeded in crushing the danger of a left-wing revolution in his country? That was surely an important achievement. Just give him time to free himself from the burden of his own inflammatory rhetoric.

As for Hungary, that country was a political freak, neither fish nor flesh nor good red herring. A monarchy without a monarch, ruled by an admiral without a fleet, defiant but isolated, revanchist but powerless. Why should anyone worry about what Hungary did? Its situation was simply further evidence of the futility to which a rejection of the democratic ideal, or at least an open rejection, was bound to lead.

The Great Depression put an end to all such comforting assumptions. Doubts regarding liberal principles and institutions, which had first emerged during the war and had then been suppressed or disguised during the brief years of stability, now reappeared in a much more dangerous form. Amid the hardships and privations of a crippled economy, while millions of people were hungry and impoverished, public opinion turned against a political system that seemed powerless to cope with the crisis confronting society. Political movements that had been dismissed a decade earlier as futile or irrational suddenly began to attract large numbers of converts desperate to find a way out of the depression.

Communism had languished during the ephemeral prosperity of the late 1920s, but now it rapidly began to gain strength, becoming once again a threat to the established order. Even more dangerous was the appearance of a new form of authoritarianism which insisted that economic collapse and social disintegration were the inevitable consequences of a liberal ideology emphasizing individual freedom at the expense of collective welfare, ranking material gain more highly than national greatness. Since liberalism was responsible for the crisis of European society, only the rejection of liberalism could overcome that crisis. The parliamentary system was nothing more than a screen for class conflict and party rivalry, for an unending struggle of selfish interests indifferent to the well-being of the community as a whole. Only a return to the traditional values of loyalty, discipline, selflessness, and patriotism could protect Western civilization against cruel, materialistic communism. The Soviet Union was a warning to all the states of Europe of what would happen if they continued on the path of popular democracy and unrestrained individualism.

The new right-wing authoritarianism assumed two distinct forms, sharing a common objective but differing in rhetoric and strategy. The more moderate one looked to the historically dominant forces in society to take the lead in the struggle against the liberal hegemony. It regarded the monarch, if there was one, as the logical choice for commander of the forces opposing the tyranny of the parliamentary system. Or a successful general or admiral, inspired by the military virtues of courage, chivalry, and hierarchical authority, might become the savior of society. Members of the old aristocracy, recently forced into the background, were likely to support a return to the historic distribution of power and influence. For that matter, many members of the bourgeoisie, frightened by the specter of left-wing radicalism, would probably welcome the restoration of a traditionalist form of government which opposed proletarian revolutionism with armed force. And then there was the established church and its faithful followers, dismayed by the "materialism" of the liberal ideology, alarmed at the spread of secularism and "immorality," eager to revive the role of religious faith in public life.

The radical wing, though more militant in rhetoric and theory than in policy or practice, was nevertheless quite different. It rejected a reliance on the traditionally conservative forces in society—crown, aristocracy, and church. It preached instead an egalitarianism under which all citizens, regardless of class or occupation, would be enlisted in the struggle for national salvation. It emphasized the importance of military strength and territorial expansion. It condemned restraint and compromise in foreign affairs as well as plutocracy and capitalism in domestic affairs, or at least too much plutocracy and capitalism. It was nativistic and xenophobic, often racist, and almost always anti-Semitic. Above all, it demanded the subordination of personal gain and class interest to the national welfare. The greatness of the state must be recognized as the prime concern of all loyal citizens.

Political organizations embracing this ideology began to appear in all the nations of Europe, even those with a long tradition of democratic government, such as England, France, the Low Countries, and the Scandinavian states. At first such organizations were regarded, especially in Western Europe, as something of a curiosity, an aberration; they were so different from other political movements, with their members wearing dark shirts or quasi-military uniforms, marching in step with soldierly precision, shouting defiant slogans, and exchanging strange greetings and salutes. To many critical observers, their processions and demonstrations resembled a noisy circus parade.

The coming of the Great Depression changed this dismissive attitude. Facing growing economic hardship and social disorder, alarmed by the radicalization of the industrial proletariat, and fearful of the spread of communism, more and more people began to see in the revival of some form of hierarchical authority the only alternative to class conflict and the triumph of the far left. For the time being the established order in Western Europe could still feel secure, but even there the increasing strength of authoritarian organizations reflected the spread of dissatisfaction with the parliamentary system. The Croix de Feu in France, the British Union of Fascists, the Rexists in Belgium, and the Nasjonal Samling in Norway were all warnings of a rising tide of disillusionment with the liberal ideas and ideals of the prewar years.

Even more ominous signs of a bitter ideological conflict could be seen in Central Europe. There the Great Depression led to the failure of the brief, tentative experiments in democracy initiated in the aftermath of military defeat. The decline of the Weimar Republic in Germany and its replacement in 1933 by a National Socialist dictatorship seemed far more disturbing than the establishment a decade earlier of the authoritarian Horthy regime in weak, isolated Hungary. This time the second most populous country in Europe, the most industrialized power on the continent, embraced the new authoritarianism in its most extreme form. The effect on other countries with a recently established, still struggling democratic government was bound to be profound. Indeed, barely a month after Hitler's victory in Germany, Chancellor Engelbert Dollfuss of Austria established a dictatorship of his own, more moderate than the one in Berlin, more in sympathy with the traditionalist authoritarianism of the old school, but equally opposed to both middle-of-the-road liberalism and left-wing radicalism.

The democratic statesmen of Western Europe were troubled, moreover, by developments in the Iberian Peninsula. The fate of Portugal may not have been one of their major concerns, even after a succession of military coups and strong-man regimes culminated in 1932 in the establishment of the dictatorship of Antonio de Oliveira Salazar, whose *Estado Novo*, or "New State," was based on a combination of moderate authoritarianism and amorphous corporatism similar in many respects to the Dollfuss regime in Austria. Yet while this turn to the right in Portuguese politics could be ignored by the rest of the continent, it did reinforce the common feeling that the direction of historical development, which had seemed to favor parliamentary democracy, was now shifting toward some form of authoritarianism.

This feeling was intensified a few years later by events in neighboring Spain. What happened in Portugal could be dismissed as a local aberration in a remote corner of Europe. There was no compelling reason to pay too much attention to it. But no one could ignore the bloody civil war raging from 1936 to 1939, which ended with the overthrow of the Spanish Republic. Not that Spain had been a model of thriving democracy during the previous two decades. There were unending struggles for autonomy or independence in Catalonia, the Basque provinces, and Morocco. There were ideological conflicts between monarchists, traditionalists, and clericalists on one side and socialists, Communists, and anarchists on the other, not to mention that the leftists fought against each other almost as fiercely as they fought against the rightists. There were military mutinies and attempted coups; there was the dictatorship or semi-dictatorship of General Miguel Primo de Rivera; then came the establishment of the republic in 1931; and then, early in 1936, the victory at the polls of various centrist and leftist parties united in the Popular Front. This led finally to the revolt of the traditionalist forces under General Francisco Franco, which, at the cost of some 750,000 lives, succeeded by the spring of 1939 in defeating the republican regime and establishing a dictatorship of the right.

What made the civil war in Spain seem so important to the rest of Europe was the feeling that here was a conflict whose outcome was bound to have consequences far beyond the Iberian Peninsula. The struggle reflected the opposing interests of the winners and the losers in the recent world war; it confronted the interests of an international order established by the peace treaties with the interests of a revisionist camp which insisted that those treaties must be repudiated. Diplomatic disagreements were further aggravated by ideological disagreements between liberal states defending the postwar status quo and authoritarian states demanding a new balance of power. That was why the civil war in Spain became a rehearsal for the world war that was about to begin, with Italy and Germany sending troops and warplanes to support the Franco forces; England and France, more restrained or more timid, siding, but only diplomatically, with the republican regime; and the Soviet Union providing the government in Madrid with financial resources and Communist volunteers to fight the enemies of the left. The victory of those enemies was a sign that the military and ideological preponderance in Europe was shifting from the liberal middle to the antiliberal right.

The most fertile soil for the ideas and policies of the new authoritarianism, however, was not Central or southern Europe but Eastern Europe. In Germany and Austria, even in Portugal and Spain, there had been serious though unsuccessful attempts to establish a democratic form of government. Beyond the Oder and the Danube, in contrast, conservatism, traditionalism, and clericalism had retained a powerful popular appeal, even while the succession states were adopting constitutions that appeared irreproachably liberal on paper. That was not surprising. Here was a region largely dominated for more than a century by czarist Russia, a region politically submissive, economically backward, and ideologically authoritarian. Among many of the oppressed nationalities there had been a yearning for independence, a hope of regaining an earlier greatness or reacquiring a lost province or territory. But except for some members of the small native intelligentsia, there was little support for popular democracy. Nationalism was more important than liberalism; patriotic loyalties outweighed parliamentary principles. The reconstruction of Europe after the First World War showed how deep-rooted the traditions of authoritarian rule and hierarchic power were in the eastern regions of the continent.

There the typical pattern of political development during the postwar period was first a halfhearted attempt to imitate the constitutional example of France or England—an attempt designed largely to win the favor of the victor states—soon followed by a relapse into authoritarianism, repression, and conformity. The earliest manifestation of this pattern could be found in Russia itself, where the transition from czarist to Communist autocracy took barely eight months, from March to November 1917. The two regimes, the old monarchical one and the new revolutionary one, may have been diametrically opposed in almost every respect—certainly in their views of state, society, economy, and faith. But in the means employed to enforce their rule there was a depressing similarity.

The succession states of Eastern Europe, which had gained or regained their independence after the First World War, conformed to the same pattern, with the important difference that their brief experiments in democracy were followed by a turn to the right rather than the left. Poland, by far the largest, with ambitions of someday being admitted to the ranks of the great powers, proclaimed the establishment of a republican form of government as soon as hostilities were over, signed a treaty guaranteeing the civil rights of the ethnic minorities which made up nearly a third of the population, and adopted a constitution modeled on that of France. But after that, it was all downhill. Financial crises, parliamentary struggles between right and left, and growing demands by the minorities for a measure of autonomy led to a military revolt in 1926 organized by the war hero Józef Pilsudski. The trappings of parliamentary government remained, but the experiment in liberalism was now over. The depression further intensified the problems confronting the government, and in 1935 a new constitution ended even the pretense of political democracy. The death of Pilsudski a few weeks later initiated the rule of the "colonels," a group of strongmen, some of them high-ranking military officers, who governed the country in the spirit of a traditionalist authoritarianism until the outbreak of the Second World War.

Romania was not, strictly speaking, one of the succession states, since it had been independent before 1918. But by the terms of various postwar settlements it had more than doubled its territory and almost tripled its population. At first the government in Bucharest, like the government in Warsaw, sought to demonstrate to the world that it was resolved to pursue the path of democratic reform and parliamentary rule. A new constitution introduced the secret ballot, the Jews received full rights of citizenship (at least on paper), and the middle-class Liberal Party assumed leadership of the cabinet. Thus Romanian politics during the early postwar period resembled Polish politics, both hoping to persuade the victorious powers that they too were committed to a free, representative form of government. But party conflicts between liberals and conservatives, growing demands of the minority nationalities for a measure of self-rule, and the devastating economic effects of the Great Depression had the same effect in Romania as in Poland. By the early 1930s, the tentative experiment in liberalism and parliamentarianism was over. In Bucharest, however, the strongman was not a prominent military leader like Pilsudski or the "colonels" who dominated the government in Warsaw but the king, Carol II. Fearing the growing strength of the far right, he initiated a policy of piecemeal reaction which culminated at the end of the decade in the establishment of what was in effect a royal dictatorship. By the time the Second World War broke out, Romania, like Poland, had embraced the doctrines and policies of the new authoritarianism.

The same pattern of political metamorphosis could be found in the smaller succession states, like Lithuania and Latvia. Here too there was at first a display of enthusiasm at the achievement of independence and support for the adoption of a democratic constitution. But the middle-of-the-road parties that predominated in the early postwar period could not deal effectively with the conflicts between right and left, with the problems of economic reconstruction, and with the bitter disputes regarding boundaries and minorities. The outcome was a steady drift toward conservatism and the eventual emergence of a strongman. All of this was familiar; only the names were different. In Lithuania the coup d'état of Antanas Smetona in 1926 initiated the steady drift of the government toward authoritarianism, culminating a decade later in the suppression of all opposition parties. In Latvia the coup d'état did not come until 1934, and the name of the man responsible for it was Karlis Ulmanis. But otherwise what happened was depressingly predictable. After all, almost every one of the succession states followed a similar course of political development.

The crucial ideological struggle in Eastern Europe, especially during the Great Depression, was thus not between democracy and authoritarianism but between moderate and radical authoritarianism. The former was generally successful in gaining and maintaining the upper hand, but the latter remained a constant threat to the established order. It criticized the traditionalists who were in power for being too cautious, too moderate, too conservative, and too deferential to established temporal and spiritual institutions. The radicals wanted a more forceful and egalitarian form of authoritarianism. They remained uncompromisingly committed to a revolutionism of the far right.

Accordingly, there arose in each of the states of Eastern Europe a political movement (sometimes more than one) demanding a policy of aggressive authoritarian militancy. In Poland it was first the Camp of Great Poland and then the Camp of National Radicalism; in Romania it was the Legion of the Archangel Michael and its organized militia, the Iron Guard; and in Hungary it was Ferenc Szalasi's Arrow Cross. None of them succeeded in gaining power before the outbreak of the Second World War, but their agitation forced the moderate traditionalists to adopt measures that were more extreme than they would have liked for fear of losing the support of public opinion.

One of the succession states, however, did not conform to the typical pattern of political development in Eastern Europe. Czechoslovakia differed in important respects from its neighbors. It had a largely industrial economy, at least in the western part of the country, and a vigorous, assertive middle class free from the political influence of a conservative, landowning aristocracy. The doctrines of secularism and anticlericalism were widely accepted, even by the Czech masses. And the leader of the republic, Tomáš Masaryk, was no Pilsudski or Horthy. He was firmly committed to the principles of parliamentary government, principles that most of his countrymen seemed to embrace as well. Here, then, was a nation regarded throughout Europe as an outpost of Western democracy in a region still in the grip of Eastern conservatism.

And yet even here there were important traditionalist forces and movements not very different from those influential in the other succession states. Czechoslovakia was a multinational country, even more so than its neighbors. The Czechs, the dominant ethnic community and the one most supportive of the new republican regime and its constitutional foundation, made up barely half the population. The others often felt neglected or ignored, some of them complaining openly that they were the victims of discrimination and that only through a fundamental alteration in the system of government could they achieve justice. There were even whispered suggestions that the dissolution of the state might not be an altogether bad idea. Many members of the German minority, for example, began to believe, especially after Hitler came to power, that only a union of the Sudeten region with the Third Reich could save them from Czech oppression. Konrad Henlein's Sudeten German Party, though officially asking for nothing more than autonomy, sought in fact outright secession. In the southeast, the Hungarians continued to hope that one day they might be able to rejoin their countrymen on the other side of the border. Some of them even became sympathizers of the Arrow Cross. And in Ruthenia, the easternmost region of the Czechoslovak Republic, the Ukrainian majority felt closer to its ethnic compatriots in Poland, Romania, and the Soviet Union than to its official countrymen.

But the most serious threat to the stability of Czechoslovakia, at least internally, was among the Slovaks. That may seem paradoxical, since they were, in theory at least, the Czechs' partners in the government and administration of the republic. But they were junior partners, clearly subordinate numerically, politically, economically, and culturally. Slovakia, largely agricultural, devout in its religious faith, still loyal to the traditions and pieties of a preindustrial society, felt slighted and sometimes patronized by the Czechs. As soon as the republic was established, some Slovak leaders began to complain that promises about the equal division of power between the two dominant nationalities were being broken, that the Slovaks were becoming relegated to an inferior position, and that only a reorganization of the republic by which Slovakia would acquire autonomy could protect its population against political subservience.

The separatist forces remained contained during the 1920s, but they were never completely silenced. Andrej Hlinka's Slovak People's Party in particular continued to oppose what it described as Czech hegemony, insisting that the promise of equality between the two major nationalities made at the time of the republic's establishment was constantly being broken. The coming of the Great Depression strengthened the various secessionist movements in Czechoslovakia, reinforcing political discontent with economic hardship. The death of Masaryk in 1937, like the death of Pilsudski in Poland two years earlier, removed from the political scene the one public figure who could still command respect even among those who disagreed with his policies. Thereafter the forces of disintegration began rapidly to gain strength, as foreign pressure, especially that exerted by the Third Reich, aggravated domestic dissatisfaction. By the time of the Munich Conference in the fall of 1938, Czechoslovakia stood helpless, confronting not only a grave military danger from abroad but a paralyzing political crisis at home.

For the Jews of Eastern Europe, the interwar years became a period of bitter disappointment. It had begun with such promise, such great hope. The constitutions of all the states in the region spoke of the equality of all citizens, whatever their religion, culture, or ethnic background. They proclaimed or at least implied that the process of emancipation which had started more than a century before was about to be completed. Jews and Gentiles alike would henceforth be free to acquire any education they proved qualified for. They would have the right to enter any profession, establish any business, choose any cultural or artistic occupation, and participate in any political or social movement. There would no longer be any limits, except talent and luck, to what a Jew might achieve. Could anyone doubt that? Were not the liberal promises of the new order in Eastern Europe clear and unambiguous? What the Jewish community had sought so eagerly and persistently in the years before the war seemed at last to have been achieved.

But disillusionment set in almost at once. It became increasingly clear that despite constitutional declarations and official promises, anti-Semitic hostility remained a powerful force in the life of the succession states, especially in times of tension, insecurity, and hardship. As soon as the war was over, the Jews found themselves involved in the conflicts of various nationalities in Eastern Europe over disputed boundaries and minority enclaves. In November 1918, after Polish troops seized Lvov, which had been briefly occupied by the Ukrainians, they embarked on a rampage through the Jewish quarter, looting, beating, and even killing some of its inhabitants. A few months later there were pogroms in Pinsk, Lida, and Vilna. During the Russian advance into Poland in 1920, the Polish high command interned some of the Jews serving in the army as a precautionary measure against espionage and betrayal. Were they not likely to be in secret sympathy with Bolshevism, like many of their coreligionists? The Polish state, its independence only recently restored, remained distrustful of the various minorities within its borders, and of the Jews most of all.

The situation in Romania was similar. Here the anti-Semitism of the masses was reinforced, as in Poland, by the anti-Semitism of the patriciate. The universities in particular were centers of opposition to the corruptive "Jewish influence." In 1922, for example, the medical schools in Bucharest, Cluj, and Iasi were disrupted by rioting students who demanded that Jews be forbidden to dissect Christian cadavers. By the end of the year these disorders had become so widespread that the government was forced to close the universities temporarily. Continuing demands that the number of Jews in institutions of higher learning be restricted, or that Jewish students be forbidden to sit next to non-Jewish students, or that Jewish physicians be prohibited from treating Christian patients reflected a profound anti-Semitic prejudice based on obsessive fears and hatreds.

One of the most common justifications for this pervasive enmity was the charge that Jews were in alliance with the foreign enemies of the state—with Bolsheviks, in the case of Poland, or with Hungarians in the Romanian kingdom. This latter charge, though exaggerated, was not entirely without foundation. Hungary had historically been far more tolerant of its Jewish minority than Romania, and after 1918 many of the Jews in Transylvania, previously Hungarian but now Romanian, regretted the change in their national status. Yet that did not always protect the Jewish minority in diminished Hungary against the same accusations that the Jewish minorities elsewhere in Eastern Europe had to face. Here too ideological conflicts, territorial disputes, social tensions, and economic hardships intensified ethnic antagonisms. The anti-Semitic rhetoric that could be heard so loudly in Poland and Romania began to spread in Hungary as well.

Thus there were growing complaints that while real Hungarians were enduring terrible hardships as a result of the war, the Jews were acquiring more and more wealth and influence. They were flooding the professions, the arts, the universities, and the press. But even that was not enough for them. They were continuing to seek political domination, to strive for control of the government. Just look at the Communist regime that the Jew Béla Kun had established in Hungary in the spring of 1919. If he had succeeded, Hungary would have become a Bolshevik state just like Russia. And though he failed, there were many others like him, with the same goals and designs, agitating, inciting, and conspiring. Where would it all end?

The Hungarian government as well as the public remained more skeptical than those in most succession states about allegations of a Jewish plot to rule Christian society. But the authorities in Budapest were well aware of a rising tide of anti-Semitism and a growing demand for action against the danger of alien domination. In 1920 they even thought it best to promulgate a law by which the percentage of students of various "races and nationalities" admitted to institutions of higher learning was to be restricted to the percentage of those "races and nationalities" in the population at large. There was no mention of Jews, and yet there could be no doubt whom the legislation was chiefly directed against. To be sure, the restrictions were never rigidly enforced and were eventually allowed to lapse. But to the Jewish community in Hungary, they were a clear warning that its members were not entirely safe from the discriminations and persecutions threatening their coreligionists elsewhere in Eastern Europe.

The anti-Semitic agitation of the immediate postwar years seemed to diminish in the middle and late 1920s. Armed conflicts over frontiers and minorities gradually came to an end—not to everyone's satisfaction, to be sure, but reflecting the growing recognition that using military force to rectify remaining grievances might prove self-defeating. The return of peace moreover had the effect of promoting economic recovery. The future began to look a little more stable, a little more secure. Not only were ethnic grievances no longer provoking armed conflict, but fundamental ideological differences were grudgingly being accepted as unalterable realities, at least for the time being. And that meant that the Soviet Union and the succession states became reconciled to an uneasy coexistence, each still suspicious of the other, but neither prepared to wage war. There were even some signs that the struggling liberalism of Eastern Europe was slowly gaining strength, becoming more confident, more assertive. Many Jews now began to believe or at least hope that the promised emancipation of their community, which had proved unattainable in the early 1920s, might still be achieved a decade later.

They were tragically mistaken. The coming of the Great Depression destroyed whatever chance there was of overcoming the forces of anti-Semitic hostility. In fact, the Jewry of Europe now faced a danger greater than any in almost two thousand years. And yet there was a certain cruel logic in the rapid intensification of ethnic bigotry during the decade preceding the Second World War. The nineteenth century had shown that the liberal doctrines of tolerance and benevolence were most likely to flourish in an atmosphere of peace, prosperity, and optimism. The twentieth century was about to demonstrate that privation, insecurity, and fear were bound to breed suspicion and prejudice. Those who had to endure hunger and suffering or the fear of hunger and suffering needed some clear, simple explanation of the crisis they were confronting. They had little patience with lectures about the intricacies of economics or the complexities of the financial market or the mysteries of supply and demand. There had to be some other reason for the dangers threatening society, a more apparent, more comprehensible reason. There had to be some plot, some scheme, some conspiracy that was responsible for the coming of the depression. And so more and more people began to believe that behind that plot or scheme or conspiracy, Jewish cunning and Jewish avarice were likely to lurk.

More than that, the result of the economic crisis was an enormous shift to the right in the politics of Eastern Europe. The contention that the various parliamentary parties represented nothing more than selfish class interests unwilling to subordinate private gain to public good began to sound plausible amid mounting unemployment and growing poverty. Perhaps it was really true that only some authoritarian form of government, disciplined, forceful, determined, and incorruptible, could save the nation from disaster. In Poland, the right-wing National Party and even the more militant National Radical Camp began to gain strength at the expense of the more traditional conservative parties. In Romania, the followers of Corneliu Codreanu, head of the Iron Guard, steadily increased in number, while two of the most virulent anti-Semites in political life, Octavian Goga and Alexandru Cuza, became for a time leading members of the cabinet. In Hungary, the appointment of the racist Gyula Gombos as prime minister did not lead to an official policy of anti-Semitism, as the Jews had feared, but the government did draw closer to Hitler's Germany and Mussolini's Italy. Ferenc Szalasi's fascistic Arrow Cross, moreover, continued to grow throughout the decade. There could be no question that the cautious, middle-of-the-road politics of Eastern Europe during the late 1920s were by the late 1930s veering more and more to the right.

Changes in the relative strength of the various political parties and movements were not the only sign of a growing tendency toward authoritarianism. More or less spontaneous expressions of mass discontent with the established order, especially with the status of the Jewish community, were an even more striking expression of the shift in public opinion toward right-wing radicalism. New outbursts of anti-Semitic violence soon exceeded in intensity any of those in the immediate postwar years. In Poland there were pogroms in Grodno, Minsk Mazowiecki, Brest, and, the most brutal of all, Czestochowa. There were other signs of rising hostility toward Jews, less violent but frighteningly ominous. Some of the institutions of higher learning, which enjoyed a measure of autonomy in their internal administration—the University of Vilna, for example, and the Polytechnical Institute in Lvov—began to require Jewish students to sit in segregated sections of the classroom, a provision that the students publicly protested against by remaining standing during lectures. Many professional organizations, especially associations of physicians and journalists, voted to exclude Jews from their membership. And then there were boycotts of Jewish banks, factories, and stores, only too familiar in the past, but never on such a scale or with such fervor.

Manifestations of this increasing enmity toward Jews could also be found in Romania and Hungary, but nowhere were they as evident or common as in Poland. Here there was a chorus of complaints about the corruptive influence of Jewish clannishness, Jewish ambition, Jewish covetousness, and Jewish radicalism. Indeed, the anti-Semitic rhetoric of the rightist parties in the succession states was indistinguishable in most respects from that of Hitler's Germany. Even in Czechoslovakia, the most liberal and tolerant of those states, the public was becoming more suspicious of the Jewish minority by the end of the decade. This was especially true of the Slovak half of the republic, which economically, socially, and culturally resembled its neighbors to the north and east more than its political partners to the west. Yet the Czechs too, once they started to feel threatened by the aggressive diplomacy of the Third Reich, began to regard the Jewish community with uneasiness and distrust.

In February 1939, George F. Kennan, at that time secretary of the American legation in Prague, reported to Washington that "the Slovak Jews . . . are the object of widespread resentment on the part of the Slovak population." Indeed, "their dress, their manners, and their habits are conspicuous and—to many Slovaks—offensive." There was a feeling "prevalent in many Slovak circles" that "the Jews have always sided with the oppressors of the Slovaks against the native population." That was why the leaders of the newly autonomous Slovak regime, in discussing the "Jewish question," made it clear "that the influence of the Jews in the political and economic life of Slovakia would have to be eliminated, and that the Slovak government would not shy at extreme measures in pursuing this purpose." Their tone was ominous, even more ominous than was recognized at the time.[1]

Most surprising was the spread of anti-Semitism among the Czechs. In July 1938, after the diplomatic crisis in the Sudeten region had raised the possibility of a military conflict but two months before the Munich agreement left Czechoslovakia defenseless, R. H. Hadow, who had recently been the British chargé d'affaires in Prague, commented on the rising animosity toward Jews. The common assumption that "there is no anti-Semitic feeling among the Czechs" was "quite incorrect," he found.

In fact, the Jews were complaining constantly that they were disliked by both sides, Hadow reported, "by the German-speaking . . . minority as anti-Germans, [and] by the Czechs as 'Germans' because they speak and use that language for business purposes, support the German (and not the Czech) opera as giving more scope for music, . . . and must—in order to live—trade with Germany." The Jews were also being accused of seeking to dominate such professions as medicine and law, not to mention the world of business, thereby earning "the most unfortunate dislike of Czech and Sudeten students alike." Hadow concluded that "in Czechoslovakia as in the other countries . . . there is a deep-seated *popular* prejudice against [the Jews] due largely to their success and 'encroachment' upon restricted fields of activity." Many of the Jews, moreover, were "only too well aware" of this prejudice, "and it is a source of great anxiety to them." They had good reasons for feeling anxious.[2]

The rising tide of anti-Semitism led almost inevitably to the adoption of measures designed to counter or appear to counter that insidious Jewish influence. In Poland, the legislature voted to prohibit ritual slaughter, a prescribed religious practice of Orthodox Judaism, as inhumane, although the government eventually suspended enforcement of this law in communities in which Jews constituted more than 3 percent of the population. Romania promulgated a law requiring that at least 80 percent of the employees in any economic enterprise be Romanians, not "foreigners." Although Jews were not specifically identified as belonging in the latter category, many of them feared, with justification, that the measure was intended to limit their participation in the workforce. In Hungary, legislation seeking to achieve the same end was more direct. All industrial, commercial, and financial enterprises were to reduce the proportion of their Jewish employees and the share of the payroll that those employees received to no more than 20 percent, while the admission of Jews to the practice of medicine, law, and engineering was to be restricted until their percentage in those professions shrank to 20 as well. Quotas of this sort were widely considered a necessary form of self-defense against the alleged Jewish preponderance in economic life about which there were so many complaints.

The most drastic of the various measures restricting the number of Jews in the professions was promulgated on the eve of the Second World War. In April 1939, only a month after Slovakia became an independent state—nominally, at least—its government issued a decree limiting the number of Jewish lawyers in the bar associations to no more than 4 percent of the membership and ordering that Jewish lawyers represent only Jews, "except in cases where there is no other lawyer." The restrictions imposed on Jews in publishing and journalism were even more severe. "A Jew may be an editor only of a Jewish periodical, that is, of a periodical which is expressly designated as such and which promotes the interest of the Jewish faith and of Jewish culture." The power to influence and shape public opinion was to be denied to those suspected of disloyalty or even subversion. How else could the nation's security be protected?[3]

To the new Slovak government, these restrictions were merely the first part of what was intended to be a comprehensive system of anti-Semitic legislation. That was clear not only to the Jewish and the non-Jewish communities but also to many outside observers. Barely three weeks after the promulgation of the April decree, Kennan wrote to the State Department that "this is, of course, only a portion of the anti-Semitic program of the Slovak leaders." The government was now preparing to deal with the problems created by the prominent role of Jews in the medical profession, by the "Jewish predominance in business and finance," and by Jewish landownership. It was clear, moreover, that the "irresponsible elements of the population . . . in Slovakia . . . will keep pace with the legislative authorities in the general endeavor to reduce the wealth and influence of the Jewish population." The next few years were to demonstrate the accuracy of that prediction.[4]

There were striking similarities between the anti-Semitic legislation adopted by the succession states and the anti-Semitic legislation of the Third Reich. But just as striking were the similarities of the rhetoric that each employed to justify that legislation. In Eastern as in Central Europe, there were complaints about Jewish guile and greed, about the growing Jewish domination of the economy, about the excessive number of Jews in the professions, and about their disproportionate role in national politics and culture. Yet, even more seriously, they were being accused of seeking to rule the native population through the power of money and the promotion of communism. They were in fact the gravest threat confronting European society. Only the most resolute measures could defeat their evil designs.

The ideological resemblance between the anti-Semitic movement in Germany on one side and in Poland, Romania, Hungary, and Slovakia on the other was in fact so close as to suggest some form of collaboration between them. They feared the same danger and opposed the same enemy. They advocated the same drastic measures to oppose the designs of world Jewry. And they claimed to protect the national interest and tradition against alien forces of subversion. Would it not have been reasonable to assume that they were consulting with one another, that they were exchanging ideas, comparing experiences, and coordinating strategies? Common interests and purposes generally lead to common strategies and efforts.

In the case of Germany and the succession states, however, important territorial disputes and diplomatic differences outweighed ideological similarities and sympathies. In international diplomacy, the Third Reich became the leader of the revisionist movement, which argued that since the peace treaties following the First World War were vindictive and unjust, they should be abrogated or at least revised. It was a contention that the losers of the conflict found irrefutable. But the winners refused to budge. Had they suffered millions upon millions of casualties, had they sacrificed so much of their wealth, only to return to the prewar boundaries? That was simply out of the question. They might have been willing to make minor concessions here and there, but the new map of Europe must remain essentially unaltered. The revisionist states had started the war, and now they would have to pay the price for their arrogance and folly.

That was the view of almost all political parties in Poland, even those that shared National Socialism's views regarding parliamentary democracy and the "Jewish question." If Hitler's demands for the abrogation of the Versailles Treaty were met, what would happen to Poland's western provinces—to Posen, West Prussia, and Upper Silesia? Would that not also encourage the Ukrainians to renew their demands for the independence of eastern Galicia? And what would then become of all those hopes of regaining the power and prestige that Poland had enjoyed in the sixteenth century? To the Romanians, talk about revising the postwar territorial settlements sounded just as ominous. It threatened their recent acquisition of Bukovina, of a large part of the Banat, and, most important, of Transylvania. Their nation might be reduced once again to the position of just another small, weak, comic-opera Balkan kingdom. And as for Czechoslovakia, revision of the peace treaties could mean something much worse than a violent disagreement over controversial boundaries or disputed provinces, much worse even than the loss of the Sudeten region. It might threaten the very existence of the republic; it might lead to its partition and destruction. Only in Hungary, the proportionately biggest loser in the First World War, did the prospect of abrogating the Treaty of Trianon meet with enthusiastic support. Here there was an obvious harmony between national interest and international anti-Semitism.

To the leaders of the Third Reich, it was clear from the outset that they could not count on sympathy among the rightist parties of Eastern Europe, not even among those that were most authoritarian and racist. A common hostility toward Jews was not enough to outweigh irreconcilable differences over the territorial status quo in the region. Therefore German policy prior to the outbreak of the Second World War was to proceed with a domestic solution to the "Jewish question" by encouraging or forcing the emigration of Jews from the Third Reich. There was no attempt to coordinate these efforts with anti-Semitic movements abroad. The underlying assumption was that a large-scale movement of German Jews to other countries would intensify anti-Semitism in those countries, and that in turn would lead to greater international understanding of and sympathy for the racial doctrines of National Socialism. The allegations in some foreign countries of ethnic brutality by the Third Reich would diminish once those countries also had to confront the problem of what to do about the pernicious Jewish influence in economy and culture.

Hitler seemed to embrace this strategy, at least as long as Europe was still at peace and he could continue achieving his objectives by diplomatic means. In November 1938, during a conversation with Oswald Pirow, the South African minister of defense, commerce, and industry, he maintained that "he was only exporting one idea." That was not the idea of National Socialism, since Germany was actually strengthened by the failure of other countries to accept the ideology of "power and creative force." The Führer was "exporting anti-Semitism." Pirow thought that "international Jewry" would be only too glad to use the "Jewish question" to incite discord between France and Britain on one side and Germany on the other. But Hitler maintained that "every state was already putting up a defense against the Jewish question." Why change a policy that was not only protecting the Third Reich against the machinations of a traitorous minority but also winning sympathy and support abroad?[5]

Two months later the foreign ministry in Berlin sent a circular to all German diplomatic missions and consulates abroad analyzing "the Jewish question as a factor in foreign policy." This was essentially an elaboration of the views that Hitler had outlined in his conversation with Pirow. While it was an important task of the Third Reich to direct and control Jewish emigration, the circular explained, "there is no reason for cooperating in the solution of this problem with other countries such as Poland, Hungary and Rumania," which were trying to encourage the departure of their own Jewish minorities. Experience had shown that "parallel interests compete with one another in such a procedure," interfering with the efforts of National Socialism to promote the emigration of German Jews. Let each nation deal with the "Jewish question" in its own way. Any attempt to rely on international cooperation in solving the racial problem was bound to prove self-defeating.[6]

The government's decision to act independently was proving a success, the foreign ministry maintained. There had been those who feared that the exodus of Jews from the Third Reich would lead to the rise abroad of "boycott nests and anti-German centers." But such timid souls had been shown to be wrong. It was now evident that "in all parts of the world the influx of Jews arouses the resistance of the native population and thus provides the best propaganda for Germany's Jewish policy." In both North and South America, in France as well as Holland, in Scandinavia as well as Greece, "wherever the Jewish migratory current flows," a marked growth of anti-Semitism had occurred. "It must be a task of German foreign policy to encourage this anti-Semitic wave." The racial doctrines of the Third Reich were not only providing protection against alien influence at home but winning sympathy and support abroad.

The circular concluded by reemphasizing that foreign criticism of the measures taken by Germany to expel the Jews, which many countries failed to understand because of their lack of experience, was only temporary. Their disapproval "will turn against the Jews themselves at the moment when visible evidence brings home to the population what the Jewish threat signifies for their own existence." As for the German government's policy of depriving the Jews of their wealth before allowing them to leave, that was not only morally justifiable but diplomatically advantageous. The poorer the emigrant Jews and the heavier the burden they imposed on their host country were, the more anti-Semitic that country would become and the more receptive it would be to National Socialist propaganda. The circular concluded with an ominous prophecy: "The goal of this German policy will be an international solution of the Jewish question in the future, not dictated by false sympathy for the 'Jewish religious minority which has been expelled,' but by the mature realization by all peoples of the danger which the Jews represent for the racial preservation of the nations."[7]

To the Jewish community of Eastern Europe, the Third Reich's decision to proceed with its racial program on its own, at least for the time being, made little difference. The anti-Semitic movement in the succession states used the same rhetoric, advocated the same legislation, and sought the same goal as the anti-Semitic movement in Central Europe. Its supporters needed no instruction from abroad regarding the danger of "Jewish subversion" or the importance of solving the "Jewish question." Indeed, popular hostility toward Jews was more profound and widespread in countries like Poland and Romania than in Germany, certainly before

1933 and perhaps even afterward. The National Socialists' arguments about the need to defend ethnic purity could be heard in a variety of forms and languages far beyond the boundaries of the Third Reich.

The coming of the Great Depression, moreover, had the same effect on the succession states as on the Weimar Republic. Rising unemployment, growing impoverishment, insecurity, fear, and bitterness all intensified a popular feeling that behind the hardships that society now had to endure lurked selfish interests and sinister forces. Liberal doctrine was merely a camouflage for class domination, parliamentary government represented only the rich and powerful, and Jewish emancipation inevitably led to Jewish domination. The result was a rapid shift in politics to the right, from an acceptance (sincere or merely professed) of parliamentary democracy to the search for a more forceful and authoritarian form of government, one that could cope with the crisis confronting the nation.

There was an important difference, however, in the form this shift assumed in Germany and in the succession states. In the case of the Weimar Republic, the Great Depression led first to a suspension of the normal functioning of the parliamentary system, officially described as only temporary, and then to brief attempts at a traditionalist right-wing regime under Franz von Papen and Kurt von Schleicher. The failure of these desperate political experiments led finally to the appointment in 1933 of Hitler as German chancellor. In the succession states, however, the conservative authoritarians prevailed over the radical authoritarians, though at a high price. Sometimes willingly, sometimes reluctantly, they had to satisfy many of the demands of the right-wing extremists. They disregarded the constitutional guarantees of parliamentary government, they suppressed political parties that seemed too far to the left, and they imposed severe restrictions on the economic and cultural role of Jews in national life. No other course was possible, they insisted. How else were they to restrain the radicals of the right, whose popular support was rapidly growing? Was it not better for the Jews to be governed by moderate anti-Semites than by fanatical racists like those in the Third Reich? The answer seemed obvious. The Jewish community should be grateful that the discrimination it now had to face was not more severe.

This was essentially the view of King Carol of Romania, according to a report that Sir Reginald Hoare, the British minister in Bucharest, sent to

London in January 1938. "His Majesty . . . was quite clear that [the Iron Guard] must be combated and that the only way to do so was to adopt part of its programme. To use force against it and so create martyrs was not the way to handle the situation, though if force became unavoidable, he would not hesitate to use it."[8]

At the same time Frank Walters, deputy secretary-general of the League of Nations, submitted to the British Foreign Office a summary of his conversation with Istrate Micescu, the Romanian minister for external affairs, whose views were essentially the same as the king's. "[He] pointed out once more that the country was in a very excited state, that the Iron Guard was expecting to increase its vote very much, and that the anti-Semite policy of the Government was absolutely necessary to enable it to prevent the Iron Guard from coming into power." Nothing was more important than that, for if the Iron Guard did come into power, the results would be disastrous. There would be a "complete volte face" in foreign policy and a "complete catastrophe" for the Romanian Jews. The avoidance of such a catastrophe, Micescu insisted, remained the objective of the government, "which was in no sense . . . fascist or totalitarian." Indeed, its goal was to oppose and defeat those who were.[9]

More than a year later, shortly before the outbreak of the Second World War, Armand Calinescu, the Romanian prime minister, was still assuring the chairman of the British section of the World Jewish Congress, Rabbi M. L. Perlzweig, that "neither he nor his Government was anti-Semitic." They had only recently suppressed the Iron Guard, an accomplishment "of great benefit to the Jews." Still, "certain elements in the life of the country" had to be taken into account. The government could not simply ignore them; it had to adopt measures "pour calmer l'opinion publique." But those measures had been introduced "deliberately in a spirit of moderation." The appeasement of popular anti-Semitism, at least to some extent, was simply unavoidable. That much was clear. The ministry, however, had consistently sought to limit its concessions to ethnic prejudice. It had remained at heart moderate and tolerant.[10]

How valid were such claims? The answer appears to be that the political leaders of the succession states were indeed by and large cautious and restrained in their view of the "Jewish question," certainly more so than the right-wing extremists for whom the Jews were the ultimate cause of all the problems facing society. Still, their acquiescence in the increasingly oppressive anti-Semitic policies of the 1930s was not simply a result of expediency. They too believed that world Jewry had gained an excessive role in economics, politics, and culture. Something had to be done to limit that role, to restrain the aspirations and ambitions of a clever, aggressive, alien minority. To be sure, they disapproved of the anti-Jewish mob violence that was becoming common in Eastern Europe. They rejected the racist rhetoric of the radical authoritarians, who demanded nothing less than the segregation and expropriation of the Jews. And yet they too felt that something must be done to loosen the grip of the Jews on their countries' wealth. They did not want to appear intolerant or bigoted, but they agreed that the most effective as well as most humane way of dealing with the problem was emigration, for the fewer Jews there were in a community, the less hostility they were likely to arouse.

In May 1937, King Carol confided to Sir Reginald Hoare his hope that "there would be no decrease in emigration to Palestine, which relieved the pressure of a most difficult problem." He had no doubt, moreover, that "a considerable number of Jewish immigrants obtained Roumanian citizenship by fraud, and he was not sure that it might not become necessary to turn them out of the country." Early the following year the king returned to the subject of Jewish emigration, sounding almost like a convert to Zionism. "With regard to the Jews, some measures must be taken to relieve the pressure," Hoare reported him as saying, "and His Majesty mentioned various parts of the world where Jews might perhaps be admitted." The best thing, however, would be "an independent Jewish state," and the king regretted that the British government "had not originally tackled the Palestine problem from that aspect." It would have made things so much easier for Romania.[11]

Emigration, however, was not the only means by which Romanian statesmen proposed to deal with the "Jewish question." There was also expulsion. Investigations conducted by the government had revealed or were alleged to have revealed that a large number of Jews had entered the country illegally, that they were therefore aliens under the law, and that they could and should be deported to wherever they had come from. At the very least, they ought to be deprived of Romanian citizenship and of whatever wealth they might have acquired by their deception. In the meeting with Rabbi Perlzweig in June 1939, Prime Minister Calinescu tried to reassure his visitor that "in the matter of the revision of nationality only a third of the cases examined had been struck off the list of citizens." The number should really have been greater, he explained, "but many cases had been viewed with an 'oeil indulgent.' " The rabbi countered that the "oeil indulgent" had apparently been closed on many occasions, upon which the prime minister promised to look into the problem more closely. But he would not retreat from the view that investigations into illegal immigration were justified and that those who had knowingly participated in it ought to be deported. How else could the country be protected against an ambitious and aggressive minority?[12]

The conviction that there were too many Jews in Eastern Europe was not confined to the rightist parties of various shades and intensities. Those who sympathized with a middle-of-the-road liberalism and even many supporters of the moderate, reformist left agreed that the deep-seated ethnic tensions in society had to be reduced. Emigration was the best way. It would enable true Poles or Romanians or Hungarians or Slovaks to regain the economic and cultural predominance that had been gradually usurped by shrewd Semitic outsiders. The necessary reduction in the number of Jews should be achieved fairly and humanely, to be sure, without excessive violence or blatant bigotry. There was no reason that the process of emigration, if carried out in a correct, professional manner, should lead to lasting resentment or bitterness on either side. Surely it must be clear to Jews and non-Jews alike that a lessening of mutual hostility through peaceful separation would be advantageous to both.

This was the view expressed in 1941 by Józef Retinger, personal secretary to the leader of the Polish government in exile in London, Wladyslaw Sikorski. Poland had by then been occupied for two years by the armies of the Third Reich. The Jewish minority had been pauperized and ghettoized; indeed, the initiation of a program of mass extermination was only a few months away. But in a book dealing with Poland's tragic situation, Retinger remained preoccupied with the problems that his nation had faced before the war and that it would surely have to face again afterward. Among the most important of those problems was "the largest agglomeration of Jews in Europe." But not only in Europe: Poland had the highest percentage of Jewish inhabitants of any country in the world. And that was bound to lead to serious ethnic frictions and hostilities. "The three and a half million Jews concentrated in Poland give the greater part of the towns and cities a specific character owing to the radically different social structure and powerful separatism of the Jewish inhabitants."

Retinger was no racist, no rabid anti-Semite. He was a typical centrist politician who disapproved not only of the genocidal program of the German National Socialists but also of the virulent xenophobia of the Polish right-wing extremists. Yet he, like most moderate statesmen in Eastern Europe, still believed that there were too many Jews in his country, that most of them were and always would be unassimilable, and that their role in economic life was excessive and detrimental. "In countries which have a preponderance of agricultural population, the concentration of two-thirds of the Jewish population within the cities and Jewish ownership of two-thirds of trade and one-fourth of industry and handicrafts cannot but lead to perturbations in the economic structure of the State." And the worst of those perturbations was that "the natural expansion of the Gentile population has been inhibited and stopped."

What was to be done? Retinger had a ready answer, the same as most of the East European political leaders before the war. "The only solution for this burning question is that offered by emigration." There had in fact been the beginning of a mass exodus of Polish Jews in the second half of the nineteenth century. But the economic crises of the interwar period had led everywhere to a closing of the gates to emigrants from the succession states. And now "the Polish Republic, the Polish nation, and the Jewish community in Poland" had to think of some way to solve the problem. "New fields for emigration must be found and the necessary capital funds must be mobilised." The "Jewish question" had ceased to be of importance only to Poland. "It has assumed an international character," Retinger insisted, "and requires the collaboration not only of Jewish circles but also of those countries which still dispose of areas available for immigrant settlement." No nation could deal with this problem alone; any solution would have to depend on the collaboration of all the nations of Europe—indeed, of the world. That solution, whatever its nature, was bound to affect profoundly not only the Jews but also all the other nationalities of Eastern Europe: the Poles, Romanians, Hungarians, Czechs, Slovaks, Lithuanians, and Latvians. All of them were waiting anxiously for an answer.[13]

On this last point Retinger was certainly right. During the late 1930s, the governments of all the succession states began to insist more and more loudly that the "Jewish question" must be internationalized, that the small, impoverished, landlocked countries of the region could not be expected to solve it without the assistance of the democratic great powers in Western Europe and the New World. That assistance might be extended through the League of Nations, through some international committee representing several states, or even through bilateral agreements between countries eager to promote the departure of Jews and countries willing to accept them. But by whatever means or procedures, the problem had to be dealt with by the international community. In the meantime, since the international community did not seem eager to assume that responsibility, the statesmen of Eastern Europe began to introduce measures designed, in part at least, to hasten or appear to hasten emigration. The authors of those measures generally recognized that their effect on the size of the Jewish population was likely to be slight. But they might serve to appease the growing anti-Semitism of the public temporarily.

In Poland, for example, the government adopted legislation in 1938 declaring that any citizen who had lived abroad for five years and "had given up all contact with the Polish state" could lose his citizenship. His passport would no longer be valid unless he obtained an endorsement certifying that his national status had not been revoked. Although Jews were not specifically mentioned in this legislation, they were clearly its intended targets. Of the 261 Polish residents in Portugal whose citizenship was annulled during the three months preceding the outbreak of war in 1939, some 85 percent had Jewish first names. But this modest achievement of the expulsion program was far outweighed by its effect on the Third Reich, which, afraid of being permanently burdened with the approximately 70,000 Jews from Poland still living within its frontiers, decided to expel all of them. The Polish government was eventually forced, though only with great reluctance and after a long delay, to readmit the resented and unwanted refugees.[14]

At about the same time the Romanian government was introducing a similar policy of civic exclusion or deprivation directed against the Jewish community. When King Carol complained in 1937 that many Jews had entered the country illegally and had become citizens by fraud, and that it might therefore be necessary to expel them, he was expressing a view prevalent not only among the masses but also among the well-to-do elite. Early the following year the authorities promulgated legislation "concerning the revision of citizenship," which had the effect of reducing more than a third of Romanian Jews to a condition of statelessness. It led to a sharp decline in the number of Jews in finance, industry, and commerce as well as the professions, becoming an important part of the exclusionary program designed to impose a quota system, the *numerus vallachicus*, on the proportion of "foreigners" in the national economy. But its effect on Jewish emigration was minimal. Not that the Jews were reluctant to leave, but where were they to go? Romania's neighbors were as eager as Romania to encourage the departure of their Jews. The last thing they wanted was to admit more of them. For better or worse, the Jews had to remain where they were.[15]

Even Czechoslovakia eventually adopted the same exclusionary policy as most of the other countries of Eastern Europe. At first it was willing to accept at least some Jewish refugees from the Third Reich. After all, they too had to face a German threat, they too were being attacked by Nazi propaganda, they too had to rely on the support of sympathetic democratic states. But the Munich Agreement of September 1938 changed all that. The Czech population, now feeling abandoned and betrayed, began to regard the Jews, especially émigrés from Germany, as responsible in part for the hostility they had aroused and for the dangerous situation of the only succession state that had offered them asylum. Early in 1939, Sir Herbert Emerson, director of the Intergovernmental Committee on Refugees, reported after a visit to Prague that there was growing resentment among the Czechs of Jewish immigrants from Germany and that the government would like to arrange for their departure. Hostility toward Jews from the Sudetenland, who had only recently managed to escape persecution by the Third Reich, was especially intense, so that the authorities were determined, "partly for racial reasons," to expel any who were not Czech citizens. Anti-Semitic prejudice in the doomed republic, only two months before its destruction, was becoming almost as bitter as in Poland, Romania, and Hungary.[16]

It soon became clear to the statesmen of Eastern Europe, however, that their efforts to encourage Jewish emigration were at best a drop in the bucket. The only way to reduce the number of Jews significantly was to provide them with areas of resettlement or colonization, preferably outside Europe, perhaps in some distant and sparsely inhabited continent or region where they could live on their own without competing against a resentful native population. But that solution required the cooperation of the great powers, especially Britain. And so throughout the late 1930s the succession states made repeated efforts to find a solution to the "Jewish question" through internationalization. The leader in this diplomatic campaign was Poland. Indeed, by the time of the outbreak of the Second World War, finding such a solution had become almost an obsession with some of the Polish statesmen. They continued to plead, argue, and threaten ever more loudly, until they themselves became victims of a cruel ethnic bigotry.

In September 1936, Colonel Józef Beck, the minister for foreign affairs in Warsaw, raised the question of Jewish emigration before the League of Nations, demanding that facilities be provided for the annual departure of between 80,000 and 100,000 Jews from Poland. In response to such demands, a commission was sent the following spring to investigate the possibility of Jewish migration to Madagascar, which was widely regarded as a suitable site for the resettlement of European Jewry, in part because it was so far from Europe. When the plan was finally abandoned early in 1938, Polish diplomacy began to consider alternatives, some of them rather surprising. In the fall of that same year, Józef Lipski, Warsaw's ambassador to Germany, reported a conversation in which Hitler had said that "he has in mind an idea for settling the Jewish problem by way of emigration to the colonies in accordance with an understanding with Poland, Hungary, and possibly also Rumania." Lipski's reply was jocular but certainly not dismissive. "I told him that if he finds such a solution, we will erect . . . a beautiful monument [to him] in Warsaw." There was no reason that even diplomatic opponents should not work together to solve a serious common problem.[17]

Polish efforts to enlist the aid of the great powers in facilitating Jewish emigration from Eastern Europe became increasingly insistent, even threatening in tone. Toward the end of 1938, *Political Information*, the organ of the Polish foreign office, criticized "certain governments" because, though having the means for solving the "Jewish problem," they underestimated its importance. Those governments should help promote Jewish emigration from countries like Poland instead of forcing them "to resort to drastic measures." The Polish ambassador in London, Count Edward Raczynski, was more explicit. "If nothing was done for the Polish Jews," he warned the British foreign office, "the Polish Government would inevitably be forced to adopt the same kind of policy as the German Government, and indeed to draw closer to that Government in its general policy." Only the outbreak of war nine months later freed the statesmen in Warsaw from the need to decide whether to carry out that threat.[18]

The views of the Polish government were widely shared by the other leaders of the succession states. They too believed that the Jews were an alien and disruptive element in the national community. They too felt that something had to be done to reduce their excessive and harmful influence. The obvious answer—indeed, the only answer—was Jewish emigration. The population of Eastern Europe was in general agreement with this opinion. If anything, the masses were even more convinced of the need to reduce the number of Jews living among them. But how was that to be achieved? There could surely be no solution other than mass emigration. Or could there?

3

A French Predicament

To most European Jews at the opening of the twentieth century, those members of their community who lived west of the Vistula and the Carpathian Mountains (barely a fourth of the total) were a favored elite. They did not have to face the injustices and discriminations that their coreligionists in Russia, Poland, Romania, and Lithuania were constantly struggling against. They were not forced to endure the insults and accusations, prohibitions and boycotts, or assaults and pogroms that were so familiar in the east. The Jewish minorities in France, England, Belgium, and Holland, even in Hohenzollern Germany and Hapsburg Austria, enjoyed rights and opportunities denied to the Jews of the czarist empire. There were no quotas restricting the number of Jews allowed to enter the universities or practice one of the learned professions or seek recognition in the arts or gain prominence in politics. To those in Eastern Europe, that seemed almost unbelievable. Only a few hundred miles from where they were living were countries in which they would be treated with respect, as citizens, as equals, in the same way as Gentiles. How could there be such a vast difference in the ethnic attitudes of neighboring states?

The difference was in fact not quite as vast as the oppressed Jewish masses in the east imagined. Beyond the frontiers of Russia, anti-Semitism was by no means unknown. Even in France and England, and certainly in Germany and Austria, there were those who regarded Jews with disdain, resentment, or alarm. But in those countries bigotry appeared mostly in an extralegal, unwritten form, in speech and conduct rather than in formal legislation. On paper, Jewish citizens enjoyed full or almost full equality, their status under the law providing them with advantages that Jews farther to the east viewed with wonder and envy. If only they could someday achieve the same status!

That was the reason that in the early years of the century, so many well-to-do East European Jews sent their sons abroad to attend a university. On the other side of the border, anyone who had the educational qualifications and the financial resources could enter an institution of higher learning. French, Swiss, Austrian, and especially German universities attracted many Jewish students from the east, not all of them from wealthy families. Even some whose resources were only modest scrimped and scraped to earn a diploma, which might open the gates of opportunity. For that matter, quite a few Jewish businessmen and professionals from Russia, Poland, and Romania settled in the nations of Central or Western Europe, where they might still be unable to acquire citizenship, but where the status of resident alien would at least provide them with the acceptance and security they were unlikely to find in their native country.

The First World War accelerated and expanded this gradual westward migration. Once it became clear that all the constitutional declarations and official pronouncements about the equality of all citizens, whatever their religion or ethnicity, in the succession states were only paper promises, the drift of the Jewish population from east to west resumed on a much broader scale. It would no doubt have been broader still if the Soviet Union had not closed its doors to emigration to the capitalistic world. Many of the Jews living there—some for ideological reasons, others because of the government's antireligious policy, and still others as a result of economic hardship and privation—would have been only too willing to start a new life on the other side of the border. But the Kremlin remained adamant. Still, even without the participation of the Jewish community of Russia, the 1920s witnessed a substantial increase in the movement of European Jews to the west.

But this time the migrants were no longer primarily well-to-do financiers, industrialists, doctors, lawyers, journalists, artists, and scholars. More and more of them came from the drab, crowded Jewish quarters of Warsaw, Vilnius, and Bucharest or from the impoverished shtetls and villages of the succession states. Their main goal, moreover, was not to gain the prominence and recognition that had been denied them in their native countries, but to earn a modest livelihood in an environment free from the prejudices and discriminations with which they had grown up. Most of them sought refuge by legal means, by qualifying for admission under the immigration laws of their host nation. But some succeeded in escaping westward by subterfuge or quasi-lawful devices, by claiming to be visitors, tourists, temporary laborers, or relatives of legal residents. Quite a few immigrated unlawfully, by using false papers or disappearing while in transit or hiring a professional smuggler. Those techniques became familiar in every European country whose standard of living was substantially higher than that of the impoverished, hungry populace of a backward neighboring state. And the chief motive was familiar as well: the quest for a stable and secure source of livelihood.

Hence the way of life of many of the postwar immigrants was entirely different from that which the prewar immigrants had sought. Refugees from the eastern ghettos had no desire for assimilation or acculturation. They had no wish to become indistinguishable from the native elite or to gain admittance to the social or cultural patriciate. They preferred to live in a modest neighborhood, among shopkeepers and skilled workers, surrounded by other immigrants from the east, conversing usually in Yiddish, the mother tongue, recalling the old days of struggle and hardship, and exchanging nostalgic stories about the way of life they had left behind. In all the countries of Cental and Western Europe, and especially in the big cities—Berlin, Vienna, Paris, London, Brussels, and Amsterdam—there were now colonies of eastern Jews, clearly distinguishable by speech, dress, and manner from the native inhabitants.

Their presence was sometimes a source of embarrassment to the local, established Jewish communities, which had only recently managed to gain acceptance, after insisting for a long time that their members were good, loyal Germans, Austrians, Frenchmen, or Englishmen. Now they suddenly saw their new-won respectability threatened by the strange, foreign-looking migrants from the east. Their uneasiness was reinforced by the inflammatory diatribes of an anti-Semitic movement warning that the invasion by the Jewish "hordes" was a threat to the culture and civilization of the

West. Long before the establishment of the Third Reich there were signs that the gradual spread of eastern Jews across Europe was arousing popular concern and opposition.

Yet throughout the 1920s the westward expansion of the Jewish community continued. Its chief motive was economic hardship and ethnic prejudice, and its most popular destination was Germany. That may seem surprising in view of what was to happen a few years later. But the Weimar Republic was eager to demonstrate to the world its firm commitment to democratic principles and ideals. And what better way to prove that commitment than by admitting impoverished Jews from the east, offering them refuge, providing them with security, and introducing them to the achievements of Western culture? The generosity of the new republican Germany should not be exaggerated: all the governments of Europe, including the one in Berlin, maintained strict limits on the number of immigrants they were willing to accept. How else were they to protect themselves against an endless flood of refugees from the succession states? But German residence laws were less rigid than most of the others, and they were less rigidly enforced. By the time of the Great Depression, all the large urban centers of the Weimar Republic, especially Berlin, had sizable colonies of eastern Jews, recent immigrants attracted by the promise of a better and more secure way of life.

All of that changed in 1933, with the triumph of National Socialism. Germany ceased to be a destination and became instead a source of Jewish refugees. Many of the migrants seeking to escape privation or persecution, now forced to look elsewhere for help, began to shift their attention to France. The logic of that shift was obvious. France had been the first nation in Europe to proclaim Jewish emancipation, almost a century and a half earlier. The republican forces there had been fighting ever since for the principle of equality for all citizens, whether patrician or plebeian, rich or poor, Christian or Jewish. Indeed, anticlericalism, secularism, and cosmopolitanism had become a measure of devotion to democracy. The struggle between liberal and authoritarian movements was a central feature of French politics throughout the nineteenth century, but the triumph of the Third Republic in the late 1870s, after a shaky start, and especially the victory of the democratic parties in the Dreyfus affair twenty years later, seemed to confirm the ascendancy of the moderate left. The success of the progressive bloc in the elections of 1902 was greeted as the culmination of a long, hard struggle in defense of the liberal ideal.

Whatever doubts may still have existed regarding the future of the republican regime were dispelled by the outcome of the First World War. The losses in manpower that France had to suffer in order to achieve victory were enormous, greater proportionately than those of any of the other belligerents outside the Balkans. But the gains were greater as well. The French Republic emerged as the most powerful of the great powers in Europe—the one with the biggest army, the largest arsenal, the most successful diplomacy, and the greatest political influence. Those terrible sacrifices on the battlefield began to seem almost worthwhile, a dreadful price that had had to be paid for a glorious triumph. Not since the days of Napoleon had France played such a decisive role in the affairs of the continent. Its hard-won ascendancy seemed to demonstrate the inherent strength of democratic principles and ideals.

To European Jewry, the triumph of the French Republic was heartening. The persecutions and discriminations it had been forced to endure in the past were invariably inflicted under some authoritarian form of government, usually under a monarch willing to tolerate or even encourage anti-Semitic prejudice. The modern republican regimes, on the other hand, whether in the Old World or the New, had proclaimed their opposition to all forms of discrimination based on race, religion, or ethnicity. Indeed, in France there seemed to be no limit to how high a Jew might rise. He could become an army officer, a high-ranking diplomat, a party leader, a cabinet member, even the prime minister. To the oppressed Jewish masses of Eastern Europe, such opportunities were simply unheard of; they seemed almost miraculous. And if that were not enough, the French were encouraging the succession states to offer the Jews the same opportunities in their own constitutions. Moreover, those efforts were apparently successful. Just look at all the laws adopted by various countries in the east proclaiming the equality of all citizens, whether Christian or Jewish. And that extraordinary achievement, which only a few years earlier would have seemed unattainable, had now become a reality, thanks largely to the democratic idealism of the French.

Democratic idealism, however, was not the only reason for the freedom that Jews enjoyed in France. Throughout Europe there was a rough but close correlation between anti-Semitic prejudice and the relative size of the Jewish community. The greater the proportion of Jews, the greater the hostility they were likely to arouse. That was why the countries along the Atlantic coast, which had the proportionately smallest number of Jews, were also the ones most tolerant toward those they did have. The proportion of Jews in France was 0.5 percent, one of the lowest in all Europe. Only Italy, Spain, Portugal, Switzerland, and the Scandinavian states had relatively fewer Jews than the French Republic.[1]

Yet the establishment of the Third Reich did not lead to any substantial increase in the size of the Jewish minority in France. Refugees from Germany and later from Austria sought asylum in various countries, in North and South America as well as in Europe, but their total did not exceed about half a million. While the Great Depression did increase the efforts of East European Jews to migrate westward, only a relative handful actually succeeded in gaining permission to settle in the French Republic. In 1931, on the eve of the triumph of National Socialism in Germany, about 200,000 Jews lived in France. Eight years later, at the time of the outbreak of the Second World War, the number had risen to some 300,000. How many of the Jewish arrivals during that decade were refugees escaping the racism of the Third Reich and how many were victims of East European anti-Semitism is hard to determine. But clearly, whether out of choice or necessity, only a small minority of emigrant Jews on the eve of the catastrophe that was about to overwhelm their community found refuge in the French Republic.[2]

Why that was so is less apparent. On the face of it, a sizable influx of refugees might have been expected to appear advantageous to both the would-be immigrants and their would-be hosts. To the former it would offer escape from the growing hostility they had to face, while to the latter it would promise to alleviate a serious demographic problem confronting the French Republic: the population of the country that had become the most powerful in Europe was lagging further and further behind that of its historic enemy. At the end of the Franco-Prussian War in 1871, there were roughly 36 million inhabitants of the recently proclaimed Third French Republic and 41 million of the newly formed German Empire. Fifty years later, in the early 1920s, the disparity between the two had grown much more pronounced. The population of victorious France was not quite 39 million, while that of the defeated and chaotic Weimar Republic was over 63 million. This growing demographic imbalance could not be ascribed to battlefield losses in the First World War, since German casualties had been almost 50 percent higher than French ones. Besides, the reacquisition of Alsace-Lorraine had added close to 2 million inhabitants to the total for France. The crucial factor appears to have been the difference in the birthrates of the two countries.[3]

This demographic disparity did not diminish during the twenty years between the two world wars. If anything, it increased slightly. The German population was a little more than 63 million in 1925 and a little more than 66 million in 1933, while the French population was a little less than 39 million in 1921 and a little more than 41 million in 1931. Clearly, the gap was not narrowing. Moreover, the statistics for the other European powers were bound to increase the concern of the government in Paris. The population of the United Kingdom, for example—a friendly nation, to be sure—rose between 1921 and 1931 from 44 million to 46 million, remaining well ahead of the French population. Even Italy, the weakest of the great powers, was catching up; in 1921 its population was not quite 38 million, about 800,000 below the French, but by 1931 the gap had narrowed to a mere 50,000. At that rate, France was likely to become the country with the lowest number of inhabitants among all the leading states of the world within a few years.[4]

Yet there was no obvious reason that that should be so. Not even the most ardent French nationalist could claim, as so many ardent German nationalists did, that his was "a people without space." The boundaries of France enclosed a larger landmass than that of any other country in Western or Central Europe. Indeed, of all the nations on the continent, only the Soviet Union extended over a broader territory. The combination of a relatively small population and a relatively large area meant that demographic pressure in the French Republic was lower than in any other major European state west of the Vistula. In the early 1930s, there were 193 inhabitants per square mile in France, as opposed to 345 inhabitants per square mile in Germany, 358 in Italy, and, far ahead of all the others, 486 in Great Britain. If any country in Europe was capable of absorbing a relatively large number of Jewish refugees, there could be no doubt which one it was.[5]

In some countries in Eastern Europe the population density was substantially lower. Although many of them complained that they had too many mouths to feed, that they were overpopulated, and that only a large-scale emigration, especially of Jews, could save them from ruin, hard figures show that in fact demographic pressure there was much lower than in Western Europe. Even Czechoslovakia and Hungary, the two succession states with the highest population density in the region, had only 270 and 242 inhabitants per square mile, respectively—far fewer than Germany, Italy, and Great Britain. As for the others, the figure for Poland was 205, for Romania 142, for Lithuania 109, and for Latvia 78. There would thus have been ample room in that part of the continent for Jewish refugees from the Third Reich. But how many refugees wanted to emigrate to one of those countries? Some of them were almost as anti-Semitic as Hitler's Germany; indeed, they were trying to get rid of their own Jews. The last thing they wanted was an influx of foreign Jews. The refugees had to look for asylum elsewhere.[6]

There was, of course, the Soviet Union, the sworn enemy of ethnic prejudice and racial discrimination, a country that proudly contrasted its avowed cosmopolitanism with the bigotry and xenophobia of its nationalistic neighbors. Its territory, moreover, even excluding the Asian member republics, was so much greater than that of any other nation in Europe. The number of inhabitants per square mile west of the Urals was only 18, not even a tenth of the figure for France. What could have seemed more logical than establishing an asylum in the Soviet Union for the victims of National Socialism, which the Kremlin condemned so loudly and bitterly?[7]

Yet here too there was a serious problem. The Soviet authorities were reluctant to admit immigrants whose political loyalties were dubious or indeterminable. Might not some of them be conservatives, capitalists, anti-Communists, perhaps even spies and secret agents? Only those whose ideological sympathies seemed beyond question were welcome in Stalin's Russia. Conversely, only a small percentage of the refugees, those whose political leanings were far to the left, wanted to emigrate to the Soviet Union. The others had serious reservations. Would they really be better off under a Communist system? Would they not have to endure ideological discriminations and economic hardships almost as harsh as those they were hoping to escape? No, it would be wiser to look for asylum elsewhere.

France seemed to be the answer. Here was a country whose ideology rejected the authoritarianism, ultranationalism, and racism of the Third Reich. Indeed, even before Hitler rose to power, many Frenchmen had concluded that Germany was an oppressive and aggressive nation, a nation to be feared and distrusted. After 1933 their sympathies were clearly on the side of the victims of National Socialism, including persecuted Jews seeking refuge from totalitarian brutality. And then there were the material circumstances that made the French Republic seem ideally suited to receive such victims: an extensive territory, a stable population, an economy well balanced between industry and agriculture, and a role in international affairs that required ample manpower. Everything seemed to point to a steady flow of victimized Jews from Central and Eastern Europe to France.

Yet that steady flow never materialized; it remained a trickle. Throughout the 1930s the French Republic contemplated, examined, agonized over, and wrestled with the "Jewish question," unable to reach a clear-cut decision. It was the same dilemma all the other democracies had to grapple with, and with the same inconclusive result. It was a conflict between theory and reality, principle and calculation, idealism and self-interest. It was a debate that went on and on, until the coming of the Second World War made its outcome irrelevant. On one side were those who appealed to the collective conscience of society, to compassion and benevolence, those who constantly reminded society of its moral duty to help the victims of cruelty and injustice. But on the other side were those (usually more numerous) who argued that charity begins at home, that the first concern of a nation should be the welfare of its own citizens, and that any attempt to assist foreigners at the expense of compatriots was bound to lead to discontent, conflict, and suffering for both. This contention was often reinforced by the view, sometimes expressed openly, sometimes only whispered, that the victims of discrimination were at least partly responsible for the harsh treatment they complained about and that in fact they might have invited the hostility they had so widely aroused.

The long prewar debate in France regarding the admission of Jews reflected this conflict of opinion. Those favoring the acceptance of political and ethnic refugees relied on familiar appeals and arguments: the obligation to help the helpless, the need to defend freedom, the courage to defy tyranny, and the duty to act with compassion. Those on the opposing side countered with arguments that sounded equally persuasive, to some even more persuasive. How wise was it to admit immigrants who were bound to compete for jobs and wages with native-born Frenchmen facing the hardships of the Great Depression? Was it really fair to aid needy foreigners at the expense of hungry, destitute compatriots? Should France alone assume the burden of assisting the victims of National Socialist oppression? Shouldn't the international community, or at least the other democratic members of that community, offer assistance as well? And wouldn't it be better to resettle the refugees in some distant territory than in overcrowded, insecure, divided Europe? The anti-immigration arguments did not sound implausible to a people frightened by the specter of economic decline and social conflict.

Supporting this line of reasoning and frequently intertwined with it was another contention, one that was voiced more circumspectly, as a rule, but that helped reinforce the opposition to admitting Jewish refugees. It argued that those refugees, especially the ones from Eastern Europe, were and would remain fundamentally different from the French. They were different in culture, language, spirit, and collective character. They would not and could not become assimilated. They would always be aliens, pursuing their own way of life, indifferent to the values and traditions of the host country in which they had chosen to live as permanent outsiders. They were a nation within a nation, a foreign element which presented an economic and cultural threat to the stability of the native community. To admit too many of them might lead to a gradual transformation of the essential nature of French society.

Those two concerns, fear of Jewish competitiveness and disapproval of Jewish separateness, formed the basis of what might be called a popular or plebeian form of anti-Semitism, familiar throughout Europe, less intense in France than in most other countries yet by no means unknown even there. Another form of hostility toward Jews was logically or ideologically more coherent: an intellectual or philosophical anti-Semitism, which maintained that the ineradicable characteristics of Jewishness were materialism, plutocracy, radicalism, and a secret resolve to predominate over non-Jews. For most lower-class anti-Semites, however, this form of ethnic prejudice was too abstruse, too analytical and complicated. They preferred the simpler variety, the one that insisted that Jewish aggressiveness and clannishness were a threat to the stability of the traditional economic and social order.

That was clearly true of France. In January 1941, barely six months after the fall of the Third Republic, SS Colonel Helmut Knochen, head of the security police in the occupation zone, reported to the military command of the German forces stationed there that it was nearly impossible to arouse anti-Semitic feelings resting on an "ideological foundation" in the French population. The prospect of "economic advantages," on the other hand, was quite useful in winning support for the "anti-Jewish struggle." That difference in the popular appeal of the two varieties of anti-Semitism was in fact apparent throughout the 1930s. The contention that the influx of Jewish immigrants, especially from Eastern Europe, was a threat to French workers and tradesmen could often be heard in everyday conversation and even appeared from time to time in the press. It was occasionally accompanied by expressions of disapproval of the persecution that Jews had to endure in the Third Reich and Eastern Europe. But that disapproval did not as a rule reach the point of a willingness to open the doors to very many victims of the persecution.[8]

In the spring of 1938, the influential Parisian newspaper *Le Temps* published a series of articles by Raymond Millet subtitled "Visits to the Foreigners in France." The author described the "sort of slaves" from the "farthest corner of Europe," immigrants who reminded him of the "legendary zombies" of Haiti. They lived twenty-five or thirty in a single apartment, they worked fifteen to eighteen hours a day, and they earned wages that were far below those of French workers. They had thus become "formidable competitors." Yet despite the harsh conditions in which they had to struggle, they managed somehow to scrape together enough money to help support their relatives back home in Eastern Europe, until they could arrange for the resettlement of those relatives in France, thereby saving them from the poverty of some distant eastern village in which only a fortunate few could afford "the luxury of an oil lamp."

But for French workers their competition had proved a disaster, Millet maintained. The hatters' association had already lost more than half its members. The furniture makers' association, the furriers' association, and the tanners' association were in trouble as well. Some of the trade unions had even begun to make preparations for a "campaign of anti-Semitism." And now the learned professions were being "invaded" by educated and well-to-do "foreigners"—Millet tried to avoid using the word "Jews"— who had succeeded in entering France openly and legally, unlike their less fortunate coreligionists who were forced to rely on various "clandestine" devices. How long would all this go on? And where would it all end?[9]

A year later the well-known novelist, essayist, and playwright Jean Giraudoux described the harmful effects of Jewish immigration much more bluntly. He saw no need to be restrained or circumspect about the Jewish threat to the economic well-being of native artisans and tradesmen. He was no far-right extremist, no avowed opponent of the democratic system of government. On the contrary, he supported the Third Republic. And yet in dealing with the "Jewish question" he displayed little of the wit and charm apparent in his plays. He complained of the "hundreds of thousands of Ashkenazis" who had escaped from "the Polish and Romanian ghettos," rejecting the "spiritual rules" of their faith but not its "particularism." Not only had they entered France by a method of infiltration that remained secret, but they were now forcing "our compatriots" out of various artisan occupations and undermining the time-honored customs and traditions of those occupations. Wherever they went, they brought with them "secret deals, embezzlement, [and] corruption." They were a growing threat to the spirit of "precision, good faith, and perfection" which characterized the French artisan class. If that were not enough, the health of many of those belonging to the Jewish "horde" was so precarious and deficient that thousands of them were entering French hospitals. Something had to be done to put a stop to this growing threat to national stability.[10]

It was not only Jewish competitiveness that aroused the concern of many Frenchmen. There was also Jewish particularism, Jewish clannishness. The Jews, or at least those immigrating from Eastern Europe during the 1920s and 1930s, seemed so different, so alien. Most of them showed no sign of wanting to become French in language, culture, behavior, and outlook. Instead they congregated in a few neighborhoods, which quickly became almost completely Judaized; they continued to speak their native "jargon"; they clung stubbornly to the strange, coarse, foreign diet of their ancestral backwaters; and they refused to embrace French culture, French custom, French speech, and French cuisine. They were an island of alienism, a nation of their own. The popular resentment provoked by their perceived economic aggressiveness was intensified by their seeming ethnic self-segregation.

Even Raymond Millet, usually restrained in his portrayal of the "foreigners" who had been pouring into France, could not disguise his distaste after a visit to the Belleville section of Paris, in which many of the recent Jewish immigrants lived. What he saw intensified his concern about "the danger of new invasions" from Eastern Europe. At an outdoor café he saw "Oriental" merrymakers buying peanuts from a "real Frenchman." Should not the roles have been reversed? Yiddish, moreover, not French, was the common language of the neighborhood. In some of the movie houses, even the characters on the screen were talking in Yiddish. A visit to a Jewish slaughterhouse was still more shocking. There were all those butchers, "with black beards, wearing black skullcaps, their black clothing stained with blood." Less repellent but nevertheless distasteful was the sight of Jewish mothers walking their children and of old men and women sitting on park benches, "looking back, perhaps with yearning, to the period of their youth." And in the cafés, even in those with a good reputation, people were discussing problems and affairs "of which an average Frenchman would not understand very much." All in all, Millet's visit to the Jewish quarter of Paris had been profoundly disheartening.[11]

Still, he was too liberal and tolerant, too much the enlightened republican, to embrace ethnic prejudice or urge the exclusion of all Jewish migrants. He asserted that for a true Frenchman, anti-Semitism was "impossible." Indeed, "each of us will continue to maintain that France cannot send to certain death the political or religious refugees who had faith in its generosity." Yet there were limits to what the nation could do. "We must take measures against the disorder." And this "disorder," he believed, was a result of the success of many of the immigrants in illegally acquiring the status of political refugees. Those who were most adept at such deception, moreover, were precisely the ones who constituted "the most dangerous, the most numerous, and the most elusive" category of immigrants, the category of "irregulars and clandestines." They were the ones against whom the authorities should always be on guard. As for the others, those who had a legitimate claim to the status of refugees, they deserved to be admitted and sheltered.[12]

Not all Frenchmen were as broad-minded, however. Many, especially among artisans, tradespeople, and shopkeepers, felt threatened by the foreigners who were competing, often successfully, with native-born workers and store owners. The longer the Great Depression lasted, the greater the resentment against the interlopers became. In the last years preceding the Second World War, especially after the fall of the leftist Popular Front, there were growing protests, demonstrations, marches, and sometimes riots directed against Jews, in particular those Jews who had recently immigrated from Eastern Europe. In September 1938, scattered outbreaks of violence against foreigners occurred, especially against foreigners who looked Jewish, not only in Paris but in Dijon, Saint-Étienne, Nancy, and several cities and towns in Alsace-Lorraine. In many countries farther to the east, such manifestations of anti-Semitic hostility would have seemed commonplace. There they were almost a daily occurrence. But in republican France, devoted in theory to liberty, equality, and fraternity, they were disturbing evidence of a widening gap between official ideology and public opinion.[13]

To the leaders of the Third Reich, of course, signs of increasing French hostility toward Jews were welcome. They suggested a greater international sympathy for the racial doctrines of the Hitler regime and, indirectly at least, a broader understanding of its political and diplomatic policies. The circular of January 25, 1939, which the German foreign ministry sent to its missions abroad described with satisfaction the spread of anti-Semitism on both sides of the Atlantic, devoting special attention to the situation in the French Republic. "The Paris City Council was to deal . . . with a motion denying naturalization to Jews in the future. The discussion of the Jewish question ended with a brawl among the speakers in the debate." A report that the ministry had received a month earlier from the consulate in Lyon was even more encouraging. Not only had "the immigration of Jewish refugees . . . lately led to unpleasant incidents here," but "the general French dislike of the new intruders for reasons of business and competition is unmistakable." Officials in the Wilhelmstrasse found such news reassuring. "This dislike [of Jews] has grown in the meanwhile to such an extent," the circular reported, "that a Jewish defense against anti-Semitism has already been organized in France." An intensification of the struggle between the supporters and the opponents of ethnic discrimination in

France was bound to please the leaders of the Third Reich. They were convinced that anything that divided and weakened the Third Republic would benefit Germany.[14]

Still, the growth of French anti-Semitism during the late 1930s must not be exaggerated. The occasional brawls and riots in Paris or Dijon or Nancy were only minor disturbances compared to the destructive fury of the Kristallnacht in Germany or the deadly ferocity of pogroms in some of the succession states. But neither should their significance be minimized. What happened after the fall of the republic a few years later demonstrated that popular hostility against Jews was more common than had been generally recognized or at least admitted before the war.

The popular or plebeian form of anti-Semitism, based on economic and xenophobic resentments, was strengthened by a patrician form emphasizing the cultural or intellectual differences between Jews and Frenchmen. To those who embraced this variety of ethnic prejudice, most of them from the educated and well-to-do bourgeoisie, what mattered above all was not the alleged economic aggressiveness or alien appearance of the Jews; it was their essential nature, their basic and unalterable character, their genetic makeup. It made little difference whether any particular Jew was a recent arrival from Eastern Europe or his family had lived in France for centuries. If anything, the latter was the more dangerous, since the recent immigrant could always be identified by speech, dress, and behavior. The assimilated Jew, on the other hand, was a serious threat precisely because he had become or seemed to have become acculturated. His appearance might be impeccable, his manners elegant, and his tone refined. But beneath that outward indistinguishability he remained unalterably foreign. His seeming acceptance of the values and traditions of his adopted country merely provided a screen for his efforts to undermine those values and traditions. Whether he was a capitalist or a Communist, a progressive or a conservative, an artist or an academic or a journalist or a politician, his overriding purpose was to dominate the society that had accepted him and offered him refuge. That was the inevitable manifestation of a deeply ingrained Jewish ingratitude.

The spokesmen for this highbrow variety of anti-Semitism did not always confine themselves to describing the spiritually and culturally destructive role of Jewry. Sometimes they too would speak of its harmful influence in economic life, of its covetousness and unscrupulousness. Yet the chief targets of their criticism were not Jewish artisans, tradespeople, and shopkeepers but Jewish academics, journalists, musicians, writers, and film producers. Here were occupations in which economic interests and cultural values converged, in which the growing presence of Jews not only threatened the numerical predominance of non-Jews in artistic and intellectual pursuits but also intensified competition for the material rewards of those pursuits. It provided another alarming example of alien infiltration of traditionally native occupations.

Even Raymond Millet, the avowed opponent of anti-Semitism, expressed concern about the growing role of Jews, especially Jewish immigrants, in the cultural life of France. He worried that they were becoming more and more prominent in professions devoted to learning, culture, and art. They were seeking employment at newspapers, for example, hoping that even if they could not become editors, they might at least be able to publish their articles. They were translating foreign works for Parisian book companies, sometimes also publishing books they themselves had written. And if that were not enough, they were "skillfully" moving into the world of the theater. As for the film industry, "they have half conquered it." That troubled Millet. "You will find few Frenchmen and few Catholics among the makeup artists in the studios or among the sound engineers." When asked about the special treatment they were receiving, those favored Jews had a ready answer: "You see of course . . . that we can succeed only in these occupations; the bosses give us preference over Frenchmen." That answer did not satisfy Millet, however. He found it disturbing that foreigners were gaining control over cultural pursuits which should rightly have been a source of livelihood for native-born citizens of France.[15]

Nevertheless, most mainstream newspapers, like *Le Monde*, dealt with the problem of Jewish immigration cautiously and discreetly, reluctant to exacerbate ethnic bigotries and animosities. But anti-Semitic hostility was in fact more common than the middle-of-the-road press was ready to admit. It could be found in the pamphlets, manifestos, and polemics of the far right. It could be heard in everyday conversation, usually in undertones or half-whispers but sometimes loud and defiant. And then there was a group of right-wing intellectuals, eloquent, assertive, defiant, and aggressive, who warned the nation against the danger of cultural and spiritual Judaization. In the prewar years they were widely regarded as gifted but misguided eccentrics, visionaries whose writings displayed literary skill but little practical judgment. After 1939, however, the early victories of the Wehrmacht won for them a brief reputation as sages and prophets, as intellectuals who had recognized and welcomed the wave of the future. But then the defeat of the Third Reich transformed them once again, this time into subversives and traitors who had formed a cultural fifth column in the service of their nation's enemy.

Robert Brasillach is a good example. A prolific writer and essayist in sympathy with Fascism, a supporter of the Action Française, an admirer of Hitler, Mussolini, and Franco, he became an apologist for the Vichy regime and a defender of Nazi racial policy after the defeat of France. Barely a year after the fall of the Third Republic he wrote an account of the prewar years that emphasized the weaknesses and corruptions of the democratic system, ascribing its failure in large measure to the insidious influence of Jews. Most of the country had unfortunately failed to recognize the extent of that influence. "The Frenchman," Brasillach explained, "is an anti-Semite by instinct, but he does not like to appear to be persecuting innocent people." The Popular Front government of Léon Blum, however, had finally helped arouse popular awareness of the danger confronting the nation. There was first of all the growing number of Jews in high government positions. That made more and more Frenchmen conscious of the threat of political Judaization. But equally important was the steady influx of Jews into important and profitable enterprises, especially in the world of entertainment. "The movie industry practically closed its doors to Aryans. The radio had a Yiddish accent. Even the most peace-loving people began to look askance at the frizzy hair and the hooknoses, of which there were surprisingly many." This portrayal was not exaggerated or biased, Brasillach insisted. "It is history."[16]

He was wrong. His portrayal was in fact both exaggerated and biased, certainly regarding the extent of Jewish influence in politics and economics. Nevertheless, the assertion that even before the war many French people were beginning to regard the Jews living among them, especially the Jews who had recently immigrated, with suspicion is generally accurate. Their concern was fed partly by xenophobia, partly by the Great

Depression, which seemed to go on and on, with no end in sight, and partly by the agitation of a patrician anti-Semitism which insisted that the national character was being corrupted by Jewish greed and aggressiveness. Throughout the prewar period, defenders of the republican system maintained—not always with complete conviction—that ethnic bigotry was a rarity in France and the overwhelming majority of French people believed in equal rights for all. But after the defeat of the Third Republic, the rapid adjustment of public opinion to the doctrines and policies of the German occupation, including those regarding ethnic origin, suggests that the French commitment to liberal principles had not been quite as firm as was officially proclaimed. It had been weakened, at least to some extent, by a group of prominent anti-Semitic intellectuals, to whom the political divisions and social conflicts that were supposedly tearing the nation apart had been initiated by an evil, sinister, alien conspiracy.

Probably the best known and certainly the fiercest, most passionate of those intellectuals was Louis-Ferdinand Céline, who had been a favorite of the far left during the early 1930s but had then turned into an obsessed, hysterical enemy of the Jews. His writings against them are one long outpouring of dire warnings and morbid fears, a brokenhearted lament for a great civilization conquered by an unscrupulous and insidious minority. He bitterly denounced the pernicious influence of the fictitious "Mr. Cohen, Mr. Lévy, [and] Mr. Jew Genialstein," not to mention the real and living "Mademoiselle [Vicki] Baum" as well as the real but non-Jewish "Mr. [William] Faulkner." They were all part of the plot. They were "plagiarizing, ransacking, [and] appropriating" the work of others. "Our Jews in the theater," moreover, "here as elsewhere, do nothing but appropriate, pillage, and resell all the folk tales and classics of the countries which they are plundering." And yet so few Frenchmen had the courage to denounce openly the crimes that those cultural parasites were committing.

Still, what good would denunciations do? Céline was convinced that the battle was over, the war was lost. "Captain Dreyfus is truly greater than Captain Bonaparte. He has conquered France and he has kept it." Could anything be done to change the outcome? Hardly. "Messieurs kikes, half-niggers, you are our gods." The great conspiracy had been successful; the evil plotters were now the rulers of France. "The earth is the paradise of the Jews. They have everything. They can allow themselves anything."

Having unburdened himself of all the phantoms and nightmares that had been haunting him, Céline could sink back in his writer's chair, breathless and exhausted.[17]

Few of the anti-Semitic French intellectuals of the prewar years were quite that vehement or obsessed or eloquent. Most were more down-to-earth, more cautious and restrained. They avoided Céline'oracular style, his visionary tone, his prophetic oratory. They preferred to describe matter-of-factly the alleged economic rapacity and cultural aggressiveness of Jewry. But many of them agreed that the qualities which had made the Jews a threat to the country were not simply acquired, not merely the result of historical experience or ethnic tradition. They were inherent and therefore ineradicable. They could not be overcome by gradual assimilation and acculturation. They were incorrigible because they were biological in nature; they were racial. The Jew, whether in Poland or France or England or the United States, was sooner or later bound to display the same genetic slyness and acquisitiveness. Nothing could be done about it. It was part of his essential nature. To ignore this hard reality was to invite a gradual corruption of the national identity.

The rhetoric of French anti-Semitism during the 1930s closely resembled the rhetoric of East European and Central European anti-Semitism. But this similarity should not obscure the fact that hostility toward Jews was much less common and intense in France than in countries farther to the east. Here there were no bloody pogroms like those in Poland, no violent riots like those in Romania, no "night of broken glass" with burning synagogues and vandalized shops like the one in Germany in November 1938. Even demands for a limit on Jewish students enrolled in the universities or for a restriction on Jews in the professions or for the establishment of a *numerus clausus* in business and finance or for the introduction of a quota system in storekeeping and the handicrafts were relatively few and subdued. To most Frenchmen they seemed too harsh and extreme, too inconsistent with the ideas and ideals of democratic republicanism.

There was one policy, however, on which all those alarmed by the seemingly growing Jewish influence in national life could agree. Something had to be done to reduce the influx of Jews into France, especially the uncouth, coarse, and outlandish Jews from the succession states. The need to restrict the immigration of such undesirable aliens seemed obvious to anti-Semites of all shades, varieties, and intensities, to moderates as well as extremists, to republicans as well as antirepublicans, and to cosmopolites as well as xenophobes. The limited scope of this demand made it all the more acceptable to the many who were reluctant to appear prejudiced or bigoted.

And yet there was no clear objective reason for support of an exclusionary policy. The total number of permanent Jewish residents in France increased during the 1930s by only about 100,000, and not all of those came from the succession states. Some were refugees from Germany and Austria, others had managed to get out of the Soviet Union, and still others were well-to-do Jews from the Middle East and North Africa. But the ones who attracted the most attention and aroused the strongest disapproval were the impoverished migrants from the East European ghettos. They looked so strange, so foreign, so incorrigibly alien. How could anyone believe that they would ever become transformed into refined, elegant Frenchmen?

Even the moderate Raymond Millet concluded his series of articles in *Le Temps* with a call for a change in the country's immigration policy. It had become clear to him that "France should attract nationalities whose blood type and whose psychology resemble ours most closely." The Dutch would obviously qualify, although they were not the only ones who could satisfy this "double requirement" for admission. In any case, it was now the task of the government to devise a plan for "selective immigration." Millet hastened to acknowledge that many foreigners and many descendants of foreigners had made contributions to "the greatness of our nation, of our history, and of our art." And yet "their worth or their glory" was not enough to alleviate "the problems created by the presence of at least three million foreigners in a nation of 40 million people, and especially by the prospect of new waves [of immigrants]." The people of France simply could not afford to stand by idly while their borders were being overrun by hordes of foreigners from the remotest corners of the globe.[18]

Millet did not direct his remarks specifically against East European Jews. In fact, he avoided even using the word "Jew" or "Jewish." In his articles, he spoke as a rule about "foreigners," without specifying their ethnic origin or religious background. He knew, moreover, that of the 3 million immigrants whom he regarded as a threat to the nation's culture and tradition, not even one tenth was from Eastern Europe. But to him, as to so many others, all those aliens pouring into the country in seemingly countless numbers, whether Syrians and Egyptians from the Mediterranean coast, Senegalese and Guineans from Central Africa, Vietnamese and Cambodians from Indochina, or Jews from Poland and Romania, were endangering the essential character and spirit of France. What made the Jews appear especially threatening, however, was their success in gaining a prominent position in economics, politics, and culture.

The growing demand for restrictions on immigration was promoted not only by ultranationalists and xenophobes alarmed by what they perceived to be the Judaization of national life. It also found support from an unexpected and surprising source—from within the Jewish community itself. To some of the established members of that community, to those whose families had lived in France for generations and even to quite a few who had once been immigrants themselves but had then become deliberately and completely Gallicized, the inflow of Jews from Eastern Europe was unwelcome. It threatened their own position. After more than a century of effort and struggle, they had recently found acceptance as true Frenchmen. They had become assimilated and acculturated, indistinguishable or almost indistinguishable from their non-Jewish compatriots. They had managed to rise to some of the highest positions among the elite of the nation. One of them had even become the premier of France. There seemed to be no limit to how far they might climb. And now all of that was being threatened by their awkward, unpolished, embarrassing country cousins. The gains they had won with such effort and at such cost were suddenly in jeopardy. What were they to do?

The dilemma faced by the Jewish patriciate of France was not unique, to be sure. It confronted well-to-do, established, and assimilated Jews in all the democratic nations. The acculturated Jews of Weimar Germany regarded the recently arrived *Ostjuden* with that same distaste and secret apprehension, until the genocidal fury of the Third Reich destroyed them all. The Jews of Great Britain, finally emerging from the shadow of Shylock and Fagin, also felt embarrassed by the appearance of their coreligionists from the east, who all too often resembled the familiar anti-Semitic stereotypes of popular bigotry. Even in the United States, the older and wealthier communities of Sephardic and German Jews looked down with disdain but also concern on the noisy rabble of peddlers, hawkers, and hustlers crowding the Lower East Side of New York. Members of the Jewish patriciate in every country were torn between uneasiness and compassion, distaste and sympathy for their uncouth, impoverished coreligionists.

The tactics adopted by many assimilated French Jews against the rising tide of ethnic hostility were similar to those employed in other countries. There was first of all the time-tested technique of avoiding direct confrontation—of not saying or doing anything that might aggravate anti-Semitic prejudice. Refusing to respond to a provocation might gradually lead to the abatement of that provocation. Such a policy had sometimes worked in the past, and it might now work again. Why not try it? In the fall of 1938, during the High Holy Days, the grand rabbi of Paris advised Jews "to avoid standing or gathering in front of places of worship." The sight of a large Jewish crowd might rouse the hostility of anti-Semites in the neighborhood. Similarly, Bernard Lecache, president of the International League against Anti-Semitism, who had become a French citizen some thirty years earlier, "repeatedly urged foreign Jews to avoid any discussions or gatherings of a political nature." The less attention they attracted, the less resentment they were likely to incur. That was the counsel of wisdom and prudence.[19]

But would that be enough? Would the avoidance of large gatherings in public places or of loud and heated debates diminish popular concern about Jewish immigration? Not likely. No matter how compliant the Jews tried to appear, no matter how unobtrusive and noncontroversial, the increasing number of refugees from Central and Eastern Europe was a constant source of provocation to those who feared that their nation was being drowned in a flood of undesirable aliens. The members of the Jewish elite were well aware of the effect that the continuing inflow of immigrants from the east was having on French public opinion. But what could they do? To advocate the exclusion of the refugees openly would be perceived by most other Jews as ethnic treason, a form of fratricide. Willy-nilly, they had to grumble and worry in private.

A non-Jew like Raymond Millet, however, could afford to say publicly what the Jewish elite was able only to whisper or insinuate. "We should not fail to mention in passing," he wrote, "that the French Israelites, those who have become integrated with our nation and who have contributed or will contribute to the defense of our soil, regard with as much uneasiness as compassion this too sudden influx, this constant flood of their coreligionists driven from Germany, from Central or Eastern Europe, by the calamities of our times." His status as a Christian, even if only a nominal Christian, enabled him to tell the world what the patrician Jews were reluctant to admit to others or even to themselves.[20]

Yet a few assimilated and acculturated Jews in France *were* willing to say openly what the others preferred to say in private. Emmanuel Berl, for example, author of the conservative newsletter *Pavés de Paris*, sounded at times almost as xenophobic as the Action Française. He described the wave of refugees during the late 1930s as a very serious problem for the nation. Something had to be done. He was convinced of the "impossibility for France to let its territory and its capital be invaded by undesirables from all countries." Those "undesirables" were pouring in incessantly, whenever they wanted to, across a porous and penetrable frontier. "That is a great misfortune, and we know it." Once the illegal immigrants entered France, moreover, the most serious penalty facing them was a month in prison. And after they were released, "various welcoming committees whose very names sound like a [charitable] appeal wait to receive them." As for the inflow of Jews, it was undeniably a significant part of "this immigration of castoffs, this residue of undesirables." How long could that go on? A few years later Berl was rewarded for his patriotic loyalty by a brief promotion to the position of speechwriter for Marshal Pétain.[21]

Yet even before the fall of the republic, opposition to the continued admission of refugees from Eastern and Central Europe began to influence government policy. Most politicians and bureaucrats remained opposed in principle to the virulent anti-Semitism of the Third Reich and the succession states. But they were also becoming convinced that France had already done as much as or more than could reasonably be expected to help the victims of ethnic bigotry. Now the time had come for other democratic countries to do their share. The authorities were still willing to admit foreigners who came as transients, visitors, or tourists, that is, those whose eventual departure seemed probable. On the other hand, refugees who were likely to attempt to become permanent residents, and that meant primarily the ones from Eastern Europe, began to be regarded with suspicion and distrust. They were perceived more and more as likely economic competitors and unassimilable cultural aliens.

The government was still prepared to cooperate with other countries in solving the "Jewish question" through emigration to some remote part of the globe. Thus in 1937 the French colonial minister agreed to send a commission appointed by the League of Nations to explore the possibility of settling a substantial number of refugees on Madagascar, which seemed sufficiently distant from France. But as European hostility toward the Jewish community became more pervasive and intense, and as pleas for an asylum for its victims became more clamorous and persistent, French authorities became increasingly fearful of being inundated by a tide of hungry, ambitious, aggressive, and incorrigibly foreign immigrants. They began to insist that the nation had reached the limit of affordable generosity.[22]

The contention that France had already done more than its share to help Jewish refugees and that the time had come for other countries to assume a larger part of the burden could be heard over and over again in the government's official political discourse. In the fall of 1938, Henry Béranger, the French representative at the intergovernmental committee formed to assist German and Austrian asylum-seekers, warned that by trying to do much more than had already been done, his nation would be risking a sharp increase in public unrest. "France has now reached the saturation point, which does not allow it any longer to receive new refugees without upsetting its social structure," he explained. "Our country went beyond the limit a long time ago." To a government wrestling with the problems of economic depression, social discontent, and diplomatic tension, the prospect of admitting tens or possibly hundreds of thousands of needy foreigners, however oppressed, however helpless, was alarming. The duty of the state, according to the prevailing view, was to look after the welfare of its own citizens first.[23]

The most authoritative statement of this position came a few weeks later, on November 24, 1938, during a meeting at the Quai d'Orsay of the highest officials of the French and British governments. Among those representing the United Kingdom were Neville Chamberlain, the prime minister; Viscount Halifax, the secretary of state for foreign affairs; and Sir Alexander Cadogan, the permanent undersecretary of state for foreign Affairs, while the spokesmen for France included Édouard Daladier, head of the cabinet, and Georges Bonnet, the minister for foreign affairs. One of the items on the agenda was the "Jewish question," and here Bonnet explained his government's position in great detail and with unmistakable clarity.

To begin with, "the French Government were much preoccupied with the question of Jewish immigration into France, particularly since the latest German measures against Jews," adopted after the Kristallnacht earlier that month. Although there were already "40,000 Jewish refugees in France," the government had not prohibited the entry of "a certain number of Jews." In fact, its policy was to grant visas to those refugees who were "in danger of death" if they remained in the Third Reich. "But France could not stand a Jewish immigration on a large scale." That was the main point. The country was "saturated" with foreigners within its borders. "The French Government were seeking a solution of this problem, but they had not yet found any means whereby any further considerable number of refugees might be settled in French territory." The limit to what the country could do had now been almost reached.

There were still a few possibilities, however, Bonnet went on to explain. American public opinion and especially the American press had recently displayed interest in the refugee problem. Still, no practical measures had been taken to help solve it. Sumner Welles, the undersecretary of state in Washington, had done nothing more than suggest that the United States might be willing to allow some refugees already in the country to obtain visas authorizing them to remain there indefinitely. How could anyone complain, then, that the French government had not done enough? It was still willing to consider "the possibility of establishing a number of Jewish refugees in a French colony." It might even allow "a few more" to enter France from Germany. "But such action . . . must be accompanied by similar efforts on the part of Great Britain and the United States." After all, the French government could not be expected to bear the burden alone.[24]

And so the debate about what to do regarding the refugee problem and how to solve the "Jewish question" went on and on, not only in France but in all the democratic nations, right up to the outbreak of the Second World War. In fact, it continued well beyond that, into the period of armed conflict between the Axis and the Allies. Its source was not primarily the unremitting virulence of the ultranationalists, xenophobes, bigots, and anti-Semites, although there were certainly enough of those. It was rather the dilemma confronting millions of ordinary people, people of generally kind intentions and generous sympathies, who found themselves torn between ideals and realities, principles and interests. Most of them felt pity for the far-off victims of ethnic cruelty, segregated, humiliated, and persecuted. But once those victims became immigrants or sought to become immigrants, the prevailing attitude toward them began to change abruptly and drastically. They ceased to be abstract symbols of man's inhumanity to man. Now they were or were about to be next-door neighbors, perhaps rivals competing with the native-born population for jobs, wages, opportunities, and rewards. And this at a time of depression, when the hungry and needy at home seemed to need help at least as much as those abroad. Here was the source of the predicament, the source of what appeared to many to be a painful choice between compassion and self-preservation.

4

Britain Wrestles with the Refugee Problem

THAT THERE WAS A CLOSE resemblance between the English and French attitudes toward the "Jewish question" during the 1930s is not surprising. The two leading democratic states in Europe were both committed to the ideals of religious tolerance and ethnic inclusivity. They had arrived at that commitment by entirely different routes, to be sure. In France, the rejection of royal absolutism during the French Revolution had led to more than a century of struggle between an authoritarian tradition and liberal reformism. Only about a decade before the outbreak of the First World War was the issue finally decided. In England, the process of change had been more gradual and less stormy. It took three hundred years to advance from a divine-right monarchy through an oligarchical parliamentarism to a system of government based on popular sovereignty. The process was peaceful, except for the civil wars of the 1640s, but the outcome was the same as in France—the triumph of egalitarian democracy.

The similarity in political ideology helps account for the similarity in the two nations' response to the victory of National Socialism in Germany. To them, the Third Reich represented a revival of the authoritarian political system and hierarchical social order that had only recently been defeated in their own countries. Their sympathy was from the outset with those who opposed the Hitler regime. Their compassion embraced all the victims of totalitarian oppression, religious and ethnic as well as political and ideological victims. And that meant that public opinion in

England and France was in general agreement that the anti-Semitic measures adopted by the government in Berlin were harsh and unjust. Even many of those who felt that the Jews had indeed acquired too much influence in European politics, economics, and culture regarded the policies of the Nazi regime as excessively harsh. Instead of solving the problem, they made it worse.

This general popular disapproval of the Nazis' racial program was not based entirely on ideological conviction. It also reflected, at least to some extent, the relatively small size of the Jewish communities in England and France. In 1933 there were about 330,000 Jews in England, about 130,000 more than in France—0.7 percent and 0.5 percent of the respective populations. Compared to the percentages in some of the succession states, these figures seemed almost insignificant. Even in Germany, where the Jewish community was much smaller than in Poland or Romania, the proportion was 0.9 percent. Thus in Great Britain, Jewish competition with non-Jewish workers, artisans, and shopkeepers or with non-Jewish bankers, industrialists, and professionals was far less intense than in Eastern or Central Europe. And that in turn helped allay the fear of growing domination by an alien minority.[1]

Before the Great Depression, England had in fact been willing to accept a fairly substantial number of Jewish immigrants from the ghettos of the continent. Between 1881 and 1930, some 210,000 foreign Jews settled in Great Britain, almost all of them from Eastern Europe. About 130,000 came from Russia, 40,000 from Austria-Hungary and Poland (mostly Galician Jews), and 30,000 from Romania. Only 10,000 had immigrated from other parts of Europe or from other parts of the globe. All in all, the number of Jews in England almost tripled in the fifty years before the Great Depression. To be sure, the total increase was not even a tenth of the roughly 2.9 million Jews who settled in the United States during the same period, the vast majority of whom arrived before the restrictive immigration laws of the 1920s. But the British authorities did admit more Jewish refugees from the autocratic eastern states than any other country in Europe.[2]

For those who found asylum in England, life became much easier than in Russia or Poland or Romania. They were now entitled, at least in theory, to almost all the rights of native-born Britons. According to law, they could no longer be excluded from the learned professions or denied access to higher education. They were free to live wherever they wanted, to practice any occupation they liked, and to seek any position to which they aspired. That was a huge difference from what they had had to endure back home in Eastern Europe. But life as an everyday experience was not always as rosy as it appeared on paper. There were occasions and situations that reminded the immigrants of the discriminations they had faced in their native countries, which they had hoped to escape. The British upper classes looked down on the newcomers as grubby and uncouth, while the lower classes often regarded them with a mixture of distrust, disdain, and amusement. They sometimes had to endure the familiar anti-Semitic slurs and epithets or even suffer a few blows now and again. This was not quite the Promised Land.

Nor did the Jewish elite in Great Britain welcome them more warmly than the Jewish elite in France. In both countries those Jews who had gained acceptance, not only on paper but in daily life, felt threatened by the new arrivals from the east. In England, Jews had been increasingly successful in gaining admittance to the ranks of the patriciate, mingling with the proud descendants of Anglo-Saxons and Normans. They were becoming more important, not only in the world of business, in which they had traditionally played a significant role, but in scholarship, literature, art, and politics. One of them had even been Queen Victoria's favorite prime minister, though at the cost of converting to Anglicanism. There was seemingly no limit to how high they might rise. But now the outlandish immigrants from Eastern Europe were threatening the hard-won gains of native Jewry. No wonder quite a few of the old-timers viewed the newcomers with distaste and resentment, usually disguised but at times quite open.

Nevertheless, before the Great Depression, Jewish immigrants were generally viewed in England with amused tolerance, as a strange and exotic but harmless minority, a little like the Gypsies, the Jamaicans, or the Indians. That attitude began to change, however, as a result of the economic hardships of the 1930s. The fears and privations that led to the establishment of the Third Reich in Germany also produced a different perception of Jewry in England. The collapse of the economy affected the standard of living in the United Kingdom almost as seriously as in the Weimar

Republic and far more seriously than in the French Republic. In 1931, the number of unemployed in France was 64,000 and in England 2,630,000; in 1935, the figure for France was 464,000 and for England 2,036,000; and in 1938, the totals were 402,000 and 1,514,000, respectively. During the decade preceding the Second World War the largest number of unemployed French workers was 470,000, in 1936, while the smallest number of unemployed British workers was 1,484,000, also in 1936. Even when the difference between the two countries was at its lowest level, unemployment in England was more than three times as great as in France.[3]

This disparity cannot be explained by the difference in size of the two populations. The number of inhabitants in the United Kingdom exceeded that in the Third Republic by not quite 12 percent, while the number of unemployed in the former exceeded that in the latter by over 200 percent. The answer lies rather in the much higher level of industrialization of the British economy, something that made it possible in good times to achieve a higher standard of living but that also left the lower classes more exposed to the hardships of a depression. And that meant also that the tensions and anxieties resulting from the industrial collapse of the 1930s began to change the popular perception of Jewish immigrants, who came to be seen less and less as quaint but harmless outsiders and more and more as hungry mouths to be fed and homeless bodies to be housed. They were increasingly viewed as competitors, rivals, intruders, and invaders. In other words, the effect of the Great Depression on British public opinion regarding Jews was similar to its effect on French public opinion. What is surprising, given the more serious impact of the economic crisis on England than on France, is that English anti-Semitism did not become more intense than it did—that it seemed, in fact, not as virulent as French anti-Semitism.

In July 1939, the British Institute of Public Opinion asked 2,000 respondents, "Among the people you know, is anti-Jewish feeling increasing, decreasing, or about the same?" The replies showed that 21 percent thought that anti-Semitism was growing, 10 percent thought that it was diminishing, and 45 percent thought that there had been no change. The rest failed to express any opinion. The overall feeling appeared to be that the increase in hostility toward Jews in England, if any, had been minor.[4]

The results of a survey conducted at the same time by the Gallup Poll seemed to point in the same direction. They suggested that people in Great Britain, alarmed by the success of Hitler's diplomacy, shocked by the Third Reich's brutal anti-Semitic policy, and frightened by the growing prospect of a new world war, were generally sympathetic to the victims of Nazi racism. On the other hand, to a country grappling with widespread unemployment and privation, the admission of a large number of Jewish refugees, not only from Eastern Europe, as before, but now also from Central Europe, was bound to appear hazardous. Under such trying circumstances, what should Great Britain do?

The replies to the Gallup Poll reflect this dilemma. To the question "Should refugees be allowed to enter Great Britain?" the answer was unambiguous. The great majority of the respondents, 70 percent, answered yes, 25 percent answered no, and 4 percent had no opinion. Yet once the issue of admitting persecuted Jews was placed in the context of the depressed state of the economy, the results became even more one-sided, but in the opposite direction. When the respondents who had declared that refugees should be allowed to enter Great Britain were then asked, "Should they be allowed to enter freely or with restrictions designed to safeguard British workers and taxpayers?" only 15 percent supported unconditional admission, 84 percent favored admission with restrictions, and 1 percent had no opinion. The results suggest a serious inner struggle in England between compassion and the instinct for self-preservation.[5]

The same struggle was going on in the other democratic nations grappling with the refugee problem. The citizens of all of them displayed pity or at least sympathy for the victims of ethnic persecution. But they also agonized over the serious economic and social problems at home: unemployment, poverty, despair, and growing popular discontent. How could a country afford to admit tens or perhaps hundreds of thousands of homeless, impoverished foreign Jews who would be competing for public assistance with native victims of the depression? The concern was understandable.

Those two forms of opposition to the immigration of Jewish refugees, the economic and the ethnic, existed side by side in all of the democracies, separate but intertwined. The stronger a country's official ideological commitment to liberal principles, the greater the likelihood that arguments against the admission of Jews would be based on economics rather than ethnicity. Yet that does not imply that those who warned against the economic consequences of an influx of refugees were actually worried about racial or cultural Judaization. Many of them, perhaps most, did in fact believe that their nation, though commendably sympathetic toward the refugees, simply could not afford to offer them asylum. And then there were quite a few in whom the economic and ethnic objections were, consciously or unconsciously, so closely connected as to be inseparable.

In the case of the United Kingdom, there seemed to be little overt hostility toward Jews. Although the British economy had suffered far more from the Great Depression than the French, open expressions of anti-Semitism were less common in Great Britain than in the Third Republic. There were no reports of mass demonstrations or street riots against the Jewish community, no vandalized stores, no broken windows, no violent assaults against Jewish shopkeepers or tradesmen. Even Sir Oswald Mosley's British Union of Fascists, whose membership never exceeded 50,000 and on the eve or the Second World War was only about 25,000, did not include racial anti-Semitism among the central planks of its program. The circular concerning the "Jewish question" that the German foreign office sent to its legations abroad early in 1939 described in considerable detail the spread of antagonism against Jews not only in France but in a number of other countries: the United States, Greece, the Netherlands, Norway, and even Uruguay. Yet there was no mention of the United Kingdom. Apparently the authorities in Berlin could find little encouraging news about the English attitude toward Jewry.[6]

Still, there is evidence that beneath the surface, people in Great Britain held views regarding the "Jewish question" not very different from those common in France or the other democratic states of Western Europe. A Mass-Observation survey conducted at the beginning of 1939, a few months before the British Institute of Public Opinion poll and the Gallup poll—less structured or focused than the other surveys, less dependent on the percentages of yeses and noes, but broader in scope and sharper in analysis—revealed a considerable diversity of attitudes regarding Jews, some of them only too familiar. One view, repeated in a variety of forms, was that "the Jews cause quite a lot of it themselves." Another maintained that "we have quite enough Jews in the country as it is and we do not want any more." One Cornishman suggested that "the Jews could have avoided their present trouble if they had less racial arrogance." A young girl of thirteen thought that "the Jews are very nice people, well mannered and kind. They are mostly well educated." But a young boy of the same age was more critical. "The Jews are very clannish. They are too rich. It is a pity the way they are persecuted, though they partly deserve it." While very few of the respondents agreed with Hitler's anti-Semitic program, several expressed at least some distrust of Jews in general. What emerged from the survey was an undercurrent of popular suspicion or even resentment against the Jewish community.[7]

This conclusion does not rest solely on responses to polls and questionnaires. It is also supported by a number of perceptive observers of English society. Malcolm Muggeridge, the well-known journalist and critic, for example, commented on the prevalence of ethnic hostility during the 1930s. "The hate Hitler generated formed a magnetic field," he wrote shortly after the outbreak of the Second World War, "which reached far; particles of hatred stirred, like iron filings by a magnet, to fall into its pattern. Even as far as England the field reached, though here, distant from the centre, the force was only faintly felt, the pattern only faintly traced." But actually, signs of widespread prejudice against Jews were not that faint. Only a paragraph later Muggeridge reported that "anti-semitic slogans were chalked on walls and in the roadway, coldly or indifferently eyed by most passers-by, but remaining until rain washed them away; windows of shops belonging to Jews were broken, and in the darkness offensive epithets shouted." In short, "anti-semitism was in the air, an unmistakable tang." Its presence was palpable.[8]

At about the same time, the writer and painter Wyndham Lewis presented an assessment of the prevailing British attitude toward Jewry which was less critical but basically not different. In a book provocatively titled *The Jews, Are They Human?*, which displayed the eccentricity apparent in many of his works, Lewis agreed that "Jews are news." But the reason for all the attention they were receiving was their growing misfortune. "It is not an enviable kind of limelight that beats upon the Chosen People. Everybody in England is talking pogroms instead of football-pools." That was because countries like Germany, Hungary, Italy, Poland, and Czechoslovakia were "freezing out" their Jewish minorities by means of what was described as "cold pogroms." The British press was full of accounts of anti-Semitic persecutions, while "the B.B.C. programmes ring with them." The "Jewish question" was now being scrutinized in England more closely than ever before.

Lewis insisted that he himself was free of ethnic prejudice. "To me a Jew is the same as any other man." In fact, "I have never experienced so much as a touch, I am glad to say, of superstitious feeling regarding this particularly subtle brand of 'foreigner,' still enveloped in an aura of mediaeval taboo." He believed that most people in Great Britain shared his own tolerant attitude. Why then were so many Germans bigoted and cruel? "It is perfectly evident that in this respect we differ extremely from our cousins across the North Sea." And yet Lewis had to acknowledge that at least some Englishmen were not always as broad-minded as he. "I have friends," he admitted, "who detest Jews, just as some people abominate cats. They cannot sit in a room with a Jew. The dark mongoloid eye, the curled semitic lip, arouses their worst passions." Many of Lewis's "cousins across the North Sea" shared the distaste of his friends for that "curled semitic lip," a distaste which, he was eager to make clear, he himself did not feel.[9]

There were even a few prominent British supporters of the cultural or patrician variety of anti-Semitism common on the other side of the English Channel. To be sure, no Célines or Brasillachs were among them, no obsessed or fanatical haters of Jews. And yet some of their views would have sounded perfectly reasonable to members of the Action Française or to readers of Julius Streicher's *Stürmer*. One of the most outspoken and certainly the best known was H. G. Wells, son of a humble shopkeeper, teenaged apprentice to a draper, the eloquent, ardent socialist, the lifelong champion of the victims of economic discrimination and oppression. His sensitivity to injustice, however, did not extend to victims of ethnic discrimination and oppression. He saw no inconsistency between his sympathy for those who were being mistreated because of their economic status and his antipathy to those who were being mistreated because of their religious or historical background. This insensitivity exemplified a certain quirkiness, an almost willful eccentricity which appeared from time to time in his thinking and writing.

Wells's analysis of the position of Jewry in the modern world, published in 1936, displayed this peculiar and unexpected shortsightedness. "What holds [the Jews] together," he argued, "is a tradition, Biblical, Talmudic and economic. Solidarity has been forced upon them by the hostility their tradition invoked. It is a tradition that stresses acquisitiveness." As a result, "they are more alert about property, money and the power of money than the run of mankind; they are brighter and cleverer with money. They get, they permeate, they control." On the continent, especially in Eastern Europe and the Third Reich, such views were widely accepted as self-evident. Even in France they would not have sounded terribly shocking.

Wells believed that an awareness of Jewish covetousness was essential for an understanding of the source of anti-Semitism. The peoples among whom the Jews lived, he explained, were naturally resentful of the material success of those clever outsiders. That success, they felt, was being achieved "at the expense of broader and finer interests, of leisure, brooding contemplation and experiment" which formed the foundation of their national culture. If the Gentiles were to hold their own, however, they would have to concentrate more on "the struggle for possession." Yet they would eventually lose that struggle, "unless they impose a handicap on [the Jew] or resort periodically to some form of pogrom." Here was the explanation for the spread of anti-Semitic hostility. "The Jew . . . grips the property, he secures the appointment. The Gentile feels he is robbed of opportunity by all this alertness. He is baffled and he gives way to anger." Was that so hard to understand?

The Jew's rapacity, according to Wells, reflected his profound estrangement from the society that had provided him with asylum and opportunity. He was not "a good citizen"; he did not give his allegiance to "the institutions, conventions and collective interests and movements of the community in which he finds himself." He was indifferent to the common welfare. "He is an alien with an alien mentality." The fountainhead of his ideology was "spoiling the Egyptians." His eager acquisitiveness, in other words, his obsession with achievement, and his indifference toward sentimental or selfless considerations were to a large extent a result of his "alien tradition," which freed him from "playing the game" according to the rules of the non-Jewish society within which he was both a member and an outsider. Wells did voice his disapproval of "the clumsy revengefulness, the plunderings, outrages and fantastic intimidations" of National Socialism. But he also maintained that a condemnation, however heartfelt, of the brutality of the Hitler regime was not enough to solve the "Jewish question" in the modern world. It merely underscored "the fundamental agelong problem of this nation among nations, this in-and-out mentality, the essential parasitism of the Jewish mycelium upon the social and cultural organisms in which it lives."

The growing anti-Semitic hostility was being exacerbated. moreover, by what Wells called the "Professional Champions," those well-intentioned, charitable Christians who claimed to be supporters and defenders of the Jews but who actually intensified popular suspicion and resentment of them by encouraging "unjust and unwise boycotts and vindictive discriminations." Such "mischief-makers" magnified any criticism of Jewish tradition into an attack against the Jewish "race," denouncing anyone who opposed the "intense isolationism" of the Jews as a "malignant enemy of a sacred and eternal tradition." They thus made more difficult the achievement of any synthesis of the opposing views of Jews and Gentiles. Thanks in part to them, "Jewish racial consciousness" had become "over-sensitised." As for "the Gentile writer who wishes to escape from the systematic hostility and detraction of a large and influential section in the literary world"—Wells was clearly referring to himself—such a writer was driven to "exaggerated and exasperating suppressions," until he finally "loses patience and explodes." To the "Professional Champions" this may seem "good business," but "it is very bad business indeed for the Jewish community."

Still, Wells believed that world Jewry's abandonment of its exclusivity and its conversion to "universalism" could not be coerced. It "must come from within, can only come from within." He agreed that "all external persecution, violence and counter-boycotting of the Jews as a race or a religion is barbaric." Persecution was not only doomed to failure but was bound to dehumanize the persecutor. Yet a Gentile writer should also be free to express the "frankest and most searching criticism of the many narrowing and reactionary elements still disagreeably active in the Jewish tradition." After all, since Jews wrote Gentile history and criticized Gentile institutions, should not Gentiles be free to write Jewish history and criticize Jewish institutions? "A man," Wells wrote—and there could be no question whom he meant—may have "the fullest apprehension of the great history and exceptional quality of the Jews," he may have "the utmost liking and admiration for individual Jews and for Jewish types and traits," he may even want "to get together with Jews in every possible way." But he could still regard Zionism and "cultural particularism" as "a blunder and misfortune for mankind."

Basically, what Wells found objectionable in Jews was not their race or religion or conduct or appearance. It was their Jewishness. He compared them to other "grievance stricken peoples" whose misfortunes had led to their alienation from the world around them. They reminded him of the "dash and brilliance of so many young Irishmen" and of the "alert nimbleness of the young Indian." He was most impressed, however, by the "immense power and penetration of so many young Jews." And yet that power and penetration were not enough to make them forget "the blunders and injustice done them by people as often as not duller than themselves." Why? Why did they allow themselves to be so "vindictive"? Why did they let those "ancient defeats" stand in the way of achieving "modern creativeness"? Why did they refuse "to be men among men"? In short, "why specialize in Erin or Mother India or Palestine, when the whole world is our common inheritance?" To those who clung so stubbornly to their separateness and uniqueness, Wells issued a ringing challenge: *Come out of Israel!"*

Here was the ultimate source of his criticism of the Jews: they refused to identify with non-Jews; they insisted on following a path different from that of the rest of mankind. And that meant that every "genuine man of science" and every "advocate of the socialist world state" was bound to recognize that his vision of the future was fundamentally different from that of the faithful adherent to Judaism. The two views of the world were irreconcilable. On one side was the Jew, who "harks back to an extremely antiquated divinity and history and is saturated with an unjustifiable racial conceit." On the other side was "the modern liberal," who "gives his allegiance to a universal order still to be attained." Was there any question to which one Wells belonged? He proudly identified himself with the progressives who "were working for the future of all mankind and not for an inassimilable tribal survival." How then could anyone accuse him of bigotry? He was in fact seeking to end anti-Semitism by ending the Jewish clannishness and exclusiveness which were the source of anti-Semitism. In his view, he was a friend of the Jews, trying to save them from themselves, from their willful, stubborn narrow-mindedness. Those charging him with ethnic prejudice were simply libelers and slanderers.[10]

Most English readers of Wells's analysis of the "Jewish question" must have felt a little uneasy. He sounded so blunt, so vehement; he was almost un-British in his intensity. Members of the educated, well-to-do patriciate wanted to be perceived as tolerant and cosmopolitan, free of the harsh prejudices so common on the continent. And many of them were indeed quite broad-minded, certainly more so than the social elite in Poland or Germany or even France. Yet there were also some (more than a few, in fact) who regarded Jews with disdain, distaste, or distrust. As a rule, however, they would reveal their prejudices in bits and pieces, in occasional hints and casual remarks, in the minor incidents of daily life rather than in bitter diatribes or dire warnings. Nevertheless, such brief glimpses of ethnic aversion suggested an undercurrent of anti-Semitism which was deeper than appeared on the placid surface of public conduct.

Sir John Simon, for example, who during the 1930s served in the cabinet successively as foreign secretary, home secretary, and chancellor of the exchequer, thought it advisable to issue a statement that despite his Biblical name, he was of Welsh descent. Lord Camrose, proprietor of the *Daily Telegraph*, brought a successful libel suit against a publication of the British Union of Fascists for implying that he was a Jew. And the well-known Anglican churchman William Ralph Inge, the "gloomy dean," suggested that the Jews were using "their not inconsiderable influence in the Press and in Parliament" to embroil Great Britain in a conflict with Germany, although he had to admit later that the evidence supporting his charge was nothing more than journalistic gossip. Such minor displays of upperclass aversion to Jews continued to pop up throughout the decade.[11]

One incident in the summer of 1938 was particularly revealing, not because of its inherent importance—it was in fact barely mentioned in the press—but because it provided a clear insight into the rising tide of anti-Semitic hostility in England. A London judge, Herbert Metcalfe, sentenced three illegal Jewish immigrants to six months in prison with hard labor, recommending in addition that upon their release they should all be deported. One was a photographer born in Russia, another was a tailor from Poland, and the third, a woman employed as a barmaid, had come from Berlin. In imposing this punishment, the magistrate stated that "as far as he was concerned, he intended to enforce the law to the fullest extent." And there were good reasons for his resolve to be stern. "It was becoming an outrage," he declared from the bench, "the way in which stateless Jews were pouring in from every port of this country." He was determined to do something about that.[12]

Here was the central issue in the long prewar debate in Great Britain regarding the increasingly pressing "Jewish question." Most English people were not greatly concerned about the possible effect of a large-scale influx of foreigners from Central and Eastern Europe on the national culture and character. In this regard there was an important difference between popular attitudes in the United Kingdom and in the French Republic. To most of the English, the chief problem regarding the immigration of persecuted Jews was its likely economic consequence. How wise was it to admit large numbers of refugees at a time when so many British workers were unemployed and so many British shopkeepers were facing bankruptcy? That concern was not only plausible; it also provided in many cases the justification for an opposition to Jewish immigration that was based as much on ethnic prejudice as on economic apprehension.

This does not mean that those who argued against the admission of refugees were motivated primarily by anti-Semitic bigotry. Nor should the tireless activities of the various humanitarian societies and organizations trying to help Jewish refugees be overlooked. Their willingness to subordinate self-interest to the ideal of a universal humanitarianism deserves recognition and respect. Yet there can be no denying that those who argued that charity begins at home and that the needs of compatriots must take precedence over the needs of aliens generally prevailed. The harsh realities of the Great Depression made any other outcome impossible.

In many cases, moreover, the contention that the admission of persecuted foreigners should not be allowed to threaten the economic welfare of fellow Britons was accompanied by warnings that a sudden influx of refugees was likely to promote the spread of anti-Semitism. Those voicing such warnings invariably insisted that they themselves were free of prejudice. They claimed that they sympathized with the victims of racism in the Third Reich and the succession states. But the broad masses of the English population, less enlightened and less compassionate, would be likely to blame the economic hardships they had to endure on Jews if the gates were suddenly opened to mass immigration. It was therefore in the interest of everyone, including the refugees themselves, to regulate and restrict the admission of needy foreigners.

There were occasions, however, when some of those opposing the admission of refugees because of its alleged economic effects and xenophobic consequences would display a half-disguised racism of their own. They generally condemned the naked brutality of the anti-Semitic policy of National Socialism. But then they would suggest, sometimes in almost the same breath, that the Jews were not entirely guiltless in provoking the hostility they encountered. Admittedly, there was no excuse for the cruelty with which the Third Reich treated them. Yet even democratic, generous nations like Great Britain had to be on guard against the unhealthy Jewish influence on society.

The economic, psychological, and ethnic forms of opposition to the large-scale immigration of Jewish refugees usually appeared independently, but sometimes they were intertwined and inextricable. The British press, for instance, was virtually unanimous in its condemnation of the violent measures adopted by the Nazi regime in dealing with the "Jewish question." They seemed so harsh, so inhumane. And yet there was very little support for the immigration of the victims of these measures. Most newspapers maintained that the depressed state of the English economy made it impossible to admit more than a very limited number of refugees. Other democratic, generous nations must do their share as well, because trying to deal with the problem singlehandedly was bound to arouse strong popular opposition throughout Great Britain.

In the summer of 1938, the weekly *Observer* wrote that deciding what should be done about the refugees from Germany and Austria presented "a problem of heartbreaking magnitude." An international conference to deal with it had just met in Evian-les-Bains in France and was about to resume its deliberations in London. But what could the English government be expected to do beyond what it was already doing? "A typically baffling illustration of the difficulty is the fact that Britain now has more Jews than Germany ever had." To admit still more would pose a serious risk. "If a further accretion of, say, 100,000 of them came into the country, how could the danger be averted of an anti-Jewish feeling here?" Obviously, the issue could not be dealt with piecemeal, nation by nation; it had to be internationalized. It would remain unresolved "unless every great country takes her proportionate share." That was the "only solution."[13]

The most persistent opposition to the admission of Jewish refugees, however, appeared in the pages of Lord Beaverbrook's *Daily Express* and *Sunday Express.* Like almost all other English newspapers, they condemned the growing oppression of the Jewish community in Central Europe, voicing their sympathy for the victims of the Third Reich's racism. But they also emphasized even more than the others the economic danger of a heavy influx of refugees who would compete with the native population for scarce jobs and opportunities. They dwelt on the likelihood of an intensified anti-Semitism in the United Kingdom. And they were far more open in suggesting that the victims of ethnic hostility, and not only in Germany, had contributed to the hostility they were facing by their antisocial mentality and conduct. They were, at least in part, the authors of their own misfortunes.

Late in March 1938, about two weeks after the Third Reich's incorporation of Austria, the *Daily Express* asked in an editorial, "Shall All Come In?" The paper had recently received from Vienna "some sad stories of the persecuted Jews." They were most distressing. But "where will it end?" There was currently a "powerful agitation" in Great Britain "to admit all Jewish refugees without question or discrimination." Under the circumstances, such a display of sympathy was quite understandable. And yet "it would be unwise to overload the basket like that." It might have an unexpected and undesired result. "It would stir up the elements here that batten on anti-Semitic propaganda." Those elements would point to the incoming tide of foreigners, "almost all belonging to the extreme Left," and ask, "What if Poland, Hungary, Rumania also expel their Jewish citizens? Must we admit them too?" The result would be even fiercer opposition to Jewish immigration. It was thus in the interest of all concerned, Jews and non-Jews alike, to avoid fostering of ethnic prejudice. "Because we DON'T want anti-Jewish uproar we DO need to show common sense in not admitting all applicants." Caution and restraint would in the long run be more effective in dealing with the refugee problem than weeping and lamenting.[14]

Three months later, the *Sunday Express* dealt with the same subject even more bluntly. Its editorial began by ritualistically condemning the racial program of the Third Reich. It spoke of the "new exodus of the children of Israel, not from Egypt but from Germany," an exodus driven by "the method of terror." As a result, "the children of Israel are sore afraid." In Great Britain, on the other hand, there was no persecution. "Indeed, in many respects the Jews are given favoured treatment here." But consequently foreign Jews were now pouring in, creating what had become a "big influx." In fact, "they are over-running the country." They were trying to enter the medical field; they wanted to practice dentistry. Was it any wonder that many English professionals "resent their living being taken from them by immigrants from foreign countries, whether they be Jew or Gentile"?

The *Sunday Express* then went on to suggest that the growing hostility toward Jews in Europe was not altogether groundless or irrational. There were reasons for it, sometimes good reasons. The Jews were being persecuted in Germany because they had become "too prosperous." Indeed, "half the lawyers and half the doctors in Germany were Jews." Their oppression was thus partly a result of their prosperity. That was nothing new, however. Some fifty years earlier "the Jews owned a great part of the agricultural land of Russia." That was when some agitator standing on a tub charged that "the Jews were using Christian blood to make their Easter bread." His accusation led to a mass pogrom that spread throughout Russia, killing 10,000 Jews. The czarist government itself had eventually joined in the persecution, confiscating the landed property owned by Jews and forcing them to live in urban ghettos.

Was there not a danger that the same sequence of prosperity and oppression might sooner or later be repeated in Great Britain? After all, the Jews were already invading medicine and dentistry. And now, worst of all, "many of them are holding themselves out to the public as psycho-analysts." That was dangerous. "A psycho-analyst needs no medical training, but arrogates to himself the functions of a doctor. And he often obtains an ascendancy over the patient of which he makes base use if he is a bad man."

The tone of the *Sunday Express* had begun to resemble that of the right-wing continental newspapers, not only German and Austrian but Polish, Romanian, Hungarian, and Lithuanian. The authors of the editorial may indeed have sensed this similarity, because in their conclusion they hastened to repeat the condemnation of National Socialist anti-Semitism and emphasize that all right-thinking Britons opposed ethnic prejudice. "The hostility to the Jews in Germany cannot be condoned," they declared dutifully. The ethnic bigotry of the Third Reich seemed all the more cruel when contrasted with the humane outlook of English public opinion. "There is no intolerance in Britain today." As a matter of fact, "intolerance is loathed and hated by almost everybody in this country." And yet there was a danger, a danger to be avoided at all costs, that the unending flood of refugees might eventually undermine the position of the Jewish community in the United Kingdom. Jews as well as non-Jews should therefore exercise caution. "By keeping a close watch on the causes which fed the intolerance of the Jews in other European countries we shall be able to continue to treat well those Jews who have made their homes among us, many of them for generations." This line of reasoning resembled the widespread contention in the French Republic that those advocating restrictions on Jewish immigration really had the best interests of the Jews at heart. They were not opponents but friends and defenders of the Jewish community. Their motives were unassailable.[15]

Not even the outbreak of anti-Semitic fury in the Third Reich during the Kristallnacht could weaken the opposition of the Beaverbrook press to the further admission of Jewish refugees. The *Daily Express* did refer briefly, almost perfunctorily, to "these unhappy men, women and children driven from the lands of their birth by terror, hatred and oppression." But it also sounded faintly annoyed by all the attention the refugees were receiving day after day in the national press. "The Jews are always in the news." It seemed that each morning there were new accounts of pogroms "here, there and everywhere," new reports of "the sufferings of the Jewish race and stories of the disabilities now being inflicted on the Jewish people." How long would this go on? Now even the British Parliament was about to start discussing the refugee problem and what should be done about it. Why? What would be the object of such a discussion? What purpose would it serve? Could it possibly be used to propose the admission of more refugees? "That is a dangerous proposition. We have already accepted our full quota of foreign Jews. We cannot assimilate any more."

Was there, then, nothing else that the government of Great Britain could do to help solve the problem of the refugees? Not quite. It could admit the Jews to the crown colonies. "There is plenty of room there and many undeveloped parts which by the sweat of man's brow and by unremitting toil would repay him a thousandfold for his labours." There was a catch—a very important catch. Would the Jews be willing to emigrate overseas? "Of course not." Some might perhaps accept resettlement in Palestine, but Palestine could not accept any more Jewish settlers. There was no way out. England had already done its share, probably more than its share. Now it could only continue to express sympathy for the victims of anti-Semitism and urge other countries to do their part in dealing with the tragic consequences of continental bigotry.[16]

In November 1938, following the violent anti-Semitic riots in the Third Reich, the House of Commons entered into a formal discussion of "Racial, Religious and Political Minorities." At the end it adopted a motion that expressed sympathy for the Jews, without mentioning them by name, and that demanded a solution for the refugee problem, without specifying what that solution should be. "This House notes with profound concern the deplorable treatment suffered by certain racial, religious, and political minorities in Europe, and, in view of the growing gravity of the refugee problem, would welcome an immediate concerted effort amongst the nations, including the United States of America, to secure a common policy." There is no record of how many members supported and how many opposed the motion, but given its noncommittal, unexceptionable wording, the vote must have been almost unanimous.[17]

Yet even on this largely ceremonial occasion there were a few expressions of uneasiness regarding the possible consequences of a commendable but overgenerous compassion for the victims of foreign prejudice. During the debate that preceded the vote, one member, Sir Archibald Richard James Southby, reminded the House that "in our desire to help this stream of refugees, we must not lose sight of the fact that there exists in the minds of many of our own people a very real fear lest there should be a tremendous influx into this country of refugees who are unable to maintain themselves and who would have to compete with our own citizens for a livelihood." A choice had to be made, a difficult yet unavoidable choice. "Many of our own people are hard put to it to find work and a means of livelihood, and our primary duty in this House of Commons is to those we represent. Our first duty is to our own people."

Southby hastened to make clear that his reservations regarding an overly benevolent immigration policy did not apply to "those refugees who are self-supporting and of good character." They represented nothing more serious than "an administrative problem with which the Home Secretary can deal quite simply." But there were others who were likely to become an added burden on a nation that was already overburdened. "The real problem is concerned with those who are not self-supporting, for whom some means of livelihood must be found, or for whom some possibility of advancement must be found elsewhere." Should not action be taken to prevent the admission of such undesirables?[18]

Sir Samuel Hoare, secretary of state for the Home Office, dealt in greater detail with the serious consequences of an unchecked inflow of impoverished immigrants into Great Britain. The country already had a very large number of unemployed. Economic competition with foreign nations had grown so fierce that "it is difficult for many of our fellow-countrymen to make a livelihood at all and keep their industries and businesses going." The result was "an underlying current of suspicion and anxiety, rightly or wrongly, about alien immigration on any big scale." But worse still—here the Home Secretary stated openly what others had only hinted at—"it is a fact, and we had better face the fact quite frankly, that below the surface . . . is the making of a definite anti-Jewish movement." That was very troubling.

Hoare hastened to assure the House that he was doing his best "to stamp upon an evil of that kind." But precisely for that reason he opposed "mass immigration which, in my view, would inevitably lead to the growth of a movement which we all wish to see suppressed." And this in turn meant that "it is essential, if we are to avoid an influx of the undesirable behind the cloak of refugee immigration, that we should keep a check upon individual cases." Such a check was in the long run best for all.[19]

The connection between the refugee problem and ethnic prejudice, between the admission of Jews and the immigration of undesirables, became even more apparent a few months later, in April 1939, shortly after the Third Reich's dismemberment of the Czechoslovak Republic, when the subject of refugees was placed once again on the agenda of the House of Commons. But this time there was no motion, not even an innocuous or noncommittal motion, regarding the fate of the victims of National

Socialism's racist policy. Instead the members revealed once more the underlying, irreconcilable conflict between generosity and prudence, between moral imperative and hardheaded realism. There was nothing ambiguous about what some of them had to say.

Godfrey Nicholson, one of the most outspoken among them, warned that "we are faced with the actual existence of anti-Semitism and the potential existence for much more anti-Semitism." Yet the government had so far refused to face the facts. Many remedies had been suggested, but "one way not to deal with the problem successfully is to allow in every Jew who applies." On the other hand, "one way to avoid creating anti-Semitism is to have at the other end a proper system of selection of the sort of Jews to admit." Careful picking and choosing was the only solution. But what sort of standard should be used to separate the desirable from the undesirable immigrants? To Nicholson the answer was clear. "An influx of Jews from Eastern Europe would naturally arouse anti-Semitism in this country, but the finest type of German Jew or, to accept Herr Hitler's terminology, of 'non-Aryan' German, will not cause anti-Semitism."

Nicholson reminded the members of the House that while it was their duty to deal with the refugee problem "as Christians and as Englishmen," they should also keep in mind that "Jews in large numbers are very difficult to assimilate into our civilisation all at once." It was thus important to reduce the problem to "managable proportions." The first thing was to map out what Great Britain could do and then do it efficiently and economically. But in addition, other countries must help. Like so many politicians grappling with the refugee problem, he had concluded that its solution had to be sought in its internationalization.[20]

This was easier said than done, however. Soon after Nicholson finished his speech, another member of the House rose to point out that other countries were just as reluctant as Great Britain to admit any more Jews, and for the same reason. Earl Winterton, the paymaster general of the United Kingdom, was also chairman of the Evian Committee, which represented more than thirty governments seeking to solve or at least alleviate the refugee problem through collective action. But experience had taught him how difficult and unlikely such collective action was. His intention, he told the members of Parliament, was to be "entirely frank" in mentioning something that was "unhappily pervasive" and that hampered all efforts to help the refugees: "It is the sub-current of anti-Semitism or anti-alienism which exists in many countries." Much of it was based on "absurd prejudices and an almost pathological credulity" regarding the evil deeds that Jews had allegedly committed. There were also several organizations, "one of which exists in this country," instigating anti-Semitic hostility. To the extent that such hostility was based on irrational ethnic hatred, it was "a wholly cruel and evil thing." There could be no justification for it.

Still, opposition to the immigration of many more Jews was not based entirely on blind prejudice. "Some of it proceeds from genuine apprehension," Winterton had to admit. There was a widespread fear, and not only in Great Britain, that "refugees admitted for permanent settlement will merely enter already crowded professions or swell the existing army of retailers and middlemen." And who could blame those alarmed by such a possibility? Indeed, if he were not the British representative on the Evian Committee, Winterton confessed, he too would oppose any further admission of refugees. After all, "the whole Evian Committee without exception is not prepared to admit the principle that they are either under a moral obligation or that it is practically possible from the point of public support in their respective countries to admit financial liability for the transfer and upkeep in the countries or for the permanent settlement of refugees."

As for the reason for this unwillingness, that was obvious. "Every one of these 32 Governments is faced with unemployment difficulties. Every one of them is frightened of the possible growth of an anti-Semitic and anti-foreign feeling if it is felt that more is being done for foreigners than for their own people." Popular opposition to Jewish immigration was too strong to be overcome by reasoning or pleading. "There is no chance of getting an alteration in that principle." Willy-nilly, the authorities had to bow to the pressure of public opinion.[21]

In the spring of 1938, a few weeks after the Third Reich's annexation of Austria, a Jewish deputation that called on Sir Samuel Hoare was told that the Home Office would have to "discriminate very carefully" in deciding on "the type of refugee who could be admitted to this country." To act hastily or rashly might prove risky. "If a flood of the wrong type of immigrants were allowed in there might be serious danger of anti-semitic feeling being aroused in this country." Naturally, that sort of feeling had to be avoided at any cost. "The last thing which we wanted here was the creation of a Jewish problem," the home secretary told the members of the deputation. And the members, according to the minutes of the meeting, assured him that they "entirely agreed with this point of view." They were in fact even more anxious than he to avoid creating a "Jewish problem."

One member even went so far as to warn Hoare against an overly generous policy regarding the admission of Austrian Jews. Otto Schiff, a well-to-do stockbroker who was himself an immigrant from Frankfurt am Main, had gained the reputation of a tireless defender of persecuted Jews seeking asylum in Great Britain. He had served as president of the Jews' Temporary Shelter during the 1920s and had then founded the Jewish Refugees Committee in 1933 to assist the victims of National Socialism. Yet during the deputation's meeting with Hoare, he offered candid though superfluous advice regarding the need to exercise caution in admitting immigrants from Central Europe. "It was very difficult to get rid of a refugee," Schiff warned, "once he had entered and spent a few months in this country." The requirement of a visa was especially important in the case of "Austrians"—he preferred not to specify their ethnic or religious background—who were "largely of the shop-keeper and small trader class and would therefore prove much more difficult to emigrate than the average German who had come to the United Kingdom." The Home Office, however, had already arrived at a similar conclusion on its own.[22]

Jewish acquiescence in government restrictions on the admission of refugees, an acquiescence designed to prevent the spread of anti-Semitism, was by no means uncommon. The established communities of West European Jews, enjoying acceptance and respectability, were reluctant to make themselves vulnerable once again to the charge that they were willing to sacrifice the common good for the sake of ethnic solidarity. Their concern, though not heroic, was at least understandable. They only had to look at Germany to see how fragile and precarious was the equality they had won at such a heavy cost. They were prepared in some cases—indeed, in many cases—to make minor concessions to popular prejudice now in order to avoid making major concessions later.

In November 1938, a few weeks after the outbreak of violent anti-Semitic riots in the Third Reich, Neville Chamberlain told the French prime minister, Édouard Daladier, during their meeting in Paris that his government was "most anxious" to help the refugees. The cabinet had already begun to discuss the problem with the British colonies and the dominions. More than that, about five hundred Jewish immigrants were being currently admitted to the United Kingdom each week. Yet that was also creating difficulties. One of the greatest was "the serious danger of arousing anti-Semitic feeling in Great Britain." The authorities could not ignore the possibility that too much concern for the victims of foreign prejudice might increase domestic prejudice. "Indeed, a number of Jews had begged His Majesty's Government not to advertise too prominently what was being done." By displaying excessive generosity toward Jewish immigrants, the government might unintentionally encourage the demand for their total exclusion.[23]

In the last years before the Second World War, the growth of anti-Semitism in Central and Eastern Europe, which steadily increased the number of Jews seeking refuge in the Western democracies, also reinforced the opposition in those democracies to the continuing admission of Jewish immigrants. But long before the Anschluss and the Kristallnacht, some political observers recognized that the growing pressure on Jews in the Third Reich and the succession states to emigrate was in the long run bound to strengthen resistance to Jewish immigration in England, France, and the United States. In March 1936, Chaim Weizmann, president of the World Zionist Organization, warned a conference of the Council for German Jewry in London against too much reliance on Western benevolence. "Jews have proved that they are an 'insoluble' element—to use a chemical term—the quantity which can be absorbed in each country proves to be small. The formula reacts quickly, and saturation point is rapidly reached." Beneath the surface of tolerance and generosity lurked ethnic hostility, even in the most progressive states. "The Jewish communities in the respective countries are always full of anxiety lest there will be too many and that anti-Semitism may be stimulated." On the basis of their own experience, those attending the conference were inclined to agree.[24]

But then, what should be done? To Weizmann the only answer was Zionism. Most refugees, however, preferred some other solution. They had little desire to go to a remote region their ancestors had left almost two thousand years before. They were reluctant to start out anew in a distant and foreign land. Above all, they had no wish to become pioneers, settlers, and farmers, no wish to adjust to a new language, a new culture, and a new way of life. What they wanted was refuge in a country in which they would be able to continue their familiar customs, habits, and occupations. They wanted to live in an urban environment, practice the skilled trades, go into business, enter the learned professions, or perhaps follow some cultural or artistic pursuit. In order to do that, they would have to emigrate to the West. But thereby they would create a dilemma for the Jews already living there. It would force those Jews to choose between generosity and expediency, between ethnic loyalty and ethnic security. It would be a very difficult choice.

They were not the only ones who had to make a very difficult choice. The governments of the democratic states confronted a problem that appeared almost insoluble. They could not simply turn their backs on the victims of an increasingly brutal anti-Semitic movement which they themselves had so often denounced—quite sincerely, as a rule. To do so would lend credibility to the accusation often made by the Hitler government that humane statesmen expressing sympathy for the allegedly persecuted Jews were only shedding crocodile tears. They were hypocrites. Just look at the barriers they were raising against the admission of refugees while condemning the Third Reich for trying to defend itself against the evil designs of those same refugees. Still, the statesmen of Western Europe, though eager to show the world how much more compassionate they were than those cruel National Socialists, could not display too much humaneness for fear of inciting some form of National Socialism in their own countries. The dilemma they had to face was the same one confronting the Jewish communities in the West.

The only way out seemed to be a cautious course midway between pity and prudence. And that in fact was the course that the British government decided to follow. In March 1938, a few days after the Anschluss, the cabinet appointed a committee of four members, headed by Hoare, to consider what should be done about the wave of Austrian refugees which was about to start flowing westward. The committee should keep in mind, according to the cabinet's instructions, "the points mentioned by the Home Secretary regarding the importance of adopting as humane an attitude as possible, and at the same time of avoiding the creation of a Jewish problem in this country." A few months later Hoare reported to the cabinet that "while he was anxious to do his best, there was a good deal of feeling growing up in this country—a feeling which was reflected in Parliament—against the admission of Jews to British territory." The government could not afford to ignore this opposition against a large-scale immigration of refugees. And a few months after that, Winterton informed a delegation representing several volunteer organizations that provided assistance to the Nazis' victims that the government was unable to grant their request for financial aid. That was simply "a political impossibility." Parliament would have to approve any such expenditure, which would then open the door to public discussion, and that in turn might lead to "an immediate outcry from all anti-alien and anti-semitic elements in this country that the Government were subsidising the admission of aliens at a time when there was widespread unemployment and economic distress among our own people." Winterton was anxious to avoid "stirring up anti-alien and anti-semitic feeling in the United Kingdom." And the members of the delegation "entirely agreed."[25]

What made the British government especially cautious in formulating its refugee policy was the fear that too much generosity on its part would encourage the states of Central and Eastern Europe to try to solve their own "Jewish question" by urging or pressuring the Jews to emigrate westward, thereby dumping the problem in the lap of countries like England. It was hard enough to cope with the continuous stream of refugees from Germany and Austria. But the possibility of having to deal with millions of refugees from Poland, Romania, Hungary, Lithuania, and Latvia—that was frightening. Any demographic shift on such a scale would soon overwhelm whatever resources were still available to help the victims of ethnic persecution. There would be thousands of refugees without work, sleeping in the streets, begging for food, dirty, ragged, and emaciated. How would that make the British government and the British nation look in the eyes of the world? Everything possible had to be done to prevent such an eventuality.

The dangers inherent in the refugee problem, moreover, inspired a flood of reports, stories, rumors, and speculations, most of them without foundation, regarding the causes and consequences of a Jewish mass migration. They were even discussed at times by high-ranking officials of the government. Thus, in the spring of 1938, Hoare reported to the cabinet that a "curious story" had reached him, which suggested that "the Germans were anxious to inundate this country with Jews, with a view to creating a Jewish problem in the United Kingdom." But neither the home secretary nor the other members of the cabinet seemed too concerned. There was no discussion of the rumor, which military intelligence had forwarded to Hoare. After all, most Central European Jews had already emigrated or were about to emigrate. Speculation about the intentions of the German government would not change the situation in any significant way.[26]

Developments in Eastern Europe, on the other hand, seemed much more threatening. Several of the governments there had made it clear that they wanted to reduce their Jewish population by promoting or coercing emigration, and that they wanted the Western democracies to assist them by resettling the emigrants. To Whitehall, that was alarming. A memorandum composed by R. M. Makins of the Foreign Office in May 1938, shortly before the meeting of the international conference at Evian, warned that anti-Semitic measures were intensifying in the succession states and that Poland in particular had been trying for a long time "to initiate some scheme of emigration in which they look for British financial support." Any plans adopted at Evian to provide asylum for East European Jews would encourage the governments in that region to increase the pressure on their Jewish minorities. The democratic states thus had to deal with more than a refugee or immigration problem. They were facing the prospect "of a mass movement of population perhaps involving some millions of people." For the British government, that would be a very serious danger.[27]

As the time the conference approached, the Foreign Office became increasingly concerned about the long-term consequences of an overgenerous policy toward East European Jews. In its instructions to the delegation that was to represent the United Kingdom, it emphasized once again that anti-Semitic measures in the succession states had recently become more severe, suggesting that especially Poland and Romania were hoping "for the assistance of other countries in disposing in part of their Jewish population." Since the political leaders of Eastern Europe were sure to follow the proceedings of the conference with great interest, it was very important that "the results of the meeting should not act as an incentive to these governments to increase the pressure on their Jewish minorities, and at the same time create an inconvenient precedent for dealing with the results of such pressure." Above all, nothing should be done to leave the impression that refugees from the succession states could find asylum in Western Europe, since that would encourage those states to act "with impunity" in forcing "sections of their population," unspecified but unmistakable, to emigrate.[28]

Once the Evian conference ended, however, the British statesmen could breathe a sigh of relief. The other participants had seemed just as reluctant to admit large numbers of Jewish refugees from Central and Eastern Europe. There was no danger after all of suddenly being inundated by hordes of hungry, desperate, pitiable victims of ethnic persecution. Whitehall's fears had been unfounded. And yet the government could not simply wash its hands of that complicated, messy refugee problem. To ignore it altogether might leave the members of the cabinet open to the charge that they were no better than those heartless bigots in the Wilhelmstrasse. Something had to be done. And since the attempt to deal with the "Jewish question" through internationalization had failed, why not try the strategy of exportation? If the French were willing to consider the resettlement of refugees in Madagascar, could the English let themselves be perceived as less generous? They had so many colonies and dependencies conveniently distant from Europe, underpopulated (at least by whites), underdeveloped, and in need of business experience, entrepreneurial skill, and financial acumen. A substantial inflow of Jewish refugees might prove of benefit to guests and hosts alike. It might turn out to be a marriage of convenience.

That was why the idea of resettling Central and East European Jews overseas was so favorably received in Great Britain, even by those or especially by those who were opposed to their admittance to the United Kingdom. The *Daily Express*, for instance, though firmly set against the immigration of Jews fleeing the Third Reich after the Kristallnacht, was prepared to welcome them to the colonies, where there was ample room and "many undeveloped parts" and where a man might be rewarded "a thousandfold" for his "unremitting toil." Similarly, Winterton stated before the House of Commons that while the Western democracies hesitated to admit any more Jewish refugees for fear of arousing anti-Semitic prejudice at home, he himself was "desperately anxious . . . to get some of these land settlement schemes actually in operation, for I believe it will be found to be the case . . . that these Jewish refugees, if properly trained and selected, will make good primary producers."[29]

Yet in fact the obstacles to exporting the refugee problem were almost as great as those to internationalizing it. The most obvious was the reluctance of most Jewish emigrants to leave Europe, even Germany or Poland or Romania, for Kenya or Guiana or even Australia or New Zealand. Indeed, the *Daily Express*, though favoring the emigration of refugees to the British colonies, doubted whether many of them would be willing to accept such a drastic change in their way of life. "Will the Jews go to these outlying countries?" it asked rhetorically. "Of course not. Except to Palestine, which cannot take in any more of them." Here was the chief, the insuperable difficulty. The great majority of the refugees, if given the choice, preferred even the crowded, grimy East End of London or the Belleville district of Paris or the East Side of New York to the most elegant neighborhood in Christchurch or Nairobi or Georgetown.[30]

Nor, for that matter, were the overseas members of the British Commonwealth eager to welcome an influx of immigrants who, while of the right color, were of a different background, a different culture, and a different collective mentality. As early as December 1933, Lord Bledisloe, the governor-general of New Zealand, though expressing sympathy for "German scientists of Semitic origin," informed the dominions secretary in London that his government would be unwilling to take any step "from humanitarian motives" that might create the impression that "German Jews of any description were being welcomed to this Dominion during a period of acute economic depression to the possible detriment of New Zealanders." This unwillingness was not a result solely of the hardships caused by the Great Depression, however. Bledisloe also feared that "immigrants from Germany might be at heart, if not openly, Communists, and spread revolutionary propaganda to the social unsettlement of the local community." That was a danger which could not be ignored.[31]

The authorities in Kenya were equally reluctant to admit a large number of Jewish refugees. The governor of the colony informed the colonial secretary in June 1938 that he would not oppose "the carefully regulated influx of Jews of the right type—i.e. nordic from Germany or Austria—for agricultural settlement in reasonably small numbers . . . in small groups of a size not too large to become part of the general economic and social life of the community." Half a year later, in January 1939, the Kenya Settlement Committee appointed by the British government submitted a report that sounded even more hesitant. It conceded that "the carefully regulated settlement of a comparatively small number of Jews of nordic type on individual holdings—the number to be governed by the absorptive capacity of the Colony—might be an advantage to Kenya." Such a settlement, however, must be privately organized and financed and must "at every stage" be subject to official approval. "Jewish immigration should, in our view, be very rigorously supervised and controlled, as . . . it would be impossible for any considerable number of artisans, clerks and professional people to be absorbed in the economic life of the Colony without seriously jeopardising the interests of existing residents." This too had a familiar ring.[32]

Plans to resettle refugees overseas thus seemed no more likely to succeed than plans to resettle them in Europe. That was the conclusion reached by the *Christian Century* in Chicago shortly before the Second World War. It described the frequent mention of Madagascar and parts of South Africa as territories where Jews could be sent to form "an autonomous society." The British prime minister, moreover, had informed Parliament that the government would be willing to open Tanganyika or British Guiana to "involuntary refugees" from Germany. And then there was Australia, which, with "a vast extent of thinly populated territory," seemed in theory to be a logical sanctuary. One serious problem remained, however: "The Australians violently object." As for South Africa, "the British and Dutch population is as anti-Semitic as Germany, and would oppose the importation of Jews to their own and probably to contiguous countries, even to the point of blocking it by force." That left only Palestine. But Palestine was also "out of the question," in view of "the failure of the British mandate to attain some *modus vivendi* as between Jews and Arabs." After all the studying, pondering, contemplating, and weighing of the refugee problem, the *Christian Century* could find no solution.[33]

Neither could the British government. The difference was that the British government could not afford to stop looking. It had to continue to sway and zigzag in dealing with Jewish immigration, carefully avoiding the extremes of open admission and total exclusion. Its policy, or lack of policy, found expression in Hoare's modest hope that he would still be able to "go on quietly considering individual cases on their merits." That meant in effect that the refugees who had the financial resources to support themselves without government assistance—mostly those from Central Europe—could generally obtain a temporary residence permit or a transit visa to the United Kingdom. For Jews seeking to leave the Third Reich, emigration was thus a possibility, though often only after considerable delay and a great deal of red tape. For the far larger Jewish community of Eastern Europe, however, finding a place of refuge was much more difficult. That was partly because its situation, though unenviable, was perceived as less precarious. But of greater importance was the fact that many of its members were poor, outlandish, and unassimilated. They were not likely to adapt readily to British customs, attitudes, values, and loyalties. And so Whitehall continued to improvise, delay, dodge, and occasionally dissemble, until the coming of the Second World War fundamentally altered the nature of the problems it had to deal with, including that perennial, frustrating, seemingly insoluble "Jewish question."[34]

5

Seeking Asylum in the New World: The United States

To Jewish refugees trying to escape persecution in Eastern and Central Europe, emigration to America seemed the ideal solution. Even the most liberal and tolerant West European nations remained burdened by inherited traditions and attitudes that made the acceptance of outsiders very difficult. They continued to cling to class distinctions and social disparities representing the legacy of a thousand years of hierarchical authority. Not even democratic constitutions or progressive laws could erase the heritage of an oligarchic past. For Jews seeking refuge, this meant that emigration to Western Europe was likely to lead to an alleviation of rather than a liberation from the prejudices they had encountered in the country of their birth.

But America was different. Here was a country where Europeans had lived for barely three centuries, a country that had never accepted the sharp distinctions separating classes and ethnicities in the Old World. Here talent and ambition were the keys to success, not wealth or status. A shoeshine boy could rise to become a millionaire; someone born in a backwoods cabin might end up in the White House. There was no limit to how high a man could rise with determination, ambition, hard work, and a little luck. To many Jewish refugees, especially from Eastern Europe, that seemed almost unbelievable. For them, the United States was a Never Land, a "golden realm." Yet they were not the only ones impressed by the opportunities America could offer the poor and underprivileged. Even some members of the European patriciate began to express approval, sometimes grudgingly, of a society free from the hierarchical rigidities and class segregations characterizing the Old World. Goethe, for example, though deferential toward traditional values and institutions, had to acknowledge toward the end of his life that "America, you have it better than our continent, the old one."

What impressed Jewish refugees almost as much as the limitless economic opportunities of the United States was its welcoming or at least tolerant attitude toward immigrants. Aliens were regarded with distrust or suspicion and occasionally with dislike even in the democratic states of Europe. They were widely perceived as not only foreign but unassimilable, in speech, custom, outlook, and loyalty. The United States, in contrast, was a nation of immigrants. The oldest and proudest families, even those descended from the Pilgrims on the *Mayflower,* had been in the country barely a few hundred years. Since then there had been countless new arrivals, year after year, from all parts of Europe—indeed, from all parts of the world. And all of them were regarded, officially at least, as Americans, with all the rights and privileges of Americans. Looming above the entrance to the harbor of the largest city in the country was a giant statue welcoming the tired and the poor of the earth, the "huddled masses yearning to breathe free," the "wretched refuse" of crowded foreign shores, the "homeless" and the "tempest-tossed." To refugees from the Third Reich or Eastern Europe, the United States seemed a nation of boundless generosity.

Still, the American acceptance of immigrants was based on more than generosity. There were also important geographic and demographic differences between the Old World and the New which explained the differences in their attitude toward foreigners seeking admittance. The United States had been through most of its history a nation of vast open spaces unsettled, uncultivated, and unexploited by whites. A rapid increase in its population through immigration would not threaten the welfare of the native-born inhabitants. On the contrary, immigration promoted economic growth. It enlarged the area under cultivation, thereby raising agricultural output. It accelerated and increased the production of coal, iron, copper, and oil. It promoted the industrialization of the economy, facilitating the establishment of shops, mills, and factories. Here was the central reason for the sharply differing views of immigrants in Europe and America, at least before the First World War. In Europe they represented rivals and interlopers threatening the economic stability of a society still closely bound to tradition. In America they became a creative force contributing to the growth of the economy and the increase in national wealth.

Even as late as Hitler's rise to power in Germany, the territorial and demographic differences on opposite shores of the Atlantic were vast. The continental United States around 1930 was almost three times as large as all the states of Western Europe combined: 2,973,766 square miles, compared with 1,042,207 square miles. The population of Western Europe, on the other hand, was substantially greater than the population of the United States, though not nearly by the same margin: 194,441,000 in Western Europe and 122,775,000 in the United States. The difference was even more striking when measured by the number of inhabitants per square mile: 41.3 for the United States, 186.6 for Western Europe. To the hungry and oppressed millions in the Old World seeking a better life, America became the Land of Promise.[1]

Jews made up a substantial part of the waves of immigrants crossing the Atlantic during the second half of the nineteenth century. In 1850, only about 50,000 of them were living in the United States, but by 1880 the number had risen to 230,000, and thereafter each successive census showed a growing increase in the Jewish population: 500,000 in 1890, 1 million in 1900, 2.2 million in 1910, 3.2 million in 1920, and 4.4 million in 1930. By the time of the establishment of the Third Reich, America had by far the largest Jewish population in the world, more than the 3,050,000 Jews in Poland or the 2,750,000 in the Soviet Union, and far more than the 900,000 in Romania or the 500,000 in Hungary. In relation to the total number of inhabitants, the percentage of Jews in the United States, 3.5, was still far behind that of most of the succession states. But it was far ahead of those of almost all the nations of Western and Central Europe: 1.7 percent in the Netherlands, 0.9 in Germany, 0.7 in Great Britain and Belgium, and 0.5 in France. Only in Austria was the proportion of Jews equal to that in the United States.[2]

The rapid increase in the immigration of Jews in the second half of the nineteenth century changed not only the size of the American Jewish community but also its origin and background. Until the 1880s, Jews crossing the Atlantic came largely from Central and Western Europe, mostly from Germany. They were generally assimilated, conversing in the language of their adopted country and sharing its customs and values. For them, the process of Americanization was relatively easy, almost as easy as for their non-Jewish immigrant countrymen. The only serious obstacle they had to overcome was religious prejudice in a strongly Protestant population. But even that was not as deep-rooted as in the Old World. The new arrivals soon learned English, they quickly became accustomed to the American way of life, and they began to play an increasingly important role in the economic life of their new motherland, especially in commerce and finance. They became living proof of the boundless opportunities that the United States could offer to immigrants of talent and ambition.

The size as well as the character of the American Jewish community started to change, however, in the last decades of the 1800s, mainly because of the explosive increase in the number of Jews entering the United States. Whereas in 1881 there were only about 8,000 Jewish immigrants, a year later the number had risen to almost 32,000. Then came a few years of relatively stable inflow, followed by a sudden jump to 36,000 in 1885, another jump to about 47,000 in 1886, a new high of 56,000 in 1887, and more than 62,000 in 1888. After a brief pause the upward climb resumed, reaching 111,000 in 1891 and nearly 137,000 in 1892. The annual totals then dropped to less than 100,000 for about a decade, only to rise to new heights: 106,000 in 1904, almost 130,000 in 1905, a record high of over 153,000 in 1906, a slight decline to 149,000 in 1907, and then another decline to 103,000 in 1908. During the next few years there was again a drop below the 100,000 mark, followed by a new rise to 101,000 in 1913 and 138,000 in 1914. The coming of the First World War finally put an end to the heavy influx of Jewish immigrants. The number did climb again briefly, to 119,036 in 1921, but then the restrictions imposed by new immigration laws reduced the admission of Jews to a level comparable to that of the early 1880s. All in all, Jewish immigrants to America for the entire period from 1881 to 1930 totaled some 2,885,000.[3]

This vast wave transformed the background and nature of American Jewry. Until a decade or two after the Civil War, most Jewish immigrants came from Germany. That began to change, however, toward the end of the century. Not only did the new German Empire enter a period of rapid industrialization, soon becoming the leading economic power on the continent; it also started to move in the direction of political liberalization and social reform. For Jews, that meant greater freedom and greater opportunity. There was now a new mood of optimism among them, which continued to grow until after the First World War. Why cross the ocean in search of liberation, they began to ask themselves, when liberation was within reach right here at home?

The decline in the number of Jewish immigrants from Central Europe was more than counterbalanced, however, by the increase in Jewish immigrants from Eastern Europe. Between 1881 and 1930, a total of 1,749,000 Jews left Russia in search of a better life in the United States. Another 597,000 left Austria-Hungary or, after 1920, the newly established Polish Republic. And then there were the 161,000 Jews who emigrated from Romania. Compared to these figures, the 114,000 Jewish emigrants from Great Britain and the 264,000 from other countries during the same period seem almost insignificant. All in all, of the 2,885,000 Jews who entered the United States during the half-century preceding the rise of National Socialism, 2,507,000, or 87 percent, came from Eastern Europe. The growing strength of an ideology based on liberalism and toleration made emigration from Central Europe seem unnecessary just as an embattled authoritarian system of government seeking to deflect opposition by inciting ethnic prejudice made emigration seem the only way out of Eastern Europe.[4]

The czarist regime in Russia, to take the obvious example, was not the first and certainly not the last in Europe to encourage the view that cunning, treacherous Jews were primarily responsible for growing popular dissatisfaction with the established order. Toward the end of the reign of the vacillating Alexander II, the government began to move steadily to the right. Under his successor, Alexander III, who came to the throne in 1881, a policy of out-and-out reaction reinforced by an undisguised anti-Semitism became official. The year in which the new czar assumed power became, not coincidentally, the year in which large-scale Jewish emigration began.

The accession of Nicholas II in 1894 did not change the policy of the imperial government regarding the political system in general or the "Jewish question" in particular. Indeed, as the twentieth century began and as resistance to the traditional form of authority gained strength, semiofficial incitement of ethnic hostility intensified. Every few years the

Jews were violently reminded that their position in Russia was deterio-
rating and they were facing increasing persecution and danger. In 1903,
a bloody pogrom in Kishinev exceeded in murderous fury any of those
in the previous twenty years. In 1905 came the publication of the forged
Protocols of the Elders of Zion, purporting to prove the existence of a
worldwide Jewish conspiracy to overthrow Christianity. And in 1911 there
was the arrest of Menahem Mendel Beilis on a charge of murdering a
Ukrainian child to obtain Christian blood to be used, allegedly in accordance with Jewish ritual, for baking matzos for the Passover holiday. Two
years later, after a trial that attracted considerable attention throughout
the continent and even as far away as the United States, Beilis was found
not guilty. But for members of the Jewish community, not only in Russia
but also in the neighboring states of Eastern Europe, such incidents were
a clear warning. More and more of them decided to seek security on the
other side of the Atlantic.

The outcome was the transformation of American Jewry, or rather,
the emergence of two distinct American Jewries. On one side was the
old, established community, constituting no more than about a tenth of
all Jews in the United States, the descendants of immigrants from Central and Western Europe. By the early 1900s they had become thoroughly
acculturated and Americanized—not always safe from the prejudice
with which much of the native population regarded non-Protestants and
especially non-Christians, but enjoying considerable affluence and social
respectability.

And then there were the other nine tenths, recent immigrants or children of recent immigrants, many of them poor and uneducated, living
in the grimy ghettos of the big city, trying to support themselves by peddling, hawking, tailoring, shoemaking, and shopkeeping. Some, usually
in the second or third generation, tried to rise above the menial occupations of most of the newcomers. They often managed to learn proper
English and acquire an education. More and more of them went into
business, becoming merchants or manufacturers. Many others earned a
law or medical degree and achieved success in the skilled professions. And
yet something, their tone or manner or style, usually betrayed their background, provoking disdain not only in Gentile society but also among the
established Jewish patriciate. The two communities of Jews in America,

the old-timers and the recent arrivals, were divided, like those in Europe, by reciprocal dislikes, one regarding the other as provincial and crude, the other resenting the first as condescending and pretentious. They practiced different occupations as a rule, they moved in different circles, they had different cultural interests, and they lived in different neighborhoods. They even had different places and forms of worship.

The influx of East European Jews diminished rapidly, however, after the First World War. Since the beginning of the century, public opinion had begun to turn against the traditional policy of unlimited immigration. The end of the frontier, which had played such an important role in shaping American history, meant that there were no longer those vast empty territories which had attracted successive generations of settlers seeking a new life in a challenging environment. Most immigrants were no longer able to earn a livelihood, as so many had previously done, by working on remote farms or in isolated mining communities. They were now crowding into the large cities, seeking employment in factories and mills, competing for jobs and wages with native workers, and being perceived as rivals and intruders rather than pioneers and settlers. The relationship between outsiders and insiders in America was beginning to resemble that in Europe.

The growing economic competition behind this change in the popular attitude toward immigration was aggravated by increasing ethnic tension. Until the last few decades of the nineteenth century, the great majority of foreigners settling in the United States had come from Western and Central Europe—from the United Kingdom, Germany, and the Scandinavian countries. Most of them were Protestants, and many had grown up speaking English. Even those who did not found it relatively easy to learn the language and adopt the customs of their new homeland. But not long after the Civil War, the chief sources of immigration began to shift to the east and south. Now most of the newcomers were Poles, Ukrainians, Czechs, Slovaks, Hungarians, Italians, and Greeks, and among them quite a few Jews. Christians still constituted an overwhelming majority, but in most cases they were no longer Protestants. Moreover, they seemed to find it more difficult than earlier arrivals to adjust to the American way of life. They tended to congregate in ethnic neighborhoods, many continued to converse in their mother tongue and to read newspapers published in

America but written in a foreign language, they celebrated strange holidays and unfamiliar anniversaries, and they sometimes displayed greater interest in political developments in their old country than in their new one. More and more native Americans began to regard them with disapproval and suspicion, as incorrigibly foreign, unwilling to become Americanized, perhaps even not altogether loyal. They were increasingly seen as examples of what Theodore Roosevelt had characterized as a "hyphenated Americanism."

Shortly after the First World War, the combination of economic tension and ethnic suspicion led to the end of the policy of unrestricted immigration into the United States. Laws of 1921 and 1924 assigned to each foreign country an immigrant quota, which was at first not to exceed 3 percent and later not to exceed 2 percent of the number of its nationals resident in the United States. By the end of the decade, moreover, the total number of immigrants was limited to 150,000 annually, with quotas for admission assigned on the basis of the "national origins" of the current American population. There could be no question about the motive or purpose of this last provision. The United States was becoming increasingly determined to defend its established cultural and ethnic character against the perceived danger of alien adulteration.

The result of the new immigration laws was a sharp decline in the number of foreigners admitted to America annually. Immigrants totaled 1,285,000 in 1907, 1,042,000 in 1910, and 1,218,000 in 1914. There were still 707,000 as late as 1924. But then came a steep drop, to about 242,000 in 1930, 97,000 in 1931, and 36,000 in 1932. The decline in the number of Jewish immigrants was even more drastic. In 1921 the figure was roughly 119,000, in 1922 it was 54,000, and in 1923 it was still almost 50,000. But by 1930 the total had fallen to no more than about 12,000, in 1931 it was not quite 6,000, and in 1932 it was less than 3,000. Whereas between 1904 and 1914 Jews had on average constituted 11 percent annually of all immigrants into the United States, for the period from 1924 to 1932 they averaged below 5 per cent. Not that the immigration laws were directed primarily against Jews seeking admission to the "golden realm." They were anti-foreign rather than anti-Semitic in intent. But by establishing quotas that favored the countries of Western and Central Europe over those of Eastern Europe, they reduced the number of immigrants from the region in which the overwhelming majority of European Jews lived. To many of the supporters of the restrictions on immigration, moreover, that effect was neither unforeseen nor undesirable.[5]

Whatever chance there was of relaxing some of the strict limitations on the admission of immigrants vanished with the coming of the Great Depression. The result of the economic crisis that began in 1929 was the same in the United States as in France, England, and the other democratic nations of Western Europe. How could a country where millions were unemployed, where hundreds of thousands had to be fed in soup kitchens, where paupers stood on street corners selling pencils or rattling tin cups, where the hungry rummaged through garbage cans looking for something to eat, and where the homeless could be seen at night sleeping in hallways or on park benches or even on sidewalks—how could such a country afford to open its doors to impoverished foreigners from distant corners of the world? Would that not increase the number of unemployed, the number of beggars, the number of the hungry and homeless? The answer was obvious; charity had to begin at home. Even 150,000 immigrants a year seemed to many Americans to be too many. The total should be reduced, they felt, not increased.

This was the situation in the United States at the time of Hitler's rise to power. The anti-Semitic policies of the new regime in Germany, even more openly proclaimed and more vigorously enforced than in Eastern Europe, aroused considerable disapproval in the New World. Indeed, the view that those seeking to flee persecution in the Third Reich faced a more serious danger than those merely trying to escape economic hardship in Poland or Romania became widespread. And American Jews generally shared that view.

But other considerations also made Jewish refugees from Germany more acceptable than those from countries farther to the east. For one thing, there were relatively few of them, fewer than 600,000, as opposed to the millions of East European Jews. And then there were the important differences in the economic position, social status, and cultural adaptability of the two Jewish communities. There was little doubt that most of the German Jews could become Americanized as quickly and easily as they had become Germanized a century earlier. But the Jews from Eastern Europe were a different story. They were generally poor, they were alien in appearance, and, most objectionable, they were so clannish, choosing as a rule to live in the Jewish neighborhoods of the big cities rather than mingling with and becoming like other Americans. Did the country really need more immigrants of that sort?

Refugees from the Third Reich seemed clearly preferable. Their only serious disadvantage was the one they shared with their coreligionists from Eastern Europe: they were Jews, or at least mostly Jews. And that meant that they aroused ethnic suspicions and resentments which, though not nearly as intense as in the Old World, were by no means unknown in the New. This explains why many of those supporting the admission to the United States of the victims of Nazi persecution—Jewish organizations, humanitarian societies, and liberal political groups—tried to universalize the refugee problem, emphasizing its breadth and diversity. They argued that the brutality of National Socialism was a threat to all defenders of freedom and justice, whether Protestants, Catholics, or Jews, conservatives, liberals, or socialists, provincialists, nationalists, or cosmopolites. And since the danger facing them transcended the categories of ethnicity or religion, the defense against it should transcend those categories as well.

This contention, however, persuaded only those who were willing to be persuaded. Most Americans believed, not without justification, that the refugee problem was mostly a Jewish refugee problem, and that the admission of victims of Nazi totalitarianism really meant the admission of German Jews. And this in turn suggests that an understanding of American public opinion in the 1930s regarding the immigration of victims of Nazi persecution depends on an understanding of American public opinion regarding Jews in general. The two were inextricably connected.

Not surprisingly, members of the Jewish community were regarded with some distaste or condescension by many native-born Americans. There was a current of anti-Semitism in the nation, not nearly as obvious or intense as in Germany or Eastern Europe but as discernible as in France or England. To be sure, other minorities were looked down upon as well, most of them also made up of recent immigrants: Italians, Poles, Czechs, Slovaks, Hungarians, Ukrainians, and Greeks. But Jews were near the bottom of the list; only African Americans and Mexican Americans ranked lower. This unfavorable view was bound to affect popular opinion regarding the admission of Jewish refugees. It reinforced the opinion that the economic hardships which so many Americans had to endure made it inadvisable to open the door to too many immigrants. And this in turn contributed to a bitter conflict between compassion and self-protection, a conflict similar to the one in Western Europe, which continued until and beyond the outbreak of the Second World War.

How strong was American anti-Semitism before the war? At first glance, the answer does not appear hard to find. In no country was public opinion measured by polls and questionnaires as often as in the United States. Moreover, the popular attitude toward ethnic minorities was a frequent subject of statistical study. Yet the accuracy of inquiries of that kind is open to challenge, especially in cases where the respondents may hesitate to express their disagreement with the orthodox or morally prescribed views on any given subject publicly.

Thus even *Fortune* magazine, which conducted numerous polls of public opinion, was reluctant to ask respondents directly whether they shared anti-Semitic feelings and beliefs. In an article published in 1936, it maintained that "indirection" provided the most accurate results, because "the use of a trial questionnaire putting the question directly showed that people are almost 100 per cent reluctant to voice an out-and-out racial antagonism." It seemed best, therefore, to ask the participants in the poll what they thought of foreign rather than domestic anti-Semitism. Accordingly, *Fortune* posed the following question in interviews with about 3,000 respondents whose age, sex, geographic region, community size, and economic status were proportionate to those of the population at large: "Do you believe that in the long run Germany will be better or worse off if it drives out the Jews?" The results showed that 14 percent of those questioned thought Germany would be better off, 55 percent thought it would be worse off, and 31 percent did not know. Since, as the organizers of the poll assumed, the views of the respondents regarding a German policy of Jewish expulsion reflected their views regarding a similar American policy, the proportion of out-and-out anti-Semites in the United States did not seem to be much more than about a tenth.[6]

Yet there is considerable evidence that while violent prejudice against Jews was relatively rare in the United States, aversion and suspicion were by no means uncommon. That conclusion is supported, for example, by a poll conducted by the Opinion Research Corporation in 1938. This time the question was not as blunt as the one *Fortune* had posed two years earlier. Respondents were asked, "Do you think the persecution of Jews in Europe has been their own fault?" The answers were more ambiguous than before. To be sure, only 12 percent agreed "entirely" that European Jewry had provoked the hostility directed against it—roughly the same proportion as had endorsed a policy of Jewish expulsion from Germany. But another 49 percent believed that the Jews were at least "partly" at fault. Only 23 percent thought that the Jews were "not at all" responsible for anti-Semitism, and 16 percent had "no opinion." The conclusion both polls point to is that while most Americans disapproved of the extreme form of ethnic prejudice embraced by the Third Reich, many shared a more moderate or restrained variety of bigotry. The prevailing attitudes toward Jewry in the United States and those in Central or Eastern Europe were clearly different, but they were not diametrically opposed.[7]

There is even evidence that as the intensity of anti-Semitism increased in the Old World, its intensity in the New World increased as well, though not nearly to the same extent. Perhaps the growing persecution of Jews in the Third Reich raised a suspicion in the United States regarding increased efforts to admit thousands of refugees. Or perhaps the growing fear of a new world war in which America might become embroiled aroused concern about the Jewish role in the worsening international situation. Whatever the reason, the intensification of anti-Semitic hostility in Central and Eastern Europe did nothing to broaden American sympathy for its victims. On the contrary, it seemed to strengthen the feeling that the Jews would try to persuade the government of the United States to assume the burden of humanitarian assistance, which the Old World was less and less willing to bear. America had to be on its guard against such efforts.

This feeling was reflected in the results of various public opinion surveys conducted in the last few years before the outbreak of hostilities in Europe. A Gallup poll in August 1937 that asked, "Do you think anti-Jewish feeling is increasing or decreasing in this country?" found opinions almost evenly divided: 29 percent thought that it was increasing, 23 percent thought it was decreasing, and the rest were undecided.

Another survey, however, this one conducted in November 1938 by the Opinion Research Corporation, showed a significant shift in the public perception of whether anti-Semitism was growing in the United States.

During the fifteen months since the previous poll there had been a dramatic change in the international situation, especially in the position of the Third Reich. Austria had been incorporated into Germany; the Sudeten region of Czechoslovakia had been annexed by Hitler; the two leading democratic states of Europe, England and France, had adopted a policy of appeasement toward the Nazi regime; and the mass pogrom of the Kristallnacht was taking place. Yet all these developments, in the view of the respondents, had only intensified hostility toward Jews in the United States. In answer to the question whether "you think anti-Jewishness is increasing or decreasing in this country," 37 percent believed it was increasing, 18 percent thought it was decreasing, and 45 percent felt it was the same or expressed no opinion. Indeed, in every such survey between August 1937 and February 1946, with the exception of the one in December 1938, the percentage of respondents who thought that American anti-Semitism was growing exceeded the percentage of those who did not, usually by a substantial margin.[8]

Many contemporary observers, moreover, some of them foreigners, commented on the extent and growth of prejudice against Jews in the United States. In October 1938, Herbert Dirksen, the German ambassador to Great Britain, reported to the Wilhelmstrasse a conversation he had just had with the American ambassador in London, Joseph P. Kennedy, who "repeatedly emphasized the sympathy which the average American felt for the German and which was greater than his liking for the average Englishman." Kennedy did not stop there, however. "As during former conversations, [he] mentioned that very strong anti-Semitic tendencies existed in the United States and that a large portion of the population had an understanding of the German attitude toward the Jews." The statesmen in Berlin were bound to be pleased.[9]

That was not the only evidence the German government received of the persistence and spread of American aversion to Jewry. A circular regarding "The Jewish Question as a Factor in Foreign Policy," which the Foreign Office sent to its diplomatic missions abroad in January 1939, dealt first with the situation in the United States. It stated with some satisfaction that "the press and official reports from North America continually speak of anti-Jewish manifestations by the population." There were hard facts, moreover, to support those reports. "It is perhaps symptomatic for domestic developments in the United States that the audience of the well-known anti-Jewish 'radio priest' [Charles E.] Coughlin has grown to over 20 million." Such developments were welcome to the leaders of the Third Reich, not only because they suggested that more and more Americans sympathized with their own racial theories, but also because they were likely to lead to greater support in the New World for Germany's diplomatic objectives.[10]

A much subtler and more perceptive analysis of American anti-Semitism appeared early in 1938 in a private report by Carl Goerdeler, the former mayor of Leipzig, who had at first been a cautious supporter of the Nazi government but had become its critic, then its opponent, and finally an important participant in a failed plot to assassinate Hitler, which led to his execution in the Second World War. A visit to the United States had convinced him that the American boycott of German goods organized in protest against Hitler's racial policies was supported almost exclusively by Jews. "It has its main center in New York. That is natural, and it grows weaker with the distance from New York." In other parts of the country, where the Jewish population was much smaller, the prevailing attitude toward Jewry was not very different from Germany's. "We must always bear in mind that there is hardly a club in the United States which accepts Jews, that in many hotels Jews are not admitted, and that indeed in all the universities the percentage of Jewish students is tacitly restricted." American anti-Semitism was really not very different from German anti-Semitism, Goerdeler concluded. The Americans, however, unlike the Germans, chose to pretend that it did not exist. "They thus harbor a certain reserve, characteristic of the Anglo-Saxons, with regard to the Jews, but they do not like to talk about it."[11]

Was that an exaggeration? Perhaps. But it was not a wild exaggeration. There were many social clubs in the United States that did exclude Jews, there were many hotels that did not welcome guests with Jewish-sounding names, and there were many universities, public as well as private, that had strict though unwritten quotas limiting the number of Jewish students. Indeed, some of the elderly and middle-aged refugees from the Third Reich would occasionally comment—in confidence, of course—that there had been less anti-Semitism in Germany under Kaiser Wilhelm than there was in America under President Roosevelt. Admittedly, in the old Hohenzollern Empire, Jews were frequently denied membership in exclusive clubs, but no hotel would refuse to accept Jewish guests. As for admission to a university, all that was required was a diploma from an accredited secondary school and enough money to pay for tuition, food, and lodging.

And yet while the prevalence of American anti-Semitism should not be ignored, neither should it be exaggerated. Despite all the prejudice and discrimination, Jews were playing an increasingly important role in government, economy, society, and culture. They still had to face serious barriers to success, but those barriers were not insurmountable. Indeed, one measure of the ability of a growing number of Jews to rise above the status of scorned outsiders was the prevalent muttering and grumbling about the ambitiousness and pushiness of these aliens, who a generation or two ago had been nothing more than peddlers and hustlers. Now they were competing more and more successfully with real Americans, whose families had been in the country for a hundred years, perhaps even longer. Should that not be a source of serious concern?

In fact many people believed that the Jews were acquiring too much influence in national affairs. But exactly what proportion of the population shared this view? And was the proportion increasing, decreasing, or stable? On this point there is no clear answer. Still, the mainstream press and most of the influential periodicals were in agreement that anti-Semitism was not a serious problem. In February 1936, *Fortune* published an article on "Jews in America" which argued that "the virus [of prejudice against Jews] has not been acclimated on this continent and . . . the efforts of the doctors to inoculate the American mind have failed for that reason." Numerous surveys of national opinion indicated either rejection of anti-Semitic dogmas or, "what is worse from the agitator's point of view," indifference to those dogmas.

Only a few months earlier, the article pointed out, a poll by the National Conference of Jews and Christians had found that 95 percent of the respondents believed that there was less anti-Semitism in their communities now than at the beginning of the depression. A subsequent inquiry conducted by *Fortune* confirmed these findings. "Few of those replying felt that anti-Semitism was a live issue. On the contrary, a considerable number felt that it was no issue at all." Why, then, all the fuss, why the dire warnings and constant alarms? There was really nothing to worry about. "American organized anti-Semitism is a poor thing indeed."

Yet that was not the end of it. The article also examined the reasons for the baseless yet common concern about popular hostility against Jews. What accounted for it? After all, "any man who loathes Fascism will fear anti-Semitism." And if he fears anti-Semitism, he will also fear "the various conditions which encourage it." And among those conditions, among the important ones, was "the apprehensiveness of the Jews themselves."

Here *Fortune* touched on an issue that appeared over and over again in the public discussion of anti-Semitism in the United States, namely, Jewish oversensitivity. Consider the average American, who certainly disapproved of the racism preached by National Socialism, according to the article. Yet even he was bound to be troubled to find his Jewish neighbor "taking offense where no offense is intended." Even he was likely to be disconcerted by "the uneasy reticence, the circumlocutions, [and] the sense of strain" of so many Jews. He was also disappointed, no doubt, to find that some of them "carry their race like an Irishman's fighting shillelagh while others resent, as though it were a deliberate insult, any reference to their blood, avoiding friends who speak of it, boycotting publications which publish it in print." Was such an attitude really warranted? Did the growing apprehensiveness of American Jewry have any basis in fact? Or was it merely the manifestation of a collective ethnic persecution complex?

Those questions led *Fortune* to its conclusion concerning the "so-called Jewish problem." It was obvious that the Jews "do not come within gunshot of running America." Their numbers were no longer increasing rapidly, so that there was no reason to fear the rise of a strong anti-Semitic movement like the one in Germany. And yet troubling issues remained. "Can this universal stranger be absorbed in the country which has absorbed every other European stock? Does he wish to be absorbed? Can he live happily and in peace if he is not absorbed? The answers must be guesses." Spanish and German Jews had in fact become largely assimilated. There were many others, however, most of them from Eastern Europe, who regarded the loss of Jewish identity as "a kind of social suicide." Their chances of preserving their distinctive ethnic character depended on toleration and mutual respect. "The first condition of their success will be the quieting of Jewish apprehensiveness and the consequent elimination of the aggressive and occasionally provocative Jewish defensive measures which the country has recently and anxiously observed." In short, there was no danger of anti-Semitism in America, nor would there be, unless the Jews themselves helped provoke it.[12]

Other influential journals dealing with public affairs agreed that an ideology based on ethnic prejudice was indeed a "poor thing," although some of them feared that it was gaining strength, especially in Europe. And the reason for its growth was the large or rather excessive number of Jews in the general population. A few months after Hitler came to power, *Harper's Magazine* published an article that spoke approvingly of the Jewish "flair for certain kinds of business," especially publishing, entertainment, music, merchandising, and banking. The Jews also contributed many "practitioners of the first quality" to medicine and law. Thus an "infusion of Jew in other stocks" was likely to be valuable. "Jewish racial material when of good quality is one of the most precious ingredients that was ever cast into humanity." How could any Jew object to such a flattering conclusion?

Unfortunately, according to *Harper's*, not all Jews were of "good quality." Less complimentary observations could be made about the "common run of nominal Jews." Indeed, they were currently being made in Germany. And whether there or anywhere else, such observations were not entirely without foundation. What determined whether the populace favored toleration or embraced prejudice was the size of the Jewish minority. In England, for instance, the Jews did better than in most countries. "[They] get what is coming to them in government, in finance, and almost everything else." But that was because they were relatively few. "[England] has never been overrun by crowds of them as has happened in southeastern Europe and elsewhere." And since Jews were so much more successful than non-Jews in acquiring wealth and influence, the more there were in any country, the greater the disparity between natives and aliens became, and the deeper the resentment aroused by that disparity grew. "Any group of people that in the long run seems to be getting more than its share of what is accessible will come in due time to be disliked by observers who are less fortunate." *Harper's*, like *Fortune*, concluded that Jews were not entirely without fault in arousing anti-Semitism. But while *Fortune* blamed Jewish apprehensiveness and oversensitivity, *Harper's* emphasized Jewish ambition, Jewish success, and too many Jews.[13]

Moreover, American public opinion and American popular journalism were reluctant, especially in the early years of the Third Reich, to accept at face value accounts of the persecution of Jews by the new government in Berlin. After all, Jewish alarmism was nothing new. Jews were always complaining about discrimination, oppression, bigotry, and injustice. Shouldn't their charges of brutality by the Nazi regime be taken with a grain of salt? Weren't similar charges made not long before against the czarist regime in Russia? And what about those endless Jewish complaints regarding anti-Semitism in Poland, Lithuania, Romania, and Hungary? Didn't that constant lamentation suggest an obsessive sense of grievance among Jews, a compulsive need to play the perpetual victim? Even some of the publications that denounced ethnic prejudice most loudly hesitated to accept Jewish accusations against the Hitler government without question. Such accusations had to be carefully studied and evaluated. They might prove to be exaggerated, perhaps greatly exaggerated. A responsible newspaper or magazine had to be on guard against distortions, whether deliberate or unintentional.

Two months after Hitler came to power, the *Christian Century*, a prominent Protestant periodical, published an editorial entitled "A Need for Light, Not Heat." It stated at the outset that precisely because the world had been shocked by the anti-Semitic policies of National Socialism, the "utmost caution" should be exercised in assessing reports of the persecution of Jews. Although the new German government's denials of physical violence were not entirely convincing, the situation in Central Europe was such that unfounded rumors could easily spread. If those rumors proved to be true, public sentiment in other countries, which currently favored equality of treatment for Germany in international affairs, would quickly turn against it. That was why it was so important to find means for "a dependable ascertaining of the facts."

The best course would be for some of the interested countries to propose a "neutral investigation" in order to ascertain to what extent ethnic persecution was actually taking place. If evidence proving that the Hitler regime supported "a systematic harrowing of the Jews" could be found, it should be made known. "Obviously a government committed to such a policy is a government wedded to the dark ages, and cannot bear a full part in the building of an enlightened world order." But if whatever anti-

Semitic excesses had recently taken place were only a "passing hysteria" which had now been brought under control and ended, that too should be made known. "The implications of the situation are of such gravity that we are sure all thoughtful persons, Jews as well as Christians, will put the tighter curb upon their emotions until the facts are beyond dispute." Wild charges by one side and outraged denials by the other would only make a bad situation worse.[14]

While the *Christian Century* advocated patience and restraint in dealing with anti-Semitism in the Third Reich, the *Christian Science Monitor* was recommending compassion and understanding. Both victims and victimizers should learn to be more tolerant. The Jews should remember what the philosopher Spinoza, an excommunicated Jew but a Jew nevertheless, once had to say: "It is rational to repay persecution with love." And the Germans in turn should remember that one of their national heroes, Frederick the Great of Prussia, had unequivocally rejected prejudice and discrimination: "In this country every man must get to heaven in his own way." According to the *Christian Science Monitor*, it was not enough for governments to restrain economic boycotts as a means of achieving a goal, even a praiseworthy goal. That would only touch the surface of the endless controversy regarding the "Jewish question." Governments could not, after all, put an embargo on hateful thoughts. Yet "it is racial and national hatreds which are at the root of today's troubles." The only way to deal with those troubles was not by political or economic measures but through spiritual values. "A better recognition of the fundamental truth that the children of God belong to one family would be the best antidote for this poison of division." The proper response to anti-Semitic hatred was the Biblical injunction to love one's neighbor.[15]

The advocacy of patience and restraint or understanding and tolerance reflected, indirectly and sometimes unconsciously, a common concern in America during the 1930s. The country was convinced that it must avoid any future entanglement in the perennial conflicts of the Old World, especially those involving Germany. Only two decades earlier, according to the prevailing view, the United States had allowed itself to be dragged into a war that was allegedly being fought to make the world safe for democracy. It had believed all the horror stories about the atrocities committed by those awful "Huns," stories about the murder of children, violation of women, and starvation of the old and helpless. And what had been the result? Instead of promoting freedom and prosperity, victory had led to the spread of authoritarianism in Italy, Germany, Hungary, Austria, and the succession states. And now the United States was in the midst of an economic depression which threatened the nation with social unrest and political instability. Could anyone doubt that the decision to take part in the First World War had proved disastrous?

Accordingly, the American public was reluctant to accept without question stories about the injustices and cruelties of the Third Reich. They sounded so much like the stories about the injustices and cruelties of the kaiser's Germany, which had turned out to be mostly propaganda. Could it be that reports of anti-Semitic persecution by the National Socialists would also prove to be exaggerated or even unfounded? Could it be that they were designed to arouse sympathy for German Jews and persuade the American government to intercede on their behalf with the authorities in Berlin? And could such intercession escalate from diplomatic complaints to military threats? There was general agreement in the United States that a direct confrontation between Washington and Berlin should be avoided at any cost.

Even a periodical like *Current History*, which had a reputation for balanced and judicious analysis of political issues, spoke with alarm about "a wave of unprecedently belligerent hysteria against Nazi Germany." That hysteria was being fanned by those who, whether they realized it or not, were in effect warmongers. "Enthusiasts of all political colors jumped without discrimination on to a careening war chariot, the hectic direction of which was unpredictable, save that it would certainly never follow the narrow primrose path of pure neutrality." And the irony of it all was "the absence of any fundamental reason for antagonism between Germany and the United States as nations." The best thing would be a "diplomatic stock-taking" on the part of both countries.

Current History was willing to concede that Americans could not and should not condone the "uncouth barbarities" of the Third Reich. But they could and should see the problem in perspective, drawing a distinction between National Socialism as an "impermanent and extraordinary form of government" and Germany as a "continuing nation." Relations between Washington and Berlin would be greatly improved if each resolved "to mind its own business." That would be in everyone's best interest. Americans would welcome a decision by the Third Reich to refrain from encouraging the Nazi movement in the United States, which in any case had "a laughingly small impact upon politics in this country." But by the same token, Americans should express their praiseworthy desire to help German Jews in uncontroversial ways, for example, "by granting a refuge to exiles." Nothing would be gained by "splenetic anti-German outbursts," which only aggravated the position of the Jewish community under National Socialism and, worse still, might let the United States be duped into a European family squabble as a result of the propaganda of the "anti-German side." Such measures as economic boycotts served merely to increase Nazi desperation. Each government should therefore avoid challenging or provoking the other. A direct confrontation could prove disastrous for both.[16]

This warning could be heard again and again during the prewar years, sometimes in a less restrained form. There was a popular perception that American Jews were using their wealth and influence to persuade Washington to exert diplomatic and economic pressure against the anti-Semitic policies of the Third Reich. They were subordinating national interest to ethnic solidarity. While non-Jewish Americans were determined to avoid entanglement in the disputes of the Old World, Jewish Americans were willing to risk dragging the country into war in order to help their coreligionists on the other side of the Atlantic.

That view, though exaggerated or distorted, was not based entirely on fantasy. The Jewish community in the United States did in fact actively engage in efforts to organize meetings, marches, and boycotts protesting the persecution of German Jewry. That was understandable. Such efforts resembled those of various Irish American associations that opposed the policies of Great Britain or of Polish American associations that opposed the aims of the Soviet Union. Many non-Jewish organizations, religious, humanitarian, liberal, and radical, also condemned National Socialism. But Jews were the most vocal and persistent among the opponents of the Third Reich. To those determined to maintain the neutrality of the United States in the face of an increasingly tense international situation, the political role of the American Jewish community appeared suspicious.

Even *Time* magazine, which could not generally be accused of ethnic bias, succumbed from time to time to the fear that Jewish influence was threatening to undermine the nation's security. In the spring of 1934 it criticized Congressman Samuel Dickstein, a New York Jew, for persuading the House of Representatives to adopt a resolution favoring the establishment of a special committee to investigate National Socialist propaganda in the United States. Having won the support of his fellow congressmen, he was now proposing "to do an even better job of spreading on the record the plight of members of his own race in Germany." He claimed that dozens of spies were coming to the United States disguised as sailors on German ships. Their mission, according to his allegations, was to spread hatred among the American people. But *Time* remained convinced that the congressman's real purpose was to persuade the nation that its safety was being threatened by the Third Reich. "If the Dickstein investigation has its way the U.S. Capitol will be turned into a public forum in which Nazis will be pilloried day after day and timid citizens will be led to believe that Chancellor Hitler is about to oust President Roosevelt." The best thing would be to ignore the alarmists, whose underlying intention was to enlist the help of the American government in the struggle against the anti-Semitism of the Third Reich.[17]

Those opposed to Washington's involvement in American Jewry's campaign against National Socialism often insisted that the hands-off policy they were advocating was actually in the best interests of the Jews themselves. Too much Jewish pressure for a condemnation of the Third Reich, too much Jewish agitation for a confrontation with the Hitler regime, was bound to backfire. Instead of restraining ethnic prejudice in Germany, it would intensify ethnic prejudice in the United States. More and more Americans would come to feel that the Jews were willing to jeopardize U.S. interests in order to defend the interests of world Jewry. And that was sure to promote anti-Semitism at home. Those urging greater caution and restraint on the part of American Jews were really not the adversaries but the friends of the Jewish community. They were trying to protect the Jews from themselves.

In the fall of 1935, for instance, Brigadier General Charles H. Sherrill, the American member of the International Olympic Committee, vigorously opposed a proposal that the United States withdraw from the Olympic games, which were to take place in Berlin the following year, as a protest against the Third Reich's discriminatory treatment of Jews in general and Jewish athletes in particular. "I am sorry that what I have done has not pleased all of my Jewish friends, many of them the most prominent Jews in New York," he declared in an interview. "But I shall go right on being pro-Jewish, and for that reason I have a warning for American Jewry." The general went on to explain why "this Olympic agitation" was so dangerous. "Consider the effect on several thousand youngsters training for this contest throughout the United States, if the boycott movement gets so far that they suddenly are confronted with the fact that somebody is trying to defeat their ambition to get to Berlin and compete in the Olympic Games." The results could be very serious. "We are almost certain to have a wave of anti-Semitism among those who never before gave it a thought, and who may consider that about 5,000,000 Jews in this country are using the athletes representing 120,000,000 Americans to work out something to help the German Jews." Couldn't those urging a boycott of the Olympics see what the consequence of their agitation was likely to be?

As a matter of fact, Sherrill maintained, reasonable and responsible members of the Jewish community shared his concern. He reported that "many prominent Jews with whom I have talked here and abroad feel the same way." They agreed that to press for a withdrawal from the Olympics "would be overplaying the Jewish hand in America as it was overplayed in Germany before the present suppression and expulsion of the Jews were undertaken." Was he voicing a friendly warning or a disguised threat? Probably a little of each. The implication of what Sherrill was saying was unmistakable, however. If the agitation for a boycott of the Olympic games persisted, "the anti-Semitism resulting here might last for years." It would therefore be in the interest of everyone, Jews and non-Jews alike, to agree to U.S. participation in the international athletic competition in Berlin. That was surely better than paving the way for some future American Hitler.[18]

Members of the social patriciate in the United States were not the only ones to view with distrust the efforts of the Jewish community to organize a militant protest movement against the racism of the Third Reich. Many of the ethnic minorities, including those from nations in Eastern and southern Europe that were threatened by the aggressive diplomacy of

Nazi Germany, also regarded the role of Jewry in their adopted homeland with suspicion. Some of their aversion was part of the cultural baggage they had brought from the old country. But much of it reflected a feeling of collective envy, a view that Jews were more ambitious, more aggressive, cleverer, and above all more successful than other immigrant communities in acquiring affluence and influence. Why? How did they manage to get ahead so rapidly? What methods, designs, devices, and tricks did they employ? And what were the secret purposes behind their appeals for justice and compassion? Indeed, distrust of the Jewish community was more common among the newcomers to the United States than among the Sons and Daughters of the American Revolution.

Even members of the oldest and most oppressed minority in America occasionally expressed bitterness over Jewish outrage at ethnic discrimination in Germany and the lack of Jewish outrage at racial discrimination in the United States. When Emanuel Celler, a Jewish congressman from Brooklyn, proposed a mass demonstration in 1933 at the arrival of the German boxer Max Schmeling as a protest against the anti-Semitic policies of National Socialism, the *New York Amsterdam News*, one of the most influential African American newspapers, objected. An article headed "America Must Go into Court with Clean Hands and a Fair Mind" sought to turn the spotlight on the subject of "America's horror when one of her favored sons is discriminated against while closing her eyes to justice where the Negro is concerned." It reminded its readers that when Hitler was reported to have said that he would try to bar black athletes from taking part in the Olympics, "not a soul moved to call Hitler to time and suggest that the games be withdrawn from Germany." But since then the situation had changed. Daniel Prenn, a Jew, had recently been dropped from the German Davis Cup team. And now "one of the moneyed factors in the United States" had become concerned. As long as only black athletes were excluded from sports like baseball, the "moneyed factors" offered no objection. But as soon as one of their own experienced the injustice of discrimination, they became outraged and began to denounce ethnic prejudice and oppression. All those piteous appeals of the Jewish community to the conscience of the world were merely self-serving.[19]

The persistent current of anti-Semitism in America accounted, at least in part, for strong popular opposition to any increase in the admission of Jewish refugees from Central Europe. Not that there was much approval for the harsh racist measures adopted by the Third Reich. But there was a growing fear that any substantial influx of Jews from abroad would increase the excessive influence of Jewry in national life. The newcomers would contribute to the financial and political resources of their ethnic community. They would strengthen the role of Jews in government, business, and the professions. Was that desirable? Would it not be a threat to most Americans? Throughout the prewar years, public opinion remained firmly opposed to lowering the barriers to the admittance of refugees from the Third Reich. As late as November 1938, only two weeks after the Kristallnacht, a poll conducted by the American Institute of Public Opinion asked, "Should we allow a larger number of Jewish exiles from Germany to come to the United States to live?" Seventy-seven percent of those expressing an opinion said no, and only 23 percent said yes.[20]

Admittedly, not all of the opposition to relaxing the immigration restrictions was based on anti-Semitic prejudice. As in the case of Western Europe, much of it reflected a concern that a large number of refugees would aggravate the hardships caused by the Great Depression, intensifying business competition and increasing lower-class unemployment. The *Christian Century* was only one of many American periodicals and newspapers arguing that "the economic condition of the country with its ten million unemployed, and the precarious tenure of millions of others on their means of earning a livelihood," made it hazardous to lower the immigration barriers. "To admit an appreciable number of Jews, all of them forced to a status of indigence before they are allowed to leave Germany, would add just that much more to the economic chaos." Though a "magnificent gesture," it would make a bad situation worse.[21]

Some surveys of public opinion seemed to support the view that opposition to an increase in the admittance of Jewish refugees was not based solely or even primarily on ethnic prejudice. While the poll conducted by the American Institute of Public Opinion in November 1938 showed that 77 percent of the respondents objected to a large influx of German Jews, a poll conducted at the same time by the Opinion Research Corporation found that when asked whether "you think the persecution of Jews in Europe has been chiefly due to unreasoning prejudice, or . . . has been largely their own fault," 52 percent ascribed the persecution to prejudice, 27 percent thought it was the fault of the Jews, and 21 percent had no opinion. The results suggest that no more than about a fourth of all Americans felt serious ethnic distrust or hostility toward Jews.[22]

Still, public opinion polls should be regarded with caution. Some respondents, even if they do not realize it, express views that are orthodox or sanctioned rather than frank or sincere. Aware of the conventional condemnation of certain attitudes and beliefs, they try to keep them hidden from others and sometimes from themselves. Those attitudes and beliefs do rise to the surface from time to time, but often disguised as the result of rational, dispassionate, objective analysis. In many cases, it is thus difficult to decide what is genuine and what is spurious, what expresses a sincere conviction and what reflects a contrived rationalization.

As for the extent of anti-Semitism in the United States, even the *Christian Century*, which emphasized the economic risk in admitting a large number of refugees, conceded that "this wicked [anti-Semitic] obsession which exists in America hardly less than in pre-Hitlerian Germany" could be whipped into "overt fanaticism" more easily than those attending round-table conferences of Jews, Catholics, and Protestants imagined. Such conferences, usually held in "the upper air of sentiment and idealism," gave the participants as well as the public at large a false conception of "the realities of our social life." Those realities were hard, even cruel, but they could not be denied. "The importation of an appreciable number of Jews at this time would become at once the occasion for which our 'Silver Shirts' and anti-Semitic 'bunds' are waiting." However noble the motives, the results were bound to be unfortunate. "It would be a tragic disservice to the Jews in America to increase their number by substantial immigration, and would hardly contribute at all to the alleviation of the anguish of the Jews in Germany." The best thing for all concerned was to leave well enough alone.[23]

Public opinion appeared to be committed to this view throughout the prewar period. How much of it expressed economic concern and how much of it reflected ethnic prejudice is impossible to determine. What is clear is that the growing persecution of Jews in Central Europe had no effect on American opposition to an increase in the admission of refugees seeking asylum. If anything, that opposition gained strength with time. On the eve of the Second World War, the well-known journalist and writer Dorothy Thompson, a tireless defender of the victims of totalitarianism, wrote in a mood of discouragement that "all democratic governments talk and protest [against ethnic persecution], but it is extremely difficult to get them to act in any large way in concert, or even separately." As for the United States, "it is sticking to limited immigration under the quota system, and it is political dynamite to touch it." Trying to change existing legislation seemed hopeless.[24]

Still, the situation of German Jews during the first four or five years of the Third Reich was serious rather than critical. Few of them recognized the fanatical intensity of Nazi anti-Semitism. Indeed, many chose at first to remain in their native country in the hope that the objectives of the new government did not go beyond the isolation and segregation of the Jewish community. Its members would be allowed to retain their possessions, practice their occupations, pursue their cultural interests, and express their moral convictions. Besides, sooner or later the nation would surely return to its senses. It would once again become the Germany of Goethe and Schiller, Kant and Lessing—humane, enlightened, and tolerant. Why yield to a sudden irrational panic?

This initial reluctance of many German Jews to emigrate made finding a place of refuge easier for those who decided to leave. There were first of all the neighboring democratic states—France, England, and the Low Countries—which, even if they did not always welcome the victims of ethnic persecution, accepted a substantial number. More important, the United States admitted many refugees despite the restrictions of the quota system. The immigration laws imposed a ceiling on the admission of foreigners, to be sure, but below that ceiling the authorities had considerable leeway in deciding whom and how many to accept. They were partly influenced in their decisions by domestic economic conditions. Yet the increase of ethnic persecution in Central and Eastern Europe combined with persistent American agitation for assistance to its victims had an important effect on the enforcement of the quota system. The gates to America were never completely shut.

The immigration statistics of the interwar period make this clear. In the years immediately preceding the Great Depression, the total number of immigrants decreased slowly but steadily, from 307,255 in 1928 to 279,678 in 1929 and 241,700 in 1930. The number of Jewish immigrants, however, remained more or less constant, rising from 11,639 to 12,479 and then dropping to 11,526, so that their percentage of all immigrants actually grew, from 3.8 to 4.5 to 4.8. The economic crisis of the next few years had a drastic effect on the admission of foreign nationals, reducing their number to less than half and then to less than a quarter of what it had previously been. The totals were 97,139 for 1931, 35,576 for 1932, and 23,068 for 1933. The number of Jewish immigrants fell sharply as well, from 5,692 to 2,755 to 2,372, the lowest figure since the beginning of the century. Their percentage of all immigrants, however, continued to rise and more sharply than before: 5.9 to 7.7 to 10.3.

Despite the depressed state of the American economy, the establishment of the Hitler dictatorship in Germany and the intensification of anti-Semitism in the succession states led to a rapid increase in total immigration and a still more rapid increase in Jewish immigration. The number of all immigrants rose from 29,470 in 1934 to 34,956 in 1935 and 36,329 in 1936, before jumping to 50,244 in 1937. The rise in the number of Jewish immigrants was even more striking: 4,134 in 1934, 4,837 in 1935, 6,252 in 1936, and a leap to 11,352 in 1937. The most remarkable change, however, was in the percentage of Jews among all immigrants to the United States: 14.0 in 1934, a small drop to 13.8 in 1935, a sharp increase to 17.2 in 1936, and finally a jump to 22.6 in 1937, the highest proportion of Jewish immigrants in almost forty years. Clearly American authorities were responding to the demand of various humanitarian organizations, non-Jewish as well as Jewish, for asylum for refugees from ethnic persecution in the Old World.[25]

Thus, during the first few years of the Third Reich, the task that confronted the German Jewish community of finding a place of refuge may have been time-consuming and nerve-racking, but it was by no means hopeless. In general, those who wanted to get out could do so, with patience and persistence. They might not always have been warmly received, but they were at least able to find asylum in Western Europe and the United States, if not as permanent residents, then as visitors, tourists, or transients. And if all else failed, there was always South Africa or the Dominican Republic. Escape from National Socialist persecution was still a possibility for those who wanted to escape.

That changed, however, beginning in 1938. In that year the Hitler regime, having consolidated its hold on political power and repudiated the military restrictions imposed by the Versailles peace treaty, initiated a policy of rigid ideological conformity at home and aggressive revisionist diplomacy in foreign affairs. Its informal alliance with the traditional conservative forces in German society was replaced by a growing Nazification of the bureaucracy and the armed forces, while its anti-Semitic program steadily expanded and intensified, culminating in the destructive fury of the Kristallnacht. In international relations, the Third Reich, having broken the "shackles of Versailles," embarked on a course of expansionism, by peaceful means if possible, by armed force if necessary. In March 1938 it incorporated Austria, in September 1938 it acquired the Sudeten region, and in March 1939 it occupied and partitioned Czechoslovakia.

The result was that the number of Jews living under the rule of Nazi Germany doubled, while the number of Jews seeking to escape that rule through emigration more than doubled. Accordingly, agitation for a place of refuge in America for those suffering ethnic persecution in Central Europe grew louder and more persistent. And that also meant that the great debate in the United States regarding the refugee problem and the "Jewish question" in general became progressively more heated and divisive, increasing in intensity throughout the prewar period, continuing unabated during the war years, and still raging long after the return of peace.

6

Seeking Asylum in the New World: Canada or Latin America?

THERE WAS AN OBVIOUS similarity and a general predictability about the attitude of the various European countries and the United States regarding the refugee problem. Those countries cannot be divided into two distinct and opposed categories, those who created the problem and those who tried to solve it. Instead, they have to be ranked within a single classification according the scope and intensity of their anti-Semitic prejudice. The Third Reich was clearly in first place, closely followed by most of the succession states. Then came the semi-dictatorial countries of the Balkan Peninsula, such as Yugoslavia and Greece, then the West European democracies, and then the nations of the Western Hemisphere, some of them liberal, some authoritarian, and some outright dictatorships. There may have been a vast difference in the degree of hostility toward Jews between the states at one end of the scale and those at the other, but the same complaints—sometimes shouted, sometimes whispered—about Jewish cunning, acquisitiveness, and subversiveness could be heard in all.

To be sure, opposition to the admission of refugees from ethnic or religious persecution was not based entirely on prejudice. The argument that the financial hardships resulting from the Great Depression made the influx of a large number of victims of National Socialism risky or even dangerous was not unreasonable. Undoubtedly many opponents of Jewish immigration had motives deriving primarily from economic considerations. But there were even more whose fear of increased unemployment or intensified competition was reinforced by a deep-seated distrust of Jews in general. Long before the hard times began, anti-Semitic hostility had been prevalent not only in Eastern and Central Europe but in Western Europe and the New World as well. That the coming of the depression aggravated that hostility is clear. But opposition to the admission of Jewish refugees did not start with the collapse of the world economy. It had existed in one form or another for centuries. Only its justifications and expressions had changed.

There was also the contention in some countries, especially in Eastern Europe, that they had already done their share, perhaps more than their share, in trying to solve the "Jewish question." It was now time for other countries to assume the burden of providing a refuge for Jews. The democracies of Western Europe and the New World, however, had no intention of opening their doors to millions of impoverished East European Jews or even to a few hundred thousand persecuted Central European Jews. They too were in the grip of the Great Depression. They too had countless unemployed workers and impoverished families to care for. And they too faced the dangers created by economic collapse and social unrest. They might be willing to admit a small number of refugees as a token of their humaneness, but to open the floodgates to masses of aliens, however needy, however pitiable—that was out of the question. So many of their countrymen were asking for help, pleading for food and housing, that too much generosity to persecuted foreigners might prove self-destructive. Noble intentions could not outweigh harsh realities.

In any case, was it actually true, as most of the succession states claimed, that anti-Semitism was essentially a reaction to the presence of too many Jews? Was it not perhaps a reflection of a cultural bias, of a traditional prejudice, rather than of a demographic imbalance? After all, in the nation with the most virulently anti-Semitic government in Europe, Hitler's Germany, Jews did not make up even 1 percent of the population, less than half the percentage in the much more tolerant Czechoslovakia to the east and only slightly more than half of that in the equally tolerant Netherlands to the west. Did that not undermine the contention that popular hostility against a Jewish minority was directly proportional to the relative size of that minority?

The crucial point was not the number of Jews but the number of Jews in relation to the size of the country in which they lived or its demographic density. And since demographic density is often both a determinant and a reflection of economic opportunity, could that not be a major factor in determining the degree of anti-Semitism? The contention that it is in fact decisive appears to be supported by concrete evidence. The emergence of the United States in the late nineteenth century as the chief refuge of persecuted European Jews, for example, suggests that geographic and demographic pressure was as important in shaping the prevailing attitude toward Jewish immigration as ideological conviction or political principle, perhaps more so. And that in turn seems to lend credibility to the endless complaints by the succession states during the interwar period that their Jewish minorities were too heavy a burden for their narrow boundaries and meager resources. It also helps explain the readiness of the United States to accept large numbers of immigrants, non-Jewish as well as Jewish, not only in the early decades of the twentieth century but even afterward. In short, the explanation makes sense.

And yet geographic and demographic factors are still not enough to account for the great difference in the intensity of xenophobic hostility and ethnic prejudice between various countries, some of them neighbors of similar territorial size and similar population density. There are bound to be other factors that explain those differences. History and tradition, culture and ideology, faith and custom—all seem to have influenced the attitude of the countries of Europe and the New World toward the refugee problem. What else can explain, for example, the difference in the response to the "Jewish question" between France, with a population density of 193 per square mile, and Great Britain, with a population density of 503? What else explains the puzzling fact that the latter, a country with one of the highest demographic concentrations in Europe, was prepared to admit a significantly larger number of Jews fleeing anti-Semitic persecution than the former, a neighboring country with one of the lowest demographic concentrations? Statistics are not enough.[1]

Even more puzzling is the difference in the policies adopted by various nations in the New World. The geographic and demographic conditions that had since the beginning of the nineteenth century made the United States willing to receive millions of immigrants could also be found in other countries in the Western Hemisphere, especially Canada. That was why, after the imposition of American restrictions on immigration in the early 1920s, more and more Europeans seeking refuge from poverty or prejudice began to look farther to the north. Canada seemed to offer almost as many advantages and opportunities as the United States. In some respects it looked even more promising. After all, the vast extent of the continental United States, excluding Alaska, 2,973,776 square miles, was easily surpassed by the total for Canada, 3,510,008 square miles.

Admittedly, not all of that area was suitable for settlement by large numbers of European immigrants. There were the great frozen wastes and isolated, barren plains of the northern territories, not to mention the long, bitter, paralyzing winters. But farther to the south, enough land to accommodate millions of newcomers could be found, especially since Canada was so sparsely populated. While the United States had 122,775,046 inhabitants in 1930, Canada had about 9,934,500. The difference in the demographic density of the two nations was even more striking: 41.3 inhabitants per square mile in the United States and 2.8 in Canada. Here then lay a vast, rich territory crying out for immigrants.[2]

To Jews in Eastern Europe, Canada looked highly appealing. They began to emigrate in increasing numbers in a pattern that resembled the growth of Jewish immigration to the United States, though on a much smaller scale. In 1850, there were only about 500 Jews in all of the Canadian provinces. But by the end of the nineteenth century the number had risen to approximately 16,400, and after that the Jewish community in Canada expanded very rapidly. In 1910 there were roughly 70,000 Canadian Jews; by 1920 the number had risen to 120,000, and by 1930 to 150,000. In the next few years, during the period between the onset of the Great Depression and the establishment of the Hitler dictatorship, the Jewish population of Canada rose to 170,000. The effects of the desperate search by East European Jews for refuge were being increasingly felt in the New World.[3]

There was a significant difference, however, between the background and character of the Jewish community in the United States and the one in Canada. Until the late nineteenth century, the former was made up mostly of German Jews, whose culture, outlook, and tradition had been shaped by the country from which they had emigrated. After that, however, they were increasingly outnumbered by Jewish immigrants from Eastern Europe, whose prevailing attitudes and customs differed in important respects. There were thus two distinct and not always compatible Jewish minorities in the United States. In Canada, however, large-scale Jewish immigration did not begin until the last years of the nineteenth century, when far fewer Central European Jews and many more East European Jews were eager to start a new life on the other side of the Atlantic. Of the roughly 125,000 Jews who emigrated to Canada between 1881 and 1930, 92 percent came from Eastern Europe—more than half of them from Russia, but sizable numbers also from Austria-Hungary, Poland, and Romania. Only about 10,000 were from other countries.[4]

That meant that the Canadian Jewish community was more homogeneous than the American one. It was not divided into Central European patricians and East European plebeians, the former regarding the latter with superiority and condescension, the latter viewing the former with dislike and resentment. In Canada, all or almost all Jewish immigrants started out as plebeians. And like their fellow plebeians in the United States, they tended to concentrate in the big cities, mostly Montreal and Toronto, settling down in Jewish neighborhoods with Jewish shops, Jewish restaurants, and Jewish social clubs. They continued to converse in Yiddish, to read Yiddish newspapers, to see Yiddish plays, and to write letters in Yiddish to relatives in the old country. They earned their living as shopkeepers, tradesmen, salesmen, small businessmen, or skilled workers. Their neighborhoods bore a close resemblance, though on a smaller scale, to New York's Lower East Side.

Before long, however, in the second and third generations, important changes started to take place, again similar to those occurring in the American Jewish community. Many of the young people, having attended public school and mastered the language and culture of their host country, began to aspire to a more elegant way of life. Many of them acquired a higher education and professional skill. Some entered the world of finance and commerce, becoming bankers, merchants, and industrialists. Others achieved success as physicians, lawyers, accountants, journalists, and teachers. They left the ghettos in which their parents and grandparents had lived, in which they themselves had grown up, and moved into more fashionable residences in other parts of the city, in the non-Jewish neighborhoods. In short, they became Canadians, indistinguishable, at least in most respects, from those whose ancestors had migrated to the country two centuries earlier.

Yet they never gained the same degree of acceptance as the American Jews. Both of the two major national communities, the French Canadians and the English Canadians, looked down with suspicion and distaste. The United States had historically been a nation of immigrants, even if the recent ones—the Italians, Poles, Greeks, and Jews—seemed more alien and less assimilable than the earlier ones—the Britons, Germans, and Scandinavians. But Canada never pretended to be ready to embrace the "huddled masses" or the "wretched refuse" from the other side of the ocean. On the contrary, the country openly announced its determination to maintain the traditional national, or rather binational, character.

That was one of the chief reasons that the Jewish community in Canada remained so much smaller than the one in the United States, not only numerically but proportionately. There were also other factors. The American standard of living was higher than the Canadian one; industrial growth was faster, economic opportunity greater. But the knowledge that Jews faced more obstacles to acceptance in Canada than in the United States also played an important part in the disparity between the two Jewish communities. Around 1930, Jews made up 3.5 percent of the American population but only 1.5 percent of the Canadian population. After the establishment of the Third Reich, therefore, most Jewish refugees thought it best to seek asylum somewhere else.[5]

Nevertheless, the extent of anti-Semitism in Canada should not be exaggerated. Many members of the Jewish community, especially those a few generations removed from their immigrant forebears, succeeded in gaining acceptance or even distinction in business, finance, and some of the professions. Yet they were rarely able to achieve the same importance as their coreligionists to the south. Their position in medicine and law was not as prominent as in the United States, their role in journalism and publishing remained far less influential, and only a few found successful careers in education, scholarship, culture, or the arts. There was no Louis Brandeis or Felix Frankfurter among the judges of the Canadian supreme court, no Henry Morgenthau or Samuel Rosenman among the advisers to the Canadian prime minister. The role of the Jewish community in the public affairs of the country was at best minor and sometimes almost nonexistent.

The barely disguised antipathy toward Jews common in Canada was not simply, as in many other democratic nations, a reflection of a general xenophobia or ethnic exclusivity. Here it was reinforced by the unique circumstances of Canada's historical development, especially the nonviolent but antagonistic confrontation of the two dominant national communities. The French Canadians—a minority, though a large minority—tended to view all immigrants as potential recruits for their traditional rivals, the English Canadians. They were right in the sense that the newcomers as a rule attended English-speaking schools, generally preferred to live in English-speaking neighborhoods, and sooner or later began to try to assimilate into the English-speaking establishment. That was understandable. The English Canadian community was politically more influential, economically more prosperous, and culturally more inclusive. The French Canadians, on the other hand, often suspicious and resentful, often on the defensive, felt that they were the rightful but dispossessed masters of the country. Anyone who had come to Canada after the tragic defeat of General Montcalm on the Plains of Abraham almost two centuries earlier was an alien, an interloper. And the more recent his arrival in the country, the less likely he was to be or to become a true Canadian.

The English Canadians were not much more tolerant toward outsiders. The long and bitter rivalry with their French compatriots tended to reinforce a conviction that they must cling to Britishness as the defining characteristic of their collective identity. Accordingly, they regarded immigrants from Eastern Europe, especially Jews, as basically unassimilable. Those aliens should, of course, be encouraged to master the English language, to adopt English manners and customs, and to learn to appreciate English culture and tradition. But they would never become authentically English. There would always be something in their appearance, manner, speech, or mentality that, no matter how hard they tried, would distinguish them from real Britons. There was no point in denying the fundamental, unalterable difference between the genuine and the spurious.

Clearly, not all Canadians, whether of French or English descent, were distrustful in their attitude toward the Jewish community. Some were tolerant, some even friendly. But there can be no doubt that xenophobia and ethnic prejudice were widespread, noticeably more so than in the United States. And the current of anti-Semitism was further intensified by the effects of the Great Depression. In Canada, as in all the countries of Europe and the New World, one of the obvious results of rising unemployment, growing privation, and mass discontent was an increase in popular opposition to Jewish immigration. There was the familiar, plausible argument that to admit large numbers of impoverished refugees was bound to increase the economic hardships so many Canadians had to contend with. There would be less food for the hungry, less housing for the poor, less employment, less income. The appeals for help for the innocent victims of ethnic persecution were always moving, they were often hard to resist. But what about the needy Canadians who were asking for help as well? Did they not have a higher claim on the compassion of their countrymen than foreigners on the other side of the ocean? In Canada as in all democratic nations, economic need reinforced ethnic prejudice in generating opposition to the admission of refugees.

In Canada, however, that opposition became stronger than in any country outside Eastern Europe. It gained force, moreover, just as the need for asylum was growing more urgent. In the early years of the Great Depression, between 1931 and 1933, close to 15,000 Jews entered Canada. But after the establishment of the National Socialist regime in Germany, the doors began to close, and they remained closed or almost closed until the collapse of the Third Reich. Between 1933 and 1945, a mere 5,000 Jews found refuge in Canada. The country's entry into the Second World War in 1939 seemed only to strengthen its determination to protect the national character and culture against the danger of adulteration.

Not that the other democratic countries welcomed Jewish refugees with open arms. In all of them there were doubts, fears, warnings, and complaints. But in none was the opposition to the admission of victims of Nazi bigotry as strong or effective as in Canada. During the period of the Third Reich, the United States accepted about 200,000 refugees, a number that many advocates of the victims of anti-Semitic totalitarianism considered pitifully inadequate but that was generous by comparison with the Canadian refugee policy. The British government admitted 70,000 refugees and allowed another 125,000 to emigrate to Palestine, at that time still a mandate of the United Kingdom. Some of the neutral countries helped as well. Argentina, with a territory less than a third the size of Canada, took in 50,000 Jews. Brazil, whose area and population were roughly equal to Canada's, accepted 27,000. Even Australia, at the farthest point on the globe from Central and Eastern Europe, found room for 15,000. The Canadian policy of exclusion was thus unique in its uncompromising strictness.[6]

As for the reason for that strictness, there was no attempt to disguise the ethnic exclusivity on which it was based. The French Canadian community in particular was frank in expressing its views. Newspapers such as *La Nation, L'Action catholique,* and *L'Action nationale* made little effort to conceal their distrust and dislike of Jews. Politicians like Wilfrid Lacroix, C. H. Leclerc, and H. E. Brunelle, members of the House of Commons representing the Liberal Party, were among the leading opponents of the admission of Jewish refugees. And various fraternal associations, mostly in the province of Quebec, like the St.-Jean Baptiste Society and the French Canadian branch of the Knights of Columbus, staunchly supported the government's exclusionary policy. Even some county councils and local banks sent letters to the government in Ottawa declaring their opposition to any relaxation of the curbs on immigration. In short, public opinion in French Canada regarded anything that might alter the existing uneasy balance between the two dominant ethnic communities, however slightly, as unacceptable.[7]

Early in 1939, for example, Brunelle, alarmed by proposals for convoking an international conference to help resettle Jewish refugees, expressed before Parliament his firm opposition to any relaxation of existing Canadian immigration laws. He spoke of the "thousands of fellow citizens whose situation is also deplorable," emphasizing that "charity begins at home." But what troubled him most was the prospect of "the entry of Jews, en masse or otherwise, into our country." He hastened to assure his fellow legislators that "I have no brief against the Hebrew race." Quite the contrary. He felt "deep sympathy for the Jews who are now being persecuted in certain countries of Europe." Yet there could be no denying that "through all the ages [Jews] have been the cause, justly or unjustly, of great difficulties in various countries." And as was generally acknowledged, "history repeats itself." Canada had to be on its guard.[8]

A week later, another member of Parliament from Quebec, Wilfrid Lacroix, submitted to the House of Commons a petition circulated by the St.-Jean Baptiste Society which bore 127,364 signatures. In essence, it repeated Brunelle's arguments. The signers protested vigorously "against all immigration whatsoever and especially against Jewish immigration." They demanded, "with all the energy inspired by the instinct of self-preservation," that the nation maintain its rigorous policy against the admission of foreigners. There were to be no exceptions. Not even members of the cabinet should have the authority to admit aliens, no matter how few, by granting them special permits providing access to Canada. Such permits were forbidden by law. The petition concluded with a request that "the Canadian government take all necessary precautions to prevent all immigration to this country." To admit ethnic elements foreign in custom and tradition might upset the delicate equilibrium between the two dominant communities. The defense of the nation's historic legacy had to be the first concern of its people.[9]

The opposition of most French Canadians to any relaxation of the restrictions on immigration for the benefit of Jewish refugees was occasionally accompanied by the contention that the dangers confronting those refugees were exaggerated. The leader of the Third Reich had been unfairly portrayed as a ruthless tyrant and aggressor. His policies were in fact not altogether unreasonable. The prominent politician and newspaperman Henri Bourassa wrote in the summer of 1938 in Le Devoir that Hitler's Mein Kampf revealed "a loftiness of thought and a breadth and variety of insights" which were impressive. The Führer did not seem to favor a policy of boundless expansionism. He sought rather to incorporate into a united Germany as many Germans of "pure blood" as possible, while carefully excluding "heterogeneous elements." He might try to annex the Sudeten region, but "under no circumstances would he want to introduce the Czech virus into the German body." Besides, "Germany is the only force capable of establishing order in the Slavic chaos. . . . What valid reason do France and England have for opposing [Hitler's] plan?" And as for Hitler's policy regarding the "Jewish question," Bourassa's readers could reasonably infer that it was motivated by a concern for ethnic purity, not by some irrational racial hatred.[10]

The English Canadians were generally more discreet in expressing their prejudices, but their prevailing views and attitudes were essentially the same. Many of the respectable newspapers, politicians, businessmen, and clergymen in the British provinces voiced the familiar ethnic platitudes regarding Jewry. Various fraternal societies, among them the Canadian Corps Association, the Orange Order, and the Knights of Columbus, as well as many farm and business organizations distrusted the Jews' role in the life of the nation. Jewish quotas, unwritten but even more rigid than in the United States, were the rule in the universities, the medical schools, the professions, and many industries. Jews were barred from acquiring property in certain neighborhoods, from vacationing in certain resorts, and from joining certain private clubs or even using the recreational facilities of those clubs. They were excluded from the governing boards of many charitable, educational, financial, and commercial organizations. There were even occasional streetfights in large cities like Toronto and Winnipeg between Jews and militant anti-Semites. The ethnic hostility in the United States seemed mild by comparison.[11]

Opposition to the admission of Jewish refugees was almost as strong among English Canadians as among French Canadians. Even the rhetoric of that opposition was essentially the same. In November 1938, barely a week after the outbreak of anti-Semitic riots in the Third Reich, the Canadian Corps Association, an organization of military veterans, came out against suggestions that the country should admit at least some of the victims of Nazi persecution. Captain W. W. Parry, chairman of the association's defense committee, urged the delegates at the monthly general meeting not to allow their country to become "the dumping ground of Europe now or at any other time." There should be no compromise, no retreat from that position. "We must be sure of the loyalty of those who live within our gates." Canada had achieved a way of life that was the envy of other nations. "Why sacrifice this heritage to those who have nothing in common with our tradition?" Sympathy for Jewish refugees should not be allowed to alter the essential character and culture of the country. "Now is no time to bring in people who have nothing in common with us, who do not want to work in the open, and who have no desire to come here other than to find a new home." Canada should remain Canadian.[12]

These views were communicated to Prime Minister Mackenzie King in a letter from Colonel Charles R. Hill, president of the Canadian Corps Association, maintaining that "the progress of democracy and civilization in Canada" would be possible only "if proper immigration laws are enacted which will ensure that our future citizens will be predominantly British." While some immigrants of a different background might be admitted as well, it was important to make sure that they were "those whose racial origin permits of rapid and complete assimilation into our social and economic life." Though condemning the Third Reich's anti-Semitic program as "iniquitous" and voicing "sincere sympathy" for its victims, the association expressed strong opposition to any influx of those victims. The veterans remained convinced that it would be in the best interests of all concerned to avoid settling refugees in areas "in which unemployment is predominant, where climatic conditions are unsuitable, and under conditions where racial origin of the immigrants is such that complete assimilation is a foredoomed failure." The letter suggested that if the British empire did decide to participate in a plan to provide asylum for Jews, its efforts should be confined to "the colonization of such areas as northeastern and eastern Africa." The Canadian opponents of immigration, like those in other democratic nations, maintained that emigrants from Central and Eastern Europe should seek refuge somewhere far away, on some distant continent or remote island, and the farther away, the better.[13]

Members of the Corps Association may have been blunter than most Canadians in expressing their ethnic antipathies, but those antipathies were widely shared in private. The feeling that Jews were fundamentally different from non-Jews in character, outlook, and conduct was not confined to the lower classes. It could often be found among members of the political and social elite, perhaps more often than among the masses. In the fall of 1938, even Vincent Massey, the Canadian high commissioner, confided to Malcolm MacDonald, the British colonial secretary, that it would be inadvisable to allow the victims of Nazi persecution to migrate to Canada. "Unfortunately the Jews were not generally good settlers on the land," he was reported as saying. "They hastened into towns and cities; and in the great cities like Toronto where there were already large numbers of Jews, any great increase would start an anti-semitic movement." How advisable was it to assist foreign Jews by endangering the security of domestic Jews?[14]

To solve this problem, Massey recommended in a confidential telegram to the Canadian Department of External Affairs that the government adopt a policy of publicly expressing sympathy for the refugees while carefully selecting the beneficiaries of that sympathy. "As a matter of tactics it might be wise for us to make a generous gesture in regard to acceptance of as many as possible Aryan Sudeten Germans from the 3,000 or so in Czechoslovakia." The reason was clear. The "Aryan Sudeten Germans" were "more desirable settlers" than "any other refugees," so that "if we could take a substantial number of them it would put us in a much stronger position in relation to later appeals from and on behalf of non Aryans." It would enable the government to exclude most Jews without appearing indifferent to the fate of refugees in general.[15]

The extent and intensity of Canadian anti-Semitic prejudice surprised some foreign observers whose own nations were no models of tolerance toward minorities, whether Jewish or non-Jewish. John Goodyear, a member of the American consular service stationed in Canada, commented in a report to the State Department on the prevalence of anti-Semitism in the country, emphasizing the rapidity of its spread. He had discovered that most people did not support Jewish immigration. On the contrary, they privately regarded the admission of Jewish refugees as a calamity. There was still some reluctance to express such views in public, but they could be heard increasingly in private conversation. The same arguments against an influx of immigrants that the Canadian Corps Association had advanced in its letter to the prime minister were also being expressed in one form or another throughout the country. Only their bluntness varied from place to place and from person to person.[16]

Nevertheless, in Canada as in the United States, there were also serious efforts to gain support for the establishment of an asylum for refugees from Nazi brutality. Those efforts were led by various Jewish organizations and societies, some of them long established, others formed only in response to the crisis confronting European Jewry. They found considerable sympathy, especially in the large cities, among non-Jewish groups—in liberal and left-wing political organizations, for example, in some church communities, mostly Protestant but sometimes Catholic, and in the trade union movement. Much of this support was based on broad ideological principles—on the conviction, for instance, that all citizens, whatever their faith or ethnicity, should be regarded as equal, or that fascistic movements like National Socialism were essentially attempts by the reactionary forces in society to maintain hierarchical rule and class exploitation. But there was also a spontaneous compassion for abused and persecuted Jewish refugees, a compassion based on private, instinctive humaneness, on a belief that the more fortunate have an obligation to help the less fortunate and that it is the duty of each and every one to aid the needy and oppressed.

For example, after the Canadian Corps Association sent its letter to the prime minister, Samuel Factor, a member of Parliament, publicly expressed his disagreement with the position the veterans had taken. "This is not immigration in the ordinary sense," he maintained. "This is an emergency." Besides, there was really no danger of a dilution or erosion of the Canadian national character and culture. "These people who are seeking refuge would be readily assimilated into the life of this country, for they represent the highest type of men and women, many of them being professional people." There were other and better arguments, however, for admitting refugees, including those who were not professional people. The ultimate reason, Factor maintained, was that "something must be done to help them, and I hope Canada will do its part." The nation had a moral obligation which it must not shirk.[17]

Other advocates of the refugees emphasized the harmlessness of a generous immigration policy. One unnamed but "prominent" member of Toronto's Jewish community tried to reassure those who feared that opening the gates even slightly would lead to a deluge of impoverished refugees. "There has never been any suggestion of 'forced mass immigration,' " he insisted. Canada would be asked only "to do something to alleviate the suffering of these people who have been deprived of their homes." Any suggestion that the country might be flooded with refugees was simply "fantastic." The newcomers would quickly adapt to their new homeland; they would soon become indistinguishable from other Canadians. As for the fear that they might take jobs away from native-born citizens or that they would compete with existing commercial and financial enterprises, that was only a specter created by the scare tactics employed by the opponents of immigration.[18]

The most impressive display of sympathy for the victims of Nazi bigotry, however, was the mass rally held in Toronto's Maple Leaf Gardens late in November 1938, with some 17,000 people crowded into the main building and an additional 3,000 at overflow meetings. The theme emphasized by all the speakers was that what was happening to the Jews of Central Europe today could easily happen to the Catholics and Protestants tomorrow. First came the mayor of the city, Ralph Day. He was followed by three Protestant clergymen: the Very Reverend Peter Bryce of the United Church of Canada, the Reverend J. F. Ward of the Church of England in Canada, and the Reverend Crossley Hunter of the First United Church in Hamilton. Catholics were represented by E. A. Conway, president of the Holy Name Society. Rabbis Maurice N. Eisendrath, Samuel Sachs, and Reuben Slonim spoke in the name of Reformed Judaism. But most striking was the silent presence of a few Orthodox Jews, "bearded and silk-hatted," sitting next to those of other faiths "in a rare excursion into a gathering of this kind," as one newspaper reporter put it. Then there was the address by the president of the Trades and Labor Council of Toronto, George Watson. And finally, messages of greeting and support from two distinguished Nobel Prize winners, Albert Einstein and Sir Frederick Banting, were read before an enthusiastic audience. It was a remarkable display of interdenominational solidarity.

The common topic at the rally was summarized by Mayor Day in his opening address. He expressed his sense of shock at the cruel ethnic persecution initiated by the Third Reich. "Today we are witnessing the spectacle of a great race being humiliated in a manner that even a few years ago seemed impossible." All people of goodwill, decency, and compassion were bound to be appalled by what was happening in the heart of Europe. "Gentiles, as well as Jews, in this city and in this Dominion are suffering at the spectacle of human beings being hounded and forced to flee to strange lands." But not only Jews were threatened by the cruelty of National Socialism. The aggressiveness and brutality of the Third Reich were a danger to international stability and "a menace to the continued peace of the world." Therefore, all nations committed to the ideal of freedom and the maintenance of peace, "peoples of all creeds in democratic countries," should unite in defense of their common fundamental beliefs. "We must band ourselves together so that none will be powerful enough to withstand us in our efforts to preserve those things we cherish." To the thousands gathered in the Maple Leaf Gardens, these words sounded very heartening.[19]

Yet mass meetings of that sort were rare in Canada. They took place mostly in the large cities, especially those with a substantial Jewish population. Canadians in general disapproved of the increasingly harsh anti-Semitic measures adopted by the Nazi regime. But to allow thousands of Jewish refugees, perhaps tens of thousands, to enter their country would aggravate the economic hardships resulting from the Great Depression.

Besides, there was a danger that mass immigration might alter the ethnic and cultural character of the nation. Those were the major reasons for the reluctance of the prime minister, the various party leaders, and most local politicians to go beyond expressing an occasional condemnation of the Third Reich's racist program. Only a few philanthropic organizations on the fringes of political life, like the Co-operative Commonwealth Federation, advocated a more generous admittance policy.

Refugees from Europe, however, found other opportunities in the New World, outside the United States and Canada. The nations of Latin America were generally more lenient in their immigration policy than their neighbors to the north. They were less concerned about protecting their national tradition and culture or defending their historic values and beliefs. Nor were they as opposed to radical ideas and movements from abroad. Their governments may have been dictatorial or semi-dictatorial, but they were often willing to tolerate small groups of left-wing intellectuals gathering in some favorite café to discuss the problems of social injustice and what to do about them. Socialists, Communists, anarchists, and Trotskyites from Central and Eastern Europe who were unable to gain admittance to the United States could find a congenial ideological environment south of the border, especially in Mexico.

Important geographic and demographic factors also helped make Latin America more willing to admit a substantial number of immigrants from the Old World. Brazil, to take an obvious example, had only 3.1 inhabitants per square mile, far below the 41.3 in the United States and not much above the 2.8 in Canada. Even Argentina, with 9.7 inhabitants per square mile, and Chile, with 14.7, were sparsely populated by comparison with many European countries. Mexico, with 21.4, had barely half the population density of its neighbor to the north. For that matter, Cuba, a small island with 81.7 inhabitants per square mile, though more populous than other nations in the Western Hemisphere, was still far behind the leading European states: France, with 193.6; Italy, with 358.2; and Great Britain, with 486.1. It is not surprising that the countries of Latin America were often willing to admit Jewish refugees, especially if they had enough money to support themselves and were prepared to offer an occasional financial reward to sympathetic immigration officials.[20]

Jewish immigration to these countries in fact began long before the rise of Hitler. Their language and culture may have seemed more alien to emigrants from Eastern and Central Europe than the language and culture of the United States or Canada, but admittance was much easier to obtain, and the economic opportunities for energetic and enterprising newcomers were very inviting. By 1933 there were 240,000 Jews in Argentina, one of the ethnically and culturally most Europeanized nations in Latin America. They constituted 2.1 percent of the Argentinian population, a far higher proportion than in Germany or any country of Western Europe. Indeed, they were the second largest Jewish community in the New World, exceeded in size only by the one in the United States. There were also significant numbers of Jews in some of the other Latin American states: 45,000 in Brazil, 12,000 in Mexico, 12,000 in Uruguay, 9,500 in Cuba, and 4,000 in Chile. The figures may appear almost insignificant by comparison with the 4.5 million Jews in the United States, but after the establishment of the Hitler dictatorship, Latin America became increasingly important as a temporary or even permanent asylum for refugees from ethnic oppression.[21]

The Jews who migrated to Latin America before 1933, however, came mostly from Eastern Europe. They were thus similar in background to those who settled in the United States, except that there was no German Jewish community among them. Of the 180,000 Jews who immigrated to Argentina between 1881 and 1930, almost 90 percent were born in Russia, Austria-Hungary, Poland, or Romania. Almost 70 percent of the 30,000 who settled in Brazil during the same period came from Eastern Europe as well. And roughly the same percentage, 20,000 of the 30,000 Jews living in the other countries of South and Central America, were emigrants from the region of Europe east of the Oder River.[22]

After 1933, however, the geographical and cultural background of the Jewish community in Latin America began to change. Many Jews from the succession states were still eager to escape growing economic hardship and ethnic hostility. But there was now also a steady flow of refugees from Central Europe who would have preferred to remain in the country of their birth but who had to face a rising tide of anti-Semitic bigotry. If possible, they would have chosen to resettle in the United States. But since the American restrictions on immigration were very hard to overcome, many of them sought asylum in Latin America, often in the hope that they might sooner or later be able to make their way north. That was why Mexico and Cuba were among the favorite destinations of the victims of persecution in the Old World. Living close to the United States would someday perhaps make it easier for them to cross the U.S. border.

The authorities in Latin America were generally aware of the personal preference of many of the Jewish refugees seeking admission to their countries. They knew that given the opportunity, the immigrants would probably have chosen some other destination. But they were willing to overlook private inclinations. What mattered was that some of the new-comers had financial resources which, while modest by the standards of the nations from which they had come, seemed substantial in the economic climate of Latin America. Others had technical or professional skills that were in short supply in their prospective new homelands. In a largely underdeveloped agricultural economy, moreover, the danger of financial or commercial competition did not appear very great. As for the fear of an alien corruption of traditional values and loyalties, the Latin American countries were much more tolerant of cultural diversity than the Anglo-Saxon democracies. They were used to a multiplicity of races, ethnicities, traditions, customs, and languages.

And another consideration often made the oligarchic governments of Latin America more willing than the democratic governments of Europe or North America to accept Jewish refugees: they had so few Jews within their boundaries. The admittance of 1,000 or 2,000 or even 10,000 was likely to be almost unnoticed. There were some exceptions, to be sure. The number of Jews in Argentina, where they constituted more than 2 percent of the population, though far behind the percentage in the United States, was well ahead of the figure for Canada. In Uruguay the Jewish community amounted to 0.5 percent of all inhabitants, and in Cuba 0.3. Elsewhere, however, in countries that were ethnically and culturally less Europeanized, the proportion of Jews was insignificant: 0.1 percent in Brazil, Mexico, and Chile. Here there could hardly be any talk of a "Jewish question."[23]

For all these reasons, the oligarchical regimes of Latin America often did more to provide asylum for Jewish refugees than the democracies, whether in the Old World or the New. To be sure, the help offered by even the most generous and humane countries seems in retrospect tragically inadequate, considering the catastrophe that was about to overwhelm European Jewry.

It is hard to argue with the contention, advanced after it was all over, that "some Jews did find refuge, but measured against the millions who were murdered and the irreparable damage their deaths caused to the spirit of humanity, the numbers sound pitifully small." Still, how could anyone before the Second World War have foreseen that the anti-Semitic fury of the Third Reich would not be satisfied with anything less than genocide? And even if it had been foreseen, would the democratic states have been willing to do much more than they actually did? Merely asking the question suggests the answer. And that answer is reinforced by the knowledge of how the democratic states did in fact respond once they discovered the terrible secret of the Holocaust while it was still in progress.[24]

In any event, the willingness of the Latin American countries to admit Jewish refugees compares favorably with the immigration policies of several nations committed in theory to the principles of democracy. Argentina accepted about 50,000 victims of Nazi anti-Semitism, while Brazil took in another 27,000. Those numbers are far less than the 200,000 who were admitted to the United States. They are smaller, for that matter, than the 70,000 who found asylum in the United Kingdom. But they are well ahead of the 15,000 who managed to gain entrance to Australia, and they seem quite generous by comparison with the total for Canada, a mere 5,000. There was thus little correlation between the political ideology or governmental system of a country and the extent to which that country was willing to accept refugees from persecution by the Nazi regime.[25]

Yet even in Latin America anti-Semitism was not uncommon. More than that, as the persecution of Jews in the Old World increased, hostility toward them in the New World increased as well. Their growing need for asylum was countered by a growing reluctance to provide asylum. The spread of ethnic prejudice was based on more than fear of the outsiders' political subversiveness, economic shrewdness, or cultural aggressiveness. It reflected an irrational, often subconscious aversion to the alien and the unknown, to the dark, mysterious forces threatening a traditional way of life, and above all to the evil designs of cunning interlopers masquerading as friendly neighbors.

Such instinctive fears account, at least in part, for the fact that hostility toward Jews was increasing in the Old World at the same time that their influence in politics, economics, and culture was declining. They also help explain why anti-Semitic suspicions and fears were spreading in Latin America, though not nearly to the same extent as in Europe. While the number of Jewish refugees seeking admittance was growing on the eve of the Second World War, the opposition to their admittance was growing too. The warnings against the destructive role of Jewry in national life that were becoming louder in Central and Eastern Europe could now be heard in the countries of Central and South America.

To the diplomats in Berlin, those were welcome signs of a rising awareness throughout the world of the danger of a Judaization of state and society. The German foreign ministry's circular regarding "The Jewish Question as a Factor in Foreign Policy in 1938" spoke with gratification about the "marked growth of anti-Semitism" in South America as well as North America, France, the Netherlands, Scandinavia, and Greece—indeed, wherever the "Jewish migratory current" flowed. The legation in Montevideo, for example, had recently reported that "for months the Jewish influx has been continuing week after week." As a result, there could be no question that "anti-Semitism is growing" in Uruguay, where the percentage of Jews in the population was small but well above the average for Latin American countries.[26]

In the spring of 1935, when James G. McDonald, the American member of the League of Nations Refugee Commission, visited Argentina, Brazil, and Uruguay to explore the possibility of resettling European victims of Nazi oppression in Latin America, what he found left him discouraged. In a letter written during his trip, he confessed that he was "more and more . . . impressed, and I must add depressed, by the accumulating evidences of the contagious character of the Nazi propaganda of anti-Semitism, often thinly disguised as ardent nationalism." There were indications that Jews were being excluded from certain professions—from medicine and police work, for example. The Argentinians were prone to copy other nations, and "unfortunately just now they are inclined to copy the Germans." Anti-Semitism had until recently been almost unknown in the country, but "now it has invaded high and influential circles, including the Governmental, the University, and the more exclusive social groups." McDonald was deeply disappointed by what he had discovered on his journey.[27]

He voiced that disappointment in the report he delivered in London before the advisory council of the Refugee Commission. He had to admit that "the general results of this tour have not been encouraging." Unfortunately, "all the countries [in the region] make it virtually impossible for foreigners to exercise any of the liberal professions in their territory." In Brazil, for instance, noncitizens were excluded from the medical profession, not only by the national constitution but also by the rules and policies of the medical association. The same restrictions applied to members of the legal profession, unless they were willing to work in some backward neighboring country like Bolivia. Moreover, "it is the definite intention of the Brazilian Minister of Agriculture that immigration should be exclusively for agricultural workers." As for Uruguay, there were "few possibilities of establishment [for refugees] on account of the bad economic conditions in the country." All in all, prejudice in South America may not have been more intense than in Western Europe or in the United States. It may actually have been less prevalent. But given the relatively small size of the Jewish community there, McDonald found the growing opposition to the admittance of refugees discouraging.[28]

That opposition could also be found farther north, in the Latin American country that was ideologically most opposed to National Socialism and that might therefore have been expected to be most sympathetic toward its victims. Mexico was the only major state in the New World to support the Loyalist cause during the civil war in Spain actively. It was also willing to admit left-wing immigrants from Central and Eastern Europe as well as the Iberian Peninsula. The Mexican intelligentsia and the Mexican artistic community were openly and defiantly revolutionary, at least in sentiment and speech. Indeed, many Jewish refugees who had been barred from entering the United States because of their radical political leanings found a congenial asylum in Mexico. Yet even here there were anti-Semitic complaints, and not only from conservative landowners and wealthy businessmen. The Federation of Mexican Farmers also urged the government to enforce the immigration laws more strictly, because "almost all of [the recent arrivals] came in under false pretenses and did not engage in work as they had promised." Instead, "they have all become merchants and gangsters."[29]

None of this alters the fact that the states of Latin America accepted more Jewish refugees than many of the nations with a more advanced economy and a stronger commitment to the principles of democracy, for even in those countries that condemned the doctrines of National Socialism most loudly there were the familiar anti-Semitic prejudices and resentments. The disparity between the democratic nations' expressions of sympathy for persecuted Jews and their reluctance to offer those persecuted Jews asylum did not escape the notice of the leaders of the Third Reich. In a speech to the Reichstag on January 30, 1939, Hitler charged his foreign critics with brazen hypocrisy. "It is a shameful spectacle," he declared, "to see today how the entire world of democracy is dripping with compassion, and yet remains heartlessly stubborn in dealing with the poor, persecuted Jewish people despite its publicly proclaimed duty to help." He may have been exaggerating the inconsistency between theory and practice, between word and deed. And yet that inconsistency was there; it was undeniable.[30]

The reasons for that inconsistency can be found partly in the economic fears and hardships spreading throughout the Western world. But there were other reasons as well, older and deeper reasons, going far beyond the refugee problem created by the Third Reich. They were rooted in a deep-seated, ancient belief that something called the "Jewish question" confronted all nations. This "Jewish question" had arisen out of the unique collective character of the Jewish people—their aggressiveness, cleverness, covetousness, and exclusiveness. They were fundamentally different from other peoples, and that difference made them unassimilable and sometimes dangerous. That view transcended national boundaries and geographic distances. It could be found with varying degrees of intensity in all countries. It was embraced most ardently by Nazi Germany, but the succession states of Eastern Europe were not far behind. It even had many adherents in the democracies of the Old World as well as the New. And that view in turn deeply influenced the prevailing perception of the refugee problem. Not until the destruction of European Jewry did it finally begin to lose its deadly force.

Adolf Eichmann during his trial in Jerusalem, 1962. Eichmann, then aged fifty-six, had become the personification of the Nazis and their nearly complete extermination of the Jews of Europe.

Adolf Hitler and Benito Mussolini in Florence in May 1938. Together they would soon plunge Europe into the Second World War.

Jewish life in prewar Poland. This is a photograph of children in the Jewish quarter of Lodz, the second largest city in Poland at the time, 1930.

France protecting its border from immigrants in 1935, including refugees from Nazi Germany.

A Jewish synagogue burns in Berlin after being set on fire by an anti-Semitic mob during the Kristallnacht, November 1938.

Jewish refugee children from Germany housed in Harwich, England. They had arrived from Germany earlier in the day when this photograph was taken in December 1938.

H. G. Wells, who wrote surprisingly intemperate anti-Semitic tracts, voiced the prejudices shared by many citizens of Great Britain.

A young Jewish woman from Austria who has just
arrived in England after fleeing her home.

Jewish refugee children from Germany arriving in New York Harbor in June 1939, just months before the outbreak of the Second World War. They were part of a small, fortunate minority.

Jewish refugee children from Poland landing in England en route to Canada in August 1939.

The United States enters the war. President Franklin Roosevelt addressing a joint session of Congress on December 8, 1941. He asked for and received a declaration of war against the Empire of Japan.

An anti–Charles Lindbergh cartoon from June 1941. Lindbergh was at first vocally sympathetic to Adolf Hitler and openly anti-Semitic. The cartoon was by Theodor Geisel, who would go on to be better known as children's book author Dr. Seuss.

Father Charles E. Coughlin, a fiery public orator and anti-Semite.

Eleanor Roosevelt working at a soup kitchen; she had occasionally voiced anti-Semitic prejudices in private correspondence.

Albert Einstein with Rabbi Stephen Wise and the author Thomas Mann in May 1938. They later urged the Roosevelt administration to take action to stop the genocide of the Jews in Nazi-occupied Europe. Their efforts failed.

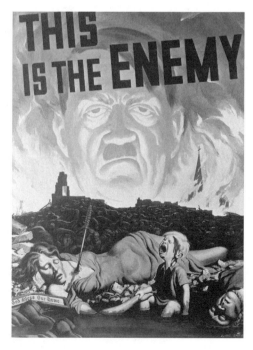

A poster from 1943 depicting the horror of Hitler's war machine.

The German SS and SD rounding up Jews in the Warsaw Ghetto in 1943. These Jews were condemned to deportation to the Nazi death camps.

Hungarian Jews being pushed off a railway car after arriving at the platform in Auschwitz.

Jewish children behind an Auschwitz barbed wire, December 1944.

The bodies of dead Jewish prisoners found when Auschwitz was liberated.

Young Polish Jews and a guardian nurse arriving in Palestine in 1943. They were among the lucky few who escaped Poland during the war.

Anti-Semitism in the United States. Five members of the Christian Front, an anti-Semitic group, pose with their rifles in 1940.

PART TWO

The Unending American Debate

The solution of the deeper and universal problem of anti-Semitism rests, we hold, with the Christian church, and with the Jewish people themselves. Democracy cannot solve this deeper problem. Perhaps religion can. But there will have to be a drastic revolution in the Christian attitude and the Jewish faith before any realistic mind can profess to see ground for hope.

THE CHRISTIAN CENTURY,
CHICAGO, NOVEMBER 30, 1938

7

In Search of a Haven

THE MAGNITUDE OF the crisis confronting the Jewish community of Europe did not become fully apparent until the late 1930s. Before then there was still hope that the liberal ideology and the international order that had become dominant after the First World War would retain their power. Admittedly, there could be no denying that the status quo was being seriously challenged. The hard times that followed the sham prosperity of the later postwar years had shaken public faith in the ideals and policies of the victor states. But that was surely no more than a temporary loss of confidence, a brief spell of pessimism which would quickly dissipate with the return of good times. There was really no reason to panic. Common sense seemed to recommend an attitude of patience and hope.

This stubborn optimism, not always entirely genuine, ignored the growing signs of a sharp shift to the right in the prevailing political sympathies of Europe. It tended to dismiss the rise of the Fascist movement in Italy as simply an expression of dissatisfaction with the postwar peace settlement. As for Mussolini, he was widely perceived to be at heart not very different from the cautious, opportunistic politicians who had governed the kingdom since its founding seventy years earlier. Similarly, the drift of the succession states toward a semi-dictatorial form of authority could be explained as part of a painful process of political maturation in a region that had never known what liberal government was. Sooner or later it was bound to recognize the advantages of such a government. And the most recent and most troubling sign of a growing rejection of democracy, the establishment of the Nazi regime in Germany, could be ascribed to the disastrous decline in the national economy. As soon as production rose and unemployment diminished, the country would return to a more traditional, more humane, and more tolerant system of government. Those who were most threatened by the shift to the right were also the ones most likely to seek comfort in glib assurances that there was really no serious danger.

German Jews were especially vulnerable to this sort of self-deception. Not only were they reluctant to admit to themselves that they had been rejected by the nation of their birth, the nation of "thinkers and poets" to which most of them remained deeply attached, but many were also convinced that the Hitler dictatorship was a fleeting phenomenon, a brief aberration. The country would soon return to its historical and cultural roots in an enlightened humaneness. In the meantime, the Jews must be patient and learn to live with the anti-Semitic policies of the new order. Besides, those policies, though unjust and humiliating, did not seem ruinous. Their purpose appeared to be the isolation and segregation of a scapegoat minority, not its destruction. Non-Aryans would still be able to engage in their customary occupations and pursuits, though under less favorable conditions. Why, then, seek a new way of life in a strange environment? Would it not be better to wait patiently until the madness of National Socialism had passed and the country returned to the traditions of reasonableness and enlightenment?

That was why the refugee problem during the first few years of the Third Reich, while serious, did not seem critical The number of Jews seeking to leave Germany remained limited. Only about 30,000 Jewish immigrants entered the United States from 1933 to 1937, at a substantially lower annual rate than during the 1920s. That was in large part a result of the restrictions imposed by the American immigration laws, but it also reflected the slow, reluctant exodus of those who were becoming victims of racist discrimination in the Third Reich. The size of that exodus was not a result of obstacles to emigration imposed by the Nazi regime. In fact, the government encouraged Jews to depart, and those who did so were often even permitted to transfer at least some of their assets to their new country of residence. It was the Jews themselves who decided in most cases to wait out the fierce storm of National Socialism.[1]

After 1937, however, the illusion that Nazism would soon pass quickly vanished. By then the Hitler regime had consolidated its hold on power, suppressing the remnants of domestic dissent and repudiating the few remaining military restrictions imposed at Versailles. It was now ready to adopt a strategy of territorial expansion through the threat of war. The leaders of the Third Reich had recognized the weaknesses of the West European democracies resulting from the Great Depression. While France and England were being torn by economic hardship and social conflict, Germany presented the appearance of a nation united in will and unyielding in determination. By exploiting the doubts and insecurities of its opponents, outwardly strong but inwardly divided, it was able to gain a series of impressive diplomatic victories—a remarkable achievement for a country that only a few years earlier had seemed on the verge of chaos. In March 1938 came the incorporation of Austria, in September 1938 there was the annexation of the Sudeten region, and in March 1939 the rest of Czechoslovakia was partitioned, the western half becoming a "protectorate" of the Third Reich while the eastern half was transformed into an "independent" Slovakia. The area and the population of Germany were now greater than in the heyday of the old Hohenzollern Empire.

For the Jewish community of Central Europe, these extraordinary diplomatic triumphs were a disaster. They meant, first of all, that despite the westward flow of refugees during the previous five years, there were now more than one and a half times as many Jews under the rule of National Socialism as at the time of Hitler's rise to power. At the beginning of 1933 there had been about 550,000 Jews in Germany; by 1938 this number had diminished, though by no more than about a third, probably even less than that. But then came the Anschluss, as a result of which the 230,000 Austrian Jews became subject to the rule of the Third Reich, and a year later they were joined by the 360,000 Jews from former Czechoslovakia, some of them directly under the rule of the Hitler regime, others indirectly through the puppet Slovak state. All of Central European Jewry was now at the mercy of National Socialism.[2]

What made the situation even more dangerous was the consolidation of Nazi control over domestic affairs, a process that paralleled and was reinforced by the German successes in foreign policy. When Hitler became chancellor, his regime was based essentially on an informal but close alliance between the adherents of the National Socialist ideology and the traditionalist conservatives of the old school. Their collaboration had begun in the last years of the Weimar Republic and continued under the Third Reich. Oligarchical right-wingers were the junior partners, but they were able to exercise considerable influence within the administrative system of the new order, and a few of them even gained important positions in the cabinet. As a rule, they played a restraining and moderating role in affairs of state.

This alliance came to an end, however, toward the end of the decade. As the radical right wing in Germany began to feel more confident, it became more assertive and aggressive. In foreign affairs that meant a diplomacy of expansion by confrontation, while in domestic affairs it led to a purge of mere sympathizers and fellow travelers from positions of leadership in the bureaucracy. Thereafter only those who were committed heart and soul to the principles of National Socialism were to hold an office of importance in the state. Early in 1938, the conservative but moderate Hjalmar Schacht was replaced as minister of economics by the true believer Walter Funk, while the unswerving loyalist Joachim von Ribbentrop took over the foreign office from the more experienced but less doctrinaire Konstantin von Neurath. It was the beginning of a process of Nazification of the administration and the judiciary, which continued without interruption until the fall of the Third Reich.

Not even the armed forces were exempt from the Nazi regime's campaign. Their traditional noninvolvement in partisan politics was challenged early in 1938, at the same time that the purge of fellow travelers from the top ranks of the government and the bureaucracy was taking place. Private scandals involving Werner von Blomberg, the minister of war, and Werner von Fritsch, the commander in chief of the army, not only led to their removal from positions of authority but also enabled Hitler to initiate the politicization of the armed forces. He himself assumed the functions of the minister of war, exercising his new responsibility through General Wilhelm Keitel, his representative at the supreme command. It would be going too far to say that the military was subjected to Nazification to the same extent as the bureaucracy, but it is clear that the vaunted independence of the armed forces from political pressures and influences was being seriously restricted.

The most dramatic manifestation of the growing militancy of the Third Reich, however, was its new ruthlessness in dealing with the "Jewish question." Until the late 1930s there had been a widespread assumption, among both Jews and non-Jews in Germany, Western Europe, and North America, that the Nazi regime sought the isolation and segregation of Jewry within clearly formulated legal limits defining the rights of non-Aryans as opposed to those of Aryans. The two ethnic communities would remain separate, each governed in accordance with its own culture and traditions and each possessing a measure of self-rule reflecting its unique historic character. For the Jews, this would mean a return to something like their status before emancipation, something resembling their semi-autonomous existence in the ghettos of the Middle Ages.

All such illusions vanished, however, in the period immediately preceding the Second World War. The growing militancy of the Nazi regime, which had become apparent in its conduct of foreign relations and its administration of domestic affairs, was displayed most dramatically in the growing ruthlessness of its racial policy. The restrictions imposed on Jews became increasingly harsh and oppressive in the course of 1938, culminating early in November in the Kristallnacht, a wave of mass riots encouraged by the authorities which were directed primarily against Jewish cultural institutions and business establishments but were often accompanied by violent assaults, some of them deadly, on members of the despised minority. Even many Germans who shared the prevailing anti-Semitic prejudices were shocked by this display of a brutal ethnic hatred, long familiar in backward czarist Russia but never before apparent in civilized, law-abiding Germany. And on top of that, the government imposed severe penalties not on the instigators but on the victims of the Kristallnacht. The Jews under Nazi rule now became an impoverished, anathematized, and terrified community of outcasts.

That was when the exodus of refugees, which had until then been a trickling stream, turned into a flood. There could no longer be any illusions among German Jews about the ephemeral nature of National Socialism or the inevitable return of the country to earlier ideals of tolerance and humaneness. Even the assumption that they would be able to lead a separate but secure existence under the Hitler regime had proved to be false. The only way out was emigration. No one, neither Jews nor non-

Jews, whether in Germany or elsewhere, suspected that the final solution to the "Jewish question" that the government would adopt was genocide. In fact, the authorities encouraged emigration, and members of the Jewish community no longer needed to be prodded. They were eager, indeed desperate, to leave. That was why during the ten months between the Kristallnacht and the outbreak of war, about 150,000 refugees left the Third Reich, roughly the same number as during the six years after the appointment of Hitler as chancellor of Germany.[3]

But the rapid growth in the number of refugees only intensified the seriousness of the refugee problem. There were far more Jews under Nazi rule in September 1939 than in January 1933—approximately 840,000, as opposed to 550,000. Almost all of them were desperately eager to emigrate. The real problem was the growing reluctance of the democratic states to accept additional refugees. They had previously been more or less willing to admit a limited number of victims of Nazi oppression as evidence of their commitment to tolerance and humaneness. But now they were becoming apprehensive. The number of Jews subject to the rule of National Socialism had increased much faster than the number of those who had managed to escape through emigration. But how many more could the democracies accept? As the refugee problem became more acute, the willingness to solve it by relaxing the restrictions on immigration gradually diminished.[4]

Relations between Germany on one side and France and England on the other were becoming increasingly tense. An outbreak of hostilities was now a distinct possibility. The destruction of Czechoslovakia finally convinced the leaders of the democratic states of Western Europe that the policy of appeasement which they had been following would not diminish German aggressiveness. Each successive concession seemed to lead only to new demands by Hitler. Having just partitioned the Czechoslovak Republic, he was now turning against the Polish Republic, demanding the annexation of Danzig and a revision of the eastern boundary of Germany. This time, however, the French and British governments were determined to resist him, even if that meant war. It would thus be very risky to admit a flood of needy refugees who would inevitably divert public attention and national resources from the essential preparations for a test of military strength.

And there was another reason for the West European democracies' reluctance to accept many more refugees—a reason that was never openly admitted but that appeared again and again in confidential government deliberations. Too much generosity toward Jews seeking asylum would play into the hands of Nazi propagandists, who claimed that Jewish wealth and influence were directing the foreign policy of France and England behind the scenes. Worse still, those charges might sound credible to some elements of the general population, especially those who were becoming alarmed at the prospect of another destructive war and who were prepared to believe that this danger was a result of the machinations of sinister and conspiratorial forces. The government authorities, anxious to avoid doing anything that might aggravate such suspicions, feared that a sudden influx of Jews was likely to arouse the hostility of domestic bigots and xenophobes. It might even lead to the spread of anti-Semitism, weakening the resolve of the nation to stand up to the Third Reich. It could prove a disaster.

The refugee problem became less pressing, or at least less immediate, after the outbreak of hostilities in September 1939. To begin with, the swift victory of the Wehrmacht in Poland led to what was in effect the partition of Eastern Europe between the Third Reich and the Soviet Union, and that meant that members of the largest regional Jewish community in the world were no longer able to escape persecution through emigration. The situation of the Jews in Central Europe was no better. Now they could not seek admittance to France or England directly, since those countries were at war with Germany. There was still the possibility of finding refuge in one of the smaller neutral democracies—in Switzerland, the Low Countries, or the Scandinavian states. But those democracies, weak and vulnerable, were reluctant to do anything that might anger the belligerents. They did not rigidly exclude all Jewish refugees, but they were very careful not to admit very many.

Even this narrow avenue of escape became almost completely closed by the summer of 1940, barely ten months after the war began. In April, Denmark and Norway were invaded and occupied by the Germans; in May, it was the turn of Belgium and the Netherlands; and by the end of June, France had been forced to surrender as well. Those extraordinary successes of the Wehrmacht, far greater than anyone in the democracies had anticipated, were a disaster for Jews who still had some hope of finding refuge in Western Europe, since most of the continent was now under Nazi control.

There was still a possibility, however, though a slim one at best, of finding a haven beyond the English Channel. If a refugee could obtain permission to enter one of the remaining neutral countries temporarily— Switzerland or Sweden, Spain or Portugal, or even the unoccupied zone of France—he might then be able to obtain a visa to some nation beyond the reach of the Third Reich. The chance, though small, did exist. Yet the handful of European governments in a position to help Jews were reluctant to risk antagonizing triumphant Germany. Switzerland and Sweden, weak and defenseless, could not afford to display too much generosity toward refugees, even if they wanted to. They might have to pay a heavy price for their compassion. Spain and Portugal, both dictatorships, both sympathetic to fascism, both on good terms with the Axis powers, were not ardently anti-Semitic, but neither were they willing to endanger their friendly relations with the Third Reich for the sake of the victims of Nazi persecution. They admitted only those who could provide evidence that they would soon be moving on to some other destination. As for Vichy France, it was at the mercy of the German occupation. In short, never before had European Jewry faced such danger.

One nation in Europe, however, was still in a position to offer asylum to Jewish refugees. England, being at war with the Third Reich, did not have to fear reprisals for displaying compassion toward those escaping ethnic persecution. The Germans were already doing all they could to defeat their last remaining military opponent. Whatever the British government might do to alleviate the refugee problem could not worsen the dangerous situation in which the country found itself. On the contrary, it would underscore England's commitment to the democratic principles of tolerance and compassion, principles that had become a central ideological justification for the struggle against National Socialism. Helping refugees would help transform a war for national survival into a crusade for universal justice.

Yet the authorities in England acted with caution and sometimes with reluctance in helping persecuted Jews, not only during the prewar years but during the war itself. Of course, thousands of victims of the Third Reich's anti-Semitism found asylum in Great Britain. But in view of the rapidly growing need for a refuge, the number of those who found it on the other side of the English Channel remained small, in part, at least, as a result of government policy. Obviously, a country fighting for its life, under constant attack by enemy submarines and warplanes, forced to import food and essential goods from distant continents, could not afford to admit large numbers of Jews, however needy or pitiful. Yet in the course of the war the British authorities did accept many refugees from allied countries occupied by the armies of the Third Reich—Poles, for example, Czechs, Serbs, and Greeks. Why, then, the persistent hesitation regarding Jews?

The answer appears to be primarily that the other refugees could be expected to return home once victory was achieved. They had no intention of remaining in England. Their hope was that sooner or later they would be able to go back to their native countries. But many of the Jews had no wish to return to communities in which they had been widely regarded as aliens or parasites or subversives. More than that, the way they had been treated by many of their non-Jewish countrymen under the German occupation reinforced their reluctance to go back to what was, in theory at least, their homeland. Most of them were likely to try to stay in Great Britain, hoping to become permanent residents enjoying a more secure way of life in a more tolerant social environment. That was the danger that alarmed the British authorities.

When Otto Schiff, chairman of the Jewish Committee for Refugees, asked the government in the fall of 1942 to admit a few hundred children and elderly men and women who had close relatives in England but were trapped in unoccupied France, Home Secretary Herbert Morrison urged his colleagues not to approve the request. "Any departure from [the government's] rigid policy of exclusion," he warned, "is liable to lead to fresh claims and additional pressure for the admission to the United Kingdom of persons who are in danger or distress." The public was already troubled by what it perceived to be the excessive number of Jewish refugees who had been granted asylum. To accept even more, he feared, might stir up "an unpleasant degree of anti-Semitism (of which there is a fair amount just below the surface) and that would be bad for the country and the Jewish community." Too much generosity was bound to prove harmful to all concerned.[5]

But it was not enough to restrict the number of Jewish refugees admitted to Great Britain. Measures had to be taken to counter the contention of German propaganda that the British government had entered the war at the instigation and in defense of world Jewry. There was fear in official circles that the charge might sound credible to some groups in England, especially among the lower classes, and so nothing should be said or done that might seem to support it. This concern appeared over and over again throughout the war years in various confidential memorandums and statements by leading officials and politicians.

In September 1939, for example, barely two weeks after the outbreak of hostilities, Sir Alexander Cadogan, the permanent undersecretary in the Foreign Office, advised the government against issuing a white paper dealing with concentration camps in Germany. First of all, he maintained, "several hair-raising reports" about the treatment of incarcerated Jews had come from the Jews themselves, "who are not, perhaps, entirely reliable witnesses." But more important, "the Germans will only say that this is further proof that the British Empire is run by international Jewry." And there would no doubt be some in Great Britain who would believe that, since "sympathy with the Jews [appears to have] waned very considerably during the last twelve months."[6]

In the spring of 1940, when someone in the Foreign Office suggested that England provide asylum in Palestine for Jewish refugees who had been trapped in the Low Countries since the outbreak of war and were facing the growing hostility of the local population, one official, J.E.M. Carvell, expressed strong opposition. "I am inclined to think that the danger of anti-Semitism in this country is as great as in Holland & Belgium. The hatred of the Jews amongst the middle & lower strata of London's population has increased greatly since the influx of German Jewish refugees." Besides, why worry about foreigners when the country was in such grave danger? "I think that the U.K. should take first place in the order of preference." Could anyone quarrel with that contention?[7]

Even in the summer of 1941, after the air battle over Britain had subsided and the Soviet Union had entered the war, the English authorities remained reluctant to dwell on the fate of European Jewry, now facing genocide. A memorandum issued by the Ministry of Information urged British propagandists to avoid too much emphasis on the brutality of the Nazi regime, especially on the chief victims of that brutality. "Sheer 'horror' stuff such as the concentration camp torture stories . . . repel the normal mind," it warned. "A certain amount of horror is needed but it must be used sparingly and must deal always with treatment of indisputably innocent people. Not with violent political opponents. And not with Jews." To dwell too much on the fate of Jews in a Europe under Hitler's domination might lend credibility to the Third Reich's contention that the war was a result of the machinations of world Jewry. It would in fact be in the interest of the Jews themselves not to draw too much attention to the genocidal policies of National Socialism.[8]

To Jewish refugees huddling on the fringes of the continent, fortunate to have escaped the Nazi regime but living in constant danger in the unoccupied zone of France, the Iberian Peninsula, Switzerland, or Sweden, terrified of being handed over to the German authorities the next day or the next week or the next month, the British policy of restricting immigration and playing down the significance of the "Jewish question" in the war was a serious setback. It was not a disaster, however. For one thing, Whitehall was not as firm and unbending in the enforcement of that policy as it tried to appear. From time to time, even in the darkest days of the military conflict, it quietly and unobtrusively, sometimes almost surreptitiously, admitted small groups of refugees—too few to attract public attention or arouse public suspicion, but enough to save several thousand from the danger of arrest by the Third Reich's secret police and deportation to the death camps of Eastern Europe.

Even more important was the growing feeling among the Jewish refugees that they must try to find asylum somewhere outside the Old World. Until the outbreak of war, Great Britain had seemed to offer a safe haven for those seeking to escape persecution. It was, after all, a country traditionally devoted to freedom and justice, toleration and compassion. Even the beginning of hostilities did not at first alter that perception. But the military victories of the Third Reich in the spring of 1940 changed it suddenly and completely. Great Britain could no longer provide Jews with the sense of security that had been so comforting only a few months earlier. Not only did the country become increasingly reluctant to admit immigrants, especially Jewish immigrants, but it could not even protect its own citizens from the perils and hardships of war. There were the endless air raids, the shortages of food and housing, and, worst of all, the constant danger of invasion by the Wehrmacht, which was only a few miles away, on the other side of the Channel. Those who had almost miraculously managed to escape the German occupation of Poland or France could no longer regard the security that England was able to provide as reassuring.

That was why the attention of Jewish refugees in search of asylum began to shift more and more to countries far from war-torn Europe. They concluded, especially after the fall of France, that safety could be found only thousands of miles away. Some of them emigrated to South Africa, others to Australia, and a few even to China. Some hoped to find a home in Latin America, while others tried to gain admittance to Canada, usually without success. The most popular destination, however, the one that seemed to offer the greatest security and the greatest opportunity, was the United States, "a nation of immigrants," a nation willing to welcome the needy and oppressed of the world, whatever their faith or origin. Could any other country seem so inviting to Jewish refugees?

The result was that between early 1938, when the Third Reich initiated its expansionist program, and the end of 1941, when the United States entered the war, the American people became increasingly involved in a long and bitter debate over what policy their country should adopt regarding the refugee problem. There was little disagreement, or at least little open disagreement, about the brutality of Nazi Germany. But what should be done about it, and more specifically, what should be done about those who were its victims? On one side were various groups and organizations, humanitarian, liberal, radical, or Jewish, arguing that the United States must demonstrate its commitment to democracy by lowering the barriers to persecuted refugees. On the other side were those who opposed all attempts to relax the restrictions for a variety of reasons, some of them economic, others conservative or traditionalist, and still others ethnic, xenophobic, or out-and-out anti-Semitic. The debate had begun even earlier in the decade, with Hitler's rise to power. But it became more urgent and vehement in the late 1930s and early 1940s, as the boundaries of the Third Reich started to expand and the number of refugees swelled. This debate continued uninterrupted throughout the war years and beyond, well into the postwar period.

What helped make it so heated was the growing connection of the refugee question with another problem that preoccupied American public opinion more and more after 1938. By then there could be no doubt that the looming diplomatic confrontation between the authoritarian great powers, Germany and Italy, and the democratic great powers, France and England, could end in a new world war. In view of that danger, what position should the United States take? Should it remain strictly neutral, determined to avoid the mistakes that had led to its involvement some twenty years earlier in the quarrels of the Old World? Or should it offer moral support, and perhaps more than moral support, to the nations that shared its commitment to democracy? Those questions were being debated with increasing intensity in America during the last prewar years, then during the early military stalemate of the opposing European armies, and finally during the crucial months before Pearl Harbor, when England stood alone against the seemingly invincible might of the Wehrmacht.

Contributing to the intensity of that debate was its unusualness, since before the late 1930s there had been no such debate and no perceived need for one. The American public was still convinced, liberals even more than conservatives, that the country's participation in the First World War had been a tragic blunder, one that must not be repeated. What was once described as a war to make the world safe for democracy had in fact undermined and endangered democracy. It had led to the rise of authoritarian forms of government, not only in Germany and Italy but in Russia, Austria, and the succession states of Eastern Europe. The only ones who had derived any benefit from the war were the "merchants of death," the munitions manufacturers and international financiers who had grown rich or richer through the sacrifice of the lives of millions of innocent young men. That must never be allowed to happen again. The politics and the politicians of the Old World were hopelessly addicted to ancient, unresolvable differences and disputes. Nothing could change that. But America should not let itself be dragged once more into that endless morass.

Toward the end of the 1930s, that view began to change. The aggressive foreign policy of the authoritarian states, first in the Far East and then in Central Europe, seemed to threaten the international order established after the First World War, creating the danger of a new military conflict among the great powers. What should the United States do in the face of that danger? Should it remain determined to avoid any involvement in the increasingly tense confrontation of the opposing camps? Or should it offer at least some support to countries threatened by the aggression of authoritarian or totalitarian regimes?

By the middle of the decade, there were already signs here and there that U.S. commitment to a policy of noninvolvement was weakening. But the first clear evidence of a shift toward a more active role in world diplomacy was the speech by President Roosevelt on October 5, 1937, responding to the undeclared war against China that Japan had initiated four months earlier. He warned his countrymen that "the epidemic of world lawlessness is spreading." What should be done about it? In everyday life a community deals with an epidemic by imposing "a quarantine of the patients in order to protect [its] health . . . against the spread of the disease." Now that same policy ought to be applied in international relations. "The will for peace on the part of peace-loving nations must express itself to the end that nations that may be tempted to violate their agreements and the rights of others will desist from such a course." In short, "there must be positive endeavors to preserve peace."[9]

This declaration, which had been intended primarily as a warning against Japanese aggression in the Far East, assumed even greater significance the following spring with the emergence of Hitler's expansionist policy in Central Europe. That initiated the long American debate about the country's proper role in the rapidly changing state of international relations. Still, at first the departure from strict neutrality that Roosevelt advocated did not seem to pose a serious risk to the security of the United States. The common assumption was that the task of restraining the Third Reich's ambitions could safely be left to France and England. As for Japan's campaign against China, that would probably prove as brief and limited as the one six years earlier. Even the outbreak of war in Europe in the fall of 1939 did not shake American confidence that the West European democracies would be able to defeat Hitler's aggressive designs without outside help.

Yet while declaring its neutrality, Washington did not hesitate to make clear that its sympathies were on the side of the democratic great powers. Not even the rapid defeat of Poland and the stalemate of the phony war could shake the widespread conviction in the United States that France and England would eventually win. The successes of Hitler's diplomacy in the last prewar years were seen as a result of the shortsighted policy of appeasement. But now that the European democracies had finally recognized their mistake and decided to stand up to Hitler's bullying, the outcome seemed clear. As for America, all it had to do was cheer them on.

Those comforting illusions were suddenly shattered in the spring of

1940. The unexpected military victories of the Third Reich meant that most of Europe had to bow, willy-nilly, directly or indirectly, to its wishes. England continued to resist, but how long could that go on? The United States suddenly faced the prospect of having to maintain its independence in a world dominated on one side by a totalitarian National Socialism and on the other by a brutal monarchical authoritarianism. Wouldn't such a world be a constant threat to the nation's traditional values and institutions? And shouldn't the nation do what it could to prevent the emergence of such a world, even at the risk of involvement in the war?

In Roosevelt's mind, there was little doubt about what course the United States must follow. Every effort had to be made to prevent an Axis victory, and that meant unstinting economic and diplomatic support for Great Britain and later for the Soviet Union in the struggle against the Third Reich. In a "fireside chat" in December 1940, the president argued that America ought to become "the great arsenal of democracy." The nation faced an emergency as grave as outright military conflict. "We must apply ourselves to our task with the same resolution, the same sense of urgency, the same spirit of patriotism and sacrifice as we would show were we at war." During the next twelve months his tone became increasingly urgent, as the United States became more and more involved in the struggle overseas. In June 1941, he declared that "we too, born to freedom, and believing in freedom, are willing to fight to maintain freedom." Indeed, "we, and all others who believe as deeply as we do, would rather die on our feet than live on our knees." And soon after that, on the eve of Pearl Harbor, he sounded even more determined. "When you see a rattlesnake poised to strike, you do not wait until he has struck before you crush him." It was obvious who the rattlesnake was.[10]

There were times, however, when Roosevelt adopted a more moderate or even conciliatory tone, especially when he sensed that too much vehemence and exhortation might prove self-defeating. A few days before the presidential election of 1940, for example, he sought to quiet the apprehension of those who were alarmed at the prospect of being drawn into the war. "While I am talking to you mothers and fathers, I give you one more assurance," he stated in a campaign address. "I have said this before, but I shall say it again and again and again: your boys are not going to be sent into any foreign wars." A political leader as sharp and experienced as

Roosevelt must have known that his assurance was a victory of wishfulness over probability, of hope over likelihood. But to him, some wishful rhetoric was the unavoidable price of defending the security of the United States against ruthless and treacherous enemies.[11]

Many Americans shared his views. Between 1937 and 1941, a large popular movement emerged based on the conviction that the growth of totalitarianism in Europe, especially National Socialism, represented in the long run a serious threat to the United States. Those who held this conviction—the advocates of "collective security" or "interventionism," as their opponents called it—maintained that the American government should support European democracy, and the more precarious the situation of European democracy became, the louder their demand that the American government should offer its support grew. On the other side, however, was another popular movement, made up of so-called isolationists, those who argued that any involvement in the quarrels of the Old World now would have the same disastrous consequences as it had had twenty years earlier. The nation should mind its own business and concentrate on coping with domestic problems, especially those created by the Great Depression. The conflict between the two movements became increasingly heated and bitter, until the attack on Pearl Harbor ended it, or at least forced it underground.

The divisions in American public opinion about Jewish refugees and the "Jewish question" in general became, logically and unavoidably, part of the debate over the country's proper role in the diplomatic and military conflict in Europe. The same groups and movements—philanthropic, liberal, radical, or ethnic—that were most opposed to the ideology of National Socialism were also the ones most sympathetic toward the Jewish victims of that ideology. By the same token, the various components of the isolationist movement—traditionalists, nationalists, localists, and xenophobes—were the ones most likely to oppose the admission of foreign refugees or to fear the influence of Jewry in national life. Admittedly, the correlation was not exact. Some advocates of the refugees believed that American involvement in the war should be avoided at all costs, and some opponents of lowering the immigration barriers argued that the United States should offer aid to embattled Britain. But by and large, support of collective security went hand in hand with at least some sympathy for the victims of Nazi anti-Semitism, while isolationism was frequently accompanied by ethnic suspicion or prejudice.

During the period between the emergence of the Third Reich's policy of territorial expansion in the spring of 1938 and the fall of France in the spring of 1940, the advocates of collective security gained strength steadily in their struggle against the isolationists, although the opposition to intervention was at the same time becoming more determined and vehement. The conflict grew even more bitter after the German military victories in Western Europe led to the increasing dependence of England on U.S. economic assistance. America now faced an agonizing choice: continued aid to the British government at the risk of being dragged into the war, or strict neutrality and the danger of the Third Reich's predominance in the Old World and its increasing influence in the New. For about a year and a half the country wrestled with this dilemma, slowly moving in the direction of increasing support for Great Britain, even if that should eventually result in military involvement.

Yet growing U.S. opposition to the doctrines and policies of Nazi Germany did not generally translate into growing sympathy for those whom those doctrines and policies threatened the most. Americans agreed as a rule that the anti-Semitism of the Third Reich was excessive and brutal. But that was not enough to overcome a widespread feeling that the Jews' role in national life was at least sometimes harmful or even destructive. The tensions and pressures of a country caught between a desire to prevent the triumph of a feared foreign dictatorship and a reluctance to become drawn into a deadly military conflict led to the reinforcement of traditional ethnic distrusts and resentments. The conjunction of democratic sympathy in foreign affairs and xenophobic prejudice in domestic affairs may have been illogical, but under the circumstances it was psychologically understandable.

Still, the increase in anti-Semitism in the United States during the period preceding its entry into the war, though noticeable, was neither startling nor alarming. A succession of public opinion polls asking whether prejudice against Jews was increasing or decreasing showed at first considerable fluctuation. In August 1937, less than a third of respondents, 29 percent, thought that it was increasing and 23 percent thought it was decreasing. By November 1938, the difference had widened, with 37 percent reporting an increase and 18 percent a decrease. But two months later, in December 1938, the results were reversed. Now 33 percent thought that "hostility toward the Jewish people" was growing, while 46 percent, the highest proportion in the entire period, thought it was decreasing. After that the pattern became more consistent and almost predictable. The percentages of those reporting an increase and those reporting a decrease in anti-Semitic prejudice were 45 and 17 in March 1939, 42 and 11 in September 1939, 48 and 13 in April 1940, 48 and 15 in February 1941, and 43 and 16 in October 1941. In short, the number of respondents who believed that hostility toward Jews was growing in the United States remained about three times as large as the number of those who did not.[12]

The evidence of a slowly rising anti-Semitism was also supported by the results of another series of polls in August 1940, February 1941, and October 1941, this one asking, "In your opinion, what nationality, religious or social groups in this country are a menace to America?" The choices before the respondents were "Jews, Negroes, Catholics, Germans, [or] Japanese." The answers showed that Jews were consistently at the top of the list, ahead of even those groups whose ancestral homelands were now regarded as a threat to the United States. Indeed, their lead increased slightly in each successive poll, from 17 to 18 and then to 20 percent. The Germans were in second place, with 14 percent in the first two polls and then 16 in the third. The Japanese were far behind, with only 6, 6, and 4. The percentage of those who regarded Catholics as a menace to the United States was also small, starting out with 6 percent and then declining to 5 and finally to 4 percent. The least threatening group, according to the survey, was Negroes, chosen by only 2, 3, and then again 2 percent of all respondents. Poor, oppressed, and segregated, they could hardly be regarded as a serious danger to the established order. Jews, on the other hand, always at the top of the list, were consistently viewed by a small but significant minority of their countrymen as a menace to the welfare of the nation.[13]

What was it that led quite a few of their fellow Americans to regard them as less loyal or trustworthy than other ethnic groups? Here again the results of public opinion polls suggest an answer, not always complete or altogether accurate, but one that indicates the extent of and the common justification for anti-Semitic prejudice in the United States. The replies to a survey asking at intervals of a few months whether Jews were as patriotic, more patriotic, or less patriotic than other citizens showed that about a fourth of the respondents believed them to be less patriotic. The percentages were 31 in March and May 1938, 26 in November 1938, 30 in September 1939 and April 1940, 25 in August 1940, 28 in February 1941, and again 25 in October 1941. At the same time, about 5 percent thought that Jews were more patriotic than most others. Thus about two thirds of the respondents and sometimes slightly more believed that there was no significant difference in the level of patriotism between Jews and non-Jews.[14]

There was a much sharper division of opinion, however, regarding another charge often made against the Jewish community in America, namely, the excessive influence in national affairs that it was allegedly able to exercise behind the scenes because of its disproportionately large share of the country's wealth. More than a third and sometimes close to half of all respondents to a public opinion poll asking whether "the Jews have too much power in the United States" believed that they did. The percentage of yeses fluctuated at first, from 41 in March 1938 to 36 in May 1938 to 35 in November 1938 and then back to 41 in February 1939. But after that the numbers started to climb almost without interruption until the eve of Pearl Harbor, a reflection of the gradual drift toward direct involvement in the war in Europe. In April 1940, 43 percent of the respondents thought that Jews had too much power; in August 1940 the percentage dropped slightly, to 42, but then in February 1941 it rose again, to 45, and by October 1941 it reached 48. The suspicion that Jewish shrewdness and deviousness were playing a major role in the politics and economics of the nation, a suspicion only too familiar in the Old World, was now gaining strength in the New World as well.[15]

To be sure, the intensity of anti-Semitism in the United States could not compare with that in Central or Eastern Europe. Even Americans who expressed dislike or distrust of Jews were unwilling in most cases to advocate policies similar to those adopted by the Third Reich. When respondents who had indicated in a public opinion poll that they thought Jews had too much power were then asked whether they would favor legislation to "restrict Jews in business," only a small minority answered yes. The percentage in the period from early 1938 to late 1941 fluctuated between a low of 18 in May 1938 and a high of 31 in April 1940. Support among the same respondents for measures designed to "keep Jews out of government and politics" was even weaker. It started out with 24 percent in May 1938, then dropped to 17 percent in November 1938, and then moved slightly up and down from 21 and 19 in April and August 1940 to 22 in February and October 1941. As for the most drastic of the hypothetical anti-Semitic laws, namely, the ones intended to "drive Jews out of the United States," they received the lowest level of support, starting with 20 percent in May 1938, dropping to 12 percent in November after the Kristallnacht, then rising again to 18 in April 1940, then dropping once more to 16 in August 1940 and February 1941, and finally climbing slightly, to 19 percent, in October 1941. The figures seem almost insignificant by comparison with the proportion of supporters of the anti-Semitic program of National Socialism in Germany, of the National Democratic Party in Poland, or of the Iron Guard in Romania.[16]

Even a poll that asked whether the respondent would be willing to support a campaign against the Jews, without specifying what measures were to be taken to counter their power, revealed a reluctance among the great majority of Americans to endorse an openly anti-Semitic policy. The percentage in favor of such a campaign started out in March 1938 with a high of 19, but then fell to 12 or 13 in the next several polls, before rising again to 15 in October 1941. Thus the fears expressed by many liberals, non-Jewish as well as Jewish, that Nazi propaganda and the growing likelihood of American involvement in the military struggle in Europe were intensifying anti-Semitism in the United States, though not baseless, appear exaggerated. The nation remained opposed to a program of organized, systematic ethnic discrimination such as the one adopted not only by the Third Reich but by a growing number of other countries on the continent as well.[17]

Still, public opinion polls do not tell the whole story. They sometimes affect a deceptive arithmetical precision which disguises private doubts, vacillations, and reservations on the part of the participants. In many cases they can only describe general trends or propensities, whose precise dimensions remain undetermined. And the chief cause of that indeterminacy lies in the hesitancy of many respondents—a hesitancy of which they themselves are not always aware—to express views generally regarded as harsh, uncompassionate, insensitive, or prejudiced. They are by and large reluctant to challenge the socially legitimized norms of behavior and thought, sometimes suppressing whatever reservations they may have about the validity of those norms. The more delicate or controversial the issue is, the more hesitant they are to violate, even anonymously, the established standards of ethical belief. None of this invalidates the general usefulness of public opinion polls, but it does raise questions about the validity of their seemingly precise mathematical results.

One such question emerges out of the disparity between the outcome of polls seeking to determine popular attitudes in America regarding Jews in general and those regarding Jewish refugees in particular. Here there was a striking difference. On the one hand, the great majority of respondents denied having anti-Semitic fears or prejudices. Most of them in fact expressed strong disapproval of the brutal treatment of Jews by the Third Reich. But on the other hand, an equally large majority opposed the admission to the United States of the victims of that brutal treatment. Indeed, the opposition remained just as strong or became even stronger at the same time that the anti-Semitic program of the Nazi regime became more and more oppressive.

What accounted for the fact that the rejection of prejudice against Jews seemed to go hand in hand with a determination to exclude Jews? Was there not an inconsistency between those two simultaneous expressions of public opinion? That question, however, may be misleading. It is perhaps unfair to equate an unwillingness to relax existing restrictions on immigration with ethnic hostility. To many of those still suffering from the effects of a long economic depression, the prospect of a sudden influx of large numbers of refugees must have seemed alarming. It must have raised fears of an even greater scarcity of available jobs, housing, and public assistance. Others may have been troubled by the likely political consequences of admitting too many foreigners. The newcomers would no doubt settle down in the big cities with congenial ethnic neighborhoods. There they would reinforce the growing strength and influence of the various established immigrant minorities, voting for the New Deal, supporting the Democratic Party, and encouraging the involvement of the United States in the war overseas. And that in turn would lead to a further diminution of the role in public affairs of real Americans, those old-stock, small-town, Protestant Americans whose ancestors had fought courageously for the independence of the United States and had then labored tirelessly to establish its greatness. To allow hundreds of thousands of new immigrants to come in would further dilute the original, true character of the nation. It would erode and weaken loyalty to inherited, traditional beliefs and values. Surely to oppose such a change in the cultural foundation of life in the United States was no proof of bigotry. It represented rather a patriotic devotion to its historic ideals and principles.

The great debate regarding the role of the United States in the conflict between democracy and authoritarianism generally avoided arguments based on ethnic fears or prejudices. The central issues were usually defined in economic, political, or social terms. And yet distrust or suspicion of Jews, though seldom openly expressed, appeared here and there, unspoken but palpable, in the course of some bitter dispute regarding the effect of loosening immigration restrictions on the country's unemployment rate or its political system or its civic faith. Obviously, not all of those who opposed the admission of refugees were motivated primarily or even partly by anti-Semitism. But at the same time, not all of those who denied being in any way motivated by anti-Semitism were in fact entirely free of prejudice. Ethnic hostilities were often so closely intermingled with economic, or political, or cultural considerations as to be inextricable.

Whatever role distrust of Jews played in the opposition to a relaxation of the restrictions on immigration, public opinion during the period of armed neutrality remained firmly against the admission of refugees outside the existing quota system. The evidence on this point is conclusive. A survey conducted by *Fortune* magazine in July 1938 asked, "What is your attitude toward allowing German, Austrian, and other political refugees to come into the U.S.?" The question did not specify the ethnic background of the refugees to be admitted, carefully avoiding the word "Jewish." But it must have been clear that most of them would in fact be Jews. And whether for that reason or not, the great majority of respondents wanted to exclude them. A few, no more than 4.9 percent, did agree that "we should encourage them to come even if we have to raise our immigration quotas," while another 18.2 percent thought that "we should allow them to come but not raise immigration quotas." On the other hand, 67.4 percent believed that "with conditions as they are we should try to keep them out." And then there were the 9.5 percent who admitted that they "didn't know."[18]

These results could not have come as a complete surprise. The pattern remained essentially the same throughout the period prior to America's entry into the war. Still, those who had hoped for a more welcoming attitude found the numbers disappointing. "So much, then, for the hospitality of our melting pot," said *Fortune* magazine. It found some consolation, however, in the response of one small segment of public opinion. "Again the Jews make a logical exception—only 18.4 percent of them are for exclusion of the refugees, and the heaviest weight of their vote is for encouraging them to come here." That too could not have seemed surprising to the readers of *Fortune*.[19]

In the fall of 1938, another public opinion poll confirmed the results of the one conducted the previous summer. Indeed, this time opposition to the admission of refugees was even stronger, although the survey was conducted shortly after the Kristallnacht. Perhaps the fact that the question posed in the new survey specified the ethnic background of those to be admitted to the United States contributed to the outcome. In any event, about 3,000 respondents were asked whether the American government should allow "a larger number of Jewish exiles" from Germany to come to live in the United States. The response was unequivocal. A small proportion, 8 percent, expressed no opinion. But of the rest, 77 percent opposed the proposal and 23 percent supported it. The outcome was even more one-sided than the one four months earlier.[20]

Was that difference due to the fact that the hypothetical refugees were now identified as Jews? Perhaps, although the results of still another survey of public opinion, conducted by the Gallup Poll in January 1939, seemed to minimize the importance of ethnic prejudice in the public attitude toward immigration. This time the question before the respondents was presented in two forms. First, "It has been proposed that the government permit 10,000 refugee children from Germany to be brought into this country and taken care of in American homes. Do you favor this plan?" And then came a second version of the same question, adding the phrase "most of them Jewish" to describe the children. The outcome was not very different from that of other polls, except with regard to the extent to which anti-Semitism appeared to influence public opinion. In their replies to the question when the ethnic background of the refugee children was not specified, 66 percent opposed their admission, 26 percent supported it, and 8 percent expressed no opinion. But when the refugee children were identified as mostly Jewish, the figures shifted—only slightly, to be sure—in favor of admission. Now the noes constituted 61 percent of the total, the yeses 30 percent, and those with "no opinion" 9 percent. What accounted for that shift? Was it a growing recognition of the deadly danger confronting the Jews of Central Europe? Was it the recent outbreak of anti-Semitic riots in the Third Reich? Was it the appeal of American humanitarian organizations? Was there some other explanation? There is no way of telling.[21]

It is clear that opposition to a relaxation of the restrictions on immigration remained strong, even gaining strength as Europe moved steadily closer to war and as the situation of the Jewish community in the Third Reich became increasingly precarious. Another survey by *Fortune*, this one in April 1939, produced results quite different from those obtained three months earlier in the poll regarding the admission of refugee children. This time the respondents were asked, "If you were a member of Congress would you vote yes or no on a bill to open the doors of the U.S. to a larger number of refugees than now admitted under our immigration quotas?" The responses were overwhelmingly one-sided, more so than in any of the previous surveys. The percentage of those who said they would vote against a relaxation of the quota system was 83.0, while only 8.7 percent favored an increase in the admission of refugees, and 8.3 percent said they didn't know.[22]

The editors of *Fortune* could not have been surprised to find that the opposition against a more generous immigration policy had prevailed, but they were taken aback by the margin of its victory. In an article headed "No Haven for Refugees," they voiced their disappointment. "Here is an American tradition put to the popular test, and here it is repudiated by a majority of nearly ten to one." The overwhelming rejection of any proposal to admit more victims of ethnic persecution appeared unalterable. "There is about this answer a finality that seems to mean that the doors of this country should be virtually closed to refugees, and should stay closed to them, no matter what their need or condition." Apparently nothing could be done about that. "The answer is the more decisive because it was made at a time when public sympathy for victims of European events was presumably at its highest." The people had now spoken, loudly and clearly.[23]

Yet the battle was not over. In fact, it became increasingly fierce and bitter. To those who believed that America had a moral obligation as well as a strategic reason to support the cause of democracy in Europe, a solution to the refugee problem was an essential part of the struggle to defend freedom. The advocates of collective security felt that the ideological justification for their position required them to aid those who were being persecuted by the ruthless racism of the Third Reich. The struggle against despotism and aggression could not be separated from the struggle against bigotry and anti-Semitism. The two were interrelated and intertwined. They were both essential parts of a noble crusade for freedom and justice. To participate in one without participating in the other would be a betrayal of the cause of democracy.

This was the contention of an article that appeared in the spring of 1941 in the *New Republic*, an ardent journalistic champion of the refugees, at a time when the United States was steadily moving closer to direct participation in the war overseas:

> This country is supposedly committed to all-out aid to another democracy, Great Britain, to be given in a democratic way. But there will be a violent contradiction between what we preach and what we practice as long as official circles in Washington continue to brush aside efforts to solve the refugee problem, calling them "mere humanitarianism" or "just relief work," something to be admired in principle and then dismissed as "inopportune." In reality, solving the refugee problem is an essential part of the war effort, especially since Germany is now fighting us by means of the "war of refugees."[24]

This became the battle cry of the advocates of collective security and universal humanitarianism as they confronted the opponents of American involvement in foreign ideologies, foreign disputes, and foreign injustices.

8

The War of Words

To THE DEFENDERS of the refugee cause, it was clear from the outset that they could not bring about a lowering of the barriers to immigration simply by appealing to democratic principles and humanitarian ideals. They had to do more. They had to convince the American public that admitting large numbers of victims of ethnic persecution would not be a threat to the economic welfare of native workers, shopkeepers, businessmen, and farmers. More than that, they had to overcome a widespread concern that the newcomers would encourage the involvement of the United States in the problems and quarrels of the Old World. And finally, they had to dispel a popular suspicion or fear, often unspoken, that the Jews were in many respects an unassimilable element, that those who were already citizens exerted a disproportionate and not always wholesome influence in national life, and that to open the door to many more would aggravate a social problem which was serious enough under existing conditions. In short, dealing with the refugee problem was bound to prove a formidable task.

Those willing to undertake that task were aware of the difficulties confronting them. But during the period before Pearl Harbor, while public opinion still vacillated between opposition to totalitarianism and adherence to neutrality, between sympathy for embattled democracy and aversion to military conflict, they tried hard to convince America that assistance to persecuted refugees was not only an expression of the democratic ideal but compatible with the country's welfare. There was no need to choose between compassion and self-interest. A more generous immigration policy, while evidence of a commitment to humanitarian principles, would also serve the material needs of society. Once people realized how irrational all those concerns about sinister alien forces were, they would see that universal humanitarianism and national interest were not mutually exclusive but mutually supportive.

The rhetoric of the advocates of the refugee cause reflected this determination to demonstrate the compatibility of idealism and practicality. Some of them emphasized the unreasonableness or injustice of ethnic bigotry, condemning in particular the vilification of Jews. Early in 1939, William Allen Neilson, the president of Smith College, denounced the "formidable anti-Semitic prejudice" that existed in the United States. "Organizations are built up to propagate it, and it is appealed to in order to block the generous impulses of those of our people who would offer refuge to the victims of persecution in Germany, Italy, and elsewhere." Such prejudice was responsible, moreover, for the "grave disabilities" imposed on Jews here at home, where many of them were excluded from hotels, resorts, fraternities, clubs, colleges, and business organizations. In fashionable social circles, there was a subtle disinclination, often disavowed, to accept them as equals.

A few months later, the *Christian Science Monitor*, which was also generally sympathetic toward the refugees, though not without some caution and hesitation, commented in an editorial on the inconsistency of countries that condemned the anti-Semitism of the Third Reich while remaining reluctant to help its victims. Their policy regarding immigration was in fact "a test of the good faith and the foresight of nations which are disposed to criticize German treatment of the Jews." There was the case of Cuba, whose consular agents abroad had recently issued visas to close to a thousand Jewish refugees, but whose government was now refusing to admit them, after they had already left Europe and were helplessly adrift on a ship off the Cuban coast. How could that be justified? And yet, how much more generous would the American government prove to be? "What will be the answer of the United States to the pleas for legislation to permit 20,000 refugee children—not all of them Jews by any means— [to enter the country] under careful provision for their adoption?" The issue, however, was even greater than the fate of these children. "Where shall [all] these people go, and what nations will see the value of taking them in?" the editorial asked. It could offer no answer.[1]

Alfred Wagg, in contrast, one of the most resolute defenders of the refugee cause, was sure of what ought to be done and why it was not being done. Writing in the *New Republic* in April 1941, he condemned what he described as the pusillanimous policy of the United States regarding Jewish immigration. The only heroes in the tragic story were "a small group of determined men, within and without the government," struggling against great odds, "in an atmosphere of opposition and suspicion and with a minimum of support from the official makers of our foreign policies," to admit the victims of Nazi racism. He did not say it in so many words, but he clearly included himself in that small group. Its endeavors were frustrated, however, by governmental indifference and out-and-out prejudice. "The refugee effort has been at best a stepchild in Washington, to be beaten and buffeted, and at worst a football for anti-Semitism and for petty bureaucrats." All the years of pleading, arguing, explaining, and demanding had failed to produce any significant results. There had been no change in the nation's immigration policy.

But now there was no longer time for quibbling or equivocating. "The time has come when our government, particularly those branches of it which have to do with our foreign policy, must fish or cut bait." The United States would either have to keep its word to the embattled democracies of Europe, "which have been promised help through relief of their refugee burden," or it would have to admit that nothing would be done, that the assurances it had been giving were only empty words, and that "for all we care, England and her allies can keep their refugees, feed and clothe them and get along as best they can without us." This would not necessarily mean a policy of excluding all immigrants. It would still leave room for the token admission from time to time of a few victims of bigotry. "We would keep the mechanism of our quotas turning, occasionally opening our doors to one or two refugees from England if transportation permits." But as for the "larger effort," the task of saving hundreds of thousands of innocent human beings trying to escape racist persecution or even mass murder, "we should have to admit that it is too much for us." And that would leave a permanent, shameful blot on the conscience of America.[2]

Appeals of this sort to the nation's sense of compassion helped arouse considerable sympathy for refugees from countries under the rule of the Third Reich. But they could not overcome fear of the economic consequences of a sudden influx of large numbers of immigrants. Admittedly, that fear was being stoked by many organizations opposed in principle to the large-scale admission of foreigners, especially Jews, to the United States. But even without their dire warnings and predictions, many Americans felt uneasy at the prospect of having to face the competition of a flood of aliens, some of them ragged and needy, some talented and ambitious, and some clever and perhaps not always honest. Shouldn't charity begin at home?

The defenders of the refugee cause were aware of those fears. They knew that popular concern about the economic consequences of lowering the barriers to immigration could not be overcome simply by appealing to the national sense of justice and humaneness. There had to be an organized, vigorous effort to allay the widespread uneasiness. Those who shared that uneasiness had to be convinced that there was nothing to be afraid of, that the newcomers would not diminish but increase opportunities for employment and livelihood, and that the national economy would be strengthened by acquiring the skills and talents of the newcomers. Accordingly, the advocates of a more generous immigration policy tried to bolster their humanitarian pleas with utilitarian arguments. The concerns aroused and fanned by bigots and racists were entirely without foundation, they maintained. The admission of refugees would benefit everyone, Americans as well as Europeans, non-Jews as well as Jews. There would be no losers, only winners.

That was the gist of an article appearing in the spring of 1939 in *Forum and Century*, which asked in its title, "Are Refugees a Liability?" The answer by its author, Frank Ritchie, was an unequivocal no. Of course they were not a liability. On the contrary, they were a valuable asset to the United States. "New avenues for foreign trade have been transferred by refugees from their native Germany." Their cultural contributions to American life, exemplified by such distinguished men as the writer Thomas Mann, the theater director Max Reinhardt, the scientist Albert Einstein, the statesman Heinrich Brüning, and "others too numerous to mention," were already recognized. But the contributions of the average man or woman who had escaped from Nazi Germany, though not as obvious or familiar, were just as important. "America can look forward to profit and new achievement from the admission of German refugees." It should therefore welcome them, not shut the door in their face, as those bigoted exclusionists were demanding.[3]

Another article dealing with "Those German Refugees," which was published at about the same time in *Current History*, also tried to allay the fear that immigrants would intensify the competition for jobs. There was no need to worry, Henry Smith Leiper assured his readers. "[The refugees] are definitely not a threat to the American workman in that their numbers are relatively small, many have special skills new to this country, and already a large number of American workers have been given employment in projects started by refugees or with refugee capital." Quite apart from the "inhumane and un-American aspects" of any policy designed to halt immigration, it would be "bad business" from a purely practical point of view not to make use of the refugee talents that had become available. "America has already gained much and stands to gain more from Germany's ill-advised and self-imposed loss." Continuing to benefit from the blind, irrational anti-Semitism of the Third Reich would be of advantage not only to the persecuted Jews but to the American economy as well.[4]

How much effect such assurances had on public opinion is not clear. They were certainly not enough to dispel the rumors and allegations that refugees were getting too many good jobs which would otherwise go to native workers and that businesses owned by Jews were hiring Jewish immigrants in preference to American citizens. The high rate of unemployment and the constant agitation of nativist and exclusionist organizations helped make those charges seem credible. Whispers, rumors, and stories about the special treatment that refugees from Germany allegedly received from companies owned by their coreligionists were especially numerous in and around New York, home of the largest Jewish community in the United States. Big department stores owned by Jews, like Macy's, Stern Brothers, Abraham and Strauss, Gimbel's, and Bloomingdale's, were frequently accused of giving preferential treatment to Jewish applicants for jobs, particularly immigrants from Central Europe, at the expense of better-qualified Christians, some of whom were actually being fired in order to make room for the newcomers. Even in a small town like

Shelton in Connecticut, with a population of no more than 12,000, there were reports of Americans being displaced from factory jobs that then went to refugees.

The accusations grew so loud and persistent that during the late 1930s, several of the companies charged with reverse discrimination—discrimination against Gentiles—thought it advisable to issue categorical denials of preferential treatment for Jewish immigrants. Delos Walker, vice president of R. H. Macy and Company, published a statement condemning the "utterly false and malicious rumor to the effect that store people in New York have been let go to hire refugees from Europe." There was not a word of truth in that. "The plain fact is that none of our employees has been displaced by a refugee." And yet the rumor would not go away. The company had thus been forced to the conclusion that "the only thing that could plant it in the minds of innocent and well-meaning people is organized and systematic propaganda, using the innocent as carriers in a whispering campaign." It was therefore best for all concerned to speak out and state publicly that "the rumor is a plain falsehood, and to say it with all the emphasis that can be placed on it." No right-thinking person should believe a vicious lie intended solely to arouse ethnic prejudice and hostility.[5]

Other department stores issued similar statements, though usually less vehemently or indignantly, denying that Jewish immigrants from Central Europe were receiving favored treatment. Richard H. Brown, vice president and general superintendent of Abraham and Strauss, declared that "to my knowledge, no employee has been discharged and replaced by a refugee from any foreign country." Elizabeth Westgate, director of personnel for Bloomingdale's, which had about 2,500 workers, stated that "the total number of people in our employ who might be classified as refugees is eleven. Of these, two were employed in 1936, seven in 1937, one in 1938, and one in 1939." How could anyone feel threatened by such insignificant numbers? Besides, "of the eleven, only one is employed in selling." More important, "not a single person has at any time been discharged from our employ in order to make room for a refugee."

Even outside New York some local officials thought it advisable to try to dispel rumors that American workers were being discriminated against for the benefit of Jewish immigrants. John C. Ready, for instance, deputy commissioner in the Connecticut Department of Labor, reported that he

could find no evidence of favoritism toward foreigners. "An investigation
. . . in six or more plants in Shelton . . . discloses that one refugee has
been employed in one of the plants as an elevator operator. This job was
created for him and no one was displaced." Similar disclaimers could be
heard in many large cities and in some of the smaller ones as well. After
all, no businessman or politician wanted to be accused of indifference to
the injustices his fellow Americans allegedly had to face.[6]

Whether such disclaimers were effective in quieting rumors about
the favored treatment of refugees is debatable. Some people were indeed
persuaded—mostly those willing to be persuaded—that the admission
of Jewish immigrants would not be a threat to American workers or
shopkeepers. Many others, however, remained unconvinced. The exact
numbers of those on the opposing sides cannot be determined, but popular resistance to lowering the barriers against refugees did not seem
to diminish appreciably. If anything, it became stronger. The argument
that an influx of foreigners from Central Europe would be an economic
danger to native labor served to reinforce a pervasive feeling that Jewish
immigrants would prove an unassimilable element in American society.
They would remain perpetual foreigners, incompatible with or perhaps
even subversive of the collective character of the people of the United
States. And the result was likely to be a spread of racist agitation, ethnic
bigotry, and anti-Semitism.

The defenders of the refugee cause tried to counter such concerns with
assurances that there was actually nothing to fear. Most of the newcomers would be men and women of intelligence and education. They would
share the American commitment to justice and democracy; they would
in fact strengthen and enrich the country's traditional way of life. Look at
what those who had already become established in the United States were
able to achieve. They had made important contributions to the nation's
economy, technology, culture, and education. They had shown themselves
to be a valuable asset to their new homeland. And besides, shouldn't America welcome them as a way of expressing the ideas and ideals on which it
had been founded and which it continued to profess and embrace?

From time to time, under special circumstances, even some of those
opposed to a relaxation of immigration restrictions became willing to
stretch the rules a little, to make an exception or two in cases that did

not threaten the basic exclusionism of the existing legislation. Thus, when a bill was introduced in Congress in 1939 to admit, over and above the existing quota, 20,000 "German" children under the age of fourteen, the *Miami News*, though an opponent of "too much immigration," expressed its approval, dismissing the economic arguments against the proposal as "extraordinary foolishness." The refugees would not take jobs away from American workers. They would in fact create jobs by increasing the number of consumers. They would be an economic asset, not a burden. The paper maintained that the valid objections against unrestricted immigration were "social and political, not economic in nature." Indeed, it shared some of those objections. "America is right in admitting no more immigrants than can be adjusted to their new environment and to our ways of thinking and carrying on." But the children entering the country under the terms of the bill would be no problem. They were "young enough, given the right chance, to be 'Americanized' with quickness and ease." They would attend American schools, master American English, and learn to like American food, American dress, and the American way of life. In short, they would become completely assimilated. As for their parents or relatives or adult coreligionists, that was a different matter. There much greater caution was required.[7]

The defenders of the refugee cause, recognizing the ethnic prejudice behind many of their opponents' contentions, did not hesitate to confront that prejudice. But they did not in most cases dismiss anti-Semitic accusations as nothing more than racist phantasms created out of thin air for the purpose of arousing hostility toward Jews. Their more common response was that while such hostility was not entirely without foundation, the seriousness of the Jewish problem should not be exaggerated. Besides, the solution to the problem was obvious and not very difficult: treat the Jews as equals, tear down the barriers to their advancement, make them feel appreciated, behave toward them in the same way you behave toward non-Jews, and all their unpleasant qualities will gradually disappear. They will become less defensive and clannish, more open and friendlier, more gregarious and affable. In short, they will become more like Christians or even become indistinguishable from Christians. The way to solve the "Jewish question," in other words, was not by repression but by acceptance.

This line of reasoning appeared over and over again in the rhetoric of the supporters of the refugee cause. The well-known economist Alvin Johnson, director of the New School for Social Research, maintained that "the conditions that give color to anti-Semitism are abating." The flood of East European Jews that had once poured into the United States was being replaced by a new Jewish generation born on American soil. "Yiddish speech and Yiddish clannishness are giving way." The concentration of Jews in commerce and in white-collar occupations was gradually diminishing. There were now quite a few Jewish farmers, "on the whole succeeding well." A fourth of the union carpenters in New York, a fifth of the electrical workers, almost half of the painters and paper hangers, almost half of the plumbers and steam fitters, half of the plasterers, and more than half of the sheet metal workers were Jews. Was that not an encouraging sign? "The unhealthy concentration in commercial pursuits forced upon the Jew by the Old World anti-Semitism, itself operating to intensify anti-Semitism, is gradually breaking up here." The stars in their course were fighting against ethnic prejudice in America. "And that is the very reason why we who love our land, and who believe in our people, and have faith in our future as the richest, the most humane, the most orderly civilization ever created by man should fight the evil intelligently and manfully." Who could resist such a stirring appeal to the American conscience?[8]

Yet Johnson also made it clear that the task of freeing Jews from the burden of prejudice could not be left entirely to Christians. Jews had to do their share as well. A "bridge of understanding" had to be built between the two communities, keeping in mind that "a bridge is always begun from both sides of the river simultaneously." Admittedly, most of the building would have to done by Christians, who, being the larger group, had more to lose from anti-Semitism. "But the Jews have to do some building, too." Here Johnson came to the heart of the matter. "There was never a persecuted race that did not develop some characteristics that seemed to give color of justification to persecution." Still, there was a way out of the deadlock created by the mutually reinforcing interaction of ethnic bigotry and ethnic exclusivity. "Abolish persecution and such characteristics disappear." Therefore, in order to find a solution to the age-old problem, an "engineering organization" representing both communities should be formed to discuss openly, "without reservations or tabus," appropriate ways "of softening the edges of inter-group conflict, of clearing away the inter-group misunderstanding." Americans owed it to their democratic heritage to do more than merely "denounce and wring our hands." But how much more could they do? Johnson concluded his analysis with a brief and mild exhortation to his countrymen: "We can try." Goodwill on both sides and mutual respect were bound sooner or later to lead to a satisfactory solution to the perennial problem of anti-Semitism.[9]

The analysis of ethnic prejudice that aroused the greatest public interest, however, was an article by Eleanor Roosevelt published at the end of 1938 in *Liberty* magazine, in reply to one by H. G. Wells which had appeared a week earlier under the title "The Future of the Jews." The well-known British author, a lifelong socialist, a sworn opponent of social injustice, had become increasingly critical of Jews, not out of racial prejudice or economic concern but because of what he perceived to be their clannishness, their stubborn refusal to identify with their non-Jewish compatriots, and their view of themselves as the chosen people, a view expressed theologically in their adherence to Judaism and politically in their support of Zionism. They were the authors of their own misfortunes, which were bound to persist until they themselves became more tolerant, more generous, and more broad-minded. In other words, they and they alone could solve the problem of anti-Semitism by changing their collective mentality.[10]

In her reply to Wells, Mrs. Roosevelt defended the traditional liberal position that the age-old persecution of the Jews had only aggravated the problem of anti-Semitism, encouraging Jewish clannishness on one side and anti-Jewish hostility on the other. The only way to deal with ethnic prejudice was to promote mutual understanding and acceptance, especially on the part of those guilty of discrimination. The key to solving the problem was mutual toleration. Once the Jews began to feel that they were no longer objects of scorn, resentment, or hostility, they would become friendlier, more outgoing, more like their non-Jewish neighbors. In short, the end of prejudice would also lead to the end of tribalism.[11]

To be sure, Mrs. Roosevelt herself had not always been free of a genteel, fashionable form of anti-Semitism common among the American patriciate. Twenty years earlier, while living in Washington, where her husband served as assistant secretary of the Navy, she had described to her mother-in-law a party for Bernard Baruch "which I'd rather be hung than be seen at. Mostly Jews." Two days later she reported that the party had been "appaling," so "appaling" that "I never wish to hear money, jewels or sables mentioned again." Later that year, after meeting Felix Frankfurter, whom her husband had invited home for lunch, she described him as "an interesting little man but very Jew." Such condescension toward the descendants of immigrants from Central and Eastern Europe, especially Jews, was widespread among members of the social elite, whose ancestors had fought in the American Revolution and had adopted the Constitution of the United States.[12]

Mrs. Roosevelt's views on politics and society gradually changed, however, during the interwar years, and by the late 1930s she had gained the reputation of a bold defender of liberal causes—bolder, in fact, than her husband. But she could afford to be bolder. She did not have to take into account the nativist predilections of many small-town voters or worry about the effect of too many condemnations of ethnic prejudice on the next presidential election. She could speak her mind freely, and in her reply to Wells she did not hesitate to express views that she shared with ardent liberals to whom anti-Semitism was a violation of the basic principles of American democracy.

Still, like many other American defenders of Jews, Mrs. Roosevelt conceded that though they were more sinned against than sinning, they were not entirely free of sin. Indeed, they were responsible, at least in part, for the hostility they so often encountered. Even some of her friends, she reported, believed that "the Jewish people . . . never allow themselves really to belong to any people among whom they live," so that they always remain "a nation within a nation." At the same time they were often perceived as "being too ostentatiously patriotic and of pushing themselves forward as nationals of this or that nation." Was there no basis for such allegations?

There was some, Mrs. Roosevelt conceded, but the Jews were not the only ones responsible. The fault rested also in part on the shoulders of Gentiles. Perhaps it was true that "on occasions the Jewish people haven't scattered themselves sufficiently through a wide area where they could be less concentrated in a racial group." Perhaps they did not always seize opportunities "to diversify their occupations." And this in turn resulted in "their concentration in certain professions which leads inevitably to resentment in those places where the predominance becomes noticeable." Yet the social and economic self-segregation of the Jews, though unfortunate, could not justify the hostility toward them which was so common in many countries, including the United States.

And then Mrs. Roosevelt offered another explanation for the existence of ethnic prejudice, a "partial" explanation, one "which we Christians may not like but which we should at least, in all honesty, face." Perhaps because "certain races" had suddenly grown aware of their own inferiority, they became "intolerant." In other words, a secret fear that the Jews were more talented or venturesome than those who wielded power over them had led to their oppression. Conversely, nations that did not persecute Jews were displaying confidence that they could successfully defend themselves and their place in the world. This insight led Mrs. Roosevelt to the conclusion that "the Jewish people, though they may be in part responsible for the present situation, are not as responsible as the other races who need to examine themselves and grapple with their own fears." Therefore, the people of Europe and the United States, having "pushed the Jewish race into Zionism and Palestine, and into their nationalistic attitude," now had the responsibility to free themselves from their irrational fears and to achieve their legitimate ends not by oppression but by a process of law.

Mrs. Roosevelt ended her article with a warning to her countrymen against following the example of certain unnamed but easily recognized countries, which were willing to sacrifice the Jews' "brains and appreciation of the cultural things in life," their "quick response to the ethical value of a situation," their "sense of responsibility in giving," and their "imaginative powers" in order to preserve an "Aryan heritage." If tyranny and fear triumphed among the American people, that would only bring out greed, cunning, and egotism in the "persecuted foreigner." It would intensify religious and racial hatred. The Jews themselves were helpless in dealing with the problem of prejudice. Only the Gentiles could decide whether the future would bring "co-operative, mutual assistance [and] gradual slow assimilation, with justice and fair-mindedness toward all the racial groups living together," or whether it would lead to "injustice, hatred, and death." The fate of the Gentile majority was inextricably linked to the fate of the Jewish minority. "It looks to me as though the future of the Jews were tied up, as it has always been, with the future of all

the races of the world, [so that] if they perish, we perish sooner or later."
Ultimately, anti-Semitism was a form of self-destruction.[13]

This conclusion reflected a profound change in the thinking of a proud, aristocratic woman. Still, though her article was widely read, its effect on American public opinion remained limited. It sounded most convincing to those who wanted to be convinced or were already convinced. Those opposed to the admission of refugees remained opposed. Indeed, the long debate regarding immigration policy and the "Jewish question" seemed to have little effect on the strength or success of either of the opposing camps. Neither the increasing urgency of the rhetoric of compassion nor the growing crisis that European Jewry faced led to a resolution of the ideological stalemate in the United States. During the years between the Anschluss and the attack on Pearl Harbor, the territory under the control of the Third Reich increased steadily and rapidly, until in the end the great majority of European Jews were at the mercy of National Socialism. But on the other side of the Atlantic, the war of words over what should be done continued without abatement or resolution.

That ethnic prejudice reinforced the reluctance of many Americans to have their government assume a leading role in dealing with the refugee problem is clear, though the intensity and extent of that prejudice is difficult to determine. Some liberal observers of public opinion were convinced that prejudice was steadily gaining strength among the population. Early in 1939, Alvin Johnson wrote in a mood of discouragement that "anti-Semitism is on the increase in America." He conceded that this was only his opinion and that various polls seeming to support it were not really conclusive. And yet, "what no one doubts may commonly be taken for pragmatically true, and no one, Gentile or Jew, doubts that there is more active anti-Semitism in present day America than there was, say, in 1930." Worse still, "no one believes that anti-Semitism has passed its peak." Admittedly, many conservative Americans who had viewed with indifference the exclusion of German Jews from public office, the universities, and the legal profession were shocked by the recent violent attacks on Jewish property. But how long would their disapproval last? "The sympathy of the propertied classes of the democracies for the Jews who have been expropriated [by the Nazi regime] is likely to prove more touching than lasting." Soon the public would once again begin to look the other way.[14]

Heywood Broun, a popular liberal columnist and political commentator, was equally pessimistic. Writing in the fall of 1939, a few weeks after the outbreak of war in Europe, he concluded sadly that the clash of ideologies on the other side of the Atlantic had only strengthened the "evil currents" on this side. "Anti-Semitism, for instance, is on the rise." And yet there was no logical reason for that. It should have become evident even to the meanest intelligence that the evil Jew of Hitler's propaganda had never been anything more than a "mythical figure." He had simply been a "whipping boy" conjured up as a sacrifice to "national sadism." That was obvious. "But is the American anti-Semite stopped in his tracks or even impelled to slow up? He is not." Among the uneducated and the credulous were many—and their number was growing—who embraced ethnic prejudice as a superficial, simplistic response to the increasingly complex problems confronting society.[15]

Was there in fact an increase of anti-Semitism in the United States during the late 1930s, or was there merely a more open expression of what had been a latent popular hostility against Jews? Did the growing racist violence of the Third Reich encourage anti-Semitic organizations in the United States to voice their opinions more loudly? Or did the American press, increasingly aware of the crisis facing European Jewry, start to pay more attention to the antagonism toward the Jewish community at home, thereby creating the impression of growing ethnic prejudice?

Some contemporary observers thought that the constant warnings by fearful liberals about the spread of ethnic prejudice were perhaps exaggerated. In the spring of 1939, for instance, an article appearing in a periodical published by the American Jewish Committee urged caution in evaluating reports of growing hostility toward Jews. The author, Norton Belth, pointed out that "dispensers of anti-Jewish scurrility, who previously worked only under the cloak of darkness, today shout their wares on the busiest street corners of New York, Philadelphia, and other large cities." This change in their tactics had created a greater public awareness of the problem and had been interpreted by many Gentiles as well as Jews as a sign that anti-Semitism was on the rise. "Among Jews this awareness is translating itself into a growing apprehensiveness." But was prejudice really increasing? Did the growing boldness of the Jew-baiters mean that they were gaining wider support among Americans? Or was it no more than a strategic maneuver designed to magnify their power? "It is important to know the truth . . . [and] there is urgent need, therefore, for a calm and thorough analysis of the strength of the anti-Semitic movement in the United States, of the forces behind it, the objectives it hopes to achieve, and the instruments it uses."

Accordingly, Belth examined some of the more important anti-Semitic organizations in the United States, whose leaders he described as the nation's "lunatic fringe," among them Fritz Kuhn's German-American Volksbund, Father Charles E. Coughlin's National Union for Social Justice, William Dudley Pelley's Silver Shirts, and Gerald B. Winrod's Defenders of the Christian Faith. None of them, he found, had appreciably gained in strength since 1933. In fact, "many . . . have declined considerably and others have completely disappeared." His conclusion was therefore that if the growth of anti-Semitic prejudice depended on organization alone, the danger would be "almost negligible." But that was the catch. While organized anti-Semitism did not seem to be on the increase, "the fact remains that there is a great deal of latent and sometimes expressed antagonism toward Jews." This spontaneous, unorganized antagonism was very difficult to analyze, Belth admitted. Even he was not quite sure whether it was growing or declining.[16]

Most other observers of public opinion were unsure as well, which is why they generally dealt only briefly with the question of whether anti-Semitism was increasing, sometimes avoiding it altogether. In November 1938, about a week after the Kristallnacht, Secretary of the Interior Harold L. Ickes described in his diary the harsh punitive decrees against the Jewish community that the German government had issued in the past few days. American disapproval had been "very much stirred up" as a result of this display of Nazi cruelty, "despite the growing feeling of anti-Semitism here." That was as far as he went, however. His attention then turned to the trouble Neville Chamberlain was having answering questions in the House of Commons.[17]

The following spring, *Fortune* magazine, commenting on the results of the public opinion poll which showed that more than 80 percent of the respondents opposed the admission of refugees outside the established immigration quotas, said nothing about the spread of anti-Semitism in the United States. It did ask rhetorically, "Would Hitler and his German-

American Bunds be safe in the joyful conclusion that Americans don't like the Jews much better than do the Nazis?" Clearly the editors of *Fortune* thought that there was a great deal of ethnic prejudice in the country. But whether it was growing or not was a question they chose not to address.[18]

Even Henry Pratt Fairchild, a prominent sociologist, avoided the subject in his comments on the prevailing attitude toward Jews in America. He readily acknowledged the existence of extensive ethnic prejudice. "Anyone who honestly recapitulates the conversations that he has heard at dinner parties, clubs, and miscellaneous gatherings within any recent period must admit that some degree of hostility or dislike of Jews in general is very widespread, even among the most broad-minded and kindly disposed of his associates." Occasionally he became dramatic in describing the intensity of hostility toward Jews in the United States. He warned the readers of the *New Republic*, for example, that "there is a powerful current of anti-foreignism and anti-Semitism in particular running close to the surface of the American mind, ready to burst out into violent eruption on relatively slight provocation." He made it sound almost as if the United States were on the verge of a Kristallnacht of its own. But was this "powerful current" of anti-Semitism becoming more powerful? Was it becoming more likely than before to burst into violence? Fairchild avoided the issue.[19]

Trying to measure changes in the intensity of ethnic prejudice in the United States by indirect methods presents difficulties as well. Opposition to the admission of Jewish refugees was expressed much more openly than antagonism toward Jews in general. That was because arguments against lowering the immigration barriers could be presented for reasons that were ideologically more acceptable than undisguised bigotry. There can be no question that the public justifications for opposing a relaxation of the existing quota system sometimes reflected a secret anti-Semitism. But it is also clear that many of those arguing against the admission of large numbers of refugees were motivated primarily or even solely by concern over the effect it would have on the opportunities of the native population to find employment and livelihood. The difference between the alleged and the real reasons for opposing changes in the immigration laws can sometimes be easily recognized, but sometimes it is almost indiscernible, and at other times there simply is no difference.

Thus in the spring of 1938, shortly after the incorporation of Austria into the Third Reich, an editorial in the *Milwaukee Journal* opposed proposals made in the name of humanity to lower the barriers against refugees from Central Europe. "What of 'humanity' to the millions of Americans who cannot now find employment in this land of ours?" it asked. "Is it humanity to jeopardize the jobs and the living standards of these still more by dropping all bars in favor of foreigners who may be unwanted in their native lands? The quotas must stay."

On the face of it, the argument sounded reasonable, even persuasive. It seemed to reflect a sincere compassion for needy fellow Americans. Who could quarrel with that? But this compassion was accompanied by a stern warning, almost a threat, to those who seemed willing to risk the welfare of their countrymen for the sake of ethnic solidarity. "American citizens of Jewish parentage who ask for special privileges for their European kin are doing neither the country, nor themselves, nor their European kin a service. They are asking something which the country, if it is to preserve the best interests of its people, cannot give." To Jewish readers of the *Milwaukee Journal* the editorial must have sounded vaguely menacing.[20]

Sometimes the opponents of relaxing the immigration restrictions used a variant of the economic argument. Instead of maintaining that the influx of thousands upon thousands of impoverished foreigners would threaten the livelihood of native-born Americans, they insisted that the United States had already done its share, indeed more than its share, in helping to solve the refugee problem. The time had come for the other democracies to assume a larger part of the burden. During congressional hearings on the bill to authorize the admission of refugee children from the Third Reich, J. H. Patten, representing the United Mechanics of the State of New York, declared that those most familiar with the problem of finding asylum for the victims of ethnic persecution would undoubtedly advise Washington "to get other governments to match the United States in what our Government is doing in receiving refugees for permanent residence." They would point out that "the United States has to date received more refugees for permanent residence than all of the other countries put together." How much more could the country be expected to do?

Not only that, the American government had been far more generous than any of the other democratic nations, Patten maintained. Those nations viewed the victims of Nazi racism as nothing more than "transmigrants," to be gotten rid of as soon as possible. Indeed, they were treating refugees not much better than prisoners in the concentration camps of the Third Reich: "At the camp in Holland refugee women and children are in uniform in a barbed-wire enclosure, and only there temporarily, as publicly stated, until they can be passed on." Congressman A. Leonard Allen of Louisiana, however, found that hard to believe. The Committee on Immigration and Naturalization had been told that Holland was accepting large numbers of refugee children as residents, he interposed. "Do you mean to say that they put them in pens like cattle?" But Patten would not retreat. "It is worse than anything we have ever created for the Indians on reservations." He insisted that instead of admitting still more refugees, the United States should urge the governments of Western Europe to be more humane. As for the Americans, they had already done as much as they reasonably could, perhaps even more.[21]

Not all opponents of lowering the immigration barriers were conservative in sympathy or nativist in outlook. Henry Pratt Fairchild, for instance, was not only a liberal; he had been variously described as "collectivistic," "socialistic," even "Marxistic" in his political leanings. He was known to be associated with various leftist causes, among them the establishment of closer relations between the United States and the Soviet Union and the release from prison of the Communist leader Earl Browder. But on the issue of admitting more immigrants his position was similar to that of the right-wing opposition, though for different reasons. He made it clear that it was not his intention to discourage philanthropic aid to Jewish refugees or to deny the obligation of countries "that are still to some extent democratic and economically prosperous" to use every reasonable means to alleviate the moral crisis confronting the Western world. But he also believed that a "realistic liberalism," a liberalism that considered the interests of all mankind now and in the future, had to recognize that a solution to society's current problems was too complicated to be achieved by an "immediate benevolence" of the old-fashioned "charitable" kind. It demanded "the most penetrating and comprehensive analysis."

That kind of analysis, Fairchild insisted, had forced him to the conclusion that the admission to the United States of hundreds of thousands of Jews could not be viewed as simply a matter of humanitarianism. There were also serious international consequences to be considered. "A wholesale readiness to accept the victims of foreign persecution inevitably acts as a standing invitation to any country that wishes to get rid of its Jewish elements to start persecuting them." As a matter of fact, there were already complaints in Poland that that country was being penalized for being too decent in the treatment of its Jews and that perhaps it should therefore start persecuting them, as the Germans were doing, in order to force them to seek refuge in countries that had previously excluded them. By trying too hard to help the victims of ethnic prejudice in Europe, Americans might unintentionally be increasing the extent and intensity of that prejudice.[22]

But for Fairchild there was still another, even more compelling reason for not admitting too many persecuted Jews, and that was the effect it might have on his own country. There was already a powerful undercurrent of anti-Semitism in the United States, just below the surface of openly expressed public opinion, ready to erupt at the slightest provocation. Would not a sudden influx of Jewish refugees make a bad situation worse? "Remembering the Native American and Know Nothing movements, the American Protestant Association and the Ku Klux Klan, it is not fanciful to feel that the sudden admission of half a million Jews might . . . cause this deep-seated emotion to burst out into action." It would be in the best interest of the Jews and the Gentiles and the victims of Nazi racism themselves not to act with too much generosity in dealing with the refugee problem.[23]

This argument was heard over and over and over again in the long debate about what the United States should do to help Jews trying to escape persecution by the Third Reich. It was embraced by some liberals as well as many conservatives, by secular organizations as well as religious societies, and by leaders of the labor movement as well as spokesmen for important business interests. The economic argument was the one invoked most frequently in the controversy. Those who worried that lowering the barriers to refugees would intensify hostility toward Jews in America generally maintained that they themselves were free and would remain free of ethnic prejudice, no matter what. But there were those others, so many of them, less tolerant, less humane, less enlightened, and less understanding, who were likely to express their deep-rooted bigotry loudly and perhaps even violently if too many Jewish immigrants were allowed to come in.

Excessive generosity would prove self-defeating. It would not alleviate but aggravate the problem.

That conclusion, though harsh, appeared to many Americans inescapable. As the *Christian Century* cautioned its readers, "The importation of an appreciable number of Jews at this time would become at once the occasion for which our 'Silver Shirts' and anti-Semitic 'bunds' are waiting. It would be a tragic disservice to the Jews in America to increase their number by substantial immigration, and would hardly contribute at all to the alleviation of the anguish of the Jews in Germany." The admission of too many refugees would only worsen a situation that was already very bad.[24]

With the intensification of the diplomatic crisis created by the confrontation of the democratic and authoritarian great powers of Europe, a new argument against lowering the immigration barriers emerged in the United States. This one was more discernibly or openly anti-Semitic than most of the others because it became part of the growing and increasingly bitter debate over the role America should play in the conflict dividing the Old World.

At first differences of opinion on the subject seemed to have little practical significance. The general assumption was that once England and France finally abandoned their policy of appeasement and decided to stand up to the Axis, they would prevail, whether by diplomatic or military means. Not even the declaration of war or the swift defeat of Poland weakened U.S. confidence that sooner or later the victors in the First World War would win the Second World War as well. But the German conquest of most of Western Europe shattered those comforting illusions. America now faced a foreign crisis greater than any in its history. To be sure, Winston Churchill seemed determined to resist the Third Reich to the bitter end. Yet it was also obvious that Great Britain could not go on fighting much longer against such heavy odds without the economic, diplomatic, logistic, and—though this was not openly acknowledged—military support of the United States. That disturbing but inescapable reality intensified the long and acrimonious debate between the supporters of collective security and the advocates of isolationism.

That debate in turn gradually broadened to include not only the refugee problem but also the entire "Jewish question." Many of the opponents of American involvement in the war became convinced that the country was being dragged into a ruinous military conflict in which it had no vital interest at least partly because of the intrigues and machinations of American Jews, to whom the protection of their coreligionists in the Old World was more important than the welfare of their countrymen at home.

The Jewish community in the United States was indeed strongly in favor of supporting Great Britain, even if that eventually led to direct American participation in the war. Many other ethnic minorities in the country—the Poles, the Czechs, the Serbs, and the Greeks, for example—also hoped that their new homeland would help save their old one from the tyranny of the Third Reich. But there was a widespread perception among vehement advocates of neutrality that the Jews were more persistent and successful than any other immigrant community in steering the nation toward involvement in the war. And that was because they were more clever and influential than the others, and sometimes more devious or cunning or stealthy or unscrupulous. They were using their important connections in business, politics, and culture to bring about a confrontation between Washington and Berlin. Their favorite hymn, according to a quip popular in many isolationist circles, was "Onward, Christian Soldiers."

This view was often also expressed in a more elegant form in lectures, articles, conferences, and mass meetings. The tone was more serious, the language more sophisticated, but the conclusion was essentially the same: the Jews were a major force behind the warmongering campaign being waged in America.

The best-known statement of this contention, the one which attracted the most attention and provoked the loudest debate, was a speech given by Charles A. Lindbergh in Des Moines on September 11, 1941. The famous aviator, still admired for his solo flight across the Atlantic, still commiserated with for the kidnapping and death of his infant son, had become a leading proponent of nonintervention. He knew that many other Americans, however, some of them powerful and influential, favored support for England in the struggle against Germany. Early in his speech, therefore, he identified the great threat to the nation's neutrality and security. "The three most important groups who have been pressing this country toward war are the British, the Jewish, and the Roosevelt administration." Those inciters of armed conflict had to be identified and resisted by all patriotic citizens who had the national interest at heart.

Lindbergh tried to make it clear that he understood why the Jews wanted to bring about the overthrow of the Nazi regime. "The persecution they suffered in Germany would be sufficient to make bitter enemies of any race." Indeed, no one with any sense of the dignity of mankind could fail to condemn the Third Reich's cruel oppression of the Jewish community. But a word of caution was also in order. "No person of honesty and vision can look on their pro-war policy here today without seeing the dangers involved in such a policy, both for us and for them." And then a familiar warning: "Instead of agitating for war, the Jewish groups in this country should be opposing it in every possible way, for they will be among the first to feel its consequences."

Tolerance was unquestionably a virtue, but one that depended on peace and strength, Lindbergh expounded. History had shown that it could not survive war and devastation. A few "far-sighted" Jews, recognizing this truth, were opposed to American involvement in the war. Unfortunately, most of them continued to support a policy of intervention. "Their greatest danger to this country lies in their large ownership and influence in our motion pictures, our press, our radio, and our government." This was standard anti-Semitic rhetoric, and Lindbergh himself seemed aware of that, because he hastened to add that "I am not attacking either the Jewish or the British people." On the contrary, "both races, I admire." Still, he would not retreat from the charge that the leaders of "both the British and the Jewish races," for reasons "which are as understandable from their viewpoint as they are inadvisable from ours"—reasons that were clearly un-American—"wish to involve us in the war." He could not blame them for looking out "for what they believe to be their own interests," but at the same time "we also must look out for ours." And then the peroration: "We cannot allow the natural passions and prejudices of other peoples to lead our country to destruction." Lindbergh did not mention the refugee problem, but the implications of what he was saying were clear. To admit large numbers of persecuted European Jews would only serve to strengthen the interventionist forces pushing the United States toward war.[25]

Others opposed lowering the barriers to Jewish immigrants not because they would help drag the country into armed conflict or because they would compete with American workers or because they would aggravate ethnic prejudice or because they would resist cultural assimilation, but because they were Jewish. These exclusionists were motivated by anti-Semitism pure and simple. To them, the inherent character or collective mentality of the Jews made them a threat to any non-Jewish community willing to accept them. The differences between Jew and Gentile were so deep-rooted, so fundamental, that no amount of tolerance on one side or assimilation on the other could overcome them. They were ineradicable.

These hard-core anti-Semites sometimes found encouragement and support in the writings of prominent intellectuals whose intention was not to reinforce ethnic hostility but to express some personal dislike or irritation. At the end of 1938, for instance, H. G. Wells, then in his seventies, more idiosyncratic, controversial, and combative than ever, presented to the American readers of *Liberty* magazine views that he had been expounding for some time to his own countrymen. As early as the First World War, he insisted, "the Jewish spokesmen were most elaborately and energetically demonstrating that they cared not a rap for the troubles and dangers of any people but their own." Aware of the persecution that the Jews now had to endure in many parts of the world, he spoke "very unwillingly" about a "certain national egotism" which they as a people displayed. This was the real source of the problem. "It is fundamental to the Jewish Question that they do remain a peculiar people in the French- and English-speaking communities largely by their own free choice, because they are history-ridden and because they are haunted by a persuasion that they are a chosen people with distinctive privileges over their Gentile fellow creatures." There was only one way to end anti-Semitism, and that was to end anti-Gentilism.[26]

Some Americans less prominent than Wells were also not afraid to appear prejudiced. They expressed their views regarding the refugee problem openly and unequivocally. During the congressional hearings on the bill to admit the refugee children from Central Europe, Mrs. Agnes Waters, who described herself as "the daughter of generations of patriots," spoke in the name of "the millions of American mothers patriotically interested in the present and future of this great Nation." She warned that "this Nation will be helpless to guarantee to our children their rights, under the Constitution, to life, liberty and the pursuit of happiness if this country is to become the dumping ground for the persecuted minorities of Europe." The ultimate source of the danger was not economic or demographic but cultural or ethnic or even racial. It could not be overcome by education and acculturation. "These refugees have a heritage of hate. They could never become loyal Americans."

That was the heart of the problem. Mrs. Waters feared that the bill would admit "thousands of motherless, embittered, persecuted children of undesirable foreigners." And the children would prove undesirable as well. They were "seasoned veterans of a revolution of hate" and "potential leaders of a revolt against our American form of government." As she became more heated in her argumentation, she became more explicit. There could be no doubt about the subversive ideology that the young refugees would embrace once they reached adulthood. "Why should we give preference in America to these potential Communists?" And then a parenthetical observation regarding not European but American Jews: "Already we have too many of their kind in our country now trying to overthrow our government." Here was still another common theme of the anti-Semitic agitation: not only were the Jews too influential in motion pictures, radio, the press, and the government, as Lindbergh claimed, but, according to Mrs. Waters, they were also trying to undermine the established constitutional system of the nation that had shown so much generosity in dealing with them. She concluded her statement with the plea to "keep America for Americans."[27]

Yet there were also those who opposed the admission of refugees not because they were likely to become Communists but because they were likely to become capitalists. Jews, according to this view, were too eager to accumulate wealth, too successful in acquiring it, and too clever in using it to gain an excessive influence in economics and politics. A few months before Mrs. Waters testified at the congressional hearing, W. J. Bott, a resident of the Bronx, a borough of New York City with a sizable Jewish population, wrote to the president urging him to worry less about the problems confronting Jews and more about the problems confronting Christians. "I realize your debt to Jewish financial backing as a result of your own case and those who you have put into office, and then again those you put into office, who in turn appoint their own 'Angels.' " But the time had come to consider other, more important obligations. "As a Christian and an American I must ask that you who are likewise an American and a Christian exercise a little concern for your own people first and worry about Russian, Roumanian, Polish and German Jews later on." Mr. Bott assured the president that he was not indifferent to the fate of persecuted refugees. Indeed, "I am deeply sympathetic of their plight." But there were limits to his sympathy. "I am far more gravely concerned about my own kind first." As for President Roosevelt, he too should save some of his compassion and generosity for suffering fellow Americans.[28]

The debate over the refugee problem went on and on, growing louder and more intense, but without any sign of an emerging agreement. As the rapid succession of the Third Reich's diplomatic and military victories made the situation of European Jews increasingly precarious, their supporters and sympathizers in the New World redoubled their efforts to provide them with asylum. Those on the opposing side would not budge, however. The debate seemed to be hopelessly deadlocked.

Yet some thought that there might still be a way out of the impasse. The refugee problem could perhaps be exported to remote parts of the globe, far from Europe and the United States, to regions that were thinly inhabited or whose population was too weak to resist an influx of persecuted Jews. In the spring of 1939, the *Christian Science Monitor*, after reporting that most countries in Latin America refused to accept any more refugees and the British government had decided to reduce drastically the number admitted to Palestine, mentioned other possibilities. George Rublee, the former director of the Intergovernmental Committee on Political Refugees, had suggested that havens might be found in British Guiana, Dutch Guiana, Northern Rhodesia, the Dominican Republic, and the Philippines. The trouble, in the opinion of the *Christian Science Monitor*, was that "most Jews apparently have no taste for the pioneering necessary in remote and undeveloped areas and do not take readily to some plans made in their behalf." This was understandable. And yet, "they may remember that other races have carved homes out of wildernesses to escape oppression." After all, even British Guiana or Northern Rhodesia was better than an East European ghetto or a German concentration camp.[29]

To many others, however, the refugee problem seemed so complicated, so hard to solve that they threw up their hands in despair. Perhaps there simply was no solution, at least no solution under existing canons of political authority and moral obligation. An editorial published in the *Christian Century* late in 1938 reflected this sense of hopelessness. The policy of the United States had to take into account not only "its sympathies and its abstract ideals" but also "the instabilities and perils" of its social order. There was, moreover, no ethical principle requiring either an individual or a nation to become exposed to a condition involving "moral overstrain." The success of the American experiment in democracy demanded that instead of inviting further complications by relaxing the immigration laws, the government should maintain or even tighten those laws. "Christian and other high-minded citizens have no need to feel apologetic for the limitations upon immigration into this country."

But what about that "Jewish problem" which had been created by "German inhumanity"? The *Christian Century* had no answer. "This editorial . . . seems to end in a blind alley." Every assistance that could be offered to the victims of ethnic persecution should be offered. The people of every nation, especially the United States, should express their "outraged protest." And those countries that could receive refugees should do so. Still, "if we seem skeptical of the practicality of many of the present proposals for mass deportation to far away and unoccupied territories, we shall rejoice if events prove that we were of too little faith." Was there no solution? Alas, there appeared to be none. "We make no attempt to disguise our bafflement."[30]

But the *Christian Century* was mistaken. There was in fact a solution, not only to the refugee problem but to the "Jewish question" in general—a direct, effective, and lasting solution. Only no one had as yet thought of it, at least not openly. It was much closer than anyone at the time realized, only a few years away. All that was needed for its adoption was a ruthless ideology and a regime powerful enough, determined enough, and pitiless enough to embrace it.

9

A Jewish Hush-Hush Strategy

MOST AMERICAN JEWS did not share the concerns regarding the refugee problem that troubled so many of their non-Jewish countrymen. To them, it was clear what their nation should do to help the innocent victims of anti-Semitic prejudice in the Old World. The United States had been founded on the principles of freedom and justice for all, whatever their faith or culture or ethnicity. The rise of a racist authoritarianism in Central and Eastern Europe was now providing a test of America's commitment to those ideals. It could return, even if only temporarily, to the policy of providing asylum to the poor and oppressed of the world, a policy that had helped the country achieve greatness. Or it could shut its eyes to the cruelties and brutalities of the Third Reich, focus its attention on its own needs and interests, and ignore the looming international crisis. How it responded to this challenge would determine how posterity judged its place in history.

What shaped the attitude of American Jews was, in the first place, sympathy for their oppressed coreligionists. Would not they themselves have become victims of that same racism if they or their parents or their grandparents had not found asylum across the ocean? It was natural for them to identify with those who remained exposed to the cruelty of anti-Semitic prejudice. But more than that, many of them still had relatives in the old country—aunts and uncles, even a wife or a husband or a child. For them, the refugee problem had great personal significance. But even those who no longer had family members overseas often remained interested in the culture and history of the country from which their ancestors had come, especially of its Jewish community. Their interest aroused a concern for the fate of that community.

And there was another reason, not as obvious as religious sympathy or ethnic identity or family connection but equally important, that helped account for the concern with which American Jews followed what was happening thousands of miles away. That reason was their identification, conscious or subconscious, with German Jews. To put it another way, many American Jews wondered, usually in private, whether what was occurring in the Third Reich might not occur in the United States tomorrow or the day after. On the face of it, this concern might have seemed farfetched and alarmist. After all, there was a world of difference between the principles and beliefs of Nazi Germany and those of the United States. But was that difference immutable or insurmountable? Could anyone really be sure? After all, if on the eve of the First World War someone had told a group of Germans, whether Jewish or Gentile, that in twenty-five years the Jews in their country would be vilified, ostracized, and segregated, they would have dismissed that prediction as preposterous. How could anything like that happen in "the land of thinkers and poets," the land of Kant, Lessing, Goethe, and Schiller? It was sheer fantasy. Germany was not czarist Russia or backward Romania. Germany was a nation of progress and enlightenment.

And yet barely a generation later Germany was in the grip of a tyrannical anti-Semitic authoritarianism. Couldn't the same thing happen in the United States? If a lost war and an economic crisis were enough to destroy German democracy, might not the same economic crisis undermine American democracy? To the Jewish community in the United States, the spread of ethnic prejudice in Europe, and not only in Germany, was a warning of what might happen on this side of the Atlantic. There were already alarming signs of a growing antagonism toward American Jews. Consider the results of a survey conducted by the Opinion Research Corporation in September 1939, which showed that about a third of the more than 3,000 respondents would support or at least sympathize with "a campaign against Jews." This was roughly the same proportion as that of the German voters who supported the National Socialist Party in the last parliamentary elections under the Weimar Republic. Could it be a sign of things to come?[1]

In retrospect, American Jews' fears about the spread of anti-Semitism in their country were exaggerated. Even most Americans who indicated that they would favor measures directed against the Jewish community could not be equated with the ardent Nazis who had helped put Hitler in power. At the time, however, Jews in the United States were by no means sure that what was happening in the Old World could not happen in the New. Wherever they looked, they saw what seemed to be a growing or at least a more openly expressed hostility, not only in Central Europe but in the authoritarian states of Eastern Europe, in the democracies of Western Europe, in Latin America, in Canada, and even in their own country. No wonder they felt uneasy.

That the extent of ethnic prejudice in the United States could not be measured with any degree of certainty only increased their concern. How was it possible to feel confident about what might happen next year or in five years or in ten? The position of German Jews during the last years of the Hohenzollern Empire or in the heyday of the Weimar Republic seemed as secure as that of American Jews on the eve of the Second World War. And look at what happened. Around the time of Pearl Harbor, a New York rabbi described the sense of vulnerability haunting the Jewish community:

> Today, as never before in their history, American Jews are apprehensive over their security. A great anxiety weighs on them. This concern is not altogether a novel phenomenon. There has always been, even in most favorable times, some uneasiness among them as to their status. But since the advent of Hitler, their disquiet has mounted steadily. Each successive triumph of fascism in Europe, each indication of anti-Semitic sentiment on the American scene has given it added force and intensity. Recent events—the Lindbergh pronouncement in Des Moines [and] the utterances of certain persons of high public position—have been all that was needed to throw the forebodings of Jews into fever heat. A vast wave of worry has swept over them of late. They are still submerged beneath it. . . . The present violence of anti-Semitism is undefinable, its future unpredictable.[2]

Stephen S. Wise, one of the most visible and vocal American Zionists, was alarmed by what he perceived to be the spread of ethnic hostility in America. Writing to a relative in May 1939, he sounded discouraged, which was for him a rarity. "What with the tragic Palestine situation and the really rising tide of anti-Semitism everywhere, I do not know what to do!" He described an incident that had made him even more aware of the danger confronting the Jewish community. "Last night, after Carnegie Hall was refused to the so-called Christian Front, made up of Coughlinites, they marched up and down 57th Street, shouting, 'Hang Rabbi Wise to a flagpole! Lynch Rabbi Wise!' — Thousands of them and the police didn't even interfere." He was very upset. In those followers of Father Coughlin, Wise saw the Brownshirts on the eve of Hitler's assumption of power, marching through the streets of Berlin, vowing death to Rabbi Leo Baeck.[3]

From time to time the Jewish sense of inferiority would rise to the surface, finding expression in jests, anecdotes, and stories about the speech or manner or behavior of low-brow Jews. Such humor was especially common in vaudeville, radio, the theater, and the movies, businesses in which, incongruously, Jews played an important cultural and financial role. Here the Jewish comic was a familiar figure, amusing and entertaining but ill-bred and a little vulgar, speaking with a singsong intonation, ostentatiously dressed or overdressed, and ignorant of proper speech and manner. He was a source of both amusement and discomfort, a caricature reinforcing a stereotype. To Jews as well as non-Jews he was a source of diversion, but while the latter generally found him credible, the former often considered him an embarrassment or even an insult.

This sense of inferiority, which was essentially a Jewish form of anti-Semitism, became apparent long before the establishment of National Socialism in Germany. As early as the spring of 1934, a Jewish graduate student at the University of Iowa published an assessment of the deep-rooted Jewish self-dislike and its role as an ethnic cohesive force in the United States. "The vast majority of Jews do not remain Jews by choice," he maintained. "Basically, the Jew hates his Jewishness, and bewails his fate." The only thing that made him stubborn and encouraged him to cling to his ethnicity was the prejudice of the outside world. "Anti-semitism is what keeps Judaism alive, and should that determinative force be removed, within a century there will be no more Jews." The elimination of ethnic bigotry would thus be not only morally justified but practically advantageous to both communities. The Christians would be rid of an age-old problem that had seemed insoluble, while the Jews would find the acceptance they had been seeking for so long. "The individual Jew will be very glad to unload his burden." And by unloading that burden, he would finally cease to be a Jew.[4]

Whatever the validity of this conclusion, it reflected a widespread self-disapproval which, combined with an awareness of Gentile prejudice, engendered a mood of constant caution among American Jews. It was important, they came to feel, not to attract too much attention among their Christian compatriots. Inconspicuousness was more than advantageous; it was essential. Therefore, in presenting a proposal or defending a cause espoused by the Jewish community, one should create the impression of a joint endeavor involving Gentiles as well as Jews. The latter might occupy a few positions of prominence; that was permissible and perhaps unavoidable. But they should be joined by as many non-Jews as possible, preferably by a majority of non-Jews. That would help counter the charge that the proposal or cause was simply an attempt by the Jewish community to promote its own interests. And creating the appearance of a collective effort should not prove very difficult. There were always quite a few sympathetic Christians, liberal, tolerant, and generous, who were ready to join Jews in opposing ethnic prejudice at home and abroad. Their participation would provide a defense against the common charge that the only causes embraced by Jews were those likely to be of advantage to them.

That was not enough, however. It was also important to show that the measures or policies advocated by Jews were designed to protect not only themselves but also the non-Jewish community. Therefore, protests against the anti-Semitism of the Third Reich often embraced other victims of Nazi bigotry: radicals, dissidents, homosexuals, Gypsies, Pentecostals, Poles, and Czechs. How could anyone then claim that such protests were designed solely to defend Jewish interests? Similarly, American Jews' condemnation of the increasingly oppressive nativism of the Romanian government frequently included criticism of its harsh treatment of non-Jewish minorities in the kingdom: Hungarians, Ukrainians, Bulgarians, and

Turks. Denunciations of ethnic prejudice in the United States, moreover, especially in the worlds of business and higher education, often identified other minorities victimized by an unacknowledged but prevalent bigotry: African Americans, Hispanic Americans, Asian Americans, Native Americans, Italian Americans, and Polish Americans. Those denunciations were at least partly an expression of the desire to generalize or universalize the struggle against anti-Semitism, to give it a broader moral and ideological foundation.

At times there was even a complete or almost complete de-Judaization of the struggle against prejudice. Jews condemning the teachings and policies of National Socialism would occasionally avoid any reference to its anti-Semitic doctrines, emphasizing instead the nonethnic basis of their opposition. They would point out that the victims of Nazi oppression included men and women of diverse political, social, and economic backgrounds and convictions. Some were liberals, others socialists, others anarchists, and still others pacifists. Among them were Protestants, Catholics, Jews, agnostics, and atheists. All of them were being vilified, all were being persecuted. To differentiate between the degrees of discrimination against the various categories of victims would be pointless and divisive. It would weaken the common struggle against the evil forces of totalitarianism. The various participants in that struggle must maintain a united front.

Most of the Jews supporting this de-Judaization of anti-Semitism were not motivated primarily by calculation or expediency. They were genuinely convinced that ethnic persecution was a danger confronting minorities of all backgrounds and faiths and that the struggle against racism had to transcend the boundaries of nationality or religion. But they were also aware that resistance to the Third Reich's racist doctrines regarding Jewry would be strengthened by broadening its basis to include other ethnic groups.

Many other Jews, however, feared that the universalization of the problem of bigotry was obscuring its true nature. The Jewish community should be less restrained and cautious; it should be more forceful and assertive. Joshua Trachtenberg, a rabbi, sociologist, and cultural historian, maintained that "it is high time we freed ourselves of the aptly categorized 'sha-sha' philosophy of Jewish polemics, which sought to turn away wrath with gentle words, to obscure the Jew from the public gaze." Such a "superficial tactic" could not in any way help solve the problem of anti-Semitism. It had failed the Jews in Germany, it had proved a broken reed in England, and it had shown itself useless in the United States. " 'Anti-defamation' campaigns and pious statistics are less than no defense."

Yet in the end, even Trachtenberg agreed that the struggle against anti-Semitism should not and could not be waged only by Jews. It had to enlist the support of other democratic, humanitarian, right-thinking Americans. "We must be prepared, in conjunction with all the progressive forces that can be mobilized on this front, to utilize every available weapon against the Fascist and anti-Jewish menace: the legislatures, the law-courts, the boycott, a relentless propaganda." The battle in defense of Jews was also a battle in defense of non-Jews. The rights of both were being threatened by the rise of totalitarianism. Therefore, those fighting ethnic prejudice were doing so "not to protect Jewish rights, but *to protect American rights*." The values they were championing were timeless and universal.[5]

For some Jews, even this formulation was not enough. They insisted that the struggle against anti-Semitism, whether in Europe or America, had to be waged first and foremost by Jews. Since they were the ones in greatest danger from racist bigotry, they were also the ones who had to assume chief responsibility for combating that danger. To remain silent in the face of the anti-Semitic threat or to work cautiously behind the scenes in opposing it or to dilute it by de-Judaization and universalization would be a shirking of duty, an abject surrender. It would be a retreat to the "sha-sha" or hush-hush strategy that Jews, submissive and fearful, had so often adopted in the past, refusing to stand up to their enemies for fear of arousing even greater hostility. The time had come to act with courage, to confront the anti-Semites directly, without subterfuge, without disguise, and if need be without the help of others.

The differences of opinion within the Jewish community between those advocating an alliance with non-Jewish democratic forces and those urging a more self-reliant stand reflected in part social and cultural differences. Recent immigrants, especially those from Eastern Europe, tended to favor an independent and assertive policy in dealing with the problem of anti-Semitism. Not fully acculturated or assimilated, still regarded by mainstream society as outsiders, they were loyal above all to their own community and were prepared to do whatever was needed to defend its interests, regardless of what the rest of the world might think. The fact that many of them still had close ties to relatives and friends in the old country strengthened their resolve. These militant Jews were the ones who participated most frequently in mass meetings and street demonstrations demanding that the American government take a stronger position against the Third Reich.

Others in the Jewish community, however, regarded public displays of ethnic solidarity with disapproval and uneasiness. They were a minority, but an affluent and influential minority, socially and economically well established, their families having come to the United States decades earlier, usually from Central or Western Europe. They were now fully Americanized in speech, appearance, manner, and thought. They had become indistinguishable or almost indistinguishable from their non-Jewish countrymen. Some had even gained entry into the more exclusive social circles, where they were treated the same as the Gentiles and where, by an unspoken agreement, their origin and background remained as a rule unmentioned. To them, anything that might strengthen the undercurrent of popular anti-Semitism or focus greater public attention on the Jewish community was unwelcome. Ideally, they would have liked to have the fact that someone was a Jew viewed in the same way as the fact that someone was an Episcopalian or a Methodist or a Unitarian. Jewishness, in their view, should be simply a description of religious affiliation, without social, cultural, or behavioral connotations.

For that reason, they were troubled to see the problem of anti-Semitism receiving special attention, whether from those who shared or those who opposed ethnic prejudice. Anything that underscored the differences between Jews and non-Jews was unwelcome to them. They had tried so long and so hard to convince their Gentile countrymen that they were just like other Americans and that they should therefore be treated like other Americans. Some of them had even succeeded in winning complete or nearly complete acceptance. And now all those gains were being jeopardized by loud demonstrations and protests designed to draw public attention to the special problems confronting the Jewish community.

Some Christians in sympathy with the Jewish cause found this timidity of the patrician, well-to-do Jews hard to understand. Toward the end of

1938, Harold Ickes entered in his diary an account of a conversation with Supreme Court Justice Brandeis in which he expressed his disapproval of Jewish fearfulness. He spoke of "the cowardice on the part of the rich Jews of America," telling Brandeis that "I would like to get two or three hundred of them together in a room and tell them that they couldn't hope to save their money by meekly accepting whatever humiliations others chose to impose upon them." As he pointed out, "the Catholic minority in this country, because it was well organized, active, and aggressive, was able to protect people of that religion and get more recognition for them than numerically they were entitled to." Why couldn't the Jewish minority also become better organized, active, and aggressive? It too would then be able to protect its people more effectively and gain more recognition for them than they were numerically entitled to.[6]

Brandeis, although a prominent member of the Jewish patriciate, his family having emigrated from Central Europe before the Civil War, agreed with Ickes. "He said there was a certain type of rich Jew who was a coward. According to him, these are German Jews, and he spoke of them with the same contempt that I feel for them." A confirmed Zionist, Brandeis maintained that in view of the triumph of National Socialism in Germany and the intensification of anti-Semitism in Eastern Europe, "there is plenty of room in Palestine to take care of all the Jews who need new homes on account of the persecution of the dictators." The homeland of their Biblical ancestors could easily absorb 50,000 refugees annually. All that was needed was a relaxation of the restrictions that the British authorities had imposed on Jewish immigration. Ickes even surmised that Brandeis had discussed these views with President Roosevelt during his recent visits to the White House. "He has always been one of the number interested in the resettlement of the Jews in Palestine."[7]

Most members of the Jewish patriciate, however, were not as bold as Ickes and Brandeis in their private conversation. They could not afford to be, or at least they thought that they could not. They remained convinced that it was in the interests of American Jewry to remain inconspicuous, to avoid attracting too much attention, even sympathetic attention. It would be better to work behind the scenes, relying on private contacts, informal connections, and unwritten and unspoken agreements. A hush-hush strategy seemed the most effective way of dealing with the problems confronting their community. Feeling surrounded by distrust and suspicion, they agreed with Falstaff that discretion was the better part of valor.

This sense of insecurity or vulnerability accounted for the reluctance of some Jews in America, especially those in positions of prominence, to be identified as Jews. They preferred to maintain a polite, prudent silence regarding their ethnic background. Thus when Roosevelt created the President's Advisory Committee on Political Refugees in 1938, some of those invited to become members declined, among them Henry Morgenthau, Sr., the banker, diplomat, philanthropist, and former ambassador to Turkey, and Bernard Baruch, the well-known financier and government adviser. It was widely believed that they did not want to have their identity as Jews publicized. There was even a story circulating in Washington that the president had asked Baruch to serve knowing that the invitation would embarrass him, as punishment for his recent testimony before a Senate committee Roosevelt disapproved of.[8]

More frequent were the behind-the-scenes maneuvers by well-to-do Jews to discourage the appointment of too many of their coreligionists to important positions in the government, because that might reinforce complaints about the growing Jewish influence in state and society. In the fall of 1938, when it became known that Roosevelt was planning to nominate Felix Frankfurter to the Supreme Court as a replacement for the retiring Benjamin N. Cardozo, a group of prominent Jews, among them Arthur Hays Sulzberger, the publisher of the *New York Times*, called on the president to try to persuade him to change his mind. They were afraid that since the appointment of Frankfurter while Brandeis was still on the bench would mean that two Jewish justices would be serving on the Supreme Court, anti-Semitic charges about the growing Judaization of the American government would increase.[9]

As it turned out, those fears were exaggerated. The Senate confirmed Frankfurter's appointment without a single dissenting vote. As long as the issue was still in doubt, however, many of his supporters expressed outrage, in most cases privately, at the meek surrender of so many prominent Jews to popular anti-Semitic prejudice. The latter were accused of being in effect allies of the Silver Shirts and the Coughlinites. Stephen Wise was one of the most vehement denouncers of this display of Jewish submissiveness. "I had known for some time that the chief pressure against

[Felix Frankfurter] is being wielded by Jews," he wrote in a letter. "These unspeakable cowards are afraid that another Jew on the Supreme Court bench may bring us hurt." Instead of standing up to the bigoted bullies who represented the most reactionary forces in American life, they were abjectly capitulating to them. That was inexcusable.[10]

Harold Ickes, though not as impassioned in his criticism of the Jewish opponents of Frankfurter's appointment, was also scornful of their timidity. What were they so afraid of? He concluded that it was "the rich Jews [who] are objecting," not because they were opposed to Frankfurter but because "they think that his appointment would increase prejudice in this country against the Jews." And that might threaten their own economic interests. "They want to be let alone to accumulate riches at any price of racial pride or prestige." Still, Ickes was less concerned about the moral or ethical implications of their timidity than about its possible political consequences. If only Brandeis, who was then in his eighties, were to resign from the Supreme Court, the president would have no difficulty in appointing Frankfurter as the only Jewish justice. However, "if Brandeis does not resign until after this Administration comes to an end and then a reactionary is appointed to succeed him, Brandeis will have something to answer for to the liberals of the country." What seemed to matter to Ickes most was not the principle that public office should be open to all Americans, but the fear that the achievements of the New Deal might sometime in the future be undone by its political enemies.[11]

The most eloquent condemnation of the unobtrusiveness that many American Jews embraced, especially those belonging to the patriciate, came from Frankfurter himself. An immigrant from Austria who had gained prominence without the benefit of inherited wealth or family connections, he did not hesitate to denounce those willing to appease ethnic prejudice in order to protect the economic and social gains they had won by their acquiescent efforts. Writing while his nomination was still being debated, he expressed "profoundest concern" regarding "the number of prominent Jews who are unwittingly embracing Hitlerism by actually sponsoring a position of political inferiority and second-rate citizenship for Jews." The suggestion that Jews should not be appointed to public office because they were Jews—Frankfurter was no doubt thinking of his own situation—seemed to him "completely indistinguishable from Nazism."

He was "shocked out of my boots," moreover, to learn that some important Jews in New York had voted against Governor Herbert H. Lehman, a fellow Jew, hoping for his defeat because they were afraid of provoking an outbreak of anti-Semitism. And he was "even more shocked out of my boots" by "the shameful case of a member of one of the leading Jewish families actually suggesting to a high, non-Jewish official in Washington that he should get rid of two of his Jewish assistants because of the hurtful effect upon business interest to have Jews in those positions." Frankfurter believed that Jews should regard themselves as Americans, entitled to the same rights and opportunities as other Americans. His position, he stated, was the same as that of the British historian R. H. Tawney, who had recently declared about Neville Chamberlain's appeasement of Hitler that "I'd rather die standing than live on my knees."[12]

Still, while bold expressions of defiance of ethnic prejudice were psychologically satisfying, they could not alter the cautious and acquiescent strategy of most Jewish leaders in dealing with the problems confronting their community. That was partly a result of their continued attachment to a traditional form of self-defense that Jews in the Old World had been employing for centuries. A subservient usefulness to Christian society had helped them cope with religious and ethnic bigotry in the age of feudalism, then in the period of monarchical absolutism, then during the emergence of the parliamentary system of government, and finally during the decade or so of illusory democracy in Central and Eastern Europe after the First World War. Why shouldn't the same strategy work now on this side of the Atlantic, in the United States?

Not only tradition, however, accounted for the circumspection and calculated unobtrusiveness of the Jewish patriciate. Bitter experience had shown that the undercurrent of anti-Semitism could not be contained either by defiant condemnations or by eloquent appeals to the ideal of democracy. Jews continued to face serious prejudice on all sides. In one form or another, it seemed to them to be everywhere. Yet it was possible to mitigate some of its effects by a policy of discretion, restraint, and inconspicuousness. It would therefore be best for Jews to avoid assertiveness or vociferousness. Too much public attention would only make a bad situation worse. In private, behind closed doors, there was room for negotiation, for compromise, for making deals. Support in elections could be traded for influence in politics; financial success might lead to social acceptance. A discreet process of give-and-take seemed the best way to counter the threat of anti-Semitism. But its effectiveness depended on the willingness of Jews to avoid confrontation, argumentation, and too much assertiveness.

Even some of the most militant leaders of the Jewish community were willing at times to subordinate their proclaimed principles to the demands of expediency. Stephen Wise, usually tireless in denouncing the weaklings and appeasers who were afraid to insist on the rights and privileges they were entitled to, occasionally displayed the same restraint or caution that he condemned in others. His bark became progressively worse than his bite. As early as January 193, he wrote to Secretary of Labor Frances Perkins expressing concern over her choice of a candidate for the vacant position of immigration commissioner. "I understand that several Jews have presented their application for the post." He found that troubling. "May I say to you, in confidence, that it is a post that no Jew ought to be called upon to fill." The reason was obvious. "The Commissioner has so much to do with the admission of immigrants, etc. including Jews, that it is really unfair to burden a Jew with that particular post."

Wise hastened to assure the secretary that he did not mean that Jews should be excluded from "any of the normal responsibilities of public life and office." But he feared that giving a Jew authority to enforce the nation's immigration laws might lend support to rumors about the growing Jewish influence in government under the New Deal. Was his advice to Frances Perkins essentially different from the advice that a group of prominent Jews gave the president two years later regarding Frankfurter's appointment, advice that Wise so vehemently condemned? In any case, the candidate whom the secretary of labor eventually recommended to the White House for the position of immigration commissioner was not a Jew.[13]

Members of the Jewish elite were not the only ones reluctant to draw public attention to their ethnic background. Many Jews of plebeian origin, those whose families had only recently arrived in the United States, who had grown up in a lower-class environment, and who had acquired prominence or wealth by their own efforts, were also often self-conscious about their ethnicity. They too were afraid that their achievements might be ascribed to the unattractive qualities and characteristics frequently associated with Jewry. Like their patrician coreligionists, they felt surrounded by hostile forces, disguised or restrained but waiting to emerge into the open when the time was right.

Sol Bloom, a well-known member of Congress, was a case in point. The son of Jewish immigrants from Poland, with little formal education and no family wealth, he had managed to become a successful entrepreneur, first in show business, then in publishing and selling music, and finally in real estate. On reaching middle age, after deciding to exchange commerce for politics, he was elected by the voters of New York to the House of Representatives. Here he rose steadily through the ranks, finally becoming chairman of the Committee on Foreign Affairs. He seemed to be an embodiment of the American success story, the self-made man who had climbed from rags to riches.

And yet he too was haunted by the insecurity afflicting so many other Jews. He recalled in his autobiography how on the evening of December 7, 1941, after the Japanese attack on Pearl Harbor, the president asked him to introduce a war resolution in the House of Representatives on the following day. He agreed. But as he was riding home and for hours afterward, he remained deeply troubled. The "honor of introducing the war resolution" seemed to him to carry "a responsibility of a peculiar sort." How would public opinion react to someone of his background, someone often described as a "Jewish warmonger," playing a highly visible role in the involvement of the nation in a life-and-death struggle? "I shrank from exposing the Jews of a future generation to the possible charge that this war had been set in notion by a Jew." After all, people full of hatred were irrational, ready to believe all sorts of suspicions, rumors, myths, and lies. "I thought about the followers of some unborn Hitler killing and torturing because the name of a Jew had been found on the declaration of a war that had been fought five hundred years before." As the United States was about to enter the Second World War, Bloom saw the specter of anti-Semitic riots and massacres centuries in the future.[14]

Especially when it came to dealing with the refugee problem, the leaders of the Jewish community were convinced of the need for caution and restraint. That was understandable. In opposing ethnic bigotry at home, they could at least claim to be defending the rights of all citizens, whatever their religion or background, rights guaranteed by the Constitution. But how could they justify efforts to persuade the government to assist the victims of ethnic persecution in foreign countries thousands of miles away by protesting to the rulers of those countries or by opening the doors of their own country to the victims? Even if they tried to defend such efforts by invoking democratic beliefs and principles, would that allay the suspicion that they were really more concerned about the fate of their coreligionists abroad than about the welfare of their countrymen at home? And would that not intensify the feelings of suspicion and resentment toward Jews that were already common in American society?

When Congressman Samuel Dickstein of New York, the Jewish chairman of the House Immigration Committee, introduced a resolution in the spring of 1934 calling for the investigation of "the extent, character and object of Nazi propaganda in the U.S. and the diffusion within the U.S. of Nazi propaganda," *Time* magazine chided him for trying to draw public attention to "the plight of members of his own race" in Central Europe. If he had his way, Congress would become a public forum in which "Nazis will be pilloried day after day," while timid souls in America would worry that "Chancellor Hitler is about to oust President Roosevelt." The House of Representatives, however, was less critical, approving the resolution by a solid majority of 168 to 31.[15]

Four years later, shortly after the Kristallnacht, Dickstein introduced a bill providing for an emergency quota for refugees of 120,000 annually, to be formed out of the unfilled portions of all regular quotas, thereby not increasing the total number of those eligible for admittance. This time the House of Representatives balked. Public opinion was now different from what it had been when Hitler came to power. Since then the situation of Jews in the Third Reich had become much worse, but the opposition to their admission to the United States had become much stronger. No amount of preaching or pleading could overcome that opposition. When after the Anschluss another Jewish congressman from New York, Emanuel Celler, proposed a temporary change in the quota system to deal with the new crisis confronting the Jewish community of Central Europe, he found no support in Congress. Indeed, some advocates of the refugee cause feared that to press too hard for a change in the immigration legislation might only strengthen the demand for a reduction in the existing quotas. Early in 1939, therefore, both bills, Celler's and Dickstein's, were withdrawn from consideration without coming to a vote.[16]

Those fears were not unfounded. Barely a month after the abandonment of the two proposals, Congress began hearings on a bill cosponsored by Senator Robert Reynolds of North Carolina and Representative Joe Starnes of Alabama. It was intended not only to limit the inflow of foreigners but to serve as a warning to those who were pushing for the admission of Jewish refugees. It provided for a reduction of all quotas by 90 percent, a halt to permanent immigration for ten years or until unemployment had fallen to 3 million, the fingerprinting and registration of all aliens, and the deportation of immigrants who were on public relief or whose presence in the United States was not in the public interest. The bill did not mention Jews specifically, but it clearly reflected not only economic concern but ethnic prejudice. Its sponsors made no effort to disguise their nativist sympathies. And while the measure failed to pass, it served the purpose of warning the proponents of the admission of refugees not to press their cause with too much zeal.[17]

Popular opposition to the admission of refugees had an effect on the White House as well. Roosevelt was generally sympathetic toward the victims of anti-Semitism in the Third Reich, and he was inclined to help them to the extent that political circumstances allowed. He knew, moreover, that the Jewish community ardently supported his administration and the New Deal, which in some circles was even labeled the "Jew Deal." But he was also a shrewd, practical politician who recognized that disregarding public opinion might cost him support at the polls. Like it or not, lofty ideals had to bow to, or at least compromise with, hard realities.

Harold Ickes left an account of a cabinet meeting in March 1938, a few days after the incorporation of Austria into Germany, at which it seemed clear that "the President thought we ought to make it as easy as possible for political refugees to come into this country, leaving it for future determination whether we could keep them here under the quota laws." Ickes himself thought it would be a "fine gesture" on the part of the United States to open its doors to "political" refugees, even if that meant a temporary amendment of the immigration laws. The nation might gain a "fine class of citizen," similar to the type who came after the revolution of 1848 in Europe. But Vice President John N. Garner had serious doubts. In his opinion, it would be impossible to amend the existing legislation. As a matter of fact, "if the matter were left to a secret vote of Congress, all immigration would be stopped." To Ickes, the thought that the United States would do nothing to help the victims of National Socialism was dismaying. "With men of ability and culture committing suicide in Austria, as the result of the annexation of that country by Germany, it seems terrible that our doors are closed." But most members of the cabinet and the president agreed with Garner that bringing the issue before Congress might only make the situation worse.[18]

In short, the growing danger faced by European Jews did nothing to weaken U.S. opposition to admitting more immigrants. Early in January 1940, James L. Houghteling, commissioner of the Immigration and Naturalization Service, reported to Roosevelt that during the previous year he had attended all the sessions of the Immigration Committees of the Senate and the House of Representatives. The experience had convinced him that "the tendency of a considerable part of Congress was toward the reduction of existing immigration quotas." This did not necessarily mean that the number of refugees entering the country was likely to diminish, but as for an increase in their admission, "the chance of any liberalizing legislation seemed negligible." Maintaining the status quo was the best that could be hoped for.[19]

Even Samuel I. Rosenman, the president's counsel and speechwriter, the son of a Jewish immigrant from Eastern Europe, thought that it would be "highly inadvisable" to urge an expansion of the immigration quotas. In a memorandum to Roosevelt in December 1938, he maintained that a modest rise in the number of refugees admitted "cannot scratch even the surface of the problem." And yet the high level of unemployment in the United States made it impossible to ask for much more, "even if guarantee is given against refugees becoming a public charge." Still, that was not the main reason for Rosenman's reluctance to press for a liberalization of the existing legislation. A proposal to that effect would undoubtedly arouse "opposition and debate" and would "delay any other comprehensive solution." Even if the quotas could be increased, which seemed unlikely, the result would be a "Jewish problem" in the countries granting the increase. What Rosenman meant was that a sudden influx of Jewish refugees would intensify ethnic tensions in the United States.

And that had to be avoided. What he recommended, therefore, was the establishment of a haven for the victims of persecution in a "new and undeveloped land" far from Europe and the United States, in Africa or South America, a place of refuge similar to that provided by the British colonies in the New World during the seventeenth century.[20]

Among many American Jews, the feeling that there was nothing they could do to help their coreligionist, that in fact they themselves were surrounded by a wall of suspicions, accusations, resentments, and prejudices, tended to create a mood of profound discouragement. To be sure, there could be no comparison between the brutal persecution of the Jewish community in the Third Reich and the ethnic aversions and discriminations common in the United States. And yet, might not those aversions and discriminations turn into persecution?

The sense of vulnerability, that "vast wave of worry" which Milton Steinberg saw as a constant reality of life for American Jews, did not dominate all of them, however. Some continued to believe that they should not yield to the forces of bigotry and discrimination, that they should resist and fight back. To them the most dangerous enemy was not the anti-Semite but the Jewish defeatist willing to acquiesce in his own subservience. An article in the weekly bulletin of the American Jewish Congress warned that "we have shown increasing signs of becoming spiritually and morally reconciled to accept this ghetto and almost voluntarily to surrender the positions won by the Emancipation." Yet nothing could be worse than meek surrender to the ethnic prejudice the Jews had been forced to endure for centuries. Were they now going to return willingly to the servility from which they had only recently freed themselves? "Our own depression and demoralization are immeasurably more dangerous to ourselves than the blows of our enemies." Their resolve to help refugees from the Third Reich was a measure of the extent to which American Jews were prepared to resist that depression and demoralization.[21]

The Jewish community was largely in agreement that the great enemy was the one within. Most of its members supported the campaign for the admission of persecuted Jews from Central Europe. A few, however, sought to avoid involvement in the bitter controversy regarding immigration barriers and quota restrictions. They were in most cases the culturally assimilated, economically successful, and socially established, the envy of their less fortunate coreligionists. But now they saw their favored status endangered. A few weeks after Hitler came to power, Henry Goldman, a former partner in the well-known banking firm Goldman, Sachs & Company and a longtime supporter of Germany, still maintained that the anti-Semitism of the Nazi regime was simply a new manifestation of a "nearly universal feeling." Hostility toward Jews was in fact no worse in the Third Reich than in the United States, "only different in form." Why, then, all the excitement about the recent change of government in Berlin? Soon afterward, however, when Goldman visited Germany, his humiliating treatment by the authorities of the new order convinced him that there really was a difference between ethnic prejudice in the Third Reich and in the United States. He returned home disappointed but wiser.[22]

Cyrus Adler, on the other hand, the distinguished scholar and educator, president of the Jewish Theological Seminary, had few illusions about the nature of National Socialism. He recognized from the outset that the hostility toward Jews in Germany was not the same as in America. Yet he too thought, at least at first, that a policy of watchful waiting by the Jewish community in the United States was preferable to a heated and contentious agitation. Too much protesting would merely draw greater public attention to the "Jewish question," probably arousing more distrust than sympathy. That was why he opposed the economic boycott of German goods which militant Jewish organizations launched soon after Hitler came to power. It would only alienate popular opinion in America without changing racist policy in Germany.

Writing in November 1933, Adler expressed concern that "there is too much public discussion [of Jewish issues] and we Jews are promoting too much of it and . . . it is not unlikely that our Christian fellow citizens will get tired of us." He feared that the anti-Semitic propaganda which National Socialism was spreading would be aided by "the constant airing of [the Jewish people's] wrongs and their sorrows and the showing of their sores [which are] wearying people and moreover are giving the impression that in the face of the difficulties and misery of the world they wish to put themselves forward as the only real problem." It would be better to lie low until the crisis had passed.[23]

More than a decade later, after the Second World War had been fought and won, after the Third Reich had been overthrown and its surviving leaders executed, Stephen Wise still could not bring himself to forgive those Jewish renegades who had pretended not to see the terrible tragedy that was about to befall their people. "It pains me as a Jew," he wrote in his autobiography, to report that while Roosevelt had from the beginning understood what was happening, "influences were at work to blur his vision and to confuse his understanding." Chief among those influences, "one is grieved to admit," were "some German Jews of status and wealth." Wise was referring to American Jews whose families had originally come from Germany. They had constantly tried to assure the president that things were "not as bad as Wise and others describe them." They claimed to be merely trying to counteract what they dismissed as "atrocity tales," but actually they were denying the "atrocious facts" of merciless persecution, which Roosevelt found very disturbing. To his dying day, Wise continued to condemn Baruch and Morgenthau and others like them for their deliberate disregard of the mortal danger confronting European Jewry.[24]

Still, the number and influence of those Jews who preferred to look the other way should not be overestimated. They constituted only a small fraction of the Jewish community in the United States. Most American Jews were determined to oppose ethnic prejudice vigorously, whether at home or abroad. But the question before them was, what strategy would be most effective? Here there was a clear division of opinion. A majority of the defenders of the refugee cause, the militants or activists, favored mass demonstrations and protests, a policy designed to make the public aware of the urgent need to provide asylum for the victims of ethnic bigotry in Europe. But to a significant minority, to the moderates or pragmatists, a head-on attack on the existing immigration restrictions seemed bound to fail. They therefore favored the tactics of compromise, negotiation, and circumvention.

This meant that the militants were the ones who organized mass meetings, marches, demonstrations, processions, and vigils designed to arouse national condemnation of the brutal racism in Europe, especially in the Third Reich. They were the ones who organized economic boycotts of goods imported from Germany and formed picket lines in front of German consulates or at the hotels in which visiting German dignitaries were staying. And they were also the ones who periodically sent large delegations to Washington to try to meet with important government officials, with congressmen and senators and even with the president himself, to plead for a more compassionate policy toward the refugees and a more forceful policy against the Nazi regime. Their goal was to focus the attention of the American people on the plight of world Jewry.

The moderates or pragmatists—the latter is probably the more appropriate term—followed a different strategy. They assumed, in most cases correctly, that mass demonstrations, while emotionally satisfying to the participants, were unlikely to have much practical effect. Public opinion was so strongly opposed to the admission of many more refugees that even sympathetic politicians were reluctant to press their cause too vigorously. That did not mean, however, that the cause itself was hopeless. It was still possible, if not to solve, then at least to alleviate the refugee problem without changing the existing legislation. Immigration officials could be urged to give special consideration to persecuted Jews within the established quotas and to fill those quotas up to the permitted limits. Refugees might be admitted as tourists, visitors, transients, or temporary workers with special qualifications. Once they were in the United States, efforts could be made to change their status to that of permanent residents. And if all else failed, American Jews should provide them with the financial support they needed to find asylum in one of the democracies of Western Europe. No single one of these alternatives nor all of them together could offer a perfect solution, yet they afforded some help, some relief, some hope. That was the best that could be achieved under existing circumstances. Even modest assistance was surely better than loud but futile protest.

The differences between the militants and the pragmatists were not only tactical and methodological; they were also social and cultural. The militants found most of their support among East European Jews, whose sense of ethnic loyalty or togetherness aroused outrage at the cruel persecution that their coreligionists in the old country had to endure. They felt a need to demonstrate, protest, and denounce the injustice with which European Jewry was being treated. The pragmatists, in contrast, belonged mostly to the Jewish elite, to those who had become accepted and established in American society. They were comfortable associating with Christian friends and acquaintances. Yet they still felt that it might be awkward or inappropriate to dwell on the differences in ethnic loyalties between them and the Gentiles in their social milieu. It would be in poor taste.

Their Jewishness was a topic that they and their non-Jewish associates preferred to avoid. If mentioning it became unavoidable, it was done tactfully and discreetly. There was a tacit agreement that the subject should be treated with delicacy.

This reticence, as well as an awareness of popular ethnic prejudice in the United States, convinced the pragmatic advocates of the refugee cause that they should minimize the fact that the great majority of those seeking asylum were Jews. It would be better to portray the doctrines and policies of National Socialism as a danger to all who disagreed with them, regardless of religion or ethnicity, whatever their political beliefs or civic loyalties. All of them were being threatened by a ruthless, tyrannical totalitarianism. The fate of the refugees was not a Jewish but a universal problem.

Felix Frankfurter, for example, maintained that it was "quite wrong" to view the opposition to the principles espoused by the Third Reich as primarily Jewish. "It falsifies the whole issue. Fundamentally the conflict is a conflict between reason and irrationality." He quoted with approval Justice Oliver Wendell Holmes's contention that "Germany has challenged civilization." That was precisely the point. "We on this side ought not to stultify the issue by reducing it to sectarian or racial dimensions." Stephen Wise made the same argument, but much more dramatically. "The horror of Nazi mistreatment of civilians should cease, whether of Jews, Protestants or Catholics, whether Poles, Czechs or Greeks," he wrote. "The greatest crime against the Jewish victims of Hitler would be to treat the crimes against the Jews differently from the treatment of crimes against French, or Czechs, or Poles, or Greeks." And in his memorandum to Roosevelt dealing with the refugee problem, Samuel Rosenman explained that his proposal to establish an asylum in some "new and undeveloped land . . . should not be restricted to Jews." On the contrary, "other persecuted or unwanted minorities should be included, e.g. Catholics, Russian, Czech, Spanish refugees." The goal was to create a haven "for all victims of persecution," whatever their faith or nationality.[25]

This tendency to deemphasize the ethnic dimension of the refugee problem, to underscore its breadth and inclusiveness, can even be seen in the names of various organizations formed to assist the victims of persecution and in the language used to describe their activities. The President's Advisory Committee on Political Refugees, established in 1938, avoided in its title any reference to the ethnicity of most of those "political" refugees. Similarly, the name of the Non-Sectarian Committee for German Refugee Children, formed to gain support for the 1939 bill to admit 20,000 underage refugees, sought to transcend the ethnic and religious boundaries of the refugee problem as well, although it failed to overcome popular and congressional suspicions regarding any proposal for a relaxation of the immigration laws.

The attempt to universalize the refugee cause was also apparent in the recruitment of sympathetic Gentiles for leading positions in the campaign to aid the victims of Nazi persecution. The bill to admit the children from the Third Reich was introduced not by one of the Jewish members of Congress but by Senator Wagner and Representative Rogers, both of them sympathetic toward the refugees, both of them representing large Jewish communities, and both of them Christian. The cochairmen of the Non-Sectarian Committee for German Refugee Children included George Cardinal Mundelein, Canon Anson Phelps Stokes, Governor Herbert Lehman of New York, the publicist and author William Allen White, and the industrialist Owen D. Young. The executive director was Clarence Pickett of the American Friends Service Committee, while the treasurer was Newbold Morris. Among other distinguished members were Helen Taft Manning, Frank P. Graham, Samuel McCrae Cavert, Harry Emerson Fosdick, Paul Kellogg, Frank Knox, Alfred Landon, William Allen Neilson, Justine Wise Polier, Cecelia Razovsky, and George Rublee. Jews made up less than a fifth of the leadership. How, then, could anyone accuse the committee of being just another self-interested Jewish organization?[26]

As a last resort, some pragmatists proposed to solve the refugee problem through the resettlement of the victims of ethnic persecution in distant and thinly populated parts of the globe. The best known was the one advanced by Samuel Rosenman, who urged the president to help create an asylum in Africa or South America. But toward the end of the 1930s, as the situation of European Jewry became increasingly precarious, plans to relocate refugees in remote regions began to multiply. They included the establishment of asylums in the Philippines, Alaska, Lower California, Australia, the Dominican Republic, and similar areas, spacious and far away and too weak to resist the pressure of the Western democracies. At the same time projects for the exportation of the refugee problem were also being recommended by various non-Jewish organizations as the best or only solution to the crisis.[27]

To most American Jews, however—to the pragmatists as well as the militants—a policy that amounted to the banishment of the victims of ethnic persecution was unacceptable. It meant that the innocent were to be punished for the crimes of the guilty. On this point Stephen Wise, whose devotion to principle was not always unbending, remained adamant. The expulsion by the Third Reich of the Jews who had been "rooted in Germany's soil" for a thousand years was "one of the most loathsome crimes of history," he maintained. The international Jewish community should not meekly yield to humiliation and oppression. "Not being a race of beggars, though we are wanderers, we must make clear to the world that we are resolved that we are not to become, nor to be dealt with, as *a refugee people*." Jews must never submit to exile to distant and isolated outposts of Western civilization. The only acceptable places of refuge were "the lands in which they have lived for centuries and millennia." Wise concluded his statement of principle with a defiant peroration. "We raise our voice today against every proposal and program which deals with Jewish migrants or exiles as if they were to be further penalized by being settled in uninhabited lands, lands of doubtful title, lands of uncertain capacity for colonization and resettlement." On this point there could be no compromise.[28]

His eloquence was moving but superfluous. Although some refugees emigrated to Australia, Mexico, and the Dominican Republic in the late 1930s, most of them moved again as soon as they could find a more congenial asylum. The majority of those trying to escape the Third Reich found refuge without great difficulty in Western Europe or North America, at least until the Kristallnacht, after which the number of refugees rapidly began to multiply. But even then it was still possible for many of those trying to leave Central Europe to find a haven in one of the democratic states on either side of the Atlantic. It was the outbreak of war ten months later that finally shut tight the doors to emigration from the Third Reich and the succession states to the east. That was when the problem of finding refuge for European Jews became transformed into the problem of insuring their survival.

The role of the United States in dealing with the refugee crisis has been the subject of a long and heated debate. There is first of all the undeniable fact that American public opinion remained firmly opposed to any rise in the number of immigrants admitted to the country, even as it became increasingly clear that European Jewry was in mortal danger. Then there is the contention that even though the United States accepted far more refugees than any other nation, some governments were, taking into account territorial extent and economic resources, more generous and compassionate. And finally, there are the troubling statistics showing that in no year before 1939 were the immigration quotas for Germany and Austria completely filled. Does not all of this suggest the ineffectualness of a hush-hush strategy, the strategy of circumspection and unobtrusiveness that the moderate leaders of the Jewish community in the United States adopted?

10

Scylla, Charybdis, and Washington, D.C.

W HAT FINALLY LED to the United States' abandonment of strict neutrality was not the Nazi regime's growing suppression of political dissent or the intensification of its anti-Semitic program. The chief reason was the unexpected change in the configuration of the diplomacy of Europe. In the first few years, the Hitler government had devoted its foreign policy to removing the military restrictions imposed on Germany at Versailles. That goal had been achieved without great difficulty. Amid the economic hardships and social tensions of the Great Depression, it did not seem to matter much that the Third Reich had reintroduced general conscription or sent its troops into the Rhineland in violation of the peace treaty. But more troubling was the conclusion in the fall of 1936 of an informal alliance between the two leading revisionist states, the Rome-Berlin Axis, committed to a complete rejection of the postwar settlement. A duality of power now replaced the hegemony of the West European democracies, particularly France, as two camps divided by ideological differences and territorial disputes began to threaten each other with the danger of a military conflict. On both sides of the Atlantic, complacency over the stability of the international order gradually gave way to a growing concern.

It was Hitler's strategy of territorial expansion through the exploitation of the fear of war that finally led the American government to abandon its policy of noninvolvement in European affairs. In the course of a single year, from March 1938 to March 1939, the Third Reich succeeded in incorporating Austria, annexing the Sudeten region, and destroying Czechoslo-vakia, all without a single military casualty. The balance of power on the continent was clearly shifting from France and England to Germany and Italy, especially Germany. To make matters worse, a momentous change was also taking place on the other side of the globe. In July 1937, Japan embarked on an undeclared war against China, which threatened to alter the balance of power in the Far East. The Great Depression, by under-mining the economic foundation of the status quo, had opened the way for a powerful movement to alter the existing structure of international relations. For the United States, this meant that the favorable diplomatic environment in which it had achieved the rank of one of the great pow-ers was now being threatened. The American government had reached a modus vivendi, an informal but comfortable understanding with the leading democracies of Western Europe. Could it feel equally secure in a world dominated by authoritarian, ambitious, and aggressive newcomers on the international scene?

This concern led the United States to take the first hesitant steps away from the policy of nonintervention. Ideological opposition to totalitar-ian oppression and moral rejection of ethnic bigotry played only a minor role. The big question was, what would be the situation of the United States in a world dominated by revisionist states like Germany, Italy, and Japan? Wouldn't the nation be isolated and perpetually on the defensive? And wasn't there also the danger of foreign infiltration and subversion? The Third Reich was already promoting the spread of National Socialism in other countries, not only among German immigrants but also among native-born conservatives and ultranationalists. It had even won a small but growing following in the United States. Could the American govern-ment afford to ignore this danger?

Such considerations persuaded Roosevelt to consider a new policy of "collective security." Americans were becoming increasingly alarmed by the successful aggression of the revisionist states. Besides, to express disap-proval of that aggression did not seem very risky. There was a widespread assumption in America, by the government as well as the public at large, that the expansionist ambitions of the Axis could be checked by France and England, once they found the will to take a firm stand. Thus, voicing support for the West European democracies would not create a danger for America. It would simply help deter the designs of Germany, Italy, and Japan without involving the United States in a military confrontation with those international bullies.

These calculations were behind Roosevelt's address of October 5, 1937, urging a "quarantine" of the aggressors who were threatening the "health of the community." He was careful not to mention by name the countries that were to be quarantined, although it was quite clear whom he meant. He made it a point to emphasize that he was not advocating the use of force against those states; his purpose was simply to help maintain security and tranquillity in a world being torn apart by economic hardships and diplomatic quarrels. "If civilization is to survive, the principles of the Prince of Peace must be restored," he declared. "Trust between nations must be revived." And if that meant that the nations opposed to aggression would have to adopt a policy of "collective security," so be it. Roosevelt concluded his speech, however, with a reaffirmation of his resolve to avoid the use of force in international affairs. "America hates war," he proclaimed. "America hopes for peace." And for that reason and that reason alone, "America actively engages in the search for peace." He was trying not only to encourage the West European democracies to resist Axis aggression but also to reassure his fellow Americans that the mistakes of twenty years earlier would not be repeated.[1]

Yet neither the West European democracies nor Roosevelt's own countrymen were entirely convinced. The governments of France and England feared, not without cause, that the burden of imposing and maintaining a "quarantine" of the Axis would fall on them and them alone. The risk of provoking a war would also be entirely theirs. America might offer moral support, praise, and encouragement, but they would be the ones doing the fighting. They decided therefore to adopt a strategy of what was disparagingly described on the other side of the Atlantic as "appeasement." They agreed to acquiesce in Hitler's expansionist program as long as it remained confined to territories inhabited by a German-speaking population willing to become part of the Third Reich.

Accordingly, they accepted, though not without considerable uneasiness, Germany's acquisition of Austria and the Sudeten region. But when in the spring of 1939 Hitler partitioned Czechoslovakia, annexing most of it against the unanimous will of the Czechs, France and England were forced to admit the failure of their policy. They announced that they would resist, by military means if necessary, the Third Reich's anticipated attempt to force Poland to cede parts of West Prussia and the province of Posen. The outbreak of war had now become almost inevitable.

This new militant stand of the West European democracies was welcomed in the United States. There was a general assumption by the American public that the military capabilities of France and England far exceeded those of the Third Reich, which had embarked on a program of rearmament only a few years earlier. What had been lacking was a resolve to defend the established international order, to resist the threat of aggression. But now that the Western European democracies had finally decided to stand up to those Axis bullies, something they should have done long ago, the outcome was not in doubt. The cause of freedom and justice would prevail. This conviction remained unshaken throughout the months leading up to the outbreak of hostilities. Not even the conquest of Poland by the German army in the first few weeks of the war weakened the general belief in the United States that sooner or later the Allies were bound to win. Confidence in the eventual victory of the French and British remained firm, moreover, throughout the period of the "phony war," the stalemate on the western front that followed the swift success of the Wehrmacht in the east. Only the extraordinary victories of the Third Reich during the spring of 1940 finally shattered the comforting illusions in the United States about the likely outcome of the war.

But by then the struggle seemed to be almost over. Admittedly, Great Britain remained determined to resist Hitler to the end. But how long would a besieged, isolated country be able to hold out against overwhelming odds? Clearly, only the involvement of the United States could prevent a total victory by the Third Reich. And so, between the middle of 1940 and the end of 1941, the American role changed from that of a sympathetic neutral to an unofficial but active belligerent. To begin with, there was the introduction of the first peacetime conscription in the nation's history. Then came legislation authorizing the president to lend or sell war supplies to any country whose security was "vital to the defense of the United States." A few months later, American troops landed in Iceland to help protect the island against the threat of invasion by the Axis. And a few months after that, Roosevelt ordered American warships to attack German submarines "on sight." Right up to the Japanese bombing of Pearl Harbor, the United States continued to maintain an official neutrality, but in fact it had become a major participant in the armed conflict long before.

The growing American involvement in the war not only led to an increase in the country's military strength and activity; it also initiated an ideological campaign designed to reinforce the strategic and geopolitical arguments in favor of resistance to the Axis. To maintain that a victory of the aggressor states in Europe and Asia would be a threat to the security of the United States no longer seemed enough. The public had to be made aware of the moral dimension of the struggle. It had to perceive the danger threatening democratic ideals and the need to defend those ideals, whatever the cost. And that meant a clear condemnation of the principles of the oppressive authoritarianism embraced by those on the other side. It meant an unequivocal rejection of their demand for unquestioning obedience, conformity, and submission. But more than that, the American people had to be made aware of the brutality with which the totalitarian regimes treated those of a different ethnic or cultural or ideological background. The struggle against the Axis was not being waged in defense of any one nation's welfare and security. It was a struggle to protect all peoples, regardless of their race or faith or nationality. Its ultimate justification embraced mankind as a whole.

Those directing this war of principles and ideals supported their arguments with concrete examples of Axis oppression. They had no difficulty providing evidence of the harsh treatment endured by the peoples conquered by the armies of the Third Reich: first the Czechs, then the Poles, then the Danes, Norwegians, Belgians, Dutch, and French, then the Serbs and the Greeks, and finally the Russians. With each successive victory of the Wehrmacht there were new stories of oppression and brutality, some exaggerated, a few manufactured, yet most reasonably accurate. But what about the earliest victims of the racist doctrines of National Socialism, the Jews? Here the strategists of the ideological war against the Axis faced a dilemma. They could not simply ignore the ethnic community that had been the first to experience the brutality of the Hitler regime and that continued to suffer a crueler oppression than any other people under its domination. Still, to focus too much attention on the crisis confronting

European Jewry might make those rumors about the behind-the-scenes Jewish influence in American politics more credible. It would therefore be best to include the Jews in the long list of victims of Nazi bigotry, but to do so unobtrusively, without too much emphasis, treating them as a people suffering no less but also no more than other peoples under German domination.

This approach won the tacit approval of the American government and of the president himself. Roosevelt was fully aware of what was happening on the other side of the Atlantic. He knew of the mortal danger threatening European Jewry, especially after the outbreak of war, and he was certainly not indifferent to it. But he also knew that ethnic prejudice was a serious problem at home as well as abroad. He recognized that Jews were among his most ardent supporters, and he rewarded their loyalty by appointing more of them to important positions in the government than any previous president had. He was too astute a politician, however, to risk his chances of remaining in office by appearing overly sympathetic toward Jewish concerns and interests. After all, if he lost the next election, the Jews too would be worse off. His successor as president, whoever it might be, would not in all likelihood prove as favorable to them. It was therefore in everyone's interests not to appear too generous in dealing with the Jewish community.

This circumspection or wariness regarding the danger of arousing popular ethnic prejudice appears time and again in Roosevelt's private conversations and confidential discussions. In the spring of 1938, Harold Ickes described in his diary a meeting with the president in which "I suggested to him the appointment of [Benjamin V.] Cohen as Under Secretary of the Treasury, where there will soon be a vacancy on account of the resignation of Roswell Magill." But Roosevelt hesitated. He said that Cohen "would be a good man but he questioned the wisdom of appointing a Jew under [Secretary of the Treasury Henry] Morgenthau," also a Jew. How would it look to have two Jews in charge of the financial affairs of the American government? Would it not be risky? Whatever the reason, Cohen did not get the job.[2]

The outbreak of war in Europe a year later made it even more difficult for Roosevelt to balance democratic ideals with political realities. The psychological tensions created by the military conflict increased the ethnic suspicions and hostilities of the Nazi regime. The refugee problem became even more urgent than before, and the American government found itself facing growing demands to provide asylum for the victims of European anti-Semitism, not only from the Jewish community but also from various liberal and charitable non-Jewish organizations. The opponents of a relaxation of the restrictions on immigration, however, became louder and more assertive as well. They knew that the victories of the Wehrmacht would increase the pleas for the admission of Jewish refugees to the United States, and they were determined to resist those pleas with unbending resolve. Roosevelt thus faced a dilemma that confronted him with increasing urgency. He decided to adopt a strategy of zigzagging, moving first in one direction, then in the other, without going too far in either. This remained essentially his policy for the rest of his administration.

Two months after the war began, Ickes had a meeting with the president, who advanced the idea of admitting 10,000 settlers annually to Alaska for a period of five years. Half of them would be from the United States, "and those from foreign lands would be admitted in the same ratio in which they can come into the country, based upon the quota law." He estimated that under this arrangement, "not more than ten per cent would be Jews, and thus we would be able to avoid the undoubted criticism that we would be subjected to if there were an undue proportion of Jews." Another reason for maintaining the quota system, according to Roosevelt, was that "a preponderating number of settlers would not come from one foreign country, thus avoiding the danger of setting up in Alaska nationalistic groups that, through adherence to their own language and customs, might resist the process of Americanization." Ickes was impressed by his chief's diligence and skill in dealing with a difficult issue, especially by "the thought that the President had given to a comparatively minor problem, from his point of view, and his cleverness in working it out." Roosevelt was clearly trying to offer some assistance to the refugees, but not too much, given the inescapable realities of the political situation.[3]

Ickes adopted a similar strategy. One of the most liberal members of the cabinet, an avowed opponent of anti-Semitism, he often criticized, at least in private, what he considered to be the timidity of the leaders of the Jewish community in opposing ethnic prejudice. But in his official capacity as secretary of the interior, he was just as cautious and circumspect, and for the same reason. To appear too sympathetic toward Jews, too willing to defend their rights as American citizens, might lend support to the charge that the New Deal was controlled by Jewish wealth and influence. It might backfire; it might prove self-defeating. The best policy was to back and fill, depending on the circumstances—to retreat in minor controversies while standing firm on major issues, to avoid the appearance of an ideologue and assume the role of a moderate, flexible liberal. The middle of the road was the wisest course.

Late in the fall of 1941, only a few weeks before the attack on Pearl Harbor, Roosevelt described at a cabinet meeting a letter he had recently received from a friend in Portland, Oregon, "who complained about some Jews on the Bonneville [Dam] staff without mentioning them." The president was not surprised by the complaint. He said that "Portland was a transplanted Maine city where Jews were not popular." Ickes was not surprised either. "I have known [all] this and have tried to keep Jewish employees down in that area." Not that the ethnic prejudice displayed by some of the residents of Portland seemed to him justified. "I am not conscious that there are enough [Jews there] to warrant objection." But there were times when popular biases and preconceptions, even if unfair, had to be appeased.[4]

A reluctance to challenge anti-Semitic prejudice was also apparent in the debates within the government concerning the refugee problem, particularly after the war began. The United States had by then become the only major country still able to offer asylum to Jews trying to escape German persecution. But this raised the prospect of a flood of impoverished refugees pouring in year after year across the nation's borders. And that was sure to arouse a storm of protest, not only against lowering the barriers to immigration but also against the politicians who seemed to support it. The danger could not be ignored. Even James G. MacDonald, who had a few years earlier served as the League of Nations' high commissioner for refugees from Germany, warned Roosevelt soon after the outbreak of hostilities in 1939 that "the injection of the problem of German refugees who are considered by the public to be predominantly Jewish" could prove risky. "Anti-Semitic spokesmen may capitalize this opportunity to accuse Jewish circles of a desire to involve the Government at a time of national emergency."[5]

Most of the leaders of the American Jewish community were as cautious as Roosevelt and his political advisers. They grieved over and sympathized with their oppressed coreligionists in the Old World. They tried to help them by raising funds for refugees who had found a temporary and precarious asylum in one of the neutral states of Europe. They pleaded with American consular officials to be more generous in granting visas to those seeking to escape ethnic persecution. But they too were afraid of aggravating anti-Semitism in the United States by displaying too much concern for fellow Jews in Europe. Even if they succeeded in persuading the government to admit more victims of Nazi oppression than the existing immigration laws allowed, wouldn't that jeopardize Roosevelt's chances in the approaching presidential election? And if he were defeated, how likely was it that his successor would be equally sympathetic toward the Jewish community in America or in Europe?

Even Stephen Wise, usually so proud of his boldness and outspokenness in Jewish affairs, admitted in a private letter in September 1940 that it would be best for all concerned not to press the refugee cause too hard. He felt that "we are in the midst of the most difficult situation, an almost unmanageable quandary." The State Department was making "all sorts of promises" and accepting lists of people in Europe who were in danger because of the recent victories of the German armies. But at the same time, reports from unofficial sources asserted that the American consuls were doing nothing. There was in fact a suspicion that the consuls were acting on private instructions from the State Department to do nothing, "which would be infamous beyond words." He surmised that behind this dissimulation was "the fear of the Skipper's [Roosevelt's] friends in the State Department that any large admission of radicals to the United States might be used effectively in the [presidential election] campaign." The word "radicals," as used by Wise in this context, was clearly a synonym or euphemism for Jews. He was therefore prepared, "cruel as I may seem," to accept the lesser of two evils. "[Roosevelt's] re-election is much more important for everything that is worthwhile and that counts than the admission of a few people, however imminent be their peril." He too felt that lofty principle had to be subordinated to cruel reality.[6]

The most vocal and persistent advocates of the refugee cause were not government officials or Jewish leaders but a group of liberal intellectuals—

journalists, publicists, writers, and academics, the great majority of them Gentiles—for whom the conflict in which the United States was becoming involved had an ideological significance greater even than its strategic or geopolitical importance. Not that they were unaware of the effect an Axis victory would have on the international balance of power. But they remained convinced that the first concern of their country should be the defense of the democratic ideals of freedom and justice against the challenge of authoritarian oppression and bigotry. And that in turn meant that America should offer protection and asylum to those who were the first and most pitiable victims of totalitarian brutality. A failure to do so would be a betrayal of the principles justifying the U.S. participation in the struggle against National Socialism.

These ideological advocates of the refugee cause were not in most cases Judeophiles; that is, they were not chiefly concerned with specifically Jewish interests or problems. They supported persecuted Jews because persecuted Jews were living proof of the fundamental evil of totalitarianism. Totalitarianism, however, was not directed primarily against any particular ethnic minority or national community. It was universal in scope; it threatened every country and society that dared oppose it; it was a menace to all of humanity. To emphasize its cruelty toward any one of its many victims would be a mistake. That was why the supporters of the asylum seekers tried to avoid identifying them as Jews. They preferred to describe them as "political refugees" or "anti-fascists," although occasionally they would also speak of persecution fed by the "seeds of anti-Semitism." The words "Jew" and "Jewish" appeared only rarely in their discourse. For one thing, those words might arouse popular suspicion over the source of the agitation for a change in immigration policy. And besides, too much attention to any one of the many victims of the Third Reich might make a recognition of the full extent of its brutality more difficult.

Those favoring an increase in the number of refugees admitted to the United States directed their criticism chiefly at the government authorities who seemed reluctant to support a relaxation of the immigration laws. The president was never included in the charges and accusations directed against officials in Washington. The advocates of the refugee cause were in fact almost unanimously in favor of Roosevelt and the New Deal. Members of the cabinet were also generally exempt from their criticism. Their main targets were officials of the State Department who were responsible for enforcing the laws, who were perceived as villains in the seemingly endless succession of problems, obstacles, delays, and technicalities that those trying to escape the tyranny of the Third Reich had to face.

Freda Kirchwey, editor of the *Nation*, wrote late in December 1940 that the State Department's attitude toward the refugee problem was "shocking." It revealed "the profound failure of leading officials of the department to understand even the elements of the conflict in which the United States is inextricably engaged." Was not the preservation of democracy at the very heart of that conflict? And if so, "surely the leaders of democratic thought and action in Europe will not be deliberately sacrificed to their— and our—fascist opponents." A firm resolve to help protect the defenders of freedom should determine every act of every official responsible for the conduct of the nation's foreign affairs.

"Instead, what do we find?" Kirchwey had been deeply troubled to learn that the State Department was appointing a new committee to supervise the admission of "political refugees." If that were really a way to straighten out "the vast tangle of conflicting jurisdictions and rulings" in which all efforts were at present bogged down, it would be a welcome change. But there was reason to fear that the only result would be "a new and far more reactionary committee" added to the official organizations already dealing with the problem. "It is difficult to believe that the President himself would knowingly countenance such a change." The danger was that a disastrous result might emerge from a plan advanced under the guise of a well-intentioned reorganization. "Beware of State Department officials bearing reforms!"[7]

Six months later, in July 1941, Kirchwey renewed her criticism of the State Department. Its officials had recently succeeded in arranging the release of twenty-one young Americans, among them her own son, who had served as ambulance drivers with the Free French forces and had been taken prisoner by the Wehrmacht. In exchange, Washington had agreed to allow German nationals in the United States to return to their homeland. Kirchwey was grateful and relieved. And yet she was also troubled by "less pleasant emotions." There was an "ugly" contrast between the resolve of the American government to rescue a few of its citizens who were captives of the Third Reich and its indifference to the fate of foreigners exposed to even greater danger. "The very assiduity which the officials of the [State] department applied to the task of freeing the Americans from the clutches of the Gestapo and bringing them home throws into relief the equal zeal with which those same officials, or their colleagues, apply themselves daily to the effort to prevent non-Americans from escaping the clutches of the Gestapo and finding safety and freedom in this country." Even a relieved mother could not overcome the feeling that those engaged in the defense of democracy throughout the world should rise above a narrow, self-centered nationalism.

Kirchwey reminded her readers that there were thousands of men and women in Europe, especially in Germany and the countries occupied by Germany, but some also in North Africa, for whom escape from Hitler's "prison-continent" was a matter of life or almost certain death. Most of them were clinging to the hope that they might eventually obtain a visa to the United States, their only guarantee of safety. But no more than a few could qualify for "that most precious and elusive document." Why? Because "the requirements of the State Department, especially in the case of political refugees, have been exacting to the point of almost total exclusion." Only a very thin trickle of "proved safe and respectable anti-fascists" had been able to pass through the "fine-meshed sieve of affidavits and investigations." And now a new barrier had been raised, an order issued a few weeks earlier excluding all applicants for admission who had close relatives in the Third Reich or in countries under the rule of the Third Reich. The ostensible reason was that those applicants might be blackmailed into becoming agents for the Hitler regime in order to save their kinsmen who had been left behind. But to Kirchwey, that explanation was simply a "canard." It had been invented to help disguise "one of the most shocking administrative rulings" ever issued by "our most reactionary department." It had to be rescinded. If not, "the doors of the United States may be considered locked not only against the 'huddled masses yearning to breathe free' but against the desperately endangered few who seek asylum in this ungenerous land." And that would be a betrayal of all the ideals and principles the nation was determined to defend.[8]

To Kirchwey, the chief villains in the tragic mishandling of the refugee problem were the bureaucrats in Washington. But to another writer for the *Nation*, the chief villains were the American consular officials in

Europe. Varian Fry had been a representative of the Emergency Rescue Committee stationed in Marseilles until the Vichy government expelled him from France in the fall of 1941. The following year, after the United States had entered the war, he published an article containing brief sketches, some of them excerpts from a diary, that illustrated the prejudices and antipathies which members of the American consular service allegedly displayed in dealing with the refugee problem. It was a bitter indictment of bureaucratic indifference and insensitivity in the face of an unparalleled human tragedy.

An entry written in Lisbon in August 1940, for example, contrasted the difference in the treatment of two applicants for the renewal of a visa to the United States. One was Elsa Schiaparelli, the well-known fashion designer, whose request was immediately granted by the consulate, so that she was able to sail for America on the next available ship. The other applicant was the sister of a prominent French Popular Front leader. It took her six weeks to get her visa renewed, although she had come to Lisbon on the same day as Schiaparelli. The vice consul wanted her to produce one document after another, first an affidavit that she had a permanent residence in the unoccupied zone of France, then a *certificat de bonne vie et moeurs* proving that she was not a prostitute, and finally a transcript of her police record, if there was one. The requirements and interrogations dragged on for so long that she gave up hope and approached the Cuban consulate for help in emigrating from Europe. When she finally did receive the renewal of her visa to the United States, she asked the vice consul why the process had taken so much longer in her case than in Schiaparelli's. His answer, at least as reported by Fry, was, "Oh, Schiaparelli will make millions in the United States."⁹

Another entry, this one in Marseilles in May 1941, described Fry's visit to the American vice consul there for the purpose of obtaining a visa for Francisco Largo Caballero, the socialist trade union leader and former prime minister of Spain. The vice consul had never heard of him. "Who's Caballero?" he asked. When told that he had been head of the Spanish government, he seemed unimpressed. "Oh, one of those reds." And when Fry assured him that Caballero had in fact been a bitter opponent of the Communists, he simply shrugged. "Well, it doesn't make any difference to me what his politics are. If he had any political views at all, we don't want him. We don't want any agitators in the United States. We've got too many of them already." The request for a visa was denied, and soon afterward Caballero was arrested by the Germans.[10]

While the *Nation* was inclined to blame bureaucratic conservatism and prejudice against foreigners, the *New Republic*, another defender of the refugee cause, pointed accusingly at ethnic prejudice, especially anti-Semitism, among the officials of the State Department. It did not deny the importance of ideological fears and suspicions, but it also emphasized distrust of Jews as a significant factor in the exclusionist views of at least some government officials at home and abroad. The charge of bigotry appeared over and over again in its analysis of the refugee problem.

At the same time that Freda Kirchwey was condemning the bureaucratic obstacles to the admission of "political refugees" who were "antifascists" and Varian Fry was deploring the denial of a visa to Largo Caballero because he was a socialist, Alfred Wagg described in the *New Republic* the Third Reich's "coldly calculated strategy" of dumping "scared, destitute human beings in great numbers across frontiers or the ocean." One of the objectives of this "clever German strategy" was "to arouse . . . in the camp of Hitler's enemies racial and religious hatreds." Unfortunately, the Nazi propaganda was proving successful. "It reaches high places in many governments including our own, places where the wish is father to the thought, and where the seeds of anti-Semitism and anti-liberalism are already sprouting." The forbidden word had finally been uttered; "anti-Semitism" was out of the bag. Those bigots in Washington and the consular offices could now be openly attacked.[11]

The *New Republic* became progressively bolder in its denunciation of the ethnic prejudices of government immigration officials. In an editorial appearing on June 23, 1941, it claimed that "there is solid evidence that some of the men in the State Department . . . are by their own profound convictions pro-Nazi or pro-Fascist." Worse still, "some of them have been charged, with formidable evidence, of anti-Semitism, of deliberately making more difficult the removal of refugees from Europe." How could people who behaved in such a reprehensible way be entrusted with the conduct of the nation's foreign affairs?[12]

A week later, on June 30, there was another editorial, this one dealing with the "anti-democratic, pro-Fascist action" of the American government in excluding refugees from Germany who still had close relatives there. The explanation that these refugees might be blackmailed was unconvincing. "The new rule is unnecessary on any practical basis." Its only effect would be to throw into despair the many thousands who had already received tentative permission to enter the United States. And to make matters worse, "there will be many people all over the world who will believe that the motive for this action comes not from genuine concern about Nazi spies but from the same little nest of anti-Semites and anti-democrats in the State Department who have in the past done so much to muddy the waters of our democratic efforts." The *New Republic* shared that belief.[13]

The following month there was still another condemnation of those "State Department appeasers" who were betraying the nation's tradition of compassion and support for the oppressed of the world. Admittedly, not all government officials were guilty. Some had displayed the good sense and sound judgment expected of civil servants holding important positions. But others were bigoted and blind to the responsibilities of their office. "Anti-democratic actions have come conspicuously from the visa division [which] has actively sabotaged the President's Advisory Committee on Political Refugees [trying] to rescue outstanding anti-Fascists from Europe." The members of the committee, however, were not the only ones to encounter the exclusionist schemes and machinations of some officials in the State Department. "Everyone else who has tried to aid the refugees has had a similar experience." It was common gossip in Washington that "there is widespread anti-Semitism in the foreign service." Indeed, "[some] consuls in Europe . . . have repeatedly been charged with putting difficulties in the way of Jews seeking American visas." These accusations of ethnic prejudice continued to grow and intensify, and the identity of its victims became increasingly explicit, changing from "political refugees" to targets of "anti-Semitism" and finally to "Jews seeking American visas."[14]

Could charges of prejudice in the State Department have been exaggerated? Could the defenders of the refugee cause, involved emotionally as well as ideologically in the effort to rescue the victims of the Third Reich's racism, have perceived plots and conspiracies where there was only an excessive bureaucratic observance of regulations? Is it not likely, moreover, that the refugees themselves, desperate to escape persecution, were inclined to suspect that their difficulty in obtaining those lifesaving visas to the United States was the result of a calculated effort by consular officials to exclude them? In the end, many of them—probably most, in fact—did manage in one way or another to find asylum in the New World. The case of Caballero, who ended up in Dachau, was seemingly an exception, not the rule.

Varian Fry described a meeting in New York in December 1941 with a consul recently stationed in Europe but now without an assignment, who enumerated the shortcomings of the former members of his staff, portraying them as often incompetent yet not particularly bigoted or reactionary. There was "old C—," for example, "good-natured but lazy as they make them. He hated nothing as much as work." Then there was W—, "a little old maid, fussy and petty. I could never get him to take responsibility for anything." T— "drank too much and ran up debts. He used to come into the office drunk almost every afternoon." P—, on the other hand, "was a faithful work horse, slow but steady. He'll never advance in the service, and he knows it." As for R—, he was "a flighty youngster, undependable." All in all, "I didn't have much support, did I?" After a sip from his glass of beer, the consul recalled a visit to his office by H— G—, the American chargé d'affaires. Having looked the staff over, he observed, "Well, Frank, you've certainly got a cross-section of the American Foreign Service here." The comment was not meant as a compliment.[15]

Yet even if the charges were exaggerated, they were not entirely baseless. There was in fact some anti-Semitism among the government officials dealing with the refugee problem—no more than in most circles of middle-class American society, but no less, either. And that common ethnic prejudice accounted, at least in part, for the delays and obstacles that many of the Jews trying to gain admittance to the United States encountered. It was not the main reason that the bulk of European Jewry, trying at any cost to escape the rule of the Third Reich, could not find asylum. But it contributed to the mental anguish and physical hardship the refugees often had to endure. In some cases it even led to their imprisonment and death.

Varian Fry, although usually reluctant to accuse consular officials of outright anti-Semitism, described a few incidents that were bound to arouse suspicion of bureaucratic prejudice. In Lisbon in August 1940, for instance, he submitted to the American vice consul in charge of visas a list of refugees who, in his opinion, should be admitted to the United States. One of the first names was that of Lion Feuchtwanger, the well-known author, whose writings frequently dealt with Jewish experiences and problems. In 1933, Feuchtwanger had decided to escape Nazi oppression by leaving Germany for France, and now, facing the same danger, he wanted to emigrate once again, this time from France to the United States. The vice consul, however, would not hear of it. "If that man should come to me and ask for a visa," he told Fry, "I'd refuse it. He put on a regular song and dance about the Soviet Union a few years ago. We don't want his kind in the United States." It was not clear exactly whom the vice consul meant by "his kind," but in any case, the story had a more or less happy ending. Although Feuchtwanger did spend a few months in a concentration camp, by the end of the year he had succeeded in crossing the Atlantic.[16]

Another incident described by Fry, also in Lisbon in the summer of 1940, seems less ambiguous. A German rabbi who had obtained an immigration visa in Berlin three months earlier was unable to leave Germany for several weeks and could not therefore book passage from Lisbon to New York before his visa expired. But the vice consul would not hear of an extension. He clung to the letter of the law, insisting that the visa would cease to be valid a few hours before the rabbi's ship was scheduled to sail. The rabbi would have to wait while the consulate in Lisbon obtained his dossier from the consulate in Berlin. It took three months for the visa to be renewed—three months during which the rabbi wondered anxiously whether he would still be able to leave for America or whether he would have to return to the Third Reich. After all, he was not Elsa Schiaparelli.[17]

While the significance of some of the incidents described by Fry may be questionable, there was at least one whose meaning was only too apparent. It concerned a Quaker relief worker in Vichy who was trying to help Jewish refugees find a way out of the unoccupied zone of France. A conversation she had with an embassy secretary in the fall of 1940 revealed an undisguised anti-Semitism. "I hope you're not helping Jews get into the United States," the secretary said to her. "What would you do with them?" she asked him innocently. His answer must have shocked the kindly Quaker, and it was no doubt meant to shock her. According to her account as reported by Fry, the secretary "hunched his shoulders in the position of a man holding a submachine gun. 'Ptt-ptt-ptt-ptt-ptt,' he said." Even if intended as a joke, the comment revealed an insensitivity to the tragedy of ethnic persecution and an indifference to the fate of its victims. It reflected a callousness unexpected in a government official representing a nation committed to the values of democracy.[18]

Were there many others in the State Department who shared the views of the embassy secretary in Vichy? The advocates of the refugee cause felt sure there were. Charges of antidemocratic and anti-Semitic prejudice on the part of those enforcing the immigration laws appeared repeatedly in liberal periodicals and journals. The same names were mentioned over and over again in the lists of officials criticized for opposing the admission to the United States of European trade union leaders, democratic politicians, moderate socialists, and Jews. Among those named most frequently as exclusionists, especially in dealing with Jewish refugees, were Leland B. Morris, the American consul in Berlin; James B. Stewart, the American consul in Zurich; Avra Warren, head of the visa division in the State Department; and particularly Breckinridge Long, assistant secretary of state. To advocates of the refugee cause, these were the chief villains among the anti-immigrationists.[19]

Long was attacked more vigorously and persistently than any of the others, not only by liberal publicists but even by some Jewish leaders who were generally reluctant to become directly involved in disputes over immigration policy. That was partly because he was the most prominent of the government officials openly opposed to admitting large numbers of refugees. But it also reflected surprise and resentment that someone of his political background would take the position he did regarding the immigration of persecuted Jews. A faithful supporter of the Democratic Party for nearly thirty years, he had been rewarded by the Roosevelt administration with an appointment as ambassador to Italy and then as assistant secretary of state. At first he found Mussolini's policies reasonable and even commendable, although before long his opinion of fascism became far more critical. As for National Socialism, he thought that Hitler's *Mein Kampf* showed considerable insight, especially regarding the connection between communism and international Jewry. That such a connection existed seemed to him indisputable.

Yet Long denied, to himself as well to others, that he was an anti-Semite or that he was in any way prejudiced against Jews. Those accusing him of bigotry were in his view only a small clique of vilifiers and schemers defaming him because he was determined to enforce the immigration laws faithfully. As for those who made up that clique, although he did not identify them, it was obvious whom he meant. In an entry in his diary at the end of 1940, he complained that "the attacks on the [State] Department and the unpleasant situation in the press over the refugee matter seems to continue." Criticism of the government's policy was growing and "seems to be joined up with the small element in this country which wants to push us into this war." To dispel any uncertainty regarding the composition of that "small element," Long added that "those persons are largely concentrated along the Atlantic seaboard, and principally around New York." Worse still, "there are elements of them in the Government here." They were the ones responsible for those unfair charges of bigotry being directed against him. "They are all woven together in the barrage of opposition against the State Department which makes me the bull's eye." He saw himself as a victim, not a victimizer.[20]

Long distrusted most foreigners, whether at home or abroad, and not only Jews. Many others seemed to him inherently incapable of becoming true, loyal Americans. There is an account in his diary of a conversation he had late in November 1941 with Laurence A. Steinhardt, the American ambassador to Russia, himself a Jew, but an acculturated, aristocratic Jew, a Jew whose ancestors had emigrated from Central Europe to America before the Civil War. Steinhardt, according to Long, was a man of "decisiveness and courage," opposed to the admission of too many East Europeans, whom he described as "entirely unfit to become citizens of this country." They were "lawless, scheming, defiant—and in many ways unassimilable." They were of the same type as "the criminal Jews who crowd our police court dockets in New York and with whom he is acquainted and who he feels are never to become moderately decent American citizens."

Long admired Steinhardt's candor and perceptiveness. "I think he is right—not as regards the Russian and Polish Jew alone but the lower level of all that Slav population of Eastern Europe and Western Asia—the Caucasus, Georgia, Ukraine, Croat, Slovene, Carpatho-Ukraine, Montenegro, etc." All those unassimilable aliens regarded public office as a "private sinecure," as an opportunity for personal enrichment. They believed that government officials could be forced or bribed to satisfy the demands of special interests. Their view of state and society was shaped by "their own unfortunate experiences abroad." In short, "[they] have a philosophy entirely foreign to our standards of government and proper conduct in public and private life." Trying to keep people of that sort from entering the country was not evidence of bigotry or anti-Semitism. It was an expression of unbending loyalty to the United States.[21]

Still, the chief obstacle to the admission of Jewish refugees was not ethnic or cultural or political bias on the part of government officials; it was the enforcement of immigration laws designed to limit the entry of foreigners seeking a better life in the New World. The quota system imposed the severest restrictions on immigrants from countries with the largest proportion of Jews in their populations, chiefly those in Eastern Europe—an effect that was neither unforeseen nor unintended. And while the immigration laws were adopted a decade before Hitler came to power, the rise of the Third Reich did nothing to weaken the resolve of the American public to maintain the limitations on the admittance of foreigners.

Why? The government of the United States had denounced openly and unequivocally the doctrines and policies of Nazi Germany and offered its moral support to the European democracies in their struggle against the aggressive diplomacy of the Hitler regime, yet most Americans seemed opposed to offering asylum to the victims of that regime. Was there not an inconsistency between America's position in international affairs and its policy regarding the refugee problem? Even the familiar argument that the admission of too many refugees would threaten the livelihood of native-born Americans no longer sounded very convincing. The diplomatic crisis of the late 1930s followed by a military conflict ended the economic depression with which most countries had been grappling for almost a decade. On one side of the Atlantic, millions of unemployed men finally found work, willingly or unwillingly, as soldiers mobilized for total war. On the other side, the growing demand for military and industrial supplies soon accomplished what the New Deal had for years been vainly trying to achieve. Those who had been desperately looking for work could now find it without much effort. And yet the undercurrent of anti-Semitism in the United States did not seem to diminish. If anything, it was growing stronger. Why?

The answer appears to be that the psychological strain of armed neutrality, of being caught between calls for resistance to totalitarianism and warnings against involvement in a deadly military conflict, outweighed relief at the return of economic stability. That strain combined with a hard core of ethnic prejudice accounted for the persistence or even intensification of American anti-Semitism during the years before the nation's entry into the war. The suspicion that the diplomacy of the United States was being controlled by a clever and unscrupulous Jewish minority was the phantasm of a deep-seated prejudice. Moreover, many, including Breckinridge Long, feared that refugees admitted to the United States might prove a threat to the nation's security. At the end of January 1941, Long insisted in his diary that while there appeared to be no collusion between the Third Reich and Franco's Spain regarding the selection of refugees permitted to emigrate, "there is no doubt in operation a systematic traffic in private hands with the connivance of the German Government." This seemed to him "sinister." He was convinced that "the German Government only gives permits to the persons they want to come to the United States." And that could prove very dangerous. "It is a perfect opening for Germany to load the United States with agents." The nation had to be on guard against efforts to use the refugee problem as an instrument of subversion.[22]

A week later, Long described a conference at the State Department dealing with the immigration question, chaired by Secretary Cordell Hull and attended by several important officials in charge of foreign affairs. Here he openly expressed the doubts regarding the admission of refugees that had troubled him for a long time, elaborating on the nature and extent of the danger. "I set out the situation existing in Russia and in Germany in showing that we no longer had control of the choice as to who should come into the United States but that the Governments of Germany and Russia respectively were choosing in their jurisdictions persons that we should receive." All over the world there were pockets of refugees who had escaped from Europe and were now applying for immigration permits to the United States—in Shanghai, Yokohama, Canada, Cuba, South America, and the Caribbean islands. There was clearly a risk that some of those refugees might be undesirables or even subversives. "The Secretary was interested but had no direct decision." The issue was therefore postponed until a future conference.[23]

But it was never actually resolved. It continued to come up over and over again throughout the period before the United States entered the war and for a long time thereafter, with some arguing that the admission of more refugees would be irrefutable proof of America's rejection of Nazi racism and others warning that it would open the door to the agents of totalitarianism.

Moreover, Long's inclusion of Russia among the possible sources of subversion reflected a growing concern over the Communist threat. To be sure, popular distrust of the Soviet Union and its American sympathizers had become apparent long before the establishment of the Nazi regime. It did diminish somewhat after the Kremlin, responding to the Third Reich's aggressive diplomacy, adopted a "popular front" policy favoring an alliance with the liberal capitalistic states against Germany. But when the Hitler-Stalin pact in August 1939 gave Berlin a free hand to attack Poland in defiance of the West European democracies, anticommunism reemerged in the United States, stronger than ever.

Suspicion over Moscow's plots and schemes also had an effect on public opinion regarding the role of American Jews in national affairs and the admission of European Jews victimized by Nazi racism. The fact that Jewish communities at home and abroad were by and large more sympathetic than the population at large to the political left intensified anti-Semitic prejudice and popular opposition to an increase in the admission of refugees. Fear of subversive conspiracies by radical immigrants was reflected in the reluctance of the American vice consul in Marseilles to issue a visa to Largo Caballero, a socialist but a bitter opponent of communism. To the vice consul, it made no difference what his political views were. As long as he had any political views at all, he was undesirable. A distrust of refugees, especially Jewish refugees, was even more apparent in the response of the American vice consul in Lisbon to the suggestion that a visa should be issued to Lion Feuchtwanger. Feuchtwanger and others like him would only increase the danger of Communist conspiracies in the United States.

Fear of subversion by the Third Reich was almost as great. But whereas in one case suspicion focused chiefly on those who were or were believed to be radical sympathizers, in the other case it was often directed against Jewish refugees. The military successes of the Wehrmacht in Western Europe had strengthened and encouraged various right-wing organizations in the

United States, arousing concern over Nazi infiltration. That concern, genuine in most cases, pretended in some, led in turn to a demand for closer
scrutiny of immigrants seeking asylum in the New World. Might not
some of them turn out to be secret agents of the Third Reich? After all,
even Jewish refugees could be forced to become spies for Berlin by threats
against their close relatives who remained trapped in Europe. And besides,
the German secret service might plant some of its agents among the Jews
admitted to the United States, where they would be free to engage in
espionage and sabotage. To ignore the danger would be irresponsible. Just
look at what had happened to France, Belgium, and the Netherlands.

That concern was usually expressed by conservatives and nativists,
to whom it offered additional justification for opposing any change in
the existing immigration laws. But even some liberals, though generally
in sympathy with the refugee cause, were worried about the spread of
authoritarianism in the New World. The defeat of democracy on one side
of the Atlantic might encourage its rejection on the other side. After all,
many of the countries of South and Central America were already governed by dictatorial regimes of the old school. It would not take much to
persuade them to embrace the ideology of Nazi Germany or Fascist Italy.
And as for the United States, the seeds of totalitarianism had already been
planted in many parts of the country by the bitter experience of the Great
Depression. As early as the spring of 1938, shortly after the incorporation
of Austria into the Third Reich, while Franco's armies were making steady
advances in Spain, Undersecretary of State Sumner Welles admitted in
a confidential telephone conversation that "our concern [is] to keep fascism from penetrating the United States." That was why "we are trying to
maintain a close understanding with the other nations in the two Ameri-
cas." The shift in the balance of power from the liberal to the authoritarian states in the Old World might have serious consequences for the New
World as well.[24]

Concern mounted as the diplomatic and military successes of the Axis
in Europe multiplied, while its right-wing disciples in the United States
were growing stronger and bolder. In the summer of 1940, Supreme Court
Justice Frank Murphy expressed to Harold Ickes his fear that "fascism will
grow in this country." Though a Catholic, he had concluded that "one
of our dangers is that the Catholic Church will stir up among its reli-

gionists here a feeling of alarm about communism," and "this will throw the Catholic Church to the fascist side." He himself saw little reason for worry regarding a Communist seizure of power, but he was less sure of the American public at large. He was thinking, no doubt, about Father Coughlin and his National Union for Social Justice. Murphy recalled that when he was running for governor of Michigan two years earlier, "not more than six priests in the entire state" had voted for him, although "I say more prayers every day than any of them." He was convinced that he had been defeated because he was perceived to be too liberal. And had not a similar irrational fear of liberalism led to the rise of fascism in Europe?[25]

Ickes shared Murphy's worry about the spread of authoritarian sympathies in the United States, but, as with many other political problems, he had a solution—a clear and simple yet unrealizable solution. On the eve of the outbreak of war in Europe, he suggested over lunch that "the only way to handle foreign propaganda and espionage was to set up counterespionage." His proposal was that "if the rich Jews, who, first and most seriously, would be affected by a movement toward dictatorship in this country, should raise a very considerable sum of money—it would probably require several millions of dollars—and place it in the hands of someone of character in whom they had confidence and then forget all about it, leaving it to him to run the show, real results might be obtained." Fifty to a hundred agents could then be hired to supervise an investigation of subversive activities in the country and report their findings to the legal authorities. But such an organization, he insisted, "would have to be absolutely independent and free from interference, even on the part of those who contributed the money." In short, while Jews should provide the financing, the leadership would have to be entrusted to a Christian in order to counter the inevitable charge that this was just another clever Jewish scheme to influence government policy.[26]

Ickes's plan never got further than a page in his diary. But it reflected an increasing fear, sometimes sincere, sometimes affected, among liberals as well as conservatives, that the nation was facing a serious danger of foreign subversion. That concern reinforced popular opposition to relaxing the restrictions on immigration. Combined with a traditional distrust of impoverished aliens, widespread ethnic and religious prejudice, and worry about being dragged into the war in Europe, it formed part of an insurmountable barrier to the admission of Jewish refugees. Even the most resolute supporters of the Nazis' victims gradually became discouraged.

Nevertheless, despite the criticisms and complaints of sympathizers with the victims of National Socialism, despite the concerns and fears in the consular service and the State Department, there was a significant though unacknowledged change in American immigration policy within the framework of existing legislation. Altogether, the United States provided asylum for roughly 200,000 Jewish refugees during the period of the Hitler dictatorship, from 1933 to 1945. Considering the magnitude of the catastrophe that overwhelmed European Jewry, the numbers seem pitifully inadequate. But at a time when fanatical anti-Semitism was raging in Europe, and not only in Germany, American policy regarding the refugee problem, though hardly generous, was neither heartless nor shameful.

PART THREE

The Destruction of European Jewry

The blood of three million Jews will cry out for revenge not only against the Hitlerite beasts, but also against the indifferent groups that, words apart, did not do anything to rescue the nation that was sentenced to destruction by the Hitlerite murderers.

JEWISH NATIONAL COMMITTEE (UNDERGROUND)
WARSAW, NOVEMBER 15, 1943

11

The Start of a Genocide

THE ENTRY OF the United States into the Second World War coincided with the opening of the final chapter in the long, unhappy history of the Jewish community in Europe. There was in fact an indirect but logical connection between those two events. The anti-Semitic program of National Socialism was based on a conviction that the crises which Germany had to face during the interwar period and after the outbreak of another worldwide armed conflict were to a large extent the result of the machinations of world Jewry. As for the German Jews, they were willing participants in those machinations, sacrificing the welfare of their Aryan countrymen in order to satisfy their own secret ambitions. All the Third Reich was trying to do was to free the nation from an alien domination to which its innocent generosity had made it vulnerable.

The Hitler regime's contention that it sought not ethnic oppression but national liberation served to justify the steady intensification of measures intended to put an end to the allegedly harmful influence of the Jewish community in German life. First came the exclusion of Jews from politics and the civil service. This was followed by their removal from all important positions in the professions, the arts, education, and scholarship. Then came a gradual restriction of their role in commerce, industry, and finance, an economic isolation which threatened them with complete impoverishment. And finally there was the increasing restriction and confinement of the Jewish minority, its segregation and ghettoization. By the late 1930s, the German Jews, once so hopeful and confident, relishing a painfully acquired prominence in national life, had become a small, frightened community of outcasts, wondering what was coming next and how all this would end.

Yet to the ardent followers of National Socialism, the growing isolation of German Jewry was not enough. They were convinced that the Hitler regime had made impressive gains thanks in considerable part to its unrelenting anti-Semitism. The problem of unemployment, which had largely contributed to the establishment of the new order, was now solved. The endless quarrels of the old political parties had been settled once and for all by a vigorous and effective dictatorship which knew what it wanted and how to get it. The result was the reestablishment of Germany, diplomatically and militarily, as one of the great powers, and that in turn made possible a series of remarkable but easy successes, which gained for the nation a broader territory and a larger population than before the First World War. Such achievements were bound to impress the most skeptical witnesses to the rise of Hitler. True, in the summer of 1939, even many nationalistic Germans experienced brief doubts and concerns when their government's expansionist policy finally led to the outbreak of a new military conflict. But the swift triumph of the Wehrmacht, first in Poland and then in Western Europe, quieted the fears of the most apprehensive citizens of the Third Reich. How could anyone now question the judgment of the Führer in dealing with international as well as national affairs?

Yet each success of the new order in Germany seemed to be followed by new obstacles and new crises. There was mounting criticism from the democratic nations in Western Europe and North America of Hitler's repressive domestic policies, especially regarding the Jews. The response to his expansionist diplomacy was even more hostile. There were charges that National Socialism was seeking to achieve hegemony on the continent by constantly defying the established order in international relations. And there were fears that it would continue to pursue a threatening and bullying diplomacy unless its opponents became more resolute in defending the existing balance of power. Indeed, France and England seemed to be shifting gradually from reluctant acquiescence to forceful resistance. But what accounted for this growing opposition to the expansionism of the Third Reich? Who was behind it? To the Nazi ideologues, the answer was clear.

The outbreak of hostilities did not seem to change the pattern of striking successes for the Third Reich followed by unexpected obstacles to a final victory. The impressive achievements of the Wehrmacht in the first two years of the war did not break the spirit of Germany's opponents. On the contrary, the British government appeared more determined to go on fighting under Winston Churchill than under Neville Chamberlain. The United States, moreover, was moving from cautious neutrality to the brink of direct participation in the conflict. The Nazi leaders began to feel like Tantalus. The closer they came to their goal, the farther it seemed to recede, always so near, yet always just beyond their grasp.

The events of 1941 destroyed once and for all the illusion of an elusive but inevitable German victory. Hitler's decision to invade the Soviet Union, the only power on the continent still capable of challenging him, was intended to achieve the decisive and final triumph of the Third Reich. The Red Army would be quickly defeated and the Communist government would be crushed and overthrown. And that would confront the British with the choice of a dictated peace or an invasion by the Wehrmacht. As for the United States, it would have to reconsider its gradual drift toward involvement in the military conflict. The grave risk of following the advice of the cunning Jewish financiers, politicians, and propagandists in America would become clear even to Roosevelt.

Yet the decision to invade the Soviet Union proved to be a fatal mistake. It transformed what had been a blitzkrieg, a war of swift and decisive campaigns, which the German armed forces had been waging so successfully since the outbreak of hostilities, into a war of attrition, in which the resources of the Third Reich were gradually absorbed, consumed, and exhausted. At first everything seemed to go according to plan. The armies of the Third Reich and its allies swiftly moved deeper and deeper into Russia, increasingly confident of an imminent victory. But then the advance slowed down and came to a standstill, and finally there was defeat and retreat—the first retreat since the beginning of the war. The Germans resumed their offensive the following summer, initially with some success. But the myth of their invincibility was now shattered. The renewed advance of Hitler's armies soon began to stagger and stumble, until it came at last to a halt. And then began a slow, steady withdrawal, which continued until the end of the war. German confidence in the ultimate victory of the Wehrmacht gradually eroded.

Even to the ideologues of the Third Reich, the 100 percent Nazis who had witnessed the rise of their movement from the fringes of domestic politics to the conquest of Europe, it became clear that the prospect of victory was dimming. Their feeling of exhilaration at the approaching triumph of their cause, a triumph which had seemed so close, began to give way to uneasiness, disappointment, and secret apprehension. Perhaps the war was really far from over. Perhaps it would go on and on, constantly demanding new resources, new efforts, and new sacrifices. Perhaps the outcome was not really as clear or inevitable as it had seemed when Warsaw surrendered and Paris was occupied. Perhaps even—although this was never openly expressed—the defeat of Germany was not an impossibility. The concerns and uncertainties grew with each new retreat of the Wehrmacht.

But how to account for this transformation of what had seemed to be an imminent victory into a stalemate and then a slow, endless withdrawal? The true believers in the Third Reich had a simple explanation for their growing worry and frustration as they contemplated the course of the war. They knew who was behind the decision of the enemy governments to continue the fight against the Hitler regime. It was the same cunning foe who had been plotting against Germany ever since the victory of National Socialism, indeed for a long time before that. The real enemy was world Jewry.

The fact that most of the Jews of Europe were now under Nazi rule—a segregated, impoverished, famished, and dying community of outcasts—did not alter the conviction of the supporters of the Third Reich that an international Jewish conspiracy was chiefly responsible for the persistence of foreign resistance to their government's policies and goals. They believed it because they wanted to believe it. It freed them from the need to consider other possible reasons for that resistance. They felt sure that the growing involvement of the United States was mostly a result of the agitation and incitement of Jewish financiers and businessmen, while in the Soviet Union the operations of the Red Army were being directed by Jewish bureaucrats in the Kremlin and Jewish commissars in the field. Even the Jews in occupied Europe, seemingly so helpless and submissive, were secretly trying to maintain contact with their fellow Jews on the other side. Jewish plots and conspiracies were everywhere, assuming various disguises of nationality, ideology, class, and religion, but all serving a single evil purpose.

This belief in the inherent depravity of the collective Jewish mentality became a psychological need, or rather a psychological obsession, for many supporters of the Third Reich. It offered them a clear, simple explanation for the growing dangers the Third Reich had to face. And by the same token, it provided a justification for the adoption of a program of ethnic extermination designed to put an end once and for all to the danger of a Semitic subversion of the Nazi cause. A genocidal solution to the "Jewish question" might seem extreme to the squeamish or softhearted, but was there any other way to counter the danger of betrayal by an inherently evil alien minority? Was the death of millions of Jews by mass execution any worse than the death of millions of Germans on the battlefield? The elimination of the Jews was essential for the protection of Aryan society. Ardent supporters of the Third Reich were convinced that a government aware of its responsibilities must have no doubt about what had to be done.

The decision to adopt genocide as the only way of solving the ethnic problem reflected in large part the mental and emotional pressures of total war. Some have argued that the leaders of National Socialism intended from the outset to exterminate European Jewry, and some prewar statements by Hitler and other leaders of the Third Reich can be interpreted in retrospect as hints or suggestions of genocide. They contain ominous warnings that the Jews will pay a heavy price for their rapacity, or that the retribution for their insatiable hunger for power will be their destruction, or that the war they were inciting would end in the extinction of their race. But there is no evidence of any specific plans for carrying out those threats before the outbreak of hostilities. What transformed violent anti-Semitic prejudice into an official genocidal policy was the war, and especially the gradual shift in the Third Reich's military fortunes. The rising sense of frustration and apprehension among the leaders of the Hitler regime found an outlet in their decision to exterminate the Jews, who were held to be ultimately responsible for the growing danger confronting Germany.

The genocide began with the invasion of the Soviet Union in June 1941, when German military units, sometimes aided by sympathizers and collaborators in the territories occupied by the Third Reich, engaged in the large-scale murder of Jews through shooting, burning, or gassing. By the end of the year, more than half a million people had been killed in these improvised local raids. Then, early the following year, on January 20, 1942, less than two months after America entered the war, while the Wehrmacht, facing a counterattack by the Soviet army, was in retreat for the first time since the outbreak of hostilities, the Wannsee Conference in a Berlin suburb coordinated and systematized what came to be known as the Holocaust. The purpose of the meeting was to give official approval to a "final solution" to the problem created by the existence of world Jewry. Since the danger to Aryan society that the Jews represented was essentially racial—that is, inherent in their collective genetic character—it could not be overcome by education or assimilation or acculturation. The only answer was extermination. Once introduced, that policy was rigidly enforced by the Hitler regime, often with the support of its foreign allies and satellites, until the conclusion of the war three years later. In the end, the destruction of the European Jewish community became the only lasting accomplishment of the Third Reich.

The German authorities never stated openly that they had decided to solve the "Jewish question" through extermination. To have done so would have lent credibility to the propaganda on the other side portraying the Nazi regime as bloodthirsty and heartless. Besides, there might be some people in the countries allied with Germany who, though agreeing that the Jewish influence in politics, economics, and culture must be curtailed, would find outright genocide repugnant. Indeed, quite a few Germans might even be shocked to learn that their government had adopted a policy of mass murder. Why risk the disapproval of those who could not bring themselves to face the hard realities of ethnic self-preservation? Thus the official explanation for the deportation of Jews from Western and Central Europe was that they were being resettled in communities of their own farther to the east, where they would have to engage in productive labor instead of exploiting and cheating their Aryan neighbors. That sounded much better than announcing that they were being sent to be killed.

Still, the Nazis' efforts to keep their genocidal plans secret were not very successful. Those who really wanted to know what was happening to the Jews deported from the Third Reich or living in areas occupied by the Wehrmacht could easily discover that the official explanation was not true. For one thing, thousands of German soldiers witnessed or at least received firsthand accounts of the widespread murder of Jews that followed the invasion of the Soviet Union. Many more heard whispered stories or rumors, not all of them accurate, about the extermination program their government had adopted. They in turn, while on furlough, often repeated what they had heard to relatives and friends back home. Admittedly, in a time of war the air was full of whispers, confidences, revelations, and secrets, some exaggerated, others distorted, and still others manufactured, so that it was hard to decide what to believe. Thus the contention of many Germans after their country's defeat that they had no knowledge of the Holocaust was at least in some cases believable. Yet anyone who really wanted to learn what was happening to the Jews could soon find out that the government's account was not trustworthy and that the truth was far more terrible than was officially acknowledged. In short, many of those who later claimed that they did not know anything about the Nazi regime's policy of genocide did not know because they did not really want to know.

In the territories occupied by the German armies, especially in the east, information about the Holocaust was easier to obtain than in the Third Reich. For one thing, there the process of extermination could be observed firsthand, in a nearby death camp, in which trains carrying human cargo arrived day after day; or in a neighboring village, where the Jews had recently been rounded up and shot; or even in the next street, where a Jewish family, along with many others, was being marched off to the woods, never to be seen again. Then there were the local volunteers and auxiliaries among "Hitler's willing executioners," helping the occupation authorities carry out their "final solution" to that perennial problem of what to do about the Jews. They too had stories to tell. And finally, the leaders of the Third Reich were far less concerned about keeping the harsh truth from conquered foreigners than from their own countrymen. After all, why should they care what those aliens thought?

As for the states allied with Germany that retained a measure of independence, their policies toward the Jewish communities within their jurisdiction varied considerably. Bulgaria steadfastly refused to follow the

Third Reich's urging to adopt an out-and-out anti-Semitic policy. Italy was willing to segregate and expropriate its Jews, but it would not go so far as to consider extermination. In most of Central and Eastern Europe, however, where the Jewish minority was much larger and ethnic hostility much stronger, genocide seemed acceptable to many people. Hungary did not actually adopt it until near the end of the war, but in Slovakia there was no need for much prodding to start the deportation of Jews to the death camps in Poland, while Romania initiated a program of raids, pogroms, and mass executions. The region east of the Oder River soon became the killing ground of European Jewry.

It is harder to determine the prevailing popular attitude toward the Holocaust. Open protests were as a rule out of the question, because of the repressive policies of the occupation authorities. Occasionally, where the citizenry was strongly opposed to genocide—in Denmark, for example—there were brief demonstrations of sympathy for persecuted Jews. But those must be balanced against the voluntary recruitment in most of the occupied countries of military units committed to the struggle against "international communism" and "world Jewry." Once the war ended, there was a predictable tendency throughout the continent to emphasize the resistance against the German occupation while minimizing the extent of collaboration with the Nazi regime. But what was the prevailing view of the Holocaust while the outcome of the armed conflict was still in doubt? The answer is complicated, partly because public opinion varied considerably from country to country, but even more because there were sharp differences in attitude within each country. Any generalization must be carefully scrutinized.

In the case of Germany, it is apparent that many people, perhaps most, had some idea—often a fairly accurate idea—that brutal measures were being taken with regard to the Jews, perhaps including genocide. But even those who were repelled by the idea of mass murder preferred not to talk about it. They felt trapped between moral principle and patriotic loyalty. Besides, to discuss the subject of ethnic extermination openly invited the risk of arrest and interrogation by the secret police. It thus seemed best to look the other way and say nothing. Yet here and there someone would find the courage to raise the subject, not only privately, not only in confidential conversation, but in a public statement or even in a communication addressed to the officials responsible for the government's policies. Those bold enough to challenge the Nazi regime publicly were in most cases churchmen, whose duty it was to keep alive among their communicants a sense of moral responsibility. Clearly, the great majority of German clergymen preferred, whether out of conviction or out of expediency, to avoid involvement in the touchy question of ethnic persecution. But occasionally one of them, especially if in a position of leadership, would speak out against the genocide. And that took courage.

In December 1942, for instance, Archbishop Joseph Frings of Cologne issued a pastoral letter which was to be read at religious services in all the parishes of the archdiocese. In it he spoke of the "inherent rights" of all human beings, which included "the right to life, to inviolability, to freedom, to property, and to a marriage whose validity does not depend on the arbitrary will of the state." Those rights could not or at least should not be denied even to someone "who is not of our blood or does not speak our language." Could there have been any question whom he meant? To emphasize the importance of respecting the spiritual freedom of every individual, regardless of ethnicity or race, the archbishop reminded his coreligionists that "the inhumane treatment of our fellow human beings is an injustice not only against a foreign people but against our own people as well." Since in God's view all human beings are equal, all of them deserve justice and compassion.[1]

Theophil Wurm, the Lutheran state bishop of Württemberg, went even further. Though at first sympathetic toward the Third Reich, seeing in it a defender of German society against secularism, materialism, and radicalism, he gradually became repelled by its oppressiveness and brutality. He too had believed that Jews were gaining too much influence in the politics, economy, and culture of the nation. But the increasingly harsh anti-Semitic measures of the Hitler regime proved too much for him. He became the most outspoken opponent of the government's genocidal program. In January 1943, he wrote to the Württemberg state ministry of the interior, protesting against "the way in which the struggle against other races and nations is being waged" and mentioning specifically "the systematic murder of Jews and Poles." The next month he sent a letter to the governor of Württemberg expressing disapproval of "all measures by which human beings belonging to other nations or races are being put to death without a judicial verdict," simply because of their "national or racial origin." And a month after that, he informed the minister of church affairs in Berlin that "the measures against the Jews adopted in Germany, especially insofar as they are being applied outside the laws in force, have for a very long time been troubling many elements of our population, especially the Christian elements."[2]

A few months later, in July 1943, Wurm wrote to Hitler himself. "In the name of God and for the sake of the German people," he pleaded with the Führer to stop "the persecution and destruction to which many men and women within the German sphere of authority have been subjected without a judicial verdict." The "non-Aryans" in the territories ruled by the Third Reich had already been largely "eliminated." But now there was reason to fear that even those who had so far been spared were in danger of being treated "in the same fashion." Wurm expressed "strong opposition" to the policy of genocide. The "exterminatory measures" directed against "non-Aryans" were in violation of God's commandment. Indeed, they undermined the foundation of all Western thought and life, "the God-given basic right to human existence and human dignity in general." There could be no misunderstanding of the bishop's views regarding the final solution to the "Jewish question."[3]

Hitler never answered the letter. For one thing, he was busy dealing with other problems, which seemed to him much more urgent. The recent German offensive on the eastern front had stalled after barely a week of fighting, and now the Soviet army was beginning to counterattack. On the Mediterranean front, the American and British forces had just landed in Sicily and were rapidly advancing toward Palermo. There were even rumors that Mussolini was in danger of being forced to resign. Why waste time on some insubordinate churchman?

But in the territories occupied by the Wehrmacht, expressing disapproval of the Holocaust was riskier. There the German authorities did not hesitate to arrest anyone who voiced criticism of their policies. Still, the harsh rule of the Hitler regime was not the only obstacle to assistance for persecuted Jews. More important was a long-existent, deep-rooted anti-Semitism, especially in Central and Eastern Europe. The loss of freedom which the nations of that region had had to endure after their defeat and the hostility toward Jews displayed by the occupation authorities reinforced the prevalent ethnic prejudices. The hardships caused by a lost war could be blamed on Jewish greed or Jewish cunning or Jewish warmongering. As for the German officials, they encouraged the view that the harsh conditions under which the defeated nations had to live were a result not of the policies of the Third Reich but of the machinations of world Jewry.

Despite all that, some people in the occupied territories risked and even lost their lives trying to help Jews. Their courage in defying not only the orders of the victorious Germans but also the prejudices of their own countrymen was remarkable. But there were also quite a few who blackmailed, robbed, or betrayed Jews trying to escape mass murder by hiding their ethnicity. And then there was the largest group of all, those who, whether out of fear or indifference, neither aggravated nor alleviated the terrible danger facing European Jewry. Their prime concern was to survive the trials of war themselves. This preoccupation with self-preservation, though not heroic, is understandable. What is less clear is the relative proportion of those who tried to help the victims of the Holocaust, those who exploited their tragedy, and those who chose to remain uninvolved. Since the issue remains emotionally charged but statistically elusive, the debate goes on and on, still impassioned, still undecided. More than half a century after the Holocaust, differences of opinion regarding guilt and responsibility remain sharp.

But it is at least apparent that the persecution of Jews during the German occupation of Eastern Europe did little to diminish the extent of anti-Semitism in the region. If anything, the physical privations and emotional tensions that the civilian population had to endure intensified traditional ethnic hostilities. The need to find villains and scapegoats tended to outweigh the compassion for sufferers and victims.

Even in the western part of what had been Czechoslovakia, in one of the most liberal and tolerant parts of occupied Europe, there were signs of growing hostility toward Jews. A report which Bruce Lockhart, head of the Political Warfare Executive in Great Britain, received from Czech intelligence sources in June 1942, after the German program of genocide had become generally known to those under the rule of the Third Reich, described the complaints of many Czechs regarding the role the Jewish community had played in national life. There were charges that its members had been, at least until Hitler came to power, advocates of the Germanization of the country's culture. Worse still, there was the familiar contention that they had acquired too much influence in political affairs and the learned professions. But that would have to change once Czechoslovakia regained its independence. The prevailing view was that after the war, Jews would not dare to engage in politics or take part in public life or become doctors or lawyers. Otherwise, there might be very unpleasant consequences. The increase of anti-Semitism could become a permanent legacy of the German occupation of Czechoslovakia.[4]

In Poland, where hostility toward Jews had been much more pronounced before the war than in Czechoslovakia, the German occupation did nothing to reduce the extent of ethnic prejudice. It may in fact have increased it. To be sure, a report from the underground received by the government in exile in November 1942 maintained that German cruelty toward Jews had aroused sympathy for the victims and condemnation of the perpetrators. As a result, the anti-Semitic attitudes common in the country during the interwar period had become less apparent. And yet, according to the same report, the demand that something had to be done to solve the "Jewish question" remained as strong as ever. Once the nation was liberated, there would have to be a sharp reduction in the number of Jews living in Poland, a goal to be achieved by voluntary or forced emigration.[5]

The members and supporters of the Polish government in exile in London were also convinced that once their country had regained its independence, there could be no return to the status quo of the prewar years. In 1941, while the execution squads of the Third Reich were initiating the mass murder of Jews, the influential advisor Józef Retinger published a book examining the past, present, and future of his country. Predictably, one section dealt with that endless "Jewish question." Its conclusion was predictable as well: "The Polish Republic, the Polish nation, and the Jewish community in Poland are faced by the vital necessity of solving this matter." As for how to solve it, that was clear. "New fields of emigration must be found and the necessary capital funds must be mobilized." The issue was no longer of interest only to Poland. "It has assumed an international character and requires the collaboration not only of Jewish circles but also of those countries which still dispose of areas available for immigrant settlement." There was no time for lengthy debate. The number of Jews in Poland had to be drastically reduced, and the sooner, the better.[6]

This view was shared by the National Council, the advisory legislative assembly of the government in exile, which largely reflected the views of the political parties of prewar Poland. Here a representative of the anti-Semitic Endecja, the National Democratic Party, introduced a resolution in May 1942 expressing the council's hope for an international solution to the "Jewish question." Though intended to create the impression of Polish approval for the Zionist cause, it was motivated primarily, as the introductory remarks in its support made clear, by the traditional ethnic prejudice of the Endecja and by its hope of bringing about the departure from Poland of as many Jews as possible once the war ended. The resolution was approved by a large majority of the National Council, but to many Jewish organizations it appeared to be an expression not of sympathy but of bias. And this suspicion was not altogether baseless. Anti-Semitism in Poland and indeed in occupied Europe as a whole did not diminish during the war. It may have actually become more intense.[7]

As for the countries allied with Germany, countries whose governments retained at least a measure of political independence, there the prevailing attitude toward the policy of genocide varied widely. In Italy there was never any official expression of opposition to the Holocaust, but considerable popular disapproval was apparent. The Jews may have had to endure humiliation, isolation, and impoverishment, but they also often received secret help from friends, neighbors, former colleagues, and even from some government officials responsible for the enforcement of the laws directed against them. There were no deportations to the death camps in Poland before Mussolini's fall from power in the summer of 1943. Although in Hungary the anti-Semitic policy of the Nicholas Horthy regime was much more rigid and oppressive, no trainloads of Jews headed north to the extermination camps prior to the German occupation of the country in March 1944. In the Slovakia of Jozef Tiso, on the other hand, there was close collaboration with Nazi Germany in the deportation of Jewish prisoners to destinations such as Auschwitz, Majdanek, Belzec, and Treblinka. And as for the Romania of Ion Antonescu and the Croatia of Ante Pavelic, here there was no need for arrests and transports. They organized a genocide of their own right at home.

Even the satellite states of the Third Reich that were reluctant to adopt a policy of extermination hesitated to voice open opposition. To do so

would be sure to arouse anger in Berlin. It would be perceived as disloyalty to the international alliance the Nazi regime had formed in support
of its ideas and ideals. It might even prove dangerous; it might invite German intervention. The best thing would be to say nothing, to promulgate
various anti-Semitic measures short of genocide and then look the other
way while the racist extremists engaged in mass murder as the only way to
solve an unsolvable problem.

To most German officials, a reluctant acquiescence on the part of some
of their country's allies was by and large acceptable. The important thing
was to avoid the appearance of a sharp division of opinion regarding ethnic
issues. Late in December 1941, Martin Luther, the Third Reich's undersecretary of state for foreign affairs, argued that "we should try to persuade
all the European states to adopt the German legislation regarding Jews."
Difficulties were to be expected only in Hungary, Italy, Spain, Sweden, and
Switzerland, countries in which, "at least as far as Italy and Spain are concerned," opposition was predictable because of "the clerical influences there
which have already become apparent." Yet that was not a serious concern.
What mattered was that most of the nations siding with the Third Reich,
especially those with a large Jewish population, seemed to accept the goals
of the Nazis' genocidal program. At least they expressed no objection. As
for a few grumblers and complainers, they could be ignored.[8]

Nevertheless, the reluctance of the German authorities to confirm the
rumors of death squads accompanying the Wehrmacht in Russia or of
extermination camps being established in Poland was understandable. It
would be best to say nothing about the Holocaust, while accusing the
enemy nations of hypocrisy for having tolerated atrocities far worse than
those for which they were condemning the Hitler regime. Where were
they when the victors at Versailles were imposing a cruel and ruinous
peace treaty on a valiant but defeated adversary? Where were they when
the Poles were humiliating and oppressing defenseless Germans in West
Prussia and Posen? Above all, where were they when Jewish capitalists
secretly allied with Jewish Communists were exploiting and corrupting a
country that had accepted them with such openhearted generosity? Those
were the real atrocities.

That the Third Reich was unwilling to disclose its program of ethnic
extermination is understandable. But the reluctance of the Allied gov-

ernments to publicize it may seem at first glance puzzling. After all, they had been maintaining for a long time, even before the outbreak of the war, that the Third Reich was ruthless, chauvinistic, and bigoted. What better proof could there be than the policy of mass murder in dealing with an innocent, helpless minority? Wouldn't a revelation of the genocide reinforce the popular conviction that the Allies were fighting for freedom and justice? And yet the leaders of these nations were very cautious, almost fearful, in disclosing that European Jewry was being exterminated. Even when they did speak of it, they preferred to subsume it under a listing of atrocities being committed against various national and ethnic minorities. Only rarely did they speak of the exceptionality or uniqueness of the Holocaust.

Why this reluctance to emphasize the mortal danger facing the Jewish community? The reason was essentially the same as during the prewar years. Now, as then, it was important to avoid saying or doing anything that might reinforce the suspicion that the struggle against the Third Reich was motivated primarily by a desire to protect the Jews or that it was in fact secretly instigated by the Jews. The hard truth was that even while the Allied governments were insisting that they categorically rejected the racist doctrines of National Socialism, they had to deal with a considerable degree of anti-Semitism in their own countries. There was a tendency among the public to ascribe the increasing sacrifice of life and wealth at least in part to the behind-the-scenes manipulations of Jewish financiers and Jewish politicians. The government authorities had to be careful not to do anything that might intensify these popular suspicions. To dwell too much on the Holocaust would probably make the situation even worse. It seemed best, therefore, to refer to the persecution of the Jews only in the context of the persecution of various other categories of victims of Nazi cruelty or, better still, avoid the subject altogether.

The first of the Allied countries to speak openly about the Holocaust was the Soviet Union. The Kremlin assumed that after twenty years of indoctrination regarding the crucial importance of the class struggle and the harmful effect of ethnic prejudice, it would be safe or even useful to make known the mass execution of Jews by the invading German forces. It might strengthen the nation's resolve to resist those cruel invaders. Accordingly, early in January 1942 a report issued by Vyacheslav Molotov, the Soviet foreign minister, spoke of the "monstrous villainies, atrocities, and outrages" that the Nazi authorities were committing in the occupied territories. At one point it mentioned Jews, along with Russians, Ukrainians, Latvians, Armenians, and Uzbeks, as victims of German brutality. Later in the report there was a brief mention of the fact that the previous summer, after the Wehrmacht had taken Lvov, a wave of mass murders of Jews and Poles had taken place. And still later the report spoke of the killing of more than 50,000 Jews in Kiev. In other parts of the Ukraine there had also been "bloody executions" of "unarmed and defenseless Jewish working people." All in all, Molotov's figures added up to about 90,000 Jews killed during the German advance into the Soviet Union, less than a fifth of the actual number in the previous six months.[9]

Soon after that, at the end of April, another report issued by Molotov dwelled on the atrocities committed by the Germans during the invasion. There were accounts of the enslavement of the native population, the destruction of national monuments, the desecration of churches, the execution of prisoners of war, and the killing of workers and peasants. But Jews were mentioned only once, included with Russian, Ukrainian, Moldavian, and other victims of Nazi persecution. Even that was more than appeared in Molotov's third report, issued in October 1942. This one spoke of the responsibility of the German invaders and their collaborators for atrocities committed against the civilian population in the occupied territories. It did not mention, however, the chief victims of those atrocities. By then the Soviet authorities had concluded that too much official condemnation of the anti-Semitic policies of the invaders might arouse more popular hostility against the Jews than against the Germans.[10]

Still, wouldn't reports of the Holocaust strengthen support for the war effort in the Western democracies, where there was reportedly a great deal of sympathy for the victims of genocide and where Jews were reputed to have considerable influence in economics and politics? That calculation may have contributed to the issuance in the summer of 1942 of a statement by the Jewish Anti-Fascist Committee in Kuybyshev, intended for publication abroad, which dealt with the murder of more than 70,000 Jews in Minsk. It appeared in British and American newspapers but not in the mainstream Soviet press. The same reasoning might also have led to the publication in December 1942 of an unsigned report distributed by the Foreign Ministry Information Bureau, which announced finally that the Germans planned "to exterminate the Jewish population in the occupied territory of Europe." In order to achieve that goal, the Nazi regime intended to send millions of Jews from all parts of the continent to concentration camps "for the purpose of murdering them." The document, though brief, presented more hard facts concerning the Third Reich's genocidal program than all the other reports issued by the Soviet government since the start of the invasion put together. That was probably because it was designed to influence public opinion in Great Britain and the United States at least as much as in the Soviet Union.[11]

The authorities in London and Washington, however, were not nearly as eager to publicize the atrocities of the Holocaust as the Kremlin imagined. The revelation that the Third Reich had initiated a program of extermination directed against European Jewry was by then no longer news to the Western democracies. Although they had at first been reluctant or unwilling to believe the reports of mass murder they were receiving from various sources, by the end of 1942 the evidence had become overwhelming and incontrovertible. It could no longer be questioned. But that created serious difficulties for the English and American officials responsible for the conduct of the war. The last thing they wanted was information from the Soviet Union confirming and reinforcing what was already well known, namely, that the Jews of the continent had been condemned by the Third Reich to mass execution. That information was bound to make their job harder.

For one thing, publicizing the Holocaust would inevitably increase demands by the Jewish community and various liberal and humanitarian organizations that something must be done to stop the murder of millions of innocent human beings. The railroad tracks leading to the death camps should be destroyed, or German cities should be bombed incessantly until the genocide stopped, or warnings should be issued that those responsible for the anti-Semitic atrocities would be treated as criminals. To yield to such demands, however, would mean that scarce national resources would have to be diverted from military operations to humanitarian efforts. Could any country engaged in a struggle for survival afford to do that? And even if it did, might that not prove self-defeating? Might it not arouse the same ethnic hostilities at home that the armed forces were supposedly combating abroad? No, the best way to end the Holocaust would be to achieve victory as soon as possible. Anything else would make the situation of the European Jews even more desperate.

The leaders of the Third Reich were aware of the dilemma confronting their democratic adversaries. Some of them believed that British and American politicians, though publicly condemning their anti-Semitic views for purposes of propaganda, secretly shared those views and at heart were in sympathy with the racist teachings of National Socialism. Joseph Goebbels, propaganda minister in the Hitler cabinet, noted in his diary in December 1942 that "the question of Jewish persecution in Europe is being given top news priority by the English and the Americans." That was nothing more than liberal hypocrisy, however. "At bottom . . . I believe both the English and the Americans are happy that we are exterminating the Jewish riff-raff." But eventually they would have to pay a heavy price for their pious displays of sham humaneness. "The Jews will go on and on and turn the heat on the British-American press." Goebbels preferred, however, not to deal with this subject publicly. "Instead I gave orders to start an atrocity campaign against the English on their treatment of Colonials." How could those cruel oppressors of natives in India and South Africa presume to lecture the Germans about the evils of racial discrimination?[12]

Still, Goebbels misjudged the attitude of the government authorities in the Western democracies toward the Holocaust. They were clearly not in sympathy with the policy of ethnic extermination. Indeed, that policy seemed to them so brutal, so heartless, that they found it hard at first to believe in the accuracy of the reports regarding its adoption. That the Hitler regime had been harsh and inhumane in dealing with the Jewish community was clear. But mass murder? That seemed almost inconceivable.

The British and American governments had less information than the Soviets about what the Germans were doing in Eastern Europe. The Kremlin began receiving accounts of the Holocaust almost as soon as the invasion of Hitler's armies began—accounts by survivors of the massacres, by local eyewitnesses, and occasionally even by prisoners of war. But the Western democracies had no direct knowledge of what was going on in Poland, Lithuania, Latvia, and the occupied regions of Russia and Ukraine. They had to depend to a large extent on vague rumors, conflicting stories, second- or thirdhand accounts, and unverified and unverifiable reports. There was thus good reason to be skeptical about some of the frightful tales coming from more than a thousand miles away.

But not only the horror of mass murder and the lack of reliable information about its extent accounted for the reluctance of the British and American governments to confirm the reality of the Holocaust. They were slow to believe that it was taking place because they did not want to believe it. They feared, not without justification, that once the Nazi extermination of the Jews became public knowledge, the task of directing the war effort would become more difficult. On one side would be those, mostly Jews and their sympathizers, who would plead desperately for some action, diplomatic or military, to halt the murder of millions of innocent and defenseless people. But to accede to those pleas, however cautiously, might create even more serious problems. There would be an immediate outcry from the exiled leaders of various other ethnic and national communities suffering under the German occupation—Poles, Czechs, Serbs, and Greeks, for example—that the Jews were receiving preferential treatment, that the Allies were showing greater sympathy for them than for the other victims of Nazi oppression. And that would inevitably weaken the resolve of the Allies to continue to fight side by side until total victory had been achieved.

In addition, how would the home front, whether British or American, react to the knowledge that the lives of the nation's sons serving in the armed forces were being jeopardized in order to protect a suffering but alien ethnic minority? Would that not reinforce the rumors that the war was being fought at the instigation of the Jews, that Christians were dying in the tens and hundreds of thousands in order to save a small but influential minority of non-Christians? And wouldn't that divert popular attention from the primary task of winning the war to a domestic dispute regarding the role of Jewry in national affairs? Would reports of mass murder by the Nazi regime even be accepted as true? After all, during the First World War there had also been stories about German atrocities. Yet once hostilities ended, it turned out that all those tales about the rape of women and murder of children in Belgium had been fabricated. Wouldn't accounts of the extermination of Jews in Eastern Europe be dismissed as a fabrication as well?

Such concerns were behind a memorandum prepared by the British Ministry of Information in the summer of 1941, barely a month after the German invasion of the Soviet Union, warning that caution must be exercised in launching propaganda directed against the racist policies of the Third Reich. "To make the material credible to the British people it is essential that . . . it should not be too extreme." Endless horror stories about the Nazi concentration camps would only repel the "normal mind." And the reason was clear. "In self-defense people prefer to think that the victims were specially marked men—and probably a pretty bad lot anyway." Admittedly, a "certain amount of horror" was helpful in spreading propaganda, but it should be used "very sparingly" and should be concerned only with "indisputably innocent people." That meant that the subject matter should not deal with "violent political opponents" of the Third Reich—with socialists and Communists, for example. "And not with Jews." The public had become tired of stories about suffering Jews.[13]

The same warning appeared even more clearly a year later, in September 1942, in a memorandum by Herbert Morrison, the home secretary, opposing a proposal to admit a few hundred Jewish refugees in Vichy France who had relatives in Great Britain. To approve such a proposal would only invite more appeals for admission from foreigners, "both Jews and others," in Portugal, in other parts of Europe, and North Africa. But how many more immigrants could the country afford to let in? Morrison was convinced that "it would not be right to make any general departure from the principle that the United Kingdom is unable, during the period of the war at any rate, to accept additional refugees." He stated the reasons for his opposition very clearly. There was, first of all, the risk that a relaxation of British restrictions on immigration would facilitate the deportation policy of the Vichy government. Then there was another, even more important consideration. "We already have a very large body of refugees here and not all sections of public opinion are enthusiastic about their presence." And then Morrison came to his chief objection. "If we got beyond a point in the admission of foreign refugees, we may stir up an unpleasant degree of anti-Semitism (of which there is a fair amount just below the surface)." That would be bad for Jews and non-Jews alike. "Discretion is therefore necessary." To devote too much attention to what was happening to European Jewry might in the long run backfire.[14]

The growing public awareness of the Holocaust and its confirmation by the Allied governments did not diminish the concern in official circles that dwelling on the danger confronting Jews under the German occupation might reinforce rather than diminish anti-Semitic prejudice at home. Even offering asylum to Jewish refugees who had so far managed to elude the grasp of the Third Reich might prove risky. In January 1943, a year after the secret Wannsee Conference had formalized Hitler's decision to exterminate European Jewry, an aide-mémoire submitted to the State Department by the British embassy in Washington maintained that "the refugee problem cannot be treated as though it were a wholly Jewish problem." There were so many non-Jewish refugees and there was so much "acute suffering" in the Allied countries that there would probably be criticism at home and abroad if "marked preference" were shown in admitting Jews from regions under enemy occupation. The result would be the one predicted by the opponents of Jewish immigration. "There is . . . the distinct danger of stimulating anti-Semitism in areas where an excessive number of foreign Jews are introduced."

There was an even greater danger in efforts to rescue Jewish victims of Nazi persecution. What if those efforts proved too successful? What if too many victims were rescued? What if the Third Reich decided to let all the Jews who wanted to emigrate do so? Wouldn't that create a major problem for the Allies? "There is a possibility," the aide-mémoire warned, "that the Germans or their satellites may change over from the policy of extermination to one of extrusion, and aim as they did before the war at embarrassing other countries by flooding them with alien immigrants." That would create a serious dilemma for Great Britain as well as the United States. After all, they had both been loudly condemning the Nazi regime for its treatment of what it regarded as inferior races and nationalities. They had both denounced it for its bigotry and cruelty. But what would happen if the Germans suddenly opened the gates and the Allies had to face a deluge of impoverished, hungry, sick refugees? Should they admit them and risk aggravating ethnic prejudice at home? Or should they exclude them, to the grim satisfaction of the Hitler government, which had always accused its enemies of shedding crocodile tears? The prospect of having to choose between those alternatives was deeply troubling to the British embassy.[15]

Fortunately, the choice did not have to be made. The fanatical racism of the hard-core Nazis generally prevailed over the expedient advice of moderates in the German government who were willing to let some Jews leave, either in return for scarce vital commodities or as a way of inciting domestic discontent in the enemy camp. What is clear is that the Holocaust had little effect on the prevailing attitudes in Great Britain about the refugee problem and the "Jewish question." There was still a great deal of sympathy, at least in the abstract, for the victims of anti-Semitic persecution. But once those victims became transformed into flesh-and-blood refugees and would-be immigrants, the popular perception of them changed drastically. Now they were often seen as outsiders, foreigners competing with the native population for food and shelter, aggravating the hardships caused by war. The Holocaust did nothing to change that view, which persisted until the end of hostilities and long after.

The prevalent attitude in the United States was essentially the same, despite the dissimilarity in the experience of the two countries during the Second World War. It made little difference that the Third Reich's initiation of genocide came a few months before America's entry into the military conflict, while Great Britain had by then been at war for almost two years. Nor were the hardships and privations accompanying the hostilities nearly as severe in the United States as in Great Britain. Thus news of the danger of extermination confronting European Jewry might have been expected to arouse greater concern among Americans than among Britons. Yet in fact that was not the case.

Of course, there was in both countries widespread abhorrence of genocide. Not even the bitterest critics of the Hitler regime had believed it capable of mass murder. But there was also, especially at first, a considerable degree of skepticism regarding the reliability of reports about the Holocaust. The Third Reich was seen as ruthless and cruel; it was clearly guilty of brutal oppression and exploitation. But genocide? That was hard to believe. Besides, even if the accounts were true, was the German treatment of other oppressed ethnic minorities much better? Should the persecution of Jews be allowed to overshadow the persecution of non-Jews? And what about the heavy loss of life in the countries fighting National Socialism? Should the Holocaust influence in any way the diplomatic policy or military strategy of the Allies? Such questions and suspicions were usually drowned out by the more acceptable expressions of sympathy for the innocent victims of Hitler's extermination program.

In the United States, the news of the Holocaust, even after its confirmation by the Polish government in exile, was regarded as dubious by many Americans, perhaps by most. A survey conducted by the Gallup Poll early in January 1943 asked a sample of some 3,000 respondents the following question: "It is said that two million Jews have been killed in Europe since the war began. Do you think this is true or just a rumor?" The replies showed that 47 percent of the participants thought that the report was true, 29 percent thought it was a rumor, and 24 percent expressed no opinion. Whatever the reason for the indecision of almost a fourth of the respondents, it is clear that close to a majority did believe in the existence and the reported extent of the Holocaust.[16]

But what about the others? What about the 29 percent who thought that accounts of the extermination of European Jewry were only rumors? Did they believe that the figure of 2 million victims was inflated? Or did they suspect that the accusation of genocide directed against the Third Reich was a wartime fabrication? And what of the 24 percent who said they had no opinion? Were they unaware of the reports in the press? Were they unable to decide whether the number of those killed was actually as high as stated in the question? Were they unsure whether any Jews were being killed, or were they simply reluctant to express their views on a touchy subject, views that some might consider callous or bigoted? Such questions remain unanswered and unanswerable.

More can be said, however, about the reasons for the considerable disbelief in the United States about the Holocaust. One was clearly a common distrust or resentment of Jews. In July 1942, six months before the Gallup Poll's investigation of prevalent views regarding the Holocaust, another survey of public opinion asked, "Do you think the Jews have too much power and influence in this country?" The replies showed that 44 percent of the respondents believed that Jews did have too much influence, 41 percent thought they did not, and 15 percent expressed no opinion. The combined proportion of those who believed that Jews were too powerful and those who would not say, 59 percent, was close to the combined proportion of those who doubted and those who expressed no opinion about the accuracy of reports of the Holocaust, 53 percent. It is reasonable to assume that there was at least some overlap between the two categories of respondents, one reflecting a shared ethnic prejudice. Indeed, many Jews as well as some liberal non-Jewish organizations charged that the noticeable reluctance to accept the reliability of the accounts of Nazi genocide was largely a reflection of anti-Semitism.[17]

Still, there was more to it than that. Even those who could not reasonably be accused of bigotry, who were in fact sympathetic toward Jewish refugees, often found it hard to believe that the Third Reich would adopt a policy of ethnic extermination. They remembered the horror stories circulating during the First World War which were later shown to be false. Since then, tales of atrocities had become an almost accepted component of psychological warfare. Such tales had to be viewed with considerable caution.

In September 1942, Vernon McKenzie, director of the School of Journalism at the University of Washington, analyzed the reasons for public wariness about reports of Nazi barbarities. "News stories from Germany before the war, even before Hitler became chancellor of the Reich, chronicled many examples of man's inhumanity to man," he pointed out. "Cruel and bestial stories were circulated, by both sides, in the previews of this present war, from Ethiopia, from Spain and from the Orient. Some were true, many grossly exaggerated." This unreliability had engendered popular distrust of reports of wartime atrocities, especially since only relatively few Americans had a direct interest in reports of that sort. The result was now apparent. "Millions were so conditioned that when the day came when Hitler invaded Poland they could say, or at least feel, that they were 'fed up by horror reports,' or that 'one side is probably just as bad as the other.' Except for the very few who were active or interested partisans there was but little attempt made to evaluate and discriminate." The country had simply grown tired of stories about the alleged crimes against humanity being committed thousands of miles away, in some remote corner of the Old World.[18]

Skepticism was also fostered by the exaggerated charges of some of the protesters against Nazi genocide, most of them Jews, who tried to add new horrors to those already widely known. Although as a rule they believed in the accuracy of what they were reporting, their judgment was often swayed by ethnic sympathy and ideological loyalty. Once their accounts proved to be erroneous, however, they reinforced doubts about the Holocaust in general.

One case that attracted considerable attention involved Stephen Wise, the fiery and tireless spokesman for the militants in the Jewish community. Writing in the fall of 1942 to John Haynes Holmes, minister of the Community Church in New York, he described the terrible news he had recently received which left him sleepless. He had learned that "100,000 Jews within the Warsaw ghetto have been massacred by the Nazis and their corpses have been used to make soap and fertilizers. . . . I am almost demented over my people's grief." He repeated this account of the massacre of Warsaw Jews and the conversion of their remains into soap and fertilizer in private letters and conversations and finally in a public statement. The news was too important, too terrible, to be kept confidential.[19]

Unfortunately, Wise's claim backfired. Since the State Department refused to support it, the incident had the effect of bolstering the suspicion of many Americans that Jews tended to exaggerate their hardships and injustices in order to win public sympathy and exploit it to their collective advantage. The inflation of the horrors of genocide provided support for popular doubts regarding the authenticity of the reports of mass murder in Eastern Europe.

Even the *Christian Century*, though often sympathetic toward Jewish refugees and clearly opposed to the racism of the Nazi regime, did not believe Wise's story. It agreed that "horrible things are happening to the Jews in Poland." It even said that it was "probable" the Nazis were transporting the Jews of Europe eastward "with the deliberate intention of exterminating them there." And yet was any useful purpose being served by the publication of the charge that Wise had recently made? To begin with, the government had "conspicuously" refrained from confirming that charge. Second, Wise's figures of the number of Jews killed differed sharply from those issued at the same time by the Polish government in exile. Third, the man whose information had been used to support the charge was the same Polish leader who was campaigning in the United States for "the complete destruction of Germany." And finally, "Dr. Wise's allegation that Hitler is paying $20 each for Jewish corpses to be 'processed into soap fats and fertilizer' is unpleasantly reminiscent of the 'cadaver factory' lie which was one of the propaganda triumphs of the First World War." The atrocities that the Third Reich was committing were terrible enough without the fabrication of nonexistent horrors.[20]

Nevertheless, many Americans, close to a majority in fact, continued to believe that the Nazi regime was indeed engaging in organized, systematic genocide. The debate about the admission of refugees now broadened to include the question of what could or should be done to save the victims of the Holocaust. The two issues, immigration and rescue, were similar in that both focused on the fate of a persecuted ethnic minority threatened with extermination. And those on the opposing sides of the two issues were similar as well. That is, opponents to the admission of Jewish refugees were also the ones most likely to question the accuracy of the reports of Nazi atrocities and the need to rescue the victims of those alleged atrocities. Conversely, the advocates of a more generous American immigration policy were frequently also supporters of U.S. attempts to rescue European Jews being deported to death camps. The differences of opinion between the two sides continued to grow throughout the war years and beyond.

Understandably, the most ardent proponents of efforts by the American government to help save the victims of the Holocaust were members of the Jewish community. How could they have remained indifferent to the terrible tragedy of European Jewry? To them, the ultimate justification of the war was a moral imperative to save millions of innocent men and women from a cruel, murderous, evil regime.

This conviction was reflected in an article that Stephen Wise published in 1942 about the collective ethical responsibility of the democratic world. "The United Nations ought once and for all make it clear to the Nazis," he pleaded, "that they themselves and their own crimes—not the Jews—are responsible for bombing reprisals and that these bombings would continue until the German people had freed themselves from their enslaving masters." The Allies must not ignore the tragic fate of European Jewry. Their silence would be interpreted as assent to the charge that the Jews were ultimately responsible for the Nazi campaign of annihilation directed against them. Yet neither Great Britain nor the United States had ever explicitly included Jews among the peoples battling for the four freedoms and entitled to the protection of the Atlantic Charter. A word of solemn warning from them might prove a deterrent against further anti-Semitic "infamies" by the Nazi regime. Most important, however, "in view of the unmeasured sufferings of Jews in all the lands of the Axis, it is become the part of inevasible duty for Britain and our own country to speak the word which is needed to lift the heart of world Jewry and to discharge a debt of honor to those who have suffered most and have least been helped." For the victims of merciless persecution who felt ignored and abandoned, evidence of support from the nations battling against the Third Reich would be a source of at least some comfort, some encouragement. It would save them from utter, hopeless despair.[21]

Still, printed expressions of compassion for the persecuted Jews of Europe, however eloquent and moving, could not provide the same emotional satisfaction as the mass meetings, attended mostly by Jews, held in many large American cities to voice a common resolve to do something to help the innocent millions threatened with extermination. Being part of a large gathering of people, men and women with shared concerns, sorrows, sympathies, and hopes, was psychologically far more heartening than any article or book. It was the sense of collective determination and common purpose that made such occasions so memorable for the participants.

One of the biggest and most impressive was the "Stop Hitler Now" demonstration on the evening of March 1, 1943, in Madison Square Garden in New York. The huge hall was filled to capacity by a crowd of about 21,000, while another 10,000 stood outside in the street, hearing the speeches through loudspeakers. Stephen Wise claimed, allegedly on the basis of police estimates, that 75,000 people had in fact tried to get in. But might that have been one of his exaggerations? With Wise, one could never be sure. In any case, the participants listened intently to several speakers deploring the tragic fate of the Jews in Europe, a few even offering concrete suggestions on how to save at least some of the victims. At the end they adopted a resolution urging the Allied governments to take measures designed to save what remained of the Jewish community under the tyrannical rule of the Third Reich.

The most specific recommendations were those advanced by Chaim Weizmann, president of the Jewish Agency for Palestine, who began his speech by reminding the gathering that 2 million Jews had already been exterminated. "The world can no longer plead that the ghastly facts are unknown and unconfirmed. At this moment expressions of sympathy, without accompanying attempts to launch acts of rescue, become a hollow mockery in the ears of the dying." Weizmann then described the "acts of rescue" which had become a moral duty for the world's democracies. First of all, "let them negotiate with Germany through the neutral countries concerning the possible release of the Jews in the occupied countries." Second, "let havens be designated in the vast territories of the United Nations which will give sanctuary to those fleeing from imminent murder." Finally and predictably, "let the gates of Palestine be opened to all who can reach the shores of the Jewish homeland. The Jewish community of Palestine will welcome with joy and thanksgiving all delivered from Nazi hands." To Weizmann, the final solution to the "Jewish question" was not genocide but Zionism.[22]

The resolution that the mass meeting adopted for submission to President Roosevelt in general followed Weizmann's recommendations. The first of its eleven proposals urged that the German government and the states it dominated or controlled be asked through neutral countries and agencies to agree to release their Jewish victims and consent to the emigration of those victims to "such havens of refuge as will be provided." There was no suggestion, however, as to how the Third Reich might be persuaded to agree to such an arrangement. The second proposal followed logically from the first. The democracies should take steps without delay to establish sanctuaries in their own or neutral countries "to serve, under agreed conditions, as havens of refuge for those Jews whose release from captivity may be arranged for or who may find their way to freedom through efforts of their own." The remaining nine proposals were elaborations or extensions of the first two, except for the sixth, which reiterated, though without much enthusiasm, Weizmann's recommendation regarding the most suitable refuge for persecuted Jews: "Overriding pre-war political considerations, England should be asked to open the doors of Palestine—the Jewish homeland—for Jewish immigration, and the offer of hospitality made by the Jewish community of Palestine should be accepted." Whether the mass meeting would have any practical effect remained to be seen, but those who participated in it returned home that night excited and elated.[23]

Jews were not the only ones expressing support for the victims of Nazi anti-Semitism. Many Gentiles, liberal and compassionate in their ideology, also voiced their condemnation of the genocidal program of the Third Reich. Some were even more outspoken than Jews. But that was at least partly because they did not have to be afraid of being charged with disloyalty to their country or with greater concern for their coreligionists abroad than for their countrymen at home. They could afford to be more outspoken.

In March 1943, for example, Freda Kirchwey denounced what seemed to her to be the do-nothing policy of the United States far more sharply than the mass meeting in Madison Square Garden two weeks earlier had done:

> The purge of the Jews is only positively a Nazi crime. In this country, you and I and the President and the Congress and the State Department are accessories to the crime and share Hitler's guilt. If we had behaved like humane and generous people instead of complacent, cowardly ones, the two million Jews lying in the earth of Poland and Hitler's other crowded graveyards would be alive and safe. And other millions yet to die would have found sanctuary. We had it in our power to rescue this doomed people and we did not lift a hand to do it—or perhaps it would be fairer to say that we lifted just one cautious hand, encased in a tight-fitting glove of quotas and visas and affidavits, and a thick layer of prejudice.

Very few Jews would have risked saying something like that in public.[24]

In addition to liberal journalists and academics, many church leaders found the extermination of innocent, helpless human beings a shocking violation of the moral convictions on which their faith rested. The archbishop of Canterbury sent a message to the "Stop Hitler Now" demonstration expressing the hope that "our two nations may unite in offering all possible aid and place of refuge for Jews now threatened with massacre and so do what we can to mitigate the most appalling horror in recorded history." The message from Cardinal Hinsley, archbishop of Westminster, was even more forceful: "It is little use uttering tirades against anti-Semitism. Jews and Christians are our fellowmen and brethren. If Christian mercy finds no place in the Nazi breast, then the lesson of stern retribution must be given in such wise that never again shall these hideous wrongs be possible." And Bishop Henry St. George Tucker, the presiding clergyman of the Episcopal Church in America and president of the Federal Council of Churches of Christ in America, declared at the mass meeting that "if we people of America really believe in the brotherhood of man, as we profess to do, we will not only be moved to indignation by the brutality of these persecutions but we will also be moved to demand that everything possible to bring it to an end shall be attempted at the earliest moment." Those witnessing this display of solidarity between Christians and Jews found it deeply moving.

And then there were the various labor leaders and prominent politicians who voiced their support for a collective effort to rescue the pitiable victims of National Socialism. The speakers at the mass meeting in Madison Square Garden included William Green, president of the American Federation of Labor, and James B. Carey, secretary-treasurer of the Congress of Industrial Organizations. Mayor Fiorello H. La Guardia addressed the audience in the name of the people of the city of New York, while Governor Thomas E. Dewey and Senator Robert F. Wagner spoke to the gathering by radio, the former from Albany and the latter from Washington. What they had to say was sincere, although there were private suspicions that their readiness to say it had been reinforced by the presence in New York of a large Jewish community. There seemed to be no extraneous considerations, however, behind the radio address of Supreme Court Justice William O. Douglas or the message sent by Wendell L. Willkie, the recent Republican candidate for president of the United States. Clearly the advocates of more vigorous measures to save European Jewry had succeeded in forging a powerful coalition transcending the boundaries of religion or ethnicity.[25]

Yet for the authorities in Washington, that coalition created a dilemma. They found themselves caught between two opposing camps, each with a large following, each determined to influence government policy. On one side were those who, while conceding (sometimes reluctantly) that reports of the Holocaust were mostly correct, maintained that the United States could do nothing about it except win the war as soon as possible. To divert manpower and resources from the struggle on the battlefield to the rescue of prisoners in the death camps would mean subordinating the national interest to an ethnic problem. It would amount to the abandonment of common welfare and collective responsibility. Those on the other side, however, insisted that the war against the Third Reich was based on principles and ideals independent of territorial boundaries or political differences. It was being waged for all of humanity, for universal beliefs and values. And what better way to demonstrate the universality of that struggle than by trying to protect the most vulnerable, the most pitiful victims of National Socialism? The effort had to be made.

Officials in Washington, including the president, were very cautious in dealing with this problem. The mounting evidence they received of the extermination of European Jewry dispelled any doubts they might have had regarding the charges of genocide, and there can be no question that most of them were genuinely in sympathy with the victims of the Holocaust. But how could they express that sympathy without arousing a backlash of criticism and resentment? The strategy they adopted, basically because they had no choice, was to voice compassion, promise eventual punishment, and suggest minor modifications in the existing restrictions on immigration. They were careful, however, to avoid any appearance of diverting military resources or risking additional casualties for the sake of persecuted Jews.

Roosevelt embraced this strategy, feeling that there was really no alternative. He knew about the Holocaust at least by the fall of 1942, perhaps even earlier. But he preferred not to become directly involved in dealing with the problem, leaving it to the State Department. Instead, from time to time he expressed his unequivocal condemnation of the brutal, fanatical anti-Semitism of the Third Reich. In July 1942, for example, he sent a letter to a mass meeting in New York organized by the American Jewish Congress expressing his appreciation of the contribution of the Jewish community to victory over the Axis. "Citizens, regardless of religious allegiance," he went on, "will share in the sorrow of our Jewish fellow citizens over the savagery of the Nazis against their helpless victims. The Nazis will not succeed in exterminating their victims any more than they will succeed in enslaving mankind." And then came a stern warning. "The American people not only sympathize with all victims of Nazi crimes but will hold the perpetrators of these crimes to strict accountability in a day of reckoning which will surely come." The knowledge that Roosevelt was on their side, that he shared their concerns and sorrows, helped make American Jews his most ardent supporters.[26]

Throughout the war, the president continued to issue similar statements of sympathy and support for the victims of the Holocaust. They were sincere as well as politically advantageous. But he preferred to leave the task of formulating an official policy to the State Department, to Secretary Cordell Hull and Undersecretary Sumner Welles. They, however, were no more eager than he to deal with what seemed to be an unsolvable problem. The issue was therefore assigned by default to the foreign service. A few years after the war, Henry Morgenthau, Jr., described this as a tragic mistake. "Hull's indulgence of such men as Breckinridge Long, who did not harass him with perplexing policy problems and with whom he could relax socially, was one of the Secretary's major weaknesses. Hull did himself particular injustice, because his subordinate failed to carry out his generous intentions on the problem of rescuing the refugees." The result was inaction in the face of a terrible tragedy.[27]

That contention was not entirely fair, however. In fact, Sumner Welles helped Stephen Wise obtain reports about the Holocaust from Gerhard Riegner, the representative of the World Jewish Congress stationed in Switzerland, although he insisted that those reports not be made public until he gave permission. After waiting at least two months following the receipt of reliable information about what was going on in Eastern Europe, Welles finally agreed to let Wise publish the confirming documents, in November 1942. "For reasons you will understand," he told him, "I cannot give these to the press, but there is no reason why you should not. It might even help if you did." What he meant was that coming from the undersecretary of state, the news might arouse a suspicion of secret Jewish influence over the government. Coming from a Jew, though, it would probably be accepted as a normal manifestation of ethnic solidarity and concern.[28]

As for the government officials entrusted with the task of dealing with Nazi genocide, Morgenthau maintained that "the typical foreign service officer lived off paper"; that is, "his instinct was always toward postponement on the hallowed theory of all foreign offices that problems postponed long enough will solve themselves." Besides, many of the bureaucrats in the State Department had little sympathy for the humble and downtrodden. "The horrors of Dachau and Buchenwald were beyond their conception." To them, decisions affecting human lives were no different from decisions affecting commercial relations.[29]

Still, Morgenthau's charges were exaggerated. American officials should no doubt have been more compassionate and generous toward the few

Jews who had found temporary refuge in the neutral countries of Europe and who were desperately trying to emigrate to the New World. But as for the Holocaust, what could they do? To agree to reduce the bombing of German cities or relax the economic blockade of the Axis in return for sparing the lives of Jews in the death camps would almost certainly back-fire. The Nazi regime might use such an action to support its contention that world Jewry was instigating and directing the war. Besides, the other national and ethnic communities under the rule of the Third Reich would demand that the United States do no less for them than for the Jews. And worst of all, many Americans would begin to ask whether the sacrifice of their sons on the battlefield was being prolonged in order to help save a persecuted but distant and alien minority. No, the best strategy appeared to be a combination of bold words and cautious deeds. There was no other choice.

12

Militant Jews, Circumspect Jews, and Doomed Jews

THE ERA OF THE Third Reich, though lasting no more than twelve years, was the most extraordinary period in the history of Germany—indeed, in the history of Europe. Never before had any political regime risen to such heights so quickly, from the depths of a ruinous economic depression to diplomatic and military dominance over the continent. And never before did any political regime suffer such a catastrophic collapse so suddenly and so disastrously. What it left behind was only devastation and suffering. No monuments have been erected in its memory, no commemorations have been celebrated, no holidays have been proclaimed, no epics have been written. The achievements of the Third Reich, which once aroused admiration among its citizens and envy among its neighbors, have long since been dismissed as specious, as mere glitter. None of them has had any lasting effect or enduring significance, except one.

It all began in the depths of the Great Depression, when a nation that had once been confident and proud confronted the mass hunger and privation caused by a global economic collapse. Social hostilities increased almost to the point of a revolutionary upheaval. As for the political system, it appeared to be in total disarray, unable to offer any solution. And then a miracle occurred. A leader emerged, a man who had until then been on the fringes of politics as the head of a small, isolated, visionary party but who now seemed to know what to do to save the country from disaster. Within a few short years he achieved the impossible. Unemployment quickly diminished and then disappeared as the economy recovered. The danger of revolution subsided as well, mostly because of the return of social stability, but also as a result of the efficiency of the secret police. And as for the new political system, a rigid, dictatorial form of authority, most Germans found it a cheap price to pay for the restoration of order and prosperity.

Whether Hitler's success in bringing about an economic recovery was the result of skill or coincidence is still a subject of debate. It was in all probability some of each. But there can be no doubt that he quickly recognized the diplomatic possibilities created by the effect of the Great Depression on the victors of the First World War, especially France and England. Torn by social tensions and political quarrels aggravated by the hard times, they were reluctant to become involved in new international conflicts arising out of the enforcement of the Versailles treaty. And Hitler knew how to exploit that reluctance. First he repudiated the demilitarization provisions imposed on his country, and then came a series of impressive territorial gains that extended the nation's frontier beyond those of the old Hohenzollern Empire—all in the space of only six years and without a single military casualty. No wonder that so many Germans, including some who initially had serious reservations about the Third Reich, became its enthusiastic supporters.

But there was still more to come, much more. The outbreak of war in 1939 at first aroused considerable uneasiness and even apprehension in Germany. How could a nation that had only recently begun to rearm and had to rely on an inexperienced and untried military force stand up to opponents who had at their command the most powerful armies in Europe? The leadership of the Wehrmacht, however, displayed remarkable skill and shrewd judgment in conducting the early campaigns. Within a month after hostilities began, Poland had been conquered. Then, only nine months later, France and the Low Countries were defeated and occupied after a series of lightning strikes whose success surprised friends and foes alike. By then there seemed to be little doubt about the outcome of the war. Neutral countries that had remained wary and aloof suddenly rushed to ingratiate themselves with the invincible victor. The few that did not, such as Yugoslavia and Greece, were quickly defeated and occupied. Not since the days of Napoleon had any nation succeeded in dominating the continent as completely as the Third Reich by the summer of 1941.

But then came an extraordinary turnabout, even more sudden and surprising than the succession of German military victories in the preceding two years. Hitler decided to crush the one state on the continent that still appeared strong enough to defy his demands. The invasion of the Soviet Union, however, proved to be a disastrous mistake. The Red Army, after suffering a series of major defeats, made a successful stand on the outskirts of Moscow and then launched a counteroffensive which forced the Germans to retreat, at least temporarily—their first retreat since the beginning of the war. And at the same time the United States, which had been gradually and indirectly becoming involved, entered the war officially. The Third Reich now faced an enemy coalition more powerful than the one it had defeated a year earlier.

After that, the decline and fall of the Hitler regime was even swifter than its rise and triumph had been. There were first of all the steady advances of the Allied armies, Soviet from the east, American and British from the south and west. Then there was the growing bombardment of German cities, which limited industrial production and created a serious economic shortage. And finally, the civilian population of the Third Reich began to suffer the same hardships long endured by the civilian population in the countries conquered by the Wehrmacht. By the time the war ended, in the spring of 1945, Germany was in ruin, its people hungry, homeless, impoverished, and demoralized, its government partitioned among the victor states, and its future hopeless. No nation in Europe had ever suffered such a disastrous defeat, and this after a succession of such brilliant victories.

Still, no matter how hard life was for the Germans under the Allied occupation, especially in the early years, there was no popular longing for a return of the Third Reich, no underground movement to revive National Socialism, no secret hope to establish a new authoritarian government under a new Hitler. There may have been a widespread desire for the end of foreign rule, for a return to self-determination and self-government, and especially for national reunification, but there was little nostalgia for the old days of discipline, conformity, victory, and harsh oppression. The successes and accomplishments of the Third Reich, hailed initially as destined to last a thousand years, were forgotten or ignored as soon as the war ended. The only enduring achievement of the Nazi regime, enduring because it could not be undone, was the final solution to the "Jewish question."

To the leaders of the Third Reich, that had been a very important objective, as important as the stabilization of political authority, the restoration of social order, and the revival of military strength. They devoted themselves to its achievement with steadily mounting resolve. The measures they adopted to counter the terrible danger in what they perceived to be a parasitical, aggressive, and unscrupulous racial minority became increasingly oppressive, in good times as well as bad, in the early years of consolidation and in the later years of triumph, in peace and in war. Their determination to deal with that problem once and for all increased throughout the era of National Socialism, culminating in genocide. Even in the last phases of the war, as defeat became more and more likely, they continued to direct desperately needed manpower, materiel, and transportation to the task of ethnic extermination. If anything, their obsession with the Jewish danger increased as their own situation became more and more perilous.

In the end, they succeeded. The only lasting achievement of the Third Reich was the destruction of European Jewry, by far the largest Jewish community in the world. At the time of Hitler's rise to power early in 1933, there were about 9,690,000 Jews in Europe, compared to roughly 5 million in North and South America (90 percent of them in the United States), 618,000 in Asia, 487,000 in Africa, and 33,000 in Australia and New Zealand. European Jews constituted 61 percent of world Jewry. By the time of the outbreak of the Second World War, to be sure, the number of Jews in Europe had diminished to approximately 8,301,000, owing to emigration motivated chiefly by concern over the growing strength and aggressiveness of the Nazi regime. But even then the European Jewish community remained the largest in the world, 52 percent of the total.[1]

By the time the war ended, however, 72 percent of the prewar Jewish population of Europe had perished as a consequence of the Holocaust— about 5,978,000 people. Even the remainder diminished rapidly, as most of the survivors emigrated, chiefly to the United States and Israel. They were driven partly by the tragic memories of what had happened during the preceding decade, partly by the unfriendly reception they often encountered on returning from hiding places or the death camps, and partly by the chaotic political and economic conditions on the continent, especially in the east. The outcome was that an ethnic community that had been an integral part of European society for almost two thousand years, that had closely interacted with the other ethnic communities in that society, and that had influenced and been influenced by the culture and civilization of its environment became marginalized and almost non-existent. Its members were relegated to the position of curious relics of a vanished age, regarded with sympathy and compassion—at least officially, if not always popularly—but irrelevant to contemporary concerns and goals. After almost two millennia, the center of world Jewry shifted away from Europe, partly to North America, partly to the Middle East. There the new Jewish communities assumed identities of their own, each with its own language, its own culture, its own values, and its own aspirations. As for European Jewry, it ceased to exist as a distinct, unique ethnic entity.[2]

The process of its destruction, however, is still not fully understood and is a subject of sometimes bitter debate, because it raises questions of guilt and innocence, complicity and responsibility. While there can be no doubt about who instigates of the Holocaust or about its consequences, there is still the question of the vast disparity in the numbers and especially the proportions of the victims of the Third Reich's program of extermination in the European nations. Why did so many Jews perish in one country while in another one so many survived? What explains the murderous success of the Holocaust in some parts of the continent and its relative failure in other parts? Those issues still need to be addressed, even if complete agreement seems unlikely.

The question that can be dealt with most easily concerns the differences in the number of Jews killed in the various countries. Here the answer is simple. The larger the community of Jews was, the more Jews were likely to be killed. In Poland, for example, which had the biggest Jewish population in Europe—3.3 million in 1939—about 2.8 million perished. In the Soviet Union, which had the second biggest Jewish population—2.7 million in 1933—those killed in the territories occupied by the Wehrmacht totaled 1.5 million. At the other end of the scale, the number of Jews in Italy was 57,000 when the war began and 42,000 when it ended. In Bulgaria, the Jewish population was 50,000 in 1939 and 43,000 in 1945. These statistics are not surprising, however. It is only to be expected that the larger communities of Jews in Europe would suffer heavier numerical losses than the smaller communities.[3]

But a more complicated issue arises in connection with not the absolute but the relative numbers of the victims of the Holocaust, for here it becomes apparent that European Jews' chances of survival varied greatly from country to country, depending on factors other than the size of their community. In Poland, for instance, whose prewar Jewish population totaled more than 3 million, 85 percent perished. But in Lithuania, where there were no more than 150,000 Jews when the war began, 90 percent had been killed by the time it ended. In neighboring Latvia, the Jewish population in 1939 was even smaller, no more than 95,000, but the percentage of those who died was almost the same as in Lithuania, 89.5. In Italy, on the other hand, 26.3 percent did not survive the Second World War, and in Bulgaria 14 percent died. As for the states that had the smallest Jewish communities—Danzig, Denmark, Estonia, Luxembourg, and Norway with a combined total of 20,000 Jews—about 30 percent lost their lives between 1939 and 1945. In short, although every Jewish community in Europe suffered tragic losses resulting from the genocide, the relative extent of those losses varied greatly.[4]

That the figures themselves are in the main accurate is beyond dispute. But how to explain the striking differences between nations? That is a much more difficult question.

One answer, plausible though not always entirely persuasive, is that the anti-Semitic measures initiated by the Nazi regime were applied much more rigorously in the countries occupied by the Wehrmacht than in the countries that, though allied with the Third Reich, retained a considerable degree of independence in dealing with their internal affairs. This would help explain the deadly success of the extermination program in Poland, Lithuania, Latvia, and even Czechoslovakia, where there had been comparatively little ethnic hostility before the war but where 82.5 percent of the Jewish population perished after 1939. Italy and Bulgaria, in contrast, were able to protect most of the Jews within their borders because they retained the authority to determine their domestic policies. For that matter, the governments of Romania and Hungary, though increasingly anti-Semitic during the interwar years, refused after 1939 to adopt a program of outright extermination, partly because of moral or religious scruples, partly because of a Jewish strategy of ransoming and bribing, but mostly because of a growing perception that the Allies were likely to win the war.

The percentage of Romanian Jews who perished during the Holocaust was 50, while the percentage of Hungarian Jews was 49.5—still tragically high, but well below the levels in Poland and the Baltic states. Clearly, there was by and large an inverse relationship between the degree of autonomy or self-determination in any country and the intensity of the anti-Semitic measures introduced in that country.[5]

This relationship, however, was not always decisive or even apparent. Some nations, though under the direct occupation of the Third Reich, were still able to save a far higher proportion of the Jews within their borders than most of the nations officially allied with the Nazi regime. In the Netherlands, for example, which had a Jewish population of 150,000 in 1939, quite a few of them refugees from Central Europe, about 90,000, or 60 percent, perished. That was a very high proportion, but well below the percentages for most of Eastern Europe. The case of Belgium is even more striking. Of the 90,000 Jews living there in 1939, some 40,000 had died by 1945—a loss of 44.4 percent, less than in Romania or Hungary, which had largely succeeded in retaining their independence. And then there was the case of Denmark, which, though occupied by the Wehrmacht early in the war, managed to save virtually all of its 6,000 Jews by secretly helping them find asylum in neutral Sweden. It was a dramatic demonstration of what could be done to protect the intended victims of the Holocaust, provided public opinion was widely and resolutely opposed to the policy of ethnic extermination.[6]

There was a close correlation between the prevalent intensity of anti-Semitic prejudice in any given country and the relative proportion of the Jews in that country who perished during the Second World War. The degree of traditional ethnic hostility was in fact an even more important factor in the extermination of European Jewry than the degree of political control exercised by the Third Reich over the various nations of the continent.

That explains why the proportion of Jewish victims of the Holocaust was higher in Eastern Europe, where anti-Semitism had been most pervasive and intense, than in Central Europe, the birthplace of National Socialism. In Germany, there were 210,000 Jews when the Second World War began and 40,000 when it ended, a loss of 81 percent. And that does not take into account the roughly 300,000 German Jews who were able to emigrate between the time Hitler came to power and the outbreak of hostilities. The contrast between the situation in Eastern and Central Europe is even more striking in the case of Austria. There, about 110,000 Jews emigrated between the incorporation of the country into the Third Reich in the spring of 1938 and the outbreak of war a year and a half later. Of the 60,000 who remained, 40,000 had perished by 1945. Thus the percentage of Jewish victims in Austria, though still appallingly high, was well below that in many of the countries farther to the east.[7]

In short, the effect of the Nazis' genocidal program depended to a large extent on the attitude of the local population toward the motives and objectives of ethnic extermination. Even in countries occupied by the Third Reich, popular opposition to the Holocaust, as in the Low Countries and Denmark, significantly limited the proportion of Jews who perished. The number of Germans to whom the government entrusted the primary task of locating and killing Jews in the occupied countries was relatively small. The Main Office for Reich Security, which was assigned chief responsibility for waging the campaign of mass murder, had fewer than 70,000 men under its command. Its effectiveness depended on the collaboration of provincial officials, county administrators, municipal clerks, and members of the police force. In many parts of Europe, moreover, it was also able to assist in organizing groups of volunteers who were ready to aid the German authorities in the killing of Jews. Indeed, those auxiliaries were often assigned the bloodiest tasks in the anti-Semitic campaign. Their collaboration made a significant contribution to the murderous success of the Holocaust.[8]

This harsh truth should not obscure the fact that in every country, even the most anti-Semitic, some people, sometimes quite a few, risked their own lives to help save those threatened with genocide. Their courageous opposition to ethnic mass murder should be fully recognized and acknowledged. But they were in most cases outnumbered by those who, with varying degrees of approval, supported the campaign of extermination being waged against Jews. And they were an even smaller minority by comparison with those who, without strong feelings one way or the other, merely wanted to survive. The exact proportions of those who actively participated in the Holocaust, those who endorsed its purpose without involvement in its execution, those who were too preoccupied with self-preservation to pay much attention to the tragedy confronting an alien minority, those who sympathized with that alien minority but dared not express their sympathy, and those who were willing to face imprisonment or even death for doing what their conscience told them to do cannot be precisely determined. Nevertheless, the subject remains the center of debate more than half a century later because it raises fundamental questions of morality and duty, of private conscience and collective responsibility. To that debate there can be no end.

Still, the intricacies and complexities of the Holocaust are largely a discovery of postwar writers and analysts. As long as the military conflict was still going on, the prevailing view in the democratic nations, including the United States, was that the Third Reich was the sole initiator and executor of the Holocaust. The National Socialist ideology had from the outset preached ethnic hatred and destruction, and now that its adherents had conquered Europe, they were simply putting into effect the pitiless doctrines they had long embraced. As for the countries under German occupation, they too were victims of those doctrines, they too had to endure oppression, impoverishment, brutality, and mass execution. How could they then be expected to do anything to help the Jews? They could not even help themselves. The evildoers responsible for the tragedy of anti-Semitic persecution and mass murder, at least the chief evildoers, were the Germans.

The great majority of Americans shared this view. But understandably, those who were most deeply affected by the tragedy of genocide were members of the Jewish community. To them, what was happening to European Jewry was an unspeakable tragedy. They felt that something had to be done to stop the mass murder of an innocent minority whose only crime was a disliked ethnicity. It was their duty to try to save millions of fellow Jews overseas. More than that, it was the duty of their country as well. Was not a resolve to put an end to genocide the morally most important reason for waging war against the Third Reich? Admittedly, there were other considerations. The Hitler regime was aggressive, dictatorial, chauvinistic, and cruel. But nothing it did was as terrible as the Holocaust. The true test of loyalty to the democratic principles espoused by countries opposed to National Socialism was a determination to put an end to genocide, whatever the risk, whatever the cost.

The Allied governments, however, did not and could not make the rescue of European Jewry the chief goal of the war. Over and over they condemned the mass murder of Jews, but almost always within the context of the atrocities being committed against various other national and ethnic communities. They feared, not without justification, that to begin making distinctions among the victims of the Third Reich would create internal rivalry and dissension. Even more important, the American public had to remain convinced that the sacrifices it was being forced to make were essential for the defense of the national interest. This fundamental difference in the way the Holocaust was perceived remained unchanged and unresolved throughout the war.

The feeling of many American Jews that there was nothing they could do to save their coreligionists in the Old World led them to suspect that their government and their countrymen were basically indifferent to the Nazis' genocide. It engendered a sense of isolation and bitterness. How could a nation committed to liberty and justice for all fail to do everything possible to end the horror?

In June 1944, a few months after the Wehrmacht occupied Hungary, an editorial in a Zionist publication in New York expressed the despair of those who, overcome by grief, had to witness from afar the mass killing of fellow Jews, unable to do anything to help them. "It seems that the murderers, far from fearing retribution at the hands of assured Allied victors," the editorial lamented, "are convinced that the destruction of their Jewish neighbors will find favor in the eyes of the liberators. They believe that the outside world hates Jews far more than it detests the most barbaric inhumanity." Worse still, "there are times when this monstrous attitude appears almost correct." After all, the Jewish communities in Poland, Czechoslovakia, Greece, the Balkans, the Low Countries, and elsewhere had been destroyed "without a hand to help them." There had been little more than a few words of condemnation, and those only "under the extreme pressure of a public opinion that could no longer be quiescent." Yet maybe now more than words would be enlisted in the struggle against barbarism. "Perhaps . . . the rulers of Hungary [will] be made to understand that wholesale Jew-murder will meet not with apathy but with vengeance on the part of the United Nations." There was still some room for hope—not much, unfortunately, but at least some.[9]

Three months later, however, an article in the same periodical voiced nothing but despair. A review of the conduct of the democratic states with regard to "the annihilation of a helpless people, suffering merely because of the accident of birth," had provided little comfort. "Most of the nations have merely locked their gates more tightly against Hitler's victims." The United States had done more than the others, but not much more. If the democracies had been willing to help, the results of the Holocaust would not have been so disastrous. "Yet little has been attempted until it was too late." Throughout the early period of the "indiscriminate slaughter of Jews," the Allied governments had insisted that they could do nothing to help them. But that was simply not true. "The will to do did not measure up to the possibilities. The world—the better world—remained cold to us, blind and deaf to our suffering."

That attitude had not changed, the article maintained. Little was being said about "the Jewish tragedy, the most fearful in human history." The press was full of stories about Hitler's V-bombs, the destructiveness of which was enough to warrant the "extermination of the German nation." But how could that "mechanical murder" be compared with "the thousands of trains loaded with Jewish men, women, and children, transported to be burnt alive in ovens of death?" The bombs were directed against belligerents, but the innocent babies being killed in their mothers' arms could not be regarded as participants in the war. "They were murdered solely because they were Jewish, because they belonged to a weak people and to a religion which had made the error of bringing civilization into the world." Yet those holding high positions in the democratic states had little to say about the gas chambers and ovens used for the slaughter of helpless human beings. "It seems that men find it difficult to speak up for the Jews, even to Hitler's discredit, at the present time." While European Jewry was being exterminated, the world preferred to look the other way.[10]

Yet the fiercest and bitterest criticism of the democracies appeared not in the United States but in Great Britain, in an article by David Ben-Gurion, who a few years later became the first prime minister of Israel. In his impassioned condemnation of what he perceived to be Allied passivity regarding the Holocaust, he portrayed the Americans and the British as not much better than the Germans:

> What have you done to us, you freedom-loving peoples, guardians of justice, defenders of the high principles of democracy and the brotherhood of man? What have you allowed to be perpetrated against a defenceless people while you stood aside and let it bleed to death, without offering help or succour, without calling on the fiends to stop, in the language of retribution which alone they would understand? Why do you profane our pain and wrath with empty expressions of sympathy which ring like a mockery in the ears of millions of the damned in the torture houses of Nazi Europe? Why have you not even supplied arms to our ghetto rebels, as you have done for the partisans and underground fighters of other nations? . . . If, instead of Jews, thousands of English, American or Russian women, children and aged had been tortured every day, burnt to death, asphyxiated in gas chambers—would you have acted in the same way?

To Ben-Gurion, the ardent Zionist, the Holocaust proved that the only way to protect the Jews of the world against future Hitlers and Himmlers was by establishing a Jewish state in the Middle East, the sacred, historic homeland of their ancestors.[11]

Most American Jews were not prepared to go quite that far. They continued to believe that there were fundamental differences between the United States and the Third Reich—ideological, ethical, and philosophical differences. Yet they too wondered at times whether their government would have tried to do more if the victims of the Nazi genocide had not been Jews. Those doubts were reinforced by the perception that anti-Semitism in America was increasing as the military conflict went on. The physical and psychological strains of war seemed to intensify traditional ethnic suspicions and prejudices in the country. Public opinion was unanimous in its condemnation of mass murder as a solution to the "Jewish question," but the feeling that Jews had indeed become too influential in national affairs appeared to be gaining strength, and to members of the Jewish community, that was deeply troubling.

Horror at what was happening in the death camps abroad combined with a concern regarding the spread of anti-Semitism at home led to a growing protest movement. Throughout the war years, American Jews held mass meetings, marches, and demonstrations demanding that the government do more to save European Jewry and to persuade the American public that more must be done. But how could that be accomplished? On this point there was no agreement, mostly because there was in fact little that could be done to deter the leaders of the Third Reich from carrying out their genocidal plans. And so the mass meetings did not generally go beyond demands that the Allies condemn the murder of European Jews more frequently or more loudly or more threateningly, and that a haven be provided, either in the United States or in Palestine, for refugees from Nazi cruelty. Too be sure, many Jewish organizations did offer specific proposals for saving at least some of those facing deportation to the death camps. But such proposals varied widely, they were often contradictory, and their effectiveness seemed doubtful at best. In their inconsistency and impracticality, they reflected the hopeless situation of the doomed Jewry of Europe.

In the spring of 1943, a confidential memorandum by R. C. Alexander of the Visa Division of the State Department spoke of the lack of any "reasonable recommendations" by "the emotionalists and the pressure groups." Their proposals could be described as nothing more than a slogan, a call for "action—not pity." Among them were suggestions to "negotiate with Hitler—break the blockade—exchange refugees for internees—relax the immigration procedure of the United States—[and] open the doors to Palestine regardless of the Arabs." At about the same time, another memorandum, this one unsigned, referred to "a flood of mail to the President and the State Department" which sought to obtain "(1) a joint declaration by the United States and the United Kingdom censuring barbarism and promising retribution; (2) opening Palestine to the Jews; (3) removing all barriers to the immigration of Jewish children and (4) exchanging Jews in occupied Europe for interned Axis nationals."

Such pleas, proposals, and demands, increasingly urgent, increasingly desperate, continued until the end of the war. As late as September 1944,

John W. Pehle, director of the War Refugee Board, reported that several Jewish organizations had urged that the Polish government in exile be asked "to direct its underground forces to destroy the death camps and free the prisoners detained there." Indeed, many Jews in the United States went on clutching at straws until the fall of the Third Reich. Perhaps something might still be done, perhaps some victims could still be saved, perhaps some miracle would eventually occur, perhaps, perhaps, perhaps.[12]

The established Jewish organizations were not the only source of efforts to persuade the government to do more to save the victims of Nazi genocide. Small groups and even private individuals who knew someone in high places or who thought they might be able to influence some important official in the State Department tried to help as well. In the fall of 1942, Breckinridge Long described in his diary a meeting with the son of Stephen Wise, who was accompanied by Nahum Goldmann, a member of the Jewish Agency for Palestine. "They asked to send food to Jews in Warsaw. I said we would agree to $12,000 a month to go to Portugal to buy food there if Treasury would license the transfer of credit. They were pleased."[13]

Similarly, in the summer of 1944, Johan J. Smertenko, the executive vice chairman of the Emergency Committee to Save the Jewish People of Europe, wrote to Roosevelt directly, urging him to adopt "measures of retaliation" against the German program of genocide. "Railways and bridges leading from Nazi-occupied territory to extermination centers in Poland can be destroyed by bombing," for example, or "the extermination camps themselves can be bombed, destroying the gas chambers where thousands of people are assassinated daily." And finally, "a specific statement can be issued that the extermination of Hebrew men, women, and children by the continued use of poison gas will be considered a provocation for retaliation in kind." Suggestions of that sort continued to appear and reappear among the endless Jewish appeals to the government to put an end somehow to the tragedy of the Holocaust.[14]

The officials in Washington generally responded with understanding and sympathy, at least publicly. To display doubt or indifference might have led to accusations of insensitivity or even prejudice. But in private they often expressed serious reservations about the practicality of the measures recommended by the Jewish protest movement. They feared that to allow the atrocities of Nazi anti-Semitism to direct or influence military strategy would undermine the country's war effort. Besides, the proposals seemed to most government officials not only impractical but incompatible. They said so in private over and over again. In his memorandum, R. C. Alexander maintained that the request by the "pressure groups" to exchange refugees for internees only served the interests of the Third Reich. "We must not permit the emotionalists, who are misled by Hitler, to mislead us. This is a time when cool heads must prevail." By exercising care and caution, the government might be able to save "a group of people here and another group there," eventually perhaps even rescuing "a large number of people." But equally or more important, "we may prevent Hitler from using the refugees once more to break through our defenses and prolong the war." The true defenders of persecuted Jews in the Old World were not the hysterical "emotionalists," with their wild recommendations and demands, but the calm, prudent, experienced officials in Washington who could tell the difference between the attainable and the futile.[15]

Another confidential memorandum contained an even more explicit account of State Department opposition to any proposal to exchange Jews in occupied Europe for Axis nationals interned in the United States. For one thing, there were not enough internees to make such an exchange feasible. But that was not the only or the chief reason for rejecting the proposal. Of greater importance was a concern that "the exile governments could be expected to object to this favoring of Jews over non-Jewish nationals." And then there was always the danger that the Third Reich might exploit American efforts to aid the victims of the Holocaust in its campaign to gain popular support in the countries under its domination. Such efforts "could . . . be used by the Germans for propaganda claims that the war is being fought for the Jews."[16]

Not even the underground resistance movements, according to the prevailing view in Washington, could always be counted on to reject the Nazis' contention that the Jews themselves were primarily responsible for the harsh treatment they now had to endure. That was why the request for the Polish government in exile to instruct its followers to destroy the death camps and liberate the prisoners was received by the American authorities with skepticism. In his report, John W. Pehle wrote that "as a matter of fact, it is very doubtful whether the Poles had the necessary forces to carry out such an operation." But that was not the only problem. "In view of the apparently deep-rooted anti-Semitism on the part of a large segment of the Polish Government and underground movement, it seemed most unlikely that the Poles would, in good faith, undertake to attack the death centers effectively unless strong political pressure involving political support were asserted." The officials in Washington, however, were reluctant to apply too much pressure on the Poles in order to save the Jews. That might intensify the divisions and dissensions in what was already an uneasy, fragile coalition.[17]

Even when occasionally granting a request for some measure designed to assist the victims of the Holocaust, the government authorities were as a rule cautious, carefully weighing the pros and cons. Late in September 1942, after agreeing to support the proposal to send food to the Jews in Warsaw, Breckinridge Long met with Secretary Hull. The latter approved the recommendation, promising to submit it to the White House for Roosevelt's consideration. But both of them remained troubled by their decision. Had they really done the right thing? "We again discussed the political reasons against the humanitarian impulses which had motivated us—and the necessity for us to take into consideration the *political consequences* if we are just to say 'no' for military reasons and oppose the humanitarian decisions of large groups of our citizens—etc." Their doubts and second thoughts were superfluous, however. Although they did not know it, close to 90 percent of the inhabitants of the Warsaw ghetto had by then been deported to the death camps. The dilemma the two American statesmen thought they were wrestling with had in fact ceased to exist.[18]

To the Jewish organizations which continued throughout the war to submit demands, proposals, and pleas to Washington, it gradually became clear that they could expect little more than sympathy and an occasional minor concession as a gesture of support. But that did not deter them. The rallies, marches, demonstrations, and vigils went on and on, mostly because the participants felt that they could not stand by idly while their coreligionists were being systematically murdered. There was a growing recognition, however, that these collective displays of protest and compassion were not likely to have much practical effect. It became apparent that the government was unwilling to let the Holocaust influence the conduct of military operations.

Many American Jews saw in the authorities' inaction a reflection of the growing ethnic prejudice in the country at large, but this concern was inflated. It expressed the collective fears of an insecure ethnic minority. But many sympathetic Christians also felt troubled by what they perceived to be the growth of hostility against Jews in the United States. Early in 1944, Senator Guy M. Gillette of Iowa wrote to Harry Shapiro, the director of the American Zionist Emergency Council, assuring him that "there are hundreds of thousands of Americans like myself who are not of Jewish origin but who are tremendously interested in the problems of these people in our own country and abroad." He expressed his feeling of shock at the "brutal destruction" of the Jews in nations dominated by the Axis, innocent men and women "marked for extermination." But what troubled the senator most was the growth of ethnic prejudice at home, in a country that officially condemned the brutal racism preached by National Socialism. "Speaking for myself, I am particularly concerned over the widespread and recently stimulated propaganda of an anti-Semitic nature which has reached a point where it is seriously threatening the peace and security of our citizens of this racial derivation." His letter was intended to express support for Shapiro, for his organization, and for all others of "this racial derivation."[19]

A similar concern continued to appear in liberal journals and periodicals throughout the war years. In the fall of 1944, an article by a Harvard psychologist in the Catholic weekly *Commonweal* sought to explain and analyze "the bigot in our midst." It pointed out that "we have always had bigots . . . and probably shall always have them." But what was especially disturbing now was "their numbers and their complexion." Public opinion polls were showing that the level of prejudice was "dangerously high." Roughly 85 percent of the population seemed ready to scapegoat some group or other, accusing its members of not contributing as much as they should to the war effort. Some Americans were "implacable Anglophobes," others expressed "prejudice against the Negro," and still others were anti-Catholic, anti-Russian, anti-labor, or anti-Protestant. While the numbers varied, the proportions were in all cases "fairly high." But "labor and the Jews are commonly blamed, and this, we know, is precisely the Nazi pattern of attack." In short, a large nucleus of people were "aggressive Antis." Some were so paranoid that they were ready to start "violent persecutions." Worse still, "recent events indicate that the strain [of big-otry], if not spreading in extent, is becoming more tense." The emotional and psychological pressures of a cruel war were producing among Ameri-cans "that pinioned feeling" which made them want to attack something, something "visible, near-lying and outlandish." Indeed, "when the con-ditions for an outbreak are ripe, anything—even a baseless rumor—will precipitate the violence." While the article was intended to be a general warning against the spread of ethnic prejudice, to Jews it had a familiar and ominous ring.[20]

Still, resentment of the supposed wealth and influence of American Jewry was not the only or even the chief reason for popular opposition to special military or diplomatic efforts on behalf of the victims of the Holocaust. As important as outright anti-Semitism was a widespread per-ception that Jews tended to be alarmists and were constantly complain-ing and lamenting. Admittedly, the Nazi regime was guilty of terrible atrocities, but the victims were not only Jewish. What about the Russian prisoners of war, starved, beaten, or even executed at the whim of the Wehrmacht? Or the Polish slave laborers, suffering and dying by the tens of thousands, defenseless against the cruelty of the conquerors? Or the innocent inhabitants of Lidice in Czechoslovakia or Oradour-sur-Glane in France, rounded up and killed by the Germans in retaliation for the forays of the underground resistance? And most important, what about the American boys in uniform, fighting and dying overseas in order to defeat the Third Reich and put an end to the Holocaust? Were not these sacrifices and losses as tragic as those the Jews had to endure? And if so, why should the Jews expect greater compassion or more help than the other nationalities and ethnicities participating in the war?

Questions of this sort were raised in a different form by some of the liberal publicists who agreed that the exterminative anti-Semitic poli-cies of the Third Reich were an unspeakable atrocity. Early in 1944, Fred Eastman, a professor of religious literature and drama at the Chicago Theological Seminary, wrote in the *Christian Century* that he was neither disbelieving nor indifferent nor without pity regarding the Holocaust. Far from it. The reports of the mass murder of Jews and "countless oth-ers" were so clearly authenticated as to be undeniable. Never before had there been such a shocking crime. "If we were disbelieving we would be fools. If we were indifferent we would be insane. If we were without pity we would be knaves." And yet Eastman could not bring himself to join those he identified as "screamers." He did not describe precisely who those "screamers" were, but it was clear whom he meant.

Why was he so reluctant to join them? Eastman offered a detailed explanation. For one thing, he and others like him had long recognized that the so-called peace following the First World War was only an armistice which would sooner or later be followed by an even bloodier military conflict. Therefore, once the Second World War was over, there would have to be a reconciliation between winners and losers. Preaching hatred of the enemy would only make that reconciliation more difficult. And besides, what exactly did the "screamers" want? Did they want more fighting? If the war was still not big enough for them, how much bigger would they like to make it? "Our sons are in the service, our incomes are mortgaged for generations to come, and the casualty lists are mounting from week to week. If the spilling of blood and the conversion of our national resources into instruments of destruction can stop the mass murders and the other depredations of Hitler's cohorts, it is being done as rapidly as the generals of the United Nations can manage it." To ask for more than that was not only unreasonable, it was irresponsible.

Still, "some people" who claimed to be more outraged than "the rest of us" about the mass killing of Jews in Europe wanted at least one other thing: more committees. "They seem to feel that something has been accomplished when another committee has been formed, another list of sponsors printed in the press, generally another full-page advertisement printed in the *New York Times* and a few other papers appealing for funds, and another opportunity granted some congressmen and senators to issue publicity statements to the effect that the Jews must be saved." Admittedly, among those pleading for a special effort to save the victims of the Holocaust were many who wanted more than an emotional outburst, more than an extension of the war, more than a new committee. But what exactly did they want? Until Eastman could be sure, he saw no reason for joining the "screamers."[21]

To some American Jews, it became apparent that the attempt to persuade Washington to oppose the Nazi extermination program by special military or diplomatic measures was getting nowhere, so they shifted the focus of their efforts to those who had temporarily managed to escape Nazi oppression. In other words, although the number of Jews who were refugees was small by comparison with the number of Jews in mortal danger under the German occupation, an effort to find a haven for the former seemed far more likely to succeed than an effort to rescue the latter. The situation of those trapped in the ghettos or the death camps appeared almost hopeless.

Yet even when it came to the refugee problem, there were sharp differences of opinion within the American Jewish community. Where exactly should the havens for victims of anti-Semitic persecution be established? The United States would be an ideal location, but public opinion was firmly against the admission of large numbers of immigrants. The government had to take that opposition into account, especially since the admission of Jewish refugees was likely to lead to demands for the admission of non-Jewish refugees as well. There was still the possibility of finding an asylum for persecuted Jews in some other part of the world, but people there seemed no more eager than those in the United States to welcome a flood of needy foreigners, alien in speech, custom, and culture. What should be done?

Many maintained that Palestine was the logical place for the resettlement of Jewish refugees from Europe. Yet that too presented problems. Would Great Britain agree to admit tens or perhaps hundreds of thousands of immigrants to a region that the League of Nations had entrusted to it for temporary administration? And how would the Arabs respond to a sudden flood of Jews pouring into a part of the Middle East they regarded as their own? And even if the refugees were permitted to enter Palestine without restriction, should that permission be valid only for the duration of the war, or should it extend beyond that? And if they were allowed to stay, should the community they would then establish be regarded as a "Jewish homeland" or a "Jewish national state"? The complications and risks of a Middle Eastern solution to the refugee problem went far beyond the fate of those seeking to escape the genocidal policies of National Socialism.

American Jews disagreed strongly about the establishment of a sanctuary in Palestine. For the officials in Washington who had to deal with the issue, it was a source of confusion and frustration. At the beginning of

1944, Breckinridge Long, whose assignment in the State Department was about to change, expressed relief in his diary at the prospect of not having to deal any longer with the refugee problem. "The Jewish organizations are all divided and in controversies of their own." The ones engaged in politics quarreled with the ones engaged in charity and relief, but they were often also in disagreement among themselves. At times they would even condemn one or another of the organizations as "anathema." In short, "there is no adhesion nor any sympathetic collaboration—rather rivalry, jealousy and antagonism." Long was delighted that all of that was almost behind him. "It will be only a few days now before I relinquish jurisdiction in connection with refugees and let somebody else have the fun." Then it would be good-bye and good riddance.[22]

Yet the inability of members of the Jewish community to form a united front was not simply a result of ideological differences or strategic disagreements. It also reflected the hopelessness of the search for some way of saving their coreligionists from the death camps. The combination of fanatical Nazi anti-Semitism, American ethnic prejudice intensified by war, and prevalent suspicion that the Jews were trying to obtain special treatment made any effective plan to rescue the victims of the Holocaust virtually impossible. To be sure, it did not stem the flow of pleas, petitions, recommendations, and demands that something must be done to prevent a terrible human catastrophe—something, anything, everything. But even those supporting such demands recognized that their efforts were unlikely to have any practical effect. What they were doing represented essentially a form of public mourning, a final rite for a dying community. The protesters felt that they could not simply remain silent witnesses to a murderous crime being committed before their eyes.

There were some American Jews, however, who did remain silent, or almost silent. They were only a minority but a well-to-do minority, culturally assimilated, socially accepted, and politically influential. Some of them were government advisers or even government officials. They had important contacts in high places in Washington, and they were well informed about what was happening to European Jewry. Their reluctance to participate in the protest movement was not the result of ignorance regarding the Holocaust. Rather, it reflected a conviction that demonstrations, marches, resolutions, and petitions would have no effect on official policy regarding the conduct of the war. If anything, they would make a bad situation worse by aggravating domestic prejudices and tensions.

The restraint of these circumspect Jews was seen by their more militant coreligionists as motivated primarily by self-interest, reflecting a reluctance to do anything that might jeopardize their position as members of the elite. That view was not altogether unfounded. The moderates did often feel uneasy and vulnerable when dealing with issues that might raise questions about their loyalty to the established values and beliefs of the American patriciate. And yet there was more to it than that. They were also sincerely convinced that the only way to save at least some of the victims of Nazi genocide was by military victory, achieved as quickly as possible. Anything that prolonged the war was bound to increase the number of those murdered in the gas chambers. And that meant that demands for a diversion of military resources to the bombardment of railroads leading to the death camps or for the negotiation of an agreement to exchange persecuted Jews for strategic materials were worse than futile. They were harmful, they were self-defeating. The only effective strategy was a single-minded, unwavering commitment to a swift victory.

There was still another reason that the moderates were reluctant to participate in the protest movement. They were almost unanimously supporters of Roosevelt and the New Deal. Not only had the president appointed more Jews than any of his predecessors to positions of importance in the government, but he seemed sincerely opposed to anti-Semitism, in America as well as in Europe. Should the Jews reward his commitment to equal treatment for all citizens, regardless of origin or religion, by making his job more difficult? Worse still, might not all those demonstrations and resolutions criticizing the government's policy with regard to the Holocaust endanger Roosevelt's chances of reelection? And if he were defeated, would his successor, whoever it might be, prove equally sympathetic toward Jews? Not likely. It seemed clear that the best thing for the Jewish community as well as for the country at large was to avoid actions or demands that might turn public opinion against the administration. The wisest course would be restraint and discretion.

This conclusion helps explain the decision of many of the circumspect Jews to discourage a display of too much activism by their militant coreligionists. A memorandum by John W. Pehle in March 1944 described a meeting with Samuel I. Rosenman, the presidential adviser, to review the draft of a declaration condemning the war crimes committed by the Third Reich. Roosevelt had indicated that he wanted the document issued in the form of a statement, suggesting also that it should be rewritten "so as to be aimed less directly at the atrocities against the Jews." Rosenman had accordingly prepared a revised draft reflecting the president's wishes. But Pehle had serious reservations. "I felt that it was a mistake to weaken the declaration in the way that it had been weakened." An earlier statement condemning Nazi atrocities had made no specific reference to the crimes committed against Jews, and "while that might not be important in the United States, it was singularly important in Germany where the people were led to believe that this country was not concerned at all about the atrocities against the Jews who were not particularly regarded as human beings." Yet Rosenman would not retreat. He said that he had advised Roosevelt not to sign the declaration because of its "pointed reference to Jews," fearing that "any such statement would intensify anti-Semitism in the United States." Pehle, the Christian, seemed more eager to denounce the mass murder of Jews in Europe than Rosenman, the Jew. But then Pehle was not as worried as Rosenman about the spread of anti-Semitic prejudice in America.[23]

Congressman Sol Bloom was equally determined to avoid any appearance of favoring his coreligionists abroad at the expense of his compatriots at home. In his autobiography, written shortly after the war, he tried to explain why he had not supported special measures on behalf of the Jews threatened with mass murder. First of all, such measures would only have worsened the situation of those they were intended to help. "The announcement that we were going to aid a particular group might lead to intensified persecutions [by the Nazis], perhaps to demonstrate that meddling from the outside could only intensify its wretchedness, perhaps to induce the payment of a huge ransom." Indeed, the Germans might even have tried "to sink a ship filled with helpless men, women, and children," thereby hoping to discourage further attempts to rescue Jews.

Besides, Bloom maintained that for him, as for all other patriotic Americans, victory was the chief objective. "The humanitarian motive to aid individuals, we had at all times to keep in mind, had to be subordinated to the greater humanitarian motive of rescuing whole peoples. Any plan that might interfere with winning the war had to be rejected." And yet, despite his unwavering support of his country's struggle against a ruthless enemy, he had to face criticism from several directions. "One group would attack me, as a Jew, for a fancied discrimination in favor of my people. And at the very same time certain Jews were upbraiding me for my failure to assert myself more vigorously in behalf of my brethren." But how could his assailants accuse him of either partiality or indifference? "I grieved that anyone believed I would do more for any one group than I would for any other group of sufferers." That was wrong and unfair.[24]

Even Stephen Wise was reluctant to say anything that might suggest he was seeking special consideration for Jews. Such a perception would intensify ethnic prejudice in the United States; it might even erode popular support for Roosevelt, the courageous defender of Jews. And that in turn might have very serious consequences for the Jewish community. He therefore made it clear in his address to the mass meeting in Madison Square Garden on July 21, 1942, that he was not seeking preferential treatment for his coreligionists. "We are asking our Government and the United Nations to serve notice upon the Nazi despots that the horror of Nazi mistreatment of civilians should cease, whether of Jews, Protestants or Catholics, whether Poles, Czechs or Greeks." And as for the contention by some Jews that Roosevelt was not doing enough to help the victims of Nazi racism, Wise insisted a few months later in a letter to a friend, Fanny Mayer Korn, that the Jewish community should in fact be thankful for what he had accomplished. "Hitler would have won the war if it had not been for our President and America." Surely Roosevelt deserved at least some appreciation and praise.

Still, there were times when Wise felt that he was being too compliant, too much of a defender of the government's policies. Perhaps he should be more demanding, more insistent, more critical. Only a week after reminding Fanny Korn that Roosevelt had prevented Hitler's victory in the war, Wise confessed to Felix Frankfurter that he was uneasy about playing the role of intermediary between the administration and the Jewish community. Indeed, he felt at times that he had let himself become an apologist for the president. "I find that a good part of my work is to explain to my fellow Jews why our Government cannot do all the things asked or expected of it." And that made him feel guilty. He wondered whether "I am getting to be a *Hofjude*," referring to the complaisant Jews who had served as financial advisers to the rulers of the Holy Roman Empire. Trying to be a protester and a conciliator at the same time was proving very difficult.[25]

The incident that revealed most clearly the ideological and strategical differences between the militants and the moderates in the American Jewish community was a march on October 6, 1943, of between four and five hundred Orthodox rabbis, who went to Washington from various parts of the country to deliver a petition asking the president to save the European Jews by arranging for their emigration to Palestine or some of the countries at war with the Axis. To Roosevelt, however, the prospect of having to receive a delegation of that sort was troubling and unwelcome. To be sure, he had previously sent greetings to various Jewish mass meetings and had even from time to time received delegations representing Jewish organizations. But those Jews had been different. They had been indistinguishable in dress, manner, and appearance from other Americans. The ones who wanted to meet with him now, however, were unmistakably Jewish. They had long beards and earlocks, they wore black coats and hats, and many of them spoke English with a pronounced Old World accent. Quite a few, in fact, resembled the anti-Semitic caricatures that the *Stürmer* was circulating among the adherents of the Third Reich. It would be best for the president not to be seen receiving visitors who were so un-American in language and bearing. As the rabbis were approaching the White House, he quietly left for Bolling Field to dedicate four Liberator bombers which had recently been acquired by the Air Force.

The task of dealing with the assembled rabbis was left to Vice President Henry A. Wallace, who received a delegation in his office and, after accepting their petition, joined the others on the steps of the Senate. He assured them that the "Jewish problem" was recognized as part of the "general problem." The group then proceeded to the Lincoln Memorial, where a prayer was offered, and then to the White House, to be greeted by Marvin H. McIntire, Roosevelt's secretary. Finally, after visiting a local synagogue, where kosher food had been prepared for them, the rabbis returned to the railroad station and started the trip back home. Washington could now breathe a sigh of relief.[26]

To the public at large, the incident was of only passing interest. Far more important were recent developments overseas, where American troops had invaded the Italian mainland and occupied Naples after the fall of the Mussolini regime. But the march of the rabbis revealed a deep divide in opinion and strategy between Jewish militants and moderates. To the latter, the procession in Washington was irresponsible; it only made the task of saving the victims of the Holocaust more difficult. By intensifying domestic ethnic prejudice and embarrassing a sympathetic president, the marchers made it that much harder for Jews who had some influence in the government to press for measures helpful to their persecuted coreligionists overseas. The only ones who had benefited from the rabbinical demonstrations were the anti-Semites.

A member of the Emergency Committee to Save the Jewish People of Europe, which had supported the march, reported a few days later that "the Jewish members of the House of Representatives . . . had done all they could to dissuade the Rabbis from making their bearded appearances in Washington." Bloom, for example, had told one of them, "as an additional inducement for not going," that "it would be very undignified for a group of such un-American looking people to appear in Washington." On the morning of October 6, before Roosevelt left the White House for Bolling Field, Rosenman assured the president that "the group behind this petition [is] not representative of the most thoughtful elements of Jewry." He added that "he had tried—admittedly without success—to keep the horde from storming Washington." Indeed, "the leading Jews of [Rosenman's] acquaintance opposed this march on the Capitol." More than four months later, at the end of February 1945, Secretary of the Treasury Morgenthau was still complaining to members of his staff that "the Orthodox rabbis have gone and done this thing on their own. They get the people out [yet] they don't tell us. But if the thing goes wrong—and not only the future treatment of Jews in Europe is at stake, but the whole question of anti-Semitism in this country—and I think that the people who are largely to blame are these Orthodox Jews." By their shortsightedness and recklessness, they had weakened the position of American Jewry.[27]

To Roosevelt, however, the march of the rabbis was no more than a minor distraction. His chief concern was waging and winning the war. Everything else had to be subordinated to the goal of defeating the country's enemies in Europe and Asia. And that meant that although he was fully aware of Hitler's extermination of European Jews, and although he was sincere in his condemnation of it, he was also convinced that the diversion of military resources not only would prolong the war but might intensify ethnic prejudice at home. That was why he carefully tried to avoid creating the impression that more was being done for Jewish than for non-Jewish victims of the Third Reich's persecution.

The president's statement of March 24, 1944, thus spoke of the need to create a world in which "all persons regardless of race, color or creed may live in peace, honor and dignity." It condemned the systematic torture and murder of civilians by the Nazis and the Japanese, citing the cruelties inflicted on "innocent Poles, Czechs, Norwegians, Dutch, Danes, French, Greeks, Russians, Chinese, Filipinos—and many others." It did make mention of the "slaughters" in Warsaw, but also of those in Lidice, Kharkov, and Nanking. Only then did it turn to "one of the blackest crimes of all history," namely, "the wholesale systematic murder of the Jews of Europe." If even more of these defenseless people were to perish on the eve of the Allied victory over barbarism, that would be a terrible tragedy. Roosevelt therefore warned that all those who were knowingly taking part in "the deportation of Jews to their death in Poland or Norwegians and French to their death in Germany" were just as guilty as the Nazis themselves. He concluded with an appeal to "the free peoples of Europe and Asia" to help all victims of oppression, again "regardless of race or religion or creed," and to rally to this "righteous undertaking" in the name of justice and humanity. The statement was broad enough and inclusive enough to withstand any charge of favoritism toward the Jewish victims of National Socialism.[28]

Roosevelt's reluctance to dwell on the extermination of European Jewry reflected a caution dictated by political realism. And yet he, like many other Americans, even liberal Americans, felt that the popular suspicions and resentments regarding Jews were not altogether baseless. The president was very careful, however, about expressing this view. The Jews were, after all, among his most ardent supporters. And yet from time to time he would say something that revealed that he too shared the common ethnic perceptions and predilections of American society. In the summer of 1939, Harold Ickes described in his diary a meeting at which he showed Roosevelt an item in a British periodical to the effect that Ambassador

Joseph P. Kennedy was telling his conservative English friends that "Jews were running the United States," even insinuating that "the democratic policy of the United States is a Jewish production." After reading the item, Roosevelt said simply, "It is true," and that was the end of it. Was he trying to protect an appointee who held an important diplomatic post? Or did he want to avoid a lengthy discussion of what ought to be done about Kennedy's indiscretion? Or did he really believe that Jews were running the United States and were responsible for the country's democratic policy? There is no sure way of telling.[29]

What Roosevelt had to say a few years later, however, in January 1943, during the Casablanca Conference, was unambiguous. In the course of a confidential conversation with General August Paul Noguès, the French resident-general in Rabat, the subject of the future of the Jewish minority in the region came up. In the president's view, "the number of Jews engaged in the practice of the professions (law, medicine, etc.) should be definitely limited to the percentage that the Jewish population in North Africa bears to the whole of the North African population." Such an arrangement would permit the Jews to engage in but not "overcrowd" the professions. General Noguès observed that it would be a "sad thing" for the French to win the war only to open the way for the Jews to control the professions and the business world in North Africa. Roosevelt tried to reassure him. The president's plan would "eliminate the specific and understandable complaints which the Germans have towards the Jews in Germany, namely, that while they represented a small part of the population, over fifty percent of the lawyers, doctors, school teachers, college professors, etc., in Germany, were Jews." Roosevelt's statistics may have been questionable, but his intentions were clear. A reasonable quota system would be best for Jews and non-Jews alike. It would protect the former against ethnic bigotry and the latter against ethnic aggressiveness. In the end, everybody would be better off.[30]

How would American Jews have reacted to the news that their favorite president was willing to impose restrictions on the economic and political opportunities open to their coreligionists abroad and perhaps even at home? They would have been surprised and disappointed, though probably not as much as might be expected. After all, though the existence of quotas was not openly acknowledged, they were common in the United States, in colleges and universities, in the arts and the professions, in business and finance, and in government and politics. Roosevelt would have seemed no worse than most Americans, in fact better. He had shown himself more willing to accept Jews as members of his administration than any previous president. He had expressed over and over again his sympathy for the victims of anti-Semitism in the New World as well as the Old. In short, Roosevelt, whatever his weaknesses, whatever his faults, was the best they could expect. Was there any alternative?

13

A Statecraft of Carefully Calibrated Compassion

THE ALLIED GOVERNMENTS' policy regarding the Holocaust was determined by a conjunction and interaction of two conflicting purposes and strategies, each with its own goal, its own logic, and its own rationale. On one side were those, most of them Jews but also quite a few Christians, to whom the chief justification for waging the war was the murderous anti-Semitic policy of the Third Reich. The Nazi regime was guilty of many crimes and atrocities: political oppression, economic exploitation, cultural exclusionism, and the cruel treatment of those regarded as ethnically inferior. The hardships that the conquered Poles, Czechs, Serbs, and Greeks had to endure reflected the brutal racism of Hitler's Germany. But since the only ones condemned to outright extermination were the Jews, their situation called for special concern and special effort. No reason offered for the military struggle against Hitler was as morally compelling or ideologically persuasive as the duty to save the lives of millions of helpless, innocent men, women, and children facing murder in the death camps of the Third Reich.

Yet those who shared this view recognized or were forced to recognize that the Allied governments would not and could not make ending the deportation of Jews to Auschwitz and Treblinka the chief goal of the war. The sacrifices in life and property of the civilian population could not be justified primarily as the price of preventing or stopping genocide. Something more had to be offered to the ones paying that price, something less remote and idealistic, something affecting them directly. And that meant that those to whom ending the Holocaust was the most important objective of the war had to agree to broaden its aims to include the liberation of other persecuted ethnic minorities, the defense of their own national frontiers, and the protection of the system of law and government under which they lived. The only question was how prominent the saving of Jews would be among the other aims and justifications of the Allied military struggle.

On the other side of this crucial debate were those, mostly high-ranking government officials, whose responsibility it was to determine the relative importance of the various demands being made on the war effort and to shape the military strategy of the nation in accordance with that determination. To them, the Holocaust was far down on the list of urgent problems and concerns. Not that they were indifferent to the extermination of European Jewry, although some of them did from time to time express commonplace ethnic biases and platitudes. Yet not even the most bigoted among them approved of genocide. What motivated them primarily was the conviction that the war effort had to be seen as essential for the defense of everyday interests and concerns, for the welfare and security of ordinary citizens. It might be useful occasionally to invoke moral principles or democratic ideals in condemning National Socialism. But to let it appear that wartime sacrifices were being made for the sake of some abstract principle or some persecuted minority could prove dangerous. It could undermine the popular determination to fight until victory had been achieved. Saving European Jewry had to be subordinated to the requirements of self-interest and self-preservation.

This is not to say that the officials determining Allied policy were blind to the consequences of the Third Reich's obsessive anti-Semitism. But their belief that displaying too much concern for the fate of foreign Jews might intensify domestic prejudice was bolstered by the conclusion that there was nothing they could do to prevent the leaders of the Nazi regime from carrying out their final solution to the "Jewish question." Hitler's devoted followers were too deeply committed to his genocidal policies to be deterred by threats or pleas or promises or bribes. Nothing could shake their belief that extermination was the only way of dealing with the terrible danger to society represented by the Jews. Future generations would undoubtedly be grateful to them for having had the courage to put an end to that danger once and for all. The leading officials of the democratic states were accordingly convinced that there was little they could do to restrain the fanatical racism of the Third Reich. The only way to save its victims was to win the war as rapidly as possible.

This view was reflected in a memorandum that Breckinridge Long submitted to Secretary Hull in the summer of 1943. What he had to say was hard to refute. He agreed that there were some Jews "outside the jurisdiction of Germany" who might still be rescued. "All the other Jews who need help are within the confines of Germany or occupied territory but there is no help that we can give them short of military destruction of German armies and the liberation of all the oppressed peoples under its jurisdiction." The United States was already doing all it could to achieve that end. As for the suggestion that the American government propose to the Germans an exchange of persecuted Jews for scarce manufactured goods or raw materials, Long dismissed that as visionary. "It is quite improbable that Germany would permit the departure of Jews even if we could bring ourselves to the point of negotiating with the enemy during the course of the conflict." His logic, though harsh, seemed incontrovertible.[1]

Yet the assumption that the Nazi regime could not under any circumstances be persuaded to abandon or modify its program of ethnic extermination was not the only reason for the Allied statesmen's reluctance to condemn the Holocaust too loudly or too frequently. After all, denunciations of genocide, even if ignored by the Germans, might prove useful for purposes of propaganda, underscoring the fundamental difference between the humanitarian ideals of the Allies and the brutal policies of the Axis. They might reinforce support for the war at home and arouse sympathy for the democratic cause abroad, in the occupied as well as the neutral countries. Yet Washington wondered also whether they might not have the opposite effect. Might they not support the Nazis' contention that international Jewry was behind the plans and policies of the Allies? And might that not in turn arouse concern among the nonbelligerents that a victory for the United States would simply mean exchanging domination by the Germans for domination by the Jews? Washington had to be careful about displaying sympathy for the victims of the Holocaust. Too little could seem to support the Third Reich's contention that most Americans secretly approved of its anti-Semitic policies. But too much could strengthen the suspicion that the Jewish community was playing a decisive role in the political life of the United States. The best thing would be a policy of caution and restraint.

In his memorandum to the secretary of state, Long drew a distinction between the situation of Jews under the rule of the Third Reich and those who were "in places of probable danger such as their precarious position in Spain." Nothing could be done to save the former except win the war. In the case of the latter, however, he seemed to suggest that there were still possibilities of rescue. At least, that is what he implied to Hull. In the privacy of his diary, however, he complained about the "Jewish faction" under the leadership of Stephen Wise, which was assiduously "pushing" the cause of the refugees "in letters and telegrams to the President, the Secretary [of State], and [Undersecretary Sumner] Welles—in public meetings to arouse emotions—in full page newspaper advertisements— [and] in resolutions." Many public officials, moreover, had signed broadsides issued by the "Jewish faction," and Senator Edwin C. Johnson of Colorado had even introduced one of its resolutions in the Senate. The members of that faction were so aggressive that "they are apt to produce a reaction against their interest."

What concerned Long most, however, was not that too much agitation by the followers of Stephen Wise might turn public opinion against the cause they were defending. It was rather the risk that "their activities may lend color to the charges of Hitler that we are fighting this war on account of and at the instigation and direction of our Jewish citizens." All that Nazi propaganda had to do was to publish Johnson's resolution and the broadsides bearing the signatures of prominent political leaders in the press of the neutral countries. That would be enough to persuade many nonbelligerents of the validity of the Third Reich's charges against the Allies. "In Turkey the impression grows—and in Spain it is being circulated—and in Palestine's hinterland and in North Africa the Moslem population will be easy believers in such charges. It might easily be a definite detriment to our war effort." In short, not only would any attempt to rescue Jews in the death camps prove futile, but even an effort to help Jews in search of refuge could prove dangerous.[2]

Yet the chief reason for the reluctance of American officialdom to display too much sympathy for victims of the Holocaust was not the effect it might have on public opinion in the Third Reich, in the occupied countries, or in the neutral nations. It was the effect it might have in the United States. What motivated the officials chiefly in dealing with the Holocaust was not personal likes or dislikes but the need to avoid doing anything that might divert public attention from the war effort and undermine the collective resolve to go on fighting until victory had been won. This did not mean that they could simply ignore the genocidal policies of the Third Reich. To do so would outrage all those to whom the Holocaust was the most terrible of the Nazis' atrocities. But to devote too much attention to the Holocaust could lead to serious domestic divisions and disputes weakening the war effort. Official compassion had to be carefully weighed and measured.

The dilemma confronting Washington was widely recognized, even by many of those who were demanding a greater effort to save the Jews of Europe. A pamphlet published in 1944 by Mercedes M. Randall of the Women's International League for Peace and Freedom urged all Americans to write to their representatives in Congress asking them to do more to help the victims of the Holocaust. But even she had to acknowledge that the unwillingness of the authorities to relax the restrictions on immigration for the benefit of Jewish refugees was largely the result of concern about the growth of domestic anti-Semitism. "Behind the reluctance of government circles to take action," she wrote, "behind the reluctance of private groups, is the fear, expressed or unexpressed, that the admission of more Jews into the United States will increase our already growing anti-Semitic prejudices." She was right.[3]

The recognition by each side that neither one could prevail led to what seemed to be a stalemate but was actually a tacit compromise. Not that their rhetoric changed in any way. Those urging a greater effort to save European Jewry continued to insist that the Allies' highest moral obligation was to save the millions of innocent human beings threatened with extermination. Those opposing such an effort went on arguing that the only way to save the victims of Nazi anti-Semitism was to win the war as soon as possible. Anything that might delay military victory should be rejected as harmful and self-defeating. Yet both sides silently agreed that it was in their common interest to avoid an open break. They might go on arguing and debating, but it was important to maintain contact, to appear to follow a policy of give-and-take, and to exchange a few concessions from time to time, even if only grudgingly.

That meant that advocates of the persecuted Jews in Europe continued to organize mass meetings and protest marches, to urge the destruction of the railroads leading to Auschwitz and Treblinka, to recommend day-and-night bombing of German cities until the Third Reich abandoned its program of genocide, and to call for the issuance of warnings of severe punishment after the war for those responsible for ethnic mass murder. Yet they recognized that requests of that sort were more likely to provide psychological or emotional satisfaction to their supporters than to have any significant effect on the policies of their government. They therefore agreed tacitly to settle for official statements of condemnation of the systematic extermination of Jews. They also hoped to be able occasionally to persuade the authorities to allow small groups of refugees to enter the United States outside the limits imposed by the quota system. But they admitted in private that this was as much as they could reasonably expect. To press for much more not only might antagonize the officials in the State Department to the point where they would refuse to make any further concessions, but it might lead to the defeat of Roosevelt in the next election. It was important to know when to stop.

The officials in Washington were equally cautious in dealing with the problem of the Holocaust. What could the United States do about it? Clearly, the government must not simply ignore the carefully planned and organized annihilation of European Jewry. Issuing an occasional denunciation of the cruelty of the Nazi regime would be safe, perhaps even useful. But at what point should this strategy stop? Supporters of the victims of the Holocaust seemed insatiable in their demand for official condemnations of genocide. No sooner did Washington issue one statement than they would ask for another and then another and then still another. There was no end to their pleas and appeals. But might not too many declarations or denunciations backfire? Wouldn't the Poles and the Czechs or, for that matter, the Dutch and the Belgians begin to feel that their sufferings were being largely ignored because of the constant complaints by the Jews in America? And wouldn't the propaganda of the Third Reich exploit the resultant rivalries and resentments in order to promote anti-Semitism on the continent? Worse still, wouldn't the display of too much concern for the victims of the Holocaust reinforce popular suspicions that the Jewish community was gaining too much influence in national affairs?

To those on the other side, however, government reluctance to become too deeply involved in the tragedy of the Holocaust reflected a callousness and insensitivity unexpected in the leaders of a great democratic nation. How could they fail to see that the policy of ethnic annihilation adopted by the Third Reich was the ultimate moral justification for the military crusade on which America had embarked? Even when they did condemn the Nazi regime's murderous racism, they often tried to avoid specifying who its chief victims were. In the spring of 1943, following the Bermuda Conference, which had been convoked to deal with the refugee problem, an article in the liberal New York newspaper *PM* complained that the delegates had "regarded [it] as almost improper to mention the word Jew despite the presence of at least 2,000,000 whose very existence is threatened in Hitler-conquered Europe." Other defenders of the Jewish cause charged that the bureaucrats in Washington and even the mainstream press preferred to use circumlocutions like "refugees," "victims," or "anti-Nazis" in describing those threatened with extermination in occupied Europe. Wasn't that likely to obscure the tragedy confronting European Jewry? Wouldn't it be better to identify loudly and clearly the intended victims of Hitler's murderous designs? To disguise the true nature of the Holocaust served only to prolong it.[4]

Nevertheless, the tacit compromise between those who favored and those who opposed a more vigorous policy was not without some achievements. The most important one was the increasing number of statements and declarations condemning ethnic persecution and threatening severe punishment for those responsible for it. These were made most frequently by local and regional officeholders, especially in states where there was a large Jewish community. Those making them were as a rule sincere, but their sincerity was reinforced by the knowledge that what they were saying could prove useful at the next election and that they themselves would not have to assume the responsibility of translating their words into deeds. Officials in Washington, on the other hand, especially those entrusted with the conduct of diplomacy and propaganda, were much more reticent. Not only were they further removed from the constant pressure of ethnic groups and organizations, but they had been taught by experience to consider carefully the likely national and international repercussions of anything they might say regarding the strategy or purpose of the war. Their caution was an inevitable result of their accountability for the conduct of the nation's foreign affairs.

Yet they too had to make some concessions. They could not afford to appear indifferent to the cold-blooded mass murder going on day after day on the other side of the Atlantic. They tried, therefore, to find some middle course, one that would express compassion for the victims but would not arouse too much resentment among the oppressed nationalities of Europe or the traditionalists and nativists in America. Those who had little to do with the formulation and conduct of foreign policy were the ones most likely to voice fiery denunciations of Nazi racism. Members of the State Department, in contrast, were among the most reluctant.

Still another important consideration influenced the issuance of official condemnations of the Holocaust, namely, the course of the war. The more doubtful the outcome of military operations, the more cautious the expression of sympathy for persecuted Jews. Conversely, as it became increasingly clear that the Allies were likely to win, statements of support for the victims became more frequent and explicit. Eventually even the leading American diplomats joined in the chorus of denunciation. The likelihood of victory made them bolder.

In March 1943, for example, only a few months after Washington's confirmation of reports regarding the genocide but more than a year after the genocide had actually begun, Congress adopted a resolution denouncing the mass murder of innocent people. It declared in the preface that Americans viewed with "indignation" the atrocities committed against the civilian population in the occupied countries, "especially the mass murder of Jewish men, women, and children," adding that "this policy of the Nazis has created a reign of terror, brutality, and extermination in Poland and other countries in Eastern and Central Europe." The text of the resolution, however, while condemning the "brutal and indefensible outrages against millions of helpless men, women, and children" as "unworthy of any nation or any regime which pretends to be civilized," did not specify the ethnic background of the millions of innocent people exposed to the "brutal and indefensible outrages" of the Third Reich.

Still, the resolution went beyond a mere denunciation of the Nazi regime's genocidal policy. It also warned of stern retribution against those responsible for ethnic mass murder. "The dictates of humanity and honorable conduct demand that this inexcusable slaughter and mistreatment shall cease and . . . it is the sense of this Congress that those guilty, directly or indirectly, of these criminal acts shall be held accountable and punished in a manner commensurate with the offenses for which they are responsible."[5]

By the time Congress issued this condemnation of the Holocaust, the tide of war had already begun to turn, but only slightly. Although the Allied forces were making important gains in North Africa, the Germans stubbornly continued to resist. In Eastern Europe, the Soviet army had broken the siege of Leningrad and won a great victory at Stalingrad, but then the Wehrmacht opened a new offensive, retaking Kharkov and Belgorod. The final outcome of the military struggle remained very much in doubt. More than a year later, however, in June 1944, when the Senate Foreign Relations Committee issued a statement urging the people of Hungary to protect the Jews living among them from annihilation in the Nazi death camps, an Allied victory seemed almost certain. Mussolini had fallen and Italy had withdrawn from the war. The American forces were about to invade Normandy, initiating the liberation of France. And the Russians, after retaking Odessa and the Crimea, had reached their prewar border with Romania. It was clear that the fall of the Third Reich was now only a question of time.

That was why the statement of the Senate Foreign Relations Committee was so much more explicit in describing the Holocaust and identifying its victims than the congressional resolution a year earlier. Issued shortly after the Third Reich had occupied Hungary and begun to deport Jews to the death camps in Poland, the declaration was unequivocal in its denunciation of the mass murder about to take place. "The news that Germany has designated the 800,000 Jews in Hungary for death horrifies the people of the United States and all freedom-loving people." It was unthinkable that the great majority of Hungarians would countenance the "cold-blooded murder of innocent men, women, and children." The country had been a haven for tens of thousands who had fled the Nazi terror in other countries. "Hungarians once shielded their Jewish fellow citizens." But now the government, under pressure from Berlin, had joined the Germans in their "ruthless determination to do away with the Jews." The conduct of the general population should demonstrate, however, that this "unholy scheme" was a betrayal of the true Hungarian spirit. "Jews can be hidden by [their non-Jewish countrymen] until such time as they may help them across the border to safety. They can refuse to buy property stolen from the Jews." In short, honorable Hungarians should use every means to obstruct the Nazis and their collaborators. But they should also prepare for a day of reckoning. "Until the time when guilt and innocence will weigh heavily in the balance, they can keep watch and remember those who are accessories to murder and those who extend mercy." They would not have to wait very long, however. "It is nearly that time."[6]

There was a vast difference in the reaction of the U.S. government to the initiation of the Holocaust in Poland in the fall of 1941 and to its extension to Hungary in the spring of 1944. Although the number of Jews threatened with extermination in the two countries varied greatly—more than 3 million in the former and about 800,000 in the latter—Washington's response was much bolder and more resolute, at least in language, when dealing with the latter than with the former. It took the American authorities well over a year to acknowledge that East European Jewry was facing mass murder. Even then they remained reluctant to state openly that the situation of the Jews was in any way different from that of the other national and ethnic communities under the brutal rule of the Third Reich. But after the Wehrmacht occupied Hungary in March 1944 and when, two months later, the mass deportation of Hungarian Jews began, protests and warnings of reprisal started almost at once.

The reason is clear. In 1941 and 1942 the Nazi regime dominated most of Europe, so it was important for American officials not to do or say anything that might support the contention of German propaganda that the Allies were serving the interests of world Jewry. The perception that Washington was more interested in the fate of the Jews than in that of the other conquered peoples might have had a serious adverse effect on public opinion on both sides of the Atlantic. It was important to avoid any appearance of favoritism toward the Jewish community. But by 1944, that had ceased to be a major concern in Washington. Now military victory seemed not only certain but imminent, perhaps no more than a few months away, a year at most. Why, then, worry about whether German public opinion might be swayed by the racist propaganda of the Nazi authorities or whether the population of the occupied countries would begin making invidious comparisons between the Allied concern for Jews and non-Jews? It no longer even mattered greatly whether ethnic prejudice at home might be intensified by too much attention to the Holocaust. The important thing was that the approaching end of the war had freed the government authorities from the need to avoid subjects likely to arouse sharp differences of opinion in Europe or America.

Even those officials in Washington who were entrusted with the conduct of foreign affairs began to speak out with a new forthrightness. On July 14, 1944, Secretary of State Cordell Hull, usually a model of diplomatic restraint, issued a fiery declaration concerning the fate of the Hungarian Jews, a declaration all the more impressive because it seemed so out of character. "Reliable reports from Hungary have confirmed the appalling news of mass killings of Jews by the Nazis and their Hungarian Quislings." The number of victims of those "fiendish crimes" was great. "The entire Jewish community in Hungary, which numbered nearly one million souls, is threatened with extermination." The president, the Congress, and many private organizations in the United States had expressed the "horror and indignation" of the American people at the "cold-blooded tortures and massacres." Indeed, all the civilized nations of the world shared that feeling. The American government would therefore try to rescue as many of the "unfortunate people" as possible. To appeal to the humaneness of the instigators and perpetrators of such outrages would be futile. Nevertheless, "let them know that they cannot escape the inexorable punishment which will be meted out to them when the power of the evil men now in control of Hungary has been broken." As his long years of service in the American government were drawing to a close, Hull began to sound almost like Stephen Wise.[7]

Six months later, on February 1, 1945, Hull's successor, acting secretary of state Joseph C. Grew, issued a similar statement warning of severe punishment for those responsible for the crimes committed against conquered national and ethnic communities. He was not as vehement as Hull, although by then the victory of the Allies seemed to be only a matter of weeks. He did, however, condemn the Nazi persecution of various minorities, even naming the one that had suffered the cruelest treatment. After quoting from some of the president's declarations denouncing the war crimes of the Third Reich and promising retribution against those responsible, Grew announced that his office was working with other government departments to draft proposals for the postwar imposition of appropriate penalties on the perpetrators. Those proposals could not as yet be made public; they were still under discussion with America's allies. But Grew wanted to state "categorically" that they were as "forthright and far-reaching" as the objectives announced by Roosevelt, objectives they were intended to implement. "They provide for the punishment of German leaders and their associates for their responsibility for the whole broad criminal enterprise devised and executed with ruthless disregard of the very foundation of law and morality, including offenses, wherever committed, against minority elements, Jewish and other groups, and individuals."[8]

But what about Roosevelt? How did he respond to the Holocaust? The answer is that his views were not very different from those of most of the important officeholders in Washington. He too found the decision of the Third Reich to exterminate European Jewry shocking and incomprehensible. How could any government, however ruthless or brutal, bring itself to adopt a policy of cold-blooded mass murder? His revulsion was reinforced by the knowledge that members of the Jewish community in the United States had stood by him through thick and thin, never doubting, never wavering. Their loyalty deserved some recognition, some expression of appreciation. To appear indifferent to the terrible tragedy confronting their coreligionists in the Old World would be not only inhumane but politically inexpedient.

Yet to display excessive sympathy for persecuted Jews could prove unwise as well. Roosevelt was too much the astute, experienced politician not to recognize that too much solicitude for any one of the ethnic minorities in the United States was likely to arouse envy and resentment among the others, especially those whose kinsmen were also suffering under the German occupation. Wasn't the Polish or the Serbian or the Greek community in America just as concerned about the fate of its former countrymen as the Jewish community? And shouldn't non-Jewish victims of Nazi racism receive as much presidential sympathy as Jewish victims? Besides, some of the longtime, long-established Americans, the "real" Americans, had for years been complaining that Roosevelt was too much under the influence of his Jewish aides and advisers. Paying special attention to the Holocaust would only reinforce those complaints. He had to be careful.

Still, Roosevelt was a master in dealing with touchy situations. He knew when to be assertive and when to be restrained, when to speak loudly and when to whisper softly. That was one of his most valuable political talents. When addressing a Jewish audience, he did not hesitate to identify the most pitiable victims of Nazi cruelty. And to those listening, his expressions of compassion sounded sincere and moving. But his tone generally changed when he addressed a more diverse public. Then he would mention the many different nationalities, often including Jews, suffering the hardships of a brutal German occupation. And there were times when he simply avoided identifying the ethnic background of the victims altogether, describing them in general terms as innocent victims, helpless prisoners, or desperate refugees. While there can be no question of the sincerity of his condemnation of the Holocaust, the form of that condemnation depended to a large extent on changing occasions and circumstances.

In his letter to Stephen Wise of July 17, 1942, for example, a letter which was to be read before the mass meeting in New York organized by the American Jewish Congress, Roosevelt voiced at the outset his deep appreciation of the contribution of the Jews in the United States to the war effort. "Americans who love justice and hate oppression will hail the solemn commemoration in Madison Square Garden as an expression of the determination of the Jewish people to make every sacrifice for victory over the Axis powers." More than that, he and all other Americans, whatever their religious faith, shared the sorrow of "our Jewish fellow citizens" regarding the cruelty of the Third Reich in dealing with its helpless victims. The president was confident, however, that the Nazis would not succeed in their program of mass murder any more than in their plan to enslave mankind. Those responsible for the crimes of the Nazi regime would be held accountable on the day of reckoning, which was sooner or later bound to come.

Roosevelt's letter concluded with the assurance that a military victory for the United States and its allies would save European Jewry. "I express the confident hope that the Atlantic Charter and the just world order to be made possible by the triumph of the United Nations will bring the Jews and oppressed peoples in all lands the four freedoms which Christian and Jewish teachings have largely inspired." To the thousands in Madison Square Garden listening to the letter, it was comforting and reassuring to know that they had a faithful friend sitting in the White House. According to the account in the *New York Times*, "[Roosevelt's] name throughout the program was the signal for an ovation."[9]

On other occasions, however, especially those pertaining to official government policy, Roosevelt sounded much more businesslike. On October 7, 1942, less than three months after his letter to the mass meeting in Madison Square Garden, he announced that it was the intention of the American government to cooperate with the British and other governments in establishing a United Nations Commission for the Investigation of War Crimes. But now there was no mention of who the victims were or what the nature of those war crimes was. Similarly, on July 30, 1943, the president issued a statement warning that "the United Nations would make use of information and evidence in respect to barbaric crimes in Europe and Asia and the instigators of those crimes would have to stand in courts of law to answer for their acts." He sounded direct and to the point. But while avoiding any appearance of ambivalence, he was also careful not to leave himself open to charges of ethnic favoritism. The important thing was to seem fair and evenhanded.[10]

And then there were occasions when Roosevelt referred specifically to the extermination of European Jewry, but only in the context of the Third Reich's crimes against non-Jews as well. An example was his statement of March 24, 1944, issued a few days after the occupation of Hungary. Here was a new development that could not be ignored. Not only was it bound to have an important effect on military operations on the eastern front, but it was also a terrible tragedy for an oppressed, frightened ethnic community which had until then been spared the horror of genocide. Roosevelt had to say something about that horror but without arousing the familiar suspicions of partiality or bias on his part.

He began therefore by referring to the atrocities being committed "in most of Europe and in parts of Asia," naming ten nationalities as victims, from the Poles and Czechs to the Chinese and Filipinos. Jews were not included. His subsequent reference to the "slaughters of Warsaw" could perhaps be interpreted as an allusion to the Holocaust, but it was followed by the names of other cities in which there had been mass murders—Lidice,

Kharkov, and Nanking—none of them with a large Jewish population. Up to that point the statement reflected a conscious effort to emphasize the broad, inclusive nature of his condemnation of totalitarian brutality.

Only then did he feel free to turn to the events of the past few days, voicing a deep concern which members of the American Jewish community had been impatiently waiting for him to express. It was terrible enough, he declared, that "the wholesale systematic murder of the Jews of Europe goes on unabated every hour." But the situation had now become even more desperate. "Hundreds of thousands of Jews, who while living under persecution have at least found a haven from death in Hungary and the Balkans, are . . . threatened with annihilation as Hitler's forces descend more heavily upon these lands." The possibility that Hungarian Jewry would be exterminated was so terrible as to be almost unthinkable. "That these innocent people, who have already survived a decade of Hitler's fury, should perish on the very eve of triumph over the barbarism which their persecution symbolizes, would be a major tragedy."

But what could the president do to prevent that tragedy? His only recourse was the issuance of warnings of severe punishment after the war for those guilty of genocide. And given the fanatical anti-Semitism of the Nazi regime, threats of retribution were unlikely to have much practical effect. Still, while ineffectual in restraining the murderous policies of the Third Reich, they would prove gratifying to public opinion in the United States. They would help create the impression that the democracies were not simply standing by helplessly while the German government was proceeding with its racist atrocities. Roosevelt reiterated his resolve that "none who participated in these acts of savagery shall go unpunished." The United States and its allies had made it clear that they would pursue the guilty and deliver them to justice. This warning applied not only to the leaders of the Nazi regime but also to their functionaries and subordinates in Germany and the satellite states. All those taking part in the deportation of Jews to their death in Poland and, the president hastened to add, all those sending Norwegians and French to their death in the Third Reich were as guilty as the Nazi executioners themselves. "All who share the guilt shall share the punishment."

In the meantime, Roosevelt appealed to those living under the rule of the Third Reich to try to do what he and his allies were unable to do. He asked "every German and every man everywhere under Nazi domination" to show the world that in his heart he did not share the "insane criminal desires" of the Hitler government. Those inwardly opposed to the evil policies of the Third Reich should hide its intended victims or help them cross the border to freedom or do whatever could be done to save them from the "Nazi hangman." And then there was one more task that each secret opponent of National Socialism should undertake. "I ask him also to keep watch and to record the evidence that will one day be used to convict the guilty."

In his conclusion the president tried to reemphasize the broad scope of his sympathies and compassions. "Until the victory that is now assured is won," he declared, the United States would continue its efforts to save the victims of the brutality of "the Nazis and the Japs." To the extent that military operations allowed, the American government would use every means at its disposal to assist in the escape of "all intended victims of the Nazi and Jap executioner—regardless of race or religion or color." He called on "the free peoples of Europe and Asia" to open their frontiers "temporarily" to all victims of totalitarian oppression. As for the United States, "we shall find havens of refuge for them, and we shall find the means for their maintenance and support until the tyrant is driven from their homelands and they may return." Roosevelt knew of course that there was strong popular opposition at home to the admission of any large number of refugees. But he hoped that the approach of the Allied victory and his assurance that those who had fled totalitarian oppression would return to their native countries after the war would limit the extent of public disapproval. In any event, he concluded his statement with a reaffirmation of his faith in the democratic cause: "In the name of justice and humanity let all freedom loving people rally to this righteous undertaking."[11]

Many of the other leaders of the coalition against the Axis were even more anxious than Roosevelt to avoid the appearance of favoring Jews—or at least they expressed their anxiety more openly. The British government, for instance, sharing the same democratic ideals and principles, was far more explicit in voicing its opposition to special consideration for any one of the national and ethnic communities exposed to Nazi brutality. And that meant no special consideration for Jews.

The differences in the official attitude between the two countries reflected in large part the differences in size and influence of their Jewish communities. Proportionately, Britain's Jewish community was much smaller than America's, constituting no more than 0.7 percent of all inhabitants, as opposed to 3.5 percent. And the differences in the economic and political influence of the two communities paralleled the differences in their size. This disparity helps account for the fact that the American government, though basically in agreement with the British that any appearance of pro-Jewish bias must be avoided, was much more outspoken in dealing with the Holocaust.[12]

Not that Downing Street was indifferent to Hitler's anti-Semitic policies. On the contrary, it often condemned the mass murder of Jews publicly and loudly. On December 17, 1942, Anthony Eden, secretary of state for foreign affairs, who had been assigned chief responsibility for dealing with the Holocaust, informed the House of Commons that the government had recently received reliable reports regarding "the barbarous and inhuman treatment to which Jews are being subjected in German-occupied Europe." The United Kingdom had therefore entered into consultations with the United States, the Soviet Union, and eight governments in exile as well as the French National Committee, leading to a joint declaration which was to be made public simultaneously in London, Moscow, and Washington. Eden then read the text of that declaration. It charged that "the German authorities, not content with denying to persons of Jewish race in all the territories over which their barbarous rule had been extended the most elementary human rights, are now carrying into effect Hitler's oft repeated intention to exterminate the Jewish people in Europe." After describing the murderous methods employed by the German authorities in carrying out their program of genocide, the declaration estimated that the number of victims of "these bloody cruelties" amounted to "many hundreds of thousands" of innocent men, women, and children. It concluded with a reaffirmation of the Allied resolve that "those responsible for these crimes shall not escape retribution."[13]

Since Eden was only one of several authors of the Allied declaration, there is no way of telling how much he contributed to its formulation or to what extent he approved of its tone and wording. But there can be no question about the authorship of the statement he issued more than a year later, on March 30, 1944, following the German occupation of Hungary. Here he condemned the "Nazi policy of extermination" as clearly and forcefully as Roosevelt had done six days earlier. At one point he even said outright that "the persecution of the Jews has in particular been of unexampled horror and intensity." To be sure, that was the only time he identified by name the victims of the Holocaust. But no one could have had any doubt about whom he meant when he later referred to Hungarian citizens expelled to "destinations named by Berlin" or spoke of "those menaced by the Nazi terror." There was nothing ambiguous, moreover, about his warning, "now that the hour of Germany's defeat grows ever nearer and more certain," that the evildoers would be brought to justice. Not only that, the satellite governments aiding the Nazi regime in its "inhuman persecution or slaughter" would also be remembered when the inevitable defeat of the "arch-enemy of Europe" was finally achieved. On the other hand, private citizens or government officials who resisted the "evil German example" would not be forgotten when the day of reckoning came. There was still the opportunity for the merciful to continue their acts of humanity and for the guilty to make amends by releasing their victims and offering them restitution. Eden concluded by calling on the nations allied with or subject to Germany to try to prevent further persecution and to protect and save the innocent. As for the British government, it would continue to do whatever it could to rescue and support "all those menaced by the Nazi terror."[14]

In confidential discussions with other government officials, however, Eden was less reluctant to refer to Jews by name and more doubtful whether anything could be done to save them from extermination. On March 27, 1943, barely three months after reading the Allied declaration condemning the Holocaust to the House of Commons, he expressed his private reservations concerning any special effort to rescue its victims. At a meeting in Washington with Roosevelt, Cordell Hull, and Sumner Welles, during which the American secretary of state raised the question of the Bulgarian Jews, who were threatened with mass murder "unless we could get them out," Eden recommended prudence and restraint. "The whole problem of the Jews in Europe is very difficult and . . . we should move very cautiously about offering to take all Jews out of a country like Bulgaria." It might lead to new demands and new problems. "If we do that, then the Jews of the world will be wanting us to make similar offers in Poland and Germany." Where would it end? And besides, the enemy would no doubt take advantage of too much Allied compassion. "Any such mass movement as that would be very dangerous to security because the Germans would be sure to attempt to put a number of their agents in the group." They had already been successful in using that method to infiltrate their spies into North and South America. They must not be given new opportunities to do so. It would be best for the Allies not to become too involved in the fate of the Bulgarian Jews.[15]

Most officials in the British diplomatic service shared Eden's concerns. Some of them were even more cautious. Early in 1943, two months before Eden's meeting with Roosevelt, Hull, and Welles, the British embassy in Washington submitted an aide-mémoire to the American State Department that warned that "many thousands of refugees continue to crowd into neutral countries in Europe, and the situation is developing with such rapidity and in such proportions that His Majesty's Government in the United Kingdom have become impressed with the necessity for consultation and joint effort in dealing with the problem." To begin with, the refugee question could not be viewed as "a wholly Jewish problem which could be handled by Jewish agencies or by machinery only adapted for assisting Jews." There were many refugees who were not Jewish, and there were many more in countries under the German occupation, millions and millions of them, all exposed to "so much acute suffering." To show a preference for Jewish victims of Nazi oppression would be bound to arouse criticism in the Allied nations. Worse still, the presence of too many Jews might provoke anti-Semitism in the countries in which they had found asylum. Besides, "there is at present always a danger of raising false hopes among refugees by suggesting or announcing alternative possible destinations in excess of shipping probabilities." And finally there came the familiar warning that the Germans might try to embarrass their adversaries by abandoning the policy of genocide and allowing all Jews to emigrate, thereby flooding the democracies with masses of impoverished aliens. That was clearly a danger which must be avoided. In short, most government officials, British as well as American, agreed that some compassion for the victims of the Holocaust was justifiable and probably even desirable. But too much could prove risky.[16]

On the other side of the continent, in the Soviet Union, there was at first far greater willingness to publicize the mass murders that National

Socialism was responsible for, including the mass murder of Jews. The Kremlin, taken completely by surprise by the German invasion, greatly alarmed by the rapid succession of the Red Army's defeats and retreats, was eager to encourage a national resolve to resist the forces of the Third Reich. And one of the obvious ways was by dwelling on the atrocities the invaders were committing, including the most gruesome of all.

But arousing hatred against the enemy was not the only reason for the publicity that the Russian authorities focused on the Nazis' genocidal policies. There was also a widespread perception in Europe, especially in the east, that American Jewry, thanks to its important role in the national economy, exercised considerable influence over government policy. To dwell on the horrors of the Holocaust would thus help win the favor of an influential ethnic minority in the United States. And that in turn would reinforce the alliance of two countries which had until recently been diplomatic and ideological adversaries.

The reasons for a shift are not entirely clear. Most of the relevant government documents remain guarded in the Russian archives, classified and unavailable for study. But a few tentative conclusions are still possible. To start with, the Kremlin began to realize that its initial assumptions about the role of Jews in determining American foreign policy had been exaggerated. The leaders of the Western democracies were far more cautious in dealing with the "Jewish question" than the Soviet diplomats had supposed. It would therefore be best, all things considered, not to appear more sympathetic or humane than the Western allies. Too much compassion might arouse distrust or resentment.

That would be even more likely in the case of the Soviet Union's neighbors. Before the war, countries like Poland, Romania, Lithuania, and Latvia had made no secret of their suspicion that Jews were playing a major role in the "Bolshevik dictatorship," perhaps even a decisive role. To devote too much attention to the Holocaust would undoubtedly reinforce that suspicion at a time when the Kremlin hoped to establish closer relations with the countries occupied or dominated by the Third Reich. Clearly, while the extermination of European Jewry could not be ignored, it should not receive too much publicity either.

Still, the shift in the Kremlin's attitude was not solely or even chiefly a result of diplomatic concerns. Equally if not more important was the problem of domestic bias and antipathy. In czarist times, Russia had been considered the most anti-Semitic country in Europe, probably in the world. Not even more than two decades of Soviet rule and indoctrination had been enough to replace a tradition of ethnic prejudice with a single-minded commitment to the class struggle. Beneath the surface of the dominant Marxist ideology, old resentments and prejudices persisted. The hardships of warfare had only reinforced them and revealed them more clearly. Almost fifty years later, some three hundred Jewish immigrants from the Soviet Union in Detroit were asked what the attitude of most non-Jews had been during the anti-Semitic mass murders under the Nazi occupation. A majority described it as hostile or indifferent. The respondents had concluded, therefore, as several of them put it, that "there is no place for me in the Soviet Union." The officials in the Kremlin must have become aware of the extent of this ethnic prejudice, and, like their counterparts in Washington and London, they concluded that it would be best not to display too much concern over the Holocaust.[17]

That became apparent also to Bill Lawrence, a reporter for the *New York Times*, who was assigned to Moscow in the summer of 1943. A year later, after visiting the Maidanek death camp, recently liberated by the Red Army, he sent a dispatch to his home office describing "the most terrible place on the face of the earth" and mentioning that "most of these victims were Jews." But the Russian censor, without telling him, deleted the ethnic identification of those killed in the camp. He learned about it only from his managing editor in New York. "Hopping mad," he confronted the Russian press official on duty, who gave him the "rather lame and halting" explanation that "some anti-Semites around the world might feel that if the victims were Jews, the murders were justified." Lawrence, however, remained dubious. The deletion, he later wrote in his memoirs, "reflected, of course, the basic anti-Semitism of so many Russians." He was in all probability right. It was a concern not about foreign but about domestic anti-Semites that had led to the censorship of his article. Yet that was something which the Soviet official responsible for the censoring could not admit. He did allow Lawrence to cable to New York that the reference to Jews which appeared in his original dispatch had been eliminated "by mistake." Whether anyone on either side of the Atlantic really believed that seems doubtful.[18]

Other foreign observers recognized the growing reluctance of the Kremlin to dwell on the Holocaust. Henry Shapiro, who was a correspondent in Moscow for the United Press during the war, described in an interview long afterward how the Russian officials gradually began to avoid including Jews among the victims of persecution by the Third Reich. In November 1943, when he and other foreign reporters went to Babi Yar, a ravine on the edge of Kiev where more than 100,000 civilians had been killed by the German death squads, there was no question that "this was a Jewish massacre and nothing else." Some eight months later, however, in the summer of 1944, after the Red Army had taken Maidanek, the Soviet authorities "minimized" the proportion of Jews among those who had perished there. And six months after that, in January 1945, when Auschwitz was liberated, the government, according to Shapiro, apparently decided that "the Jewish role—both as victim and as Soviet hero—was to be forgotten." Now that the Kremlin's armies had crossed the country's prewar frontiers and were advancing deeper into the neighboring states, it was more important than ever to show that the Kremlin was not a tool of world Jewry, as Nazi propaganda had maintained.[19]

The strategy the Soviet authorities therefore adopted was to refer to Jews who had perished during the Holocaust only in the context of the other victims of Nazi brutality, and without mentioning them too frequently or prominently. On February 2, 1945, shortly after the liberation of Auschwitz, *Pravda*, a leading Russian newspaper, reported that the Red Army had saved "several thousand tortured, emaciated inmates of the Germans' greatest 'murder factory' at Oswiecim [Auschwitz] in southwest Poland." The article went on to say that fragmentary information indicated that at least 1.5 million prisoners had been "slaughtered" in the death camp (far below the actual number, which was close to 4 million). During 1941, 1942, and early 1943, the report continued, five trains had been arriving daily at Auschwitz, "with Russians, Poles, Jews, Czechs, French and Yugoslavs jammed in sealed cars." The mention of five non-Jewish categories of victims of ethnic persecution was apparently enough to make it safe to mention Jews as well.[20]

By the time the war ended three months later, however, not even that appeared to be enough to overcome popular suspicions about a special concern for the victims of the Holocaust. Now the treatment of Jews as an indistinguishable component of the dominant nationality of the country in which they lived became the common practice, without regard for differences of ethnicity, religion, or culture. On May 7, 1945, while a delegation of high-ranking military officers representing what remained of the German government was signing the unconditional surrender of the Third Reich, the Soviet Union's Extraordinary State Commission published its report on Auschwitz, where the slaughter exceeded "in barbaric intention and method" not only "the greatest brutalities of such infamous conquerors as Genghis Khan" but even Germany's own record in such centers of mass murder as Maidanek, Dachau, and Buchenwald. More than 4 million "citizens" of "the Soviet Union, Poland, France, Belgium, the Netherlands, Czechoslovakia, Yugoslavia and other countries, including the non-Allied lands of Hungary and Rumania," had been put to death in Auschwitz. The means employed to perpetrate that atrocity were "shooting, famine, poisoning and monstrous tortures." And this in turn meant that the Germans had had to build gas chambers, crematories, surgical wards, laboratories, and clinics around Auschwitz in order to create their "mass-production monstrosity." The commission's report was the most detailed account up to that time of the deadliest of the Third Reich's extermination centers. Yet it failed to identify the ethnicity of at least half of those who had perished there. The war was now over and all of Eastern Europe was under the direct or indirect rule of the Kremlin. But the authorities were still determined to maintain the policy of avoiding as much as possible any distinction between Jewish and non-Jewish victims of Nazi genocide.[21]

The leaders of the Western democracies did not try to persuade the Soviet government to modify that policy. They acquiesced in it, and at times they even adopted it themselves. On November 1, 1943, following the Moscow conference of the foreign ministers of the three leading members of the coalition against the Axis, a declaration regarding German war crimes was issued by Roosevelt, Stalin, and Churchill. It contained the by then familiar warning that once victory had been achieved, those responsible for or participating in "atrocities, massacres and executions" would be sent back to the countries in which their "abominable deeds" had taken place to be judged and punished. Lists of the perpetrators would be obtained from the Soviet Union, Poland, Czechoslovakia, Yugoslavia, and Greece, including Crete and other islands, as well as from Norway, Denmark, the Netherlands, Belgium, Luxembourg, France, and Italy. The declaration went on to identify the various categories of innocent victims of the Third Reich's murderous brutality. "The Germans who take part in wholesale shootings of Italian officers or in the execution of French, Dutch, Belgian, or Norwegian hostages or of Cretan peasants, or who have shared in the slaughters inflicted on the people of Poland or in territories of the Soviet Union . . . will know that they will be brought back to the scene of their crimes and judged on the spot by the peoples whom they have outraged." Their punishment would be strict but just.[22]

The authors of the declaration knew about the Holocaust, but they agreed more or less willingly that it would be best not to include Jews specifically. Anyone reading their statement, however, would have known who the main targets of those "slaughters inflicted on the people of Poland or in the territories of the Soviet Union" were. Still, at a time when the balance in the military conflict was beginning to shift in favor of the Allies, when American and British forces were advancing in southern Italy and preparing to invade France, and especially when the Red Army was approaching the prewar frontiers of its country's neighbors, it seemed inadvisable to say anything that might stir up the traditional fears and prejudices of the peoples of Eastern Europe. Even more important, a dispute among the Allies concerning the Holocaust might create frictions and divisions at a time when maintaining unity was of the utmost importance. The most liberal of the government officials in the democratic nations had to agree that nothing, not even the tragedy of mass murder, must be allowed to weaken the sense of common purpose of the coalition against the Axis.

Most countries in the New World were as reluctant as those in the Old World to draw special attention to the terrible danger confronting European Jewry, and this reluctance was reflected in their policy regarding the admission of those seeking to escape the danger. The Canadian declaration of war against Germany, like the American declaration of war, did little to alter the prevailing attitude toward refugees or the "Jewish question." If anything, the loss of life and the decline in the standard of living that resulted from the military conflict intensified popular suspicion and distrust of alien minorities, especially Jews. In the spring of 1943, an editorial in the *Winnipeg Free Press* admitted regretfully that "all the old bigoted, prejudiced, narrowly nationalist conceptions which, before the war broke out, made our borders almost impossible for [refugees] to cross" were still common. That was deplorable and yet undeniable. "Gross prejudice and gross exaggeration sadly mark every discussion of that historic and fateful 'Jewish problem.' " There had been no change in the public perception of this problem, despite the military struggle against Nazi totalitarianism. "Anti-semitism, shameful though it must be to admit it, has far too large a footing among Canadians." The time had come to adopt a more generous and humane attitude toward Jewish refugees.[23]

The political leaders of the country, however, were reluctant to follow that advice, whether out of conviction or out of expediency. To most of them, the prewar objections to a relaxation of the immigration barriers still seemed valid. In the summer of 1944, when the Hungarian government, cautiously encouraged by the United States, made an offer allowing Jews threatened with deportation to the death camps to leave the country, High Commissioner Vincent Massey dismissed the plan as merely an attempt by the Roosevelt administration to gain support in the coming presidential election. American politicians "apparently wanted the Jewish vote without taking in more Jews," he declared at a meeting of dominion officials in London, "because if they allow more Jews in they would lose the Roman Catholic vote." Why should Canada let itself become involved in the domestic politics of the United States?[24]

Not even the return of peace diminished opposition to the admission of Jewish refugees. As late as October 1946, more than a year after the defeat of the Axis, there was still considerable anti-Semitic prejudice in the country. Asked "if Canada does allow more immigration, are there any of the following nationalities which you would like to keep out?" 49 percent in a sample of between 2,000 and 2,500 respondents said they would exclude Jews. That was less than the 60 percent opposed to the admission of Japanese immigrants, but it was much higher than the disapproval of other hypothetical candidates for entry: 34 percent against German immigrants, 33 percent against Russian immigrants, and 31 percent against Negroes. Then came a substantial drop in the opposition to immigration: only 25 percent against Italians, 24 percent against Chinese, no more than 16 percent against Middle Europeans, 15 percent against Ukrainians, and 14 percent against Poles, while 18 percent of the respondents were opposed to all immigrants, whatever their nationality or ethnicity. Clearly the war years and the extermination of most of European Jewry had not significantly altered the prevailing popular attitude in Canada regarding either Jews or Jewish immigration.[25]

Nor did the Second World War lead to a relaxation of the immigration barriers in the countries of Latin America. If anything, the longer the military conflict continued, the greater their reluctance to assume the burden of providing refuge for new immigrants became. Yet they did not have to endure the same hardships as those participating directly in the war. Some of them were nominally belligerents, having declared war against the Axis but without actually engaging in combat. Others remained officially neutral, though in most cases expressing support for the Allied cause, partly out of conviction, partly out of calculation. But none of them faced the same dangers and sacrifices as the countries fighting in the front lines. Still, they too were deeply affected by the world conflict. Their economies were in serious disarray, since the traditional markets for their exports had shrunk and the importation of essential goods from abroad had declined. Then there were the political pressures to which they were increasingly exposed, demands on one side that they participate more actively in support of the Allied cause and warnings on the other side that any deviation from strict neutrality would lead to swift retaliation by the Axis. Finally, uncertainty regarding the outcome of the war and the nature of the new international order once hostilities ended imposed a growing burden on public opinion in all the nonbelligerent nations, including those of the New World.

In the fall of 1942, a report by the American Unitarian Service Committee described the reluctance of Latin American countries to issue immigration permits to Jews living in constant fear and peril in unoccupied France. Because of the difficulty of obtaining visas to the United States, the committee had investigated the possibility of finding a refuge for them farther to the south. But government authorities there were no more willing than those in Washington to open their doors to large numbers of immigrants, some of them without means of support, some perhaps in need of medical care. "Cuban and Mexican [visas] are unobtainable," the report complained, and "South American [visas are obtainable] in only rare cases." For example, "[no more than] one visa from Lisbon to Argentina has been granted." For those with money, the chances were some-what better. "There are rumors of Ecuador visas for $300 which are being explored." And then there were opportunities for those with special quali-fications. "Our New York office telephoned of the possibility of Chilean visas for scientists to teach in universities." But only a month later the military forces of the Third Reich moved into the unoccupied zone of France, and then even those Jewish refugees who had $300 or who had been trained as scientists were trapped.[26]

The weekly reports of the American War Refugee Board in the spring of 1944 provide a more detailed account of Latin American policies. By then it had become clear that the Allies were gaining the upper hand and that their victory was only a question of time. More than that, numerous accounts in the press and repeated statements by the Allied governments had revealed to the world the Third Reich's plan for the extermination of world Jewry. The Holocaust was no longer a secret. And yet the gen-eral reluctance to accept refugees seeking to escape mass murder did not diminish. After all, wouldn't an influx of hungry, homeless Jews aggravate the shortage of goods to which the native population had access? Wouldn't those foreigners soon begin competing, perhaps too successfully, with local businessmen, merchants, and professionals? And once the war was over, would they be willing to return to wherever they had come from, or would they remain as a perpetually alien and unassimilable minority?

Doubts and suspicions of this sort are clearly reflected in the War Refugee Board's reports. One report, issued in March 1944, summarized information recently received from the American mission in Havana, to the effect that "immigration into Cuba has practically ceased since the early part of 1942 as a result of a decree forbidding the granting of visas to nationals or natives of the Axis countries." Certainly the mission in Havana had no trouble identifying those "nationals or natives of the Axis countries" eager to obtain Cuban visas. It characterized the attitude of the Cuban authorities toward the "refugee problem" as "indifferent, if not slightly hostile, with little more than lip service being accorded to its humanitarian aspects."[27]

Two weeks later, that same attitude was described in a report dealing with Nicaragua's "willingness to rescue refugees." The U.S. embassy there had been informed by the Foreign Office that before making any promises or commitments, it would have to have information regarding the "practical steps" needed to put the American government's plan for the resettlement of victims of the Third Reich into effect. Specifically, the authorities in Managua wanted to know more about "the probable number of persons to be received by the United States, the facilities for transport which may be available, the time of the expected evacuations, the nationality of the refugees, etc." As for the chances that the Nicaraguan government would be willing to issue a public statement on the subject of refugees, "our Embassy believes that embarrassment might result from our requesting such a statement at this time." Not only might the request be rejected, but the statement, even if issued, would probably be so ambivalent as to be worse than no statement. It might therefore be best not to press the issue.[28]

The unwillingness of Latin American nations to admit what they believed to be too many refugees was based to a considerable extent on social as well as economic considerations. A sudden flood of immigrants might aggravate class tensions or even provoke mass riots. And then there was the danger that the newcomers, once they had become established in the host country, would cease to be pitiable victims of ethnic prejudice and become shrewd businessmen, clever financiers, successful professionals, or prominent publicists. That would be bound to lead to the spread of anti-Semitism among the native population. Was that not what had happened in Central and Eastern Europe? The governments of the region had to be on guard against too much compassion.

Some of the Latin American states hesitated to express such concerns openly, preferring to disguise them behind a veil of evasions, generalities, and euphemisms. But others were willing to reveal what was on their mind. While they usually expressed themselves indirectly or obliquely, there was no mistaking their meaning. A report by the War Refugee Board contained information received from the American mission in Colombia that the government there, while prepared to cooperate in a general way in extending "humanitarian assistance" to refugees, would offer such assistance only in accordance with its national immigration policy, the purpose being to protect the nation against "any uncontrolled influx of undesirable refugees." Those reading the report easily recognized who the "undesirable refugees" were likely to be. At the same time, the American embassy in Lima was offering an assessment of "the Peruvian attitude toward the rescue and relief of the Jews of Europe and other victims of enemy persecution" which sounded very familiar. Pending a formal reply on refugee policy from the Peruvian Ministry for Foreign Affairs, "which the Embassy expects to be noncommittal or negative as well as delayed," little assistance or sympathy could be expected from the government authorities.[29]

Finally, a few countries in Latin America made no effort to hide their ethnic fears and suspicions. They openly used words like "Jew" or "Jewish," something their more discreet neighbors preferred to avoid. Among those outspoken countries were some in which Jews were a rarity. The American mission in Ecuador, for example, reported that there were no restrictions there on the entry of Jews based on racial or religious prejudice. But "they, like other immigrants, are admitted only if they will engage in certain specified pursuits." That was the real problem. "The Ecuadorian Government believes that the entry of further Jewish refugees who would probably settle in the two principal cities of the country would lead to a strong anti-Semitic feeling." The American mission, conceding that "this might be true," recommended therefore the establishment of temporary camps for Jewish refugees for the duration of the war. On the other hand, "non-Jewish refugees who are fit for agricultural labor would be welcome in Ecuador." They did not pose any threat to the native population.[30]

In Bolivia, the prevailing attitude was similar. Here too the number of Jews was very small; most Bolivians had never actually met one. Yet many Bolivians feared that the admission of too many would upset the country's economic balance, especially in the cities. The American embassy in La Paz reported the existence of a "general resentment" of Jewish refugees who had entered the country in recent years. The newcomers "have competed with established Bolivian merchants and small shopkeepers when many of these immigrants were officially admitted with the understanding that they were to engage in agriculture." That was a source of distrust. If they had only been willing to settle down in the hinterland and work as farm laborers, they would not have been regarded differently from native members of the rural proletariat. It was their insistence on gaining entry into the urban bourgeoisie that accounted for the hostility they aroused.[31]

That hostility was likely to be even greater in nations with a highly developed industrial economy. In a country like Bolivia, Jewish immigrants competed mostly with a small class of native tradesmen and shopkeepers. But in Chile, which had a proportionately far larger urban population and a much higher level of economic development, the rivalry between outsiders and insiders was bound to be more intense and the ethnic resentment more bitter. The American embassy in Santiago reported that since the outbreak of war, "rigid rules" had been enforced by the Chilean government regarding the admission of immigrants, and that "there have been charges of discrimination in their application, particularly with respect to Jews." It was the ambassador's opinion that the chief obstacle to "large-scale immigration to Chile, especially to Jewish immigration," was the fear that the newcomers "will become concentrated in the urban centers." Such a concentration would lead to increased competition in commerce and industry—a competition in which the position of native businessmen might be endangered by overambitious outsiders.[32]

This fear of Jewish economic aggressiveness helps account for the fact that the loudest opposition to the admission of refugees could be heard in Argentina, the nation with the most developed economy and the highest proportion of Jews in Latin America (higher, in fact, than in any state of Western Europe). Here, according to the American embassy, the consensus of those active in Jewish rescue and relief work was that "so long as the present regime remains in power, no assistance whatsoever can be expected from the Argentine Government in refugee matters." Jewish organizations in the country were said to own large tracts of land able to support thousands of refugee families. Indeed, the nation as a whole seemed capable of absorbing millions of immigrants. And yet "no conceivable political change would make possible the willing acceptance of a very large proportion of Jews among those proposed millions." The prevailing view was that Argentina already had more than enough Jews. To admit still more would only make a bad situation worse.[33]

Most American Jews, however, refused to abandon the struggle. To them the Nazi extermination of European Jewry was one of the most important moral justifications for the war, perhaps the most important. Nothing should be allowed to obscure its horror. The Jews in Great Britain and the Soviet Union generally shared this view, but they were too few, too weak, and too insecure to protest against their governments' policies. The Jewish community in the United States, however, had fewer inhibitions. No sooner had the Allied declaration of November 1, 1943, been issued than protests from individuals, groups, and organizations like the American Jewish Congress and the Emergency Committee to Save the Jewish People of Europe began to pour into Washington. Didn't Jews facing the Holocaust deserve at least as much attention as the Cretan peasants who had been specifically mentioned in the declaration? The Germans were already half convinced that it would be safe to kill Jews. Wouldn't the omission of any reference to anti-Semitic mass murder reinforce that impression? Would it not suggest to the Nazi authorities that the Allies were indifferent to Hitler's intention to exterminate all of European Jewry? The failure of the leaders of the coalition to refer to the Holocaust in their statement seemed inexcusable.[34]

These protests made an impression on Washington. It was one thing to remain silent about the killing of Jews in a joint declaration by the Allies, which had to take into account the divergent views of several governments. But to face a storm of criticism from some of Roosevelt's most loyal followers, who felt betrayed by his acquiescence in a seemingly insensitive, cold-hearted public statement, that was something entirely different. The damage had to be repaired as soon as possible. On November 18, 1943, less than three weeks after the issuance of the declaration, Secretary of State Hull tried to make amends for the omission in a report to a joint session of Congress. Toward the end of his speech he referred to "the bestial and abominable crimes" committed by the Nazi regime, crimes against "the harassed and persecuted inhabitants of occupied territories—against people of all races and religions." So far, that was standard rhetoric. But then Hull went on to say that "Hitler has reserved for the Jews his most brutal wrath." Unlike the usual formulation, there was no mention of any of the other victims of Nazi cruelty. Hull's exclusive reference to the Holocaust was a form of atonement. Even the most ardent supporters of the Jewish cause were now bound to feel at least somewhat mollified.[35]

Yet the bitter controversy over the Allies' official attitude toward the Holocaust had a symbolic and psychological rather than practical significance. The leaders of the Third Reich were too deeply committed to their struggle against the specter of Semitic dominance of state and society to be deterred by threats of postwar retaliation. As for the Allied condemnations of mass murder, they may have been emotionally satisfying to those to whom the Holocaust was the most terrible of the Nazis' atrocities. But those who argued, for whatever reason, that winning the war was the only way to save what was left of European Jewry were essentially right. Threats of ultimate punishment for the perpetrators of genocide did have some effect in the smaller countries aligned with the Axis, especially after the military balance began to shift in favor of the Allied coalition. Even there, however, the main reason for a change in attitude was the likelihood of military defeat.

Nevertheless, the Allies' attitude toward the Holocaust had at least one practical effect. While it could not help save the millions of Jews who became prisoners of the Nazi regime following its military victories early in the war, it did affect the thousands of Jewish refugees who had managed to escape persecution by the German authorities but were now living precariously just beyond its grasp, mostly in the Iberian Peninsula, the Balkans, and North Africa. Shouldn't something be done to save them? The Allies were constantly condemning Nazi tyranny and brutality. Here was their chance to demonstrate their commitment to the democratic principle of compassion for the weak and oppressed. Having confirmed the unofficial accounts of the mass murder of Jews, they were under constant pressure to do something to assist those seeking to escape imprisonment and execution. To the millions facing death under the German occupation, the Western democracies could offer nothing but condemnations of genocide and promises of punishment for the perpetrators. But the relatively few still able to emigrate, desperately searching for refuge, they could serve as living proof of the humane ideals motivating the coalition against the Axis. All that had to be done was to provide them with shelter and protection.

But that was much more difficult than it sounded, more difficult even than finding an appropriate expression of disapproval for the Holocaust. Here too there had to be a careful balance between too much and too little compassion, a constant awareness of the effect of what was said or done on Nazi propaganda, on the other oppressed ethnic communities under German occupation, and on domestic public opinion. The situation had to be handled with great care—not completely ignored, but not allowed to interfere with the war effort, either.

The solution that was adopted, at least for the time being, was the organization of an international conference in Bermuda to consider the refugee problem. Its recommendations would not be binding, though they were to be carefully studied by the governments of the Alliance. The conference was intended essentially to demonstrate the concern of the democratic governments for the victims of National Socialism without in any way restricting their freedom of action in dealing with the problem.

In March 1943, a month before the conference met, a confidential memorandum summarizing the views of the American government stated at the outset that "the refugee problem should not be considered as being confined to persons of any particular race or faith." The Nazi persecution of minorities had led to the flight of people "of various ethnic and religious backgrounds" as well as of some who were in danger because of their political beliefs. The refugee problem was thus not limited in scope to "persons of any particular race or faith who may be subjected to oppression, persecution, or extermination by the Nazi-Fascist Governments and their satellites." Steps taken solely in behalf of—here the word "Jews" was crossed out and replaced by "any separate race or nation"—would be open to criticism by "other unfortunate peoples," whose plight also deserved the most earnest consideration. Nazi propagandists had made false charges intended to distort the broad humanitarian interest of the Allies into "a sole interest in certain minorities." The participants in the conference should therefore try to avoid any "possible implication" that might be useful to the propagandists.[36]

Not only enemy propaganda, however, was a source of concern to officials in Washington. On the eve of the conferenc, another confidential memorandum, this one circulating among the American delegates, made it clear that "the United States Government does not wish to be accused of admitting large numbers of refugees to fill the gap caused by American boys abroad, since this might cause serious domestic disunity." The meaning was unmistakable. The conference should avoid recommending measures that might aggravate anti-Semitic prejudices and hostilities at home.[37]

The British government was essentially in agreement with the American position. Nevertheless, early in the conference a member of its delegation emphasized economic risks and transportation problems rather than ethnic prejudice as the main reason for not admitting too many refugees. A large proportion of those seeking asylum were "empty mouths for which Hitler has no use." He might even conclude that there were 20 or 30 million people who were a liability rather than an advantage to him, and he might therefore be glad to get rid of them. If the Allies were to admit these "useless people," it would relieve him of a burdensome obligation. And if he did decide to release a large number of old people and children, "we should be placed in a ridiculous position because we could only take between 500 and 1,000 a month." To open negotiations with Hitler and have him agree that the Allies could take as many refugees as they wanted, and then for the Allies to be forced to admit that they could not accept those refugees after all, would place the Western democracies in "an impossible situation." In fact, "we know that both our Governments would never agree to such a recommendation even if this Conference should recommend it." The practical obstacles were simply too great.[38]

Yet problems of transportation and accommodation were not the only reason for Downing Street's reluctance to agree to accept large numbers of refugees. Equally important, perhaps more important, was the fear of intensifying ethnic hostilities at home and abroad. The aide-mémoire that the British embassy had submitted to the American government three months earlier emphasized that the refugee question should not be treated as "a wholly Jewish problem." There were many refugees who were not Jewish, and there was acute suffering in the general population of the nations under German occupation. To show preference for Jews in providing assistance to the victims of Nazi persecution would be sure to arouse criticism in the parts of Europe conquered by the Wehrmacht. Worse still, "there is also a distinct danger of stimulating anti-semitism in areas where an excessive number of foreign Jews are introduced." And that danger existed not only in the remote regions of Africa and Australia but also here at home, in Great Britain and the United States. It must be avoided.[39]

Even some American and British Jews agreed with this line of reasoning, concluding that anything which might weaken the war effort by arousing domestic tensions and dissensions should be rejected. Congressman Sol Bloom was a delegate at the Bermuda Conference, partly to serve as a refutation of charges that it was indifferent to the fate of European Jewry, but partly because as a devoted follower of Roosevelt, he was unlikely to support measures unacceptable to the administration. As it turned out, he met all those expectations. In his autobiography, he explained that he and the other American delegates faced a situation that was "urgent, complex, and delicate." They had to remember at all times that the humanitarian motive of aiding individuals was subordinate to the even greater humanitarian motive of rescuing entire nations. "Any plan that might interfere with winning the war had to be rejected. We could divert no force, not a single ship, in direct use against the enemy to succor any of his victims."

There was the danger, moreover, that a report that the Allies were planning to aid "a particular group" might lead to increased persecution of that group, perhaps to show that meddling from the outside would only intensify the wretchedness of the intended beneficiaries or perhaps to extort the payment of a huge ransom. And then there was always the possibility that the Germans would make a special effort to sink a ship full of "helpless men, women, and children," thereby hoping to discourage future attempts at rescue. Too many demands to save the refugees would only make the situation worse. "No one could guess how long the war might last, and every effort must be spent that could shorten it by even as little as a day." The only way to end the horror of the Holocaust was through military victory.[40]

The Bermuda Conference did not disappoint the hopes and expectations of the government officials who had organized it. It condemned the atrocities being committed in the name of National Socialism without offering specific proposals for ending or alleviating them. Its only concrete results were a decision to reactivate the Intergovernmental Committee on Refugees and a recommendation to establish a camp in North Africa for the victims of persecution who had found a temporary haven in Spain, thereby making it possible for others to seek asylum in the Iberian Peninsula. The leaders of the Western democracies could now breathe more easily. The meeting in Bermuda had not led to any awkward proposals or demands.

A few days after the conference, Secretary of State Hull wrote to Roosevelt asking for his approval of a recommendation against any significant changes in the existing policy regarding the refugee problem. First of all, a "scheme" advocated by "certain pressure groups" for moving an undetermined number of persons from an undisclosed place to an unknown destination "is, of course, out of the question," although the government might be willing from time to time to pay a share of the cost of moving a specific number of persons from a particular place to a designated destination. That was no more than a reaffirmation of the established guidelines in dealing with proposals for the rescue of refugees.

More important was Hull's warning against any attempt to change the existing immigration legislation. The quota system, he maintained, was flexible enough to accommodate a large number of refugees from Central Europe, who could qualify under current rules. On the other hand, "any attempt to bring refugees into the country without compliance with the immigration laws, or in excess of quota limitations, would be likely to result in throwing the whole refugee question into Congress, where there is a prevailing sentiment for even more drastic curtailment of immigration into this country in time of war when our own citizens are going abroad to lay down their lives, if necessary, for their country." Any proposal to revise or circumvent existing legislation would only make the situation worse. Accordingly, Hull's letter concluded with the statement that "I cannot recommend that we bring in refugees as temporary visitors and thus lay ourselves open to possible charges of nullification or evasion of the national origins principle embodied in the quota laws." To tamper with the established system of admission would only lead to demands for more severe restrictions on immigration.[41]

The president did not have to be convinced. He had already come to the same conclusion. In his reply a week later, he agreed that "we [cannot] do other than comply strictly with the present immigration laws." North Africa might serve as a temporary shelter for refugees from Europe, but not as a place of permanent residence without the approval of all the appropriate authorities. Although there was "plenty of room" in North Africa, "I raise the question of sending large numbers of Jews there." That would be "extremely unwise." Roosevelt shared Hull's view, moreover, that "we cannot open the question of our immigration laws." And as for allowing temporary visitors to enter the United States, "we have already brought in a large number." To bring in any more might prove politically hazardous.[42]

This remained essentially the position of the American government throughout the war. From time to time, especially as the likelihood of victory grew, the administration responded to the urging of the Jewish community and its sympathizers by introducing a few modest measures designed to assist refugees from National Socialism. But at the same time it emphasized that those measures did not represent an effort to alter in any way the existing quota system, that they were designed to assist all refugees, without regard for religion, ethnicity, or nationality, and that those admitted under special dispensation would be returned to their native countries immediately after the war. That was as far as Washington was willing to go.

On June 12, 1944, Roosevelt referred in a message to Congress to "the systematic persecution of helpless minority groups" by the Nazis. He described "the unprovoked murder of innocent people simply because of race, religion, or political creed" as "the blackest of all possible crimes." He even identified by name the chief victims of that unprovoked murder. Although the hour of the final defeat of Hitler's regime was drawing closer, he said, its "insane desire to wipe out the Jewish race in Europe" continued undiminished. Still, that was only one instance of Nazi barbarity. There were others that should be mentioned. "Many Christian groups are also being murdered." The Third Reich's policy of mass extermination was a result of hateful doctrines which the Allies must destroy or the war would have been fought in vain. That was why the government was admitting to the United States a thousand refugees, mostly women and children. But "upon the termination of the war they will be sent back to their homelands." In the meantime they would be quartered in a vacated army camp, where, the president emphasized, they were to live "under appropriate security restrictions." The nation had to show sympathy for the victims of Nazi cruelty, but only within reasonable limits.[43]

Nevertheless, the reasons offered by the Allied leaders for their caution in dealing with the Holocaust were not baseless. Allied expressions of concern for persecuted Jews were in fact often used by Nazi propaganda to foment anti-Semitic bigotry. At times they also aroused envy and resentment among the other oppressed nationalities and ethnicities under the German occupation. And even in America and Great Britain, they occasionally provoked muttered complaints that the war was being prolonged in order to protect a far-off alien minority. As for proposals for an exchange of scarce commodities for victims of persecution, would that not protract the military conflict and increase the loss of life? And even if an agreement with the Third Reich could be reached or Hitler did decide to release hundreds of thousands of Jews, what would the Allies do with them—where would they house them, how would they feed them?

Those were real concerns, based on rational, reasonable calculations. Yet beneath them was an undercurrent of popular ethnic suspicion which had become almost traditional, not only in Eastern Europe but farther to the west as well, on both sides of the Atlantic. The statesmen of the Western democracies, now involved in a devastating war, had to take into account public prejudices and predispositions. Very few of them were outright anti-Semites, although some did display a patrician condescension toward Jews. But they could not ignore popular opinion, which had become increasingly hostile toward aliens and outsiders under the pressure of a destructive military conflict. Members of the British delegation to the Bermuda Conference reported to Anthony Eden the existence of "the present combination, in so many countries, of pity for Jews under German control and extreme reluctance to admit further Jews into their borders." That was a perceptive observation. Under those circumstances, the leaders of the coalition against the Axis had no choice but to continue to pursue a statecraft of carefully calibrated compassion.[44]

14

Should More Have Been Done to Stop the Holocaust?

T HE PASSAGE OF TIME has decided, rightly or wrongly, the outcome of most of the controversies and disputes regarding the
Nazi genocide during the Second World War. There is now general agreement, at least in the United States, that the extermination of
European Jewry was the most terrible of the Third Reich's many atrocities. There are still some countries in Europe, especially in the east, where
doubts about the validity of this conclusion persist, but they are usually
expressed cautiously and unobtrusively. Why invite bitter debate about an
issue that is now of only symbolic significance and that has been overshad-
owed by more immediate problems?

The reluctance to revive old arguments accounts in part for a general
readiness to concede that the unwillingness of the authorities in Washington to admit large numbers of refugees from German persecution reflected
their awareness of prevalent popular aversions and prejudices. And as for
the uneasy feeling before and during the war, even among sympathizers
with the victims of the Third Reich's anti-Semitism, that the Jews were
not entirely without fault in arousing ethnic hostility—that their ambitiousness or aggressiveness or clannishness helped account for the resentment they often encountered—that too has come to seem not only unfair
but essentially irrelevant.

Yet a few controversies arising out of the Second World War simply refuse to go away. The horror of the Holocaust is so great that even
many of those born long afterward, Christians as well as Jews, continue

to wonder why more was not done to stop the Nazi genocide. The questions they ask are the same as those asked while the genocide was still in progress. Why couldn't the Allies negotiate with the German government to release Jews in the death camps in return for financial inducements or economic concessions? Why couldn't they announce that the air raids destroying German cities would continue and increase until the genocide had stopped? And, most important, why couldn't they bomb the railroad tracks leading to the death camps or the death camps themselves? Some of the prisoners would undoubtedly have been killed, but not nearly as many as died in the course of a slow, orderly, methodical process of ethnic extermination. Why did the Allies do so little?

That question was asked with new persistence after the Second World War. As the Holocaust ceased to be a contemporaneous event and became more and more a subject of investigation and contemplation, the issue of what could have or should have been done to stop it arose with new urgency. In 1979, Henry L. Feingold maintained in an article asking "Who Shall Bear Guilt for the Holocaust?" that "thousands of Hungarian and Slovakian Jews might have been saved [in the spring and summer of 1944] had the American 15th Air Force, stationed in Italy and already bombing the synthetic oil and rubber works not five miles from the gas chambers [of Auschwitz], been allowed to [bomb the camp]." By the fall of that year, moreover, Auschwitz was easily within the range of Russian dive bombers. Why then did the American assistant secretary of the army, John J. McCloy, insist that attacking the death camp would be of "doubtful efficacy"? Why did the Soviet authorities refuse to approve plans for destroying the railroad tracks on which hundreds of thousands of innocent victims were being sent to their death? "All that was required was a relatively minor change in the priority assigned to the rescue of Jews." The reluctance of the Allied leaders to use military force to stop the Nazi genocide resulted in "the most horrendous inhuman acts by witnesses during the years of the Holocaust." Even now they seemed unforgivable.[1]

Yehuda Bauer, writing at about the same time, was somewhat more restrained in his criticism of Allied policy. Part of the blame, he argued, had to be placed on the Jewish relief organizations in America, which did not use their resources as wisely and responsibly as they should have. In the case of the Joint Distribution Committee, for example, "some of the expenditures of scarce . . . dollars were, to judge with the benefit of hindsight, less than judicious." Hundreds of thousands were poured into a visionary venture to resettle Jewish refugees in the Dominican Republic, which turned out to be a total fiasco. Hundreds of thousands more were given to the Russians in the hope that they would make a determined effort to save the Jews of Eastern Europe. If that money had been allocated to the Jewish community in Slovakia or Hungary instead of the Kremlin, it might have made "a real difference." As it was, the resources were simply wasted.

Nevertheless, Bauer concluded, most of the JDC's limited funds went where they were needed, and the results were in many cases exactly what had been hoped for. Without those funds, "the hiding of the children in France, the rescue from starvation in the Transnistrian ghettos, the feeding of the Jews beleaguered in the Swiss and Swedish houses in Budapest," and many other forms of assistance would have been impossible. Admittedly, there were limits to what the Joint Distribution Committee had been able to accomplish, limits imposed by its legalistic approach to the rescue problem and its lack of adequate resources. Yet there was also another obstacle, a very important one, namely, "an Allied policy that aimed exclusively at military victory rather than at both victory and the saving of lives." If the nations fighting against the Axis had shown greater concern about the mass murders, hundreds of thousands of Jews who perished in the death camps, millions perhaps, might have survived the war.[2]

Almost twenty years later and more than half a century after the Second World War, Peter Novick was still wrestling with the question of what could have and what should have been done to stop the Holocaust. But what could have been done seemed less important to him than what should have been done. "A much more energetic program of rescue on all fronts might have reduced the overall toll by perhaps 1 percent, conceivably 2 percent." That would have meant saving possibly as many as 120,000 lives; it would have been a major humanitarian achievement. But tragically, the realization that not even the most heroic efforts could save more than a small fraction of the victims of Nazi racism had the effect of discouraging what little might have been done. "The perception that the overall impact of American efforts would be marginal probably served to inhibit action by government officials—and by American Jews." Perhaps it should not be so, Novick sadly reflected, but it seems that people become energized only when they feel that they can make a big difference. "The (in my view) dim practical possibilities for substantial rescue are relevant to the consequences of American inaction, not to its morality."

Here was the crux of his argument. Military intervention to try to stop the Holocaust was justified not because of its practical consequences, not because of its chances of success, but because of its underlying rightness, its moral significance. To stand by while a monstrous crime was being committed against millions of guiltless, defenseless human beings was a violation of the basic humanitarian ideals of democracy.[3]

Yet in a time of war, when soldiers were dying in battle day after day, when civilians were forced to endure hunger and privation and air bombardment, when the very existence of the nation was at stake, the practical results of military action had to be regarded as more important than its moral justifications. That was why the requests of various American Jewish organizations were generally restrained.

Still, there were some exceptions to the common strategy of prudence. The letter of July 24, 1944, that Johan J. Smertenko sent to Roosevelt in the name of the Emergency Committee to Save the Jewish People of Europe was fierce in tone and uncompromising in content. The railways and bridges leading to the death camps should be bombed, he urged, and the government should proclaim that "this action is taken in order to prevent the transportation of the Hebrew people of these Axis countries to Hitler's slaughter houses." Air raids directed against the gas chambers "would enable the Hebrew people gathered in these camps to escape and offer them an opportunity to join the underground resistance forces where they can be of help in sabotage and resistance activities." And finally, a statement should be issued that the extermination of Jews by poison gas would be considered a justification for a policy of retribution. Indeed, "the threat of widespread use of the same medium upon the German population will contribute to the disaffection of the German people and may result in a speedier collapse of Hitler's home front." There was nothing cautious about such proposals.[4]

They were an exception, however. Most of the suggestions submitted to Washington regarding the rescue of European Jewry were much more restrained. For example, in a letter sent to Sumner Welles on April 14,

1943, in the name of the Joint Emergency Committee for European Jewish Affairs, Stephen Wise outlined the measures that should be taken "if the remnants of European Jewry are to be saved from destruction," which were cautious to the point of timidity, especially in view of the recent official confirmation of the Nazi regime's program of racist extermination. He proposed first of all "negotiations with the Axis Powers through neutral governments to permit the exit of Jews from Axis-occupied countries." Second, the Allies should create "temporary and permanent sanctuaries" for the refugees from Nazi persecution. And finally, "in view of the fact that planned starvation is one of the methods of accomplishing the extermination of the Jewish populace of Europe," the Allies should provide food for those Jews who were unable to obtain permission to leave the occupied countries. That was as far as Wise thought it advisable to go.[5]

Why was he, like so many of the other leaders of the Jewish community in America, reluctant to urge the government to adopt a more forceful policy regarding the Holocaust? The Allies had by then revealed to the world the Nazis' genocidal program. Trains were carrying thousands of victims to the death camps in Eastern Europe day and night. The total number of those gassed, shot, or starved had already reached well over a million. Yet Wise still hesitated to suggest anything more than negotiating with the Nazi regime for the release of those facing extermination or for the provision of food to the intended victims in the event that the Nazi regime would not let them go. Why this timidity?

Part of the answer was the general skepticism in the United States about reports of the mass murder of European Jewry. That the Nazi authorities were treating Jews harshly seemed credible, to be sure. There might even have been some cases of deadly violence against innocent civilians. But planned, systematic genocide? That was hard to believe. The Germans were, after all, a civilized, cultured people. Those who had crossed the Atlantic to settle in the United States were no worse than Americans of other backgrounds. In fact, they appeared better than some. That those who remained in the Old World would now engage in organized, methodical genocide seemed unlikely.

Besides, psychological warfare had recently become an essential part of military conflict. During the First World War, the Germans had been accused of mass rapes and murders in occupied Belgium, only to have those charges dismissed afterward as unfounded rumors or deliberate lies. At the same time, the Turks had been condemned by their foes for committing atrocities against defenseless Armenians. In 1920, during the invasion of Poland by the Bolshevik armies, there were similar stories about Russian soldiers engaging in robbery, rape, and the murder of civilians. During the brief period of political and economic stability later in the decade, there were very few reports of atrocities. But with the renewed international tensions of the 1930s, charges of murderous cruelty by those on the other side reappeared, more frequent and more graphic than ever. The Japanese were torturing and killing helpless Chinese; the Italians were oppressing and enslaving conquered Ethiopians; and in Spain, followers of Franco were executing supporters of the republican regime and supporters of the republican regime were executing the followers of Franco. No wonder that after the outbreak of the Second World War, many Americans were inclined to view reports of the Holocaust with suspicion. Those reports seemed no more credible than the horror stories that opposing sides had been hurling at each other for almost thirty years.

Skepticism about the Holocaust was reinforced by another common perception, namely, that Jews saw themselves and wanted to be seen by others as victims of prejudice and injustice. Their hunger for sympathy was much older than the war or even than the Hitler regime. It had originated centuries earlier, at a time when the Jewish community was segregated, isolated, and persecuted. Liberation and enfranchisement had not lasted long enough to overcome the psychological effects of a long history of oppression. Those effects were still being widely felt. They were even a source of stories and jokes about the cliquishness or the oversensitiveness of Jews. Such qualities were widely seen as the manifestation of a stubborn Jewish addiction to victimhood.

That some Jews had been killed under the German occupation was generally, though not universally, acknowledged. But the number of those killed was widely disputed during the war years. The results of a Gallup poll conducted in January 1943, a few weeks after the official Allied confirmation of the Holocaust, reflected this disagreement. The question asked of the respondents was preceded by a straightforward statement of fact: "It is said that two million Jews have been killed in Europe since the war began." Then came the controversial part. "Do you think this is true or just a rumor?" The replies revealed a sharp difference of opinion. Only 47 percent thought that the statement was true, while 29 percent thought it was only a rumor and 24 percent preferred not to express an opinion. Did those who doubted or expressed no opinion believe that the number was exaggerated, or did they think that no mass murders had taken place? As for those who believed that some Jews might indeed have perished, but not 2 million, what number would they have found credible? And what of those respondents, almost a fourth of the total, who remained silent? Were they indifferent or undecided or reluctant to express views that might be considered insensitive? There is no answer.[6]

But the next Gallup poll dealing with the Holocaust, conducted almost two years later, in November 1944, was more inclusive and more revealing. It asked two important questions. First, "Do you believe the stories that the Germans have murdered many people in concentration camps?" No specific figure was given for the number of victims of the German genocide, and no reference was made to the ethnic background of those victims. By then the Wehrmacht had been forced to retreat from eastern Poland and several of the death camps had been liberated by the Soviets. The evidence of anti-Semitic mass murders by the Third Reich seemed irrefutable. Yet 12 percent of the respondents were still unconvinced, and another 12 percent expressed no opinion. In short, almost a fourth of the total remained dubious about the actuality of the Holocaust. More than that, the combined percentage of skeptics—that is, those who did not believe that the Third Reich had engaged in genocide and those who preferred not to express an opinion—did not vary greatly in the various parts of the United States, ranging from a high of 27 in the Middle Atlantic states to a low of 16 in the western states, the only region with less than 20 percent. There was little correlation between the proportion of Jews in the population of any given region and popular belief in the validity of the official reports.

The answers to the second question were perhaps even more revealing. Those who had indicated that they believed the Germans had indeed "murdered many people in concentration camps," 76 percent of the respondents, were then asked, "Nobody knows, of course, how many may have been murdered, but what would be your best guess?" By that time, the total number of victims of the Holocaust was approaching 6 million.

But most of the participants in the poll underestimated the actual figure by a wide margin. Of the approximately 3,000 respondents, including those who doubted that many people had perished in the death camps, 27 percent thought that at most 100,000 had been killed, 5 percent thought that the number was 100,000 to 500,000, 1 percent thought it was between 500,000 and 1 million, and 6 percent thought it was 1 million. Only 8 percent were closer to the actual figure: those whose estimates ranged from 2 million to 6 million. Then there were the 4 percent who overestimated the total, some by a narrow margin, others by a wide margin. And finally, a large proportion of the respondents, 25 percent, were "unwilling to guess." All in all, 12 percent, at most, estimated correctly or overestimated the number of victims of the Holocaust.[7]

Even the end of the war in Europe did not substantially change the popular perception of the extent and intensity of the Nazi genocide. By the time of the next poll, conducted in May 1945, Hitler was dead and the Allies had occupied all of Germany. Auschwitz, Treblinka, Maidanek, Chelmno, and the various other death camps had been liberated by the Red Army. There could no longer be any question regarding their purpose or function. And yet doubts about the Holocaust persisted. The median estimate of the number of victims was 1 million, well above the figure in the poll taken six months earlier but still far below the actual total. The percentage of respondents who thought that the reports of Nazi genocide were true had risen to 84, but even now more than a tenth of the participants still had some reservations and suspicions. The victory of the Allies had not been enough to dispel them.[8]

This persistent disbelief was partly a result of popular skepticism about the stories of wartime atrocities that had been multiplying since the First World War. It was partly also the reflection of a common perception that Jews tended to be malcontents and complainers, exaggerating or even fabricating the injustices which they allegedly had to endure. Yet there was more to it than that. Some of those who did not believe in the Holocaust—many, perhaps—did not want to believe in it, whether consciously or subconsciously. They feared that acknowledging the accuracy of the reports would intensify the demand that the American government do something, and the result would be that a war being fought to defend the United States against aggression and invasion might become transformed, at least partially, into a crusade to save a persecuted minority thousands of miles away in the Old World. Was that really in the national interest? Should American soldiers be asked to risk their lives in order to protect a foreign ethnic community threatened with genocide? The answer seemed clear. The chief concern of the government should be the defense of the country and the security of its citizens.

This does not mean that the opponents of special efforts to rescue the victims of Nazi anti-Semitism were indifferent to the fate of those victims. On the contrary, they were almost unanimously in agreement that genocide was a cruel and unacceptable way of dealing with the "Jewish question." Many of them believed, however, that Jews had indeed acquired too much influence in politics and economics, and not only in the United States. They suspected, moreover, that members of the Jewish community were trying to persuade the American government to use its diplomatic, financial, and military resources to save their coreligionists in Europe. Those efforts had to be resisted. The program of ethnic persecution that the Third Reich had adopted was admittedly extreme and inhumane. But demands that the United States sacrifice members of its armed forces in order to rescue the victims of National Socialism had to be rejected. The chief concern of the American government should be the welfare of the American people.

This view was shared by most of the politicians and officials in Washington. They preferred not to express it openly, since that might leave them vulnerable to charges of heartlessness or bigotry. But from time to time, especially when the Holocaust became a subject of debate, there was no mistaking how they felt. In November 1943, after a resolution was introduced in Congress urging the creation of a commission "to formulate and effectuate a plan of immediate action designed to save the surviving Jewish people of Europe from execution at the hands of Nazi Germany," Congressman Karl E. Mundt of South Dakota, a member of the House Foreign Affairs Committee, expressed serious doubts. "As a general policy for this country," he maintained, "it is not good practice for us to establish a precedent, or if the precedent is already established, to emphasize it, whereby we pass legislation which singles out groups of people by their religion or by their color or their faith or their political affiliations, either for special consideration or for special penalty. . . . That would be treading a pretty dangerous path. It is sort of doing the Hitler thing in reverse. The repercussions at home, at least, are bound to be insidious." The congressman did not identify by name any of the "groups of people" who should not receive special consideration, but anyone hearing or reading his statement could guess whom he had in mind.[9]

Most government officials, especially those in the State Department, were in agreement with Congressman Mundt, and no one more so than Breckinridge Long. He had felt for some time that the Jewish community was pressing too hard for special efforts by Washington to save European Jewry. And the longer the war continued, the more convinced he became. In the spring of 1943, reflecting in his diary on the Bermuda Conference, he complained that Stephen Wise and his followers had been "so assiduous in pushing their particular cause" that they were gradually arousing public opposition. They were lending credibility to the enemy charges that Jews were secretly controlling the American war effort, thereby weakening the national resolve to continue the military struggle until victory had been won. Not only that, they were unwittingly supporting popular suspicions about their aims and activities. Their constant pleas and demands could easily prove detrimental to their cause. To oppose their efforts, therefore, would be not only in the national interest but also in the Jewish interest.[10]

A few months later, in his testimony before the House Foreign Affairs Committee regarding the establishment of a commission to help rescue the remnants of European Jewry, Long was not quite as outspoken as in his diary. After all, he had to be careful about what he said openly, especially since he was already being widely accused of anti-Semitic bias. But he could at least support the views of Congressman Mundt concerning the inadvisability of singling out any particular ethnic or racial group for special consideration. "The State Department has maintained that attitude all through," he explained to the members of the committee, "but the situation has come to a state of publicity today where I think the Jewish interests have emphasized the fate of the Jews as such." His formulation was cautious enough to withstand accusations of prejudice but clear in its reservations about proposals perceived as too favorable to Jews on either side of the Atlantic.[11]

Nevertheless, the popular fear that leaders of the Jewish community were trying to persuade the government to take military measures to stop the Holocaust was exaggerated. A few did advocate the use of armed force to destroy the railroad tracks leading to the death camps or the death camps themselves. But most recognized that requests of that sort were not only futile but likely to backfire, as they would in all probability intensify the widespread suspicion about the patriotism of American Jewry. It might be worth the risk to propose the resettlement of Jewish refugees either in the United States or in some of the neutral countries or colonial territories outside Europe. It might even be safe to try to provide food for the starving Jews in the ghettos of Poland. But urging the government to divert its military resources to rescue prisoners in the death camps—that would be dangerous.

Even Stephen Wise, whom Breckinridge Long regarded as the leader of a militant "Jewish faction," hesitated to urge the use of American military resources for the liberation of the victims of Nazi racism. From time to time, especially when addressing an audience of Jews, he did display a combativeness that came close to a demand for the rescue of countless innocent men and women. Addressing the American Jewish Conference, for example, he urged his audience "solemnly to demand of the United Nations that not another hour be lost in rescuing from the lands in the hands of Hitler the remaining Jews, the less than 3 million survivors of the 8 million Jews who lived in pre-Hitler Europe. Any further delay of rescue would doubtless mean that there would be no Jews to save in what was Hitler's Europe." It was clearer than ever, he argued, that some way of saving the victims of the Holocaust could be found, "provided the United Nations, led by our own, have the will to rescue our harassed, despoiled, tortured brothers." To do so was more than an expression of humaneness, more than the fulfillment of a moral obligation. It was an act of atonement, a form of reparation. "Such rescue of the surviving may in part redeem the world's shame of the years 1933–1939."[12]

Those listening to Wise's speech did not have to be persuaded. But convincing government officials in Washington was something else. Not that they were unaware of the Holocaust. They knew very well what was going on in Eastern Europe, and most of them were shocked by the sheer cruelty of the Third Reich. They had to deal, however, not only with American Jews eager to save fellow Jews overseas but also with other Americans who as a rule condemned genocide yet also saw, day after day, long lists of their countrymen killed or wounded in combat. They were reluctant to increase the number of casualties by trying to rescue victims of the Holocaust. The authorities thus faced a dilemma to which only one response was possible. Whatever their personal inclinations, they could not afford to endanger the lives of American soldiers for the sake of European Jews. To do so would create domestic dissension and weaken the war effort.

Most Jewish leaders, recognizing that there was really no solution to the problem, did not press the government very hard for a change in official policy. They concentrated their efforts on issues that were less controversial—on the resettlement of refugees, for example, or on economic assistance to the starving ghettos in Eastern Europe. Even Wise, when dealing with important officials in Washington, avoided preaching about the world's responsibility for the tragedy confronting his coreligionists across the Atlantic. Instead he talked about negotiating with the Axis to allow Jews to emigrate or about finding sanctuaries overseas or about providing food for those who were denied permission to leave. Such proposals, though still contentious, were not likely to arouse nearly as much opposition as demands for air attacks against Auschwitz and Treblinka.

Besides, to argue for the use of military force against the Nazi genocide might create a serious predicament for Roosevelt, the friend and protector of the Jews. Instead of helping, it might hurt the Jewish cause at home and abroad. "Hitler would have won the war," Wise explained in a private letter, "if it had not been for our President and America." To weaken Roosevelt's position by making impossible demands would be disadvantageous to both. The wisest course was to save any talk about the shameful international behavior before the war or about the use of armed force to rescue prisoners in the death camps for speeches before organizations like the American Jewish Conference.[13]

Jews holding important positions in the government were also reluctant to appear to support special measures in favor of the victims of the Holocaust. Leaders of Jewish organizations in the United States, men like Stephen Wise, were expected to plead and argue for efforts to help their coreligionists abroad facing extermination, but those entrusted with the defense of the national interest had a responsibility to rise above any exclusive consideration for a particular religious or ethnic or national minority. Their obligation was to protect the welfare of all of their countrymen, without regard for personal preferences or loyalties. And prominent Jewish officeholders, aware that some of their fellow Americans viewed them with suspicion and distrust, were especially careful not to display too much concern for the victims of the Holocaust.

Even Henry Morgenthau, secretary of the treasury, an old friend of Roosevelt's, felt that he had to be cautious in dealing with questions affecting European or American Jewry. His closeness to the president would only intensify the misgivings of quite a few of his countrymen about his role in the administration. At the end of February 1945, when the Third Reich was on the verge of military defeat and political collapse, he still hesitated to approve negotiations between a Jewish organization in New York and the German government for the release of some "non-Aryans" in exchange for a substantial financial ransom. "The thing is this," he explained at a meeting with his staff. "The *Chicago Tribune* has about got this, and the story they are talking of running is that Henry Morgenthau, the Jew, is dealing with Himmler to bring out Jews, and Jews only, see, that I am dealing with Himmler." How would that make him look?

Some of those at the meeting tried to reassure him, but Morgenthau remained uneasy. "Suppose they print that story," he worried. "I never could catch up to them. . . . I mean, the facts are known." He read a letter he had received to the effect that Himmler wanted Jews, and Jews only, to be released, so that when they reached the countries recently liberated from German rule, the local population would be struck by the fact that "there were no Christians among them." That would surely intensify anti-Semitic prejudice in those countries and, Morgenthau feared, perhaps in his own country as well. It would be best not to press for negotiations.[14]

Even Gentiles in important government positions who were sympathetic toward Jewish causes thought it prudent to emphasize, at least in public, that the war was being waged in defense of all the national and ethnic communities persecuted by National Socialism. Harold Ickes was a case in point. There can be no question about his unqualified rejection of anti-Semitism, whether in the Third Reich or in the United States. Indeed, he often criticized the leaders of American Jewry, at least in confidential conversation or in the privacy of his diary, for being too timid in asserting the rights of Jews as American citizens. What were they so afraid of? Why did they hesitate to condemn the ethnic prejudices and discriminations unfortunately too common in a nation committed to the principles of democracy? Why did they not stand up for their rights more boldly? And yet he too was reluctant to say or do anything that might intensify domestic discord or weaken patriotic resolve. The important thing was to maintain national unity. Everything else, even the struggle against social injustice and ethnic bigotry, had to yield to the demands of military conflict.

As late as December 1944, Ickes remained reluctant to express in public views that might be perceived as favorable toward Jews. Having learned that several Jewish organizations were working on a book to be titled "Jewish Black Book," he sent a letter to an acquaintance expressing doubt about the advisability of such a work. "The Jews do not have to be told about atrocities against the Jews and others might only have their prejudices stimulated or increased." The result would be a reinforcement of the perception that the Jewish community was always complaining, always pleading for sympathy, without much concern for other ethnic or national communities also suffering cruel persecution.

Ickes therefore offered a counterproposal, namely, that a book should be written on some subject such as "No Soft Peace." A work of that sort could still deal in detail with the cruelties being committed by the Third Reich, "but they should be treated not as atrocities against Jews as much as atrocities against people in general, including not only Jews but Catholics and Protestants, Hollander, French, Belgian, Filipinos, etc. I really think that a book of this nature might be really helpful right now." Ickes added that he wished he were free to write such a book himself, but he already had proposals before him for four other books, "including the one on coal which I never seem to be able to finish." Still, a "very effective" work dealing with the approaching postwar settlement could and should be written, a work "that might influence the thinking of people and strengthen their resolve against a soft peace." A book analyzing how to punish Germany for its crimes would also be more useful than just another long recital of the injustices committed against Jews. There were already enough of those in print.[15]

The resolve of American government officials to dispel any popular perception that the war effort was even in part a crusade to save European Jewry appears repeatedly in their rejection of demands for the bombing of the death camps in Poland. For one thing, the Germans would be sure to point to such air raids as proof that the Allies were following the orders of cunning Jewish manipulators and wire-pullers. The countries occupied by Germany might also become suspicious of the role played by Jews in determining American policy. Were not the Poles, the Czechs, the Belgians, and the Norwegians just as much victims of Nazi brutality as the Jews? All the traditional ethnic biases of the Old World, which the war had clearly not diminished, were bound to be intensified. Worst of all, how would the American public react to reports that American airmen were risking their lives in an attempt to save some of the Jews imprisoned in the death camps? It was obvious that direct military intervention to stop the Holocaust could have a serious adverse effect on the war effort. It would be best not to try it.

Still, to say so openly was risky as well. It would be an implicit acknowledgment that the American public did not always support the principles and ideals to which the nation officially subscribed and which were constantly being invoked to justify the struggle against the Third Reich. Therefore, the argument usually advanced was that in the long run, the use of armed force to attack the death camps would be not only ineffective but detrimental. The only way to save what was left of European Jewry was to defeat the Third Reich as quickly as possible.

The logic of that argument seemed irrefutable, which is why it was so frequently invoked. Those invoking it did not generally have any private doubts about its validity. On the contrary, most of them believed wholeheartedly in what they were saying. Yet they also feared that to agree even to an occasional symbolic bombing of railroad tracks or gas chambers might open the floodgates. An air raid on Auschwitz would no doubt lead to demands for an air raid on Maidanek and then Treblinka and then Belzec and then Chelmno. There would be no end to requests and pleas, ever louder, ever more insistent. And then wouldn't the resistance movements in the occupied countries begin requesting similar raids against the prisons and detention camps holding captured members of the underground? Surely they deserved as much Allied sympathy and support as Jews in the death camps. And then there were the various governments in exile, each eager to influence the Allied military strategy in favor of the prompt liberation of its countrymen. Were they not likely to begin asking the American authorities for the same special efforts as those being made on behalf of the victims of Nazi anti-Semitism? No, the best policy was to leave Pandora's box alone.

In June 1944, when a representative of the War Refugee Board stationed in Switzerland urged the bombing of railway lines from Hungary to Auschwitz because "there is little doubt that many of these Hungarian Jews are being sent to the extermination camps," the authorities in Washington rejected the proposal. As Assistant Secretary of War John J. McCloy explained to John W. Pehle, "the War Department is of the opinion that the suggested air operation is impracticable." It could be carried out only by "the diversion of considerable air support essential to the success of our forces now engaged in decisive operations." Even if an air attack on Auschwitz were approved, "it would . . . be of such very doubtful efficacy that it would not amount to a practical project." The armed forces had more urgent tasks before them.[16]

The War Refugee Board did not give up easily, however. A few months later, in November, Pehle wrote to McCloy once again urging air raids against Auschwitz and nearby Birkenau even more forcefully than before. He recommended that the War Department give serious consideration to "destroying the execution chambers and crematories in Birkenau through direct bombing action." Such action would be clearly justifiable "if it is deemed feasible by competent military authorities." But there was the rub. In his reply, McCloy reported that the operations staff of the War Department had rejected the proposal because the target was too far away to be reached by dive bombers and fighter bombers stationed in England, France, and Italy. While heavy bombers could probably fly to Auschwitz and back, they would have to travel 2,000 miles over enemy territory without an escort. That would be too risky. "The positive solution to this problem," McCloy concluded, "is the earliest possible victory over Germany."[17]

The reluctance of government officials to use military force to stop the Nazi genocide also reflected a concern that it might weaken the morale of the armed forces. After all, a citizen army was bound to share the sympathies and antipathies of the citizenry at large; that was an inevitable result of the deprofessionalization of warfare, of the democratization of armed conflict. And that meant that the men in the ranks were as likely as civilians, perhaps even more likely, to be disturbed to learn that they were being ordered to engage in deadly combat so that European Jews facing extermination could be rescued. They were prepared to face the dangers of battle to defend their nation and to protect their families, friends, and countrymen. But to be exposed to deadly peril in order to rescue a distant, often mistrusted ethnic minority might raise troubling questions in the minds of some soldiers. It might weaken their resolve and loyalty. It was something to be avoided.

Even McCloy, who insisted that his opposition to proposals to bomb the death camps rested solely on a conviction that military victory was the quickest way to end the Holocaust, occasionally admitted that he was also troubled by the prevalence of anti-Semitic prejudice in the armed forces. Writing in April 1943 to Elmer Davis of the Office of War Information, he reported the comments of a young army officer he knew. "There is one persistent worry I have had from the first day I got into the Army," McCloy's friend confessed. Did the American people really know what they were fighting for? "In the majority of the soldiers' minds lies only deep mistrust of England even more than Russia, as well as the Hitlerian idea that the whole war was started by Jewish capitalists. It is unbelievable that Americans should believe these things, but they do, and are willing to believe anything involving race prejudice." As for the reasons, at least one was obvious. "Isolationism is so deep rooted."[18]

McCloy agreed with the young officer that distrust of Jews was common in the armed forces, and he too regretted its prevalence. But what could he do about it? "This is perhaps primarily an Army problem and one that I hope we shall be able to deal with," he told Davis. But he was by no means sure. "I do not believe we can divorce Army thinking from national thinking." It seemed to him unlikely that the armed forces could be taught to reject ethnic prejudices while the public in general continued to embrace them. Clearly, "if the men come into the Army with those prejudices, it is going to be hard to eradicate them." The military authorities should of course encourage greater tolerance, greater understanding. But they could not afford to ignore the common aversions and bigotries of the men in the ranks who were risking their lives day after day in battle with the enemy.[19]

The determination of the army leadership not to appear partial to the Jewish victims of Nazi atrocities was reflected not only in its opposition to proposals for the bombardment of the death camps. Even in situations where there was no danger of suffering casualties, where the risks were emotional or psychological rather than physical, the armed forces hesitated to create the impression that they felt special concern for or focused particular attention on Jews. There was always the fear of arousing latent prejudices or reinforcing secret suspicions in the ranks. Nothing should be done, no matter how innocuous or well-intentioned, that might weaken the morale of the men in uniform.

In the fall of 1944, Sergeant Richard Paul, a reporter for *Yank* magazine, received an assignment to write a "German atrocity story" designed to reveal to American soldiers the true nature of the enemy they were fighting. During an interview with Pehle at the War Refugee Board, the sergeant received copies of two reports from prisoners who had recently escaped from Auschwitz, which he then used in writing his article. But almost immediately obstacles and problems began to appear. On or around November 10, Paul reported to Pehle that he was "very much discouraged about the progress of his story." The editors of *Yank* had concluded that "our reports were too Semitic" and had asked him to get a story "from other sources." He had then gone to the Pentagon to get permission to publish his story overseas, but "he had been sent from one officer to another in quick order and had found a very negative attitude." The consensus of those he talked to was that what he had written was "a hell of a hot story," meaning that it was so controversial that it "would have to move through the highest military channels for approval." The sergeant came away deeply disappointed.

The Treasury Department official who took his telephone call and summarized it for Pehle tried to console him. His article was sound and certainly appropriate. "Inasmuch as the whole Nazi extermination program was more than 90 percent Jewish, it was most unlikely that he could get any stories that did not deal principally with Jews." This reasoning failed to sway the editors of *Yank*, however. A few days later, Paul telephoned to report that "New York again had asked him to try to get a less Jewish story." And on November 16 he telephoned a third time, to say that his story was still being held, although he had sent a long memorandum to the main office repeating all the arguments for using the reports about Auschwitz and informing the editors that those reports were now being released to the press. But New York would not budge. "The Acting Managing Editor said that because of latent anti-Semitism in the Army, [Paul] ought, if possible, to get something with a less Semitic slant." In the end, the story was never published.[20]

At the same time, another soldier of much higher rank was encountering similar difficulties. General of the Army Dwight D. Eisenhower, supreme commander of the Allied Expeditionary Forces, had been urged by Washington to issue a statement warning the Germans against the mass murder of prisoners in the concentration camps. By then there was no longer any doubt about the outcome of the war. The Red Army had driven the Wehrmacht out of the occupied territories in the Soviet Union and was now standing at the gates of Warsaw. On the other side of the continent, American and British forces had liberated France and Belgium, even crossing the prewar frontier of Germany and taking the city of Aachen. Final victory was in sight. As for the Holocaust, almost two years had elapsed since the Allies had officially confirmed reports of the systematic extermination of European Jewry by the Third Reich. There was a danger, however, that the Nazi regime, recognizing its impending defeat and driven by ethnic hatred, might accelerate the mass murder of those it regarded as deadly enemies. Something should be done to warn the perpetrators against continuing their policy of anti-Semitic genocide. Even if that did not deter the Nazi zealots, it might at least have a favorable effect on public opinion at home.

On October 30, 1944, Acting Secretary of State Edward R. Stettinius, Jr., sent a telegram to chargé d'affaires George F. Kennan at the American embassy in Moscow informing him of a plan to have Eisenhower issue a statement warning the Nazi authorities not to kill innocent civilians. Would the Soviet government be willing to issue a similar warning? It would be of great help. Washington had recently received reliable information that the Germans were preparing "a last minute slaughter in forced labor and concentration camps, of thousands of United Nations nationals and stateless Jews held by them." This plan was the culmination of "the program of mass murder and terror" that the Third Reich had inflicted on the peoples of the world. While the Allies were determined to impose just punishment on those committing the crimes, they also wanted to take every possible step to prevent "last minute atrocities."

That, Stettinius explained, was why the president, with the concurrence of the British government, had requested Eisenhower's statement of warning. Arrangements were now being made to meet this request. The telegram then reproduced the draft being considered by the authorities in Washington as well as by the leaders of the armed forces in Europe. After opening with "Attention Germans!" it spoke of the large numbers of prisoners in labor battalions and concentration camps. And then came a stern admonition: "Germans, these are my orders. You shall disregard any order from whatever source to molest or otherwise harm or persecute any of these people regardless of their nationality or religious faith." The Allied armies were now on German soil. As they advanced, they would expect to find the prisoners alive and unharmed. Anyone responsible for their mistreatment, "directly or indirectly, in large measure or small," would be subject to severe penalties. "Those now exercising authority, heed this warning!"[21]

There was a small but significant difference, however, between Stettinius's description of those threatened by "a last minute slaughter" and the description in the draft statement that he included in his telegram to Kennan. He himself spoke of "thousands of United Nations nationals and stateless Jews" facing mass murder. The draft statement referred to the same likely victims of Nazi persecution as "people regardless of their nationality or religious faith."

Controversy over the ethnic identification of a large part of those in danger of execution continued for weeks before Eisenhower's statement was issued. On one side were those, many of them active in efforts to deal with the refugee problem, who maintained that Jews would be among the first victims of Nazi vengefulness. Precisely for that reason, Jews should be mentioned specifically in the warning. Lawrence Lesser of the War Refugee Board, for example, submitted a draft in which Eisenhower would warn the citizens of the Third Reich not to obey any order to harm the prisoners in labor battalions or concentration camps, "without regard for their nationality and whether they are Jewish or otherwise." To ignore this warning would lead to severe penalties. "Those now exercising authority, take heed!"[22]

On the other side were those, some of them holding important positions in the armed forces, who were equally determined in their opposition to singling out any particular ethnic group, meaning Jews, for special mention in the statement. The danger was that any special mention might backfire. It might make the situation of the Jews under Nazi rule even more precarious by intensifying anti-Semitic hostility. On October 14, 1944, the Supreme Headquarters of the Allied Expeditionary Forces at Versailles sent a message to the War Department in Washington explaining that "we have no objection to issuing a statement similar to that urged by the executive director of the War Refugee Board, provided the words 'or religious faith' are substituted for 'whether they are Jewish or otherwise.'" As for the reason, "Psychological Warfare Division believes that original wording would give Germans powerful propaganda line." It would seem to support the contention of the Nazi regime that international Jewry was inciting and prolonging the military conflict.[23]

The dispute over the wording of the statement continued behind the scenes for at least a month. There is no way of telling exactly who all the participants were, what each of them said, or even what role Eisenhower played in the outcome. What is clear is that the statement finally issued on November 7 warned the Germans not to molest, harm, or persecute prisoners in concentration camps and forced labor battalions, "no matter what their religion or nationality may be." That the omission of any mention of Jews reflected a concern about the prevalence of anti-Semitic prejudice among the Germans seems clear. But could there also have been concerns about the effect that a display of special sympathy for Jews might have on public opinion in the occupied countries of Europe or perhaps even in the United States? That is a distinct possibility.[24]

The same consideration appears even more clearly in the attitude of the British authorities. Like the officials in Washington, they were reluctant to do or say anything that might lend support to the German contention that the war was being deliberately prolonged because of Jewish agitation. But while the Americans tended to emphasize the effect that special sympathy for the victims of the Holocaust might have on public opinion at home, the British were more likely to express uneasiness, especially in private, about its effect on popular fears and suspicions in the occupied countries. At a time when so many nationalities and ethnicities had to endure the cruelties of war, it seemed inadvisable to emphasize the sufferings of any single one.

Still, not all observers recognized or at least acknowledged the underlying reasons for the British government's reluctance to condemn the Nazi policy of anti-Semitic genocide more forcefully. Early in 1944, the writer and journalist Arthur Koestler, a disillusioned Central European leftist who had found refuge in England shortly after the outbreak of war, complained in an article in the *New York Times Magazine* that although he had been lecturing to British troops for three years, the prevailing attitude in the military regarding Nazi atrocities remained unchanged. "They don't believe in concentration camps, they don't believe in the starved children of Greece, in the shot refugees of France, in the mass graves of Poland; they have never heard of Lidice, Treblinka or Belzec." He had been able to convince his listeners for an hour or so that all those stories about the cruelties perpetrated by the Nazis were true. But then they would shake themselves and their mental self-defense would begin to work. "In a week the shrug of incredulity has returned like a reflex temporarily weakened by a shock."

This refusal to recognize the depths of the human capacity for evil had become, according to Koestler, part of the collective mentality of the British people and even of the British government. "They carried on business-as-usual style, with the only difference that the routine of this business included killing and being killed. Matter-of-fact unimaginativeness has become a kind of Anglo-Saxon racial myth." It was often opposed to "Latin hysterics" and praised for its value in times of emergency. Yet the myth did not explain what might happen between emergencies. Indeed, it was responsible for the failure of the government to prevent the recurrence of emergencies. Too little emotionalism could prove as dangerous as too much. That was the problem which England confronted in dealing with the Holocaust.

Who should be held responsible for that problem? To Koestler, the answer was clear. The British authorities, especially those whose job it was to maintain public awareness of the moral issues underlying the war, had failed to make clear to the people of England that more than national welfare or even national security was at stake. The Ministry of Information and the British Broadcasting Corporation had proved competent in dealing with some aspects of the task; for almost three years they had kept England going on nothing but defeats, until now at last they could boast of at least some successes. "But at the same time they lamentably failed to imbue the people with anything approaching a full awareness of what it was all about, of the grandeur and horror of the time into which they were born." That failure accounted for the reluctance of the British public to believe the reports of the Holocaust or to recognize fully the tragic significance of the destruction of European Jewry.[25]

There was more to it, however—more than Koestler recognized or was willing to admit. The statesmen in Whitehall knew as much about the Holocaust as those in the White House and the State Department. It was not a lack of information or a skepticism inherent in the Anglo-Saxon mentality that kept them from responding more forcefully to the news of the Nazi genocide. On both sides of the Atlantic, there was reluctance to display too much sympathy or grief at what was happening to the Jews in the death camps for fear of arousing resentment among the non-Jewish populations under the German occupation. The deadly success of the Third Reich's program of ethnic extermination had done little to diminish the intensity of anti-Semitic distrust and hostility on the continent. If anything, the hardships of a cruel war had increased that distrust and hostility.

A resolve to avoid dissension among the members of the coalition against the Axis helps explain the British government's response to a letter that Chief Rabbi Joseph Hertz sent to Churchill on May 8, 1944. The occupation of Hungary by the Wehrmacht a few weeks earlier had initiated the deportation of members of yet another Jewish community to the extermination centers in Poland. Under the circumstances, Hertz proposed a plan that reflected his horror and despair at what was happening. He urged the prime minister to issue a proclamation stating that since the British government had for almost thirty years taken special interest in "the fate and future of European Jewry," and since the Nazis had now separated the Jewish minority from the general population under their rule, condemning it to "torture and mass extermination," the United Kingdom was declaring all Jews in enemy territories to be "British protected persons," offering them the assistance available to such persons, including "the provision of travel-documents, facilities for exchange and place of refuge." Hertz hoped that Churchill and perhaps the prime ministers of the dominions as well would give "due consideration" to his suggestion. By doing so, they would at least demonstrate their firm commitment to "the great human causes" the nation was so valiantly defending.[26]

The government's response was predictable. How could the officials agree to make a special effort to help Jews without also making a special effort to help Poles, Czechs, Belgians, or the French? It was out of the question. That was the substance of the letter that Pierson Dixon of the Foreign Office sent on May 16 to John Martin, Churchill's private secretary. The various departments consulted about Rabbi Hertz's proposal had all agreed that it was "impracticable" for a variety of reasons. For one thing, the governments in exile allied with England would be sure to criticize, "if not actively resent," a declaration stating in effect that while some of their nationals were "British-protected persons," others were not. Besides, the Germans were unlikely to agree to abandon or even modify their anti-Semitic policies, and even if they did, "we have probably not enough eligible German civilians to exchange for British subjects in German hands," not to mention "the very limited shipping facilities available for the purpose of exchange." The practical obstacles to Hertz's proposal were simply too great to be overcome by humane motives and honorable intentions.

And then Dixon came to the heart of the matter. "We have always taken the line that although the Germans have attacked the Jews with especial ferocity, they have also attacked and murdered many hundreds of thousands of non-Jews (in Poland the proportions are said to be about equal)." To provide Jews with an exclusive opportunity to escape persecution by giving them special protection would be sure to arouse resentment among the other victims of Nazi oppression. Moreover, "we doubt whether it would be appreciated by the U.S.S.R." It might actually intensify anti-Semitism in the countries under German occupation, and by stereotyping the "Jew" as a category, it would perpetuate the Third Reich's racist doctrines, which England was determined to stamp out. Thus the best reply to Hertz would be that not only was his proposal unlikely to be accepted by the Nazi regime, but it would probably bring many disadvantages to the Jews themselves. The nations allied in the war against the Third Reich were determined to help "*all* the victims of German tyranny" without making a futile gesture of "declaring one category of persons to be British-protected."[27]

Downing Street did not need much persuading. British officials had already decided that it would be a serious mistake to adopt special measures on behalf of any one category of victims of Nazi brutality. On June 12, Anthony Eden informed the War Cabinet officially of Hertz's proposal, adding that the difficulties created by its acceptance would be "unsuperable." Nor would it in any way improve the situation of the Jews. The prime minister, however, wanted the members of the War Cabinet to be aware of his decision before a letter of refusal was sent to Hertz. The members of the War Cabinet in turn offered their unanimous support for the prime minister's position, agreeing without debate that "a negative reply should be sent to the Chief Rabbi."[28]

In his letter to Hertz two weeks later, however, Eden tried to sound conciliatory. He assured the chief rabbi that his proposal had received "the most careful and sympathetic consideration by the Ministers concerned." The negative reply that the foreign secretary unfortunately had to communicate was certainly not a reflection of any lack of deep concern by the government over the fate of his coreligionists on the continent. But a futile gesture would clearly have no effect, except perhaps to lead the Germans to adopt even harsher measures against their victims. Besides, "to offer Jews, and Jews only, priority of escape as British-protected persons would be to overlook the fact that German brutality has been directed very extensively, above all in Poland, against non-Jews." The government did not want to arouse resentment among allied countries where large numbers of non-Jews were also in danger. The only solution was to work patiently, in conjunction with the Allies, especially the United States, using all practical means to rescue the Jews threatened with mass murder. Eden concluded with an assurance that by relying on a flexible strategy of assistance, "we are having a measure of success which, although out of proportion to the whole enormous problem, is not inconsiderable." The chief rabbi might find some solace in that knowledge.[29]

The proposal to extend British protection to Jews living under German occupation was only a minor incident in the long debate within the British government regarding an appropriate response to the increasingly harsh anti-Semitic policies of the Third Reich. Less than two months elapsed between the time the chief rabbi wrote to Churchill and Anthony Eden's letter rejecting his plea. The rejection, moreover, could not have come as a surprise to anyone, not even to the chief rabbi himself. Its significance lies not in any effect it had on official policy regarding the Holocaust but in its revelation of the motives and purposes underlying that policy. To British as to American officials, it was of the greatest importance to avoid any action that might arouse dissension among members of the coalition against the Axis. Despite constant assurances that the Allies were firmly united in their resolve to go on fighting against the Third Reich until victory was achieved, a continuation of prewar frictions and rivalries threatened their sense of common purpose. This meant that policies likely to exacerbate the tensions between them must be avoided, and this in turn suggested that any special effort to protect the Jews under German rule might create a danger of reinforcing traditional ethnic suspicions and resentments.

That was why Downing Street, like the White House, was so reluctant to adopt measures designed specifically to save the Jewish victims of Nazi persecution. And that was also why the various governments in exile hesitated to instruct the resistance movements in their countries to make a special effort to prevent the deportation and execution of members of the Jewish community. To American and British military authorities, a special effort meant sending bombers more than a thousand miles over enemy territory to attack the death camps in Poland. That was as much as they could do. Members of the underground, however, especially in Eastern Europe, were in a position to obstruct the mass murder of Jews by acts of sabotage—by blowing up railroad tracks leading to the gas chambers, by demolishing the walls of the prisons in which the victims were held, or by helping the residents of the ghettos to escape and form guerrilla bands of their own. The resistance movements did in fact occasionally try to rescue Jews facing mass murder. As a rule, however, they were reluctant to make any special attempt to save the victims of the Nazi genocide. Their policy was to draw no distinction between Jewish and non-Jewish victims of German oppression. After all, to draw such a distinction might reinforce ethnic prejudices among their countrymen, prejudices which, truth to tell, they sometimes shared. To the leaders of the Western democracies, it therefore seemed best not to press the governments in exile too hard for assistance.

Poland, the largest of the Central and East European nations under the rule of the Third Reich, with the second largest Jewish population in the world, provided a good example of the conflicting views and sympathies regarding the Holocaust. The Polish government in exile in London was generally willing to do what it could to help save the victims of Nazi genocide. It played a major role in revealing and publicizing the Third Reich's adoption of a program of ethnic extermination. Its sympathy for persecuted Jews reflected in part the influence of the prewar liberal and socialist movements whose representatives were included in its governing body. It maintained close relations with Jewish organizations in Great Britain and the United States, including a few Jewish members in its advisory assembly. There was little evidence in its ethnic policies of the suspicions and resentments common in Polish politics before the war.

While there can be no doubt that the official rejection of anti-Semitism by the government in exile was sincere, it was also reinforced by a belief that the pleas for Allied help in saving the victims of Nazi racism might benefit the non-Jewish population of Poland as well. Bombing the railroads to and from the death camps could prove useful to the Polish underground. Raiding German military installations would be bound to assist the resistance forces. Even providing food for the starving Jews inside the ghettos might help feed the hungry Poles outside. And there was still another consideration. The widespread belief in Europe, especially in the east, that Jews exercised considerable influence over the policies of the White House encouraged the government in exile to maintain good relations with the Jewish communities in the Western democracies. In short, both principle and expediency favored the collaboration of Poles and Jews in America and England in the struggle against the Third Reich.

The prevailing attitude inside Poland, however, was different. Here the underground largely reflected authoritarian, xenophobic, and often anti-Semitic views of the prewar conservative and nationalist movements. The war had done little to diminish hostility toward Jews. If anything, that hostility had increased. There were exceptions, but by and large the leaders of the resistance remained convinced that there had been too much Jewish influence in national affairs before the German occupation and this influence must not be allowed to reemerge once the occupation ended. The best solution would be the emigration of Jews, whether voluntary or coerced. But whatever the solution, there could be no return to the prewar status quo.

For the Allies, this meant that using armed force to halt or impede the Holocaust was narrowly limited. Although there remained the possibility

of using air power to bomb the railways leading to the extermination centers, that was not only risky but of limited effectiveness. Guerrilla attacks
against the death camps seemed much more promising, since they could
liberate the prisoners directly and enable them to form resistance groups
of their own. But that was something which the underground was reluctant to attempt. To risk the lives of Polish volunteer fighters in order to
rescue persecuted Jews seemed almost irresponsible. The chief concern of
patriotic Poles should be the liberation of Poland.

In short, the obstacles to any attempt to save the victims of the Holocaust by military action appeared so great that it was rarely proposed as
long as the war was still going on. The debate over its desirability became
heated only after the military conflict had ended, when the full extent of
the Nazi genocide was finally recognized and it became psychologically
easier to maintain that more should have been done to stop the extermination of European Jewry. That was when the argument grew louder that
the Allies should have bombed the death camps—as a symbolic gesture, if
nothing else—and that paratroopers should have been sent into combat
to save Jews condemned to the gas chambers, even if only a handful could
be saved, as a way of showing the world that the Allies were not indifferent
to the Holocaust. What better way was there to demonstrate their commitment to democratic values and principles?

As long as the war was still going on, however, even loyal supporters
of the Jewish cause were cautious in suggesting that an opportunity to
rescue at least some victims of Nazi racism was worth the risk of battlefield casualties. On September 6, 1944, after the Wehrmacht had occupied Hungary, John Pehle reported to Henry Morgenthau that "several
Jewish organizations" had proposed that, in order to prevent the further
deportation of Hungarian Jews, "the railway lines leading from Hungary
to known death camps be bombed and that the death camps themselves
be attacked by paratroops and bombed." But he had not forwarded that
proposal to the military authorities. "At this stage of the war, it did not
seem proper to suggest to the War Department the diversion of military
equipment or military personnel to nonmilitary purposes. Furthermore,
aerial and paratroop raids of this kind must entail casualties on the part
of the raiders and we did not feel justified in asking the War Department
to undertake a measure which involved the sacrifice of American troops."

Pehle added that Allied air attacks against the death camps might actually help accomplish the German objective, the extermination of Jews, more rapidly and effectively than the Germans themselves could, especially in view of the swift advance of the Russian armies. Military victory would be the best way, indeed the only way, to put an end to the Holocaust.[30]

Pehle was also critical of another proposal advanced by Jewish organizations, namely, that the Polish government in exile be asked to instruct its underground forces to destroy the death camps and free the imprisoned Jews. The War Refugee Board decided not to submit this request to the Polish authorities in London. More than two months earlier, on June 27, 1944, Ignacy Schwarzbart, a Jewish member of the Polish National Council, had urged Prime Minister Stanislaw Mikolajczyk to send similar instructions to the resistance in Poland. But Mikolajczyk had simply ignored the proposal, and the reason was clear: "In view of the apparently deep-rooted anti-Semitism on the part of a large segment of the Polish government and underground movement, it seemed most unlikely that the Poles would, in good faith, undertake to attack the death centers effectively unless strong political pressure involving political support were asserted." And then Pehle mentioned, almost as an afterthought, another reason for not urging the Polish underground to attack the death camps: "As a matter of fact, it is very doubtful whether the Poles had the necessary forces to carry out any such operation." What would be the point, then, in asking them to try to do the impossible?[31]

In summary, what emerges from a comparison of the official attitudes toward the Holocaust in the United States, Great Britain, and the other members of the coalition against the Axis is that all of them seemed to combine a resounding condemnation of ethnic mass murder with an obvious reluctance to commit military resources to an effort to save the victims of that ethnic mass murder. The argument that they commonly advanced, whether out of conviction or expediency, was that the only way to end the Nazi genocide was by defeating and overthrowing the Third Reich. Any policy, however humane or well-intentioned, that delayed the victory of the Allies was ultimately a disservice to all, Jews and non-Jews alike, who were engaged in the life-and-death struggle to defend democracy against tyranny.

But what about the argument that the Allies had a moral duty to do whatever they could to prevent the destruction of European Jewry? Even if it meant heavy military casualties, shouldn't they have made an effort to rescue the victims of Nazi racism? And that raises another fundamental question. Could armed force have stopped the Holocaust? Since the question is hypothetical, the answer has to be hypothetical as well. But the available evidence strongly suggests that the obsessive anti-Semitism of the Third Reich, its conviction that the Jews were an unrelenting and deadly menace to Western society, was too strong to be overcome by aerial bombardments or paratrooper raids. Even after the death camps were liberated by the Soviet armies, the Nazi program of ethnic genocide continued in the form of starvation, disease, exhausting labor, death marches, brutal beatings, and mass executions. Paradoxically, those who maintained that only victory on the battlefield could save the Jews were in essence right. The tragedy was that by the time victory came, so few Jews were left to be saved.

PART FOUR

From Victimhood to Martyrdom

The trouble with [the Nazi war criminal Adolf Eichmann] was precisely that so many were like him, and that the many were neither perverted nor sadistic, that they were, and still are, terribly and terrifyingly normal. From the viewpoint of our legal institutions and of our moral standards of judgment, this normality was much more terrifying than all the atrocities put together, for it implied . . . that this new type of criminal . . . commits his crimes under circumstances that make it well-nigh impossible for him to know or to feel that he is doing wrong.

HANNAH ARENDT,
Eichmann in Jerusalem, 1963

15

The Twilight of European Jewry

THE MILITARY STRUGGLE raging between 1939 and 1945 marked the end of five centuries of European predominance in the world. During that long period, a combination of four or five European states played the leading role in international affairs, militarily, politically, economically, and culturally. The balance of power shifted from time to time between Spain, France, England, Germany, and Russia. But whether individually or collectively, directly or indirectly, they were able to extend their rule over almost the entire globe. Here and there some overseas region settled by European colonists would rebel against the mother country, establishing an independent state: in North America during the eighteenth century, for example, and in South and Central America during the nineteenth. But even these newcomers to the international community remained linguistically, religiously, and culturally attached to the Old World. At the opening of the twentieth century, Europe still seemed to be the dominant force in world affairs.

The First World War initiated a process of decline which ended three decades later with the disintegration of Europe's central role in international relations. To be sure, there had for some time been signs of growing dissatisfaction with the predominance of the great powers—in India, for example, in Japan, and in South Africa. But the outbreak in 1914 of a mutually destructive war hastened the end of Europe's centrality in world affairs. The reestablishment of peace four years later briefly created the illusion of a "return to normalcy." The disarmament of Germany and the isolation of the Soviet Union combined with the seeming revival of prosperity in the middle and late 1920s suggested that perhaps little had actually changed or that any change that had taken place was really for the better. But that illusion quickly vanished with the coming of the Great Depression at the end of the decade.

The 1930s demonstrated beyond any doubt that the old Europe, based on a balance of power among its leading states, generally supporting the principle of representative government, embracing the economy of free enterprise, and endorsing the doctrine of equality before the law regardless of class, religion, or ethnicity, was finished. In its place came a new and different Europe, a Europe trying to steer a middle course between the growing radicalism of the lower classes, forced to endure the hardships of a shrinking economy, and the right-wing authoritianism of various fascistic movements, which were hierarchical, ultranationalist, and usually anti-Semitic. The divisions within as well as between the European countries favoring a democratic form of authority and those favoring a dictatorial one led in 1939 to the outbreak of a new and even more ruinous war, which changed the balance of power in the world once and for all.

The Europe that emerged was fundamentally different from the one that thirty years earlier had proudly marched into the First World War or even from the one that had more recently stumbled into the Second World War. By 1945, it was clear that the center of authority in the world had shifted dramatically. Now the great powers were the United States, separated from the Old World by a vast ocean, and the Soviet Union, a country European only in part. The nations lying between those two new superpowers were forced to ally with one or the other. They had no choice. On one side were the countries of Western Europe, still loyal to the democratic principles they had embraced before the war but now dependent on American support and therefore forced to accept American leadership. On the other side were the secondary states of Eastern Europe, all of them anti-Communist during the interwar period but then compelled to form governments submissive to the Soviet Union. On both sides of the "iron curtain" separating the two alliances there was dissatisfaction with the diminished role of nations that had once been proudly independent. But now they had to bow to a harsh reality. For those in the west, defiance of the United States might invite Russian aggression, while for those in the east, opposition to the Kremlin was likely to lead to an invasion by the Soviet army.

For most of the world, however, the end of the age of European predominance meant liberation. The struggle against colonialism, which had been gaining strength throughout the interwar period, finally achieved victory after the Second World War. With the leading imperialist states now playing a diminished role in international affairs, native independence movements became bolder and more assertive. Within a decade after the war ended, a "Third World" emerged. Countries that had nominally retained sovereignty but had actually been dependencies of the great powers, such as China and Egypt, were able to become independent, often defiantly independent. Those that had been outright colonies of European states, such as India and Indonesia, achieved a new status as sovereign nations. The age of European imperialism was over. That did not by any means solve all the political, economic, and social problems confronting the newly liberated peoples of the world, but they were now free to deal with those problems without foreign supervision or interference.

There was also another important result of the Second World War, not as momentous as the end of European dominance in international politics or the emergence of the Third World as a major force in foreign affairs but the most tragic—namely, the destruction of the Jewish community in Europe. That community had been a part of European society for almost two thousand years, isolated and segregated for most of that time and yet widespread, conspicuous, and influential in the economy and culture of the continent. Its emancipation, beginning in the nineteenth century, had had the effect of increasing its importance in society as well as the hostility that that importance aroused. The organized, systematic extermination of the Jews of Europe during the Second World War, unprecedented in Western history, was a direct result of their achievements, reflecting pervasive popular prejudice and resentment. They had to pay a terrible price for the freedom they had briefly enjoyed. Many of those who survived the Nazi genocide concluded in retrospect that the road out of the ghetto had led not to emancipation, as they had once assumed, but to Auschwitz and Treblinka.

The high proportion of European Jews killed in the course of the Second World War was not only a measure of the extent of anti-Semitic mass murder but also a reason for the large-scale emigration of the survivors after the return of peace. Approximately 8.3 million Jews lived in countries occupied by or allied with the Third Reich at the outbreak of the war. By the time hostilities ended, close to 6 million of them had been killed—about 72 percent. Including the Jewish communities in Great Britain, the unoccupied parts of the Soviet Union, and the neutral countries, about 9.7 million Jews had lived in prewar Europe, so roughly 62 percent perished during the Second World War. The destruction of European Jewry thus became the only one of the Third Reich's fundamental goals that was largely and permanently achieved.[1]

The decline of the Jewish community in Europe did not end with the overthrow of the Third Reich, however. It continued for at least another decade, and even afterward there was a steady exodus of Jews, partly to the Middle East, partly across the Atlantic. The center of world Jewry, which had been in the Old World for almost two millennia, suddenly shifted to the United States and to the new state of Israel. This shift represented more than a geographical or environmental change in the world's Jewish community. It also led to a fundamental transformation of its character, psychology, and outlook.

That transformation began as soon as hostilities ended in the spring of 1945. In defeated Germany there were hundreds of thousands of foreigners, Jews as well as Gentiles, most of whom had been forced against their will to leave their native countries. They included released inmates of concentration camps, liberated political prisoners, slave laborers, conscripted workers, and voluntary migrants who had been employed as servants, craftsmen, factory workers, or farmhands. The Allies provided these "displaced persons" with shelter in refugee camps or temporary residences until they could be repatriated. Most of them did return to their homelands within a year, although some hesitated because of the Soviet occupation of Eastern Europe. The Jews, however, were as a rule unwilling to go back to the scene of their brutal persecution during the German occupation, and not only by Germans. They preferred to remain displaced until they could emigrate to the New World or Palestine. Memories of what had happened during the war made it very difficult for many of them to return to their native countries.

The Jewish survivors temporarily in Germany were not the only ones who thought it best to emigrate. Most of those who had left their prewar homes to find asylum or to go into hiding decided afterward that there was no going back to their old way of life. There were too many reminders of what had happened, reminders of the hardships they had had to endure and of the behavior of some of their neighbors during their ordeal. Worse still, even now they continued to encounter hostility among their countrymen. Especially in Eastern Europe, there was still considerable anti-Semitic prejudice, fed by a concern that the returning Jews would attempt to regain what had been taken from them during the occupation. They would no doubt try to get back the homes that had once been theirs but that were now occupied by Gentiles. And what about the shops, stores, and businesses they had owned before the war? What about their savings accounts, their investments, their stocks and bonds? What about the positions they had held in journalism, education, scholarship, and the arts? Were they not likely to demand the restoration of those as well? And what would then happen to their non-Jewish compatriots who had gained or regained what many believed was rightfully theirs? Jews returning from hiding places or imprisonment or exile often found a cool reception or worse. The extermination of close to two thirds of European Jewry had not significantly diminished the traditional ethnic hostilities and prejudices of the Old World.

There was another important reason for the persistence of anti-Semitism in Europe in the postwar years. Especially in the east, where the Soviet Union imposed Communist governments on the countries freed from the German occupation, many people believed that the unpopular political shift to the far left was supported or even engineered by Jews, who were more loyal to the Kremlin than to the country of their birth. This charge was nothing new. The interwar period had seen bitter complaints that the Jewish community was in sympathy with communism, that it conspired to overthrow the established political order, and that its ultimate goal was to gain dominance over a society in which it was only a small minority. The adage that "where there's a Jew there's a Communist, and where there's a Communist there's a Jew," frequently heard during the 1920s and 1930s, especially in Eastern Europe, grew even louder and more persistent under the German occupation. In the immediate postwar period, while the Soviet Union was tightening its grip on reluctant neighbors, the perception that the Jews were agents of the Kremlin, supporting its goals and serving its interests at the expense of their non-Jewish countrymen, remained widespread.

This belief was reinforced by the fact that the leadership as well as the membership of several of the Communist parties in Europe did include a disproportionate number of Jews—a reflection, in part at least, of their conviction that the overthrow of the capitalistic system would end the age-old anti-Semitic prejudices in Western society. Yet it was also obvious that the great majority of Jews, including those in the east, opposed communism. There were first of all the masses of Orthodox Jews, to whom the materialism and atheism of the Marxist ideology were anathema. But even secular Jews, those to whom traditional Judaism had ceased to be of major importance, were mostly either middle-of-the-road liberals or moderate socialists. The proportion of Communists among Jews was higher than among Gentiles, but not nearly as much as anti-Semites claimed. The great majority of Jews remained opposed to the doctrines and policies of the Kremlin.

To many ardent nationalists, however, who feared the expansionism of the Soviet Union after the war, all this made little difference. Some of those who once accused the Jews of being behind the spread of capitalism now accused them of being behind the spread of communism. Quite a few even accused them of being behind both. Their psychological need for villains and scapegoats made a rational assessment of the postwar international situation impossible.

That meant that for the first two or three years after the Allied victory, open displays of anti-Semitic hostility were not uncommon in Eastern Europe. Sometimes they even assumed the form of violent attacks against Jews, not very different from the pogroms of the czarist era. Especially in Poland, the largest of the states occupied by the Red Army in the later stages of the war and the one most bitterly opposed to Soviet domination, there were frequent assaults against Jews, some of them deadly. Between September 1944, while the Wehrmacht still occupied western Poland, and

September 1946, 327 authenticated cases of the murder of Jews by mass violence took place. The bloodiest was the anti-Semitic riot in Kielce on July 4, 1946, in which 51 Jews died. But there were others as well. In April 1946, racist riots in Cracow resulted in the death of 20 Jews. In Lublin, 15 Jews were murdered in June 1945, a month after the end of the war, and another 12 were murdered in March 1946. In the city of Lodz, the highest monthly number of victims of anti-Semitic violence in any given month was 8, in May 1945. But in Rzeszow the corresponding figure was 19, in August 1945, and in Warsaw that same month it was 11. The figures may seem insignificant by comparison with the genocide that had been going on only a year or two earlier, but they reflect the persistence of ethnic hostility long after the defeat and overthrow of the Third Reich.[2]

As the Soviet Union consolidated its hold on the neighboring states, the intensity or at least the expression of anti-Semitic hostility in the east declined. According to the ideology of the Communist movement, ethnic prejudice was artificially and deliberately stimulated by capitalism in order to create dissension in the ranks of the proletariat and divert attention from the exploitation of the working class, on which the traditional economic system rested. Prejudice against Jews was therefore officially condemned. But beneath the surface it continued to simmer, finding an officially sanctioned outlet after the establishment of the state of Israel. As the Kremlin began to support the Palestinian cause in the Middle East, condemnation of the policies of the newly established Jewish state became ideologically acceptable in the Communist countries. In theory, the adversary was not Jewry but Zionism. This, however, was often a distinction without a difference. For many secret opponents of the new order in Eastern Europe, "Zionist" became a synonym, or rather a euphemism, for "Jew." They could once again organize demonstrations, as they had done in the prewar years, but this time under the slogan "Zionists to Palestine" instead of "Jews to Palestine." The basic meaning remained the same.

In the Soviet Union itself, the situation was different. Thirty years of Communist rule had reduced, though not entirely eliminated, the common anti-Semitism of the czarist era. Here it was possible to talk disapprovingly about the destruction of European Jewry by the Nazi regime without arousing popular resentment. Indeed, throughout the war years the Kremlin often publicized the anti-Semitic atrocities that were being committed under the German occupation, usually in order to influence foreign rather than domestic public opinion, and especially in order to win the support of Jewish communities in the Western democracies. As late as 1945 and 1946, the Extraordinary State Commissions for Establishing and Investigating the Crimes of the German Fascist Occupiers continued to issue reports on the crimes of the Third Reich, including the mass murder of Jews. The Kremlin could in fact become quite explicit in its description of the brutal anti-Semitic policies the Hitler government had adopted.

During the long international debate that preceded the establishment of the state of Israel, moreover, the Soviet Union took a position favorable to the Zionist cause. On November 26, 1947, Andrei Gromyko, the Kremlin's delegate to the United Nations, delivered a speech before the General Assembly supporting the division of Palestine into two states, one Arab, the other Jewish. Even the most ardent Zionist would have agreed with what Gromyko had to say. He rejected the contention of the Arab states that partitioning Palestine would be a "historic injustice." That contention was, in his view, "unacceptable." After all, "the Jewish people has been closely linked with Palestine for a considerable period in history." More than that, the United Nations should not ignore the tragic fate of the Jews during the cruel military conflict that had only recently come to an end. "It may not be amiss to remind my listeners again that, as a result of the war which was unleashed by Hitlerite Germany, the Jews, as a people, have suffered more than any other people." Still, responsibility for the destruction of European Jewry rested not only on the Third Reich. "There was not a single country in Western Europe which succeeded in adequately protecting the interests of the Jewish people against the arbitrary acts and violence of the Hitlerites." Not many Jewish leaders would have risked saying something like that in public.

Gromyko, however, did not justify partition as the only solution to the "Palestine problem" by dwelling solely on the suffering of the Jews during the war. Even now, he maintained, in the postwar world, the creation of an independent Jewish state would have a "profound historical significance." It would meet "the legitimate demands of the Jewish people," hundreds of thousands of whom "are still without a country, without homes, having found temporary shelter only in special camps in some western European countries." There was no need for him to describe in detail the conditions under which the displaced persons were forced to live. "These conditions are well known." They had already been portrayed before the United Nations by representatives of other governments that shared the Soviet delegation's point of view and which therefore supported the plan to divide Palestine. The reestablishment of an independent Jewish nation in the Middle East after almost two thousand years would be more than an act of atonement for the injustices that European Jewry had had to endure in the past. It would also be a means of ensuring that those injustices did not recur in the future.[3]

Could anyone listening to Gromyko's speech have guessed that within only a few years the Kremlin's policy on the Palestine issue and the "Jewish question" in general would become completely reversed? That turnabout, however, was not an isolated shift in the Kremlin's diplomacy. Rather, it was one aspect of the dissolution of the wartime alliance between the Soviet Union and the Western democracies. It was part of what soon came to be called the "cold war." As the opposing camps confronted each other—the Kremlin and its satellites in Eastern Europe on one side and the United States, Great Britain, and most of Western Europe on the other—Israel aligned itself with the latter. The geography, economy, politics, and culture of the new nation made that the only choice possible.

But it also meant that the Soviet Union became increasingly committed to the Palestinian cause. With the intensification of the cold war, the Kremlin's criticism of Zionism grew sharper and louder. The same Gromyko who in 1947 urged the establishment of a Jewish state in the Middle East as a form of atonement for the cruelties the Jews had had to endure during the war began to argue a few years later that Israel was responsible for the same sort of cruelties against the Arabs. The Kremlin never went so far as to suggest that all or even most Jews were Zionists. But the Soviet public began to assume more and more that there was little difference between the two.

The spread of popular distrust of Jews was strengthened, moreover, by the unacknowledged but obvious anti-Semitic prejudice of Stalin in the last years of his dictatorship. The suspicions that he indirectly revealed about the role of Jews in Soviet society were widely recognized, reinforcing the undercurrent of ethnic bigotry which had never been entirely suppressed. That undercurrent was less apparent than in the satellite states, where public opinion remained unreconciled to the cosmopolitan doctrines of the official postwar ideology. But it was clear that even in the Soviet Union, Jewishness was increasingly becoming an obstacle to advancement in government service, the learned professions, the fine arts, and the world of scholarship.

On the other side of the iron curtain, the level of ethnic prejudice had traditionally been much lower, and its intensity diminished significantly after the war, partly because the number of Jews had been drastically reduced, but partly also out of sympathy for the victims of the recent anti-Semitic mass murders. And yet the survivors of the Nazi genocide were not always welcomed when they returned from the death camps, foreign asylum, or domestic hiding places. In Western as in Eastern Europe, there was a concern, generally unexpressed, that those coming back would try to regain their properties and possessions. While in principle that might seem fair, it would also be hard on those being deprived of what had briefly been theirs. Not surprisingly, many returning survivors of the Nazi genocide found a cool reception.

There is little direct evidence of the degree or extent of that coolness, but the recollections of Jews in Western Europe during the early postwar period often mention the indifference or even hostility of some of their neighbors. In countries only recently freed from a cruel foreign occupation, still having to endure the hardships of a devastated economy, the prospect of a large influx of impoverished survivors of anti-Semitic persecution was bound to be troubling. On the one hand, people sympathized with those who had suffered so terribly under a brutal foreign occupation that had also oppressed the general population. But on the other hand, they were struggling to survive in a Europe still trying to recover from the effects of a military conflict that had impoverished winners and losers alike. In such an environment, there was not much room for pity.

It is hard to measure with any precision public opinion in Western Europe regarding the Jewish survivors of the Nazi genocide. People appeared to be torn between compassion and self-interest, between the condemnation of ethnic mass murder and a search for economic security. Sometimes those contradictory emotions were expressed simultaneously. The official statements of the postwar governments generally spoke approvingly of the return of surviving Jews and their reintegration into the nation's political and cultural life. But in their reminiscences, many of those survivors recalled the indifference, coolness, or even covert hostility they sometimes encountered after returning to their homelands. To determine which of the many reports or accounts are reliable and which are not is not easy. Very few public opinion polls regarding the "Jewish question" were conducted in Western Europe after the war, partly as a matter of deliberate policy. The results might have proved awkward to countries officially condemning Nazi racism.

One of the few exceptions was postwar Germany—not the eastern part, which was in the Soviet zone of occupation and obediently followed Soviet policy, but the western part, especially the American zone. Here the military government authorized a survey of public opinion regarding the anti-Semitic policies of the Third Reich in October 1945, five months after the war in Europe ended. The participants were asked which of the three following statements they regarded as generally true: "(1) The treatment the Jews received under Hitler was just what they deserved. (2) Hitler went too far in his treatment of the Jews, but something had to be done to keep them within bounds. (3) The anti-Jewish measures were absolutely unjustified." The responses were unanimous in condemning the genocide. Not a single one of the participants agreed that the mass murder of Jews was what they deserved. Only 19 percent believed that while Hitler's policy of extermination went too far, something should have been done to limit the influence of Jews in national life. But 77 percent felt that the anti-Semitic measures of the Third Reich were unjustified. Even taking into account the possibility that some of the answers reflected what the respondents thought was expected of them rather than what they actually believed, there can be no doubt that the overwhelming majority were sincerely opposed to the Nazi genocide.[4]

A poll conducted at the end of March 1946 produced a similar but less one-sided result. The question it asked appeared in two somewhat different forms. According to the first, "it was also said that international Jewry alone would profit from the war. Now that the war is over, do you think that is true?" The second version began not with "it was also said" but with "Hitler also said." The outcomes were slightly but significantly different. When the assertion that only Jews profited from the war was attributed to unidentified individuals or organizations, 14 percent of respondents agreed with it, 74 percent disagreed, and 12 percent expressed no opinion. But when Hitler was named as the source of the assertion, the percentage agreeing with it dropped to 11, while the percentage disagreeing rose to 77. The figures suggest that while the great majority of Germans rejected the anti-Semitic charge that the Jews had benefited from the war, those who believed it to be valid were somewhat more likely to express their agreement if it was not identified with Hitler, the man responsible for their country's catastrophic defeat and partition.[5]

Other public opinion polls support the conclusion that while most Germans after the war opposed discrimination against Jews, a minority continued to favor at least some anti-Semitic measures, and the less harsh the measures, the larger the minority. There was clearly no wish to return to the virulently racist policies of the Nazi regime. But there was some apprehension about a restoration of full legal equality for Jews, which in the days of Weimar had led to envy and resentment and indirectly to a brutal dictatorship.

A poll conducted in the American zone of West Germany and Berlin on April 26, 1946, reflected this ambivalence or ambiguity. The participants were once again asked the same question in two different forms, suggesting an awareness by the American occupying authorities of the vacillation in the ethnic attitudes of many Germans. One version asked whether "Jews should have the same legal rights as members of the Aryan race," while the other asked whether "Jews shouldn't have the same rights as those belonging to the Aryan race." On the face of it, the answers to the two formulations might have been expected to be diametrically opposed. That is, those who favored equal rights for Jews could logically be assumed to oppose the denial of those rights, and vice versa. But that is not how it turned out. When asked whether Jews should have the same rights as Aryans, 85 percent of the participants said yes, 10 percent said no, and 5 percent expressed no opinion. But when the same question was asked in a reverse form, that is, whether Jews should not have the same rights as Aryans, 33 percent of the participants agreed, 62 percent disagreed, and 5 percent still expressed no opinion. In other words, although a substantial majority of the respondents consistently opposed denying equal rights to Jews, a significant minority remained of two minds, torn between humanitarian principle and popular prejudice.[6]

In brief, the more extreme an anti-Semitic opinion or proposal was the less approval it was likely to receive, and conversely, the milder the form or expression of anti-Semitic sentiment was the more approval it was likely to receive. Clearly the great majority of Germans after the war rejected prejudice against Jews in any form. But there was also the bitter memory of the hardships and humiliations the nation had suffered under the Weimar Republic. The crisis that had led to the establishment of the Nazi dictatorship was, or course, not the fault of the Jews. And yet there could be no denying that after the coming of the Great Depression, countless Germans were driven to poverty and despair, while Jews in general appeared able to cope with the economic crisis. Some of them even seemed to thrive. Their success helped undermine the fragile basis of the German experiment in democracy. Was there, then, not a danger that the restoration of the Jewish community to the status it had enjoyed before 1933 might lead in the future to the rise of a new racist totalitarian movement and a new Hitler?

This concern could not be characterized as anti-Semitic in the same sense as the proposition that what had happened to the Jews was what they deserved or that international Jewry had profited from the war. And yet even those who wholeheartedly condemned the racist measures introduced by the Nazi regime had occasional doubts about the advisability of reestablishing a Jewish community in Germany. In view of all that had happened in the previous twenty years, how wise would it be to return to the dangerously generous policies of Weimar? The question, though unavoidable, was deeply troubling.

This ambivalence appeared clearly in a poll conducted in December 1946. The participants were asked whether "the Jews [should] be helped to emigrate to Palestine or to rebuild their life in Germany." The issue was not a theoretical one. Large numbers of German Jews were still living abroad in refugee camps and temporary asylums, not sure of what their future would be, some of them even wondering whether they should not try to return to their homeland. At the same time, a bitter conflict was going on in the Middle East over the establishment of a Jewish state in Palestine. For the participants in the poll, the question posed a dilemma almost as troubling as the one confronting the refugees themselves. The results showed that 43 percent wanted to help the Jews emigrate to Palestine, 15 percent wanted them to return to Germany, 38 percent gave "qualified answers," and 4 percent expressed no opinion. But what precisely were those "qualified answers"? The published results provide no details, but it seems safe to assume that enough of the replies at least indirectly favored Jewish emigration to Palestine to constitute, in combination with those favoring it directly, a clear majority of all the responses. Most Germans, including those who rejected all forms of ethnic prejudice, apparently thought it best to encourage Jewish refugees to resettle in a country of their own rather than return to Germany. After all, who could be sure of what might happen someday if they did return?[7]

There is less information about public opinion elsewhere in Western Europe regarding Jewish refugees, but what information there is suggests that the prevailing attitude in other countries was no more favorable toward the acceptance of Jews, whether native-born or foreign, than in Germany. There were everywhere the familiar official condemnations of racist brutality and ethnic mass murder. Yet there was also an unexpressed but widespread popular concern over the economic consequences of a sudden reappearance of those who a few years earlier had been deported to the death camps. They would undoubtedly demand the return of what had once been theirs. But while a restoration might in principle seem no more than right, in practice it would mean a substantial shift in the economic and social status of non-Jews as well as Jews. Those who would have to pay the price for such a shift did not always welcome the return of the survivors of the death camps.

And then there were the ultraconservatives, who even before the war had been in sympathy with the racist doctrines of National Socialism. They had been only a small minority in the democratic states of Western Europe, but their number had increased considerably under the German occupation. Some of them became fellow travelers of the Third Reich—allies, auxiliaries, Vichyites, and quislings. Some even formed military units fighting side by side with the Wehrmacht during the invasion of the Soviet Union. The defeat of the Third Reich had meant their defeat as well. Their leaders had been tried as collaborators and condemned to imprisonment or execution, but the rank-and-file had survived, its members now powerless, scattered, and regarded with distrust but still unrepentant, authoritarian, and anti-Semitic. Was there not a danger that someday they might regain power? That seemed very unlikely. But then again, who after the First World War could have foreseen the coming of Hitler?

Those were all important considerations which persuaded many survivors of the Nazi genocide, in Western as well as Eastern Europe, that it would be best to leave the Old World. When the Nazi regime was finally overthrown, there was a prevalent expectation that the survivors would return to their native countries and try to rebuild, though on a much smaller scale, the Jewish communities that had been destroyed in the course of the war. It soon became apparent, however, that in fact most of them, especially those from the east, had no wish to return permanently. For one thing, their experience during the war had shown them that quite a few of their countrymen agreed that ethnic extermination, though brutal, was the only way to solve the "Jewish question" once and for all. The reception they met upon returning often reinforced their impression that at least some of their neighbors would be pleased if they could find refuge elsewhere or even if they did not return at all. That impression, though frequently exaggerated, was not baseless. In Eastern Europe especially, it was clear that traditional ethnic prejudices had not diminished as a result of the war.

Fear of the persistence of anti-Semitism was not the only reason that many Jewish survivors decided to emigrate from the Old World. Those in the countries occupied by the Soviet Union in the latter stages of the military struggle were alarmed by the growing pressure from the Kremlin to establish Communist regimes in the "liberated" states. To Jews who had been businessmen, mill owners, shopkeepers, and traders, this meant that they would be unable to regain the properties they had owned before the German invasion. They might even be regarded by the new order as former capitalists. Many Orthodox Jews feared the avowed godlessness of Marxism even more than the religious hostility of the established churches during the prewar years. And finally, the secular Jews who embraced a middle-of-the-road liberalism or an anti-Stalinist form of radicalism—democrats, socialists, anarchists, and Trotskyites—were in even greater danger than the capitalistic or pious Jews. In short, the forces behind the Jewish exodus from Eastern Europe became almost irresistible.

Farther to the west, the situation of the surviving Jews was much better. There they were free to return to the occupations they had pursued before the German invasion. They could practice their faith without interference from political or religious authorities. And as for their ideological convictions, no one investigated them or seemed to care what they were. Not even the unfriendly attitude of some of their compatriots was a major problem. The chief obstacle to the reestablishment of the Jewish communities, more important even than the harsh economic conditions in postwar Europe, was a feeling of insecurity kept alive by the memory of what had happened under the Nazi occupation and by the fear that something like that might happen again. Nothing could quiet that fear. The only way to overcome it seemed to be emigration.

But where? For many European Jews, finding a place of refuge after the war was almost as difficult as it had been during the war. There were, to begin with, neutral countries like Switzerland, Spain, Portugal, and Sweden, which had not been occupied by the Wehrmacht and had in fact admitted modest numbers of refugees while the armed conflict was going on. Some had even expressed tacit disapproval of the genocidal program of the Nazi regime, but always with caution, afraid that too much criticism might invite reprisals by the Third Reich. As for the Jews they had admitted, there was a clear understanding from the outset that once the war was over, the refugees would have to go back to their native countries. After the Allied victory, most of them were in fact required to leave and find permanent residence elsewhere. Admitting additional survivors of the Nazi genocide once peace was established was out of the question. After all, they were no longer in danger. They were free to return to their homelands. It would be unreasonable to expect the neutral states to accept large numbers of needy Jews, admittedly suffering hardship and privation but no more so than their non-Jewish compatriots.

The prevailing attitude in Great Britain was essentially not very different. As long as the war was still going on, the government had been willing to admit tens of thousands of Jewish refugees. This was partly an expression of sympathy for victims of the murderous policies of the Third Reich, but it was also an attempt to demonstrate to the world the fundamental difference between humanitarian democracy and brutal totalitarianism. Yet even then mutterings and grumblings could be heard about the additional burden that Jewish refugees imposed on the population. Now that hostilities were over, there was no reason to accept any more of them.

They were no longer in danger of extermination. Let them return to the countries they had come from and reestablish their communities there.

Some even maintained that the Jews who had found asylum in Great Britain during the Hitler regime should also be required to go back to their homelands. Barely a week after the war in Europe ended, Herbert Morrison, secretary of state for the Home Office, declared at a meeting of the War Cabinet Committee on Refugees that foreign Jews "should eventually go back whence they came." Otherwise, they might become an "explosive element," especially "if the economic situation deteriorated." This view was shared, though not always openly, by many of his countrymen.[8]

Most survivors of the Nazi genocide, however, were unwilling to go back to their native countries for a variety of emotional, psychological, ideological, and economic reasons. They had concluded that it would be best to leave the Old World for good and seek a new life elsewhere. The result was that in the decade following the Second World War, there was a large-scale migration of Jews to the west and south. Not that there were no longer any Jews left on the continent, but they ceased to be a distinct and integral component of European society. The millennial history of Europe's Jewry had come to an end. In a few countries, Great Britain and France in particular, the Jewish community retained a sense of common tradition and shared destiny. Elsewhere, however, the consciousness of a separate ethnic identity largely dissipated. A fundamental change in the nature and composition of world Jewry was now taking place.

The exodus of Jews from Europe was not easy. In Palestine, a bitter conflict raged between Jews and Arabs, while Great Britain, which had a mandate from the League of Nations to govern the region, tried to steer a middle course between the opposing sides. The limits which it imposed on Jewish immigration, however, were not always strictly or effectively enforced. Especially during the Second World War, Palestine had seen a significant influx of refugees, and even afterward a steady stream of illegal immigrants continued to flow across the Mediterranean despite the efforts of the British authorities. Nevertheless, for European Jews trying to leave the Old World, emigration to Palestine was not an easy choice. Once there, they would find themselves among fellow Jews, but first they would have to evade the surveillance of armed patrol boats on the lookout for illegal immigrants. Then they would have to face the danger of deadly clashes with Arabs, which were becoming increasingly frequent. And finally, even if they managed to surmount those obstacles, what then? Life in the Middle East would still be difficult, not only because of the constant risk of Arab attacks but also because of the unending hardships of a backward economy. Was getting out of Europe really worth the price?

The situation of the Jews in Palestine improved in the spring of 1948, with the end of the British mandate and the proclamation of an independent state of Israel. But that was immediately followed by a war with the Arab League, which lasted for more than a year. The uneasy truce concluded in the summer of 1949 was widely recognized as little more than a temporary interruption of an armed conflict which was likely to continue on and off for the foreseeable future. The economic problems the new Jewish state had to contend with, moreover, could not be expected to diminish, considering the probability of future military struggles with the Arab states. And as for Zionist appeals to Jewish pride or patriotism, they did not always have much effect on the emotionally exhausted victims of years of oppression and persecution. To many of those who had survived the Nazi genocide, what mattered most was a way of life free of stress, a calm, secure, and reasonably comfortable existence. The prospect of still another long struggle against another bitter enemy was more than most of them could face.

That was why the first choice for most European Jews was emigration to North America. There they could find a congenial environment in which to build a new life not very different from the one destroyed by the Third Reich. They could feel at home in the political and economic system on the other side of the Atlantic. Even the mentality and culture over there would not seem very foreign to them. Equally important, they would find an ethnic milieu they could adjust to without difficulty. The Jewish community in the United States, the largest in the world even before the war, constituted 3.5 percent of the total population. And while Jews made up no more than 1.5 percent of all Canadians, even that was well above the percentage in most of the European countries after 1945. Besides, the majority of Jews in North America had come from Eastern Europe, which was also the prewar home of the great majority of the survivors of the Nazi genocide. Those trying to emigrate to the New World could expect to find there a familiar and congenial environment.[9]

The trouble was that the New World was not nearly as eager to embrace them as they were to embrace the New World. The experience of the war years and the knowledge of what had happened to European Jewry did little to diminish popular opposition to the admission of Jewish refugees. That was true of North America as well as Europe. And the reasons were similar as well: fear of economic competition, uneasiness about alien political influence, concern regarding cultural adulteration, and outright ethnic prejudice. Expressing sympathy for the victims of Nazi persecution was one thing. Offering refuge to those victims was something entirely different. This difference had become apparent even before the war, and it continued for a long time after the war.

Early in October 1946, a survey of Canadian public opinion regarding the admission of Jewish immigrants started out by reminding the participants that "Britain is interning Jewish refugees who have attempted to enter Palestine without permission." It then asked whether "you think Canada should allow some of these refugees to settle here or not." The results were clear and unmistakable. Almost two thirds of the respondents, 61 percent, felt that "no, [Canada] should not allow," 23 percent felt that "yes, should allow," 10 percent were undecided, and 6 percent gave "qualified answers." The figures were roughly comparable to those in the poll conducted two months later in the American zone of occupation in Germany. Both surveys revealed strong popular opposition to the immigration of Jews unable or unwilling to find refuge in Palestine.[10]

As for the reasons for that opposition, the results of a poll conducted on October 30, 1946, showed that traditional ethnic prejudice was an important factor in the reluctance of most Canadians to admit Jewish refugees. The participants were asked whether, if the country did allow more immigration, there were any among ten specified "nationalities" whom they would like to keep out. The answers revealed that the Japanese, recent enemies of Canada, were at the top of the list of undesirables, named by 60 percent of the respondents. But not very far behind, with 49 percent of the responses recommending their exclusion, were members of the Jewish "nationality." Germans, on the other hand, also recent enemies of Canada, were rejected as immigrants by 34 percent of the participants, while the Russians, allies during the war, were rejected by 33 percent. Negroes were regarded as not very desirable either, with 31 percent of the participants favoring their exclusion. The Italians and the Chinese were more acceptable, with only 25 and 24 percent, respectively, of the unfavorable evaluations. At the bottom of the list were Middle Europeans with 16, Ukrainians with 15, and Poles with 14 percent. Unspecified "others" were chosen for exclusion by a mere 3 percent of the respondents, while 18 percent favored the admission of all of the named "nationalities." (Since the participants could each offer more than one answer, the percentages add up to considerably more than 100.)[11]

The conclusion to which these two polls point is that unwillingness to admit Jewish immigrants to Canada was to a large extent the result of popular anti-Semitism. A year and a half after the war, distrust of Jews remained as widespread as before the war. No one justified or approved of the mass murder of European Jews. But Canadians' general condemnation of the Nazi genocide did not translate into a willingness to accept its survivors as immigrants.

The dominant view in the United States was similar. The same popular doubts, suspicions, resentments, and fears that had been common before the war persisted afterward. Victory over the Axis did not appear to have had much effect on the general opposition to any change in the existing immigration legislation. There was, however, a widespread awareness of the problem created by the hundreds of thousands of displaced persons and stateless refugees in the Old World, living in constant fear and anxiety, unwilling to return to their homelands but unable to find a suitable place for resettlement. Clearly something had to be done to help those victims of racist persecution.

There was some talk about drafting an international plan for the relocation of refugees. American public opinion, however, remained opposed to any proposal involving the admission of large numbers of immigrants. A survey conducted at the end of August 1946 which asked whether "you [would] approve or disapprove a plan to require each nation to take in a given number of Jewish and other European refugees, based upon the size and population of each nation," showed that 37 percent of the respondents were willing to support such a plan, 48 percent were unwilling, and 15 percent expressed no opinion. But when the hypothetical plan involved an exclusively American effort to solve the refugee problem by relaxing the restrictions on immigration, the opposition increased sharply. The second part of the survey began by informing the participants that "President Truman plans to ask Congress to allow more Jewish and other European refugees to come to the United States to live than are allowed under the law now." Did they approve or disapprove of the idea? This time the response of the participants was unequivocal. Only 16 percent supported it, while 72 percent opposed it and 12 percent expressed no opinion. In short, the public at large might perhaps have been persuaded to support participation in some international plan to help resettle Jewish survivors in various parts of the world outside Europe. But for the United States to assume the burden alone? That was unacceptable.[12]

Public opinion continued to reflect the strains and stresses of the war long after the return of peace. That conclusion is supported by a series of polls taken between August 1940 and March 1959 asking whether "you [have] heard any criticism or talk against the Jews in the last six months." The results showed an uninterrupted increase in popular disapproval of Jews in America, starting with the early stages of the military conflict and ending in the immediate postwar period. In the first poll, conducted in the summer of 1940, 46 percent of respondents reported hearing criticism of Jews recently. That number rose to 47 percent in February 1941 and then to 50 percent in October 1941 and December 1942. By May 1944 the percentage had reached 62, and it remained at that level as late as March 1945. Then, in February 1946, after the Allied victory, it climbed once again, to 64, its highest point.[13]

The polls also asked those who reported that they did hear criticism of Jews to describe its content. The results were revealing, because they specified the reasons or rationalizations for popular ethnic prejudice. They included most of the traditional complaints about the role of Jews in national life: "too many in government," "clannishness," "aggressive pushiness," "avoiding army, getting soft jobs in army," and simply "Jewish 'race' disliked." But the most frequent and persistent charges pertained to Jewish "unfairness in business, unscrupulousness," "control of business, property, finance," and the familiar "too much power." There was nothing unusual about any of these charges. They were widespread in Europe as well as North America. They had been heard over and over again before and during the war. They were in fact common in popular thought and opinion on both sides of the Atlantic, helping to shape the prevailing attitude in the Old World as well as the New regarding the admission of the survivors of the Nazi genocide.[14]

The obstacles facing European Jews eager to emigrate after the defeat of the Axis seemed almost insurmountable. There was first of all the popular opposition in America to any change in the quota system; then there was the decision of the British government to restrict the admission of refugees to Palestine; and finally there was the constant danger of Arab attacks against Jewish settlers and settlements in the Middle East. How could those who had barely managed to survive the racist mass murders organized by the Third Reich now be expected to face the prospect of exclusion or detention or even death in battle against a sworn enemy? The wisest course seemed to be to remain in the Old World and try to rebuild the ethnic communities destroyed by the Nazi genocide.

Yet, in fact, a massive Jewish exodus from Europe began almost as soon as the war came to an end. The statistics regarding this migration differ measurably but understandably, given the chaotic conditions during the military conflict and the immediate postwar period. Still, according to data gathered by the American Jewish Committee, which appears generally reliable, the Jewish population of Europe dropped from about 9.74 million in 1939 to about 3.92 million by 1947. By 1955, the number, including Jews in Turkey and the Asian parts of the Soviet Union, had shrunk still further, to 3.45 million. In other words, close to half a million Jews left the continent in the decade following the end of the war.[15]

Most of the emigrants came from Eastern Europe, which is not surprising, since the great bulk of European Jews had lived there before the rise of the Third Reich. But determining how many came from each country is far more difficult, because of the territorial changes following the military conflict. The Soviet Union acquired large parts of the neighboring countries that had a sizable Jewish population: the Baltic states, eastern Poland, Ruthenia, northern Bukovina, and Bessarabia. In dealing with the decline in the number of Jews in the nations of Eastern Europe, it is therefore hard to determine precisely how much was a result of the change in national frontiers and how much was caused by the outflow of Jewish emigrants. But it is at least clear that most of the decline was due to the westward movement of large numbers of Jews.

In the case of Poland, which had a Jewish population of more than 3 million before the war, only about 500,000 survived the Nazi occupation. By 1947 the number of Jews living there had diminished to roughly 105,000, and by 1955 it had dropped to 45,000. In Romania there was a similar decline. In 1939 the country had close to 900,000 Jews, about half of whom perished in the course of the next few years. But of the approximately 425,000 who survived, no more than 225,000 were still in Romania a decade later. Some had become Soviet citizens as a result of the Kremlin's expansionist policy, but most had emigrated. The pattern in Czechoslovakia was essentially the same. Of the more than 300,000 Jews living there when the war began, between 60,000 and 90,000 were still alive when it ended. While the estimates vary somewhat, by 1955 the number remaining in the country had dwindled to 17,000. The sizable Jewish community in Ruthenia was incorporated into the Ukraine, but the great majority of the surviving Czech and Slovak Jews emigrated from Europe.[16]

The only nation east of the iron curtain with a large Jewish population was the Soviet Union. Not that the Jews living there had been spared the horrors of the Nazi occupation. Of the roughly 3 million at the outbreak of the war, only about half were still alive when the war ended. But by 1947 the number had risen again to 2 million, making up the bulk of what remained of the Jewish population of Europe. This increase in the proportion of European Jews living in the Soviet Union, a proportion which had been about a third before the war, was partly a result of the expansion of the country's boundaries following the defeat of the Third Reich. But it also reflected an official policy restricting or rather indirectly prohibiting emigration. Those applying for permission to travel abroad knew that they would have to overcome endless bureaucratic requirements, delays, and obstacles. Worse still, they would arouse suspicion that they were secretly in sympathy with the opponents of the Soviet regime. And that could prove dangerous.[17]

In the other states east of the iron curtain, emigration was much easier, at least at first. In the immediate postwar period, before the establishment of the Communist governments and their acquisition of unrestricted power,

Jews were free to leave. Their departure was in fact discreetly encouraged, since it would reduce the risk of a revival of prewar ethnic prejudices and hostilities. Those emigrating could not, of course, expect any compensation for the properties or possessions they were leaving behind. But at least there were no bureaucratic obstacles to their departure. Not until the coming of the cold war did it become difficult for East European Jews to seek refuge abroad. But by then most of them had already left.

The situation in Western Europe was different. For one thing, here the nations freed from the German occupation reestablished a democratic form of government, something that almost all the Jews who survived the war welcomed. An economic system based on free enterprise seemed inviting to those who had once been active in commerce, industry, or finance. But most important, the attitude of the general population toward the Jewish victims of persecution had been more sympathetic than in the east, and it remained more sympathetic after the war. Thus for the great majority of Jews, the political and social environment in Western Europe was more congenial than that in Eastern Europe.

Yet here too there was a steady outflow of Jewish emigrants during the early postwar years. This reflected partly the psychological effect of the systematic extermination of European Jewry by the Third Reich. But there were also practical motives and considerations: the growing intensity of the cold war, the economic recession lingering after the fall of the Nazi regime, and the disguised but unmistakable persistence of popular ethnic prejudice. The result was an exodus of large numbers of Jews from the countries west of the iron curtain. In the Netherlands, the Jewish population of 150,000 in 1939 was reduced to about 60,000 by 1945 and to 25,000 by 1955. In Belgium, the number of Jews dropped from 90,000 in 1939 to 50,000 in 1945 and 42,000 in 1955. France was an exception; although the Jewish population there, which had totaled 300,000 on the eve of the war, fell to 210,000 by 1945, a decade later it once again reached 300,000. A sizable number of emigrants from Eastern Europe had concluded that a safe refuge could still be found in the nation that had been the first on the continent to grant Jews full civic equality.[18]

Yet the country in Western Europe with the largest Jewish population, larger than in any other European state outside the Soviet Union, was Great Britain. To many of the survivors of the Nazi genocide, this was the only nation in the Old World that could still offer peace and security to refugees traumatized by a terrible collective tragedy. It had displayed extraordinary courage in defying and resisting the threat of a German invasion. It had proved firm in its commitment to the principles and ideals of democracy. And it had remained relatively free of the ethnic prejudice which became common in the countries under the German occupation. To Jews haunted by the memory of what had happened during the war, here was a nation that could still provide some assurance of safety and stability.

That perception was largely a result of wartime experience. When Hitler came to power in 1933, there were no more than about 330,000 Jews in Great Britain. Five years later, the number had dropped to 300,000, partly a consequence of the economic depression, but partly also a reflection of the growing fear of another world war. Then, after hostilities began and especially after the early victories of the Wehrmacht, the Jewish population began to increase rapidly because of the influx of refugees. Once peace was restored, however, the number diminished again, to 345,000 in 1947, only to be followed by another increase even larger than the one following the German occupation of the continent. By 1955 the figure reached 450,000, the highest in the history of Great Britain. The postwar situation of European Jewry had led to a greater inflow of refugees than the wartime persecution by the Third Reich.[19]

Still, the preferred destination of the great majority of Jewish emigrants was not England or France but the New World or the Middle East. To be sure, millions of Jews remained in the Old World, but except in a few countries like England and France, the Jewish communities there lost their sense of collective character and destiny, the feeling of a common tradition and experience which had been the basis of their ethnic identity. The postwar European governments, moreover, encouraged this transformation. They adopted a policy of equal treatment for all their citizens, regardless of background, faith, or ethnicity. But in return they expected all their citizens to renounce the particularistic loyalties and convictions that reflected differences in collective mentality or character. In short, the price of complete acceptance was complete assimilation. There was no objection to continuing to identify someone as being of Jewish or Turkish or Moorish descent, but to make that identification the foundation of a separate ethnic or cultural or ideological community would be divisive and should therefore be avoided. In Europe's postwar environment, Jewishness ceased to be regarded, officially at least, as a determinant of faith or ideology or conduct and became a purely physical characteristic, like skin color or hair length. The rejection of collective identity was even more important than emigration in marking the end of European Jewry as a separate and distinctive ethnic community.

Still, the shift of the center of Jewish life from the Old World to North America and the Middle East represented more than a geographic or demographic change. It led also to a fundamental alteration in the nature of world Jewry, involving not only language but also collective experience, outlook, and faith. The long history of the Jewish community in Europe as an alien and scorned minority had led to the emergence of a common defensive mentality in confronting a hostile world. Jewish awareness of widespread popular resentment and hostility, sometimes exaggerated, had the effect of engendering a sense of insecurity and defensiveness, not only in Eastern Europe but in Western Europe as well. However, that outlook began to change after the war with the emergence of new centers of world Jewry shaped by new experiences, new opportunities, and new goals.

The most dramatic of those changes was the reestablishment after more than two thousand years of an independent state by and for Jews. Before the war, most of them had regarded Zionism as a bold but ineffectual response to the discrimination they so often encountered. They made frequent contributions to the Zionist cause, but out of sentimental attachment rather than ideological conviction. Even in Eastern Europe, the great majority hoped to gain freedom and equality by other means, the Orthodox Jews by waiting for the coming of the Messiah, the secular Jews by becoming assimilated, by supporting democratic reform, or by embracing some form of Marxism. To try to create a Jewish homeland in Palestine seemed touching and commendable but unrealistic. Why abandon a cozy, familiar way of life for something so visionary?

The Second World War changed that perception. By a cruel irony of fate, Hitler became the source of a fundamental change in the prevailing Jewish attitude toward Zionism. Those who survived the mass murders under the German occupation began to feel that emigration from Europe was the only way to build a Jewish community capable of providing its members with physical and emotional security. To many of them, Palestine, the ancestral homeland of the Jews, seemed a logical destination. But getting there was easier said than done. There were the restrictions on immigration, the attacks by Palestinian Arabs, and the hardships of building a new life in a strange and barren part of the world. Those were daunting obstacles.

In one way or another, however, legally, semilegally, or illegally, large numbers of European Jews began to emigrate to Palestine, before, during, and especially after the war. In 1933 the number of Jewish settlers in the mandate was only 230,000. By 1938, partly as a result of anti-Semitic persecution by the Third Reich, the number had almost doubled, to 424,000. In 1947, after the war ended but before the establishment of a separate Jewish state, the number was 622,000. And finally, in 1955, a few years after the proclamation of the independence of Israel, its population, including Arabs as well as Jews, reached 1.6 million, slightly more than the combined number of Jews in all the states of Europe outside the Soviet Union. A new center of Jewish life had emerged, different from the old one in spirit, character, and culture.[20]

But the most eagerly sought destination of Jews who decided to leave the Old World was the United States. Here was a country with a flourishing economy, a country of boundless opportunity. More than that, immigrants could find a congenial environment in the largest Jewish community in the world, most of its members, like most of those seeking refuge, originally from Eastern Europe. For about eighty years, ever since the Civil War, Jews had been pouring into the "golden realm," increasing from a few hundred thousand to several million. Even anti-Semitic prejudice, though by no means unknown, was far less intense in the New World than in most of the countries of Europe, especially in the east. The only obstacle to the admission of Jewish refugees, but a very serious one, was the legislation narrowly restricting immigration.

The statistics regarding the growth of the Jewish population in the United States are impressive. In 1878 there were 229,400 Jews in the country, no more than 0.5 percent of the total population. But by 1907 the number had risen to 1,776,700, and 2 percent of the population. The figures continued to climb steadily. In 1913 there were 101,330 Jewish immigrants, and in 1914 there were 138,051. During the First World War came a sharp drop, but by 1921 the influx had returned to its prewar level, with 119,036 Jews entering the United States.

That was when Congress decided, chiefly for economic reasons but with an admixture of ethnic prejudice, that enough was enough. The laws of 1921 and 1924 imposed strict limits on immigration, limits reflected in a drastic decline in the number of Jews admitted to the country during the years that followed: 10,267 in 1925, then a slight rise to 11,483 in 1926, and then another slight rise to 11,639 in 1927. The coming of the Great Depression further reduced the influx of Jewish immigrants, chiefly through a more rigid enforcement of the limitations on admission: 5,692 in 1931, 2,755 in 1932, and 2,372 in 1933. After the establishment of the Third Reich, however, the authorities began to relent. Growing sympathy for the victims of Nazi persecution combined with pressure by Jewish organizations in the United States led to a mounting increase in the number of admitted Jews: 11,352 in 1937, then 19,736 in 1938, and finally 43,450 in 1939, the highest figure since the adoption of the legislation restricting immigration almost two decades earlier.[21]

The outbreak of the Second World War followed by the German domination of the continent led to a further relaxation of the official attitude in Washington regarding the immigration problem, particularly the admission of Jewish refugees. But now the chief obstacles were the restrictions imposed on Jews by the Nazi regime. At first it was still possible for those who had found temporary asylum in one of the neutral or unoccupied countries to find some way of reaching America. The number of Jews entering the country was 36,945 in 1940 and 23,737 in 1941. But then, after Pearl Harbor, came a sharp drop, to 10,608 in 1942 and 4,705 in the first half of 1943. For the next few years only rough estimates are available, but approximately 18,000 Jewish immigrants entered the United States between July 1943 and December 1945. All in all, close to 140,000 Jews were admitted in the course of the war, although this estimate has to be viewed as tentative. Figures vary, sometimes considerably, in part because of the imprecise nature of the statistical data available during a bitter military struggle, but in part also because of the difficulty in distinguishing between the various categories of those admitted: immigrants, refugees, visitors, temporary residents, and scientific or technological experts. Any figure should be regarded as only an approximation.[22]

Statistical information regarding immigration to the United States during the immediate postwar period is more reliable. It shows that as soon as the military conflict ended, Jewish refugees began to enter the country in numbers comparable to those during the last years before the outbreak of hostilities. In 1946 there were 15,535 immigrant Jews, in 1947 there were 25,885, and between January and October 1948 there were 12,300. That, however, was only the beginning. Close to half a million Jewish refugees entered the United States in the decade following the end of the war. According to the figures of the American Jewish Committee, the number of Jews in the country rose from 4,770,647 in 1947 to 5,200,000 in 1955, an increase of about 9 percent. But even more striking was the increase in the proportionate size of American Jewry as part of world Jewry. In 1938 the Jewish population of the United States was already far larger than that in any other country, constituting about 30 percent of all Jews. By 1955, however, it had not only increased its numerical superiority over the other Jewish communities, but its percentage of world Jewry had risen to 43. Its sheer size seemed to many of the displaced persons in Europe to offer the promise of stability and security.[23]

Yet the most striking aspect of the transformation of American Jewry was not its growth. As a matter of fact, although the number of Jews in the United States had been rapidly increasing for almost a century, their percentage of the entire population of the country had begun to decline even before the Second World War. The highest proportion was reached in 1927, with 3.6 percent of all Americans. By 1955, despite the admission of hundreds of thousands of refugees following the fall of the Third Reich, the percentage had dropped to 3.1, and a generation later, in 1986, it was even smaller, 2.5 percent. A relatively low birthrate and, far more important, a heavy influx of non-Jewish immigrants, mostly from Latin America but also from Asia and parts of Africa, led to a significant decrease in the relative size of American Jewry.[24]

That did not turn out to be a disadvantage, however. On the contrary, the steady decline in the popular perception that the national character was being altered or undermined by an unending flood of impoverished Jews from Eastern Europe made it easier for members of the Jewish community to gain acceptance, to become assimilated and acculturated, to achieve "Americanization." The social and cultural barriers that had confronted them before the war began to shrink and disappear. There were no longer serious restrictions on the admission of Jews to higher education, either as students or as teachers. They also became eligible for membership in all or almost all social clubs and organizations, even the most exclusive ones. Their role in politics was no longer largely confined to that of unofficial, behind-the-scenes aides and advisers. In growing numbers they were becoming congressmen and senators, members of the cabinet; even the vice presidency did not seem beyond their reach, while rising to the presidency itself appeared to be only a matter of time. Two or three decades earlier, during the Great Depression, would anyone have believed that possible?

Still, the growing acceptance of Jews into mainstream American society also meant the gradual decline of what had been regarded as typical manifestations of the uniqueness and individuality of their community. The Jewish neighborhoods that had once been part of almost every large city in the United States became transformed, as their original inhabitants began to move to more fashionable places of residence, while recent non-European immigrants rapidly replaced them. The number of Jewish stores and kosher restaurants diminished as well, and even the remaining ones often became careless about observing the strict dietary prescriptions and prohibitions of Orthodox Judaism. Yiddish newspapers and periodicals stopped publishing, the Yiddish theater stopped performing, and Yiddish films stopped appearing on the screens of neighborhood movie houses. Even popular vaudeville jokes about Jews, usually told with a foreign accent and in a singsong inflection, became no more than an embarrassing memory for those now increasingly part of the establishment in America. Most significant, however, was the steady drift of Jewish religious observance from rigid adherence to the traditional rules and commandments of orthodoxy to a reformism similar to the one spreading in American Protestantism, by which rituals and ceremonials became subordinated to humanitarian beliefs, principles, and ideals. To the Jewish immigrants from Eastern Europe who had arrived in the United States only a few generations earlier, all of this would have seemed unbelievable.

The changes in the character and outlook of European Jewry after the war were as drastic as those of American Jewry. There were still millions of Jews living in the Old World, but except for a few communities in the Western democracies, they had lost their sense of ethnic togetherness. They were no longer facing the discriminations and oppressions that had been common before the war, but as a token of appreciation of their new acceptance, they were expected to abandon their Jewish sympathies and loyalties. There was popular acknowledgment and condemnation of what they had suffered under the German occupation. But that was all in the past. The distinctive Jewishness of the prewar era came to be regarded as a sort of historical anachronism, an archaelogical fossil. It might still be of some cultural or sociological interest, but it should no longer be regarded as a unifying ethnic force transcending territorial boundaries and national loyalties. Its renunciation was the price of emancipation. That was the bargain to which both sides implicitly agreed. And that also meant that the long chapter in Jewish history that had begun in Roman times, a chapter in which European Jewry played the central role, was now at an end.

16

The Emergence of the Holocaust

THE DRAMATIC CHANGE in the popular perception in America of Jewry and the "Jewish question," that emerged after the Second World War also had a profound effect on the prevailing attitude toward the Nazi genocide. While the military conflict was still going on, there was general agreement that even although the Jewish population under the German occupation had to endure hardship and oppression, occasionally even mass execution, that was not very different from what other peoples conquered by the Third Reich had to endure. They were all victims of the racist brutality of National Socialism. What was happening to the Jews, though terrible, was just one of the many atrocities being committed by the Nazi regime. The only way to put an end to all of them was military victory.

The public was also inclined to believe that reports of the organized, systematic extermination of the Jewish population of Europe were exaggerated. Persistent skepticism about the extent of the genocide continued until the end of the war. In May 1945, after Hitler's suicide, after the fall of the Third Reich, even after the occupation of all of Germany by the Allies, there was still considerable doubt about how many people had been murdered in the name of National Socialism. A poll asking, "What do you think of the reports that the Germans have killed many people in concentration camps or let them starve to death—are they true or not?" showed that 84 percent of the respondents believed the reports to be true. Another 9 percent believed them to be "true, but exaggerated," while 1 percent thought they were "doubtful, hard to believe," and 3 percent thought they were "not true." Finally, there were the 3 percent who simply "can't decide."

This poll did not ask the participants to choose between several differing estimates of the number of victims. Instead, they were told at the outset that "nobody knows how many have been killed or starved to death." And then, "What would be your best guess?" The results showed that the median average of the estimates was 1 million, a figure that was only a fraction of the actual number. As the war was drawing to a close, Americans became increasingly convinced that the Third Reich was indeed guilty of mass murder in the occupied countries. The extent of that mass murder, however, continued to be largely underestimated.[1]

Such polls did not generally mention that Jews were proportionately the most numerous victims of these atrocities. They spoke instead of the "many people" who had been killed in the concentration camps, without specifying the national or ethnic background of those people. That subject had already become a source of considerable controversy. But in the years immediately following the war, it grew increasingly clear that while all the nationalities under the German occupation had suffered oppression, privation, and at times even mass murder, Jews had been the only ones condemned to organized, systematic extermination. There were the widely publicized trials of the war criminals, or at least of those who had survived. Then there were the accounts and reminiscences of the liberated prisoners in the concentration camps, non-Jewish as well as Jewish. And finally, the testimony of many residents of the countries that had been conquered by the Third Reich, sometimes even of the Germans themselves, helped provide a generally accurate picture of what life and death in occupied Europe had been like.

It became apparent that out of a worldwide Jewish population of 15,748,000 in 1938, a total of 5,978,000—38 percent—perished in the course of the war. The number of Jews in Europe who perished was of course much higher, around 60 percent. No other national or ethnic community suffered proportionate losses even close to those of European Jewry. The highest estimates of those losses while the war was still going on, estimates that had been popularly viewed as greatly exaggerated, were shown to be accurate in the decade that followed. Not only the proportion but also the number of Jews who died during the Nazi genocide far exceeded that of non-Jews in all the countries under German rule with the exception of the Soviet Union. The statistical evidence on this point is indisputable.[2]

There was a reason for the disparity. The Third Reich did not envision or seek the indiscriminate destruction of the peoples of occupied Europe. Admittedly, they were to remain permanently subordinate to their German conquerors, politically, economically, socially, and culturally. They were condemned to a position of perpetual inferiority. Those prepared to accept such a position, however, would be able to lead a segregated but more or less peaceful existence as artisans, laborers, farmhands, and servants. Some could continue to be shopkeepers, mill owners, moneylenders, or small businessmen. A few might even be allowed to become doctors, teachers, financiers, and industrialists. But in return they had to accept the status of submissive vassals of the Third Reich, following its orders and bowing to its wishes. They had to agree to accept the restrictions and requirements of permanent subordination.

Those resigned to living under the domination of the Hitler regime were thus in general free to go on with their traditional way of life. The oppressive measures of the occupation authorities were directed chiefly against those resisting or suspected of resisting their rule. The Germans were generally not very meticulous in distinguishing between the appearance and the reality of opposition—between the ones who were members of the underground, the ones who might be members of the underground, and the ones who could perhaps become members of the underground. There can be no question that many innocent people were imprisoned and executed on the basis of mere suspicion. It is also clear that many more died as a result of famine, epidemic disease, and forced labor. Yet the great bulk of the population in the occupied countries, including those in Eastern Europe, survived the war.

The situation of the Jews was fundamentally different. In their case, it did not matter whether they were submissive or defiant, assimilated or segregated, pious or secular or converted to Christianity. Their Jewishness alone was enough to make them a deadly menace to society, a menace that could be overcome only by genocide. Other ethnic communities—the Gypsies, for example—were also viewed by Nazi ideologues as a threat to be countered by mass execution. Only in the case of the Jews, however, was ethnic extermination adopted as a secret but official policy. Nothing less than total destruction could protect the world from the designs and machinations of an inherently evil race.

This form of anti-Semitism was essentially different from the earlier varieties that had emerged in the wake of Jewish emancipation. In czarist Russia, for example, the far right had often attacked Jews in language that resembled the later rhetoric of National Socialism. They were greedy, parasitical, unscrupulous, devious, and subversive. They represented a danger that must be overcome, and the only way to overcome it was by segregation or emigration. The Jews should therefore be forced to return to the ghetto, where they would have less opportunity to exploit their kindly but naive Christian neighbors. Better still, they should be persuaded to leave Europe and resettle in some distant part of the world where they would no longer pose a threat to the country of their origin. Their departure might be encouraged by occasional mass riots, even by a pogrom here and there. But out-and-out ethnic extermination was something that not even the most virulent anti-Semites of the old school were prepared to advocate.

For that matter, the Nazis were also reluctant to advocate genocide publicly. But during the war they adopted a program of ethnic mass murder which, though never openly acknowledged, became widely known in the occupied countries and even in the Third Reich itself. It rested on the conviction that putting an end to the Jewish menace in Germany or even throughout the continent would not be enough. The Jews were a danger wherever they lived, a danger to the entire world. To destroy them only in Europe would therefore be insufficient. The threat they represented was global in scope, so that a defense against it had to be global as well. For the time being, the battlefield was the European continent. But sooner or later the struggle would have to expand throughout the world. There was no other way to overcome the terrible danger confronting mankind.

The obsessive nature of Nazi anti-Semitism was no secret to the Allied governments. They were fully aware of the ongoing extermination of European Jewry. Yet the fall of the Third Reich did not at first change the popular perception that the destruction of European Jewry, though an act of unparalleled brutality, had been only one of the many atrocities of the Hitler regime. More than a decade was to elapse before the Nazi genocide gradually became transformed into "the Holocaust."

While anti-Semitic prejudice in the United States actually increased during the military conflict and remained prevalent even after victory, by the late 1950s a significant shift in public opinion was becoming apparent. A series of polls asking whether "you [have] heard any criticism or talk against the Jews in the last six months" showed a steady increase in yeses, from 46 percent in August 1940 to 62 in March 1945 and 64 in February 1946, half a year after the defeat of the Axis. By November 1950, however, the percentage of those who reported hearing criticism of Jews had dropped sharply, to 24. And after that the proportion of respondents who had recently heard anti-Semitic comments continued to diminish steadily, with only a few brief interruptions: 16 percent in April 1951, 21 percent in July 1953, 14 percent in November 1954, 13 percent in November 1955, 11 percent in November 1956 (the lowest figure since the surveys began nearly two decades earlier), and 12 percent in March 1959. Clearly a remarkable change in popular attitudes was taking place.[3]

What was even more striking was the decline in criticism of the weaknesses and vices that had in the past been considered typically Jewish. When the participants who reported hearing criticism of Jews recently were asked, "What kind of criticism or talk was it?" the replies indicated that the complaints concerned chiefly the Jewish role in the economic life of the nation. The most frequent criticism pertained to "unfairness in business, unscrupulousness." That was mentioned by 27 percent of the participants in August 1940, by 31 percent in February 1941, and by 21 percent in October 1941. After the United States entered the war, it gradually climbed to 30 percent in May 1944. But the high point, 39 percent, was not reached until November 1950. Then came a steady decline, to 29 percent in April 1951, 20 percent in November 1954, 18 percent in November 1956, and finally 10 percent in March 1959.

A similar pattern emerged in the second most frequently mentioned criticism of Jews, namely, "control of business, property, finance." Here the proportion of respondents who had heard that criticism in the previous six months remained essentially unchanged during the prewar period and most of the wartime years: 20 percent in August 1940, 21 percent in February 1941 and October 1941, a slight drop to 18 percent in December 1942, and a slight rise to 22 percent in May 1944. The approach of victory, however, and the end of the war led to a sharp decline in the level of reported popular disapproval of the Jewish role in financial affairs: 13 percent in March 1945, 17 percent in February 1946, and 13 percent again in April 1951. This was followed by another rise to 20 percent in July 1953, November 1955, and November 1956, followed in March 1959 by the lowest percentage in the entire series of polls, a mere 6 percent.

Still another complaint appeared over and over again, this one pertaining to Jewish influence in politics as well as finance. Jews had "too much power," which changed in November 1950 to "too much political power." Here the pattern resembled that of the two other common complaints. At first the percentage of those expressing concern about Jewish influence remained relatively steady: 10 percent in August 1940, 12 percent in February 1941, 9 percent in October 1941, 11 percent in December 1942, and 10 percent in May 1944. The approaching victory of the Allies had little effect, with 11 percent of the respondents still reporting complaints in March 1945. But then came a sharp decline in the percentage of those hearing recent expressions of concern regarding Jewish influence: 6 percent in February 1946, 5 percent in November 1950, then a modest increase to 8 percent in April 1951, and then a sharp decrease to 3 percent in November 1954, November 1956, and November 1959. Here was further evidence that a remarkable change in public opinion about the role of Jews in national affairs was taking place.

There had to be a special reason, therefore, for the ups and downs of public opinion regarding "Communist leanings [or] spying" by Jews. Throughout the 1940s, reported criticisms of Jewish subversiveness remained at 1 percent. But that changed abruptly after the war. In November 1950 the percentage rose to 8, in April 1951 it was 18, and in July 1953 it reached a high of 26. The cause, however, was clear. The "Communist scare" and the congressional investigation of "un-American activities" led by Senator Joseph McCarthy aroused concern over American left-wing supporters of the Soviet Union. In the fearful atmosphere of the early years of the cold war, it was easy to believe that at least some of those supporters were guilty of subversion. And among the ones suspected, rightly or wrongly, of being in sympathy with the Stalin regime were a disproportionate number of Jews. This accounted largely for the sharp rise of anti-Semitism in the early 1950s.

But as the excesses of the McCarthy campaign against communism became apparent and the popular fear of left-wing plots and conspiracies began to subside, the level of popular suspicion of Jewry declined as well. By 1954 the percentage of reported complaints concerning the "Communist leanings" of Jews had dropped to 11, followed by another sharp decline, to 2 percent in November 1955 and 4 percent in November 1956. By March 1959 the proportion of reported criticisms of the Jewish community based on its alleged political disloyalty fell to the lowest point, less than 1 percent. The fear of left-wing subversion caused no more than a brief interruption in the continuing decline of anti-Semitic prejudice in the United States.[4]

This conclusion is reinforced by more direct evidence, that is, not only by what participants in public opinion polls had recently heard others saying but by what they themselves felt and believed. There was in fact little difference between the results of the two kinds of surveys of popular feelings and attitudes regarding the "Jewish question." When asked the usual "Do you think the Jews have too much power in the United States?" 35 percent of the respondents answered yes in November 1938, a percentage that rose to 48 by October 1941, shortly before Pearl Harbor. Once America entered the war, the proportion of those who thought that Jews had too much power continued to climb steadily, from 47 percent in February 1942 to 51 percent in December 1942 and 56 percent in May 1944 and March 1945. Popular disapproval of Jewish power reached its high point in June 1945, a month after the end of the war in Europe: 58 percent. As late as February 1946 that disapproval was still at 55 percent. Then came a long interruption in the surveys of public opinion regarding Jewry, until in 1962 a new poll revealed that the percentage of those concerned about the extent of Jewish power had dropped to 17. That was a remarkable change.[5]

Even more impressive was the decline in the proportion of respondents who agreed that "there [are] objectionable qualities which . . . Jews generally have to a greater extent than other people." The available statistical information, which makes possible a comparison only of the years 1940 and 1962, shows that while 63 percent of the respondents on the eve of America's entry into the war believed that Jews had "objectionable qualities," two decades later the percentage was no more than 22, barely a third of what it had been. Here was further evidence that the level of anti-Semitism in the United States steadily dropped after the victory over the Axis.[6]

The most sensitive measure of the shift in American public opinion of Jews, however, was not the extent of reported criticism of their power or the popular perception of their influence in national affairs. It was, rather, prevalent attitudes about personal relations with members of the Jewish community in the workplace, higher education, the neighborhood, and marriage. Here the decisive factor was not a perception of abstract forces in state and society, as distinct from private feelings and concerns. Instead, the respondents were asked to describe their own attitude toward a close association with Jews—toward meeting with them, sitting next to them, conversing with them, and even entering into an intimate personal relationship with them. That was far different from expressing an opinion about their influence in national affairs or their power in commerce, finance, and industry.

But here too there was a striking decline in the level of distrust of or uneasiness about Jews. A comparison of the results of two public opinion polls, the first in 1940, the second in 1962, each asking whether "it would make a difference to [you] if a prospective employee were Jewish," showed a sharp decline in anti-Semitic prejudice. In the first poll, 43 percent of the respondents indicated that they would prefer not to have a Jewish employee or coworker whom they would have to meet with on a more or less regular basis. In the second poll, however, the percentage of those opposed to sharing the workplace with Jews fell to only 6. This drop in ethnic discrimination was similar to the drop in the less personal and more abstract forms of popular intolerance.[7]

A comparable decline appeared in surveys asking the participants whether "you think colleges should limit the number of Jews they admit." This issue affected a far smaller proportion of the general population than the one regarding the employment of Jews. Before the war, a quota system intended to restrict the admission of Jewish students had been widespread in American higher education. The more elite an institution of academic learning was, the stricter the exclusion of Jews was likely to be. This patrician form of anti-Semitic discrimination as a rule remained unadvertised. Its existence was in fact denied at times. Yet even before the war there had been considerable opposition to such exclusionary policies, and afterward that opposition became irresistible. In a poll conducted in 1938, the great majority of the respondents—65 percent—thought that there should be no restrictions on the admission of Jews to colleges, while 26 percent supported at least some restrictions. By the time of the poll conducted in 1962, public opinion on this issue had become one-sided almost to the point of unanimity: 88 percent against and 4 percent for restrictions. Now almost no one seemed to object to Christians and Jews sitting side by side in the same lecture hall.[8]

There were similarly few objections to living in the same neighborhood. A series of polls soon after the war asked the participants, all of them Christians, whether they would be willing to accept Jews as neighbors. "Suppose a Jewish family were going to move in next door to you. Would you say you wouldn't like it at all, or that you wouldn't like it but it wouldn't matter too much, or that it wouldn't make any difference to you?" The answers closely resembled those in reply to the question about admitting Jews to colleges and universities. That is, only a small minority of the respondents were unwilling or reluctant to have Jewish neighbors, and that minority declined steadily almost to the vanishing point. The percentage of those who would not like having Jews as neighbors "at all" dropped from 10 in 1950 to 7 in 1953, then to 3 in 1954, 5 in 1955 and 1956, and finally 2 in 1959. There was a similar decline in the proportion of respondents to whom having a Jewish neighbor would not matter "too much," from 20 percent in 1950 to 12 in 1953, to 8 in 1954, to 6 in 1955, to 7 in 1956, and to 8 again in 1959. Conversely, the percentage of those to whom the presence of Jews in the neighborhood "wouldn't make any difference" rose rapidly, from 69 in 1950 to 80 in 1953 and 88 in 1954, before dropping slightly to 87 in 1955 and 86 in 1956 and 1959.

The most striking decline in the level of opposition to Jewish neighbors, however, was recorded in the poll conducted in 1962. Now those who were strongly opposed and those who were somewhat opposed to Jews in the neighborhood together accounted for no more than 3 percent of the total, while the proportion of those to whom having Jews in the neighborhood made no difference rose sharply, to 95 percent. The proportion responding with "don't know," a response given by 1 percent of the participants early in the 1950s, 2 percent in the middle of the decade, and 4 percent toward the end, dropped again to 2 in 1962. The unacknowledged but persistent and widespread exclusion of the Jewish community from the more fashionable residential areas was finally at an end.[9]

The most sensitive but also most ambiguous measures of the level of anti-Semitic prejudice in American society were the polls of 1950 and 1962 asking the participants "How would you feel about marrying a Jew?" They were offered four choices in their responses: "I definitely would not marry a Jew," "I would rather not marry a Jew but it wouldn't matter too much," "It would make no difference to me," or simply "No opinion." What makes the interpretation of the results difficult is that they reflect not only the extent of willingness to enter into a close personal relationship with a Jew but also the level of commitment to a particular religion. To put it another way, the reluctance of a devout believer, whether Christian or Jew, to marry someone outside his or her faith may express a conviction that such a marriage would be a betrayal of that faith. It may be evidence not of ethnic prejudice but of religious loyalty. It is impossible, however, to determine the underlying motive merely on the basis of the reply to a question asked in a public opinion survey. The issue is too complex for that.

Still, these surveys should not be dismissed out of hand. They suggest, especially in conjunction with other surveys assessing the level of anti-Semitism, the direction in which ethnic prejudice in the United States was moving. Even without knowledge of the basic religious convictions of the respondents, the results reinforce the conclusion that hostility toward American Jewry was diminishing. The number of participants in the polls who reported that they would definitely not marry a Jew declined from 57 percent in 1950 to 37 percent in 1962. At the same time, however, the proportion of those who would prefer not to marry a Jew but to whom "it wouldn't matter too much" rose from 16 to 25 percent, reflecting a shift in opinion by some of those who had previously been out-and-out opponents of intermarriage. The percentage of those who declared that "it would make no difference to me" rose from 22 to 30, a far lower proportion than was willing to work alongside Jews or study alongside Jews or live alongside Jews. As for those who expressed no opinion, their percentage rose from 5 to 8, another sign of the difficulty in overcoming the last barriers between two traditionally separate religious communities.[10]

Assessing public opinion regarding the "Jewish question" in postwar Europe is more difficult. For one thing, surveys of popular beliefs and attitudes were not nearly as common in the Old World as in the New. And that in turn reflected the fact that the American political system was or at least appeared to be more sensitive and responsive to shifts of public opinion than the political system in Europe. Especially on the continent, government authorities tended to be more elitist, not as susceptible to the pressure of popular preferences and demands. The views of the population at large about current events had comparatively little direct influence on official policy.

More than that, government authorities on the continent were generally reluctant to measure and analyze public opinion too closely. They were uneasy about what surveys of the prevailing popular attitude regarding state and society might reveal. The official position in Eastern as well as Western Europe was that most citizens of the countries occupied by or allied with the Third Reich had been firmly opposed to the policies of the Nazi regime. But what could they do? Oppressed and powerless, they had had to look on in silent disapproval while the conquerors imposed a reign of terror on helpless millions longing for liberation. What would happen now, however, if public opinion polls were to reveal that a minority, perhaps even a sizable minority, still continued to support some of the authoritarian measures introduced by the Third Reich? And what about the changes in the prewar frontiers that Hitler's government had imposed, many of them welcomed by the revisionist states but revoked after the Allied victory? Would not surveys of public opinion show considerable popular opposition to the restoration of the prewar borders? It would be best to avoid close scrutiny of popular beliefs or sympathies and continue to maintain that there was general public support for the postwar settlement in foreign as well as domestic affairs.

That same policy was adopted in dealing with popular attitudes toward Jews. While the war had been going on, there was at least some support for the Nazi genocide in the countries allied with or occupied by the Third Reich. That support assumed various forms, from revealing Jewish hiding places to serving as guards in the death camps. Considerable anti-Semitic prejudice had been apparent, especially in Eastern Europe, even among those who did not participate directly in the destruction of the Jewish community. That prejudice persisted after the overthrow of the Third Reich. There was evidence of its existence, for example, in the mass riots in Poland that occurred immediately after the war. But even farther to the west, some of the prewar and wartime ethnic fears and resentments continued. It was therefore important to avoid the risk of providing additional evidence of continuing anti-Semitism through public opinion polls. There was no telling what those polls might reveal. The wisest course would be to go on insisting that the Germans and the Germans alone were responsible for the destruction of European Jewry.

There was one thing, however, that the governments of Europe could do to reinforce the contention that their countries had never supported the Nazi genocide. In the years following the war, most of them adopted legislation prohibiting the open expression or display of ethnic prejudice. That meant that anti-Semitic newspapers and journals were suppressed, anti-Semitic parties and organizations were dissolved, anti-Semitic views in books or lectures were banned, and political agitators advocating anti-Semitic measures were arrested and imprisoned. The severity of this legislation far exceeded that of the legislation in force in the United States. But then again, the burden of guilt weighing on the European states was much heavier.

All of this meant that Jewish communities on both sides of the Atlantic now reached a level of acceptance they had never before been able to attain. Both the psychological and material effect of the Nazi genocide were to free world Jewry at last from the oppressions and discriminations it had been forced to endure for almost two thousand years. The extermination of more than half of Europe's Jews meant that the role of the survivors in the economy, politics, and culture of the continent diminished almost to the point of nonexistence. They could no longer be considered a threat even by the most distrustful of their non-Jewish countrymen. The much smaller decline in the relative size of the American Jewish community had the similar effect of reducing popular concern about the influence its members had acquired in national life. Yet an equally important factor in the achievement of full equality by Jews after the war was an unacknowledged but common sense of guilt for not having done more to save the victims of a fanatical ethnic hatred.

Such was the emotional environment in which the Nazi genocide became transformed into "the Holocaust." This change in terminology reflected a growing recognition or acknowledgment that the mass murder of European Jewry was unique and fundamentally different from the many other atrocities committed in the name of National Socialism. In the late

1950s, as the differences in the underlying motivations and goals of Nazi persecution of Jews and non-Jews gradually became clearer, the popular perception of them began to change and the term "the Holocaust" began to appear. The change was intended to emphasize the unique character of the genocide, as opposed to such other ethnic or national holocausts such as the Armenian holocaust, the Gypsy holocaust, and the American Indian holocaust. Those too were unspeakable atrocities, but they could not compare in extent and intensity with "the Holocaust." This one was beyond comparison.

Its uniqueness found expression in several forms of remembrance and commemoration. The most common was the erection of memorials—more of them in America than in Europe, but a growing number in Europe as well—dedicated to the millions who had perished in the Nazi mass murders. Then there were the museums designed to portray the way of life of the victims of the Holocaust, their homes, their possessions, their customs, and their beliefs. There were also solemn observances, secular as well as religious. And on special occasions such as the anniversary of the uprising of the Warsaw ghetto, mass meetings were held to express a collective grief at the destruction of European Jewry and to vow that never again would such an atrocity be allowed to happen.

The Holocaust also became the subject of serious scholarly study and research. A growing number of colleges and universities in America began to offer courses dealing with the extermination of Jews in the Old World. A few even established academic programs devoted entirely to the examination of the background, course, and outcome of the anti-Semitic policies of the Third Reich. The Holocaust became part of the history curriculum in many high schools and some elementary schools. In short, after the 1950s, the public on both sides of the Atlantic, but in America more than in Europe, became increasingly sympathetic toward those who had faced mass murder as a result of ethnic prejudice. That prejudice began to seem more and more irrational and unjust, a hateful obsession unworthy of an enlightened people.

There was a close correlation between the growing public denunciation of the Holocaust and the general decline of popular anti-Semitism in Western society. Both reflected the abjuration of bigotries and animosities that had been prevalent in the Old World since the Middle Ages. Without knowing it, the victims of the Holocaust had paid with their lives for the opening of a new era in the history of world Jewry. Their tragic fate had indirectly made possible the reestablishment of an independent Jewish state in the Middle East. But more than that, it finally led to an unqualified acceptance of Jewry on both sides of the Atlantic. The diaspora, which had begun in the days of the Roman Empire, now came to an end, at least in its traditional form.

Yet some unanswered questions about the origin and cause of this momentous change in the history of the Jewish community still remain. If the Holocaust led to increasing popular awareness of the injustice of ethnic persecution, why was that awareness so slow to emerge? Why wasn't there greater condemnation of the mass murder of Jews while that murder was going on? Open protests in the countries under German occupation obviously would have invited brutal repression and retaliation. But what about the United States and Canada? Could they not have done more to denounce the barbarity of the Holocaust? Especially after the war, when there was no longer any danger of Nazi reprisals, why did it take the Western democracies a decade or more to fully acknowledge the murderous extent of the Holocaust? Those questions still call for close examination.

In his book *The Holocaust in American Life*, Peter Novick identified and analyzed some of the reasons offered for the slow recognition of the motivation and effect of the Holocaust. For one thing, the coming of the cold war changed the prevalent view about the identity of the United States' chief opponent. The Russians ceased to be "indispensable allies" and became "implacable foes," while the Germans were suddenly transformed from "implacable foes" into "indispensable allies." The same Americans who cheered in 1945 when Soviet forces attacked Berlin organized an airlift in 1948 to protect Berlin from Soviet expansionism. "The apotheosis of evil—the epitome of limitless depravity—had been relocated, and public opinion had to be mobilized to accept the new worldview." As a result of this reversal of the international situation, it seemed advisable to the United States and its European allies to condemn the misdeeds of their present rather than their former enemy. Otherwise, the united front they had formed against a common danger might begin to unravel.[11]

But what happened afterward that led to the emergence of "the Holocaust" more than a decade after the end of the war? The usual explanation is that an unexpected conjunction of several important events in the early 1960s drew public attention to the destruction of European Jewry. The first was the trial of Adolf Eichmann, the high-ranking Nazi official who had been put in charge of the Third Reich's program of anti-Semitic extermination, who had managed to escape to South America after the Allied victory. Found and seized by Israeli secret agents in the spring of 1960, he was smuggled out of Argentina and transported to the Middle East to be tried for his role in organizing the wartime genocide. Found guilty, he was executed in 1962. His trial attracted worldwide attention, not only because of the testimony presented to the court regarding the imprisonment, deportation, and execution of millions of Jews but also because of the insight it provided into the mentality of those entrusted with the task of enforcing a program of mass murder.

A year later, Hannah Arendt published *Eichmann in Jerusalem: A Report on the Banality of Evil,* a book that aroused almost as much interest and debate as the trial itself. Its focus was not the policies and actions that had been central in the court proceedings but the men responsible for the initiation of those policies and the implementation of those actions. Arendt's conclusion, at least the one that attracted the most attention, was that those who had carried out the destruction of European Jewry, Eichmann being a prime example, were not as a rule fanatical anti-Semites but rather colorless bureaucrats to whom the enforcement of a program of genocide did not seem essentially different from the enforcement of customs regulations or immigration restrictions. The ordinariness with which the Holocaust was viewed by many of those responsible for its execution, their routinization of ethnic persecution and extermination—that was the most striking feature of the book. It attracted attention to an aspect of the Second World War that had until then usually been seen as only one of the many atrocities the Nazi regime had committed.

In 1963, the same year, another work appeared which, though different in form and theme, also aroused considerable public interest in the Holocaust, namely, Rolf Hochhuth's play *The Deputy.* That interest was in part a result of the author's nationality: he was German. More important, he dealt with an aspect of the Nazis' anti-Semitic policies that had until then been discreetly avoided or mentioned only briefly: the attitude of the Roman Catholic Church toward the destruction of European Jewry, which had generally been described as one of restrained but unmistakable disapproval. Could the Vatican have done more? Its relations with the Third Reich were already so strained that any intercession in behalf of the victims of racist persecution would only have led to an open break with the Hitler government without in any way helping those victims. Under the circumstances, the only thing the Church could do was remain silent.

Hochhuth, however, profoundly disagreed with this contention. A religious faith that claims to represent moral principles and values, he insisted in his play, cannot and must not look the other way while those principles and values are being violated, even if protests can have no practical effect. Opposing evil, though in vain, is better than meekly acquiescing. In the postwar mood of growing regret and guilt, the appearance of *The Deputy* hastened the emergence of "the Holocaust."

According to Novick, there was still another reason for the gradually rising public interest in the destruction of European Jewry. The supporters of Israel, he argued, both Jews and non-Jews, were convinced that remembering the Holocaust would strengthen the widespread resolve to defend the new Jewish state against its Arab enemies. It would reinforce the growing determination to prevent a repetition in the Middle East of what had happened a few decades earlier to the Jewish community in Europe. "American Jews' anxiety about Israel's security, and their viewing Israel's situation within a Holocaust framework, was the single greatest catalyst of the new centering of the Holocaust in American Jewish consciousness." Especially after the Six Day War of June 1967 and the Yom Kippur War of October 1973, there was an increasing conviction among Jews in the United States that the Holocaust was not only the greatest tragedy in the history of their people but was also in a sense an appeal to the entire world never to allow that tragedy to occur again. In other words, keeping alive the memory of what had happened to European Jewry was more than a form of commemoration. It was also a strategic weapon in the struggle for the survival of Israel.[12]

All these explanations for the emergence of the Holocaust as the most terrible atrocity of the Second World War and as one of the most closely studied events of that war seem plausible. And yet a careful scrutiny is likely to arouse at least some doubts. Are those explanations really enough? Do they in fact account entirely or even largely for the broad interest that the mass murder of European Jews continues to attract more than half a century after its occurrence? Is there something else that underlies that interest? Indeed, could it be that the traditional explanations deal primarily not with the causes but with the effects of a changing popular view of the Holocaust? The more closely one examines the familiar reasons given for the shift in public opinion, the less satisfactory or convincing those reasons appear to be.

For example, there is the contention that the emergence of the cold war in the late 1940s diverted attention from Nazi atrocities to those committed by the Soviet regime. According to this contention, it seemed inadvisable to the Western democracies to dwell on the crimes of the Third Reich when the support of the recently established German Federal Republic in confronting the Kremlin was of major importance. But how to explain, then, the emergence of the Holocaust in the early 1960s? The diplomatic conflict between Washington and Moscow was then just as bitter as it had been ten years earlier. Yet in America as well as in Europe, public interest in the persecution of Jews during the Nazi regime continued to grow. There was seemingly little conflict between the increasing awareness of the anti-Semitic program of the Third Reich and the increasing acceptance of the new West German state as an ally in the struggle against totalitarianism.

And what about the effect of the Eichmann trial, or of Hannah Arendt's book concerning the banality of evil, or of Rolf Hochhuth's play about the Catholic Church's passive attitude toward the extermination of European Jewry? Did they not help raise public awareness of the atrocities committed twenty years earlier? Though they clearly did, the question remains, why? The testimony at Eichmann's trial in 1961 was not essentially different from the testimony at similar trials conducted immediately after the war, which found the leaders of the Third Reich guilty of various crimes and atrocities. In short, what the trial of Eichmann revealed was already generally known as a result of earlier legal investigations and proceedings. The difference was not in what was learned later but in the public reaction to what was learned later. Something had happened to alter the prevailing view.

The same question arises in connection with the argument that Israel's struggle for survival in the wars of 1967 and 1973 reminded the world, and Jews especially, of the destruction of a defenseless and helpless ethnic minority by a fanatically anti-Semitic totalitarian regime. Yet here too serious questions and troubling doubts persist. If the successful defense of Israel two decades after its establishment had the effect of increasing popular interest in the Holocaust, why didn't the proclamation of an independent Jewish state two decades earlier and the resultant military struggle against the Arab League have the same effect? With pictures of the death camps and gas chambers still vivid in the world's memory, with newsreels of piles of corpses and emaciated survivors appearing on movie screens in every country, interest in the Holocaust and compassion for its victims might have been expected to emerge much sooner than it did. Yet in fact a decade or more elapsed before the systematic extermination of European Jewry began to be perceived as not simply one but the greatest of the atrocities committed by the Third Reich. Why?

The reason appears to be that it took a decade or more for most people to recognize that the "Jewish question," which had been a source of concern and controversy in Western society for such a long time and had resisted so many attempts to find a satisfactory answer, was finally solved. What the old monarchical order had tried to attain by isolation, segregation, and discrimination and the democratic system had hoped to achieve by toleration, emancipation, and assimilation, Nazi totalitarianism succeeded in accomplishing by mass murder. The Holocaust not only ended the long chapter in Jewish history that had begun with the diaspora in Biblical times. It also solved a problem that had been troubling and worrying Western society for almost as long, namely, what to do about an ethnic minority which remained stubbornly different, unwilling to accept the faith and tradition of the national community it was part of, and yet able to play an important role in the economy, culture, and politics of that community. What to do about this problem now ceased to be an issue. It had at last been resolved or rather eliminated.

That was at first not apparent, however. In the years immediately following the war, there was still a popular expectation or concern, in America as well as Europe, that the survivors of Nazi persecution would soon reappear in the form of a human deluge, demanding the return of their confiscated possessions and the restoration of the positions they had once held in business, government, learning, and the arts. The statistics regarding the number of those killed during the Holocaust were not enough to overcome an uneasy feeling that many of those who had been deported during the Nazi occupation were still alive and might eventually come back to the countries in which they had previously resided. The presence of thousands of displaced persons in occupied Germany reinforced a concern, especially in Eastern Europe, over the reemergence of the "Jewish question." Once the Jews returned, the old familiar disputes and resentments regarding their role in society would return as well. Wouldn't it be best to try to avoid such an eventuality?

This concern was intensified by the westward shift of what was left of European Jewry after the war. Between 1948 and 1955, the Jewish community in Belgium increased by 7,500, or 22 percent. In France during the same period, the number of Jews increased by 95,000, or 46 percent. And in Great Britain, the nation with the largest Jewish population in Western Europe, the increase was numerically the largest as well, 105,000, though proportionately, with 30 percent, it was still behind France. In retrospect, the westward flow of a few hundred thousand Jews does not appear excessive or threatening, but in the uneasy, insecure environment of the postwar years, it aroused a disguised but palpable popular concern. How long would the flow of Jewish refugees from the east continue? What effect would it have on the economy and society of the host countries? And even more threatening, what would happen if the Soviet Union suddenly decided to allow some or perhaps even most of its 2 million Jews to emigrate? The result would be disastrous. Concerns of that sort had the effect of restraining European expressions of sorrow and sympathy for the victims of the Holocaust.[13]

Those same concerns emerged at the same time and with the same effect in the New World. The United States had been spared the cruel experience of enemy occupation and tyrannical Nazi rule. But there too participation in the war had exacted a heavy price in manpower and wealth. The losses at home tended to overshadow or obscure the losses suffered by other countries and other communities, including the Jews. By the time the military conflict ended, the destruction of European Jewry had become widely known in America. Yet public sympathy remained dispersed among the many foreign victims of the Hitler regime's brutality or focused on fellow Americans who had sacrificed their lives in defense of the nation.

As for the admission of the survivors of the Holocaust, that was simply a new form of a problem the country had been grappling with for close to a century. That the "golden realm" remained the favorite destination of Jews seeking to emigrate from Europe was not surprising. But neither was the continuing opposition to a relaxation of the restrictions on immigration. The tragic experience of those who had been forced to live under the Nazi occupation, though viewed with considerable sympathy, was not enough to overcome a popular unwillingness to relax the established quota system.

Despite all that, there was a significant flow of European Jews into the United States during the immediate postwar years, an inflow made possible not by the adoption of new laws but by a loose interpretation or even indirect evasion of the existing ones. Between 1948 and 1955, the size of the American Jewish community increased by about 429,000, or 9 percent, a result almost entirely of the immigration of refugees from Europe. The number of Jews admitted by the United States was about twice the number admitted by the democracies of the Old World. But at the same time, the American population as a whole was also increasing rapidly, because of the influx of large numbers of migrants from various foreign countries, especially in Latin America, so that the percentage of Jews actually declined from 3.7 in 1947 to 3.1 in 1957. In any case, the number of survivors of the Holocaust who found asylum in the New World, though considerable, was far smaller than the number of survivors who continued to look for asylum.[14]

What finally solved the problem of what to do about the hundreds of thousands of Jews trying to leave Europe was the establishment of the state of Israel. Not that resettlement in the Middle East was the ideal solution for all of them. Many, perhaps even most, would have preferred to cross the Atlantic and find refuge in the New World. But since that was proving increasingly difficult, Israel became, partly by choice, partly by necessity, the destination of the great majority of European Jews trying to emigrate. Once an independent Jewish state was proclaimed in the spring of 1948, barriers to the admission of Jewish immigrants fell. The Holocaust led indirectly to the emergence of the Middle East as one of the two new centers of world Jewry.

The statistical evidence of this momentous change is irrefutable. In January 1933, when Hitler rose to power, only about 200,000 Jews lived in Palestine, most of them ardent Zionists willing to endure hardship and privation or even risk their lives for what appeared to be a noble but unattainable ideal: the establishment of an independent Jewish state in the ancient homeland of the Jews. By 1938, however, their number had more than doubled, to roughly 424,000, a result in large part of the growth of National Socialism in Central Europe. There was a further increase to 622,000 during and immediately after the war, despite the continuing efforts of Downing Street to restrict the admission of Jewish immigrants. And finally, after the proclamation of Israel's independence, a flood of refugees increased the total population of the new state to 1,615,000, the great majority Jewish, by 1955. The number of Jews who found refuge in the Middle East after the war was almost twice the combined number of those who emigrated to Western Europe and those who emigrated to the New World. Israel's Jewish community became the third largest in the world, exceeded only by the one in the United States and the one in the Soviet Union.[15]

This shift in the distribution of world Jewry had a profound effect, not only in the Middle East but in Europe and America as well. By the late 1950s, it had becoame clear that the question of what to do about the survivors of the Nazi genocide had been answered. More than 3 million Jews were still living in the Old World, but they could not or would not emigrate. A small minority remained attached to the culture of their native country or still felt at home in its social environment or continued to participate actively in its economic life. They had no wish to leave. The majority, however, mostly those living in Eastern Europe, recognized as soon as the cold war began that any attempt to emigrate to the democratic states on the Atlantic coast or in the New World would not only arouse the suspicion of the Communist authorities but could lead to severe penalties. Trying to leave became very risky. That was why, after more than a century, the westward flow of European Jews finally came to an end.

The growing realization in Europe and America during the late 1950s that the problem of Jewish refugees had now been solved—indeed, that the "Jewish question" in general had ceased to exist—made possible the transformation of the Nazi genocide into the Holocaust. Those who had survived the anti-Semitic mass murders initiated by the Third Reich gradually ceased to be seen as an endless flood of hungry, impoverished, demoralized, and desperate victims of persecution demanding compensation for what they had lost and what they had suffered, insisting on the return of the property and status that had been theirs before the war, and pounding on the gates of the prosperous democratic states on both sides of the Atlantic, seeking admission without regard for economic limitations or legal restrictions. As it became apparent that the quest of many Jewish survivors of the German occupation for indemnification, asylum, and security was only temporary, that in one way or another most of them had been able to find a new and stable way of life, it also became easier to express sympathy for all they had been forced to endure.

The underlying reason for this change was not always recognized, however. Those who witnessed the gradual fading away of the "Jewish question" were as a rule not aware that this was making possible the emergence of the Holocaust as the central atrocity of the Second World War. Yet in retrospect the connection seems clear. It helps explain why the trials soon after the war of the most important leaders of National Socialism failed to arouse as much popular interest in the destruction of European Jewry as the trial sixteen years later of an obscure bureaucrat who insisted that he was only carrying out the orders he had received from his superiors. It helps explain why Israel's desperate struggle to achieve independence during the 1940s failed to attract as much attention or sympathy in the Western democracies as Israel's victorious wars in defense of independence during the 1960s and 1970s. But most important, it helps explain the growing significance of the Holocaust in the popular perception of the atrocities committed by the Third Reich, a significance reflected in a steady increase in the number of monuments, remembrances, and commemorations dedicated to the Jewish community of Europe which had been so cruelly destroyed.

Still, the emergence of the Holocaust as the most tragic single event of the Second World War was not only the result of a determination to keep alive the memory of a terrible crime committed against millions of innocent victims. It also expressed an often subconscious psychological need of the ethnic compatriots or heirs of those victims to demonstrate to the world the evil consequences of intolerance and prejudice. Keeping alive an awareness of the murderous consequences of anti-Semitic bigotry during the Second World War was likely to encourage the rejection and suppression of that bigotry. In other words, commemoration of the Holocaust was not only a way of remembering a tragic past. It was also a means of ensuring a more tolerant and humane future. It was meant to have subtle but important social consequences.

This conclusion was eloquently expressed in Charles S. Maier's book *History, Holocaust, and German National Identity.* "Former perpetrators and victims," he maintained, "have been locked into a special relationship." Whatever public debts or material compensations were paid did not really matter. "Confessional memory is demanded as the only valid reparation." The victims' anguish provided a claim on "official memory" and thus came to be perceived as a "valuable possession." And because of that, other peoples also began to seek the "status of victimhood." After all, Jews were not the only minority in America that had had to endure hostility and discrimination. Weren't African Americans, Native Americans, Latin Americans, Japanese Americans, Arab Americans, and Southeast Asian Americans also victims of intolerance and oppression? Did they not also have to suffer racist insults and violent attacks? No wonder that some of those minorities began to claim a Holocaust of their own, also spelled with a capital *H*.[16]

A few years later, Maier elaborated on this theme in an article contending that the commemoration of the Holocaust was a branch of what might be called the "memory industry." Formal remembrances of historic tragedies are not intended solely to remind the present generation of what happened to a previous generation. They are also a condemnation of current grievances and injustices, whether real or imagined. Imposing museums built to "teach the lessons of the Holocaust," though devoted in some respects to the study of history, are also part of a "memory industry." In other words, "it is the aftermath of memory and only secondarily the pursuit of history that motivates their construction." Their primary purpose is not to recapture the past but to shape the present.[17]

The goal of winning respect, attention, and validation is shared by many minorities in the United States. "Jews, of course, are not the only group demanding attention from others." American politics, according to Maier, has arguably become a competition for "enshrining grievances." Every ethnic community, every social minority wants to gain its share of public honor and public funds by advertising the disabilities and injustices that it has suffered and continues to suffer. "National public life becomes the settlement of a collective malpractice suit in which all citizens are patients and physicians simultaneously." Memories of the past become inseparable from aspirations for the future.[18]

The effect of the Holocaust on public opinion in the Old World has been similar. There is general agreement that the destruction of European Jewry was a terrible crime, unforgettable and unforgivable. Whereas in the United States remorse or guilt derives from an uneasy feeling that the country should perhaps have done more to help save those threatened with extermination, on the continent, especially in the east, remembering the Holocaust also means remembering the collaboration of many local authorities and some local inhabitants in the roundup and deportation of Jews to the death camps. Those are unpleasant memories, accusatory and troubling. Why bring them up? Yet with the passage of time, even the European countries that were allied with the Third Reich and willingly collaborated in the Holocaust began to erect monuments and museums in memory of those who were once seen as devious, unscrupulous aliens but who have now become innocent, pitiful victims.

Yet an unexpressed uneasiness about the growing commemorations on both sides of the Atlantic persisted in the Old World. That the anti-Semitic mass murders committed during the war were a terrible atrocity was acknowledged almost as soon as the war was over. Still, they were not the only atrocity. There were many, many more. Didn't the Germans also kill millions of non-Jews in Eastern Europe? Even in Western Europe, in France and Belgium and the Netherlands, countless innocents died cruelly and unjustly under the German occupation. Did they not deserve as much sympathy, as much remembrance as the Jews who perished during the Holocaust? And still other questions, usually unspoken, accompanied the spoken ones. Could it be that Jews are more experienced and skilled in using the injustices they have endured to gain compassion and compensation? Could it be that they are simply better than non-Jews at squeezing advantage out of hardship and misfortune? Questions of that sort continued to be asked, though only in whispers, at the same time that monuments and museums were rising and spreading on the continent.

Still other reasons, practical rather than psychological or emotional, account for the widespread remembrances in the Old World and the New of the destruction of European Jewry. The overthrow of the Third Reich and the reestablishment of democratic government in the western half of the continent initiated a long quest for restitution by those who had been deprived of their possessions by the Nazi regime. In most cases the process was simple, because the evidence of ownership was clear. But there were also numerous legal disputes over property that might have been obtained by the German authorities through coercion or confiscation. Some of those disputes continued to drag on through the legal system for half a century and more.

Here, commiseration with the victims of the Holocaust proved useful to those or the heirs of those who sought the return of possessions that they claimed were rightfully theirs. It meant that German, Austrian, or Swiss banks involved in litigation over accounts that might have belonged to murdered Jews often yielded in order to avoid the charge that they were still trying to profit from the Nazi genocide. Even works of art that had changed hands three or four times since the war occasionally became a subject of contention, with the heirs of the original Jewish owners seeking the return of what they believed legally belonged to them. Although the paintings, sculptures, or furnishings in such cases had as a rule been bought by museums or private collectors in good faith, without knowledge of their origin or history, they were often restored to the descendants of their original owners as an expression of condemnation of the Holocaust. No one wanted to be seen as the beneficiary of National Socialism.

Indeed, many of the slave laborers, both Jewish and non-Jewish, who had been forced to work for companies manufacturing supplies for the German war effort sought and received compensation for what they had suffered. For that matter, some business establishments in the neutral countries and the United States that had had financial dealings with the Third Reich during or even before the war decided to make periodic contributions to organizations assisting the survivors of the Holocaust or supporting the cause of Israel. Their policy was at least partly a form of insurance against possible charges of indifference to the horror of Nazi genocide.

Still, postwar atonements and reparations for the Holocaust were only an incidental result of the final solution to the "Jewish question." The most important effect was a fundamental change in the composition of world Jewry, whose center now shifted, partly to the New World, partly to the

Middle East. The United States, with its large population of Jews, became the heart of the international Jewish community. Not only the numbers of American Jews but also their increasing acculturation, their growing acceptance, and their rising influence in the most powerful nation in the world assured them a dominant position.

Yet the steady assimilation of the Jewish community also altered its traditional character. The end of the long influx of Jews from Europe, especially from Eastern Europe, hastened the adaptation but also the integration of Jews in America. They became increasingly like other Americans in appearance, speech, manner, and outlook. More and more of them were now accepted as part of the establishment. The unique qualities of Jewishness, which had once been a source of popular humor or even ridicule, became less pronounced, less apparent, while the caricatures of those qualities in cartoons, movies, and vaudeville acts steadily declined, not only because of greater public tolerance for ethnic differences but also because of the diminishing display of those differences by Jews. The goal of assimilation and acceptance as equals which American Jews had so diligently but unsuccessfully tried to attain before the war had finally been achieved.

But that achievement also required the abandonment of many characteristically or specifically Jewish forms of belief and conduct. Not only did Jews begin to resemble their non-Jewish compatriots in dress, style, behavior, and thought; they also drew much closer to mainstream America in their values, beliefs, ideas, and ideals. The rigidly orthodox form of Judaism that most immigrants had embraced was now largely replaced by a new reformed variety, similar in many respects to the reformist branches of Protestant Christianity. The left-wing radicalism that many others had brought with them from czarist Russia was gradually replaced by a less militant, more moderate and restrained liberalism. Most important, the religious or ethnic loyalty that had been the foundation of Jewish exclusiveness gradually eroded to the point where marriage between Jews and Christians became fairly common. Partly as the result of a relatively low birthrate, partly as a consequence of marriage with members of other religious or ethnic communities, and partly because of an outright renunciation of Judaism in any form, the size of the Jewish community in America, though numerically slowly increasing, began to diminish proportionately.

As for remembering the East European origin of most American Jews, that became largely limited to the occasional humorous use of some Yiddish word, to the playing of klezmer music for amusement, and to the display of a few fading photographs of exotic-looking ancestors in some Polish or Russian shtetl.

The situation in Israel, the other center of contemporary Jewry, is different. Here Jews are not an accepted and acculturated minority; they are a majority and are determined to remain a majority. To them, the experience of the Jewish community in Europe is a warning, something to be avoided at any cost. That experience had bred a meek compliance and abject submissiveness which those in the newly reestablished Jewish homeland are determined never to accept. Israel is deliberately different from the Jewish communities elsewhere in the world—different in language, culture, character, and belief. Its relatively low birthrate and a diminished influx of immigrants have left it vulnerable to the attacks of neighboring Arab states. But a spirit of resolve and an attitude of unbending militancy have provided it with a level of security that large numbers alone could not achieve. The future of Israel as a center of world Jewry is, or at least seems to be, assured.

In any case, it is beyond doubt that the final solution to the "Jewish question" during the Second World War put an end to a long, tragic chapter of Jewish history characterized by vain hopes and failed aspirations. As for the new chapter that is now beginning, may it have a happier ending than the old one.

Notes

Introduction

1. Maier, "A Surfeit of Memory?," pp. 136, 143.
2. Ibid., pp. 136–37.
3. Ibid., p. 147.
4. Stember et al., *Jews in the Mind of America*, p. 128.
5. Ibid., p. 121.
6. Novick, *Holocaust in American Life*, pp. 85–86.
7. Ibid., pp. 144–45.
8. Ibid., pp. 159–060.

Chapter One: The Siren Song of Emancipation

1. Goldhagen, *Hitler's Willing Executioners*, p. 71.
2. Luther, *Luther's Works*, vol. 47, p. 266.
3. Dohm, *Ueber die bürgerliche Verbesserung der Juden*, pp. 28, 34.
4. Voltaire, *Works*, vol. 10, p. 284.
5. Voltaire, *Correspondence*, vol. 49, pp. 131–32.
6. Dostoyevsky, *Diary of a Writer*, vol. 2, 650.
7. B. Bauer, *Jewish Problem*, p. 63.
8. Marx, *Zur Judenfrage*, pp. 42–43, 45, 49.
9. Mommsen, *Reden und Aufsätze*, pp. 414, 424.
10. Hartenau [Rathenau], "Höre, Israel!," p. 458.
11. Chamberlain, *Foundations of the Nineteenth Century*, vol. 1, pp. 330–31.
12. Drumont, *France juive*, vol. 1, pp. 527, 530.
13. Dühring, *Judenfrage als Frage des Racencharakters*, pp. 2, 4.
14. Meinecke, *German Catastrophe*, p. 32.
15. Ruppin, *Jews in the Modern World*, pp. 26–27.

Chapter Two: Eastern Europe in Crisis

1. Kennan, *From Prague after Munich*, pp. 50–51.
2. Vago, *Shadow of the Swastika*, p. 324.
3. Kennan, *From Prague after Munich*, pp. 152–55.
4. Ibid., p. 150.
5. *Documents on German Foreign Policy, 1918–1945*, vol. 4, pp. 340–41.
6. Ibid., vol. 5, p. 930.
7. Ibid., pp. 931–33.
8. Vago, *Shadow of the Swastika*, p. 268.
9. Ibid., p. 269.
10. Ibid., pp. 412–13.
11. Ibid., pp. 224, 268.
12. Ibid., p. 413.
13. Retinger, *All about Poland*, pp. 65, 67–68.
14. Engel, *In the Shadow of Auschwitz*, pp. 98, 254–55.
15. Vago, *Shadow of the Swastika*, p. 224; Starr, "Jewish Citizenship in Rumania," p. 77.
16. Sir Herbert Emerson, "Report on visit to Prague," January 17, 1939, GBNA, T 160/1324 pt 2 ff 13577/05/3.
17. Parkes, *Emergence of the Jewish Problem*, pp. 140–41; Jedrzejewicz, *Diplomat in Berlin*, p. 411.
18. *New York Times*, December 22, 1938; Strang memorandum, December 9, 1938, GBNA, FO 371/22540.

Chapter Three: A French Predicament

1. Ruppin, *Jews in the Modern World*, p. 26.
2. Ibid.; Mendes-Flohr and Reinharz, *Jew in the Modern World*, p. 696.
3. Mitchell, *European Historical Statistics*, p. 20.
4. Ibid., pp. 20–21, 24.
5. *Statesman's Year-Book, 1931*, pp. 12–13, 16, 67–68, 841–42, 917, 1013, 1016.
6. Ibid., pp. 772, 990, 1072, 1081, 1192, 1222.
7. Ibid., p. 1232.
8. Marrus and Paxton, *Vichy France and the Jews*, p. 209.
9. *Le Temps*, May 19, 1938.
10. Giraudoux, *Pleins pouvoirs*, pp. 65–66.
11. *Le Temps*, May 15, 1938.
12. Ibid.
13. Marrus and Paxton, *Vichy France and the Jews*, p. 40.
14. *Documents on German Foreign Policy*, vol. 5, p. 932.
15. *Le Temps*, May 22, 1938.
16. Brasillach, *Notre avant-guerre*, p. 189.

17. Céline, *Bagatelles,* pp. 181–82, 232, 329.

18. *Le Temps,* May 28, 1938.

19. Centre de Documentation et de Vigilance, *Bulletin d'information,* p. 7.

20. *Le Temps,* May 7, 1938.

21. *Pavés de Paris,* November 11, 1938, p. 13, and December 9, 1938, p. 11; Marrus and Paxton, *Vichy France and the Jews,* p. 43.

22. Parkes, *Emergence of the Jewish Problem,* p. 141.

23. Centre de Documentation et de Vigilance, *Bulletin d'information,* p. 15.

24. *Documents on British Foreign Policy,* pp. 294–95.

Chapter Four:
Britain Wrestles with the Refugee Problem

1. Ruppin, *Jews in the Modern World,* p. 26.

2. Mendes-Flohr and Reinharz, *The Jew in the Modern World,* p. 705.

3. Mitchell, *European Historical Statistics,* pp. 169, 171.

4. Cantril, *Public Opinion,* p. 381.

5. Gallup, *Gallup International Public Opinion Polls,* vol. 1, p. 22.

6. *Documents on German Foreign Policy,* vol. 5, p. 932.

7. Mass-Observaton Archive, "Mass-Observation: Anti-Semitism Survey," February–March 1939, ed. Tom Harrisson, pp. 32, 40, 56, 65, in *Mass Observation Archive,* microfilm. (Brighton, England)

8. Muggeridge, *Sun Never Sets,* pp. 286–88.

9. Lewis, *The Jews, Are They Human?,* pp. 7, 17.

10. Wells, *Anatomy of Frustration,* pp. 176–83.

11. Muggeridge, *Sun Never Sets,* p. 287.

12. *Times* (London), August 20, 1938.

13. *Observer* (London), July 31, 1938.

14. *Daily Express* (London), March 24, 1938.

15. *Sunday Express* (London), June 19, 1938.

16. *Daily Express* (London), November 21, 1938.

17. Great Britain, *Parliamentary Debates,* p. 341:1483.

18. Ibid., p. 341:1458.

19. Ibid., p. 341:1468.

20. Ibid., pp. 345:3068–69.

21. Ibid., pp. 345:3082, 3084.

22. Home Office, minutes of the Home Secretary's meeting with a Jewish deputation, April 1, 1938, GBNA, HO 213/42.

23. *Documents on British Foreign Policy,* vol. 3, p. 295.

24. Central British Fund for World Jewish Relief, "Speeches."

25. Cabinet Conclusions 14/38, March 16, 1938, GBNA, CAB 23/93; Cabinet Conclusions 33/38, July 20, 1938, CAB 23/94; Home Office, Williamson memorandum, October 25, 1938, HO 213/1636.

26. Cabinet Conclusions 14/38, March 16, 1938, GBNA, CAB 23/93.

27. Foreign Office, Makins memorandum, International Assistance to Refugees, May 23, 1938, GBNA, FO371/21749, C5319/2289/18.

28. Foreign Office, Instructions for the delegation to the Evian conference, July 5, 1938, GBNA, FO371/22529, W8885/104/98.

29. Great Britain, *Parliamentary Debates,* p. 345:3082. Cf. *Daily Express* (London), November 21, 1938.

30. *Daily Express* (London), November 21, 1938.

31. Dominions Office, Lord Bledisloe to J. H. Thomas, December 22, 1933, GBNA, DO 57/175/14414/11.

32. Foreign Office, R. Brooke-Popham to Malcolm MacDonald, June 18, 1938, GBNA, FO 371/22534, W12288/104/98; Foreign Office, *Settlement Committee Report* (Nairobi, 1939), p. 72, FO 371/24088.

33. "Demonic Germany," p. 1456.

34. Cabinet Conclusions 33/38, July 20, 1938, GBNA, CAB 23/94.

Chapter Five:
Seeking Asylum in the New World: The United States

1. *Statesman's Year-Book, 1931,* pp. 12, 67–68, 81, 443, 673–74, 784, 842, 1013, 1016, 1086, 1113, 1145, 1202, 1277, 1296, 1312.

2. Mendes-Flohr and Reinharz, *Jew in the Modern World,* p. 707; Ruppin, *Jews in the Modern World,* p. 26.

3. Mendes-Flohr and Reinharz, *Jew in the Modern World,* p. 472.

4. Ibid., p. 705.

5. Ibid., p. 706.

6. *Fortune,* January 1936, pp. 46, 157.

7. Stember et al., *Jews in the Mind of America,* p. 138.

8. Ibid., p. 79.

9. *Documents on German Foreign Policy,* vol. 4, p. 636.

10. Ibid., vol. 5, p. 932.

11. Carl Goerdeler, report on the United States, January 2, 1938, pp. 38–39, NL Goerdeler, 22. Bundesarchiv.

12. "Jews in America," pp. 79, 85, 141.

13. Martin, "Nazis and the Jews," p. 126.

14. "A Need for Light, Not Heat," p. 443.

15. *Christian Science Monitor* (Boston), April 4, 1933.

16. "Noise over the Nazis," pp. 25, 30.

17. *Time,* April 2, 1934, p. 10.

18. *New York Times,* October 22, 1935.

19. *New York Amsterdam News,* April 26, 1933.

20. Cantril, *Public Opinion,* p. 385.

21. "Demonic Germany," p. 1457.

22. Stember et al., *Jews in the Mind of America*, p. 138.
23. "Demonic Germany," p. 1457.
24. Thompson, "Escape in a Frozen World," p. 168.
25. Mendes-Flohr and Reinharz, *Jew in the Modern World*, p. 706.

Chapter Six: Seeking Asylum in the New World: Canada or Latin America?

1. *Statesman's Year-Book, 1931*, pp. 12–13, 16, 841–42.
2. Ibid., pp. 282, 443.
3. Mendes-Flohr and Reinharz, *Jew in the Modern World*, p. 707.
4. Ibid., p. 705.
5. Ruppin, *Jews in the Modern World*, p. 26.
6. Ibid.; Abella and Troper, *None Is Too Many*, p. vi; *Statesman's Year-Book, 1931*, p. 699.
7. Abella and Troper, *None Is Too Many*, pp. 17–18.
8. Canada, *Official Report of Debates*, vol. 1, p. 305.
9. Ibid., p. 428.
10. *Le Devoir* (Montreal), July 28, 1938.
11. Abella and Troper, *None Is Too Many*, pp. 50–51.
12. *Globe and Mail* (Toronto), November 19, 1938.
13. Ibid., November 21, 1938.
14. Dominions Office, Malcolm MacDonald memorandum of meeting with Vincent Massey, November 29, 1938, GBNA, DO 121/2.
15. Canada, Department of External Affairs, *Documents-External Relations*, vol. 6, 1936–1939, p. 837. (National Library of Canada, Amicus #4321887, Ottawa
16. I. Abella and H. Troper, *None Is too Many*, p. 51.
17. *Globe and Mail* (Toronto), November 21, 1938.
18. Ibid.
19. Ibid.
20. *Statesman's Year-Book, 1931*, pp. 12, 16, 67–68, 282, 443, 655, 699, 718, 765, 841–42, 1013, 1016, 1088–89.
21. Ruppin, *Jews in the Modern World*, pp. 26–27.
22. Mendes-Flohr and Reinharz, *Jew in the Modern World*, p. 705.
23. Ruppin, *Jews in the Modern World*, pp. 26–27.
24. Abella and Troper, *None Is Too Many*, p. vi.
25. Ibid.
26. *Documents on German Foreign Policy*, pp. 931–32.
27. High Commission for Refugees (Jewish and Other) Coming from Germany, letter from James G. McDonald to Felix M. Warburg, April 30, 1935, Box 3. Baeck.
28. High Commission for Refugees (Jewish and Other) Coming from Germany, "Summary Report of the Meeting of the Advisory Council of the High Commission, Held in London on July 15th, 1935," p. 3. Baeck.

29. Goldberg, "Immigration Attitudes of Mexicans," p. 3.
30. Domarus, *Hitler: Reden und Proklamationen,* vol. 2, p. 1056.

Chapter Seven: In Search of a Haven

1. Mendes-Flohr and Reinharz, *Jew in the Modern World,* p. 472.
2. Ruppin, *Jews in the Modern World,* p. 26; Marrus, *Holocaust in History,* p. 27.
3. Marrus, *Holocaust in History,* p. 27.
4. Ruppin, *Jews in the Modern World,* p. 26.
5. War Cabinet, memorandum by the Home Secretary, September 23, 1942, GBNA, CAB 66/29/18.
6. Foreign Office, minute by Alexander Cadogan, September 16, 1939, GBNA, FO 371/23105/C16788.
7. Foreign Office, minute by R.T.E. Latham, April 4, 1940, GBNA, FO 371/25240, and Minute by J.E.M. Carvell, April 8, 1940, FO W 2812/38/48.
8. Ministry of Information, memorandum: Plan to Combat the Apathetic Outlook of "What Have *I* Got to Lose if Germany Wins," p. 2, July 25, 1941, GBNA, INF 1/251.
9. Roosevelt, *Public Papers and Addresses,* vol. 6, pp. 410–11.
10. Ibid., vol. 9, p. 643; vol. 10, pp. 226–27, 390.
11. Ibid., vol. 9, p. 517.
12. Stember et al., *Jews in the Mind of America,* p. 79.
13. Ibid., p. 128.
14. Ibid., p. 116.
15. Ibid., p. 121.
16. Ibid., p. 123.
17. Ibid., p. 131.
18. *Fortune,* July 1938, p. 80.
19. Ibid.
20. Cantril, *Public Opinion,* p. 385.
21. Stember et al., *Jews in the Mind of America,* p. 149.
22. *Fortune,* April 1939, p. 102.
23. Ibid.
24. Wagg, "Washington's Stepchild," p. 592.

Chapter Eight: The War of Words

1. *Christian Science Monitor,* June 2, 1939.
2. Wagg, "Washington's Stepchild," p. 594.
3. Ritchie, "Are Refugees a Liability?," p. 320.
4. Leiper, "Those German Refugees," p. 63.
5. Ibid., pp. 19–20.

6. Ibid., p. 20.
7. U.S. Congress, *Admission of German Refugee Children: Joint Hearings*, pp. 22–23.
8. Johnson, "Rising Tide of Anti-Semitism," p. 116.
9. Ibid.
10. Wells, "Future of the Jews," pp. 6–7.
11. E. Roosevelt, "Mrs. Roosevelt Answers Mr. Wells," pp. 4–5.
12. Letters from Eleanor Roosevelt to Sara Delano Roosevelt, January 14, January 16, and October 16, 1918. FDR Library.
13. E. Roosevelt, "Mrs. Roosevelt Answers Mr. Wells," pp. 4–5.
14. Johnson, " Rising Tide of Anti-Semitism," p. 113.
15. Broun, "Shoot the Works," p. 298.
16. Belth, "Problems of Anti-Semitism," pp. 6–7, 18.
17. Ickes, *Secret Diary*, vol. 2, pp. 503–4.
18. *Fortune*, April 1939, p. 102.
19. Fairchild, "Are Refugees a Liability?," p. 317; idem, "Should the Jews Come In?" p. 344.
20. *Milwaukee Journal*, March 30, 1938.
21. U.S. Congress, *Admission of German Refugee Children: Hearings before the Committee on Immigration and Naturalization*, pp. 244–45.
22. Fairchild, "Should the Jews Come In?," pp. 344–45.
23. Ibid., p. 344.
24. "Demonic Germany," p. 1457.
25. *Des Moines Register*, September 11, 1941.
26. Wells, "The Future of the Jews," p. 6.
27. U.S. Congress, *Admission of German Refugee Children: Joint Hearings*, pp. 197–99.
28. Breitman and Kraut, *American Refugee Policy*, p. 110.
29. *Christian Science Monitor* (Boston), June 2, 1939.
30. "Demonic Germany," p. 1457.

Chapter Nine: A Jewish Hush-Hush Strategy

1. Stember et al., *Jews in the Mind of America*, p. 132.
2. Steinberg, "First Principles," pp. 587–88.
3. Wise, *Selected Letters*, p. 233.
4. Levitan, "Leave the Jewish Problem Alone!," p. 555.
5. Trachtenberg, "Stop Fascism," p. 33.
6. Ickes, *Secret Diary*, vol. 2, p. 510.
7. Ibid., pp. 509–10.
8. Stewart, *United States Government Policy on Refugees*, p. 285n1.
9. F. D. Roosevelt, *Roosevelt and Frankfurter*, p. 481.
10. Wise, *Selected Letters*, pp. 229–30.
11. Ickes, *Secret Diary*, vol. 2, pp. 470–71.

12. Letter from Felix Frankfurter to Jacob Billikopf, November 15, 1938. Frankfurter Papers, LOC.
13. Letter from Stephen S. Wise to Frances Perkins, January 7, 1937. Wise Papers, AJHS.
14. Bloom, *Autobiography,* p. 260.
15. *Time,* April 2, 1934, p. 10.
16. Lookstein, *Were We Our Brothers' Keepers?,* p. 97.
17. Ibid., pp. 96–97.
18. Ickes, *Secret Diary,* vol. 2, pp. 342–43.
19. Memorandum from James L. Houghteling to Franklin D. Roosevelt, January 5, 1940. FDR Library.
20. Memorandum from Samuel I. Rosenman to Franklin D. Roosevelt, December 5, 1938. FDR Library.
21. Steinberg, "First Principles," p. 587; Lestschinsky, "Where Do We Stand?," p. 5.
22. Stewart, *United States Government Policy,* pp. 4–5.
23. Letter from Cyrus Adler to Abram C. Joseph, November 22, 1933. AJC.
24. Letter from Felix Frankfurter to Charles E. Wyzanski, April 18, 1938. Wyzanski Papers, Harvard Law.
25. Wise, *Challenging Years,* p. 238.
26. Letter from Felix Frankfurter to Jacob Billikopf, January 8, 1935. Frankfurter Papers, LOC; Wise, *As I See It,* pp. 123–24; Memorandum from Samuel I. Rosenman to Franklin D. Roosevelt, December 5, 1938. FDR Library.
27. Stewart, *United States Government Policy,* pp. 523–24.
28. Memorandum from Samuel I. Rosenman to Franklin D. Roosevelt, December 5, 1938. FDR Library.; Hand, *Counsel and Advise,* p. 307n35.
29. Wise, *As I See It,* p. 109.
30. Mendes-Flohr and Reinharz, *Jew in the Modern World,* p. 706.

Chapter Ten: Scylla, Charybdis, and Washington, D.C.

1. F. D. Roosevelt, *Public Papers,* vol. 6, pp. 410–11.
2. Ickes, *Secret Diary,* vol. 2, p. 389.
3. Ibid., vol. 3, pp. 56–57.
4. Ibid., p. 644.
5. Memorandum from James G. McDonald to Franklin D. Roosevelt, September 26, 1939. FDR Library.
6. Wise, *Selected Letters,* p. 242.
7. Kirchwey, "State Department versus Political Refugees," p. 649.
8. Kirchwey, "Scandal in the State Department," p. 45.
9. Fry, "Our Consuls at Work," p. 507.
10. Ibid., p. 508.
11. Wagg, "Washington's Stepchild," p. 594.
12. "Don't Appease Japan!," p. 843.

13. "Slamming the Door," p. 873.

14. "State Department Appeasers," p. 106.

15. Fry, "Our Consuls at Work," p. 509.

16. Ibid., p. 507.

17. Ibid.

18. Ibid., p. 508.

19. "State Department Appeasers," p. 106.

20. Long, *War Diary,* p. 162.

21. Ibid., pp. 225–26.

22. Ibid., p. 174.

23. Ibid., p. 175.

24. Ickes, *Secret Diary,* vol. 2, p. 352.

25. Ibid., vol. 3, p. 229.

26. Ibid., vol. 2, pp. 695–96.

27. Thompson, "Escape in a Frozen World," p. 168.

Chapter Eleven: The Start of a Genocide

1. Corsten, *Kölner Aktenstücke zur Lage der katholischen Kirche,* p. 269.

2. Schäfer, *Landesbischof D. Wurm und der nationalsozialistische Staat,* pp. 159–61.

3. Ibid., pp. 164–65.

4. Laqueur, *Terrible Secret,* p. 164.

5. Engel, *Facing a Holocaust,* pp. 37–38.

6. Retinger, *All about Poland,* pp. 67–68.

7. Engel, *In the Shadow of Auschwitz,* p. 123.

8. *Akten zur deutschen auswärtigen Politik,* vol. 1, pp. 132–33.

9. Laqueur, *Terrible Secret,* p. 69.

10. Ibid., pp. 69–70.

11. Ibid., pp. 70, 245n5.

12. Goebbels, *Diaries,* p. 241.

13. Ministry of Information, memorandum: Plan to Combat the Apathetic Outlook of "What Have *I* Got to Lose if Germany Wins," p. 2, July 25, 1941, GBNA, INF 1/251.

14. War Cabinet, memorandum by the Home Secretary, September 23, 1942, GBNA, CAB 66/29/18.

15. *Foreign Relations of the United States: Diplomatic Papers,* 1943, vol. 1, p. 134.

16. Cantril, *Public Opinion,* p. 383.

17. Stember et al., *Jews in the Mind of America,* p. 122.

18. McKenzie, "Atrocities in World War II," p. 270.

19. Wise, *Personal Letters,* pp. 260–61.

20. "Horror Stories from Poland," pp. 1518–19.

21. Wise, *As I See It,* p. 121.

22. *New York Times,* March 2, 1943.

23. Ibid.
24. Kirchwey, "While the Jews Die," p. 366.
25. *New York Times*, March 2, 1943.
26. Wise, *Challenging Years*, p. 227.
27. Morgenthau, " Morgenthau Diaries VI," pp. 22–23.
28. Wise, *Challenging Years*, p. 276.
29. Morgenthau, "Morgenthau Diaries VI," p. 22.

Chapter Twelve: Militant Jews,
Circumspect Jews, and Doomed Jews

1. Ruppin, *Jews in the Modern World*, pp. 26–27; Mendes-Flohr and Reinharz, *Jew in the Modern World*, p. 696.
2. Mendes-Flohr and Reinharz, *Jew in the Modern World*, p. 696.
3. Ibid.; Ruppin, *Jews in the Modern World*, p. 26.
4. Mendes-Flohr and Reinharz, *Jew in the Modern World*, p. 696.
5. Ibid.
6. Ibid.; Ruppin, *Jews in the Modern World*, p. 26.
7. Mendes-Flohr and Reinharz, *Jew in the Modern World*, p. 696.
8. Theodore S. Hamerow, "The Hidden Holocaust," *Commentary*, March 1985, p. 33.
9. *Jewish Outlook*, June 1944, p. 4.
10. Bublick, "The Year 5705," pp. 5–6.
11. Ben-Gurion, "Before the Tribunal of History," p. 3.
12. Wyman, *America and the Holocaust*, vol. 2, p. 267; vol. 3, p. 11; vol. 8, p. 44.
13. Long, *War Diary*, p. 283.
14. Johan J. Smertenko to Franklin D. Roosevelt, July 24, 1944. FDR Library.
15. Wyman, *America and the Holocaust*, vol. 2, p. 267.
16. Ibid., vol. 3, p. 11.
17. Ibid., vol. 8, p. 44.
18. Long, *War Diary*, p. 283.
19. Wyman, *America and the Holocaust*, vol. 8, p. 232.
20. Allport, "Bigot in Our Midst," pp. 582–83.
21. Eastman, "A Reply to Screamers," pp. 204–5.
22. Long, *War Diary*, p. 336.
23. Wyman, *America and the Holocaust*, vol. 9, pp. 4–5.
24. Bloom, *Autobiography*, pp. 273–74.
25. Wyman, *America and the Holocaust*, vol. 1, pp. 79, 225, 228.
26. Hassett, *Off the Record with F.D.R.*, pp. 209–10; Wyman, *America and the Holocaust*, vol. 5, p. 82.
27. Wyman, *America and the Holocaust*, vol. 5, p. 82; vol. 8, p. 166; Hassett, *Off the Record with F.D.R.*, p. 210.
28. Wyman, *America and the Holocaust*, vol. 9, pp. 14–15.

29. Ickes, *Secret Diary*, vol. 2, p. 676.
30. *Foreign Relations of the United States: Conferences at Washington and Casablanca*, p. 608.

Chapter Thirteen: A Statecraft of
Carefully Calibrated Compassion

1. *Foreign Relations of the United States: Diplomatic Papers*, vol. 1, p. 321.
2. Ibid.; Long, *War Diary*, p. 307.
3. Wyman, *America and the Holocaust*, vol. 8, p. 56.
4. *PM*, April 30, 1943.
5. U.S. Congress, *United States Statutes at Large*, pp. 721–22.
6. *Foreign Relations of the United States: Diplomatic Papers*, 1944, vol. 1, pp. 1064–65.
7. *New York Times*, July 15, 1944.
8. Ibid., February 2, 1945.
9. Wise, *Challenging Years*, p. 227; *New York Times*, July 22, 1942.
10. Wyman, *America and the Holocaust*, vol. 6, pp. 316–17.
11. Ibid., vol. 9, pp. 14–15.
12. Ruppin, *Jews in the Modern World*, p. 26.
13. Great Britain, *Parliamentary Debates*, 1942–1943, 5th ser., pp. 385:2082–83.
14. Great Britain, *Parliamentary Debates*, 1943–1944, 5th ser., pp. 398:1561–63.
15. *Foreign Relations of the United States: Diplomatic Papers*, 1943, vol. 3, p. 38.
16. Ibid., vol. 1, p. 134.
17. Laqueur, *Terrible Secret*, pp. 69–70.
18. Gitelman, "Soviet Reactions," p. 18.
19. Lawrence, *Six Presidents*, pp. 100–101.
20. Lipstadt, *Beyond Belief*, p. 261.
21. *New York Times*, February 3, 1945.
22. Ibid., May 8, 1945.
23. *Foreign Relations of the United States: Diplomatic Papers*, 1943, vol. 1, p. 769.
24. *Winnipeg Free Press*, April 3, 1943.
25. Dominions Office, Note of Meeting with Dominion High Commissioners, August 10, 1944, GBNA, DO 121/14.
26. Cantril, *Public Opinion*, p. 309.
27. Wyman, *America and the Holocaust*, vol. 1, p. 164.
28. Ibid., vol. 11, p. 39.
29. Ibid, p. 66.
30. Ibid., pp. 65–66, 75.
31. Ibid., p. 75.
32. Ibid., p. 65.
33. Ibid., p. 75.
34. Ibid., pp. 129–30.
35. Feingold, *Politics of Rescue*, pp. 228–29.

36. U.S. Congress, *Congressional Record*, Part 7, p. 9679.
37. Wyman, *America and the Holocaust*, vol. 3, p. 70.
38. Ibid., p. 18.
39. Ibid., p. 80.
40. *Foreign Relations of the United States: Diplomatic Papers*, 1943, vol. 1, p. 134.
41. Bloom, *Autobiography*, p. 273.
42. *Foreign Relations of the United States: Diplomatic Papers*, 1943, vol. 1, pp. 177–78.
43. Ibid., p. 179.
44. U.S. Congress, "Caring for Refugees," pp. 1, 3.
45. Foreign Office, United Kingdom Delegates to the Bermuda Conference on the Refugee Problem to Mr. Eden, June 28, 1943, GBNA, W 7541/6711/48.

Chapter Fourteen: Should More Have Been Done to Stop the Holocaust?

1. Feingold, "Who Shall Bear Guilt," p. 271.
2. Y. Bauer, *American Jewry and the Holocaust*, p. 458.
3. Novick, *Holocaust in American Life*, p. 58.
4. Letter from Johan J. Smertenko to Franklin D. Roosevelt, July 24, 1944. FDR Library.
5. Wise, *Selected Letters*, p. 258.
6. Cantril, *Public Opinion*, p. 383.
7. Gallup, *Gallup Poll: Public Opinion*, vol. 1, p. 472.
8. Stember et al., *Jews in the Mind of America*, p. 141.
9. U.S. House of Representatives, Committee on International Relations, *Selected Executive Session Hearings of the Committee, 1943–50*, vol. 2, *Problems of World War II and Its Aftermath*, part 2 (Washington, D.C.: Government Printing Office, 1976), pp. 15–16, 196.
10. Long, *War Diary*, p. 307.
11. U.S. House of Representatives, *Problems of World War II*, p. 196.
12. Wise, *As I See It*, p. 77.
13. Wise, *Selected Letters*, p. 258; Wyman, *America and the Holocaust*, vol. 1, p. 255.
14. Wyman, *America and the Holocaust*, vol. 8, p. 153.
15. Ibid., vol. 13, p. 215.
16. Telegram from American Legation, Bern, to Secretary of State, Washington, June 24, 1944; Letter from John J. McCloy, Assistant Secretary, War Department, to John W. Pehle, Executive Director, War Refugee Board, July 4, 1944. FDR Library.
17. J. W. Pehle to John J. McCloy, November 8, 1944; McCloy to Pehle, November 18, 1944. FDR Library.
18. Letter from John J. McCloy, Assistant Secretary, War Department, to Elmer Davis, Director, Office of War Information, April 21, 1943, USNA, RG 208, Entry 1, Box 3, Folder "Motion Pictures 1943."
19. Ibid.

20. Wyman, *America and the Holocaust*, vol. 13, pp. 108–9.

21. *Foreign Relations of the United States: Diplomatic Papers, 1944*, vol. 1, pp. 1174–75.

22. Wyman, *America and the Holocaust*, vol. 9, p. 18.

23. Ibid., p. 20.

24. Ibid., vol. 11, p. 418.

25. Koestler, "Nightmare," pp. 5, 30.

26. Foreign Office, Letter from Chief Rabbi J. H. Hertz to Churchill, May 8, 1944, GBNA, FO 371/42758.

27. Premier Papers, Letter from Pierson Dixon to John Martin, May 16, 1944, GBNA, PREM 4/51/8.

28. Premier Papers, War Cabinet's Endorsement of a Negative Response to Chief Rabbi J. H. Hertz, June 12, 1944, ibid.

29. Foreign Office, Letter from Anthony Eden to Chief Rabbi J. H. Hertz, June 28, 1944, GBNA, FO 371/42758.

30. Wyman, *America and the Holocaust*, vol. 8, pp. 43–44.

31. Ibid., vol. 8, p. 44.

Chapter Fifteen: The Twilight of European Jewry

1. Mendes-Flohr and Reinharz, *Jew in the Modern World*, p. 696; Ruppin, *Jews in the Modern World*, p. 26.

2. Engel, "Patterns of Anti-Jewish Violence in Poland," pp. 49–50.

3. United Nations, General Assembly, p. 125.

4. Cantril, *Public Opinion*, p. 384.

5. Ibid.

6. Ibid.

7. Ibid., p. 388.

8. Minutes of the War Cabinet Committee on Refugees, May 16, 1945, GBNA, CAB 95/15.

9. Ruppin, *Jews in the Modern World*, p. 26; *World Almanac and Book of Facts, 1949*, p. 204.

10. Cantril, *Public Opinion*, p. 388.

11. Ibid., p. 309.

12. Ibid., p. 387.

13. Stember et al., *Jews in the Mind of America*, pp. 60–61.

14. Ibid.

15. *World Almanac and Book of Facts, 1949*, p. 204; *World Almanac and Book of Facts, 1957*, p. 328.

16. Mendes-Flohr and Reinharz, *Jew in the Modern World*, p. 696; *World Almanac and Book of Facts, 1941*, p. 510; *World Almanac and Book of Facts, 1949*, p. 204; *World Almanac and Book of Facts, 1957*, p. 328.

17. Mendes-Flohr and Reinharz, *Jew in the Modern World*, p. 696.

18. Ibid.

19. Ruppin, *Jews in the Modern World,* p. 26; *World Almanac and Book of Facts, 1941,* p. 510; *World Almanac and Book of Facts, 1957,* p. 328.
20. Ruppin, *Jews in the Modern World,* p. 27; *World Almanac and Book of Facts, 1941,* p. 510; *World Almanac and Book of Facts, 1949,* p. 204; *World Almanac and Book of Facts, 1957,* p. 328.
21. Friesel, *Atlas of Modern Jewish History,* p. 132; Mendes-Flohr and Reinharz, *Jew in the Modern World,* p. 472.
22. Mendes-Flohr and Reinharz, *Jew in the Modern World,* p. 472.
23. Ibid.; *World Almanac and Book of Facts, 1949,* p. 204; *World Almanac and Book of Facts, 1957,* p. 328.
24. Friesel, *Atlas of Modern Jewish History,* p. 130.

Chapter Sixteen: The Emergence of the Holocaust

1. Gallup, *Gallup Poll,* vol. 1, p. 604.
2. *World Almanac and Book of Facts, 1941,* p. 510; Mendes-Flohr and Reinharz, *Jew in the Modern World,* p. 696; Ruppin, *Jews in the Modern World,* p. 26.
3. Stember et al., *Jews in the Mind of America,* pp. 60–61.
4. Ibid.
5. Ibid., p. 121.
6. Ibid., pp. 54, 65.
7. Ibid., p. 94.
8. Ibid., p. 104.
9. Ibid., p. 96.
10. Ibid., p. 106.
11. Novick, *Holocaust in American Life,* pp. 85–86.
12. Ibid., p. 168.
13. *World Almanac and Book of Facts, 1949,* p. 204; *World Almanac and Book of Facts, 1957,* p. 328.
14. *World Almanac and Book of Facts, 1949,* p. 204; *World Almanac and Book of Facts, 1957,* p. 328; Stember et al., *Jews in the Mind of America,* p. 354.
15. Ruppin, *Jews in the Modern World,* p. 27; *World Almanac and Book of Facts, 1941,* p. 510; *World Almanac and Book of Facts, 1949,* p. 204; *World Almanac and Book of Facts, 1957,* p. 328.
16. Maier, *The Unmasterable Past,* pp. 160–61.
17. Maier, "A Surfeit of Memory?," p. 143.
18. Ibid., p. 147.

Bibliography

ABBREVIATIONS OF SOURCES OF ARCHIVAL MATERIAL

AJC	American Jewish Committee Archives YIVO Institute for Jewish Research, New York, New York
AJHS	American Jewish Historical Society, New York, New York
Baeck	Leo Baeck Instititute, New York
Bundersarchiv	Bundesarchiv (German National Archives), Koblenz
FDR Library	Franklin D. Roosevelt Library, Hyde Park, New York
GBNA	National Archives of the United Kingdom, Kew
Harvard Law	Harvard Law School Library, Special Collections Department, Cambridge, Massachusetts
LOC	Library of Congress, Washington, D.C.
USNA	National Archives of the United States, College Park, Maryland

Abella, Irving, and Harold Troper. *None Is Too Many: Canada and the Jews of Europe, 1933-1948*. New York, 1982.

Akten zur deutschen auswärtigen Politik, 1918–1945. Series E. Göttingen, 1969-1979. 8 vols.

Allport, Gordon W. "The Bigot in Our Midst: An Analysis of His Psychology." *Commonweal*, October 6, 1944.

Bauer, Bruno. *The Jewish Problem*. Translated by Helen Lederer. Cincinnati, 1958.

Bauer, Yehuda. *American Jewry and the Holocaust: The American Jewish Joint Distribution Committee, 1939-1945*. Detroit, 1981.

Belth, Norton. "Problems of Anti-Semitism in the United States." *Contemporary Jewish Record*, May-June 1939.

Ben-Gurion, David. "Before the Tribunal of History." *Zionist Review*, September 22, 1944.

Bloom, Sol. *The Autobiography of Sol Bloom.* New York, 1948.

Brasillach, Robert. *Notre avant-guerre.* Paris, 1941.

Breitman, Richard, and Alan M. Kraut. *American Refugee Policy and European Jewry, 1933-1945.* Bloomington, 1987.

Broun, Heywood. "Shoot the Works: I Can Hear You Plainly." *New Republic,* October 18, 1939.

Browne, Lewis. "What Can the Jews Do?" *Virginia Quarterly Review,* Spring 1939.

Bublick, Gedaliah. "The Year 5705." *Jewish Outlook,* September 1944.

Canada. Department of External Affairs. *Documents-External Relations.* Vol. 6: 1936-1939. National Library of Canada, Amicus #4321887, Ottawa.

Canada. House of Commons. *Official Report of Debates.* 4th session, 18th Parliament. 1939.

Cantril, Hadley, ed. *Public Opinion, 1935-1946.* Princeton, N.J., 1951.

Céline, Louis-Ferdinand. *Bagatelles pour un massacre.* Paris, 1937.

Central British Fund for World Jewish Relief. "Speeches Delivered at the Anglo-Jewish Conference Convened by the Council for German Jewry at the Dorchester Hotel on Sunday, March 15, 1936." In *The Jewish People from Holocaust to Nationhood: Archives of the Central British Fund for World Jewish Relief, 1933-1960.* Reading: CBFWJF, 1989, Microfilm Collection, Reel 4, File 15.

Centre de Documentation et de Vigilance. *Bulletin d'information,* October 6, 1938. New York: Jewish Theological Seminary.

Chamberlain, Houston Stewart. *The Foundations of the Nineteenth Century.* Translated by John Lees. London, 1911.

Corsten, Wilhelm, ed. *Kölner Aktenstücke zur Lage der katholischen Kirche in Deutschland, 1933-1945.* Cologne, 1949.

"Demonic Germany and the Predicament of Humanity." *Christian Century,* November 30, 1938.

Documents on British Foreign Policy, 1919–1939. 3rd series, vol. 3.

Documents on German Foreign Policy, 1918-1945. Series D, vols. 4 and 5. Washington, D.C., 1949-64.

Dohm, Christian Wilhelm. *Ueber die bürgerliche Verbesserung der Juden.* Berlin, 1781.

Domarus, Max, ed. *Hitler: Reden und Proklamationen, 1932-1945.* Wiesbaden, 1973. 2 vols.

"Don't Appease Japan!" *New Republic,* June 23, 1941.

Dostoyevsky, F. M. *The Diary of a Writer.* Translated by Boris Brasol. New York, 1949. 2 vols.

Drumont, Édouard. *La France juive.* Paris, 1986. 2 vols.

Dühring, Eugen. *Die Judenfrage als Frage des Racencharakters und seiner Schädlichkeiten für Völkerexistenz, Sitte und Cultur.* 5th ed. Berlin, 1901.

Eastman, Fred. "A Reply to Screamers." *Christian Century,* February 16, 1944.

Engel, David. *Facing a Holocaust: The Polish Government-in-Exile and the Jews, 1943-1945.* Chapel Hill, N.C., 1993.

———. "Patterns of Anti-Jewish Violence in Poland, 1944-1946." *Yad Vashem Studies* 26 (1998).

————. *In the Shadow of Auschwitz: The Polish Government-in-Exile and the Jews, 1939-1942.* Chapel Hill, N.C., 1987.

Epstein, M., ed. *The Statesman's Year-Book: Statistical and Historical Annual of the States of the World for the Year 1931.* London, 1931.

Fairchild, Henry Pratt. "Are Refugees a Liability? A Debate: I--New Burdens for America." *Forum and Century,* January-June 1939.

————. "Should the Jews Come In?" *New Republic,* January 25, 1939.

Feingold, Henry L. *The Politics of Rescue: The Roosevelt Administration and the Holocaust, 1938-1945.* New Brunswick, N.J., 1970.

————. "Who Shall Bear Guilt for the Holocaust: The Human Dilemma." *American Jewish History,* March 1979.

Foreign Relations of the United States: The Conferences at Washington, 1941-1942, and Casablanca, 1943.

Foreign Relations of the United States: Diplomatic Papers, 1943.

Foreign Relations of the United States: Diplomatic Papers, 1944.

Friesel, Evyatar, ed. *Atlas of Modern Jewish History.* New York, 1990.

Fry, Varian. "Our Consuls at Work." *Nation,* May 2, 1942.

Gallup, George H., ed. *The Gallup International Public Opinion Polls: Great Britain 1937-1975.* New York, 1976. 2 vols.

————. *The Gallup Poll: Public Opinion, 1935-1971.* New York, 1972. 3 vols.

Giraudoux, Jean. *Pleins pouvoirs.* Paris, 1939.

Gitelman, Zvi. "Soviet Reactions to the Holocaust, 1945-1991." In *The Holocaust in the Soviet Union: Studies and Sources on the Destruction of the Jews in the Nazi-Occupied Territories of the USSR, 1941-1945.* Edited by Lucjan Dobroszycki and Jeffrey S. Gurock. Armonk, N.Y., M. E. Sharpe, 1993.

Goebbels, Joseph. *The Goebbels Diaries, 1942-1943.* Edited by Louis P. Lochner. New York, 1948.

Goldberg, Nathan. "Immigration Attitudes of Mexicans: An Insight." *Rescue: Information Bulletin of the Hebrew Sheltering and Immigrant Aid Society (HIAS),* July-August 1945.

Goldhagen, Daniel Jonah. *Hitler's Willing Executioners: Ordinary Germans and the Holocaust.* New York, 1996.

Great Britain. House of Commons. *Parliamentary Debates: 1938–1939.* 5th ser.

————. *Parliamentary Debates: 1942–1943.* 5th ser.

————. *Parliamentary Debates: 1943–1944.* 5th ser.

Hand, Samuel B. *Counsel and Advise: A Political Biography of Samuel I. Rosenman.* New York, 1979.

Hartenau, W. [Walter Rathenau]. "Höre, Israel!" *Die Zukunft* 18 (1897).

Hassett, William D. *Off the Record with F.D.R., 1942-1945.* New Brunswick, N.J., 1958.

"Horror Stories from Poland." *Christian Century,* December 9, 1942.

"Humane Judenbehandlung durch Demokratien?" Der Weltkampf: Monatsschrift für Weltpolitik, völkische Kultur und Judenfrage in aller Welt 16 (1939).

Ickes, Harold L. *The Secret Diary of Harold L. Ickes.* New York, 1953–1954. 3 vols.

Jedrzejewicz, Waclaw, ed. *Diplomat in Berlin, 1933-1939: Papers and Memoirs of Jozef Lipski, Ambassador of Poland.* New York, 1968.

"Jews in America." *Fortune,* February 1936.

Johnson, Alvin. "The Rising Tide of Anti-Semitism." *Survey Graphic,* February 1939.

Kennan, George F. *From Prague after Munich: Diplomatic Papers, 1938–1940.* Princeton, N.J.: Princeton University Press, 1968.

Kirchwey, Freda. "A Scandal in the State Department." *Nation,* July 19, 1941.

———. "State Department versus Political Refugees." *Nation,* December 28, 1940.

———. "While the Jews Die." *Nation,* March 13, 1943.

Koestler, Arthur. "The Nightmare That Is a Reality." *New York Times Magazine,* January 9, 1944.

Kushner, Tony. *The Holocaust and the Liberal Imagination: A Social and Cultural History.* Oxford, 1994.

Laqueur, Walter. *The Terrible Secret: An Investigation of the Suppression of Information about Hitler's "Final Solution."* London, 1980.

Lawrence, Bill. *Six Presidents, Too Many Wars.* New York, 1972.

Lewis, Wyndham. *The Jews, Are They Human?* London, 1939.

Leiper, Henry Smith, "Those German Refugees." *Current History.* May 1939.

Lestschinsky, Jacob. "Where Do We Stand?" *Congress Bulletin,* June 16, 1939.

Levitan, Albert. "Leave the Jewish Problem Alone!" *Christian Century,* April 25, 1934.

Lipstadt, Deborah E. *Beyond Belief: The American Press and the Coming of the Holocaust, 1933-1945.* New York, 1986.

Long, Breckingrudge. *The War Diary of Breckinridge Long: Selections from the Years 1939-1944.* Edited by Fred L. Israel. Lincoln: University of Nebraska Press, 1966.

Lookstein, Haskel. *Were We Our Brothers' Keepers? The Public Response of American Jews to the Holocaust, 1938-1944.* New York, 1985.

Luther, Martin. *Luther's Works.* Edited by Jaroslav Pelikan and Helmut T. Lehmann. St. Louis, 1955–1976. 54 vols.

Maier, Charles S. "A Surfeit of Memory? Reflections on History, Melancholy and Denial." *History and Memory* 5, no. 2 (1993).

———. *The Unmasterable Past: History, Holocaust, and German National Identity.* Cambridge, Mass., 1988.

Marrus, Michael R. *The Holocaust in History.* New York, 1987.

Marrus, Michael R., and Robert O. Paxton. *Vichy France and the Jews.* New York, 1981.

Martin, Edward S. "The Nazis and the Jews." *Harper's Magazine,* June 1933.

Marx, Karl. *Zur Judenfrage.* Edited by Stefan Grossmann. Berlin, 1919.

Mass-Observation Archive. "Mass-Observation: Anti-Semitism Survey." Edited by Tom Harrisson. Brighton, England: Mass-Observation, February–March 1939.

———. "Mass-Observation: Post-Mosley Questionnaire." Edited by Tom Harrisson. Brighton, England: Mass-Observation, January 1944.

———. "Report on British Attitudes toward Various Nationalities, December 10, 1940." Edited by Tom Harrisson. File Report 523B. Brighton, England: Mass-Observation.

McKenzie, Vernon. "Atrocities in World War II: What Can We Believe?" *Journalism Quarterly*, September 1942.

Meinecke, Friedrich. *The German Catastrophe: Reflections and Recollections.* Translated by Sidney B. Fay. Cambridge, Mass., 1950.

Mendes-Flohr, Paul, and Jehuda Reinharz, eds. *The Jew in the Modern World: A Documentary History.* 2nd ed. New York: Oxford University Press, 1995.

Mitchell, B. R. *European Historical Statistics, 1750-1970.* New York, 1975.

Mommsen, Theodor. *Reden und Aufsätze.* Berlin, 1905.

Morgenthau, Henry, Jr. "The Morgenthau Diaries VI—The Refugee Run-Around." *Collier's*, November 1, 1947.

Muggeridge, Malcolm. *The Sun Never Sets: The Story of England in the Nineteen Thirties.* New York, 1940.

"A Need for Light, Not Heat." *Christian Century*, April 5, 1933.

Neilson, William Allan. "'Minorities' in Our Midst." *Survey Graphic*, February 1939.

"Noise over the Nazis." *Current History*, May 1937.

Novick, Peter. *The Holocaust in American Life.* Boston: Little, Brown, 1999.

Orwell, George. *The Collected Essays, Journalism and Letters of George Orwell.* Edited by Sonia Orwell and Ian Angus. London, 1968. 4 vols.

Parkes, James. *The Emergence of the Jewish Problem, 1878-1939.* London, 1946.

Retinger, J. H., ed. *All about Poland: Facts, Figures, Documents.* London, 1941.

Ringelblum, Emmanuel. *Polish-Jewish Relations during the Second World War.* Edited by Joseph Kermish and Shmuel Krakowski. Jerusalem, 1974.

Ritchie, Frank. "Are Refugees a Liability? A Debate: II—America Needs Them." *Forum and Century*, June 1939.

Roosevelt, Eleanor. "Mrs. Roosevelt Answers Mr. Wells on the Future of the Jews." *Liberty*, December 31, 1938.

Roosevelt, Franklin D. *The Public Papers and Addresses of Franklin D. Roosevelt.* Edited by Samuel I. Rosenman. New York, 1938–1950. 13 vols.

———. *Roosevelt and Frankfurter: Their Correspondence, 1928-1945.* Edited by Max Freedman. Boston, 1967.

Ruppin, Arthur. *The Jews in the Modern World.* London, 1934.

Samuel, Maurice. *The Great Hatred.* New York, 1940.

Schäfer, Gerhard, ed. *Landesbischof D. Wurm und der nationalsozialistische Staat, 1940-1945.* Stuttgart, 1968.

"Slamming the Door on the Refugees." *New Republic*, June 30, 1941.

Starr, Joshua. "Jewish Citizenship in Rumania (1878-1940)." *Jewish Social Studies* 3 (1941).

"State Department Appeasers." *New Republic*, July 28, 1941.

Steinberg, Milton. "First Principles for American Jews." *Contemporary Jewish Record*, December 1941.

Stember, Charles Herbert, et al. *Jews in the Mind of America.* New York, 1966.

Stewart, Barbara McDonald. *United States Government Policy on Refugees from Nazism, 1933-1940.* New York, 1982.

Thompson, Dorothy. "Escape in a Frozen World." *Survey Graphic*, February 1939.

Trachtenberg, Joshua. "Stop Fascism: Preserve Democracy." In *How to Combat Anti-Semitism in America*. New York, 1937.

U.S. Congress. *Congressional Record. Admission of German Refugee Children: Joint Hearings before a Subcommittee of the Committee on Immigration United States Senate and a Subcommittee on Immigration and Naturalization House of Representatives*. 76th Congress, 1st Session. April 20 and 22, 1939.

U.S. Congress. *Congressional Record. Admission of German Refugee Children: Hearings before the Committee on Immigration and Naturalization, House of Representatives*. 76th Congress, 1st Session. June 1, 1939.

U.S. Congress. *Congressional Record.* 78th Congress, 1st Session. Vol. 89. Washington, D.C.: Government Printing Office, 1943.

U.S. Congress. House of Representatives. "Caring for Refugees in the United States." 78th Congress, 2nd Session. Document No. 656, June 12, 1944.

U.S. Congress. House of Representatives. Committee on International Relations. *Selected Executive Session Hearings of the Committee, 1943-50*. Vol. 2: *Problems of World War II and Its Aftermath*. Washington, D.C., 1976.

U.S. Congress. *United States Statutes at Large*. 78th Congress, 1st Session. Vol. 57, part 2: Concurrent Resolutions. Washington, D.C.: Government Printing Office, 1943.

United Nations. General Assembly, 125th Plenary Meeting, November 26, 1947, A/PV.

Vago, Bela. *The Shadow of the Swastika: The Rise of Fascism and Anti-Semitism in the Danube Basin, 1936-39*. London, 1975.

Voltaire. *Voltaire's Correspondence*. Edited by Theodore Besterman. Geneva, 1953-1965. 107 vols.

———. *The Works of Voltaire*. Translated by William F. Fleming. Paris, 1901. 42 vols.

Wagg, Alfred, III. "Washington's Stepchild: The Refugee." *New Republic*, April 28, 1941.

Wells, H. G. *The Anatomy of Frustration: A Modern Synthesis*. London, 1936.

———. "The Future of the Jews." *Liberty*, December 24, 1938.

"Why Are We in This War?" *Yank*, January 28, 1944.

Wise, Stephen S. *As I See It*. New York, 1944.

———. *Challenging Years: The Autobiography of Stephen Wise*. New York, 1949.

———. *The Personal Letters of Stephen Wise*. Edited by Justine Wise Polier and James Waterman Wise. Boston, 1956.

———. *Stephen S. Wise, Servant of the People: Selected Letters*. Edited by Carl Hermann Voss. Philadelphia, 1969.

World Almanac and Book of Facts. New York, 1941, 1949, 1957.

Wyman, David S., ed. *America and the Holocaust*. New York, 1989-1991. 13 vols.

Index

Page numbers in *italics* refer to illustrations.